From Merchants to Emperors

Pratapaditya Pal and Vidya Dehejia

From Merchants to Emperors

British Artists and India
1757 – 1930

*

Cornell University Press

Ithaca and London

FROM MERCHANTS TO EMPERORS
BRITISH ARTISTS AND INDIA · 1757–1930

*

ORGANIZED BY
THE PIERPONT MORGAN LIBRARY
AS PART OF THE
FESTIVAL OF INDIA

*

PRESENTED AT
THE MORGAN LIBRARY · NEW YORK
1 MAY – 31 JULY 1986
AND
LOS ANGELES COUNTY MUSEUM OF ART
9 SEPTEMBER 1986 – 4 JANUARY 1987

*

*

FIRST PUBLISHED IN 1986 BY
CORNELL UNIVERSITY PRESS
124 ROBERTS PLACE
ITHACA · NEW YORK 14850

*

INTERNATIONAL STANDARD BOOK NUMBER
CLOTH 0-8014-1907-7
PAPER 0-8014-9386-2
LIBRARY OF CONGRESS CATALOGUE CARD NUMBER
85-048273

*

PUBLISHED IN THE UNITED KINGDOM BY
CORNELL UNIVERSITY PRESS · LTD
ELY HOUSE · 37 DOVER STREET
LONDON WIX 4HQ ENGLAND

*

PRINTED AND BOUND IN JAPAN

Contents

Foreword by Charles Ryskamp
7

Preface by Pratapaditya Pal
9

Introduction
11

1. Transporters of Picturesque Beauties
21

2. Strangers in the Land of Regrets
45

3. In Search of Romantic India
97

4. Native Artists and Exotic Art
153

5. India Through the Lens
181

Notes
213

Glossary
217

Bibliography
219

Index
223

Franklin Jasper Walls, who died in 1963, bequeathed his residuary estate to The Pierpont Morgan Library to establish a lecture series in the fine arts, iconography, and archaeology, with the provision that the lectures be ultimately published in book form.

Throughout his life, Mr. Walls was interested in the fine arts and in the study of art history. When the Association of Fellows of The Pierpont Morgan Library was organized in 1949, he became one of the founding members. He was particularly concerned with the Library's lecture program, and served on the Association's Lecture Committee. Without ever revealing his testamentary plans, he followed with keen attention the design and construction of the Library's new Lecture Hall, completed a few months before his death.

Lectures given by Dr. Pal and Dr. Dehejia, interpretations of the material in this book, are the seventh series of the Franklin Jasper Walls Lectures to be published.

Foreword

In a fascinating narrative and through watercolors, drawings, sketchbooks, illustrated books, prints, and photographs, this volume tells the story of the British in India over nearly two hundred years. No colonial power or group of artists has left a comparable portrayal of a ruling class in its adopted country. Many of the artists are amateurs; some are draftsmen, surveyors, engineers, and architects. Others are distinguished painters and printmakers like Tilly Kettle, William Hodges, Johann Zoffany, Thomas and William Daniell, Arthur William Devis, and George Chinnery. In various kinds of works of art, we can see the British governing and playing, their public and private lives, their social customs and domestic arrangements. We have a detailed visual record of the British themselves–through their own art and native Indian watercolors and drawings; we as well have a view of nearly all aspects of Indian life.

The book, *From Merchants to Emperors*, is published in connection with an exhibition of the same name held during 1986 at The Pierpont Morgan Library in New York and the Los Angeles County Museum of Art. Most of the works in the exhibition, and the illustrations in this book, are drawn from the collection of Paul F. Walter of New York, and have not previously been seen by the public. Mr. Walter is an extraordinary collector–from the ancient to our contemporary world, a connoisseur of paintings, drawings, photographs, sculpture, and furniture. India has for many years been a very special interest of his. In the last decade or so he has assembled a remarkable collection of Rajput painting as well as the early photography by the British in India. In 1979, The Pierpont Morgan Library, in collaboration with the Gallery Association of New York, showed part of his Indian holdings: eighty miniatures of the Rajput school. This exhibition, *The Classical Tradition in Rajput Painting*, traveled to seven other museums in the United States, giving a very large number of persons an opportunity to appreciate the color and line, and the representation of Indian myth and history, so brilliantly realized in the Rajput school of painting.

Even before the Festival of India had been announced, Mr. Walter agreed with the Morgan Library that the art of the British in India during the time of their hegemony deserved special attention. We are pleased that the scholar and author of the catalogue of our exhibition of Rajput painting, Dr. Pratapaditya Pal, Senior Curator of Indian and Southeast Asian Art and Curator-in-Charge of West Asian Art of the Los Angeles County Museum of Art, and Adjunct Professor of Fine Arts at the University of Southern California, could choose, with Dr. Vidya Dehejia, Adjunct Associate Professor of Art History of Columbia University, those works of art from Mr. Walter's collection and from other sources, that represent the period of the British in India from 1757 to 1930.

Our gratitude goes first of all to Mr. Walter and to the authors of this volume. We are also indebted to those who graciously permitted us to reproduce works in their collections: The Asiatic Society (Calcutta), Balfour & Newton Libraries of the University of Cambridge, Edwin Binney, 3rd, Fogg Art Museum and Houghton Library of Harvard University, Niall Hobhouse, India Office Library and Records of the British Library, Kenneth J. Lane, Leger Galleries, Los Angeles County Museum of Art, The Pierpont Morgan Library, Lord Romsey, Charles Ryskamp, Spink & Son, Victoria and Albert Museum, Victoria Memorial Hall, Thomas John Willis, and the Yale Center for British Art. We are grateful to Marvin Hoshino, who designed this handsome volume, and to Pamela Barr for editing it.

Three other persons have played a crucial role in the organization of the exhibition and the planning and editing of this book: Priscilla C. Barker, Francis S. Mason, Jr., and Lynn Thommen. Others of the staff of the Morgan Library who have been of special help are: Anna Lou Ashby, Robynne Dinkelaker, Timothy Herstein, David Loggie, Patricia Reyes, Frederick C. Schroeder, Nancy Seaton, Edward Sowinski, Diane Stiles, Deborah Winard, Elizabeth Wilson, David W. Wright, and Jeanne L. Wright, and at the Los Angeles County Museum of Art, Earl A. Powell, III, Anita Feldman, John Passi, and Myrna Smoot. Many thanks are also owed to Terrence Abbott, curator of the Paul Walter collections.

Generous support for research and travel came from the Walter Foundation. The Franklin Jasper Walls Lecture Fund has supported the printing of this book, and the Charles Engelhard Foundation has aided its publication through endowed support for all Morgan Library publications.

Charles Ryskamp · Director, The Pierpont Morgan Library

Preface

WHEN Paul Walter asked me to organize an exhibition based on his collection of works by British artists who visited India in the eighteenth and nineteenth centuries, I was rather hesitant. I had indeed studied British Indian history in both high school and as an undergraduate, but I was only marginally familiar with the art of the period. As a child, I had seen works by British artists at the Victoria Memorial in Calcutta, which was the principal repository of such material in India, but it was not until the early sixties, when I was at Cambridge University, that I really became acquainted with the works of such artists as William Hodges and the Daniells. The challenge, however, seemed worthwhile, and has indeed proven to be so; I have subsequently acquired some familiarity with material that is nothing short of fascinating.

Since the Paul Walter Collection is in New York, I invited Dr. Vidya Dehejia, who is Adjunct Associate Professor of Art History at Columbia University, to be the co-curator of the exhibition and to co-author the book with me. Like me, she was born during the Raj and is a Tamil Brahman from a small town not far from Madras. Thus, I felt that the material would be reviewed by two Indians who were from two of the important Presidencies of British India, Bengal and Madras, which would also contribute toward the scholarly integration of the perceptions of the north and the south. I decided to write the chapters dealing with the British in India, their imperial image, their institutions and way of life, and to examine the response of the native artists to the British presence and patronage. I suggested that Vidya Dehejia write about the British artists' perceptions of India and the Indians, and consider the British photographers' views of the country.

Although both of us were born in British In-dia, our upbringings were quite different. I was raised in a very conservative, nationalistic home. My father had been incarcerated by the British government several times for his political views, once with a broken head. I remember vividly the excitement of the "Quit India" movement of 1942, the exhilaration of Japanese attacks on the Calcutta harbor–as if they were the harbingers of Indian freedom–and the tragic famine of 1943, when Calcutta was filled with millions of starving refugees from the countryside. The bloody riots that preceded India's independence from the British in 1947 are also indelibly etched in my memory. Yet, in 1946, my father, who wore nothing but homespun cotton all his life, packed me off to a prestigious English-speaking boarding school in the hills. While at school for the greater part of the year, I was molded into the caricature of a young English gentleman, who loved reading P. G. Wodehouse and playing cricket, but when I returned home for the holidays I reassumed my native guise.

Vidya Dehejia was raised as a true baba sahib, as she was the daughter of one of the first Indians who was permitted to join as an officer the thus far (as late as the thirties) entirely British "Indian Police." Her childhood days were spent in pukka British-Indian manner, generally in the company of British children, under the vigilant eyes of ayahs and sepoys. Riding lessons played a prominent part in her life, and annual visits to hillstations were a matter of form. Evenings were spent at the gymkhana playing badminton, while her parents sipped gimlets and played bridge before returning home to a meal of soup, roast fowl or mutton, and a steamed pudding served with a custard sauce. As the burra sahib of a local district, her parents once entertained the viceroy and his spouse at their home whose walls were decorated with prints by Gainsborough and Constable.

Thus, in different ways, for both of us British India is not really part of history, but an integral part of our childhoods. In many ways, writing this book involved reliving these vivid experiences. Nothing in life is clearly black or white, and we are aware that our appreciation of the British artists' perceptions of India may reflect our own ambivalence about the British Raj.

While the idea of the exhibition was initiated by Paul Walter, it was Dr. Charles Ryskamp, the director of The Pierpont Morgan Library, who suggested that we write a book on the subject. We generally chose to exhibit graphics and photographs taken largely from Mr. Walter's collection; however, the text covers many works that will not be on view. This book is intended as a general overview of the subject in a single volume, rather than as a specialized study of a single aspect of the art of British India—that is the prerogative of Dr. Mildred Archer.

Apart from Paul Walter and Charles Ryskamp, without whose collaboration neither the exhibition nor the book would have materialized, Mildred Archer's is the first name that comes to our minds when it is time to express our gratitude to individuals. As soon as we began working in the field, we realized that we couldn't take a single step without consulting her writings (which are voluminous as the bibliography demonstrates). As the footnotes will indicate, we have borrowed liberally from this cornucopia of scholarship on British Indian art and artists. In addition, she has very kindly read the entire manuscript, and her suggestions and criticisms have proved invaluable. We would also like to thank Dr. Marjorie Munsterberg of the Columbia Society of Fellows in the Humanities, who generously shared her specialized knowledge of British art and of the field of photography. Mr. Giles Eyres, Mr. Niall Hobhouse, and Mr. Robin Garton, all of London, have provided us with valuable information and bibliographical references. Mr. Aditya Dehejia kindly translated the Latin verse, composed by Trevelyan, which is quoted in the book. In India, mention must be made of Mr. Jagmohan Mahajan of New Delhi, one of the few Indians working on British Indian art, and Dr. Samir K. Mukhopadhyay, of Calcutta University, who helped us acquire some photographs.

In his foreword, Dr. Ryskamp has thanked our friends and colleagues in various institutions. We must mention Ms. Eleanor Garvey at the Houghton Library, Harvard, Mrs. Pauline Rohatji at the India Office Library, and Dr. Duncan Robinson and his staff at the Yale Center for British Art. In addition, we thank the noted collector Dr. Edwin Binney, 3rd, who was his usual, generous self, and Mr. Thomas John Willis, who, like Paul Walter, has been seduced by the charms of British Indian art and allowed us to use some of his material. We are indebted to them, as well as to all those who are acknowledged in the foreword.

We would also like to thank Dr. Charles Ryskamp and his staff, and Dr. Earl A. Powell, III, the director of the Los Angeles County Museum of Art, as well as his staff for their cooperation and assistance. A special word of appreciation is due to Ms. Myrna Smoot, Assistant Director of LACMA, Larry Reynolds, the institution's chief photographer, and his colleagues, and the staff of the museum's Research Library, who cheerfully met my incessant requests for interlibrary loans. David Loggie, the photographer for the Morgan Library, who is responsible for more than half of the illustrations in this book, deserves special thanks.

Finally, it is always a pleasure to work on a project with Paul F. Walter, whose enthusiasm for collecting is exceeded only by his forebearance and generosity. He already owns most of the pictures reproduced in this book; we would also like to dedicate the text to him.

PRATAPADITYA PAL · Senior Curator of Indian and Southeast Asian Art and Curator-in-Charge of West Asian Art, Los Angeles County Museum of Art

Introduction

It certainly is curious, and highly entertaining to an inquisitive mind, to associate with a people whose manners are more than three thousand years old; and to observe in them that attention and polished behaviour which usually marks the most highly civilised state of society.

WILLIAM HODGES — 1793

"Do you like India?" Mrs. Bristow asked me.
"Oh, yes. I think it's marvellous."
"And what do you think of the people?"
"I like them very much, and think them most interesting."
"Oo, aren't you a fibber! What was it you said the other day about 'awful Anglo-Indian chatter'?"
"But I thought you were speaking of the Indians just now, not the Anglo-Indians."
"The Indians! I never think of them."

J. R. ACKERLEY — 1932

I

IT seems singular, but as far as our enquiries have gone, our possessions in the East appear to have attracted none of our artists, till towards the end of the last century. Then there came a shoal of them; and afterwards the fancy died away. . . .[1]

These observations are from the introduction of an article about British artists in India published in the Indian newspaper *Pioneer* sometime around 1880. Substantial excerpts from the article comprise the chapter on art in India in W. H. Carey's 1882 *The Good Old Days of Honourable John Company*, a compilation of curious reminiscences about the dominance of the East India Company from 1600 to 1858. In his introduction to the chapter, Carey remarks, "Art seems to wither amid the arid plains of Hindostan," and "the generality of the artists who have figured among the Calcutta or Mofussil community, have confined themselves almost wholly to portrait-painting, finding that more lucrative than subjects of a more laborious and lofty description."[2]

Carey's criticism is unduly harsh. Although the majority of the twenty-two artists described in the 1880 review were portrait painters, a

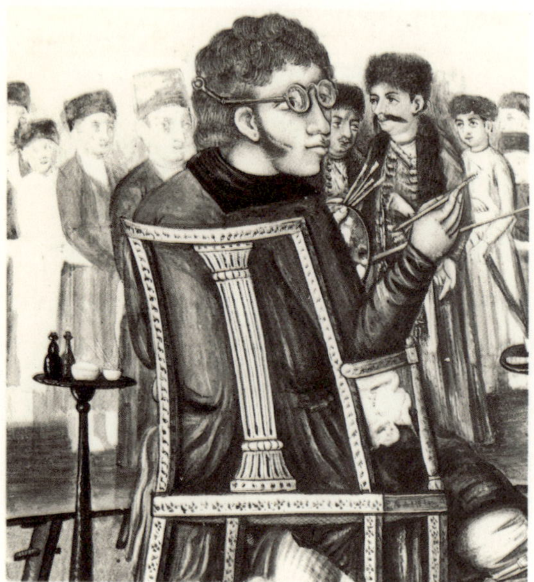

1. *Tilly Kettle*, detail of fig. 157.

number of them also painted subjects that Carey would have found more deserving of praise. By the end of the eighteenth century most eminent British artists, such as Tilly Kettle (1735–86), William Hodges (1744–97), Johann Zoffany (1733–1810), Thomas (1749–1840) and William (1769–1837) Daniell, Arthur William Devis (1762–1822), and Francesco Renaldi (1755–c. 1799), had already visited India for a few years and returned home with or without their fortunes.[3] Robert Home (1752–1834) arrived in 1791 and remained until his death. Others, like George Chinnery (1744–1854), did not arrive until the early nineteenth century. Hodges and the Daniells were not portrait painters, and several of the others, notably Zof-

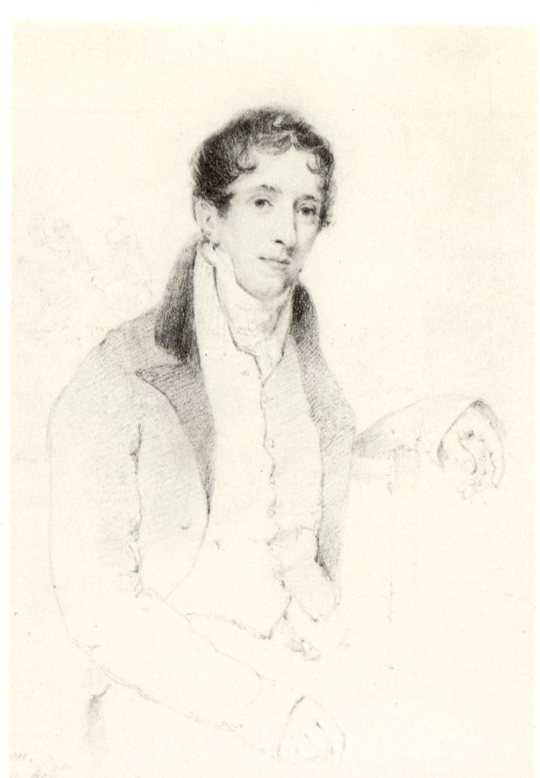

2. William Daniell. *Portrait of a Sporting Artist, possibly W. B. Daniell.* 1811. Pencil. Yale Center for British Art, Paul Mellon Collection.

fany, Devis, Home, Chinnery, and James Wales (1747–95), were busy observing and re-creating the landscapes and monuments of the country, though they earned their livings by painting portraits. Although Zoffany is remembered primarily for the latter, landscapes were his true interest. Two of his well-known conversation pieces show several landscapes which appear not to have survived. Among all of the professional portrait painters who visited India, Chinnery was certainly the finest limner of the countryside and its people. Portrait painting was not only exacting but very likely boring as well and even Gainsborough, that master of the genre, remarked, "I am sick of portraits and wish very much to take my viol-de-gamba and walk off to some sweet village, where I can paint landskips and enjoy the fag end of life in quietness and ease."[4]

The same thought must have occurred to many of the painters who went to India for a

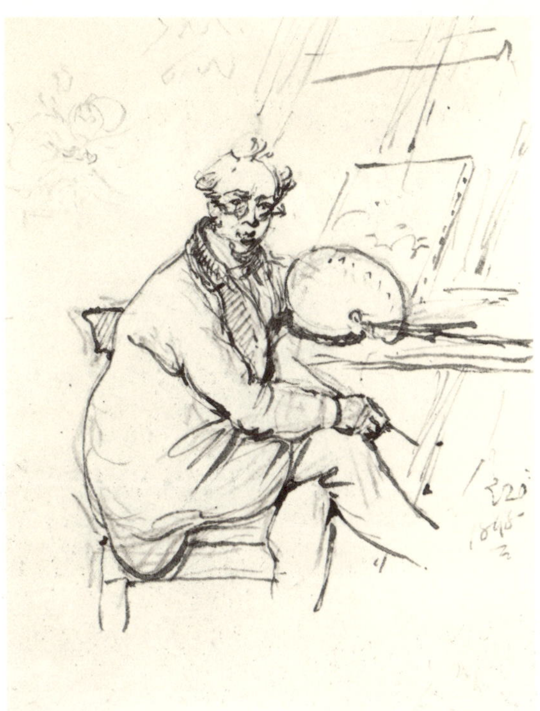

3. George Chinnery. *Self-Portrait.* 1848. Pencil, pen, and brown ink. Yale Center for British Art, Paul Mellon Collection.

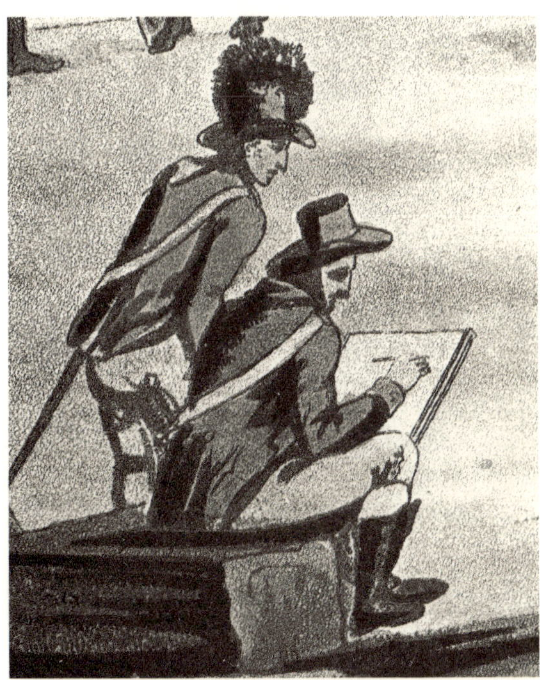

4. J. C. Sadler after James Hunter. *Amateur Artist at Work.* Detail from *The Mysore Gate at Bangalore* from *Picturesque Scenery in the Kingdom of Mysore.* 1804. Colored engraving. The Thomas John Willis Collection.

few years to make their fortunes so they could return to their homes and live, if not in affluence, at least in comfort. It meant working hard and long hours in an enervating climate, undertaking arduous journeys, partaking of an active social life that involved much eating and drinking, scrambling for commissions, and pleasing eccentric clients. Though more lucrative than in England, earning a living as a professional artist in India was not easy. It is not surprising, therefore, that by 1825, the "fancy died away," and one would be hard pressed to name even half a dozen eminent artists who succumbed to the lure of India during the last century of British rule in the subcontinent.

In addition to professional artists, a large number of draftsmen, surveyors, engineers, and talented amateur artists—Sir Charles D'Oyly (1781–1845), James Forbes (1749–1819), Robert Grindlay (1786–1877), Emily Eden (1797–1869)—who made the journey have bequeathed to us a vast body of material that may not always be as technically accomplished as the works of the professionals, but is no less spontaneous and delightful. At their best, several of them were so gifted that their drawings and watercolors, unless signed, are virtually indistinguishable from those rendered by professional artists. Many of their original sketches were redrawn by such artists as Bopley Fielding and J. M. W. Turner back home for the engravings that illustrated books about India. Some of them also wrote and published personal reminiscences that were enlivened by aquatints and lithographs based on lively, on-the-spot sketches and drawings that express a variety of levels of British tastes and interests. While most professionals were engaged in painting portraits of the nabobs and sahibs or composing history pictures of imperial interest, the amateur artists were able to cast their nets much wider. The works of professional artists had to satisfy their clients and sell in a fairly competitive market. The sketches and drawings of the amateurs, however, were meant primarily for the artists themselves, were executed more freely, and are more intimate observations of the Indian scene.

13

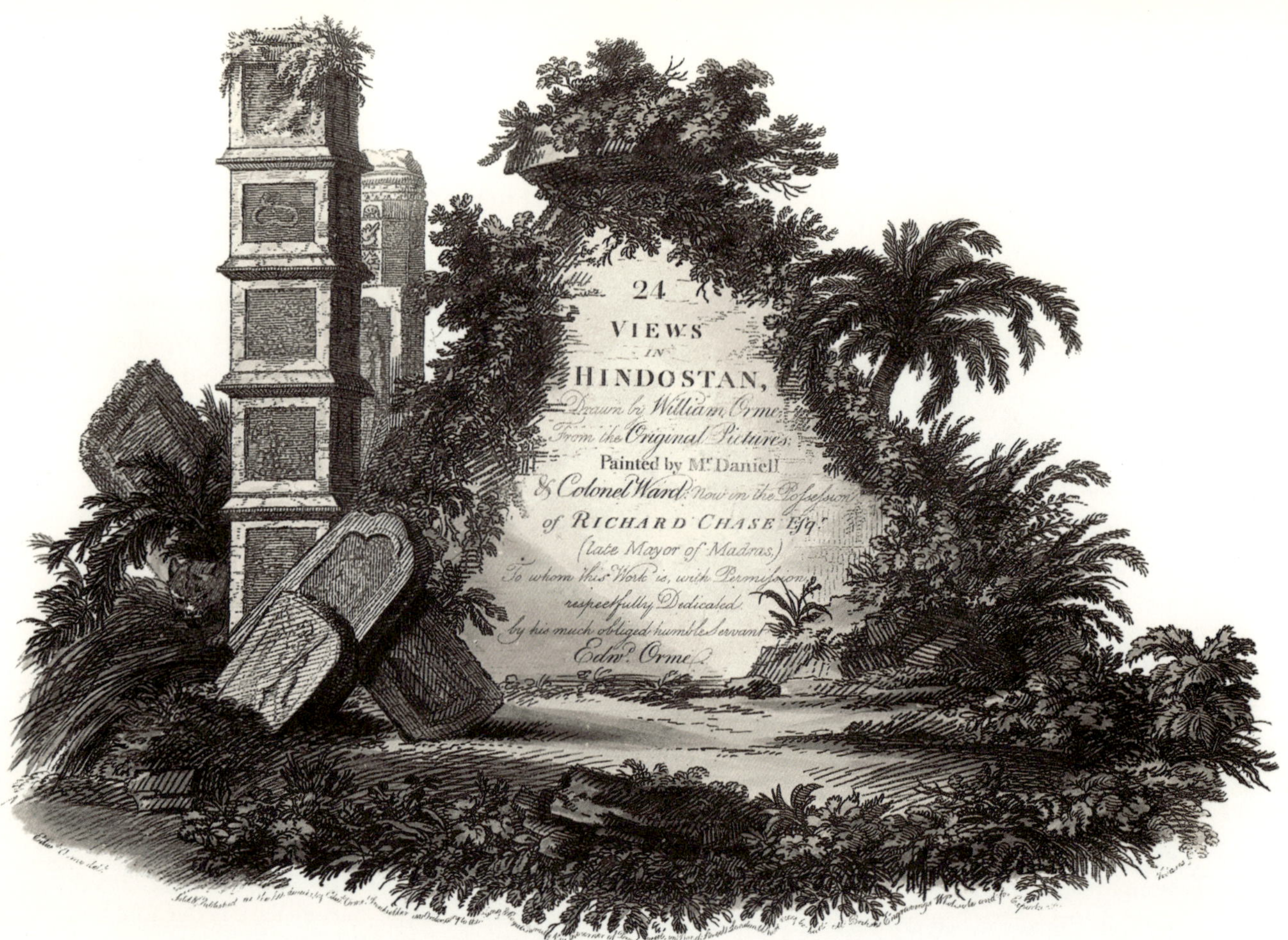

5. Edward Orme. Frontispiece, title plate from *A Brief History of Ancient and Modern India*. 1805. Engraving. The Thomas John Willis Collection.

Few professionals had the resources or opportunities to study the land and people as closely as the employees of the East India Company, or an amateur like Emily Eden, whose brother Lord Auckland was the governor-general.

Starting in the mid-eighteenth century, drawing formed an essential part of a liberal education, especially of the British upper and middle classes. A private drawing master was as common as a music instructor, and taught both men and women either in schools or at home. Indeed, the demand was so great that professional watercolorists published drawing books and teaching manuals, in addition to giving lessons. Thus, many of the British who went to India during the Georgian and early Victorian eras were well trained. Drawing skills were a prerequisite for the engineers, surveyors, and gunners of the army. The East India Company's college at Addiscombe was well staffed by a talented drawing master of the day. The curriculum at Hailebury College, where members of

the Indian Civil Service were trained, also included drawing. It is known from contemporary newspaper advertisements that drawing lessons were given by professional artists in India, as well. The best known and most admired teacher was George Chinnery, whose many students included Sir Charles D'Oyly. Chinnery's profound influence on amateur artists was felt long after he had left India. These amateur artists were extremely prolific; of the more than ten thousand items preserved in the India Office Library in London, less than one-tenth are by professional artists.[5]

Whatever else may be said of British imperial rule in India, no other colonial power in history left such a vast amount of visual material recording the life and perceptions of the ruling class with such fidelity or in such graphic detail. There were many other colonial powers in Asia during the Victorian age, and the British themselves ruled territories other than India. But, nowhere else can one experience the domestic

14

and official lives of the British as intimately as one can through their pictures, drawings, lithographs, and photographs of India. We can observe precisely how they lived with their army of servants and complex domestic arrangements; their private chores and their public charades; their social customs and amusements; their clubs and their *gymkhanas*; their love of sports and their craze for hunting; how they dressed and transported themselves across the vast subcontinent; what their fears and foibles were, their aspirations and obsessions. No other race or nation has left such accurate documentation of their imperial venture as the British.

Equally perceptive though far more romanticized are the British views of the Indian scene. With the rapid expansion of their authority in India after the Battle of Plassey in 1757, the British back home became increasingly curious about their unexpected windfall. While only the wealthy could afford the oil paintings of the professionals, and the sketches and watercolors of the amateurs gratified the artists' relatives and friends, illustrated books and portfolios were more accessible. These books were lavishly illustrated, first with aquatints and then with lithographs based on the sketches, drawings, and watercolors brought back to England by both professional and amateur artists. Aquatint was an expensive process, while copperplate engraving, though cheaper, was laborious. By the 1830s, lithography had become the vogue; less expensive than aquatint, illustrated books could now be produced for a less affluent and therefore wider public. Hodges's *Views on India* (1785–88), the Daniells' *Oriental Scenery* (1795–1808), Forbes's *Oriental Memoirs*

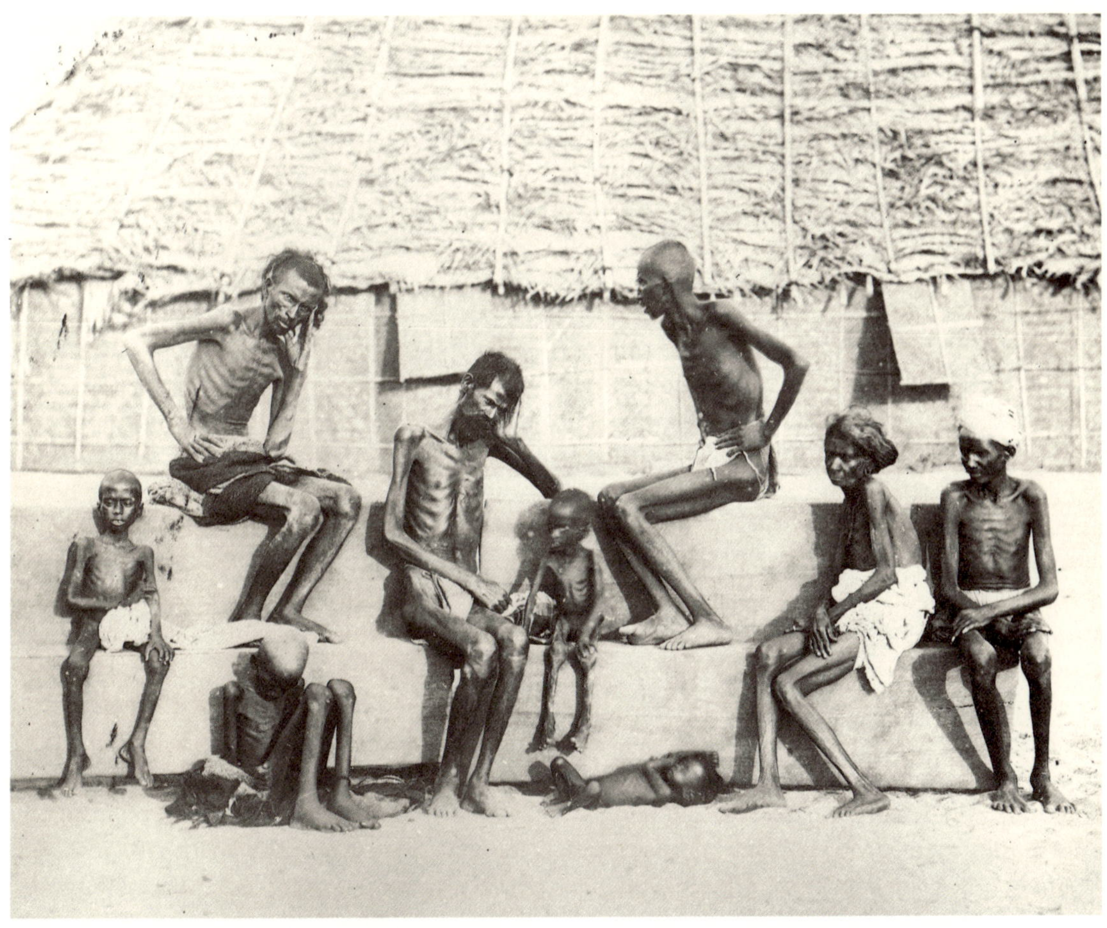

6. Captain Willoughby Hooper. *Madras Famine*. 1877-78. Albumen print. Walter Collection.

(1813), Captain Thomas Williamson's *Oriental Field Sports* (1819), D'Oyly's *Costumes of India* (1830), and Emily Eden's *Portraits of the Princes and Peoples of India* (1844) are unsurpassed examples of their genre.

Books and portfolios with picturesque illustrations based largely on impressions sketched by amateur artists continued to be popular through the mid-nineteenth century. This romance with the "Indian" India, however, withered as rapidly in the second half of the century as it had begun in the first half. A major contributing factor was the tragic events of 1857 which dramatically altered the British attitude toward India. India was no longer a mysterious and unfamiliar country; the British public's curiosity had been well satisfied. With the widening social gulf between the rulers and the ruled, there was a marked decline in interest in the country's peoples and cultures. Fewer professional artists were inspired to visit India after it officially formed a part of the empire where the sun never set. A second important reason was the invention of photography, which came to India early. While in many ways the early professional photographers pursued the same interests as the early painters, their medium could produce more candid, direct images and was less time consuming. While the picturesque and romantic India so evocatively and effusively evoked by the painters of the earlier period may have captivated the British imagination and satisfied their curiosity about the exotic, it was the realistic images of photographers that awakened their audience to the reality of an India that was not always so palatable.

Official photography was restricted mostly to historical occasions of splendor such as the grand durbars and viceregal visits to the grandees of the empire (the effete legendary nawabs and maharajas), while professionals once again catered to a select and wealthy clientele, concentrating on portraits, landscapes, and monuments. But, pictures taken by amateurs are often far more telling about the grim realities of India. Indeed, photography played a major role in recording the horrors of the 1857 mutiny and arousing the British public at home. It was only through brutal images frozen through the lens that the same British public learned that India was more than just a country of sahibs and memsahibs, of maharajas and snake charmers, of polo and pigsticking, of romantic hillstations and magnificent ruins. It was also a land of abject poverty and starving masses, of floods and famines, of devastation and death. One gleans almost no idea of how the majority of Indians lived from looking at highly sanitized and selective views left behind by the British artists of pre-1857 India. Only photography brought the real India too close for comfort.

In general, Anglo-Indian life was depicted with astonishing detail and humor by British artists. Indian trades and occupations, costumes and customs, exotic tribes and those more familiar, the majestic mountains and the awesome rivers, all of nature's creatures great and small, and the picturesque temples and mosques were sketched and painted with fidelity and sympathy. Even though the definition of realism as perceived by the British artists, both professional and amateur, was limited and narrow, in a little over half a century they succeeded in documenting much more vividly and with much greater breadth the peoples and landscapes of India than was done by Indian artists in the previous four millennia. Nevertheless, the picture remains incomplete, and while the images do not lack elements of "truth," they catered essentially to the prevailing tastes and requirements of the Anglo-Indian patrons in India or British patrons at home. Except as ethnological curiosities there was very little attempt to represent the subordinated people. The "realities" that were portrayed were for the most part "fashioned" to assert British beliefs and values.

When the first group of British artists arrived in the last quarter of the eighteenth century, India was already a myth and in many ways remained so until the British left in 1947. As the imperial image came into sharper focus during the nineteenth century, the sense of illusion became keener and the background fuzzier. Like the imperial policymakers, artists, too, despite

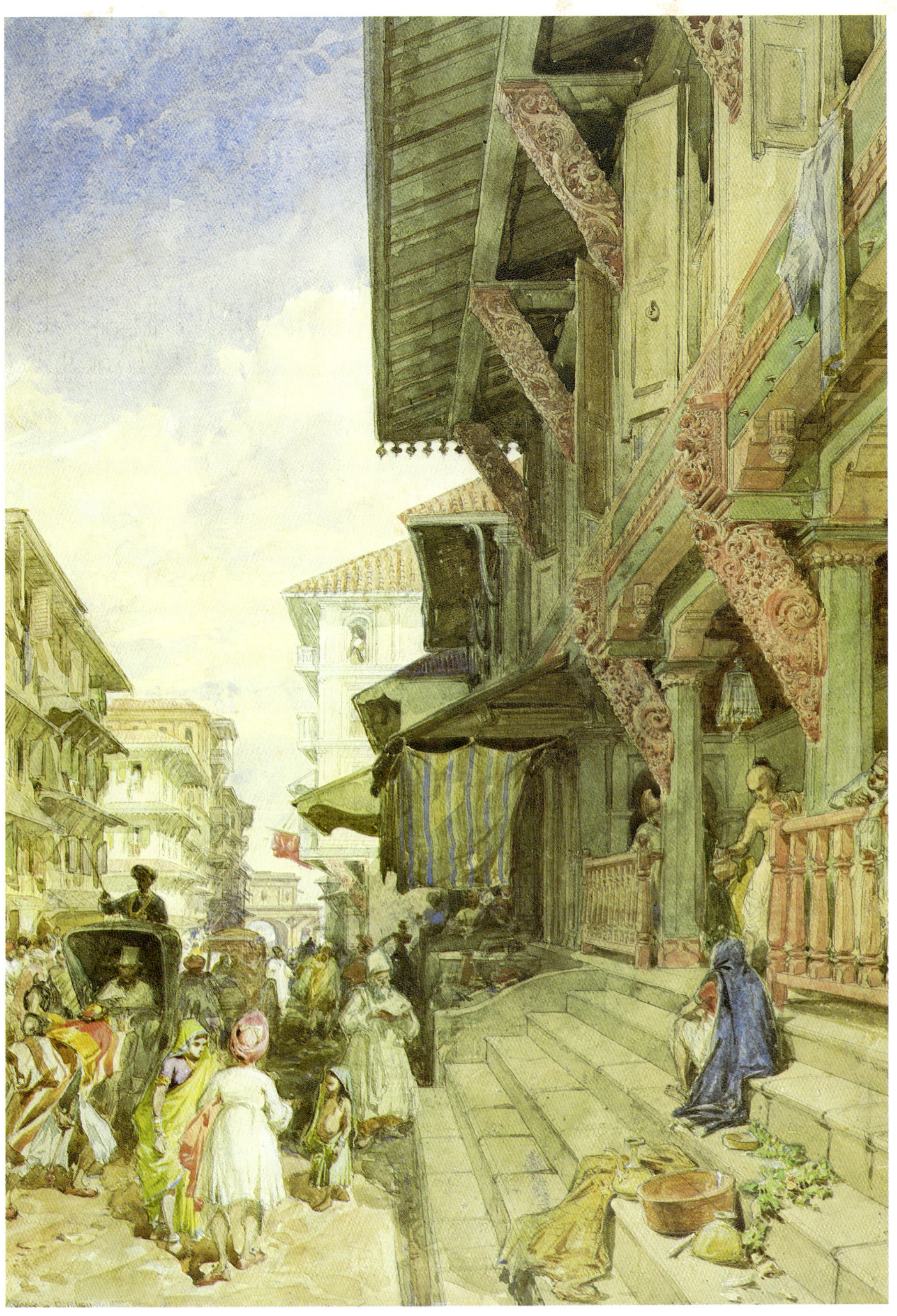

COLORPLATE 1.
William Simpson. *Street Scene in Bombay.* 1862.
Watercolor.
Walter Collection.

their personal perceptions and predilections, shared in that dream and illusion and helped perpetuate the myth. So, while the artists, both in India and Britain, vied with one another to depict the British triumphs, none cared to portray the horrors of war. Hodges revealed his feelings of despair upon witnessing in July 1780 multitudes of refugees abandoning their villages, "bearing on their shoulders the small remains of their little property, mothers and infants at their breasts, fathers leading their horses burthened with their young families, others sitting on the miserable remains of their fortunes on a hackery, and dragged through the dust by weary bullocks."[6] It was not, however, an appropriate subject for visual representation.

Similarly, the impressions of the rebellion of 1857, whether visual or verbal, were grossly unbalanced in favor of the imperial authority and provide us with hysterical accounts and vivid images of the sufferings of the British with grudging admissions of the horrors of British retribution. In February 1858, the Swedish artist Egron Lundgren (1815–75) was sent by Thomas Agnew and Sons of Manchester specifically to record the events of the revolt. Although, like Hodges, he did not altogether ignore the realities of the situation, his reactions were muted. As the art historian Sten Nilsson has observed, Lundgren's diary does "reveal that he sensed the questionable element in their [the British] actions" and was horrified by "the cruelties he was forced to witness," but he shied away from discussing this because "he did not want his reporting to create a stir and political debate."[7] Had he been more courageous, he might have helped upset the myths about the revolt that the British so assiduously nurtured for almost the next century. Similarly, William Simpson (1823–99), of Crimean War fame, recorded some of the unsavory aspects of Indian realities, as in a dramatic ink sketch of a famine (fig. 116), but comparison with a later photograph of the victims of the Madras famine of 1877–78 by Hooper demonstrates how much more graphic, grimly vivid, and immediate a portrayal was possible (fig. 6).

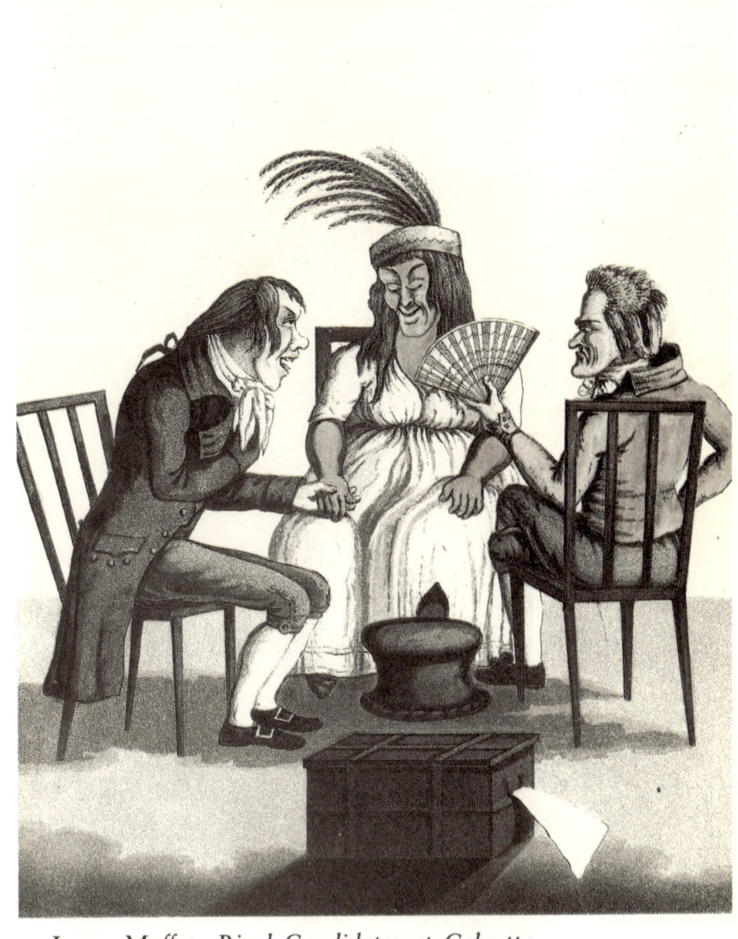

7. James Moffat. *Rival Candidates at Calcutta.* c. 1800. Colored engraving. Walter Collection.

The British satirical social and political cartoons about British India have received little attention. Georgian England from the 1780s through the 1820s was particularly fertile soil for cartoonists. "From Hogarth forward" writes Robert L. Patten, an authority on English literature, "moralizing satirical prints depicting contemporary scenes were a staple of London (and some provincial) book and print dealers."[8] What better fodder for the caricaturists' cannons than the avarice and sloth of the merchants and officers of the East India Company, the wealthy nabobs. The Anglo-Indian may have taken himself very seriously in India, but in

Britain he was an easy target for the satirist and caricaturist. Most of the caricatures discussed here were created in Britain for a local public, but the genre was quite popular in nineteenth-century India. G. F. Atkinson's (1822–59) classic *Curry and Rice*, first published in 1859, was still in demand in the early twentieth century. The anonymous *Indian Charivari Album* was another popular example which was first published in Calcutta in 1875.

By and large, British homes in India were decorated with works by British artists, but a few housed collections of Indian paintings, especially of the Mogul style. This was particu-

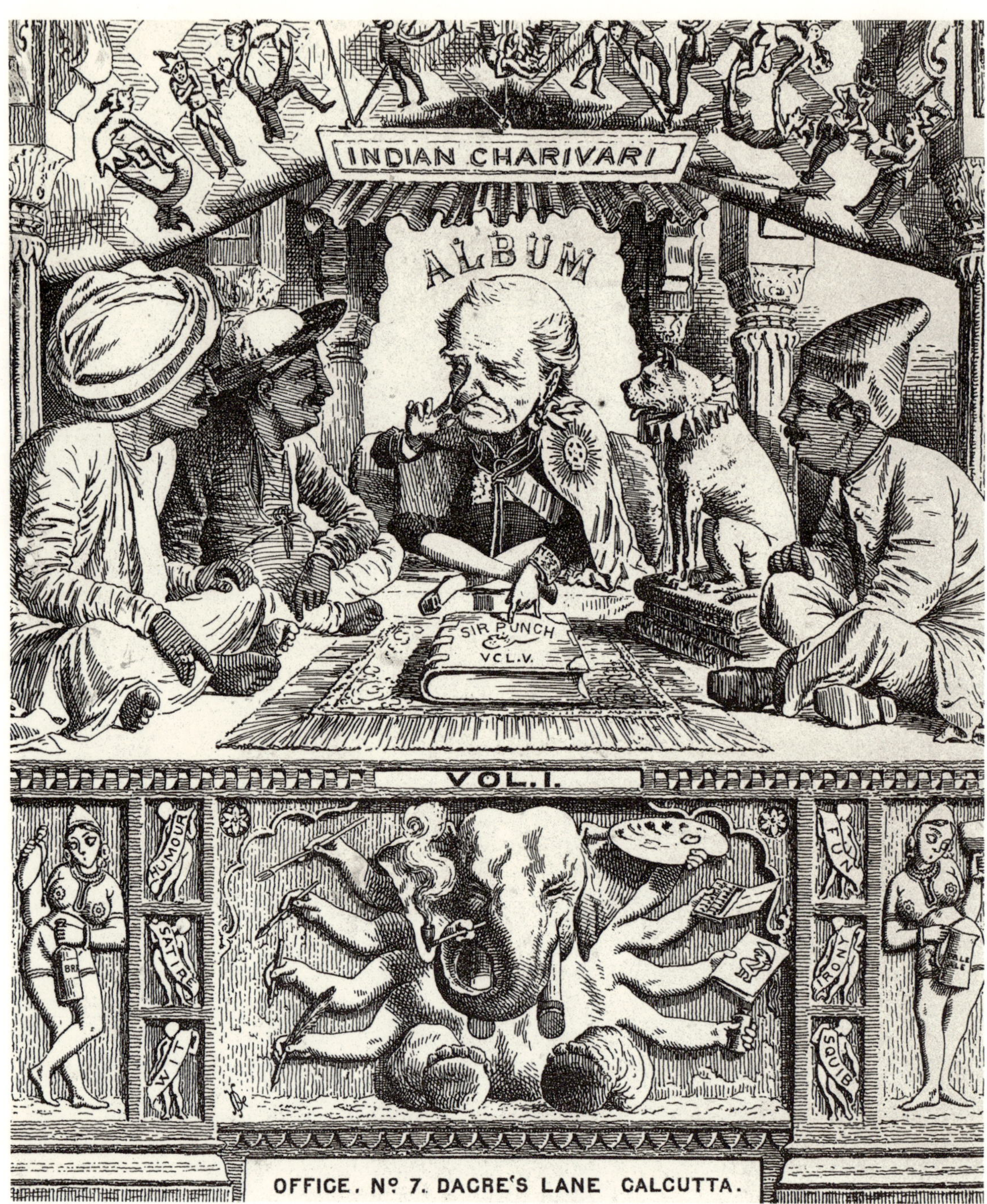

8. Title page from *Indian Charivari Album*. 1875. Engraving. Walter Collection.

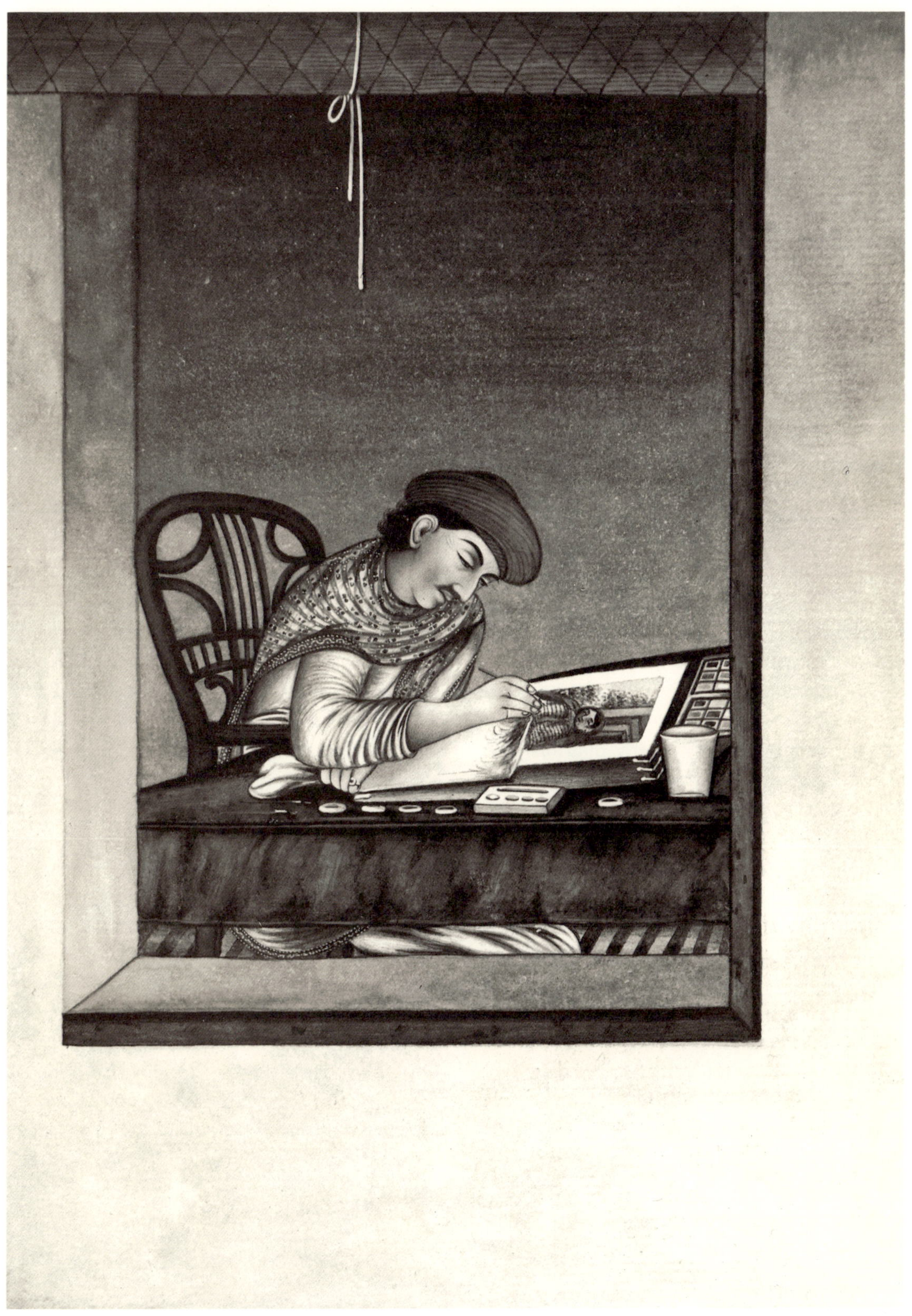

9. Anonymous. *An Indian Artist at Work.* c. 1815–20. Watercolor. Reproduced by permission of the India Office Library and Records (British Library).

larly true in the eighteenth century when Clive, Hastings, Richard Johnson, and others decorated their homes with collections of Indian paintings. Many Britons commissioned works from the leading Indian artists of the day. Lady Impey, the wife of Sir Elijah Impey, the first chief justice of the supreme court in Calcutta (1774–82), was one of the earliest and best known patrons of Indian artists. Indeed, much work was done by Indian artists in Calcutta, Murshidabad, Patna, Lucknow, and Delhi for British patrons. The works of many of the British painters who worked for the courts in Lucknow and Murshidabad were copied by Indian artists who were influenced in their choice of subject matter and technique, namely the use of watercolors instead of gouache. This led to the development of the distinctive, if hybrid style of the Company school, which flourished for about a century. This, too, began to wither after 1857, although their miniatures on ivory and delicate pictures on mica remained popular with British patrons as gifts and souvenirs.

Another lively group of artists who gathered in Calcutta around 1830 was the Kalighat school. Its patrons were mostly pilgrims who visited the city's famous shrine to the goddess Kali, but it also produced works for the educated middle class of the city. These works show the influence of the British taste for secular subjects and, to some extent, British drawing methods. Nevertheless, its was a highly original style and its works were collected by the British as well.

The British introduced printmaking into India, an indirect result of the introduction of the printing process in general. Indian artists seem to have been rather lukewarm in their reception of both engraving and lithography. Not only were they slow in adopting European methods, but by the time they did in the second half of the nineteenth century, they simply imitated the foreign techniques without any originality or inventiveness. Both printing and printmaking, however, appear to have attracted Indians from all castes, even Brahmans.

The Indians who worked for British patrons came from families of professional artists. Although they modified their techniques to suit British tastes by cultivating a more heightened sense of realism than they were accustomed to, they were overshadowed in the second half of the nineteenth century, first by photographers and then by "gentlemen" artists. Art in India had always been a hereditary profession and, by and large, the artist/craftsman had rather a low social position, certainly in Hindu society. Ideally, Moslem society was casteless, but no matter how much an artist's work was admired by his patron, it is unlikely that the two had much social interaction. The professional British artist, on the other hand, was very much a part of the Anglo-Indian society and his company was much sought after unless he was a crashing bore. Such exalted personalities as Lady Amherst, the wife of a governor-general, and Emily Eden, the sister of another, were freely sketching and drawing without sacrificing their social status or dignity.

This social acceptibility of the artist made it easier for Indians from all walks of life to practice art on professional and amateur levels. Art schools sprang up in the major Indian cities; the one in Bombay was founded by the Parsi philanthropist Jamshedji Jijibhoi in 1857. John Griffiths (1837–1918), considered the greatest Victorian painter to visit India, arrived with Lockwood Kipling, Rudyard Kipling's father, in 1865. Griffith's original works, as well as his splendid copies of the ancient Buddhist murals of the cave temples of Ajanta published in 1896, exercised considerable influence upon the academically trained gentleman artists of the period.

1. Transporters of Picturesque Beauties

Yet to India, artist sail,
And if judgement there abide,
India will thy talents hail,
Cheering thee with bounteous pride.

Nor dost thou by parts alone
Strive for favour, wealth, and fame;
Wheresoe'er thy heart is known,
Virtue will support thy claim.

Then adieu, ingenious friend,
And if rough old Ocean prove,
Doubt not fortune will attend
Him whom taste and virtue love.

ANONYMOUS — 1796[1]

I

WHEN Tilly Kettle, the first British portraitist to visit India, arrived in Madras in 1769, the East India Company, familiarly known as the "John Company," was well-entrenched as the major political force on the subcontinent. The British were the last to join the European scramble for the riches of the East in the 1500s. By the close of the century they had made some headway on the west coast of India by establishing trading posts, and the charter for the East India Company was granted by Queen Elizabeth I in 1600. The contemporaneous ruler of India was Akbar (r. 1556–1605), the third member of the Mogul (Mughal) dynasty, a name that has become synonymous in English with fabulous wealth.

Throughout the seventeenth century, the British and their East India Company remained content with trading, but the situation changed dramatically after the death in 1707 of Akbar's great-grandson, the last great Mogul emperor, Aurangzeb. His successors in Delhi were weak and the consequent absence of a strong central authority forced the British to enter the political arena. The merchants of a trading company found themselves increasingly entangled politically with regional Indian rulers, who had taken advantage of the rapid decline of Mogul power

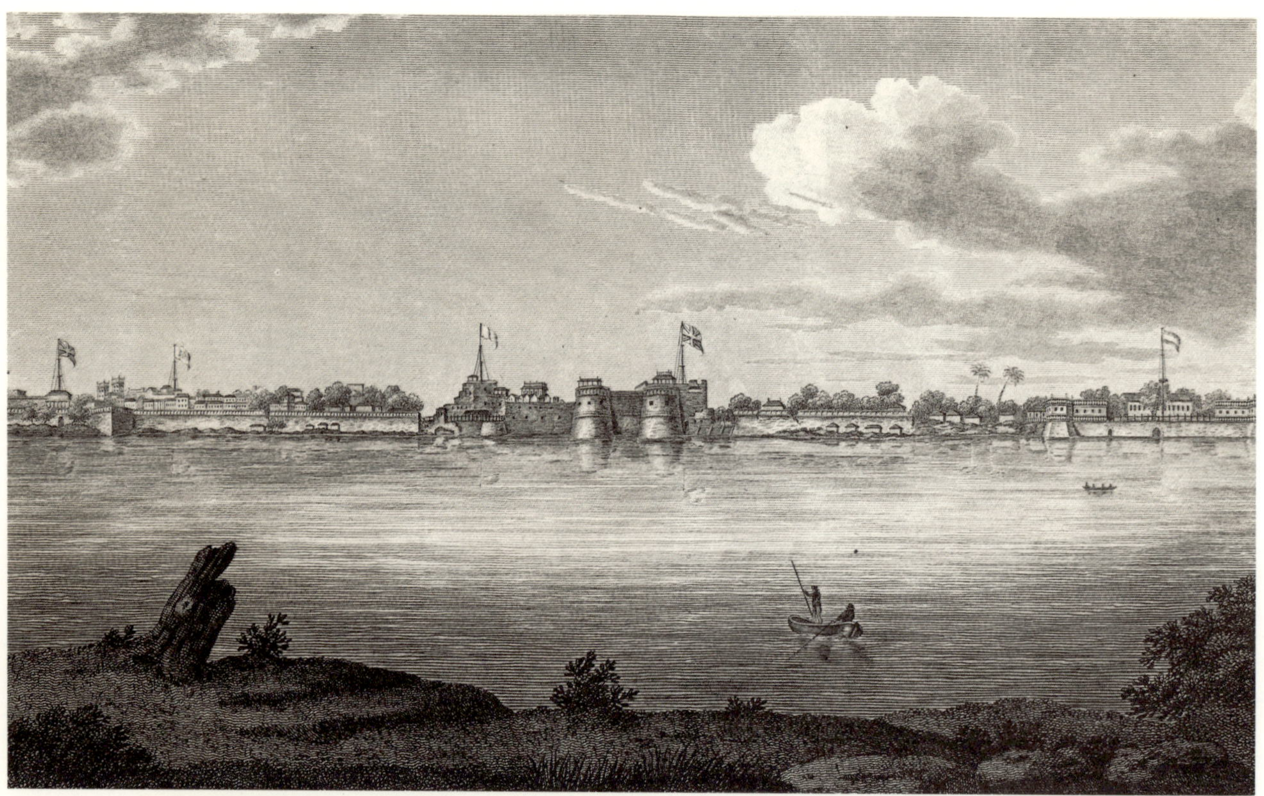

10. James Forbes. *Surat on the Banks of the Tappee* from *Oriental Memoirs*. 1813. Engraving. The Thomas John Willis Collection.

and become independent, and with other Europeans on the subcontinent, particularly the French.

At the time of Aurangzeb's death, the principal British trading centers were Surat in Gujarat, Madras on the southeast coast, and Calcutta near the mouth of the Hoogly River in Bengal. Subsequently, Bombay, which the British Crown acquired from Portugal in 1660 as part of a marriage settlement, eclipsed Surat as the leading city in the west. Calcutta was founded almost accidentally by Job Charnock, a Company servant, in 1692 and remained the political and commercial hub of British India until 1911. All three cities—Madras, Bombay, and Calcutta—were created by the British and always regarded as the three principal seats of the Presidencies of British India.

Before the end of the eighteenth century, the East India Company had ceased to be a mere commercial venture and had become the paramount political power in the land. Although Queen Victoria was not proclaimed the empress of India until 1877, by 1800, when Governor-

General Wellesley built his palace in Calcutta, the merchants of John Company were well on their way to becoming empire builders. The foundations of that empire were laid first in the south and then in Bengal by a young man named Robert Clive, who, like Tilly Kettle, had arrived in Madras as a friendless and penniless civil servant of the Company. Before he was thirty, Clive had proved his military genius by roundly defeating the French at Arcot (1751), not far from Madras. Clive's victory over Siraj-ud-daula, the ruler of Bengal, in a mango grove at Plassey in 1757, in what Phillip Woodruff calls, "surely the most miserable skirmish ever to be called a battle,"[2] marked a turning point in the history of India for almost the next two centuries. By the time Tilly Kettle arrived in India, the John Company was effectively administering an area larger than the British Isles.

II

No professional British artist is known to have visited India before 1757. During the last quarter of the eighteenth century, however, they came in large numbers. Indeed, the change was so dramatic that all manner of professionals were drawn to the subcontinent as William Hickey (1780s), a member of the Calcutta bar and an extraordinary diarist, observes in his delightful memoirs:

During the period that Mr. Cleveland and I lived together, a young Jewess of the name of Isaacs [Martha Isaacs, in India 1778–1822] arrived in Calcutta, to exercise the profession of miniature painting. Cleveland, having known her family in England, interested himself to promote her success. He, therefore, observed to me that, as he had heard me say I meant to send my picture to a favourite sister, he should be obliged if I would sit to his friend. I accordingly did so. . . . This lady, two years afterwards, married Mr. Higginson, a gentleman high in the Company's civil service and of large fortune.[3]

British artists flocked to India after the mid-eighteenth century for many reasons. As the historian Percival Spear has observed, "Between 1750 and 1785 there occurred in India a radical change in the English life and outlook, a metamorphosis from the secluded if not always elegant life of the factories, to the fevered cosmopolitanism of later Calcutta, a brilliant if slightly tawdry imitation of the world of the 'First Gentlemen of Europe.'"[4] The British were no longer merely traders; their growing political power and influence called for a different kind of man, one more educated and cultured. The stature of the Presidency towns, especially of Calcutta, grew and more cities and settlements were created. Residencies were established in the native states, and as territorial annexations continued at a rapid pace well into the nineteenth century, the illusion of permanence seemed to be a reality. The number of Europeans, both military and civilian, official and nonofficial, male and female, increased significantly.

The influx of British women was one of the most significant factors in the change in attitude that gradually took place in the nineteenth century. Prior to 1757, few women went to India. However, the opportunity to "catch" a wealthy husband brought the British women out in

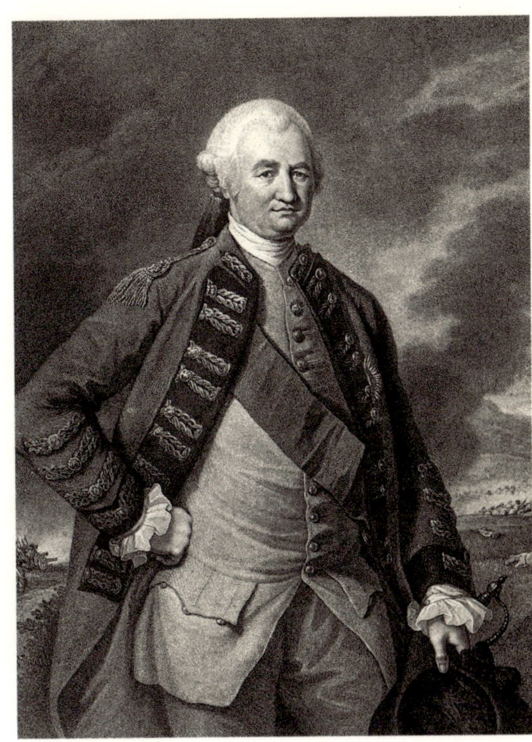

11. F. Bartelozzi after Nathaniel Dance. *Lord Clive.* 1788. Engraving. Walter Collection.

boatloads during the last quarter of the eighteenth century. They were uncharitably referred to as girls of the "Fishing Fleet" and those who returned home unsuccessful were called "Returned Empties." An anonymous British caricaturist seized upon the idea of this "sale of English beauties" (colorplate 2).

With the growth of political power, there was a corresponding boom in corruption and a new class of wealthy British. They were sarcastically known as "nabobs," a corruption of the title nawab used by Moslem rulers. The more stable social order in the British settlements manifested itself in the building of enormous mansions in the cities, towns, and countryside. By the time Warren Hastings, the first governor-general of British India, returned to England in 1785, Calcutta had already become known as the "City of Palaces."

All of these palaces and mansions had walls that needed decorating and hence the demand for artists. One of the most curious features of British Indian history is that the British interest

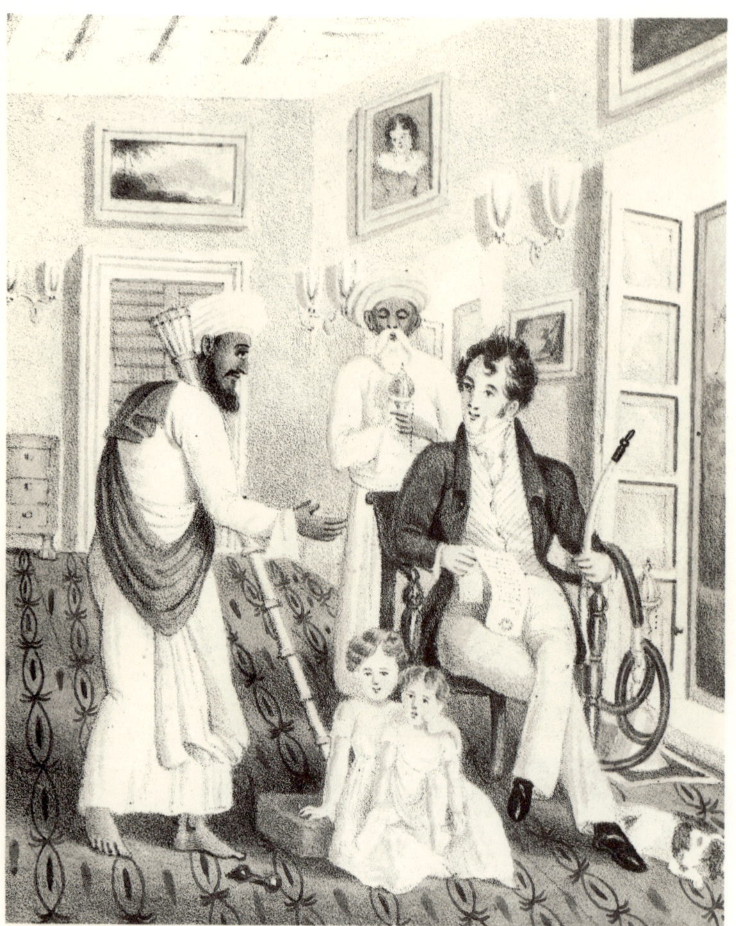

12. Sir Charles D'Oyly. *An Assaburdar or Long Silver-Stick Bearer* from *The European in India*. 1813. Colored lithograph. Walter Collection.

in things Indian, whether material or cultural, diminished in proportion to the imperialist expansion. Although some Britons remained interested in Indian history, literature, and the arts, by the end of the eighteenth century, the Indian lifestyle was eschewed for a more British way of doing things. Every settlement became a replica of a British town, and but for the inescapable heat, indispensable servants, invincible mosquitoes, and spacious verandas, the memsahib could forget she was in India once inside her home. While some Anglo-Indians collected Indian paintings and patronized Indian artists, most preferred to decorate their houses with works by Europeans.

In 1767, when Clive departed from India, "The Town of Calcutta," wrote a Mrs. Kind-

ersley, "is likewise daily increasing in size, notwithstanding which, the English inhabitants multiply so fast, that houses are extremely scarce. Paper or wainscot are improper, both on account of the heat, the vermin and the difficulty of getting it done; the rooms are therefore all whited walls, but plastered in pannels, which has a pretty effect, and are generally ornamented with prints, looking-glasses, or whatever else can be procured from Europe."[5] Presumably the British were already importing or bringing prints with them to decorate their homes. Extant literary and pictorial evidence shows that by the end of the century, however, most Anglo-Indian homes were decorated with etchings and engravings by British artists depicting a wide variety of *Indian* subjects as well as with small portraits in oil, while the walls of the wealthier residences were crowded with more ambitious paintings.

III

WHILE, in general, the patrons of the British artists who visited India were *nouveau riche* nabobs, administrators, civil servants, and the wealthier captains and colonels of the army, most of whom commissioned portraits or bought engravings to decorate their Indian homes and to take back to England as mementos when they retired, many works of art were commissioned by various local authorities and public organizations to honor government and community leaders. Paintings of the judges of the high court were commissioned by members of the bar, and government buildings were adorned with ceremonial portraits of governors-general and viceroys as well as with historical pictures. Artists also received commissions to commemorate special occasions. For instance, for the anniversary of a British victory at Seringapatam (1792), the Calcutta Theatre was decorated by Devis and the Belgian artist Balthazar Solvyns (1760–1824). "In front of the eastern door of the house was a grand transparent view of Seringapatam, by Messrs. Devis and Solwyns, from a drawing of Lieutenant Colebrooke. Over the windows were light transparent views of the principal forts taken from the enemy . . . , painted by Mr. Solwyns, from drawings of Lieutenant Colebrooke."[6] The streets and parks in the various cities and towns were adorned with a wide variety of commemorative sculptures of the heroes of the British government and army. One particularly impressive example, erected after 1857, was the magnificent equestrian portrait of General Outram, one of the heroes of the Mutiny, at the intersection of Park Street and Chowringee in Calcutta (fig. 13).

Although in the eighteenth century, most artists landed in Madras, as ships anchored there on their way to China, it was Calcutta that provided painters with the chance to make their fortunes. (However, a few artists such as Kettle, George Willison [1741–97], Thomas Hickey [1741–1824], and Chinnery did thrive in Madras.) When the aged Catherine Read (1723–78) arrived in Madras in 1777, a certain Mr. Bruce of Calcutta wrote the following to a friend of hers there:

I am clear for her coming round to this settlement immediately, where she will find such employment as she chooses, and of course, if not increase, prevent the diminution of her fortune. We have had one tolerable good painter here named Kettle, who acquired a good independency in three years. We have now another nam'd Paxton, but he is a very indifferent hand, and yet gets employment.[7]

Others also suggested she go to Calcutta where, as a Major Kyd wrote in February 1778, "I am confident (not in my own opinion alone, but on Mrs. Hastings' also) that you will have every reason to be satisfied in point of emolument from the exercises of painting, but also enjoying a society far more numerous, not less respectable and much less divided by party spirit, and if I mistake not from your description of things, of more liberal sentiments."[8]

Mrs. Hastings, referred to in Kyd's letter, is, of course, the wife of Warren Hastings, the first governor-general of British India. A remarkable man, Hastings was one of the most enlightened patrons of arts and letters, both European and Indian, in the entire history of British India. His

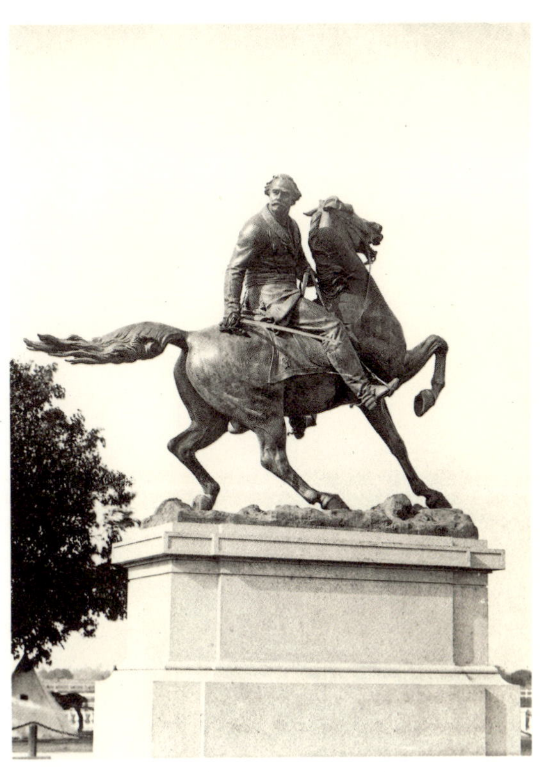

13. Bourne and Shepherd. Detail from *Statue of General Sir James Outram, Calcutta.* c. 1870. Albumen print. Walter Collection.

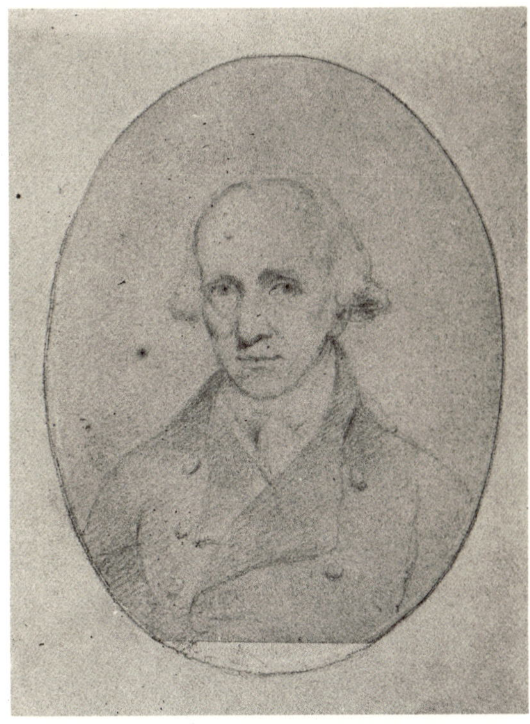

14. William Daniell. *Warren Hastings.* 1795. Pencil. Reproduced by permission of the India Office Library and Records (British Library).

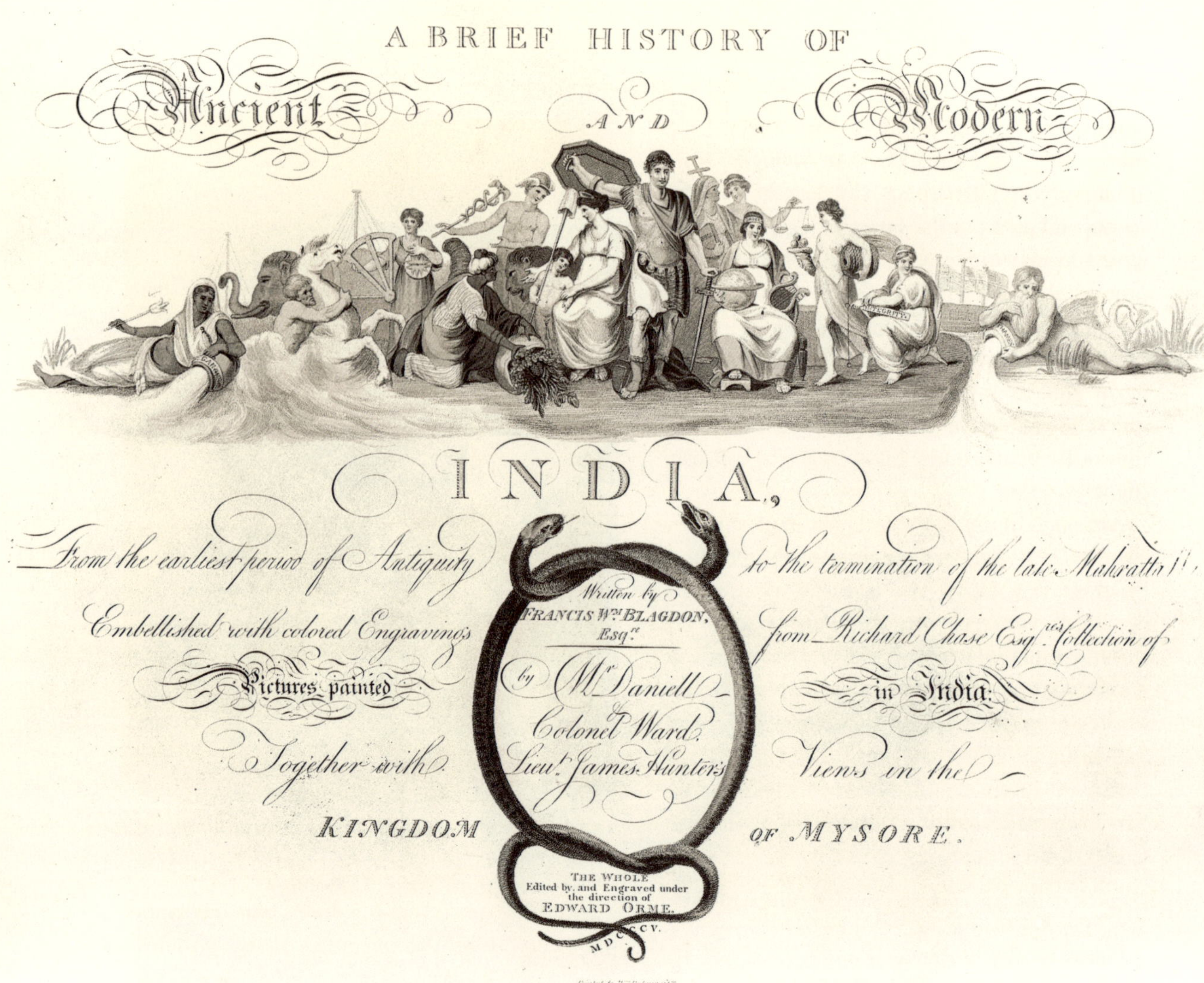

15. Edward Orme. Second title plate from *A Brief History of Ancient and Modern India*. 1805. Engraving. The Thomas John Willis Collection.

collection included both Indian and British art and not only did he himself commission works from visiting British artists but always found time to recommend them to others. Once a pet of the British royal family, Zoffany fell out of favor with the queen and left England in 1783. After brief sojourns to Madras and Calcutta, he arrived at the court of Oudh in June 1784 when Hastings was on an official visit there. According to Mildred Archer, a preeminent historian of British Indian art:

It is symptomatic of Hastings' desire to help Zoffany that on the evening of the very day following Zoffany's arrival he was taken by Hastings to start a portrait of the Prince [the Mogul prince Jawan Bakht who had come to Lucknow to meet Hastings]. Three further sittings in the presence of Hastings followed on June 12, 16 and 17. The same anxiety on Hastings' part to establish Zoffany with the court had induced him to take the artist with him to paint Asaf-ud-daula.[9]

Although Nawab Asaf-ud-daula himself was not much interested in English artists, his father Shuja-ud-daula had been a generous patron of Tilly Kettle. Other Indian courts patronized British artists, especially those of the nawabs of Carnatic in the south and of Murshidabad in Bengal. In the nineteenth century, many of the rulers and princes continued to patronize European painters and photographers, commissioning portraits and works recording the state visits of their British overlords.

The greatest lure of India was wealth. There was also a growing desire among the British public to have an artist's eye-witness account of the country rather than the pictures of fantasy that were conjured up by European engravers who had never visited the subcontinent. But, most professional artists who undertook the rigorous journey to India did so to amass private fortunes just like the nabobs who returned home with enormous wealth much to the chagrin and envy of the landed gentry, the commercial middle class, and the politicians. The mid-eighteenth century was not a particularly felicitous time for British artists in England, nor were there fortunes to be made in America. Under the circumstances, ambitious painters had little choice but to turn to India.

While Warren Hastings was laying the solid foundations of the British empire in India, the American colonies were engaged in their war of independence. It is understandable that the British public at home developed a taste for pictures depicting their nation's glorious triumphs on the various battlefields of India and why so many artists in Britain, who never set foot on Indian soil, painted pictures that blatantly celebrated British imperialism. It was the East that offered its abundant riches to Britannia, as symbolically depicted in an engraving of the pediment in the East India House on Leadenhall Street in London (fig. 15).

IV

It took considerable courage for a British artist to venture forth to India in the last quarter of the eighteenth century. Even before he could undertake the long, difficult, and tedious journey around the horn of Africa—*if* he could find a berth in an East Indiaman—he had to seek permission from the Company, pay a not inconsiderable deposit, and equip himself completely, with his personal effects and with all of the necessary tools of his craft, for the latter were not readily available in India. In 1786, when the unfortunate artist John Alefounder (1758–94) was recovering from a suicide attempt, Devis sold his friend's materials to help him settle his debts, which infuriated Alefounder. In the *Calcutta Gazette* of September 21, 1786, he pub-

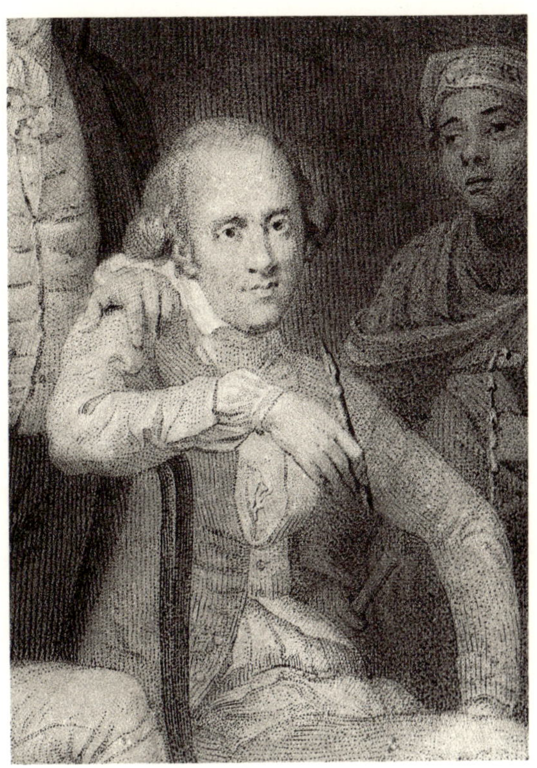

16. Johann Zoffany. Detail of fig. 65.

licly complained that Mr. Devis was not authorized to sell his pictures or his painting utensils and urgently requested their return, especially his *fitch* pencils, "as none could be procured in Calcutta, and he had none to paint with."[10]

Once they arrived in India, usually in Madras, most artists headed for Calcutta. In order to become successful, which meant receiving commissions, the artist needed the right introductions which he brought with him from home or procured from influential Anglo-Indians he befriended on the boat on the way to India. But, letters of recommendation alone did not guarantee success. An artist also had to lead an active social life and be well liked by the right people. Even the celebrated Zoffany, who was introduced to Calcutta society by none other than Lord Macartney, the governor of Madras, could hardly have succeeded if Hastings had not characterized him as "the greatest painter that has ever visited India, unless Alexander brought Appelles with him," and not found him ". . . gentle, lively, possessed of a high sense of honour, of a sound judgement, an uncommonly quick penetration, and a well-cultivated understanding, with a spirit of resignation and an equality of temper almost exceeding any within reach of my knowledge or recollection."[11] Even the eccentric and hypochondriacal Chinnery, "when not under the influence of low spirits," entered William Hickey in his diary, "was a cheerful, pleasant companion," who was seen at all the right parties.[12]

Even with enthusiastic letters of introduction and social charm, gaining commissions was not an easy task. Competition was stiff, especially when several artists were in the same settlement. During the last quarter of the eighteenth century, only Madras and Calcutta had the means and the taste to sustain a large number of British artists. Bombay never really entered the picture and except for James Wales and Robert Mabon (in India 1791–98), no professional artist of any merit or renown appears to have worked there. Even Calcutta became much too crowded at times, although occasionally an artist found himself alone in the city and did quite well. Ozias Humphry (1742–1810), one of the most distinguished miniaturists who visited India, was at first quite ecstatic about the response from the citizens of Calcutta but quickly became disillusioned and discouraged. Before leaving for the upcountry, he bitterly complained that the people of Calcutta

are ignorant of everything but likeness and smooth finishing. They require as much as they would in London and more. In proportion as they grow poor they grow nice and want good pennyworths—besides they see here daily the best and most finished pictures of Smart, Meyers, Cosway and all the best miniature painters whereas they never see one oil picture and Mr. Hickey a very weak painter is their best in oil except Zoffany who is soon to return."[13]

Hickey was alone in Calcutta, for Zoffany was away in Lucknow, where Humphry and Charles Smith (1749–1824) arrived at the same time. The simultaneous presence of the three artists in Lucknow had even the resident worried: "I know not what to do about Mr. Humphry and Mr. Smith, the painters. . . . If I

was to wish my greatest enemy the most perplexing situation, I should for the present make him Governor-General's Agent at the courts of the Shahzade and Vizier."[14] Several months later, Humphry was still complaining that he had not earned a rupee. He did subsequently receive commissions in Lucknow, and later in Benares, but returned to England a disappointed man.

Although some artists prospered more than others, India did not turn out to be the Eldorado that British artists hoped it would. Even those who earned a good deal found living in India quite expensive. As socializing was a necessary part of the routine, the artists had to return social favors at great expense. Neither housing nor food were cheap. The rent for a modest house in Calcutta was 500 rupees* a month and brandy and claret, which were consumed in great quantities, were costly, as they had to be imported from Europe. It was apparently a very serious matter when, during their journey through the south, a porter tripped and broke two bottles of William Daniell's madeira. In order to attract clients, artists had to live in a certain amount of luxury. They often had to have their houses built from scratch and it cost William Hickey 12,000 rupees just to furnish his. A large number of servants had to be maintained and journeys upcountry were not only laboriously long but also expensive. Even those who were successful in India did not necessarily return home rich.

The tragic career of the hapless artist Alefounder, who took his own life, is an example of how difficult it could be for the British artist in India. Alefounder tried everything to make a go of it. He cleaned Zoffany's altarpiece for the vestry of St. John's Church (cleaning old pictures was one way British artists supplemented their incomes; another was painting transparencies for festivities and backdrops for theatrical performances); he made engravings to accompany

*Here and following, costs are given in eighteenth-century figures. An exact equivalent in today's standards is virtually impossible to establish. The reader is provided with these figures for comparative purposes only.

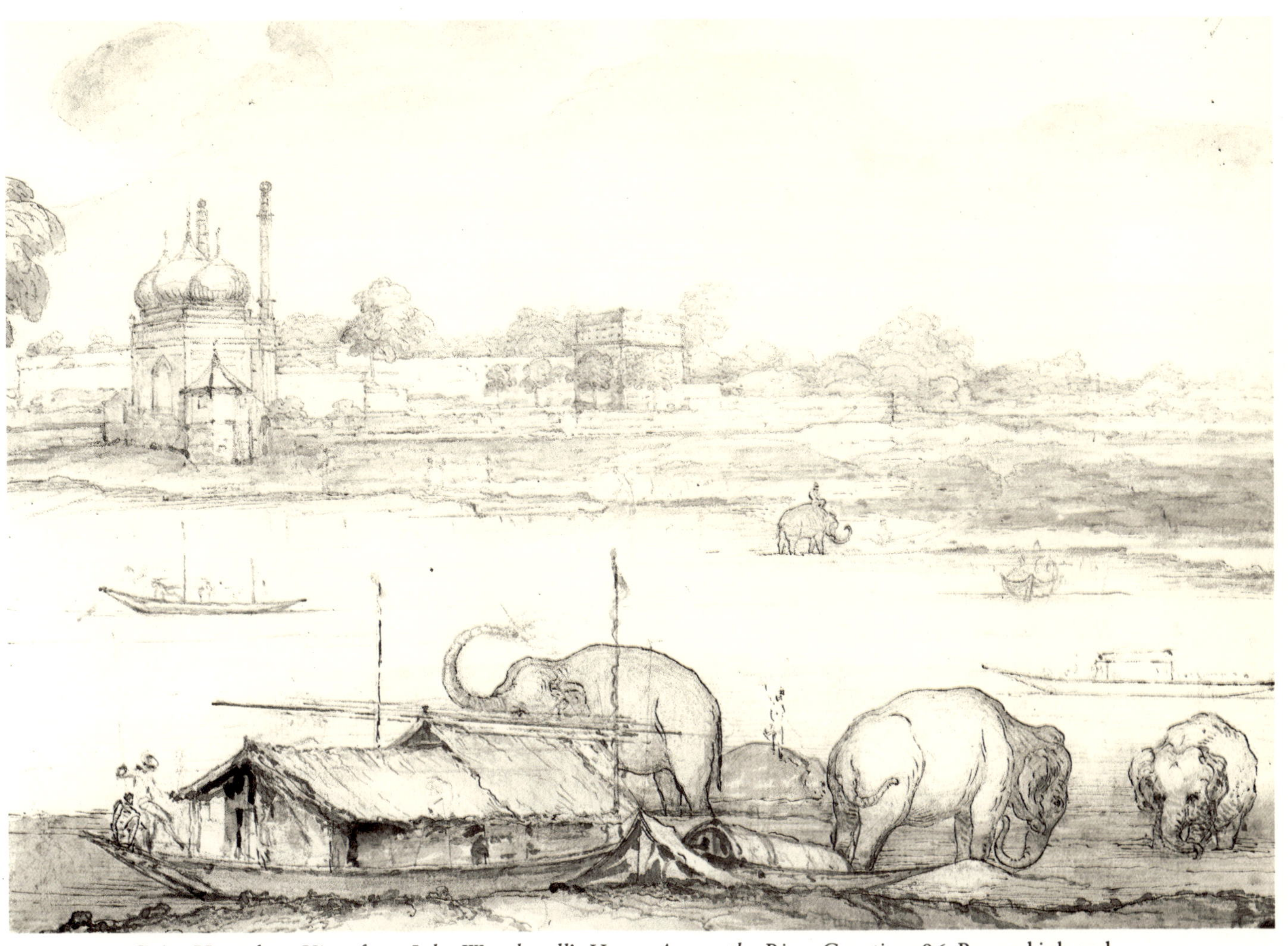

17. Ozias Humphry. *View from John Wombwell's House Across the River Gumti.* 1786. Pen and ink and wash. The British Library.

articles published in the *Asiatick Researches*; he even attempted to etch Sanskrit letters for Sir William Jones. He gave up portraiture and tried his hand at conversation pieces. He organized lotteries of his paintings (which was not an uncommon way for artists to diminish their stock), and drastically reduced his prices (indeed, a kind of a price war among artists of Calcutta was a familiar economic ploy). Alefounder's story may not be typical, but even successful artists like Devis and Chinnery never made their fortunes. Despite a long and enormously busy career, which had a profound influence upon a generation of many gifted amateurs, Chinnery was so heavily in debt that, abandoning his wife, he quietly sailed for

Macao on July 13, 1825, where he spent the rest of his life.

V

THE John Company was not very interested in supporting the arts; they rarely commissioned works and only occasionally bought any. When Hickey was in Madras he approached the Company with a proposal to visit the various regions and record the landscapes, monuments, races, and customs of the country as well as "British political and military transactions" so as to emphasize the development of the British as "imperial rulers of this eastern world."[15] The Company, however, was not interested and turned down Hickey's proposal. "However much,"

29

they wrote, "we wish the promotion of the useful and ingenious arts, the pursuits marked out by Mr. Hickey must be left to the exertions of voluntary enterprise and the encouragement of private patronage." Public memorials and monuments in most cities and communities were funded by the residents. While in matters of trade the Company was fiercely monopolistic, they recommended free enterprise in the arts.

Most commissions were obtained by the artists from the wealthier members of the community through direct contacts. Frequently, however, the artists resorted to newspaper advertising to secure business. In the *Madras Courier* of July 19, 1792, Devis advertised his "proposals for publishing by subscription a series of prints illustrative of the arts, manufactures and agriculture of Bengal from paintings taken from nature."[16] During their stay in India, the Daniells frequently placed advertisements in the local newspapers for their various series of landscapes and views of monuments. The following advertisement, which appeared in a Calcutta newspaper in 1798, provides a very clear idea of what the average charge was for a portrait:[17]

PORTRAIT PAINTING—Mr. Morris having taken a house in Wheeler Place, directly behind the Governor's house, begs leave to inform such ladies and gentlemen who may be inclined to favour him with their sittings, that he is ready to paint them at the following prices:

A head size,	15 gold mohurs
Three quarters,	20 gold mohurs
Kit cat,	25 gold mohurs
Half-length	40 do
Whole-length	80 do

Mr. Morris was not a well-known portraitist, and his charges were not exorbitant. While he was charging about 1,500 rupees for a full-length portrait, Zoffany had billed Warren Hastings 2,500 rupees for a similar size portrait of Mrs. Hastings and a hefty 15,000 rupees for a history painting. On the other hand, one could pick up an engraving by R. Brittridge of Calcutta of one of Zoffany's portraits of Warren Hastings for the relatively modest price of 32 rupees. It should be noted that in 1772, the East India Company in London paid Edward Penny only £210 for the historic picture of Clive receiving military funds (see fig. 36). In July 1789, Alefounder reduced his price to about 1,500 rupees for a full-length portrait but demanded advance payment. George Willison charged about 1,200 rupees for a full-length portrait but more than doubled his fee for an Indian ruler. Thus, the portrait prices varied depending on the reputation of the artist as well as the size of the patron's pocketbook. In general, however, only the wealthy could afford the better artists. As a Mrs. von Dankelman wrote to a friend, "Doubtless you will never guess the place from which I am writing to you. It is in the house of a painter where Lady Chambers is having her portrait done and I am wretched at not being rich enough to have a copy of it done for me, as although the painter's taste is ravishing, his price is extravagantly high. It is a Mr. Devis who is doing it and the likeness is perfect."[18]

Apart from direct sales, many works of art changed hands through public auctions and lotteries. As early as 1784, the *Calcutta Gazette* reported that, "the valuable collections of paintings, late the property of Augustus Cleveland, [William Hickey's friend and a patron of the miniaturist Martha Isaacs] deceased, would be sold by public auction on the 24th instant, consisting of the most capital views in the districts of Monghyr, Rajmahal, Boglipore, and the Jungleterry by Mr. Hodges."[19] Artists themselves frequently had to sell their works through similar auctions or resort to lotteries. In 1786, George Carter (1737–94), who visited India for only a year, and like Alefounder, was something of a social misfit, advertised a lottery of his paintings at 100 rupees a ticket. Even more successful artists like the Daniells and Devis had lotteries, which, however, did not generally prove very lucrative.

Public subscriptions were another way artists sold their works. Most engravings were sold by subscription. In the *Madras Gazette* of 1795, the following announcement appeared about Devis's prints of various Indian occupations: "Materials for completing the splendid under-

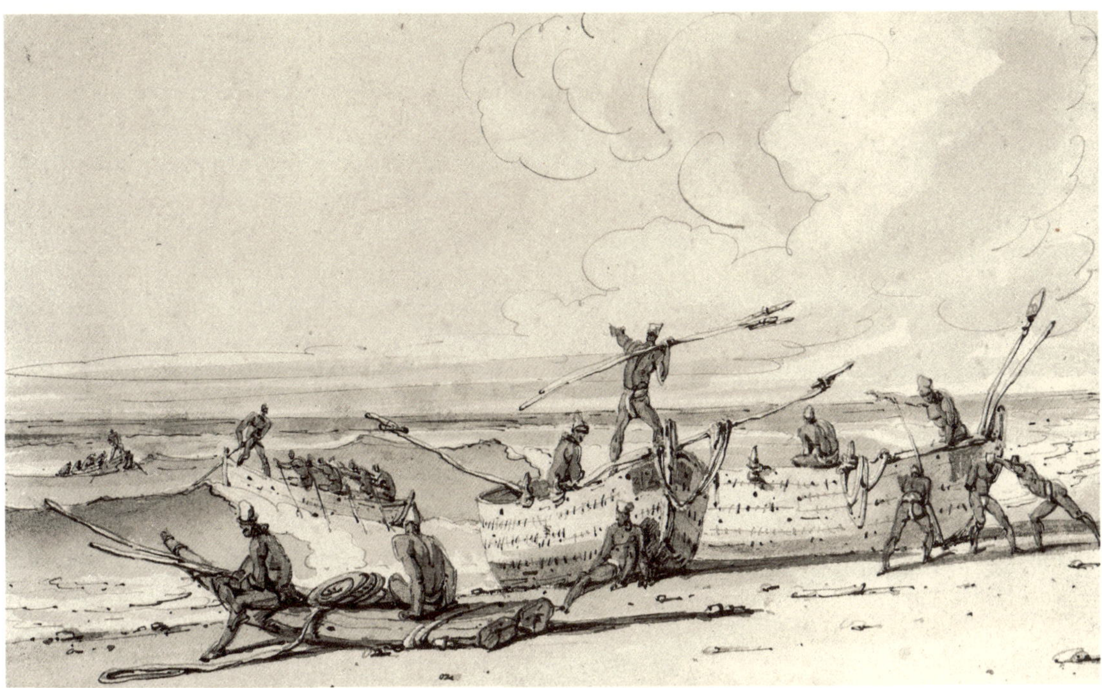

18. George Chinnery. *Surf Boats on the Beach, Madras.* 1807. Pen and ink and wash. Reproduced by permission of the India Office Library and Records (British Library).

taking of which this gentleman commenced nearly three years ago have been carefully collected and arranged. The views of the different arts, manufactures, and agricultural processes of the natives are all nearly finished, and the subscribers to the engravings to be executed from those views may expect copies in the course of twelve or fifteen months." [20] Chinnery tried the innovative approach of a serial advertised in the *Madras Courier* of November 26, 1806:

Proposals for publishing monthly a work to be entitled the "Indian Magazine and European Miscelany" . . . Mr. George Chinnery as Joint-Proprietor of the work, will furnish an etching monthly. The first number will exhibit a view of Madras, from the beach; and every succeeding publication will contain either a landscape from nature or figures illustrative of the character, and occupations of the natives; to be accompanied by a description of the plate. [21]

Altogether Chinnery managed nine etchings for the magazine which did not survive for long after he departed for Calcutta the following year. The etchings, however, are among the liveliest renderings of Madras done by any British artist in India, even if the figures are highly classical rather than Indian in form (fig. 18).

Many of the portraits of civilian and military officials and the works of art in the various public buildings and squares in the cities and settlements of British India were paid for by public donations. Public meetings were generally called to select the artist and the amount of money to be raised. These meetings were open both to the local Europeans and wealthy and prominent Indians. At a meeting called in 1793 to commission Devis to paint a portrait of Governor-General Lord Cornwallis, the fee was set at a generous 20,000 rupees, presumably because one of the speakers felt that the artist, "stands in need of our bounty only from having too often given way to those generous sentiments in support of others which I now call forth on his behalf." [22] In contrast, Chinnery was paid only 5,000 rupees in 1822 when some of the Indian lawyers of Calcutta commissioned a portrait of J. H. Harrington who had just retired as chief justice. In December of the same year, a meeting was held in Calcutta's town hall to discuss how to commemorate the impending retirement of

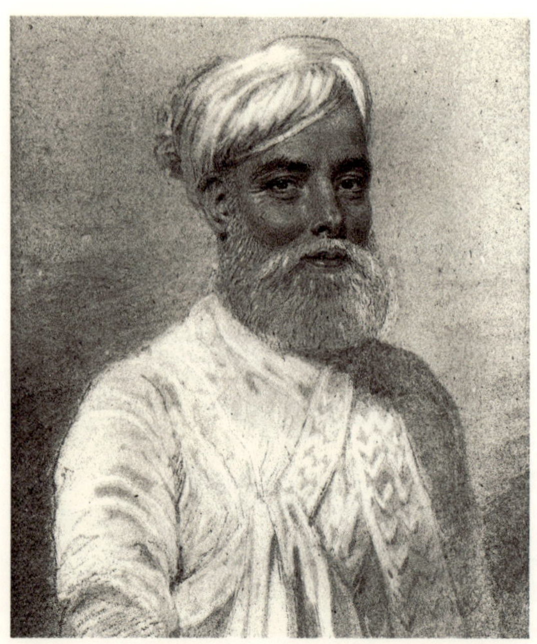

19. John Smart. *Muhammad Ali, Nawab of Arcot.* c. 1788. Miniature on paper. By courtesy of the Board of Trustees of the Victoria and Albert Museum.

the governor-general, the Marquis of Hastings (in office 1813–22). Apparently, the public wanted to commission a bronze equestrian statue, but the Marquis felt this would be too costly. They therefore decided upon a portrait and a marble statue to be installed in the town hall. While both the British and the Indian communities often joined together in commemorating retired or departed governors and generals, the Indians often independently commissioned British artists to render portraits of enlightened Britons who had been particularly enthusiastic about Indian causes. Thus, when H. H. Wilson, the great Orientalist and Sanskrit scholar, left for England in 1830, a dozen prominent Bengalis led by Prince Dwarakanath Tagore raised 1,500 rupees for a portrait by George Beechy (1797–1852).

VI

THE merchant princes of Calcutta were not the only Indian patrons of British artists between 1757 and 1857. In Madras, the Nawab of Arcot, Muhammad Ali, had quickly become an Anglo-

phile and not only employed an Englishman, George Paterson, as his advisor in 1770, but filled his palace with furniture, mechanical toys, and other bric-à-brac from England (fig. 19). He also affected British mannerisms and took breakfast and afternoon teas with his family. Muhammad Ali began a trend that has left a permanent impression on India. European-style furniture, even though no longer imported from the continent, remains an essential part of the Indian lifestyle, and although the Indian may not relish kippers and kidneys for breakfast, drinking tea and coffee remains as yet another legacy of the British.

Muhammad Ali was also probably the first Indian ruler to patronize British artists. His first commission was given to Francis Swain Ward (c. 1734–94), who worked for the Company. He also acquired portraits by Tilly Kettle that are among the finest renderings of Indian rulers by British artists. Muhammad Ali commissioned his own and his family's portraits from British artists as gifts. In 1774–75, he persuaded George Willison to paint six portraits, two of which were sent as presents to King George III and the East India Company offices in London. Willison more than doubled his normal charges for these royal commissions. When the artist left for England, the nawab still owed him £1,400, though he had already received as much as £20,000 while in Madras. As Mildred Archer has noted, Muhammad Ali may have purchased subjects other than of his family from Willison. Apparently, the miniaturist Smart also had difficulty getting his fee from Muhammad Ali, even though he painted for the royal family from 1785 to 1795. In 1801, Thomas Hickey was commissioned by Nawab Azim-ud-daula, Muhammad Ali's grandson, for a portrait which was a gift for Lord Clive, the governor of Madras.

Another local court that patronized British artists was that of Murshidabad in Bengal, whose last independent king was the impetuous Siraj-ud-daula, betrayed by his generals and defeated at Plassey by Clive in 1757. Several British artists visited Murshidabad to paint both

32

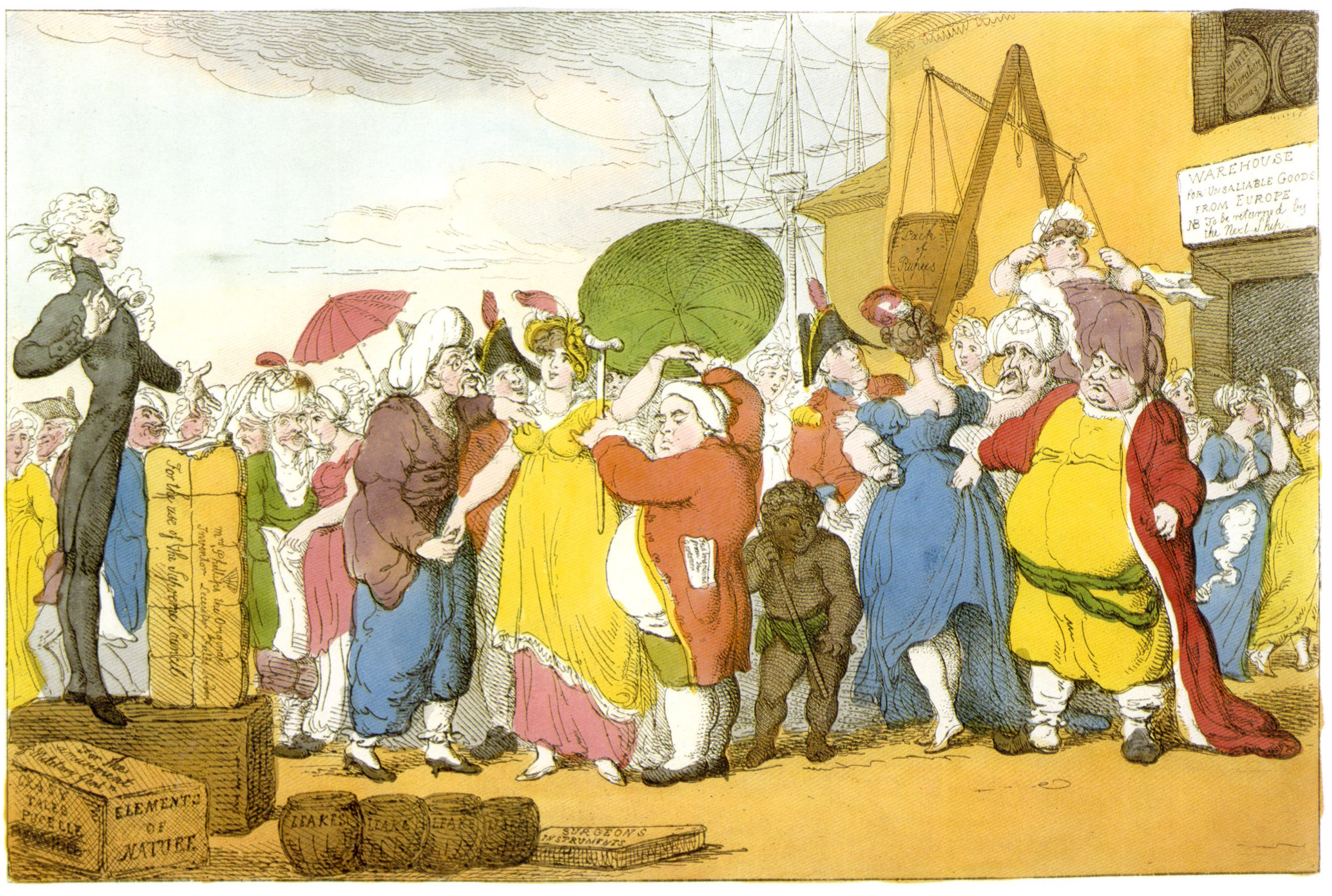

COLORPLATE 2.
Anonymous. *A Sale of English Beauties in the East Indies.* c. 1800.
Colored engraving. Walter Collection.

for their countrymen living there as well as for the court. The residency of Murshidabad was a highly desirable assignment. As William Hickey sardonically observed, the post was particularly lucrative not only because "the whole stipend or salary allowed by Government to the Nabob passed through such Resident's hands, in which channel a considerable portion of it always stuck to his fingers," but also because the resident served as the sole agent for "purchasing and paying for every European article the Nabob wished to have."[23] No wonder Robert Pott paid Sir John D'Oyly a persuasive £34,500 to relinquish the post early. Kettle appears to have been the first artist to visit Murshidabad where the nawab's mother commissioned a portrait of her son for Warren Hastings. The nawab was also painted by George Farington (1752–88) who reached Calcutta in 1783 but seems to have left for Murshidabad in 1785, having found too much competition in the capital from Zoffany, Charles Smith, and Thomas Hickey.

On the west coast, James Wales became the painter at the Mahratta court at Poona through the courtesy of Sir Charles Malet, resident from 1786–97. A military people, the Mahrattas had little interest in the arts, but were quite generous in their patronage of Wales, perhaps in hopes of pleasing the British or giving the appearance of being cultured. They not only commissioned several portraits of themselves, but pictures of women and animals as well. Between Malet and the Mahrattas, Wales was kept so busy that he often dispatched his assistant Robert Mabon to sketch for him. Mabon's sketches are fascinating for their rich details, lively spontaneity, and subtle humor. Mahratta dominance ended in 1818 after two wars with the British, during which many of Wales's paintings appear to have been destroyed.

Ironically, the court that proved to be the most troublesome for the Company also provided the British artists with their most sustained and rewarding patronage. This was the court of Oudh in the glittering city of Lucknow. Warren Hastings was impeached upon his return to England because of his dealings with

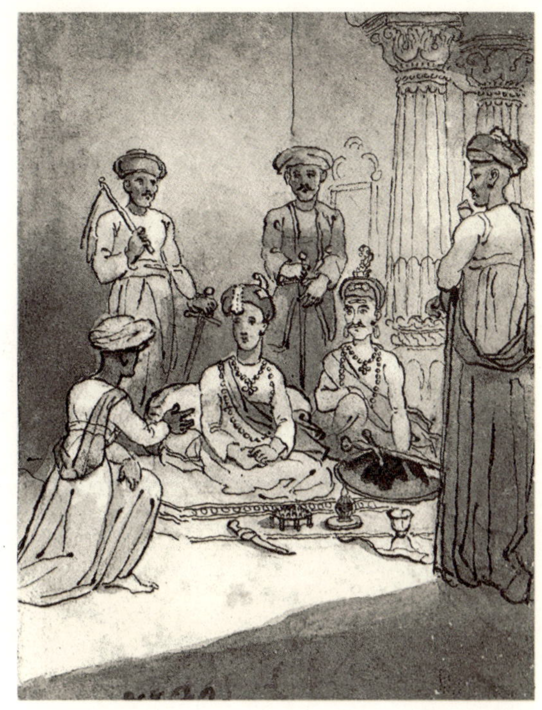

20. Robert Mabon. Preliminary sketch for Wales's projected painting of the *Mahratta Peshwa and his Ministers*. c. 1792. Pen and ink and watercolor. Yale Center for British Art, Paul Mellon Collection.

Oudh while governor-general and Lucknow again loomed large in the British imagination during and after the events of 1857. Kettle, Zoffany, Smith, Home, Humphry, Renaldi, George Place (d. circa 1809), and George Beechy were among the many British artists who worked for the court. Home and Beechy were employed by the court as Painters to the King of Oudh.

Indeed, until 1857, Lucknow was no less lively a center for British artists than Calcutta and Madras. Notwithstanding his addiction to frivolities and his attachment to "low, ill-born and base-minded associates," Nawab Asuf-ud-daula's (ruled 1775–97) was a remarkably lively, cultured, and cosmopolitan city with a sizeable European community. Apart from the British officials, there were several important Europeans such as Colonel Antoine Polier (1741–95) and Major Claud Martin (1735–1800) in the nawab's employ. When Polier, a

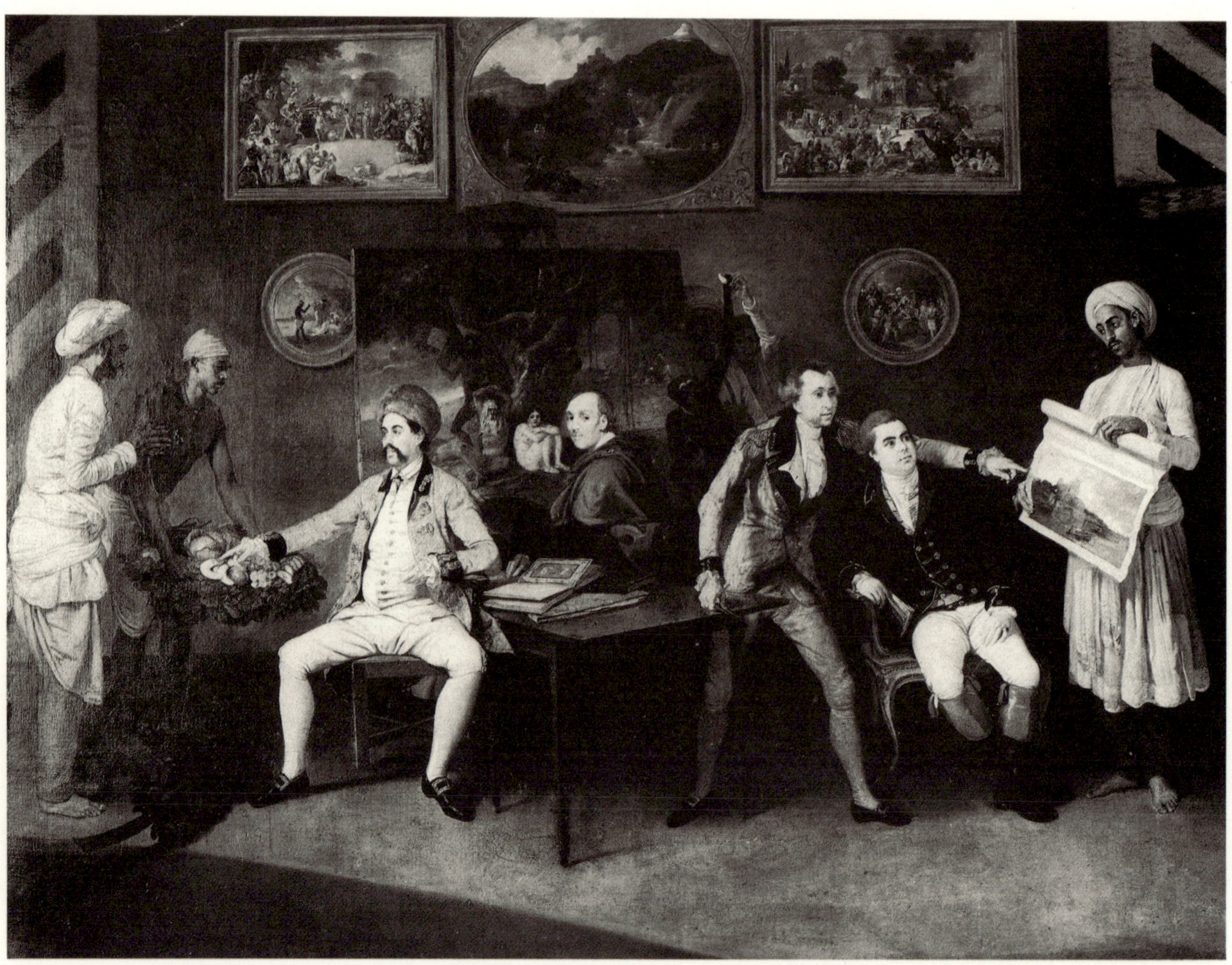

21. Johann Zoffany. *Colonel Antoine Polier with his Friends Claud Martin, John Wombwell and the Artist.* 1786. Oil on canvas. Victoria Memorial Hall.

Swiss architect and engineer, left India, none other than Sir William Jones, the British judge and great Orientalist, remarked, "A better disposed or better informed man never left India." Martin was a French adventurer who worked for the Company until 1779 when he joined the nawab's services; he remained in Lucknow until his death. An extremely rich man, he was a keen naturalist, bibliophile, and munificent philanthropist. Both Polier and Martin were enthusiastic collectors of art, European as well as Indian. John Mordaunt, a son of the Earl of Peterborough, was another colorful Englishman who shared the nawab's inordinate fondness for cockfights, immortalized in Zoffany's paintings and engravings that capture so eloquently the cosmopolitanism and gaeity, the freedom and laxity, that prevailed in Lucknow at that time.

VII

APART from the works of the British artists in India, much British and some continental European art came into the country through trade. Newspaper advertisements and accounts provide us with some idea of the kind of art that was sold in eighteenth-century Calcutta. Some of the works that found their way into the Indian marketplace were brought over by the artists themselves. One, George Carter, "whose spirit," according to Farington, "is not of a common kind," brought a group of his own paintings of English subjects that he was apparently unable to sell while in India. On returning to England, however, he continued to paint with an eye on the British-Indian market. He sent one such painting, a portrait of Cornwallis with Tipu's sons, to Calcutta in 1792,

34

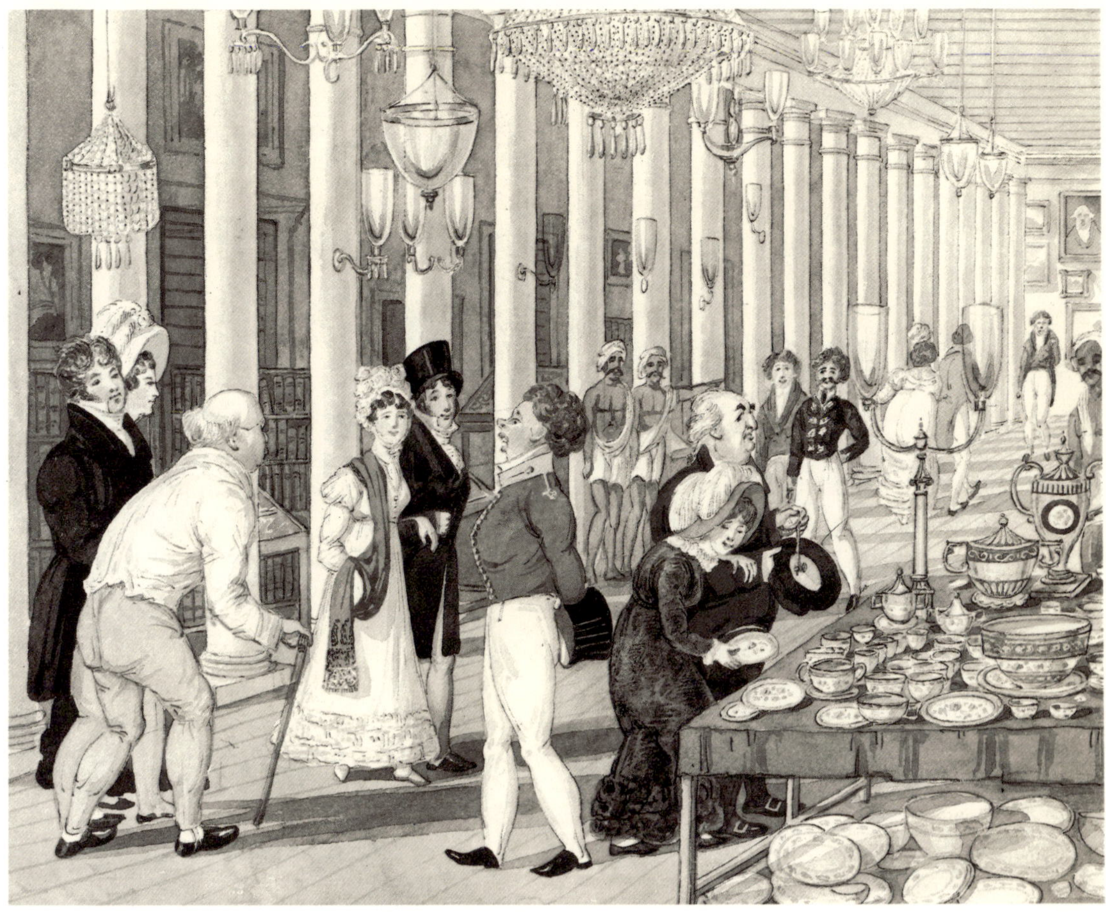

22. Sir Charles D'Oyly. *Taylor's Emporium, Calcutta*. c. 1825–28. Watercolor. By courtesy of the Board of Trustees of the Victoria and Albert Museum.

and although the *Bombay Courier* touted it as combining "the brilliancy of Titian with the softness of Correggio," it failed to sell. Old Masters and Baroque pictures were never the rage in the Calcutta market. The Calcutta establishment Pengelly, Mortimer and Co. organized many sales of artworks which they frequently advertised in the local newspapers. Sir Charles D'Oyly's *Taylor's Emporium, Calcutta* provides us with a good idea of what these art dealing establishments were like (fig. 22).

On January 30, 1826, Pengelly, Mortimer and Co. proudly announced that they had received "the immense painting of the Battle of Waterloo; which, having been exhibited to the admiring thousands of the British Metropolis, has been sent to the city of palaces for the gratification of the Indian community." [24] The admission price to view the painting was set by "several scientific gentlemen" at four rupees per person. However, anticipating that many viewers would return frequently, a monthly ticket was available for ten rupees. The 13½-by-8½-foot painting in its gold frame could be purchased for £900. The advertisement further informed the public that the monumental canvas was the combined effort of three gentlemen: Alexander Sauerweid was responsible for the design, George Clint, A. R. A. for the portraits, and Abraham Cooper, R. A. for the painting. The ultimate fate of this picture is not known. It is interesting that as early as 1826, a Calcutta commercial gallery was charging such a high admission price in anticipation of a "blockbuster" exhibition. The usual fee was much less, as seen in an 1831 newspaper announcement of an exhibition of drawings and paintings organized by the Brush Club at the town hall which lists the price of a single admission ticket for a gentleman at two rupees and a season ticket at four (ladies were gallantly admitted free of charge). This is the earliest extant record of a publicly organized exhibition in Calcutta, if not in India, and presumably, the objects were borrowed from local private collections. After the 1850s, regular exhibitions were organized by the various schools of art founded in the three Presidencies.

Indian rulers and wealthy merchants, especially of Calcutta, had large collections of European paintings and furniture. The taste for things European was already evident by the eighteenth century, and became even more fashionable after 1857. Toward the end of the nineteenth century, most maharajas abandoned their traditional palaces and practices in favor of a more European lifestyle complete with plumbing and chandeliers, paintings and sculptures, all of which were imported from Europe by the boatload. The Marble Palace of the Mullicks in Calcutta and the Salar Jung Museum in Hyderabad are among the two most glaring examples of this new cult of Europeanization.

VIII

THE vast amount of Anglo-Indian literature consisting of memoirs, travelogues, poetry, and fiction constitutes an incredibly rich source of information about the British perception of India. Some of the artists also left behind fascinating accounts of their own experiences in India which are no less interesting than their sketches and paintings. Many also wrote notes and com-

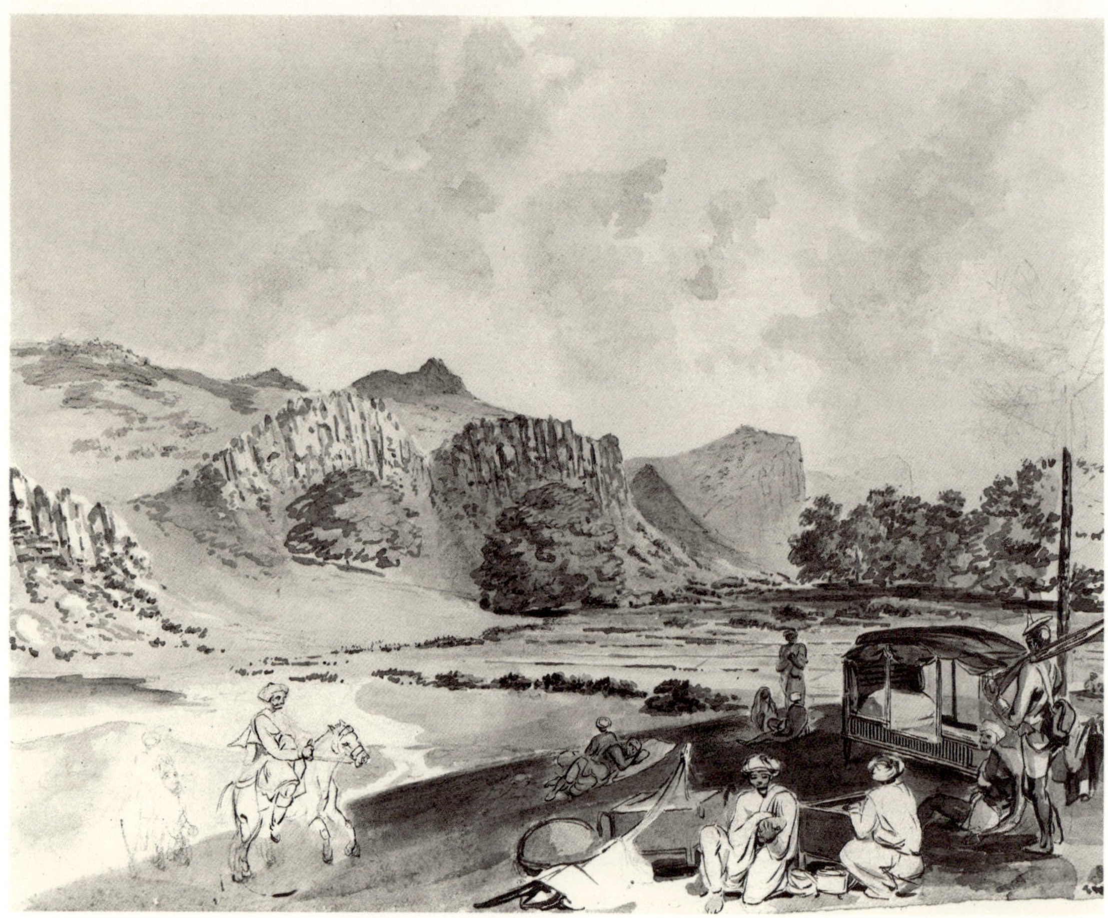

23. Samuel Davis. *In India, On the March*. c. 1785. Gray wash and watercolor over pencil. Yale Center for British Art, Paul Mellon Collection.

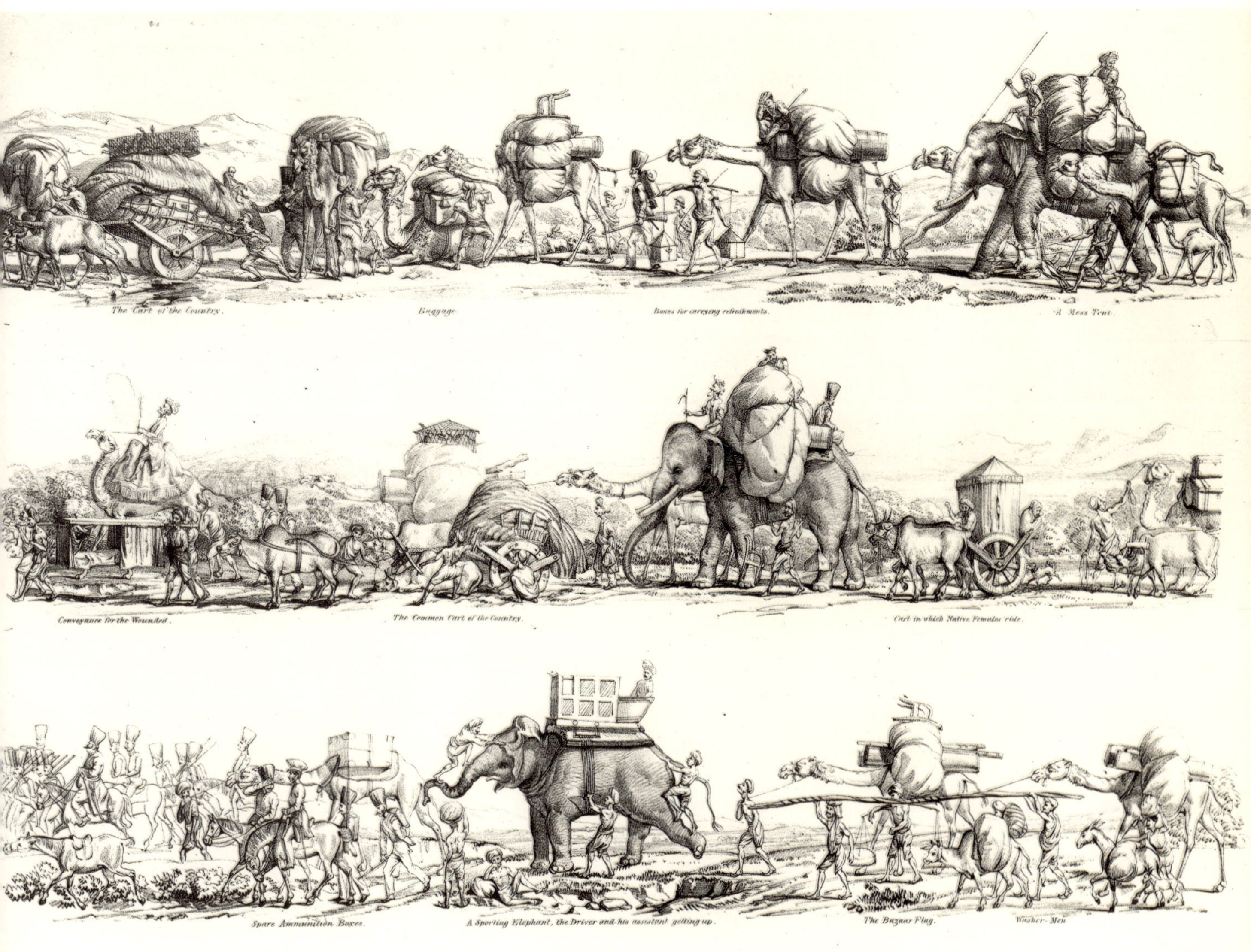

24. Anonymous, *Bengal Army on the March*. c. 1845. Lithograph. Walter Collection.

ments to accompany their prints which are highly informative and remarkably sensitive and insightful.

From the detailed accounts left by the Daniells, for instance, we know what it was like to travel across India almost two centuries ago. Before the days of steamboats and railways, the river Ganga (Ganges) was the main thoroughfare for journeys between Calcutta and the up-country, and so it loomed large in everyone's imagination. There is perhaps no other river in the world that has inspired so much literature and art, especially from foreign visitors. These journeys were undertaken in large, comfortable boats known as budgerows. One eyewitness account of a flotilla of three hundred boats that left Calcutta for a journey up the river reads:

With budgerows, horse boats, baggage boats, cook boats, hospital and soldier boats, the scene was the most extraordinary that can be conceived. Every officer had a sort of Noah's ark attached to his budgerow, and the uproar to fill it with its various animals was terrible: unwilling horses, and obstinate cows, with goats and sheep, running in all quarters; men, women, and children, of all colours and costumes; carriages, gigs, palanquins, coops of poultry,

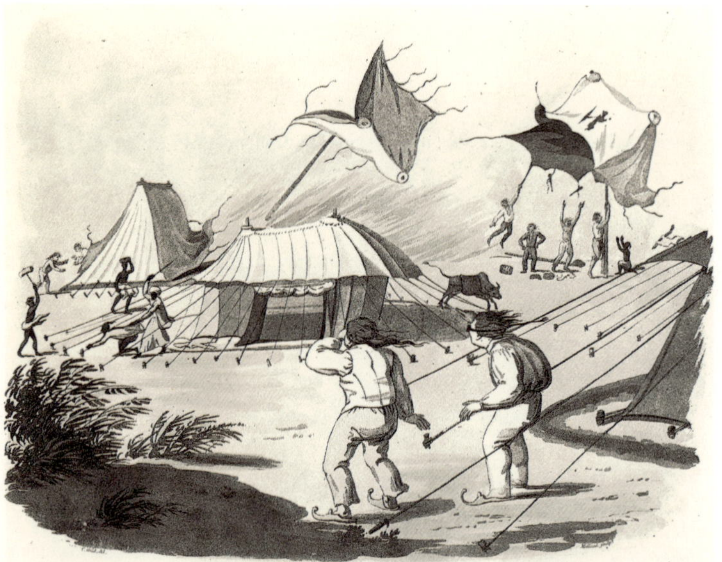

25. Charles Gold. *Tents Blowing up in a Storm.*
c. 1806. Lithograph. Private Collection.

ducks, geese, and turkeys, scattered about, cackling
and hissing with all their might were to be seen in
every direction.[25]

Where the journey involved traveling over
land, the artists prudently joined up with a
company of British soldiers who were on the
march. It was necessary to travel in the company of British forces for the territory traversed
by the artists was often not under direct British
control. Hodges had to abandon his plans to
travel beyond Agra for precisely this reason.
Furthermore, travelers were frequently the targets of large groups of brigands. On their journey through northern India, the Daniells were
attacked twice by robbers. These marches were
elaborate and expensive. *Bengal Army on the
March* (fig. 24) provides a good idea of what
was involved as does the following description
of the Daniells' preparations for a trip through
the south:

Their entourage consisted of forty-seven people including eleven bearers each for two palanquins, a
syce (or groom) each for two horses and four drivers
for a bullock cart, besides three bullocks for the carriage of their tents and baggage. Seven porters were
engaged to carry the provisions (including one for
"Fowls etc.") and four porters for transporting the

drawing tables and a cot. Among their personal attendants were a major domo, a *dubash* to look after
money matters, a cook, two peons, one armed guard,
a Portuguese and a Mussulman boy.[26]

Despite all of the preparations and precau-
tions, mishaps and misadventures commonly
occurred. Much of the journey involved going
through dense jungles and crossing rivers without bridges but the artists were undaunted in
their search for the unknown and the exotic.
Visiting Sher Shah's mausoleum in Bihar,
Hodges noted, "This being the season of the
rains, it was with difficulty I could pass in my
palankeen; in many places the bearers waded
above their middle in water, and the whole
ground was one continued swamp."[27] Writing
about their trip to Srinagar in the mountains of
Garhwal, the Daniells observed, "In these high
situations the traveller encounters no villages;
he must carry with him the means of subsis-
tence, or perish. Taka-ca-munda is a solitary
resting place; a plain stone building erected
near the barren summit of one of the highest
mountains, for the accommodation of benighted
wanderers, or to afford an occasional shelter
from the storms that vex these cloud-enveloped
hills."[28] Storms of one kind or another were always a menace, as we see in a very lively rendering by Charles Gold (d. 1842), based no doubt
on his own experience (fig. 25). Another amateur artist, James Baillie Fraser (1783–1856),
who has left us some delightful views of the
Himalayas, wrote in his journal, "Our encamp-
ing ground for the night was not far from
hence, at the top of the glen: it was a cave under
a large stone, called Bheem-ke-Udar; in a dry
night it is sufficiently comfortable, but rain
would readily beat in. In this cavern, and under a few other large stones around it, there
was some shelter though scanty, for our company. . . ."[29]

The artists were dedicated and sincere in
their desire to know the country; in the words
of Thomas Daniell, "to acquire some local ideas
of those distant regions which it has been the
good fortune of our friends or relatives to explore." In many ways the eighteenth-century

38

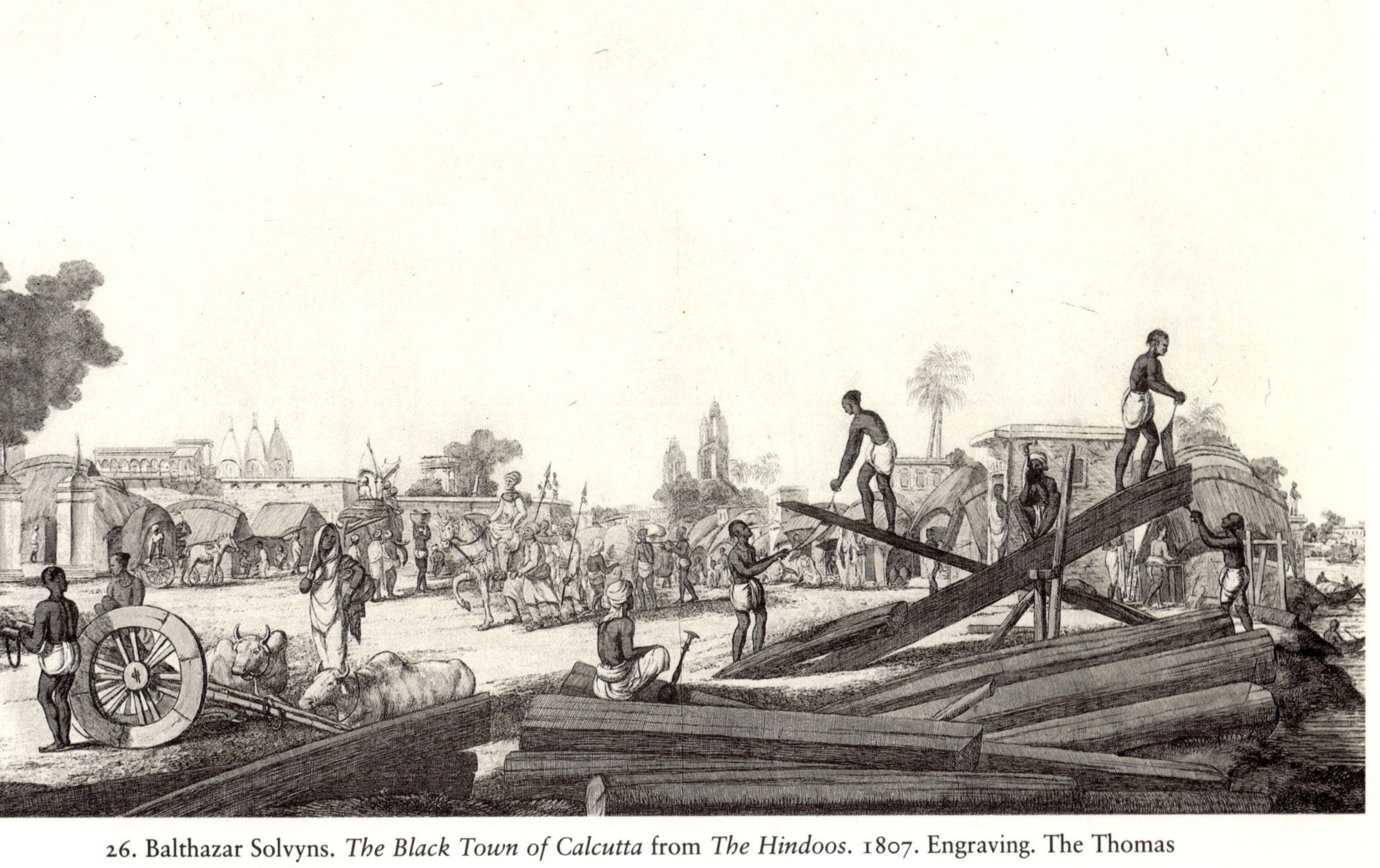

26. Balthazar Solvyns. *The Black Town of Calcutta* from *The Hindoos*. 1807. Engraving. The Thomas John Willis Collection.

British artists were pioneer explorers who accomplished the same things that generations of official surveyors and organized expeditions achieved in a more scientific way. In fact, the Daniells' exploration of uncharted areas of the Himalayas and searches for the source of the Ganges were of considerable help to the Company's cartographers. In such instances, financial reward was not the principal motivation. As Thomas Daniell wrote in an eloquent passage in his introduction to *A Picturesque Voyage to India by the Way of China*, published in 1810:

It was an honourable feature in the late century, that the passion for discovery, originally kindled by the thirst for gold, was exalted to a higher and nobler aim than commercial speculations. Since this new era of civilisation, a liberal spirit of curiosity has promted undertakings to which avarice lent no incentive, and fortune annexed no reward: associations have been formed not for piracy, but humanity; Science has had her adventures, and philanthropy her achievements; The shores of Asia have been invaded by a race of students with no rapacity but for lettered relics: by naturalists, whose cruelty extends not to one human inhabitant; by philosophers ambitions for the extirpation of error, and the diffusion of truth. It remains for the artist to claim his part in these guiltless spoliations, and to transport to Europe the picturesque beauties of those favoured regions.[30]

IX

AMONG the early British artists, Hodges, the Daniells, Forbes, Fraser, and D'Oyly were especially perceptive and often ecstatically responsive to the sights and smells, the colors and shapes of their environment. Some of their com-

39

ments and observations verge on the poetic, while others are amusing and illuminating in a most unexpected manner. Certain sights and monuments so fascinated the artists, such as the Ganges, Benares, the banyan tree, women by the river or the well, that they have become almost stereotypes of British art with Indian subjects. The monuments and ruins, the temples and mosques, were another source of joy for the landscape painters and the amateurs.

Apart from seeking their fortunes and the "higher and nobler" aims mentioned by Thomas Daniell, artists had varying reasons for going to India. Solvyns reiterates that he embarked upon his monumental project to record the customs and manners of the country partly for sentimental reasons. "The work was undertaken under the Idea, that a delineation from Nature of such objects in Hindostan, as are interesting from their beauty or novelty to an European, or any way elucidatory of the habits, manners and features of the various tribes . . . would be acceptable to the Public."[31] He goes on to say that he hopes his pictures will bring back memories of their sojourn in India once the Anglo-Indians were back home in Britain. This remained a principal motive behind the voluminous quantity of depictions of human interest subjects by amateur British as well as by Indian artists.

An amateur who also served in the army, Colonel Charles Ramus Forrest (active 1802–27) appears simply to have been charmed by the romantic landscape of India and wanted to transport his sense of exhilaration to his fellow countrymen. In his preface to his *A Picturesque Tour along the Rivers Ganges and Jumna*

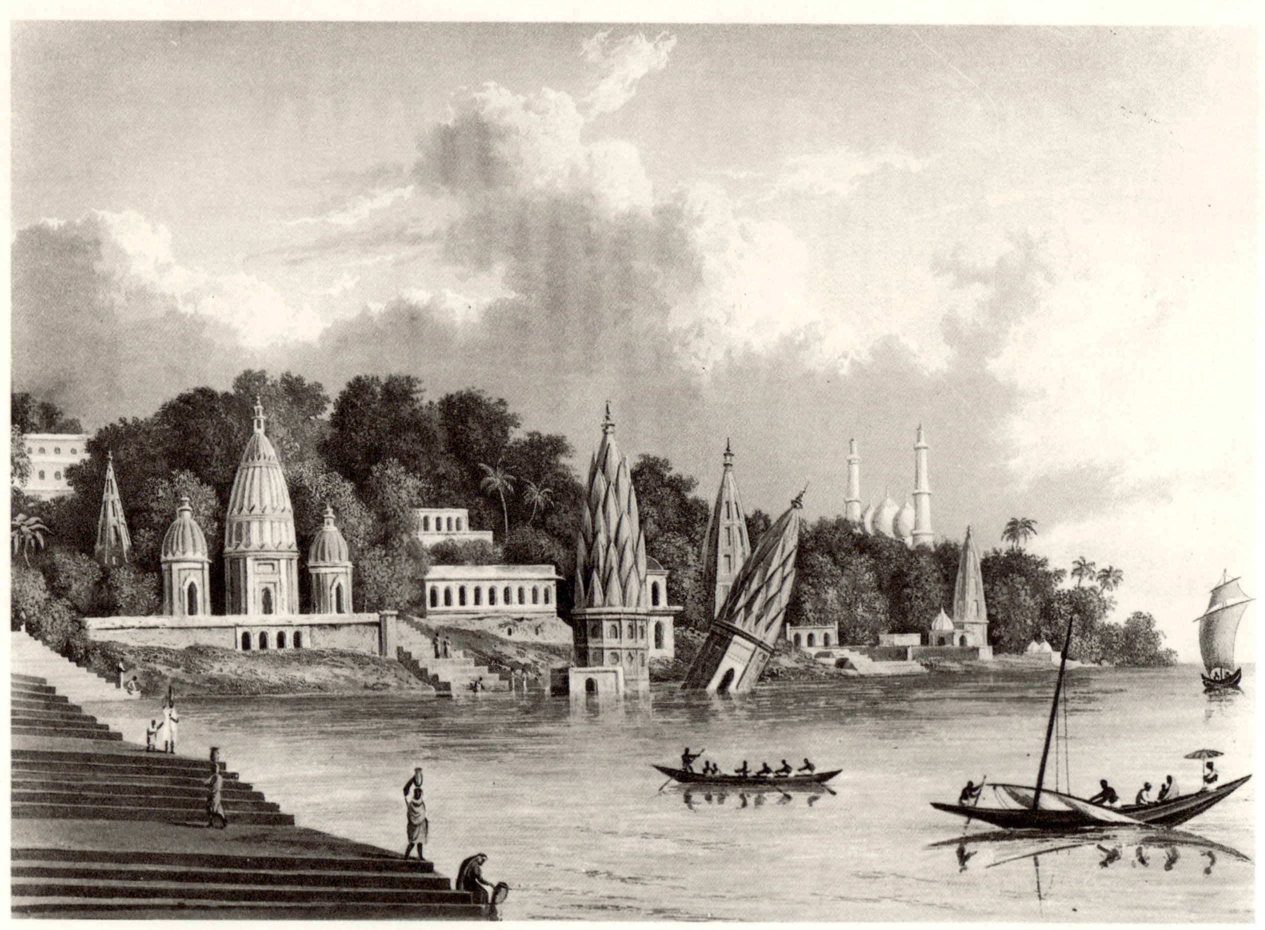

27. Colonel Charles Ramus Forrest. A view from *A Picturesque Tour Along the Rivers Ganges and Jumna*. 1824. Engraving. By courtesy of the Board of Trustees of the Victoria and Albert Museum.

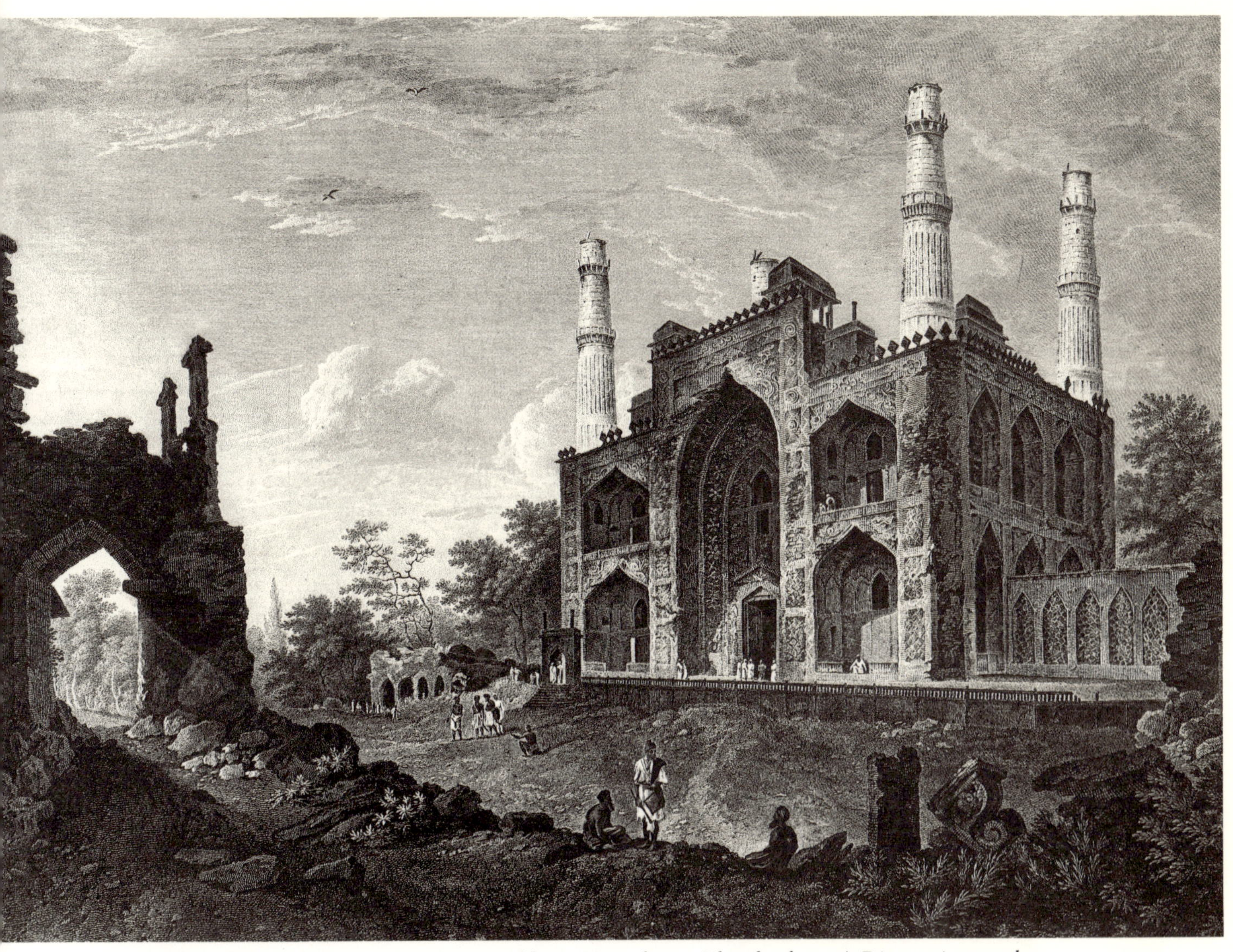

28. William Hodges. *Entrance Gateway to Akbar's Mausoleum, Sikandra* from *A Dissertation on the Prototypes of Architecture, Hindoo, Moorish, and Gothic.* 1786. Aquatint. Reproduced by permission of the India Office Library and Records (British Library).

(1824), he not only tells us how he always drew, and often colored, on the spot "while the magic effects of the scenes represented were still impressed on his mental vision," but also hopes that "the reader will recollect with indulgence, that the colouring of the views, which so far exceeds that of the scenery of Europe, is but a just portrait of the enchanting features of India, eternally glowing in the brilliant glory of the resplendent Asiatic sun."[32]

James Forbes's reasons for painting India are among the most moving:

The manuscripts from which these volumes are compiled, and the drawings which illustrate them, have formed the principal recreation of my life. The pursuit beguiled the monotony of four Indian voyages, cheered a solitary residence at Anjengo and Dhuboy, and softened the long period of absence from my native country: it has since mitigated the rigour of captivity, and alleviated domestic sorrow. Drawing to me had the same charm as music to the soul of harmony.[33]

After 1857, fewer professional artists visited India and those that did usually went with spe-

41

cific commissions. For instance, William Simpson was sent by Day and Son, the principal lithographers in London, to do a series on the Mutiny, although by the time he arrived, it was over. Simpson wrote:

The public were interested in the cause of the Mutiny, and in everything connected with the people of India. More interest had been excited in England about that country than had existed before. Mr. William Day and I talked all this over, and finally it was determined that I should go out with the purpose of making drawings for a large and important work that should do justice to such a subject.[34]

Interestingly, Simpson also tells us that before leaving for India he "spent a considerable time in the library of the India House, then in Leadenhall Street, looking over books about India, such as Daniels' [sic], to see what had been already done, and to get hints as to places I ought to visit."[35] Just as the Daniells had retraced Hodges's journey, Simpson closely followed that of the Daniells in his fourteen thousand-mile trip by land and water across India. And like the Daniells, he visited some uncharted areas of the Himalayas, had some exciting adventures, and was captivated by the isolation and charm of the mountains.

Simpson returned to India some years later with the Prince of Wales as an official artist attached to the prince's retinue. Other artists were summoned from England on special occasions to serve as visual chroniclers and court artists. Valentine Prinsep was sent by the queen in 1877 to record the durbar and draw the princes. Edward Lear appears to have been one of the few professionals who visited India for personal reasons.

X

OF the many British artists who left accounts of their travels through India, William Hodges remains one of the most sensitive and poetic. His writings are as delicate and romantic as his paintings. He was as impressed by the "inexpressible grandeur" of the Ganges as he was charmed by the "simplicity and primitive appearance" of the people. Admiring the river, he wrote, "the meandering of the river Ganges through the flat country, and glittering through an immense plain, highly cultivated, as far as the extent of the horizon, where the eye is almost at a loss to discriminate the termination of the sky and land."[36] Upon seeing a group of Moslem women visiting tombs at night, he wrote, "It is both affecting and curious to see them proceeding in groups, carrying lamps in their hands, which they place at the head of the tomb: the effect, considered in a picturesque light, is highly beautiful; with that of sentiment, it is delightful." He was ecstatic about the conditions of light in India which gratified the eye and filled his mind with both gaeity and tranquility. "It was not uncommon to see the manufacturer at his loom, in the cool shade attended by his friend softening his labour by the tender strains of music."

Hodges seems to have been ambivalent about Indian sculpture. On one occasion he clearly could not be enthusiastic and wrote, "Considering these works, as I do, with the eye of an artist, they are only to be paralleled with the rude essays of the ingenious Indians I have met with in Otaheite, and on other islands in the South seas." However, he admired the Hindu artisans' skillful carving of architectural ornaments, which he found superior to that of the Moslems. "Some of the sculptures in their buildings are very highly to be commended for their beauty of the execution; they may, indeed, be said to be very finely drawn, and cut with a perculiar sharpness." Hodges was much more responsive to Indian architecture. He was, of course, ecstatic about the Taj Mahal. "The effect is such as, I confess, I never experienced from any work of art. The fine materials, the beautiful forms, and the symmetry of the whole, with the judicious choice of situation, far surpasses anything I ever beheld." At Sikandra, overwhelmed by the great mausoleum built for the Mogul emperor Akbar, Hodges remarked, "A blazing eastern sun shining full on this building, composed of such varied materials, produces a glare of splendour almost beyond imagination of an inhabitant of these northern climates to con-

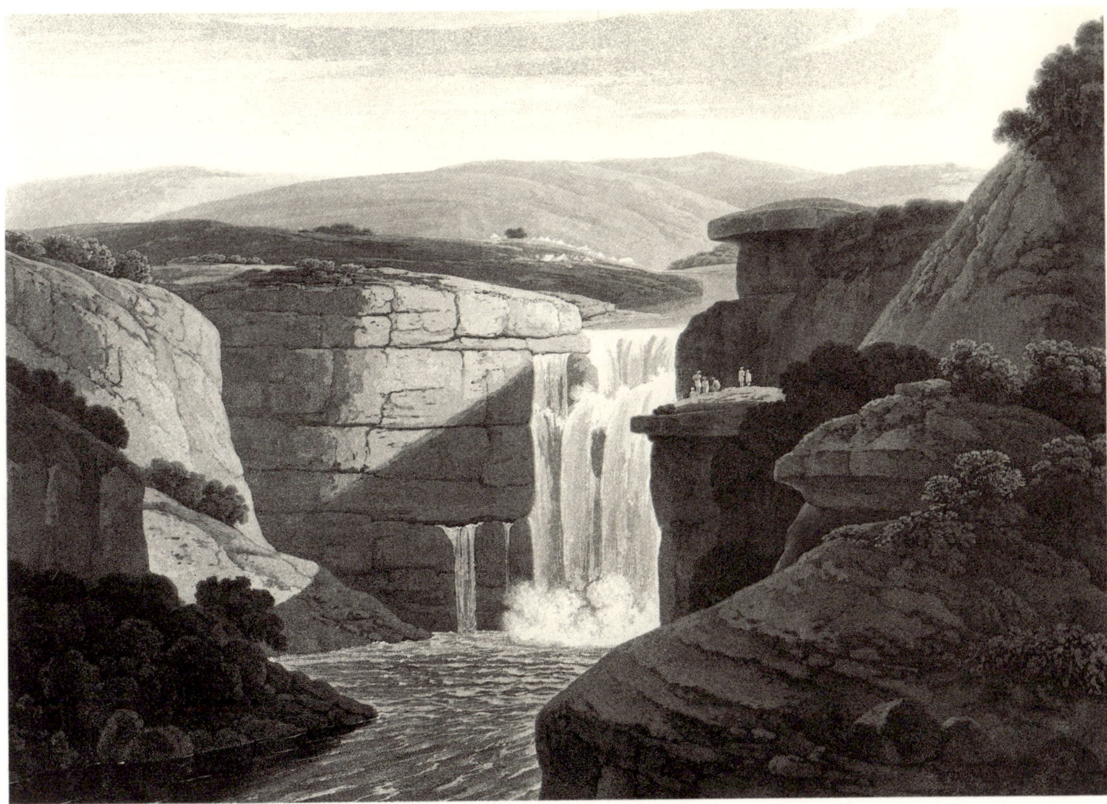

29. Thomas and William Daniell. *Dhuah Koonde* from *Oriental Scenery; Twenty-four Views in Hindoostan.* 1795-1808. Aquatint. The Pierpont Morgan Library.

ceive; and the present solitude that reigns over the whole of the neglected garden, excites involuntarily a melancholy pensiveness." He was even more philosophical upon seeing an artist's renderings of the great temples of western India:

There is an almost universal tradition which characterizes rocks and caverns as the haunts and sacred habitations of the Gods; and in consequence of which the form and gloom of such caverns have been universally imitated in the oldest temples. Their external forms and appearance is in the spiry rock, the towering cliff, and the mountain in its immense extent: How varied! How grand! . . . In grottos and caverns gloom and darkness are common and desirable to both, for Fancy works best when involved in the veil of obscurity.

The reaction of the British to Indian sculpture was a curious mixture of fascination and a classically oriented criticism of form. James Forbes, upon viewing the sculpture of Ellora and Elephanta, wrote that while they "may as-

tonish a common observer, the man of taste looks in vain for proportion of form and expression of countenance." However, despite his academic reservations, he was filled with a sense of mystic wonder at such sites. In his *Oriental Memoirs* he describes the reaction of an eminent English artist whom he had escorted to the Elephanta caves off the coast of Bombay:

I had been lavish in its praise . . . . We remained for several minutes without speaking . . . at length . . . I expressed some fear of having been too warm in my description . . . he soon relieved my anxiety by declaring, that, however highly he had raised his imagination, on entering this stupendous scene he was so absorbed in astonishment and delight as to forget where he was. He had seen the most striking objects of art in Italy and Greece, but never anything which filled his mind with such extraordinary sensations.[37]

This sense of wonder and an almost mystical rapport with the Indian scene is evocatively expressed in a remarkably lyrical passage by James

43

Baillie Fraser as he stood high in the Himalayas at the source of the Jumna River:

Between the two banks, the view is closed by the breast of the mountain, which is of vivid green from perpetual moisture, and is furrowed by time and the torrents into numberless ravines; and down these ravines are seen trickling the numerous sources of this branch of the Jumna. Above this green bank, rugged, bare and dark, rocky cliffs arise, and the deep calm beds and cliffs of snow, towering above all finish the picture. Noble rocks of varied hues and forms, crowned with luxurient foliage, and the stream foaming from rock to rock, forms a foreground not unworthy of it.[38]

Ruminating over the ruins of the ancient city of Kanauj, Thomas Daniell wrote:

It is impossible to look at these miserable remnants of the great city of Cannoge without the most melancholy sensations, and the strongest conviction of the instability of man's proudest works. . . . The plains of India indeed present to mankind many a sad proof of the uncertainty of human glory.[39]

Daniell's observations about the importance of water in Hindu thought and civilization are quite insightful. Attracted both by rivers and waterfalls, which he characterized as "those magnificent circumstances in nature," he was aware that in hot climates water was "an obvious source of endless comforts and advantages" and therefore naturally appealed to the "fabricators of mythological systems." He understood very well why Indians accord water divine attributes, because

the sacred fluid was believed capable of washing away the blemishes of sin, we cannot wonder that the unreasoning multitude . . . should behold the foaming torrent, falling in thunder down the precipice, with equal dread and veneration; and imagine the holy haze that fills the surrounding atmosphere must give an extraordinary degree of sanctity to such situations, and consequently a superior efficacy to their ablutional rites. They approach the sacred stream as into the presence of a superior being; and while their corporeal members are really cleansed, they piously believe, that by so close a contact with the divinity their spiritual part must necessarily acquire a corresponding purity.[40]

Daniell captured, so succinctly and yet with such insight, the essence of what India is all about—the mystique of the civilization that invariably makes a mystic out of all of its admirers. Hodges had perceived this when he wrote, "Gentlemen who have resided long in India lose the idea of the first impression which that very curious country makes upon an entire stranger; the novelty is soon effaced, and the mind, by a common and natural operation, directs its views to more abstract speculation; reasoning assumes the place of observation, and the traveller is lost in the philosopher."[41]

2. Strangers in the Land of Regrets

We do not, we cannot, associate with the natives.
We cannot see them in their houses and their families. We are necessarily very much confined to our
houses by the heat; all our wants and business
which could create a greater intercourse with the
natives is done for us, and we are in fact strangers
in the land.

LORD WILLIAM BENTINCK—1807[1]

1757–1857

I

REGARDED as one of the most liberal impe-
rialists of his day, Bentinck envisioned a
society in India where the two races would mix
freely, even intermarry. When he spoke these
words in 1807, he was the governor of Madras,
which had been strictly segregated, with its no-
torious Black Town, from the very beginning.
Calcutta, which had been somewhat more liberal through the 1780s, had begun to change by
the close of the century, and when Bentinck returned to India as the governor-general in 1827,
the gulf between the British and the Indians had
become unbridgeable.

The British were only the last in India's long
history of foreign domination; beginning with
the Aryans around 1500 B.C., the Persians,
Greeks, Parthians, Scythians, Kushans, Huns,
Afghans, and Moguls had successively invaded
the land and their cultures had been assimilated
in the melting pot of Indian civilization. The
British alone retained a separate identity, essentially by remaining aliens or exiles in what
Alfred Lyall called the "Land of Regrets." Two
years after his return from his second assignment Bentinck wrote:

In many respects the Mohammedans surpassed our
rule; they settled in the countries which they conquered; they intermixed and intermarried with natives; they admitted them to all privileges; the interests and sympathies of the conquerors and conquered
became identified. Our policy has been the reverse of
this; cold, selfish and unfeeling; the iron hand of
power on the one side, monopoly and exclusion on
the other.[2]

One might not agree with Bentinck's "enlightened" view of Moslem rule in India, but it is
true that they became far more assimilated than
the British.

When Warren Hastings became the first governor-general in 1772, Indo-British relations

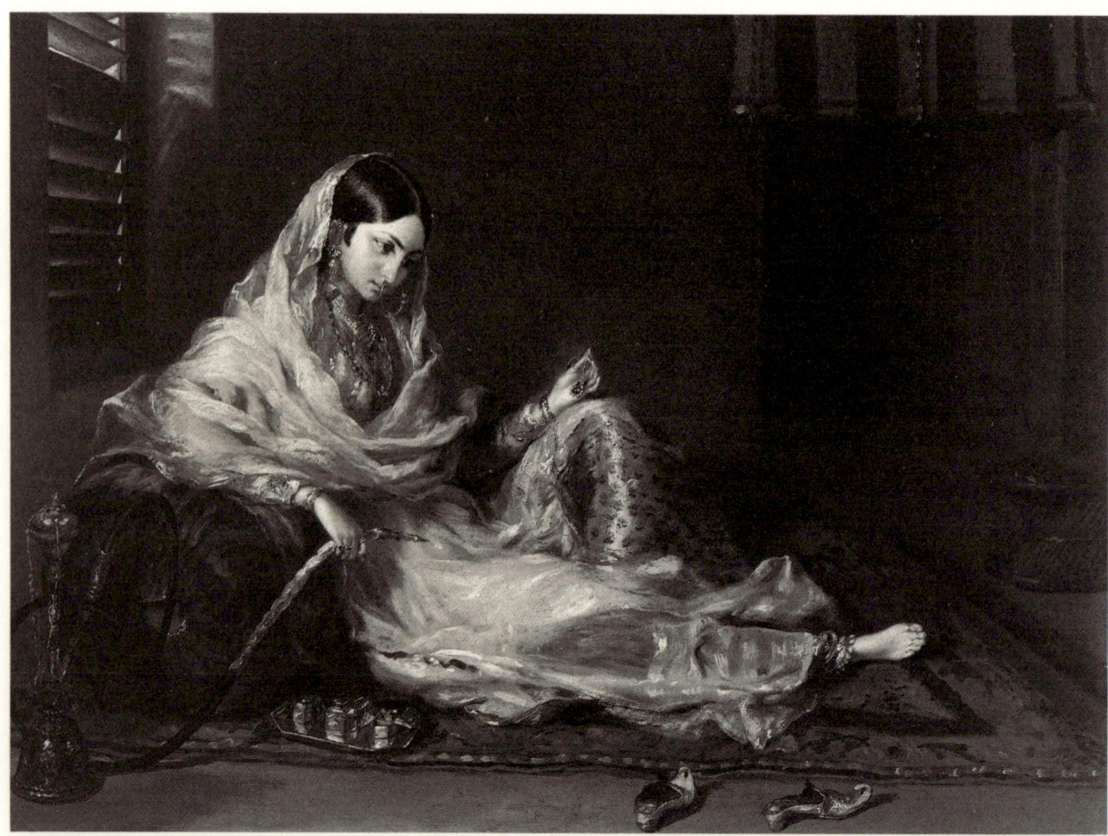

30. Francesco Renaldi. *Indian Girl in an Interior*. 1789. Oil on canvas. Yale Center for British Art, Paul Mellon Collection.

were still civil, but the situation changed by the close of the century. For instance, taking an Indian wife (*bibi*) had been common among Europeans. Kettle had two daughters by his Indian *bibi* during his stay in Lucknow. By the time Chinnery arrived in 1802, however, this practice was frowned upon. By the 1830s, children of such mixed marriages had become social outcasts. Despised both by the Europeans and Indians, they had their own distinct communities until 1947.

Many paintings of the period have survived that show the intimacy that prevailed between the Anglo-Indian nabob and his Indian *bibi* in the last quarter of the eighteenth century. William Hickey's account of his life with his beloved "Jemdanee" in his *Memoirs* is as memorable as Thomas Hickey's sensitive portrait of this beautiful lady. Much admired by William Hickey's friends, she mixed freely with them and was evidently a lady of both sophistication and charm. Francesco Renaldi was perhaps the most sympathetic painter of the nabobs and

their *bibis*. His shimmering, glowing portraits of Moslem women and honest, dignified portrayals of Europeans with their Indian families evoke the time when Indo-British relations had yet to be tainted by arrogance and prejudice (figs. 30, 31). The European and his son are dressed in the Indian fashion, and he gazes wistfully into the eyes of his *bibi* at his side. How different this was from the later British attitude as recalled by J. R. Ackerley, who visited India in 1927 as a secretary to a maharaja:

Talking of snakes, Mrs. Montgomery once told me that once she nearly trod upon a krait—one of the most venomous snakes in India. She had been very ill at the time, suffering from acute facial neuralgia, "so that I didn't care if I trod on fifty kraits. I was quite stupid with pain, and was going back in the evening to my bungalow, preceded by a servant who was carrying a lamp. Suddenly he stopped and said 'Krait, Memsahib!'—but I was far too ill to notice what he was saying, and went straight on, and the krait was lying right in the middle of the path! Then the servant did a thing absolutely without precedent in India—he touched me!—he put his hand on my shoulder and

46

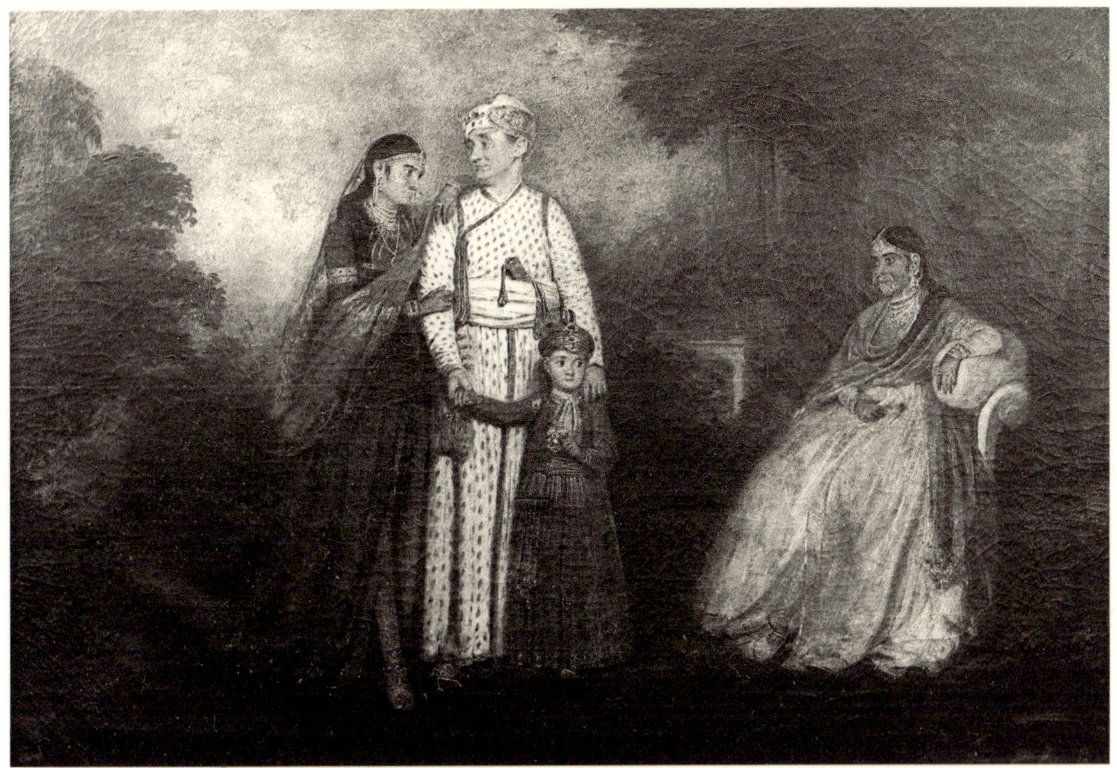

31. Francesco Renaldi. *A Hindustani Family*. c. 1794–95. Oil on canvas. The Asiatic Society.

pulled me back. My shoe came off and I stopped. Of course if he hadn't done that I should undoubtedly have been killed; but I didn't like it all the same, and got rid of him soon after."[3]

Thus, in William Hickey's India, the bridge that the earlier generations of Anglo-Indians had built between themselves and the Indians was already showing signs of instability and would collapse by the time Lord Bentinck arrived. The gulf widened steadily during the first half of the nineteenth century and culminated in the rebellion of 1857. Even though Queen Victoria informed her first viceroy, Lord Canning, that her Indian subjects "should know that there is no hatred to a brown skin, none," for the most part, until their departure from India in 1947, most Anglo-Indians lived and behaved, according to Sir Henry Cotton, one of the more sympathetic and enlightened civil servants, "as though they were not in India at all."

While to the Indians, every European male, whether he was a gentleman or not, was a *sahib* and every female, whether a countess or a bar-maid, a *memsahib*, ironically the Anglo-Indians developed a class system that was far more brutal than the one they had left behind. This system of Anglo-Indian social stratification has often been compared with the more rigid Indian caste system which the British found objectionable and frequently blamed for social problems in general, and race relations in particular. Following this analogy, the Brahmans of the Anglo-Indian society were the civil officials of the government (the competition-wallahs of Trevelyan). The next level were the military officers who corresponded to the second Indian caste, the warriors or *Kshatriyas*. The third group, like the Indian *Vaisyas*, were the merchants, though there was a sharp division between commerce and trade. Traders were derided as box-wallahs and were unlikely to be invited to a dinner for the commercial types. The fourth group consisted of the ordinary British soldiers, the Tommies. Lower still were the Eurasians, corresponding to the Indian *Sudras*.

This "caste system" of Anglo-Indian society

47

is nowhere more pathetically expressed than in a satirical ballad of 1852:

> On the banks of Ganges' water
> When the wind blew fierce and hot,
> Was the Planter's lovely daughter,
> Fairest of the lot:
> For his bride a soldier sought her,
> But Pa and Ma said nay,
> And the Planter's lovely daughter
> Might not disobey.
>
> On the banks of Ganges' water,
> When the rainy season fell,
> There I saw the Planter's daughter
> All called her the belle;
> Now another lover sought her,
> A rich civilian he,
> On the banks of Ganges' water,
> None so sad as she.
>
> On the banks of Ganges' water,
> When the pleasant winter came,
> Still was seen the Planter's daughter,
> And her soldier flame;
> But the Planter's lovely daughter
> From thoughts of him were free,
> On the banks of Ganges' water,
> A Judge's bride was she.[4]

Just as the hierarchy and rules of the caste system evolved by Anglo-India were scrupulously followed, correct behavior was imperative at all times. The following verse by Noel Coward, penned in 1945, shows that the situation had not changed much even as the British were about to leave India:

> Have you heard any word
> Of that bloke in the "Third,"
> Was it Southerby, Sedgewick or Jim?
> They had him thrown out of the Club in Bombay
> For, apart from his mess bills exceeding his pay,
> He took to pig-sticking in *quite* the wrong way.
> I wonder what happened to him![5]

There was even a right and a wrong way to stick a pig!

However, when it came to confronting the natives, the Anglo-Indians could never be faulted for not sticking together, whatever the class distinctions among them. The most vivid incidence of this was probably when, on April 13, 1919, Brigadier-General Dyer and his men butchered, in a matter of minutes, over three hundred innocent people and wounded over a thousand in Amritsar. The subsequent outpouring of sympathy, even approbation, for Dyer, who came to be known to the Indians as "the butcher of Amritsar," by the British community in general was typical of their survival-of-the-pack mentality.

II

FOR the British, it was a natural assumption that the men who founded and ruled the empire in India were heroic figures. Despite the loss of their American colonies, the concept of empire was still quite valid to the British in the last quarter of the eighteenth century. As early as 1764, the achievements of Clive were seen as comparable to those of a Roman emperor as is evident from a marble statue portraying him as such (fig. 34). Others were commemorated in a similar fashion: John Bacon's (1740–99) statue of Marquis Cornwallis dressed in Roman military attire in the Calcutta town hall, and Sir Richard Westmacott's (1775–1856) 1830 marble statue of Warren Hastings as a Roman senator (now in the Victoria Memorial Museum, Calcutta). An even earlier anonymous engraving shows an oval, half-length portrait of Warren Hastings placed on a high plinth, on either side of which are a Moslem with his sword and a Hindu, who clearly give the reverent impression of being before a divine image (fig. 35).

The analogy between the British and Roman empires was used quite pervasively at the time. The decor at a military ball held in Calcutta on March 27, 1793, in commemoration of a victory at Seringapatam, caught the attention of a local newspaper: "On each side of the vestibule in the approach to the temple were placed in basso-relievo the busts of Augustus and of Trajan; above that of the former emperor was represented the restoration of the Roman standards and eagles, which had been seized from Crassus; above the bust of Trajan, the Dacian chief was represented imploring the clemency of his imperial conqueror."[6] In keeping with the

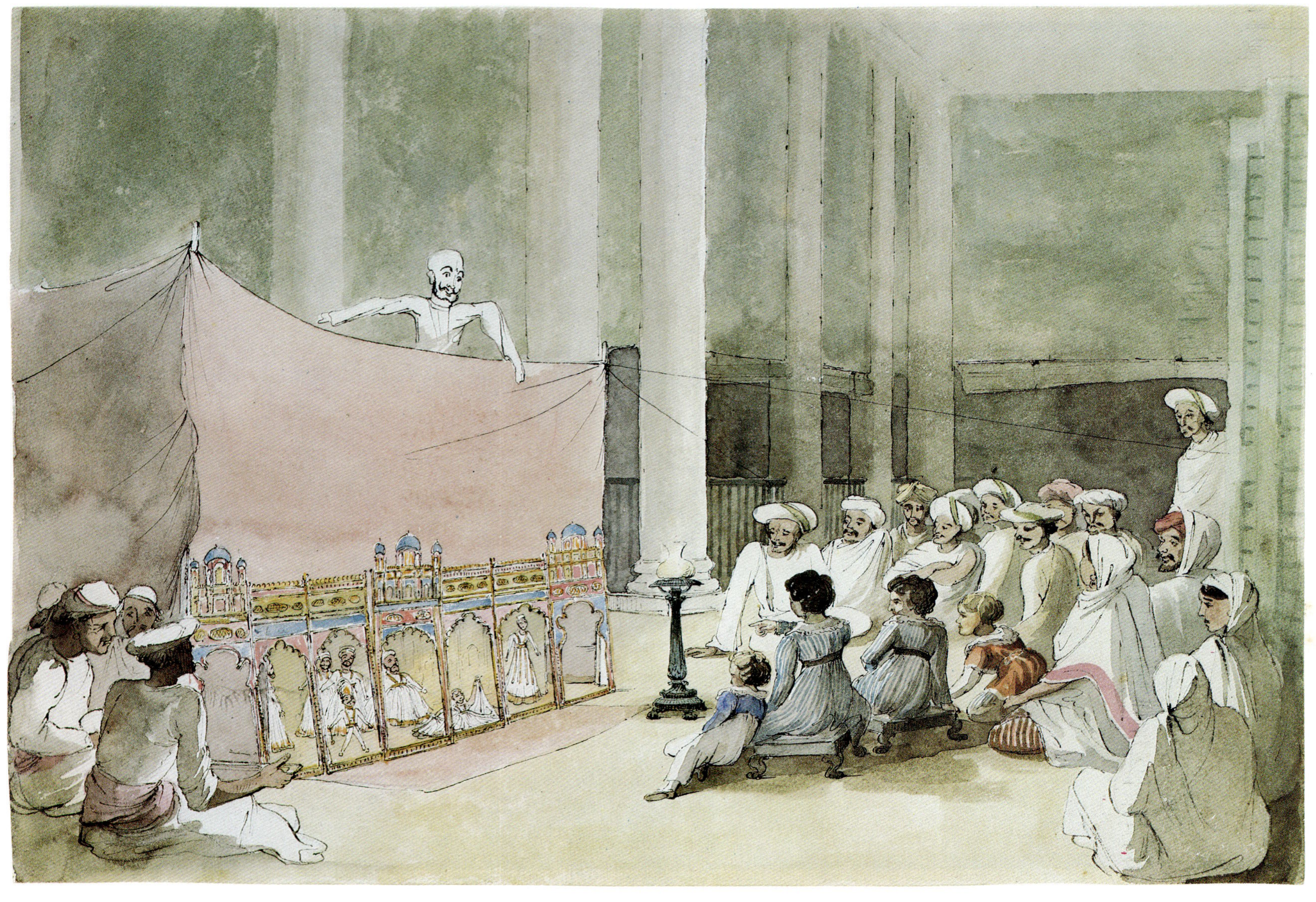

COLORPLATE 3.
William Prinsep. *Kutpootlee Nautch, Alias Fantoccini–On My Verandah*. c. 1827.
Pen and ink and watercolor.
Formerly in the collection of Spink & Son, Ltd.

spirit of the times, at the St. Andrew's Dinner the following year, one of the toasts offered was, "May the British constitution pervade the earth and trample anarchy under foot."

The idea of placing pictures of governors-general and (after 1857) viceroys in public buildings, and of adorning the streets, squares, and parks with statues of public figures was a novelty in India. There was no precedence for this practice on the subcontinent. Even the autocratic Moguls did not flout the Islamic laws by displaying their portraits in public. Few of their subjects probably knew what the emperors looked like. The British were the first imperial power on the subcontinent who fully appreciated the enormous propaganda value of using artworks to enhance their public image.

There were no British artists in India to record Robert Clive's many triumphs either against the French or in Bengal. So, upon returning home, Clive himself commissioned several commemorative pictures of some of the historic occasions in which he had participated. In an unusual expression of gratitude to the founding father of the empire, in 1772 the Company commissioned Edward Penny to paint a highly romanticized and symbolic picture of Clive receiving a legacy for the Company's military fund from the nawab of Murshidabad (fig. 36). In the center of the painting is a madonna-like widow with four children, while the heroic Clive stands to her right, pointing to a group of five, rather depressed-looking soldiers. No less symbolic though more stately is Benjamin West's depiction of the historic moment in 1765 when Clive accepted from the Mogul emperor Shah Alam the grant or authority to collect revenue from the states of Bengal, Bihar, and Orissa, which constituted the first conscious step toward an empire (fig. 37). Although commissioned by Clive, the picture was not finished in his lifetime. The scene is imaginary, for Clive's encounter with the grand Mogul took place in a tent, while West, possibly with Clive's encouragement, has made the occasion an imperial durbar. As one contemporary critic observed, "As the scene is Asiatic, we think the buildings in

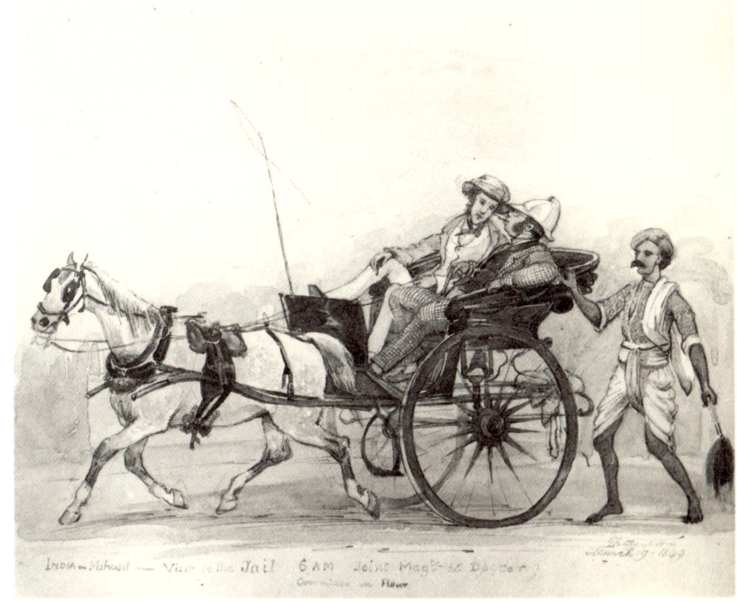

32. Anonymous. *Visit to the Jail*. 1849. Drawing. Walter Collection.

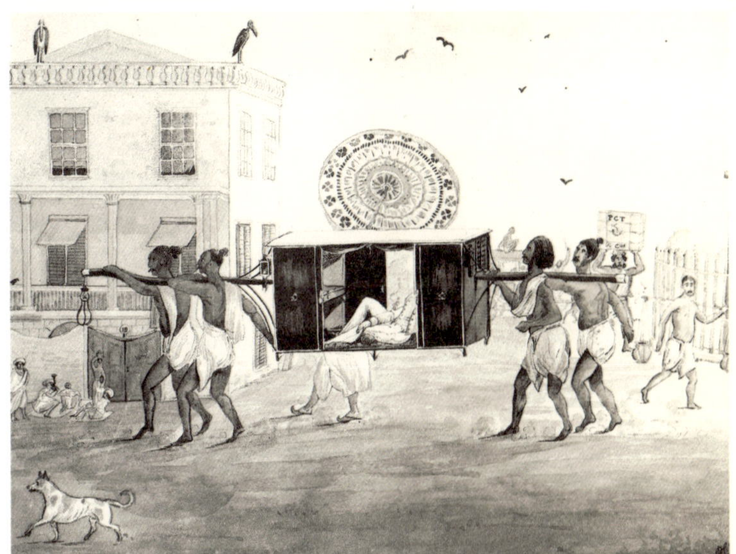

33. P. C. French. *Sahib Being Carried in a Palanquin, Corner of Writers' Building*. 1828. Drawing. Walter Collection.

the background are not sufficiently in *costume*, for the main structure bears too strong a resemblance to our venerable dome of St. Paul."[7]

Such criticisms, however, could not be leveled against historic pictures by British artists who were actually in India. One of the most monu-

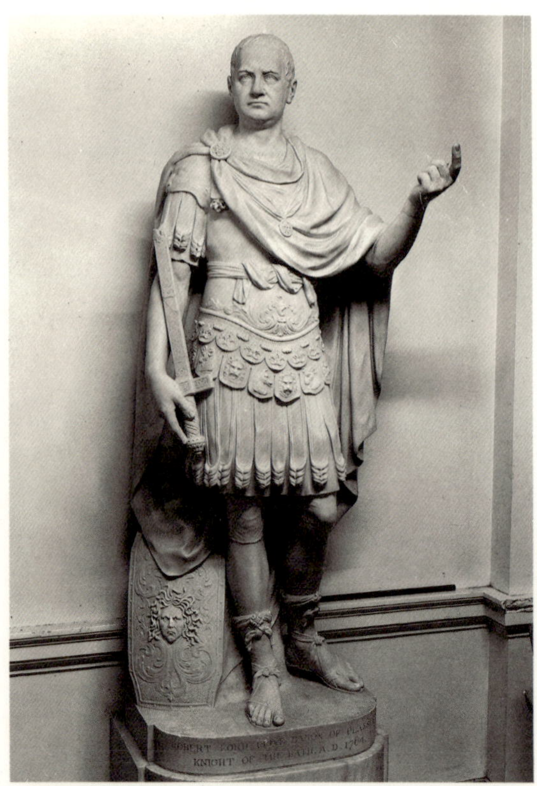

34. Anonymous. *Clive as Roman Emperor*. Reproduced by permission of the India Office Library and Records (British Library).

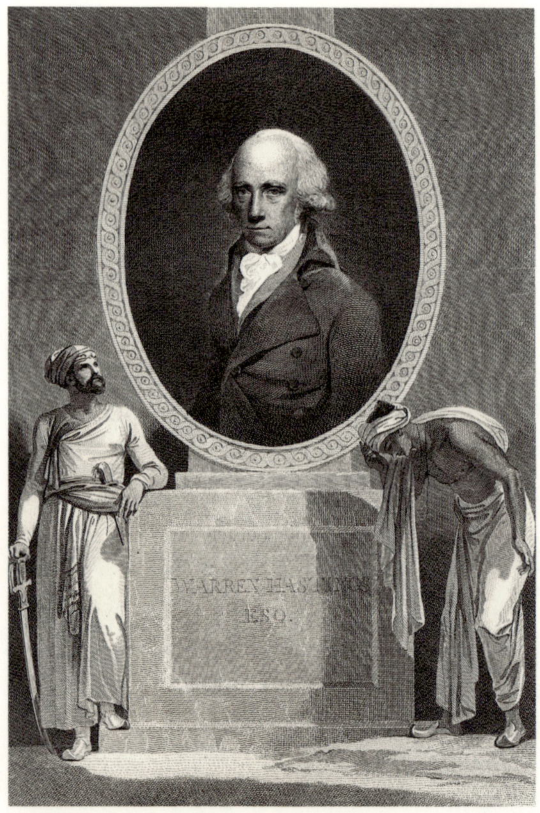

35. Anonymous. *Warren Hastings*. 1797. Engraving. Walter Collection.

mental and dramatic of these is Zoffany's 1795 depiction of Haider Beg Khan's embassy to Lord Cornwallis (fig. 38). Zoffany himself was part of the march from Lucknow to Calcutta and is seen on a horse next to the second elephant. The picture graphically captures the panic and commotion caused by the magnificent elephant in the center. The animal had abruptly turned against his *mahout* whom he has caught in his trunk and is about to crush to death. The painting itself remained unsold until the artist's death, but engravings must have been well known in the nineteenth century for newspaper accounts from as late as 1880 refer to it. The heroic composition is clear testimony to Zoffany's acute powers of observation, his uncanny sense of melodrama, and his empathy for Indian subjects. As Mildred Archer has remarked, "The picture with its immense number of Indian figures, its magnification of the enraged elephant and its brusque relegation of Kennaway [on the

second elephant] and Zoffany himself to minor positions in the rear demonstrates with what avidity Zoffany had observed Indian life during his journeys up and down the Ganges and how deeply 'Indian' India had penetrated his being."[8]

III

THE events that galvanized the British toward the end of the eighteenth century were the various Anglo-Mysore wars and the ultimate defeat and death of the Mysore ruler Tipu Sultan in 1799 (fig. 39). Known as the "tiger of Mysore," Tipu was an implacable enemy of the British and unlike most other contemporary monarchs obstinately refused to compromise with them. By 1784, the British had suffered a number of humiliating defeats, first at the hands of Tipu's father Haidar Ali, who died in 1782, and then of Tipu himself. Both men appear to have been ruthless in torturing and killing British pris-

50

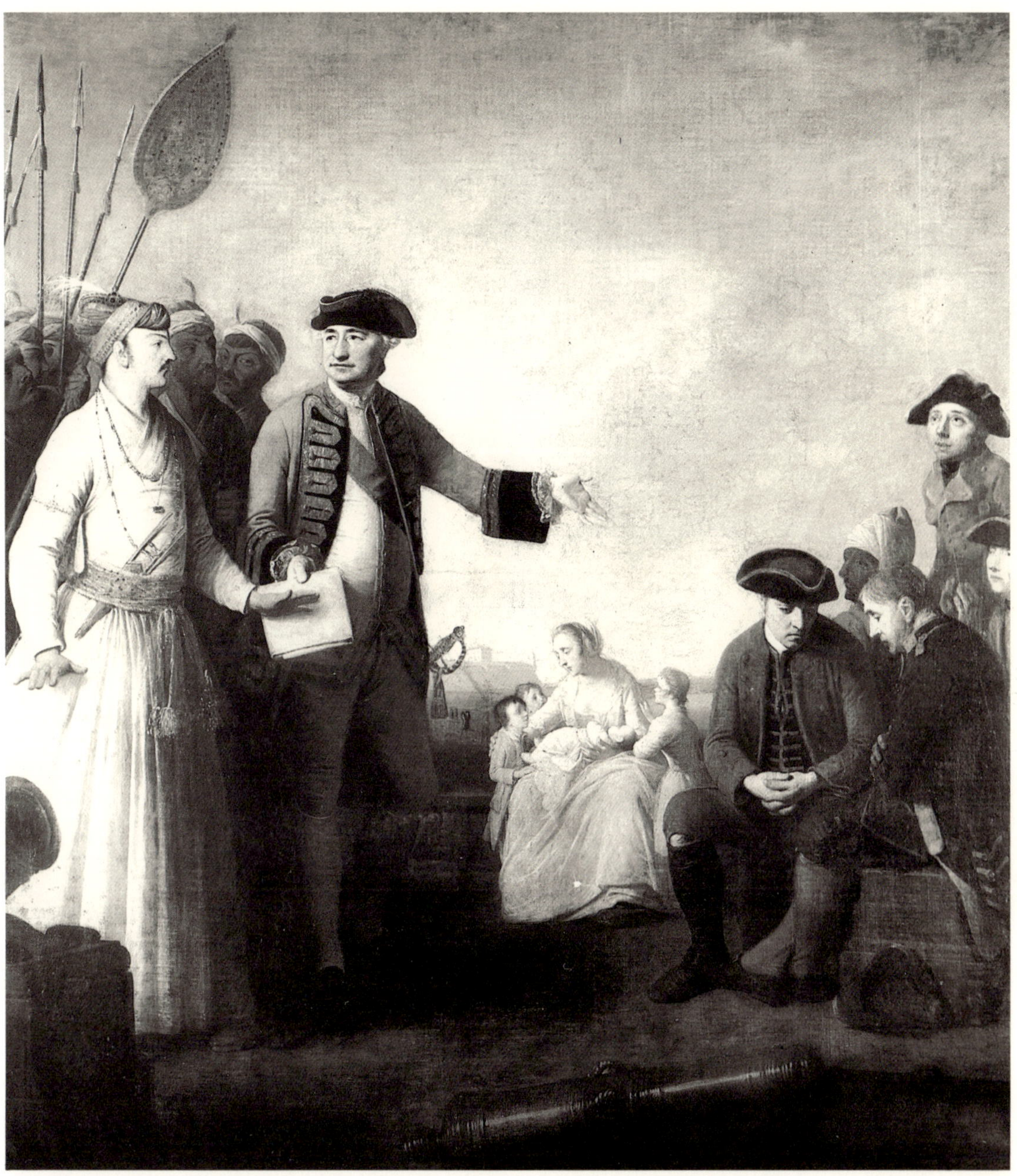

36. Edward Penny. *Clive Receiving a Legacy from the Nawab of Murshidabad*. 1772. Oil on canvas. Reproduced by permission of the India Office Library and Records (British Library).

oners. Grisly stories about their apparent excesses freely circulated in Britain and had the same effect of outrage and indignation as the much embroidered accounts of the so-called Black Hole of Calcutta massacre had had in 1757. In 1792, Lord Cornwallis defeated Tipu and forced a very harsh treaty upon him. In order to insure that Tipu abided by the terms of the treaty, Cornwallis took two of the ruler's sons as hostages. In 1799, the British stormed the fort at Seringapatam, the capital of Tipu's realms. Tipu was killed and among those who discovered his body was Arthur Wellesley, the future hero of Waterloo.

The British obsession with Tipu Sultan continued for generations and was evident in both

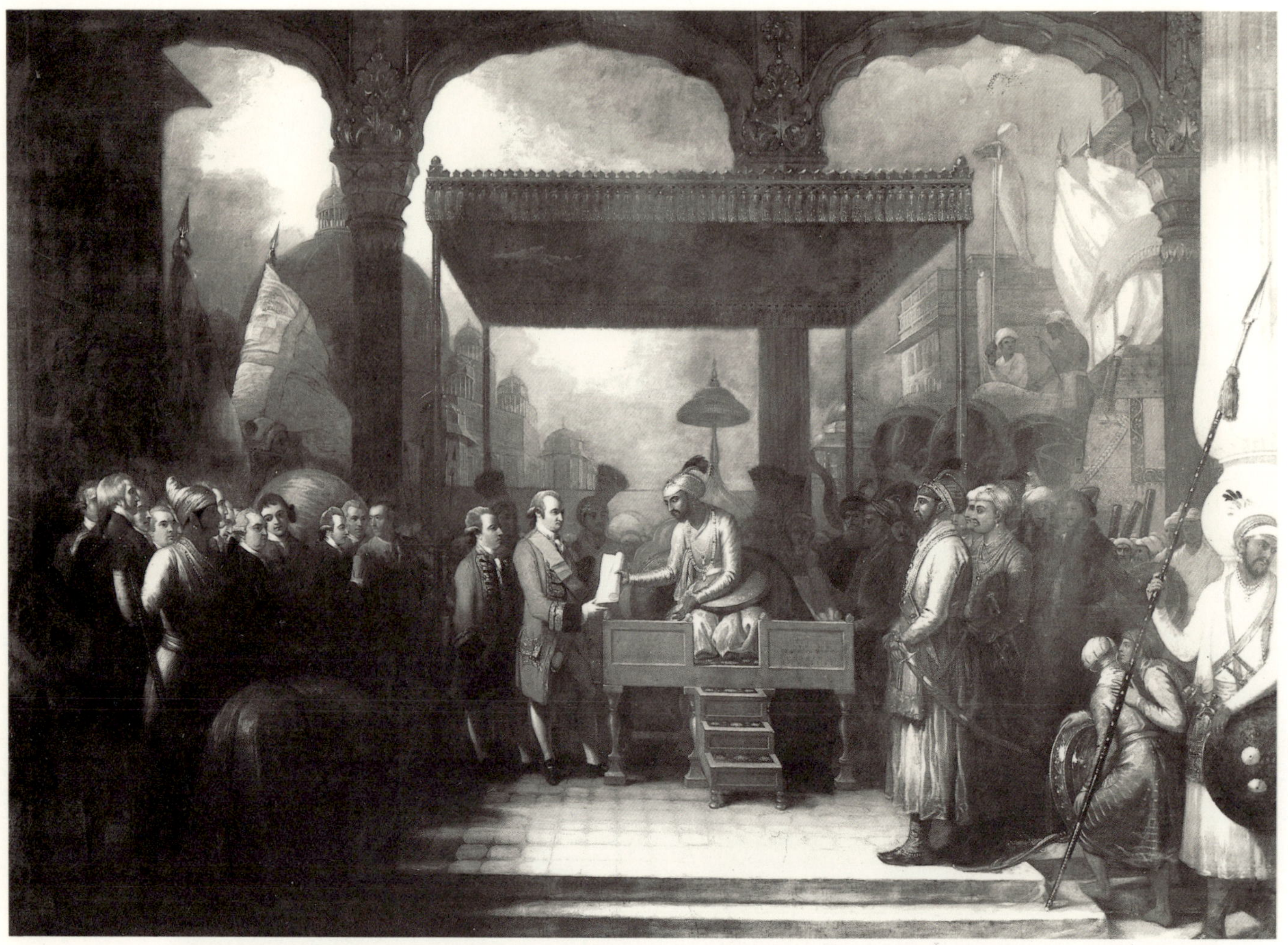

37. Benjamin West. *Clive Receiving the Grant of the Diwani of Bengal from the Mogul Emperor Shah Alam.* c. 1818, after an earlier painting by West, c. 1795. Oil on canvas. Reproduced by permission of the India Office Library and Records (British Library).

literature and the visual arts. Indeed, events connected with the Anglo-Mysore wars and Tipù Sultan constituted by far the most popular historic subject for painters in the entire history of British India. The topic remained popular until the mid-nineteenth century and was treated by artists such as Sir David Wilkie (1785–1841), Henry Singleton (1766–1839), and Sir Robert Kerr Porter (1777–1842) in England and Arthur William Devis, George Carter, and Robert Home in India. Even the American painter Mather Brown (1761–1831), who had arrived in England around 1780, painted several versions of the two young princes being taken as hostages. His first two paintings were exhibited at the Morland Gallery in London accompanied by the following announcement: "Two high-finished cabinet pictures of India subjects, one representing the departure of the two sons of Tipoo Sultan from the zenana; the other where the royal children are delivering the definitive treaty of peace into the hands of Earl Cornwallis, at the time the princes were hostages in his Lordship's camp of Seringapatam: in which pictures the artist received every assistance by drawings made in India."[9]

Looking at an engraving after one of Brown's versions of the subject, it is difficult to believe the artist had actually seen drawings made in India (fig. 40). The figural forms as well as the costumes conform much more to European ideas of Oriental subjects than to what one would have actually encountered in Tipu's palace in Mysore. Much more convincing are Robert Kerr Porter's renderings of the discovery of Tipu's body and the storming of Seringapatam (figs. 41, 42). The original monumental painting of the siege was destroyed by fire (after the East India Company had refused to buy it), but Porter had done a smaller version that was published as an engraving. Unlike Brown, Porter probably did have Indian drawings at his disposal. However, the scene of the discovery of Tipu's body is romantically unrealistic; for a man who had been shot and stabbed several times, Tipu seems remarkably unscathed.

IV

ANGLO-INDIAN life between 1757 and 1857 has been chronicled in extraordinary detail, but perhaps the most succinct and humorous description is in G. F. Atkinson's preface to *Curry and Rice*, a satirical work that deservedly enjoyed prolonged popularity after the author's

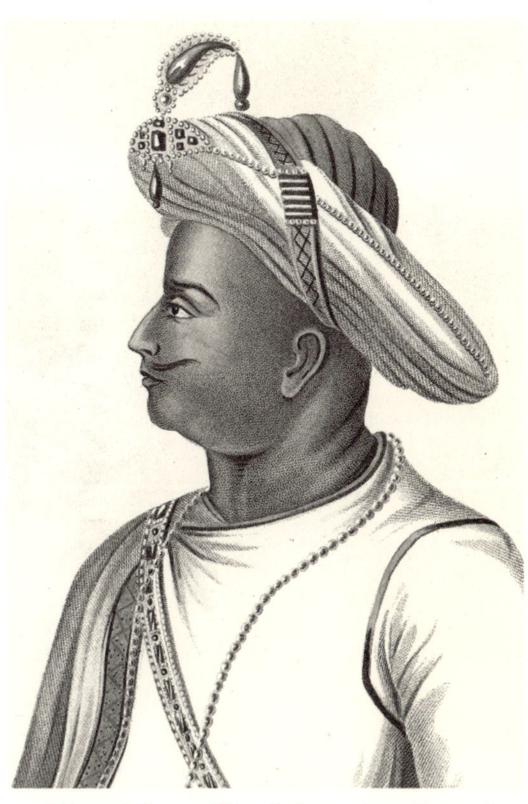

39. Edward Orme. *Tipu Sultan*. 1805. Engraving. The Thomas John Willis Collection.

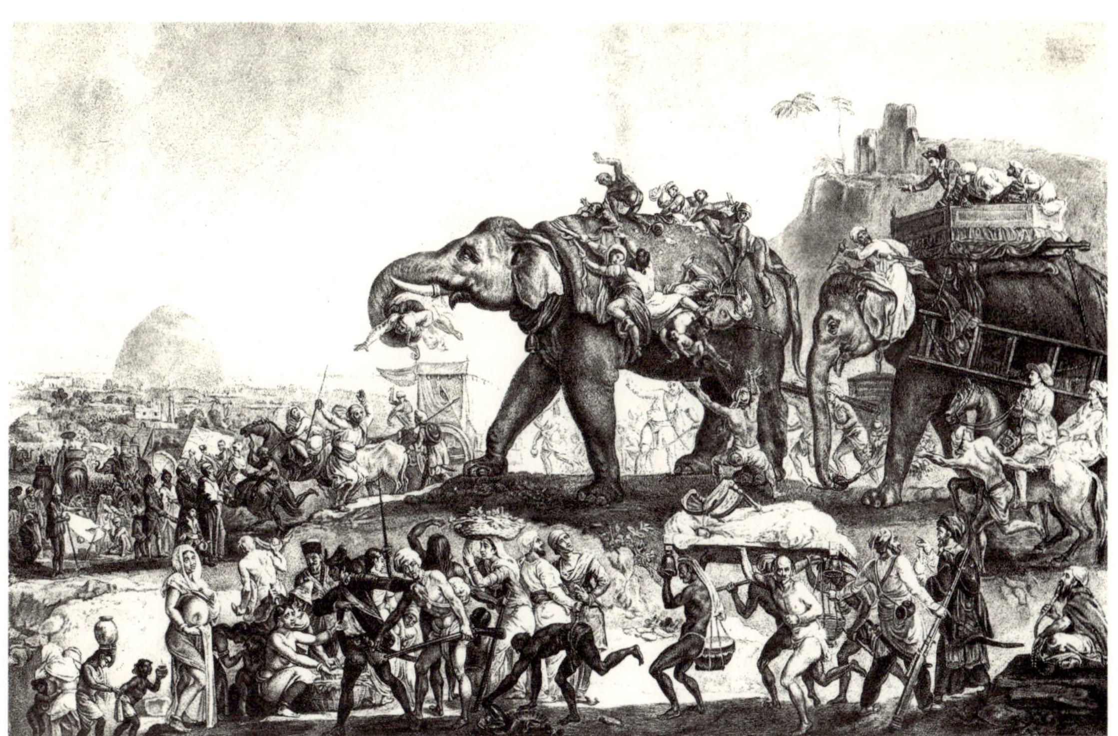

38. Richard Earlson after Johann Zoffany. *Embassy of Hyderbeck*. 1800. Engraving. Walter Collection.

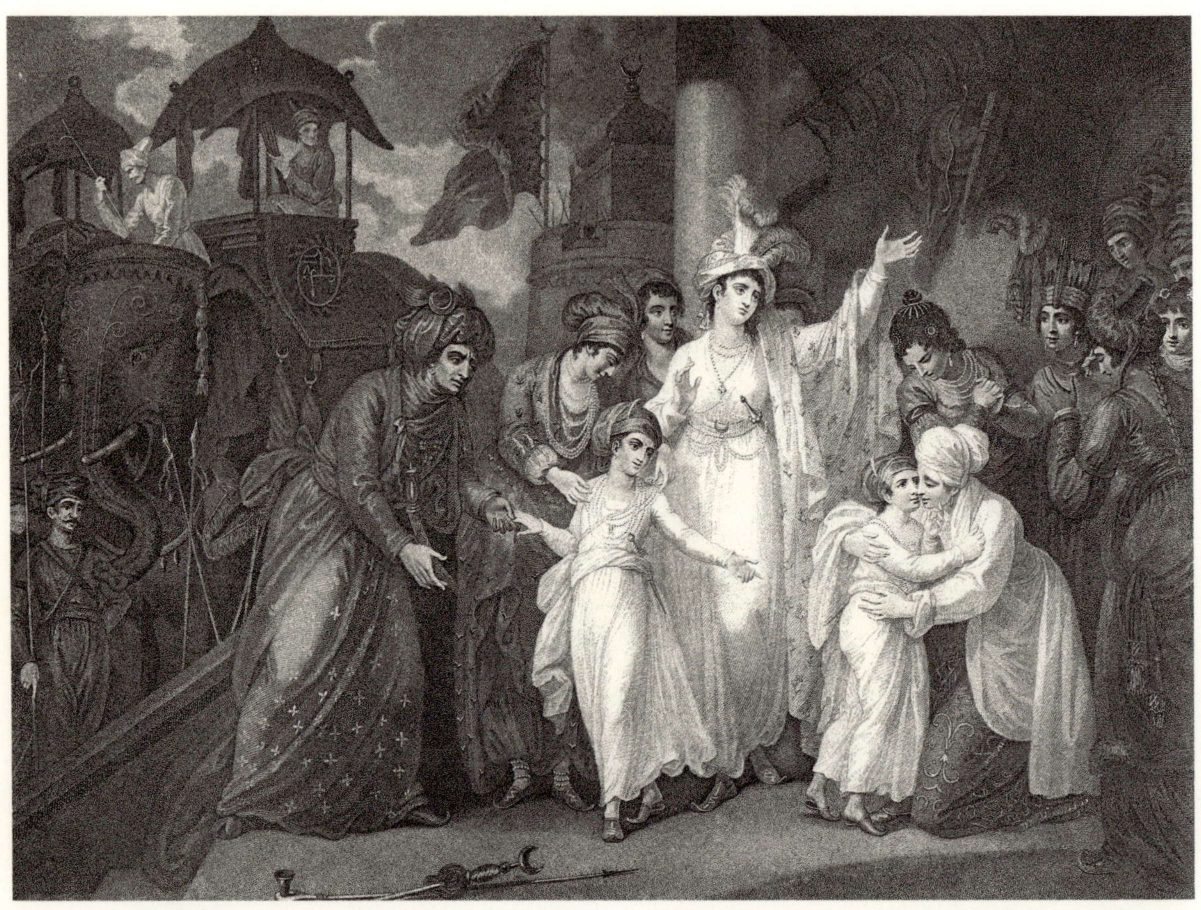

40. Mather Brown. *Departure of the Sons of Tipu from the Zenana.* 1793. Engraving. Walter Collection.

premature death in 1859 at the age of thirty-seven:

What varied opinions we constantly hear
Of our rich Oriental possessions;
What a jumble of notions, distorted and queer,
Form an Englishman's "Indian impressions"!

First a sun, fierce and glaring, that scorches and
    bakes;
Palankeens, perspiration, and worry;
Mosquitoes, thugs, cocoanuts, Brahmins, and
    snakes,
With elephants, tigers, and curry.

Then Juggernut, punkahs, tanks, buffaloes, forts,
With bangles, mosques, nautches, and dhingees;
A mixture of temples, Mahometans, ghats,
With scorpions, Hindoos, and Feringhees.

Then jungles, fakeers, dancing-girls, prickly heat,
Shawls, idols, durbars, brandy-pawny;
Rupees, clever jugglers, dust storms, slipper'd feet,
Rainy season, and mulligatawny.

Hot winds, holy monkeys, tall minarets, rice,
With crocodiles, ryots, or farmers;
Himalayas, fat baboos, with paunches and pice,
So airily clad in pyjamas.

With Rajahs—But stop, I must really desist,
And let each one enjoy his opinions,
While I show in what style Anglo-Indians exist
In Her Majesty's Eastern Dominions.

Apart from laying the foundations of the empire in the mango groves of Plassey in 1757, Clive also began the era of the nabob. Avarice and corruption formed the credo of the nabob, and Clive himself was a shining example of this new breed of Anglo-Indian. Not satisfied with amassing wealth for its own sake, they used it to buy both power and prestige. They antagonized the British gentry by buying their country estates and the politicians their seats in Parliament. Considered upstarts, they and the Com-

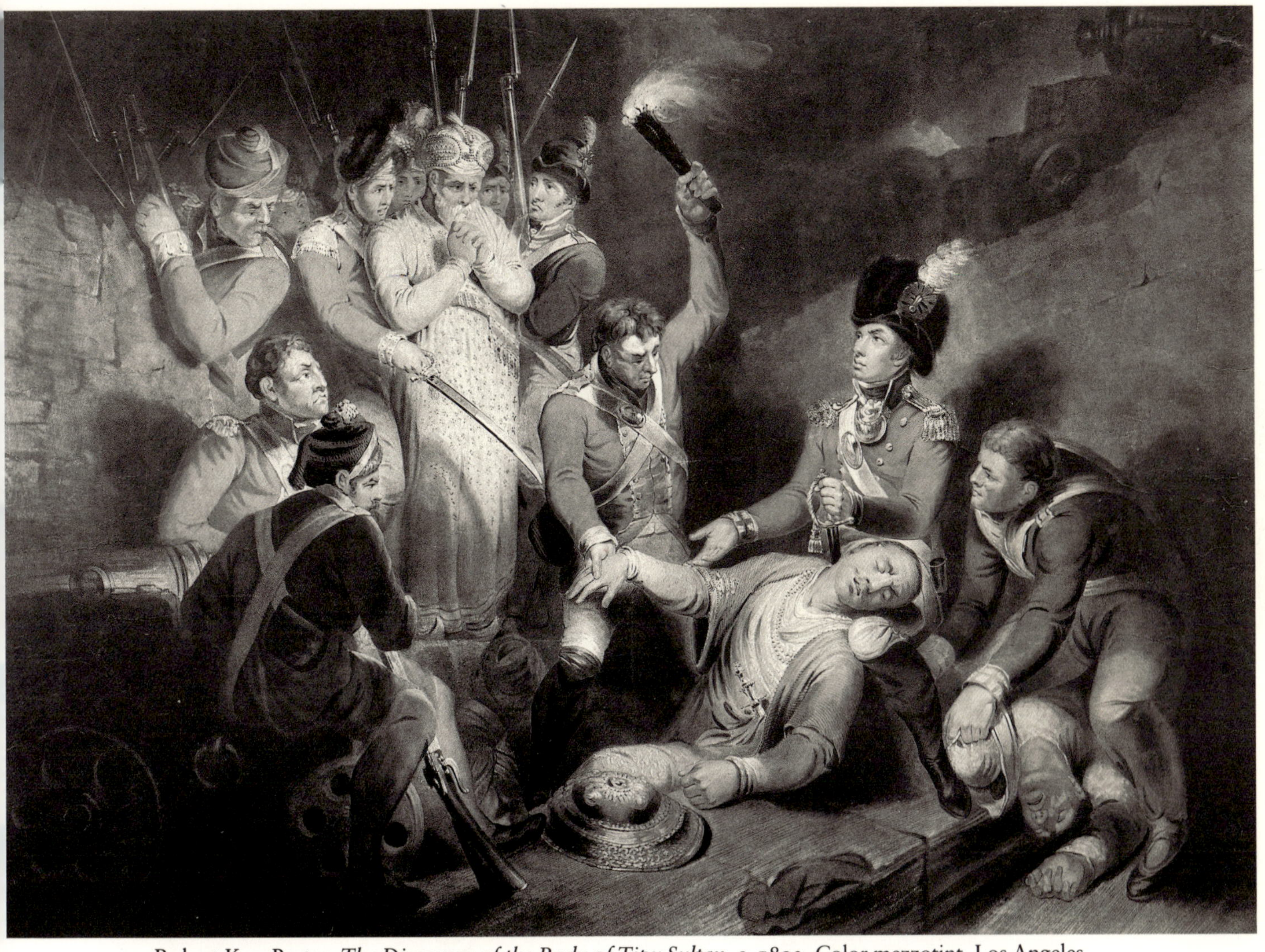

41. Robert Kerr Porter. *The Discovery of the Body of Tipu Sultan*. c. 1802. Color mezzotint. Los Angeles County Museum of Art. Gift of Irene Salinger in memory of her father, Adolph Stern.

pany were both envied and derided by their compatriots and became easy targets for caricaturists. Most of these cartoons had only one aim—to expose and ridicule the sloth and avarice of the Company and its nabobs.

Warren Hastings's impeachment generated a great deal of public interest and inspired a considerable number of satirical cartoons. Hastings was one of the most enlightened of the men who administered British possessions in India and yet, ironically, was derided as a tyrant and oppressor of the natives. A large number of caricatures about Hastings appeared; one shows him as a political bandit masquerading as the savior of India (fig. 45). One of the charges against him was his unfair and unduly harsh treatment of Chait Singh, the ruler of Benares, whom he mistreated and ultimately deposed. The public was reminded of this unfortunate and highhanded action by a caricature of Chait Singh's ghost appearing before the impeached administrator, inspired no doubt by Shakespeare's Hamlet (fig. 46).

The demand for such caricatures was so great that certain establishments, such as William Holland of 11 Cockspur Street in London, specialized in caricatures about the East India Company. The principal themes were the venal-

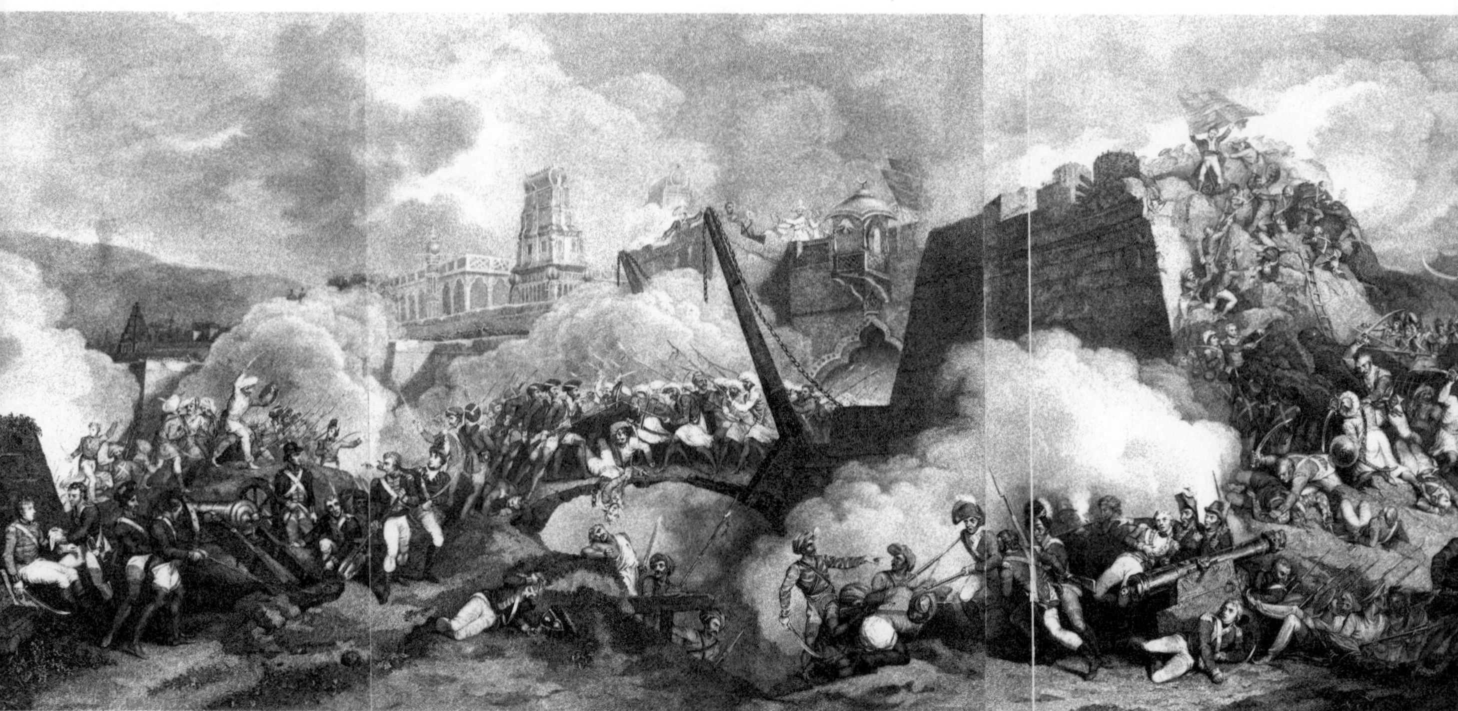

42. Robert Kerr Porter. *The Storming of Seringapatam*. 1802. Lithograph. Walter Collection.
   Below: Detail of figure 42.

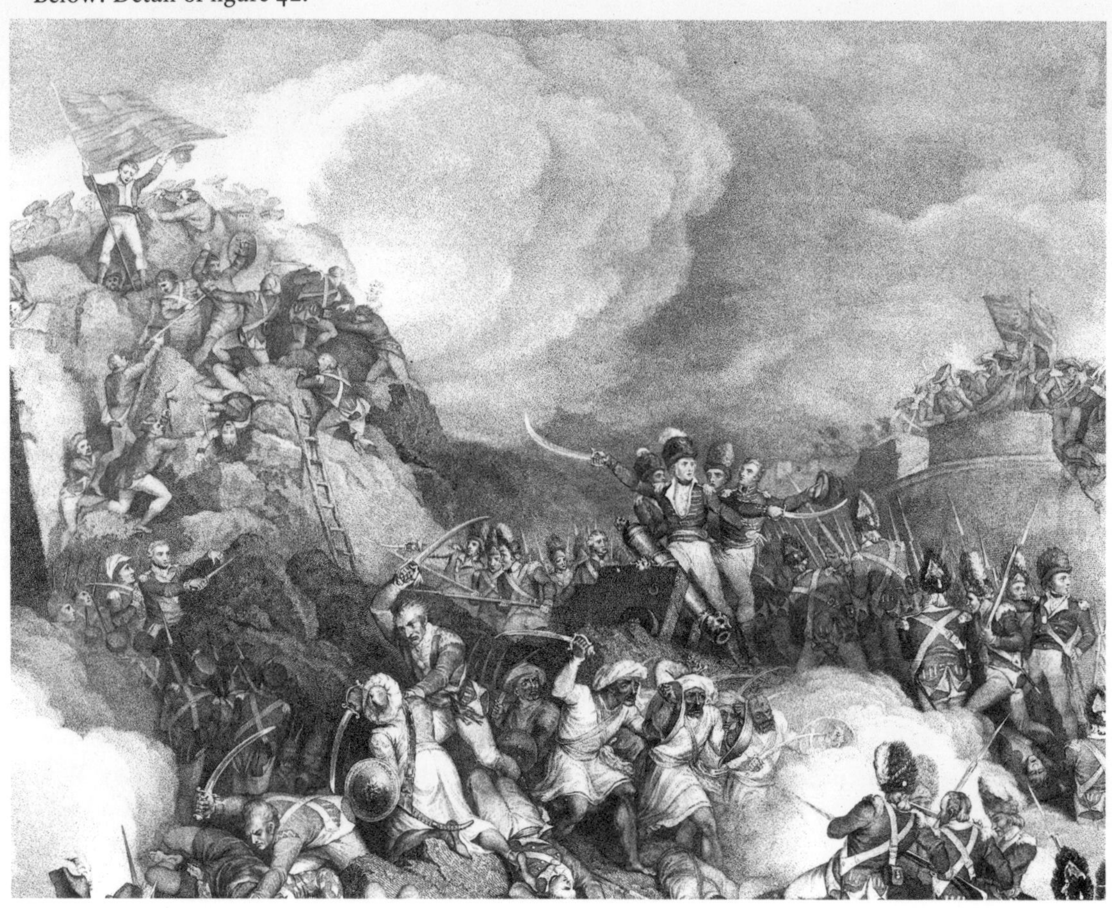

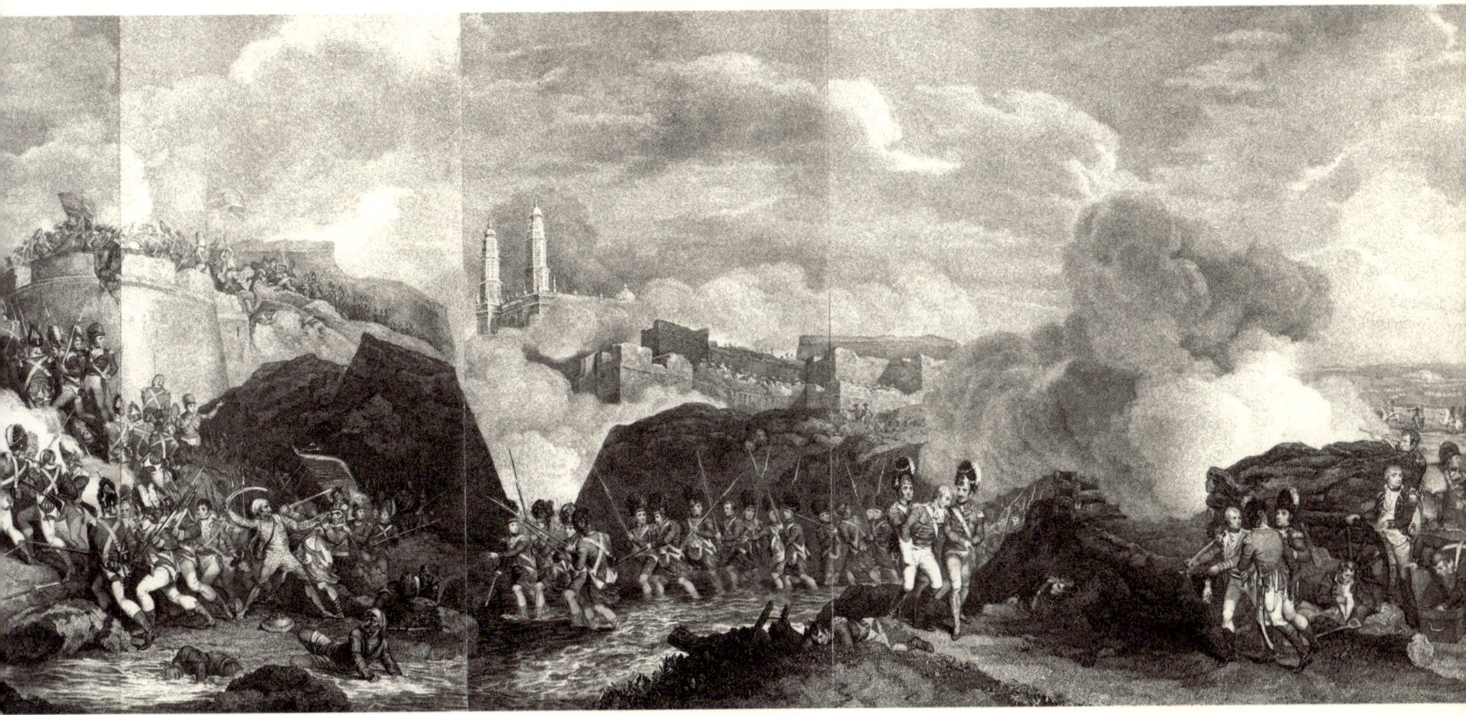

ity, dishonesty, and corruption among traders and the fashions and foibles of the nabob as a social misanthrope.

Only a few of the many young Britons who sought their fortunes in India returned home as nabobs in the century between 1757 and 1857, but they all shared common experiences. Even in the highly class-conscious Anglo-Indian community, perceptions of India and the Indians were remarkably uniform, although the graphics, journals, and travelogues of the period deal mostly with the upper echelon of society. James Moffat's caricature of an arrogant, nonchalant young Englishman smoking his hookah, which is being kept alive by one servant as another fans the master and a third presents him with bills, is a most amusing and accurate representation of the plight of an aspiring nabob (fig. 48). Throughout their stay in India, the British enjoyed the privilege of signing "chits" for all of their material needs, and by the end of the month, their debts had usually caught up with them.

The passengers who sailed up the eastern coast to disembark at Madras had their first glimpses of the seminaked natives rowing their small boats to the East Indiamen to unload both human and inanimate cargo. As is clear from contemporary pictures, there were no docks or jetties and the boats anchored a good distance from the shore. Even though the long voyage around the horn of Africa (and later a much shorter one through Egypt) had allowed the passengers to become acclimatized, the sounds and smells, the heat and dust, and the clamoring of the strange languages must have created a profound sense of bewilderment and doubt. Sir Elijah Impey, the first chief justice of the Calcutta high court, upon arriving at Calcutta and observing the nakedness of the Indians, is said to have remarked that they were an oppressed people indeed since they could afford neither socks nor boots. Soldiers often mistook the Indian traders dressed' in flowing robes for women, but were soon disillusioned.

By far the most difficult aspect of the British experience in India was the climate. For the greater part of the year, the entire country is hot and humid. Respite in the north comes with winter, between November and February, which

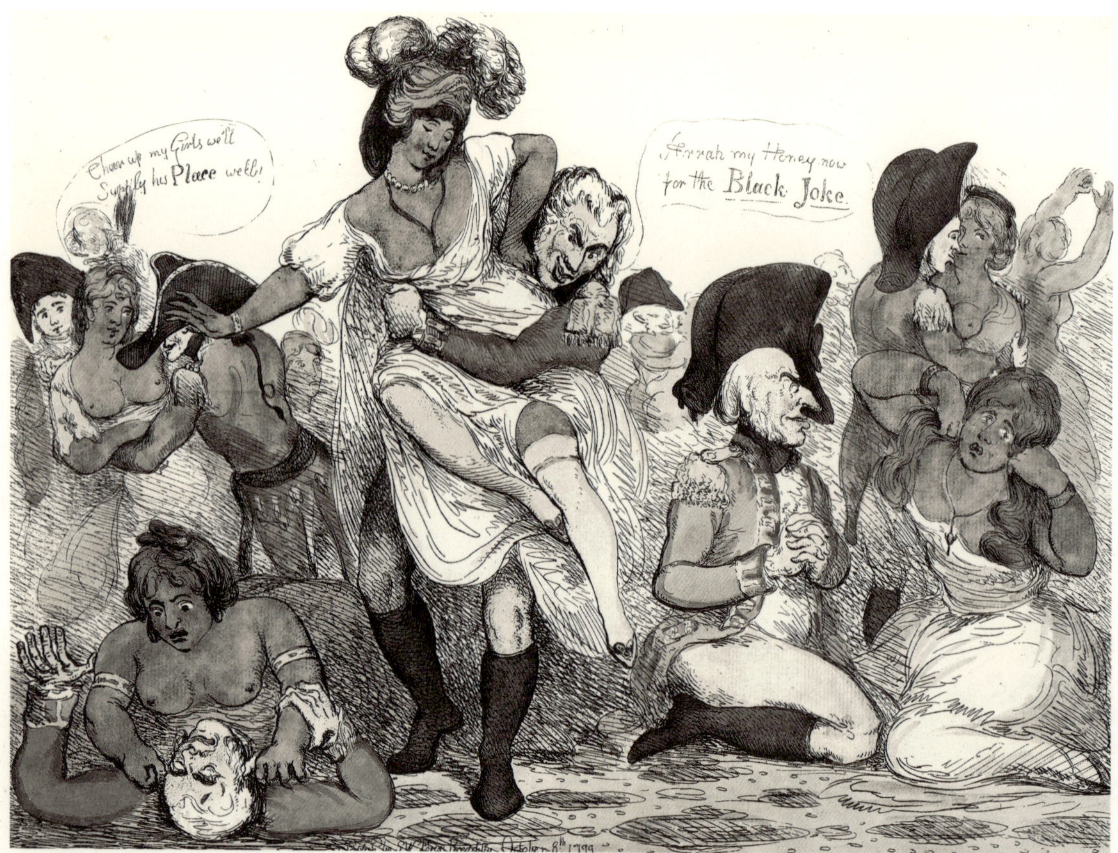

43. Thomas Rowlandson. *The Death of Tippoo, or Besieging the Haram.* 1799. Colored engraving. Walter Collection.

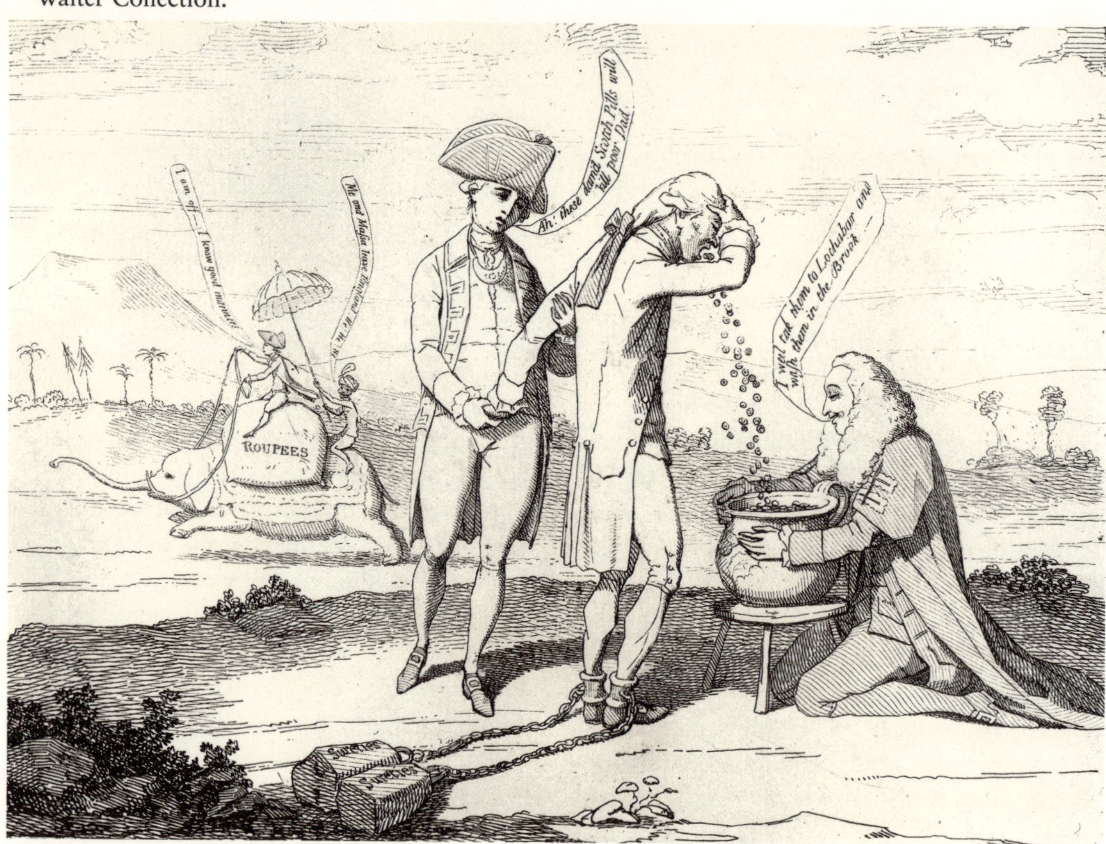

44. Anonymous. *The Nabob Rumbled, or A Lord Advocates Amusement.* 1783. Engraving. Walter Collection.

Shipping Instructions for JEFSTARK

Print this Packing Slip and enclose inside the front cover of the book.

Please ship this item no later than Thu Jul 16, 2026.

Ship to:

ALIBRIS APEX DC 76524214-30
APEX
800 AVONDALE AVE.
GRANDVIEW HEIGHTS, OH 43212-3473
UNITED STATES

PN #	Item ID	Alibris ID	Media Type	Title / Author	Seller List Price	Order Date
76524214-30	054993	B083664356	BOOK	From Merchants to Emperors; British Artists and India 1757-1930 Pal, Pratapaditya	$12.50	Jul, 6 2026

76524214-30

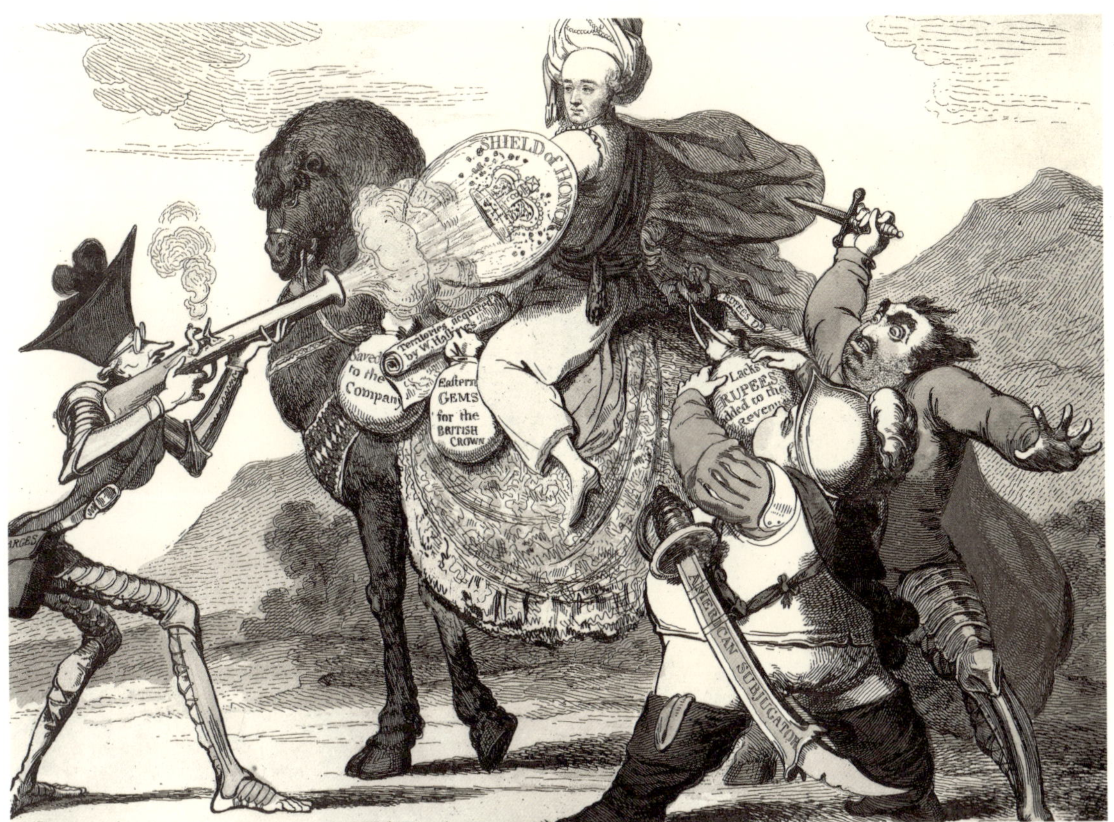

45. Anonymous. *The Political Banditti Assailing the Saviour of India.* 1788. Colored engraving. Walter Collection.

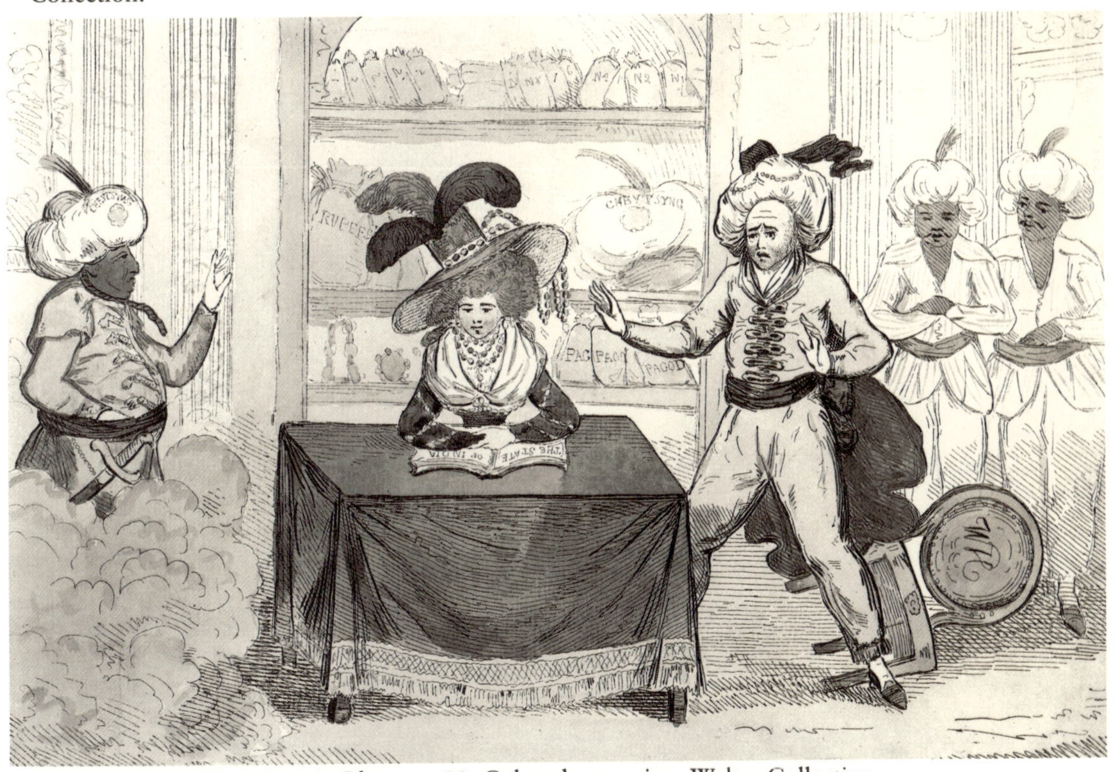

46. Anonymous. *Cheyt Syng's Ghost.* 1788. Colored engraving. Walter Collection.

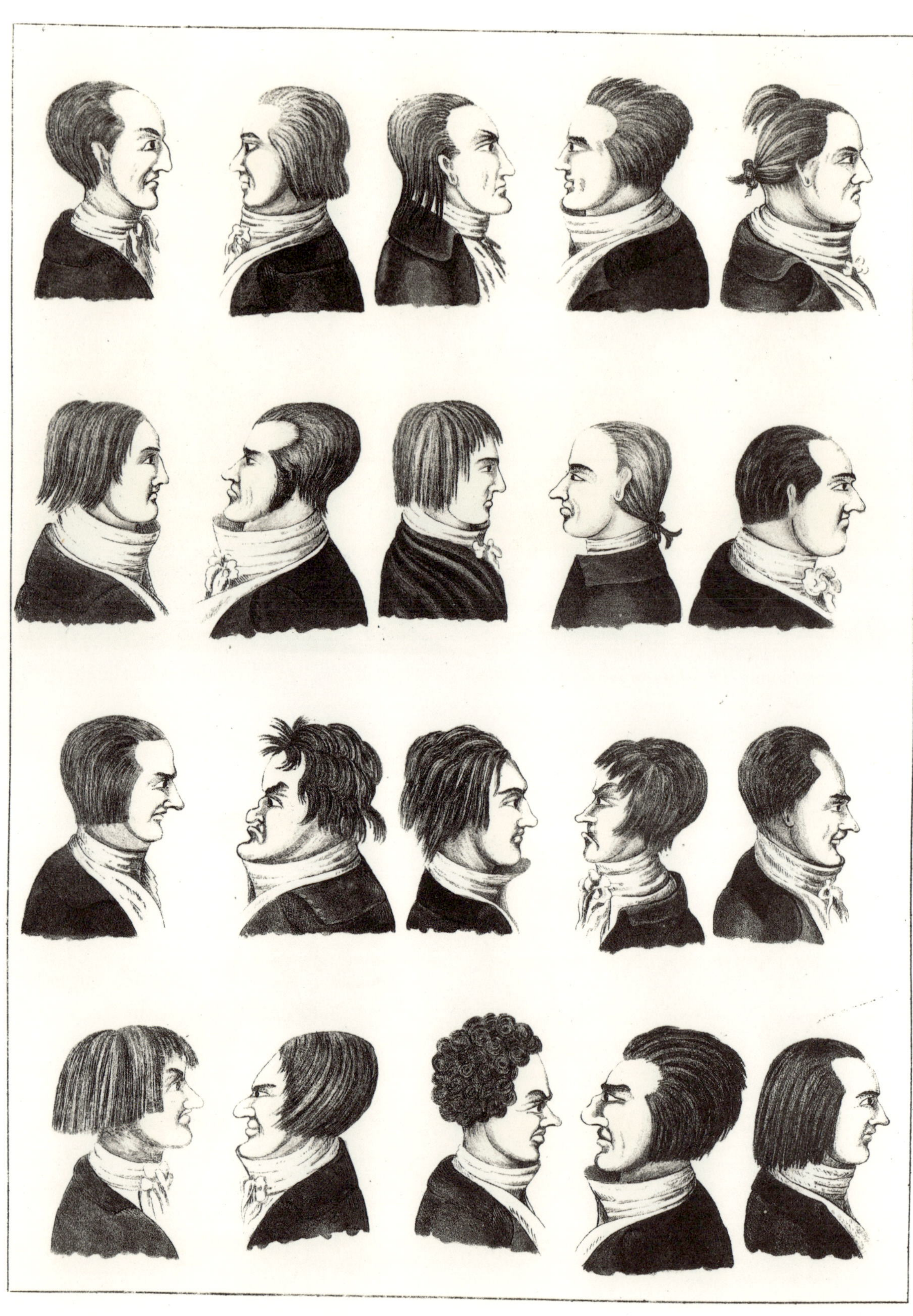

47. Anonymous. *Nabobs*. 1811. Colored engraving. Walter Collection.

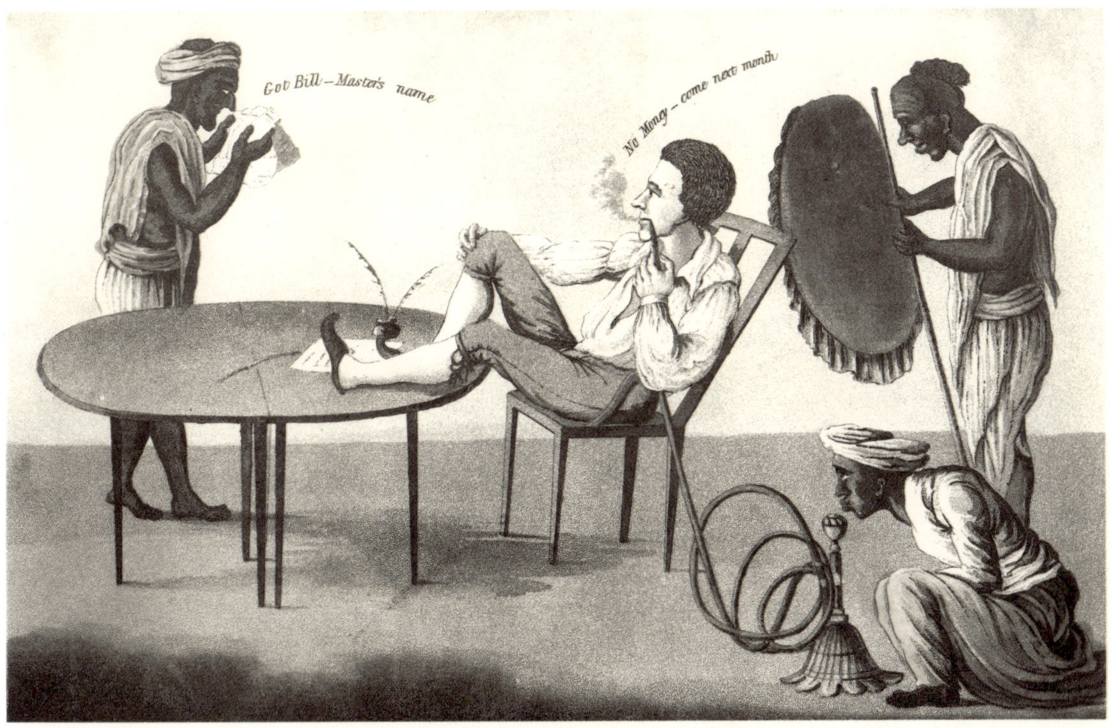

48. James Moffat. *Scene in the Writers' Buildings, Calcutta.* c. 1811. Colored engraving. Walter Collection.

is traditionally the season for enjoyment. Only the wealthy could afford a *punkhah*, the swing fan that was pulled by hand, and the *tatties*, the grass screens that covered all of the doors and windows during the day and had to be continuously sprayed with water. Ice was unknown until it was imported from Boston after 1834 thanks to the ingenuity of an American apothecary.

Not only did every diarist and writer dilate upon the discomforts of the climate, but the subject also inspired some amusing caricatures in London. One shows a new arrival who is inappropriately dressed for the climate being urged into a liquor store by a veteran of the British Indian army to purchase a popular "cure" for the heat (fig. 50). Another that deals with the climate also portrays the snobbery prevalent among Anglo-Indians and the Indians' perception of the strange behavior of the foreigners (fig. 51). While the pirouetting soldier considers the land fit only for monkeys and salamanders and the women as black as the devil, the Indians regard him as a wild man from the woods and the snotty lady reclining in her palanquin finds him an animal curious enough to be a good companion for the baboon in her menagerie.

Neither their costumes nor their inordinate fondness for drinking were conducive to alleviating the Anglo-Indians' discomfort from the oppressive heat. While the early settlers had made some concession to the climate by wearing Indian loose fitting, airy garments at home, after the establishment of the empire the Anglo-Indians gradually became much more "British" in such matters, wearing totally inappropriate, uncomfortable, and even unhealthy clothing that had been designed to be worn in the climate of the British isles. They seemed to believe that clothes make the man and that the imperial image could hardly be upheld if they went around dressed in Indian attire. It was not uncommon for a British gentleman even in remote outposts to eat dinner alone at home in full dress solely for the benefit of his servants. (Incidentally, the dinner jacket was designed by Edward VII while he was sailing to India in 1875 in consideration of the climate.)

The eating and drinking habits of the Anglo-

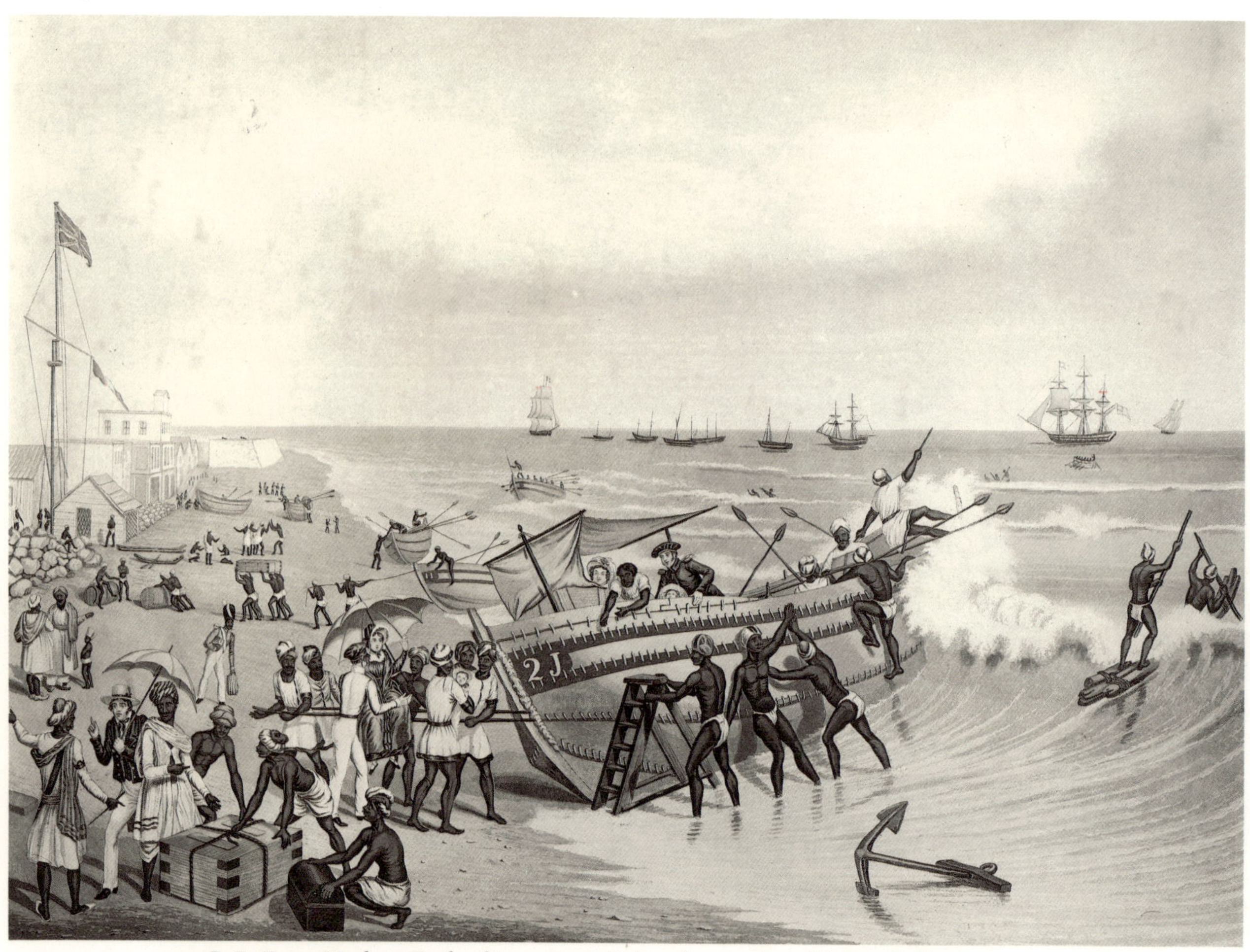

49. G. B. East. *Madras, Embarking*. 1856. Colored engraving. Walter Collection.

Indians were not particularly adaptive either. Like the Romans, they indulged their imperial appetite for food and wine with extraordinary imprudence. It was common for a well-to-do Anglo-Indian to consume generous portions of two or three kinds of meat at each of three meals a day and drink a great deal of brandy and claret at both dinner at noon and supper at night. In 1874, the artist Edward Lear (1812–88) spoke about his dinner one evening at a Benares hotel: "Soup good, and a boiled fowl with rice just tolerable. Nothing else, however, at all eatable, mutton quite raw, stewed ducks hard. I may except, though, a bread and butter pudding." [10] By the close of the nineteenth century, excesses in eating habits had been somewhat curbed, but heavy drinking, especially of whiskey, remained a favorite pastime. Excessive drinking was no doubt a diversion from boredom and the misery of life in exile. Alcohol was also considered good medicine for many stomach-related disorders. Thomas Rowlandson (1757–1827) did not think much of this theory as his cartoon shows (fig. 52). The bottle of *lal shraub*, red wine, that the man recommends to his suffering friend will be of highly questionable benefit. As much as seventy-eight years later, Edward Lear wrote in his diary, "Cross, unwell and wretched . . . Had some cold meat and beer in my room, the latter medicinally to set digestion right and was utterly miserable." [11] In any event, in the annals of drinking, many delectable concoctions remain today, a legacy of Anglo-India: punch (from the Hindustani word for "five," corresponding to the number of ingredients), gimlet, Pim's cup, and gin and tonic.

62

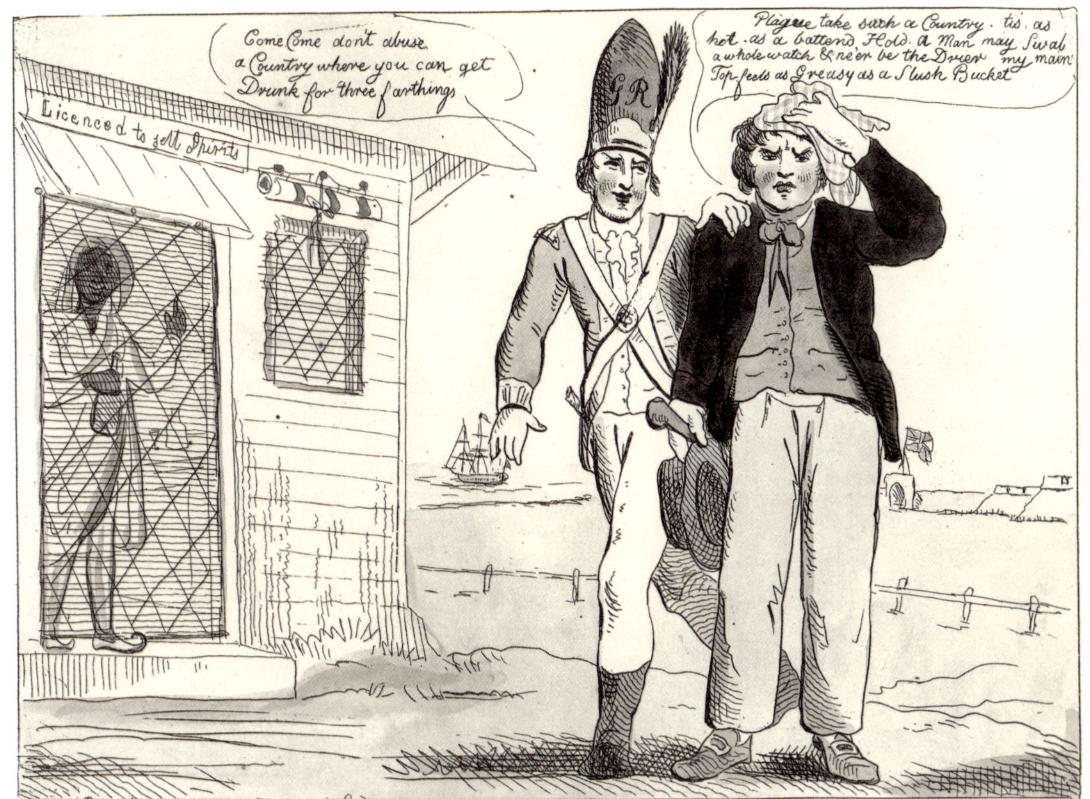

50. Anonymous. *The Bengal Soldier's Defence of a Hot Climate.* c. 1800. Colored engraving. Walter Collection.

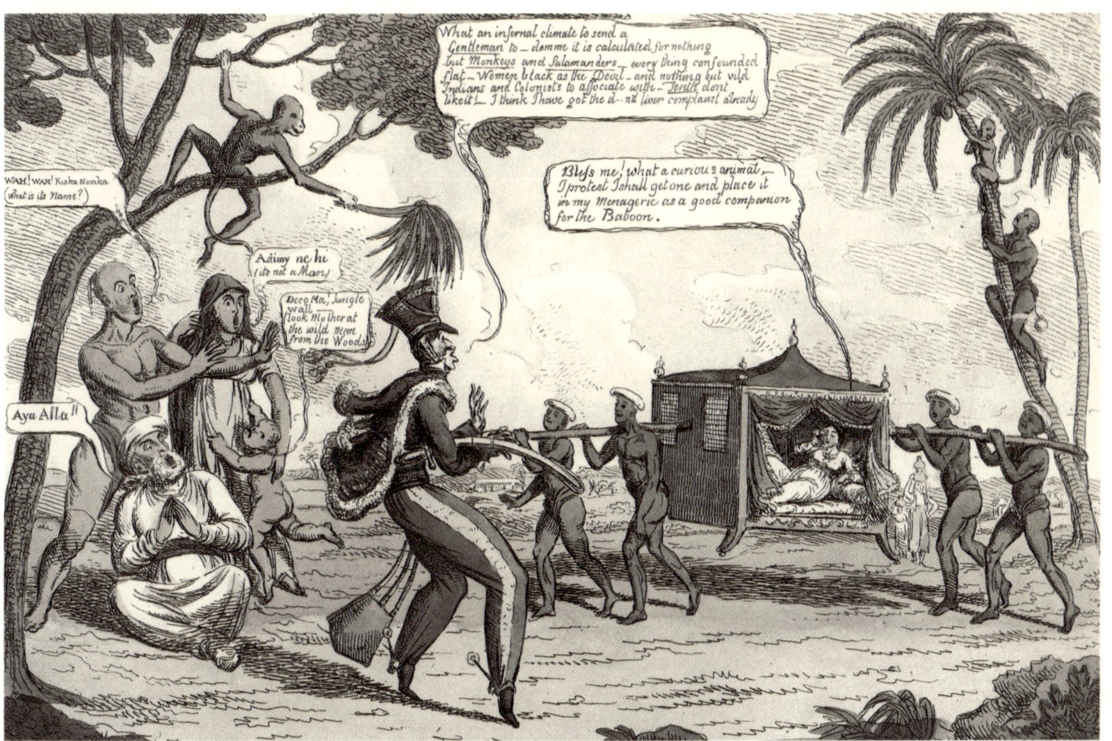

51. Anonymous. *Hot Quarters for the Tenth, or a Curiosity for India.* 1824. Colored engraving. Walter Collection.

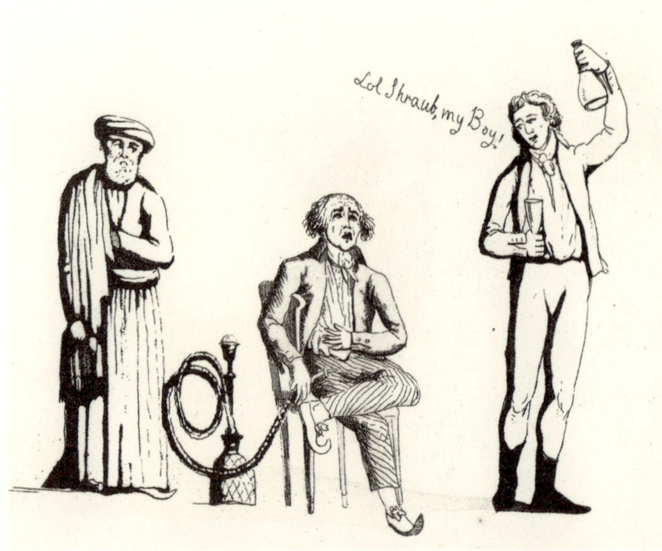

52. Thomas Rowlandson. *A Bengal Remedy for the Bile*. 1797. Colored engraving. Walter Collection.

Hardships notwithstanding, the average Anglo-Indian lived a life of abundance and luxury, both mentally and physically insulated from the natives except for his servants. Anglo-India has often been called the land of "qui-hais" (or "who's there," which was the way servants were summoned) and "brandy-pawnee" (pawnee = *pani* = water). The servants, whether domestic or official, and the clerks (the much ridiculed *babus* in Bengal and everywhere else the empire expanded) were the twin pillars without which the edifice of the empire would have weakened long before the cause of independence was espoused by the Western-educated Indians in the 1880s. The British imperial machine operated via an intricate bureaucracy. This is yet another unfortunate and seemingly permanent legacy of British rule in India; the clerk remains today as he was in British India, a petty but indispensable part of the machinery. And now, as then, bribery is the only grease that makes the equipment work. Anglo-Indian literature has equally maligned both the *babu* and the domestic servant, and the artist has generally ignored the former and immortalized the latter. In formal portraits and in sketches and drawings by amateur artists, servants of both sexes are ubiquitous. Indeed, in some portraits and conversation pieces, servants were introduced like props to enhance the Indian atmosphere.

Sir Charles D'Oyly's lively renderings of the domestic bliss of Anglo-Indian life, whether of a sahib smoking his hookah in the company of his children and the family dog or a memsahib adorning herself at her vanity with the aid of two *ayahs* (maids), are as interesting for their depictions of the costumes and attitudes of the masters as they are of the servants (fig. 53). It was often said that the memsahib was bored because she had few domestic chores to perform. Neither she nor the master of the house ever visited the market, and looking at Atkinson's picture of a kitchen from his famous *Curry and Rice* (fig. 54), the mistress seems blissfully unaware of the state of affairs there as well. Equally humorous is the story about a lady who did happen to visit her kitchen once and found the cook straining the soup through one of her husband's socks. Noticing her surprise, the clever cook quickly reassured his mistress that the sock was clean.

Even though most children of Anglo-India were shipped back home for schooling before they reached ten, while in India their only companions were the servants who pampered and spoiled their *chota* (little) sahibs or their missy *babas*. The dominating figure of the nursery was the *ayah* but a host of other servants were available at all times to serve the child. A charming picture by William Prinsep (1794–1874) shows four English children and thirteen servants watching a puppet show on the veranda of their house (colorplate 3). Riding in the early mornings was a compulsory part of the daily routine for the children as well as for the adults and the *syce* or groom became a close acquaintance (fig. 55).

Differences in language must have contributed to the Briton's sense of exile in India. India was, and still is, a country where fourteen major languages and countless dialects are spoken. In the days of Warren Hastings, many Britons took private lessons in Persian, which was the Mogul court language, but most had to retain native interpreters for taking care of their personal and

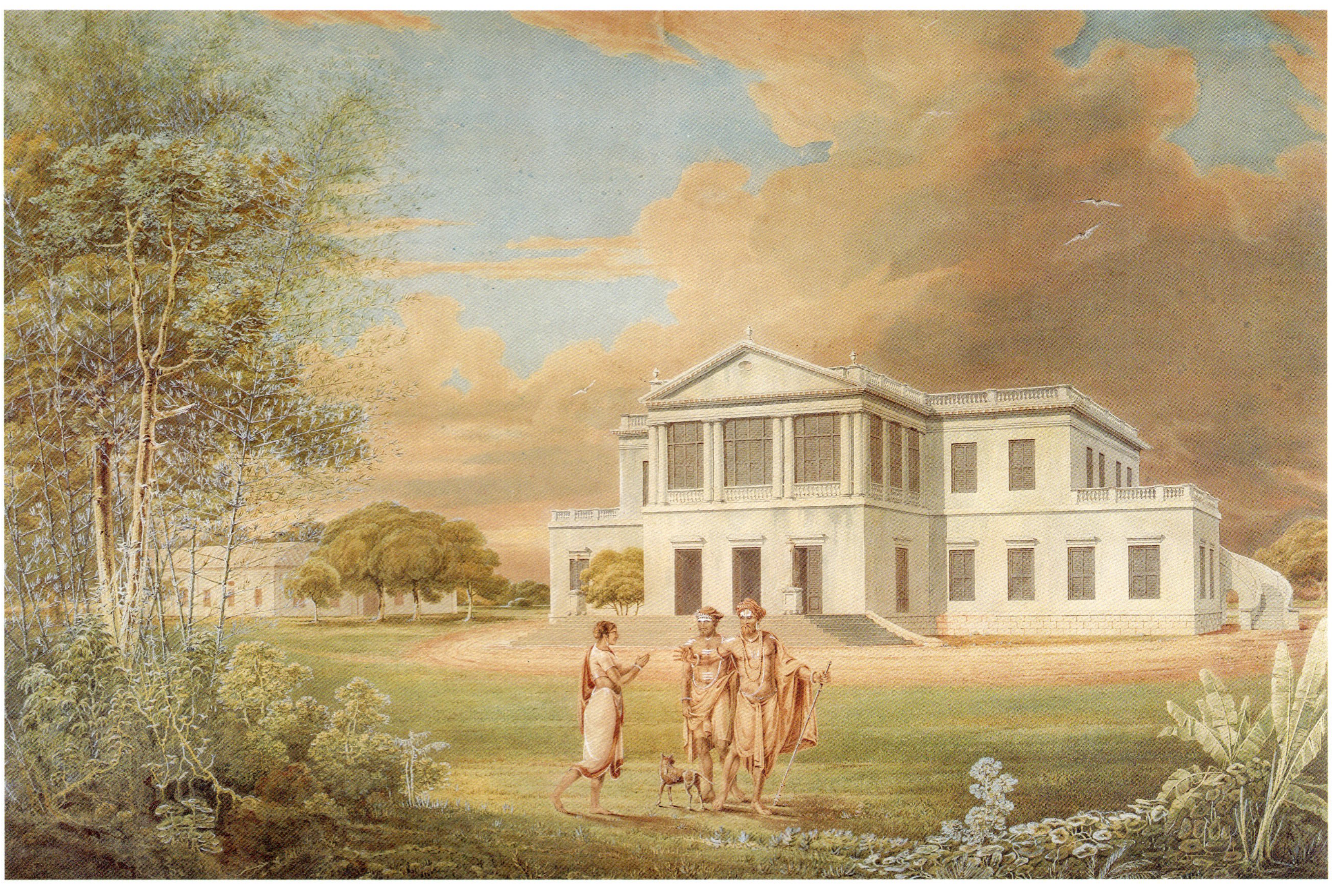

COLORPLATE 4.
Captain John Young Porter. *Sir Thomas Strange's House.* 1811. Watercolor.
Walter Collection.

business affairs. These middlemen proved to be the undoing of many a Company servant. Although aspiring civil servants were given language training in the administrative colleges in Britain after 1857, and although throughout the history of British India the study of Indian languages was assiduously pursued by gifted Britons (including Sir William Jones, the famed Orientalist), by and large language was a significant factor in keeping the rulers and the ruled apart. The adoption of English as the official administrative language, largely due to the efforts of Thomas Babington Macauley, who served on Bentinck's Supreme Council from 1834 to 1838, partly solved the administrative problem. Macauley's recommendations affected India more deeply and permanently than many other measures adopted by the British. The change in attitude between Macauley's day and the end of the nineteenth century is best illustrated by comparing D'Oyly's 1813 lithograph of a language

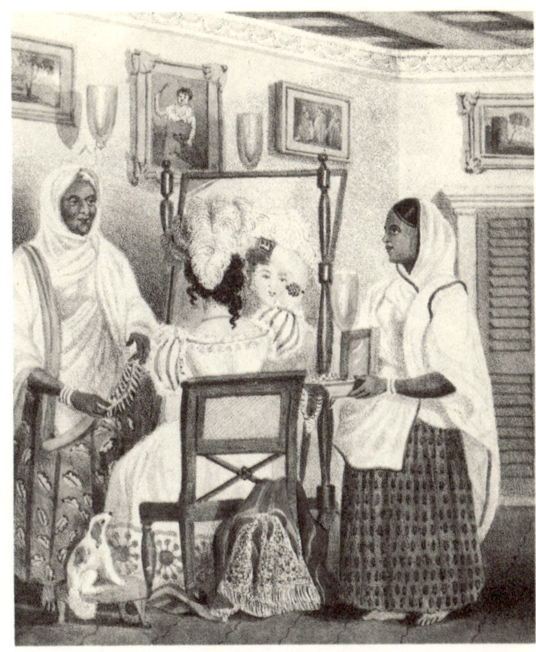

53. Sir Charles D'Oyly. *Female Attendants* from *Costumes of India*. 1830. Colored lithograph. Walter Collection.

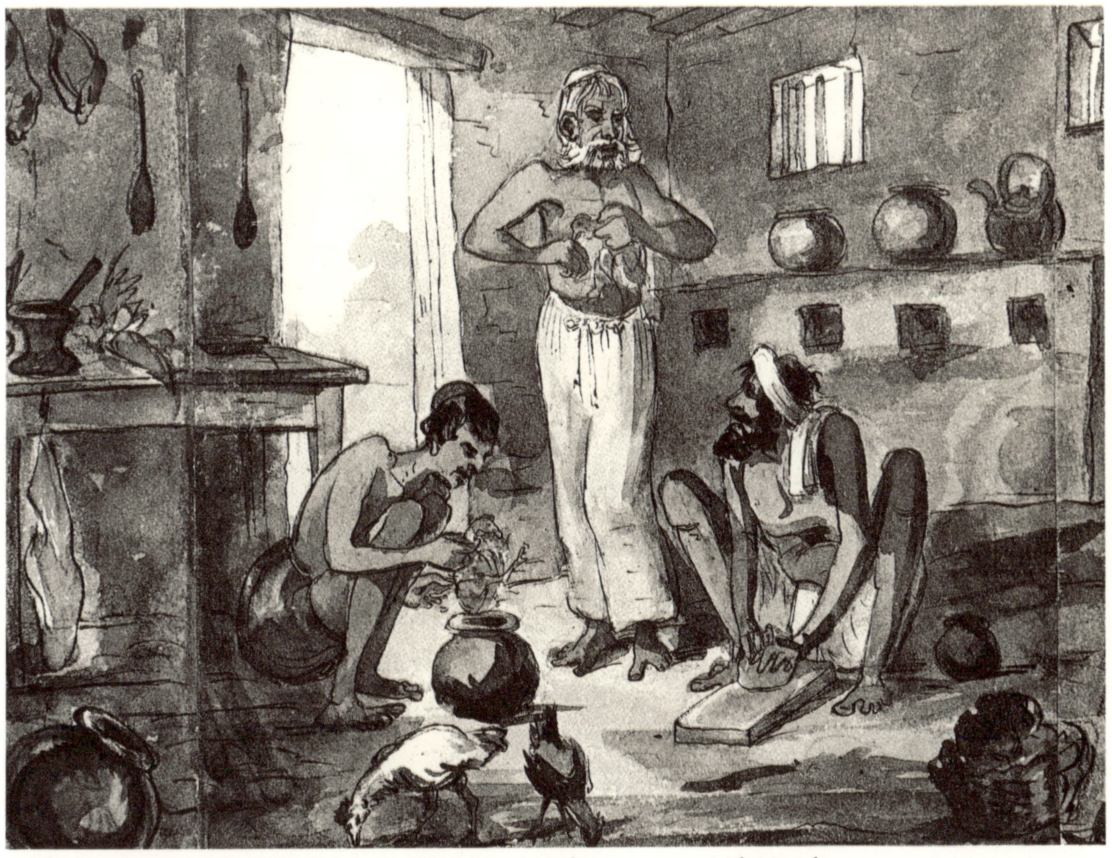

54. G. F. Atkinson. *Our Cook Room* from *Curry and Rice*. 1859. Lithograph.

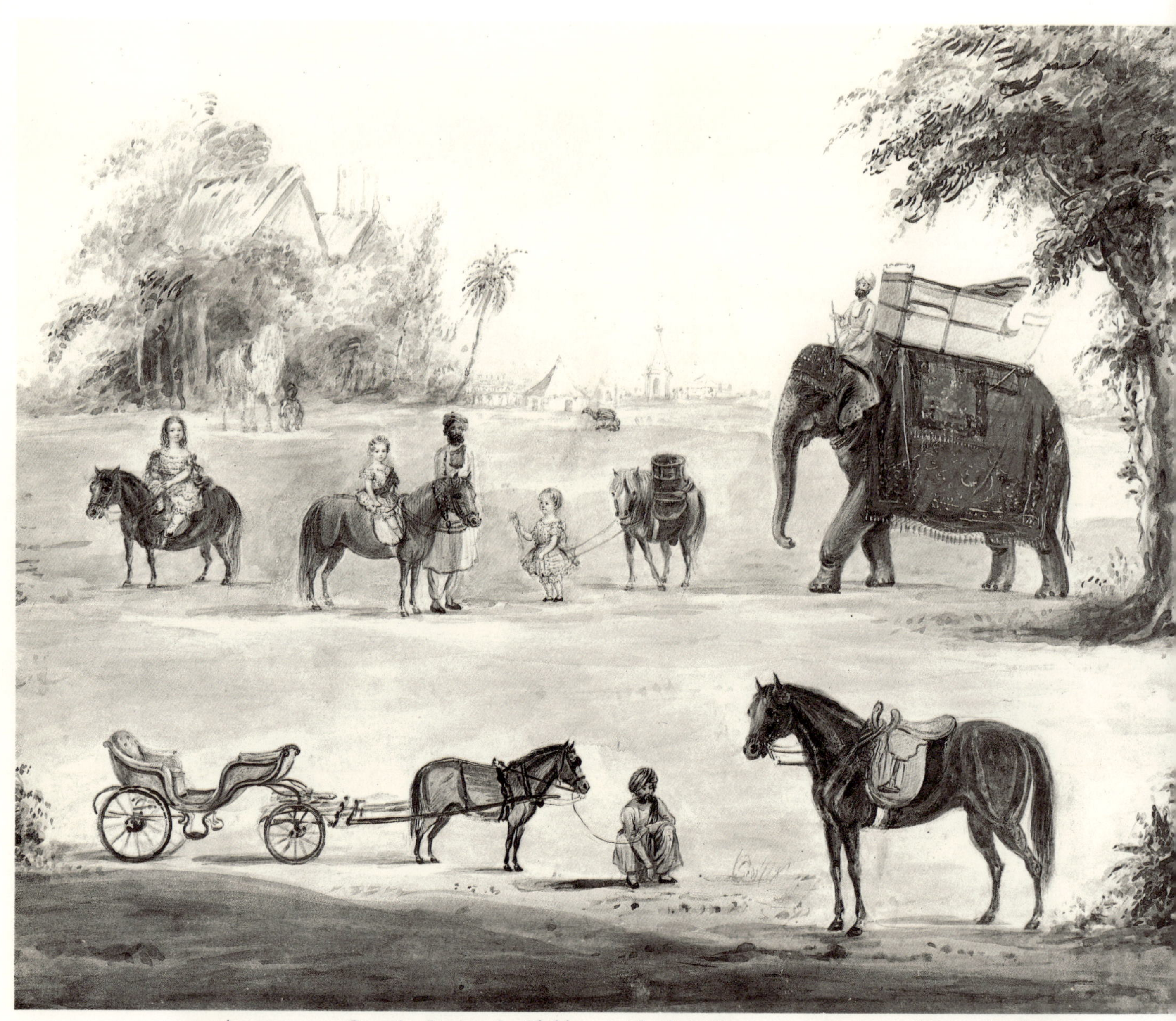

55. Anonymous. *Captain Simpson's Children with their Ponies.* c. 1840–50. Watercolor. Walter Collection.

lesson (fig. 56) with a lithograph by Atkinson from 1859 (fig. 57). The disdainful attitude of the student toward the *munshi*, or teacher, is now clearly evident in the later caricature. Atkinson, who served with the Bengal Engineers between 1840 and 1859, was a talented artist who must have been encouraged early in life, for his mother had studied with Chinnery in Calcutta. He also appears to have been considerably influenced by D'Oyly.

V

UNTIL the seat of government was transferred to Delhi in 1911, Calcutta was the commercial and political capital of British India and Burma. Its residents had far more privileges and diversions than those who lived elsewhere. Amateur theaters and concerts, dinners and balls, horse races and parades, as well as colorful Indian festivals such as Durga puja, Charak (hook-swinging), and Mohurrum offered rich fare for the varied

66

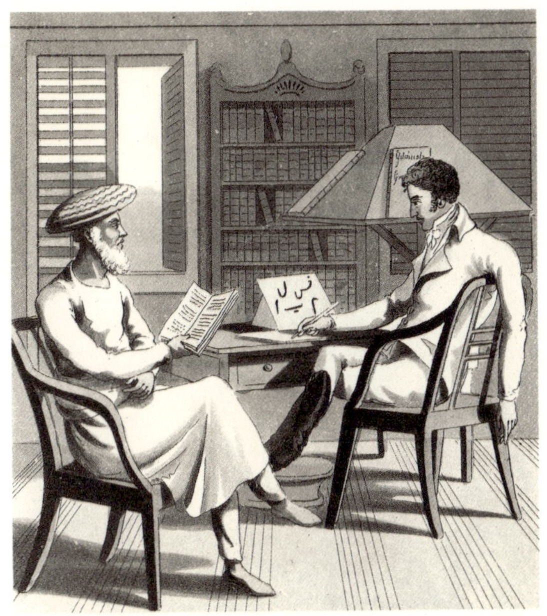

56. Sir Charles D'Oyly. *English Gentleman and his Munshi or Native Professor of Languages* from *The European in India*. 1813. Colored lithograph. Walter Collection.

tastes of the cosmopolitan society. Generally, the "season" began with the cooler days of autumn, early in October, when the government officials and most memsahibs returned from the hillstations, and lasted until the next exodus sometime in late March. The sahibs often had to return to their duties in the plains long before their families did.

The season consisted of one long series of dinners and dances, not only in Calcutta but in most Anglo-Indian settlements. The climax was the grand feast (*burrah-khana*) in the governor-general's palace in Calcutta followed by a ball, which usually took place around Christmas. Fancy dress balls were particularly popular both in government circles as well as in the clubs and *gymkhanas*. Even the children had their own little fancy dress parties. "The English ladies," wrote a journalist in the 1790s, "are immoderately fond of dancing, an exercise ill calculated for the burning climate of Bengal. Imagine to

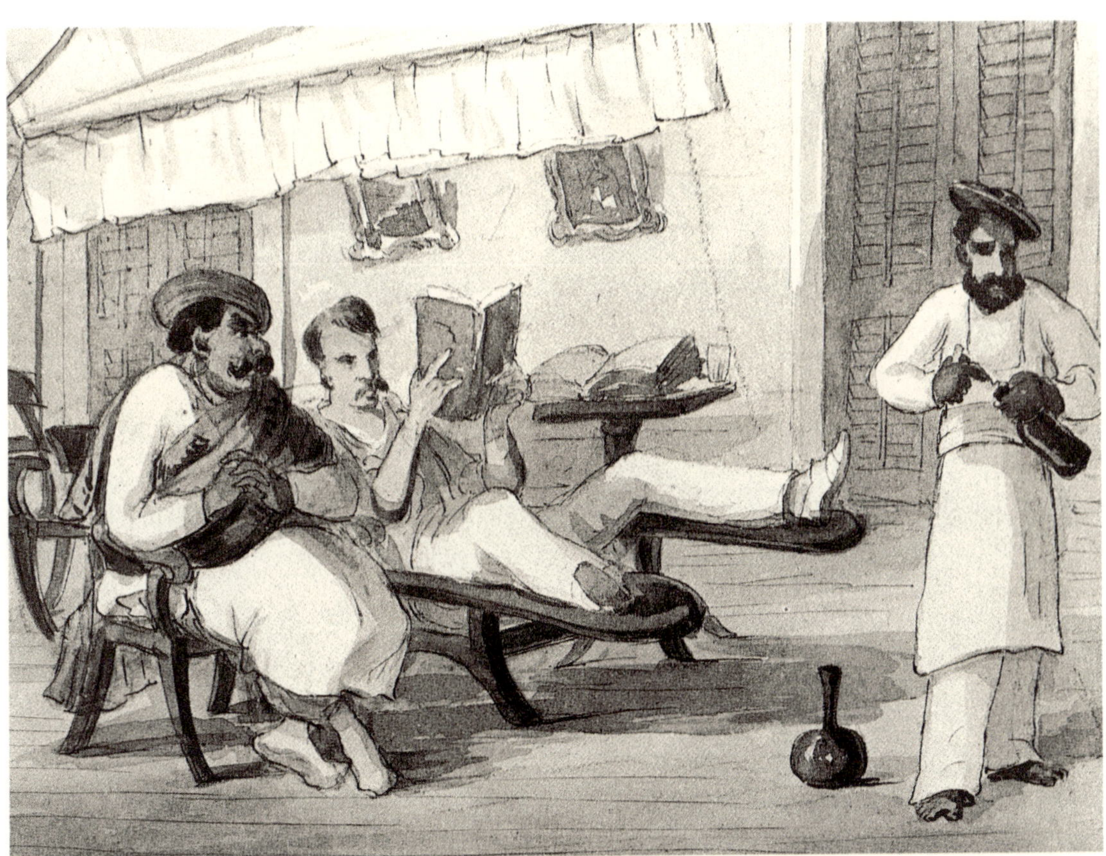

57. G. F. Atkinson. *Our Moonshee* from *Curry and Rice*. 1859. Lithograph.

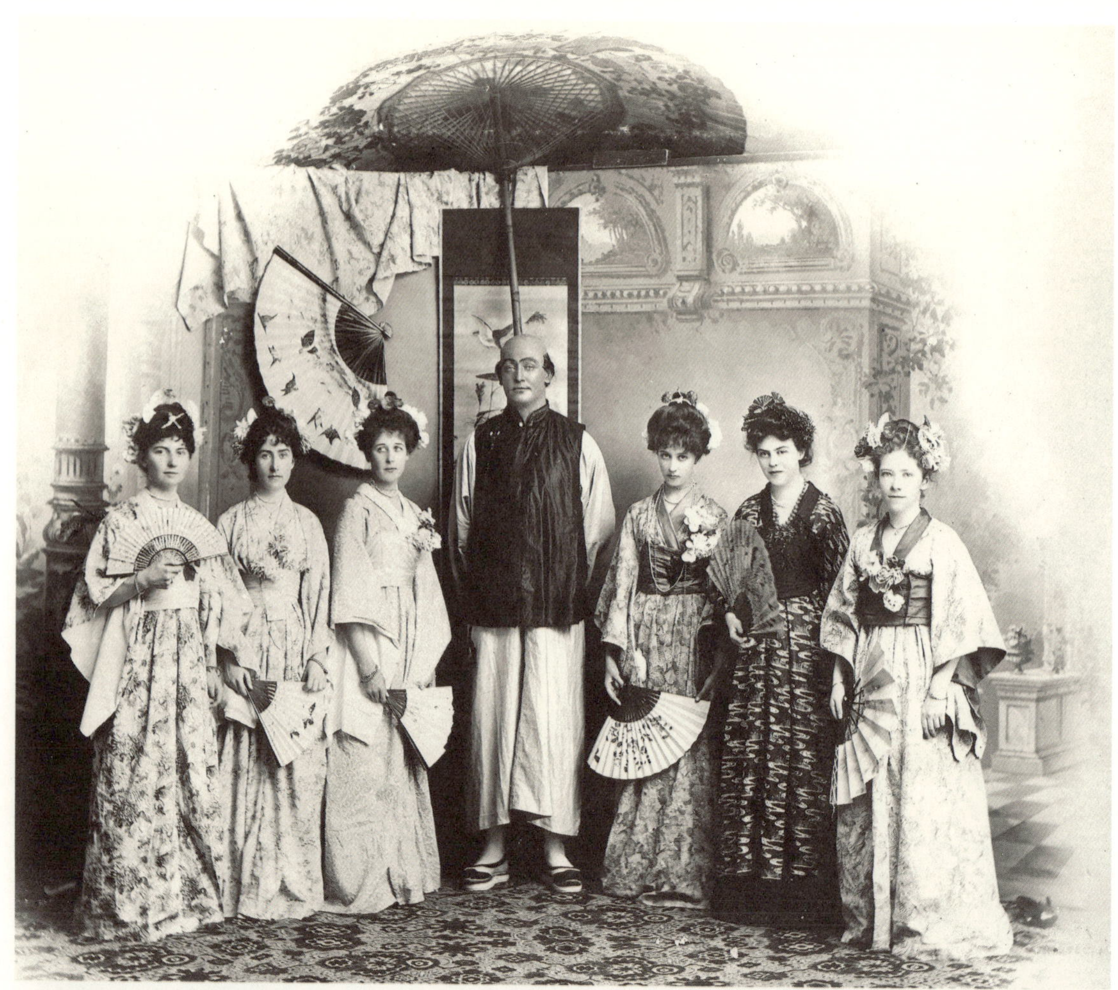

58. Anonymous. *Scene from San Toy Performed at Poona*. 1900. Gelatin-silver print. Walter Collection.

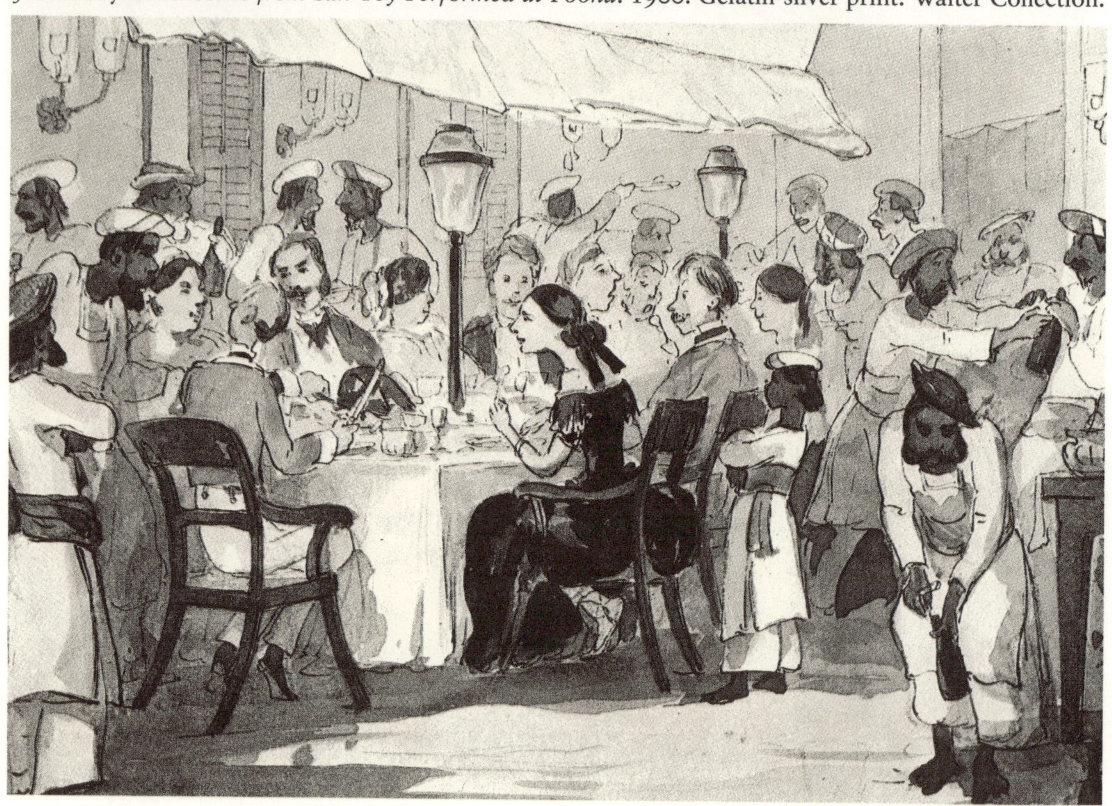

59. G. F. Atkinson. *Our Burra-Khanah* from *Curry and Rice*. 1859. Lithograph.

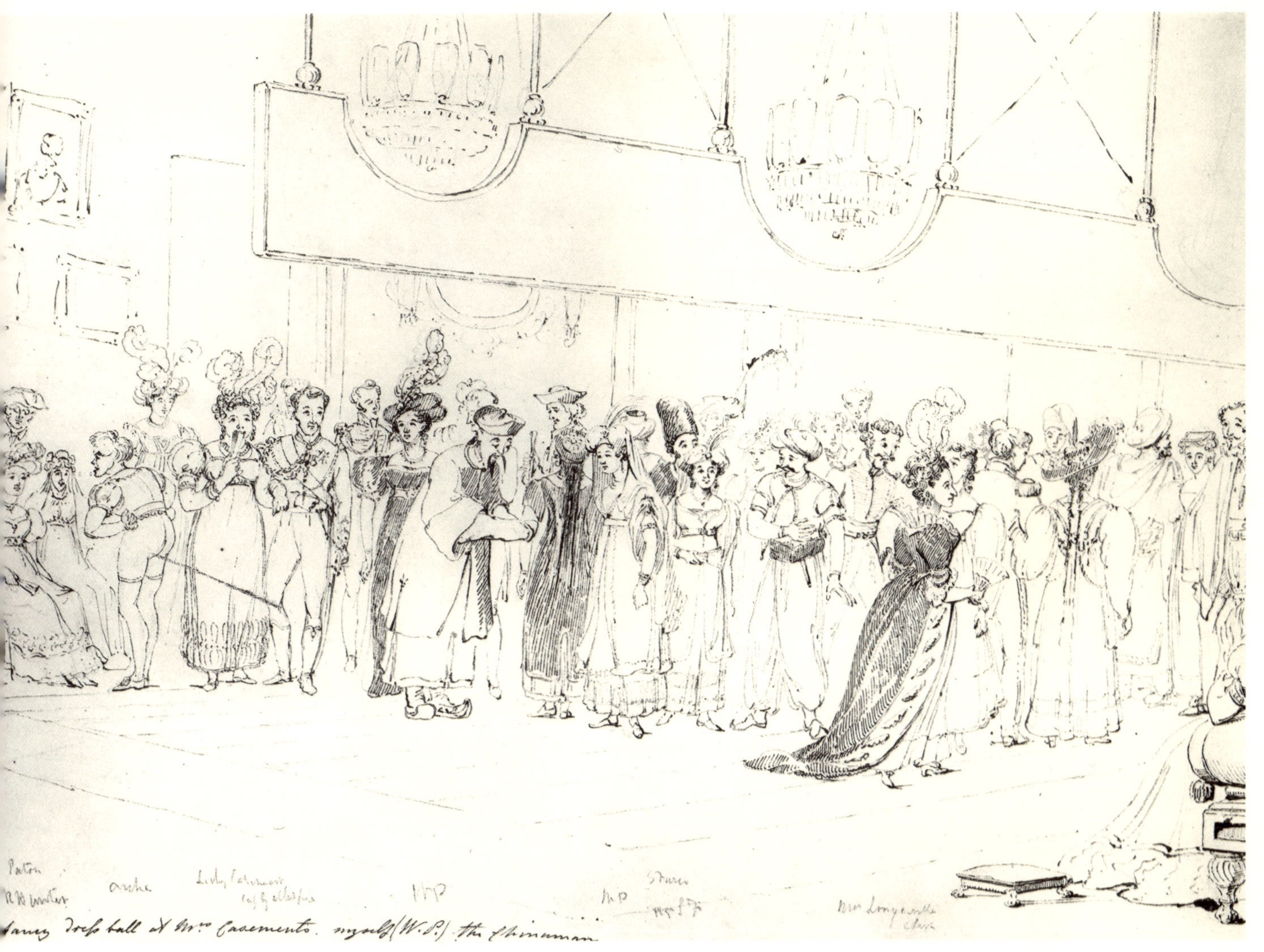

60. William Prinsep. *A Fancy Dress Ball at Mrs. Casement's.* c. 1824. Pen and ink. Walter Collection.

yourself the lovely object of your affections ready to expire with heat, every limb trembling and every feature distorted with fatigue, and her partner with a muslin handkerchief in each hand employed in the delightful office of dipping down her face, while the big drips stand impearled upon her forehead."[12]

Naturally, most of the dinners and parties did not include the Indian community. While the nawabs of Oudh or the Sikh ruler Ranjit Singh ate freely with the British, most Hindus were afraid of being ostracized by their community leaders if they shared a meal with the foreigners. The situation was so strained, even in the cosmopolitan society of Calcutta of the 1830s, that Dwarakanath Tagore, a merchant prince who did a great deal of business with the British, had to set up a completely separate household for western-style entertainment, for which he was never forgiven by his wife. Tagore's garden house situated in the outskirts of the city was frequently used by newly married British couples for their honeymoons. Indian women were still in *purdah* and would not have dreamed of appearing before strange Indians, let alone foreigners. Indeed, not until after World War I did Indian women begin to appear in public and attend dinners and dances, and even then, such behavior was restricted mostly to royal families, civil servants, and a few highly westernized Indians, many of whom married a liberated second wife to fulfill their social obligations in order to advance their careers.

Indian food taboos also contributed to the social estrangement between the two societies. Moslems do not eat pork, while most Hindus do not eat meat of any kind. In the 1830s, some of the Hindu boys of the Hindu College in Calcutta began to defy convention by eating chicken and drinking wine which became the subject of a heated debate in the Bengali newspapers of the period and literally shook the very foundations of Bengali society. The middle-class Indians were extremely conservative in matters of dress as well, as is evident from an article in a Bengali newspaper of 1825 which discusses a couple of Bengali boys who were seen in the streets wearing European dress, and questions the propriety of such behavior, which was found frightening to women and a disgrace to their fathers, should they be mistaken for English youth.

Before dancing became popular, which coincided with the "importation" of British females, a dinner in the Anglo-Indian community was usually followed by a nautch performance. The word nautch is an early Anglicization of the Indian word *nach*, meaning dance, and among the many Indian customs adopted by the eighteenth-century Anglo-Indian, watching a nautch and smoking the hookah were by far the most popular. Dancing girls have formed an integral part of Indian culture since very ancient times. The encounter between the courtesan and ascetic is a stock motif in Sanskrit literature. At the Moslem courts, especially under the Moguls, dancing was an essential component of royal entertainment; until recently, it was part of Indian religious practice as well.

The British became quite infatuated with the Indian dances, as a Martha Mary Sherwood noted disapprovingly in the early nineteenth century:

The influence of these nautch-girls over the other sex, even over men who have been brought up in England, and who have known, admired and respected their own country-women, is not to be accounted for. . . .

It steals upon those who come within its charmed circle in a way not unlike that of an intoxicating drug, being the more dangerous to young Europeans because they seldom fear it. . . .[13]

Mrs. Sherwood's observations could well be applied to the wealthy and influential Bengalis of Calcutta as well, many of whom squandered their fortunes and even shed blood pursuing the ephemeral pleasures provided by their favorites. Nautches remained popular with the Indians as an invariable part of the entertainment they provided for the Anglo-Indian community, both at the courts and in Calcutta.

Indeed, no *Durga puja*, the autumn festival of the goddess celebrated with great pomp in Calcutta, was complete without a nautch organized for the invited European guests. The Russian visitor Prince Alexis Soltykoff's rendering of the *Durga puja* is set in a Bengali house and shows

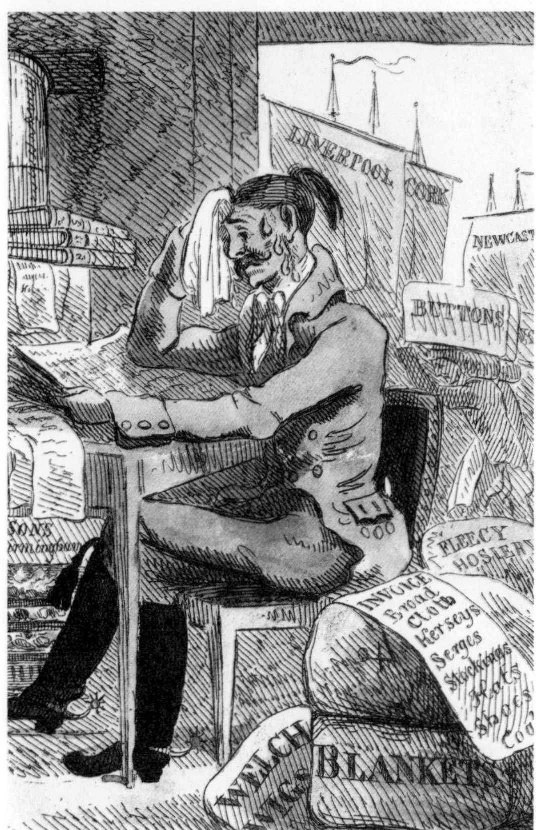

61. Anonymous. *A Native Merchant in the English Costume.* c. 1812. Colored engraving (page from a scrapbook). Walter Collection.

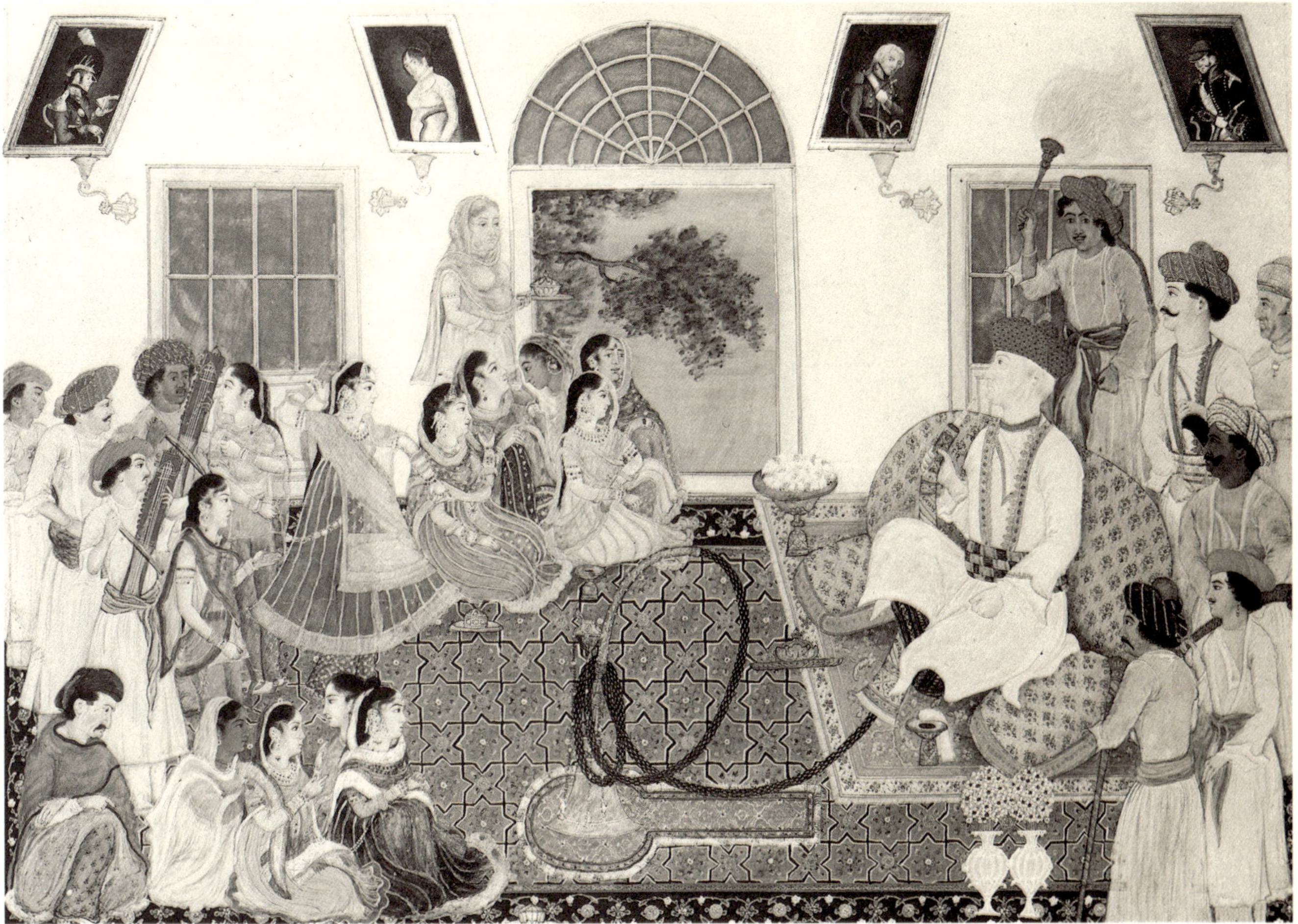

62. Anonymous. *Sir David Ochterlony Watching a Nautch*. c. 1820. Watercolor and gold. Reproduced by permission of the India Office Library and Records (British Library).

a nautch being performed in front of the image of the goddess beneath a swinging *punkah* hanging from the ceiling (fig. 63). Interestingly, the group of Europeans includes women, though presumably the ladies of the house did not appear to receive them. It is curious that foreigners were allowed to enter the sacred area but were otherwise not permitted inside houses or Hindu temples.

The Anglo-Indians of Calcutta passed a good deal of time in coffee houses and taverns. A visitor of 1780 recalled:

I was, en passant, shown a tavern, called The London Hotel, where entertainments are furnished at the moderate price of a gold mohur a head, exclusive of the desserts and wines. At the coffee-houses your single dish of coffee costs you a rupee (half a crown); which half a crown, however, franks you to the perusal of the English newspapers, which are regularly arranged on a file, as in London. . . .[14]

A curious form of amusement that was invented and enjoyed by early Calcutta society was the practice of pelleting each other with morsels of bread at the dinner table. As noted by William Hickey, with obvious disapproval:

In this party I first saw the barbarous custom of pelleting each other with little balls of bread, made like pills, across the table, which was even practised by the fair sex. Some people could discharge them with such force as to cause considerable pain when struck in the face.[15]

Fortunately, however, this strange and childish custom "fitter for savages than polished so-

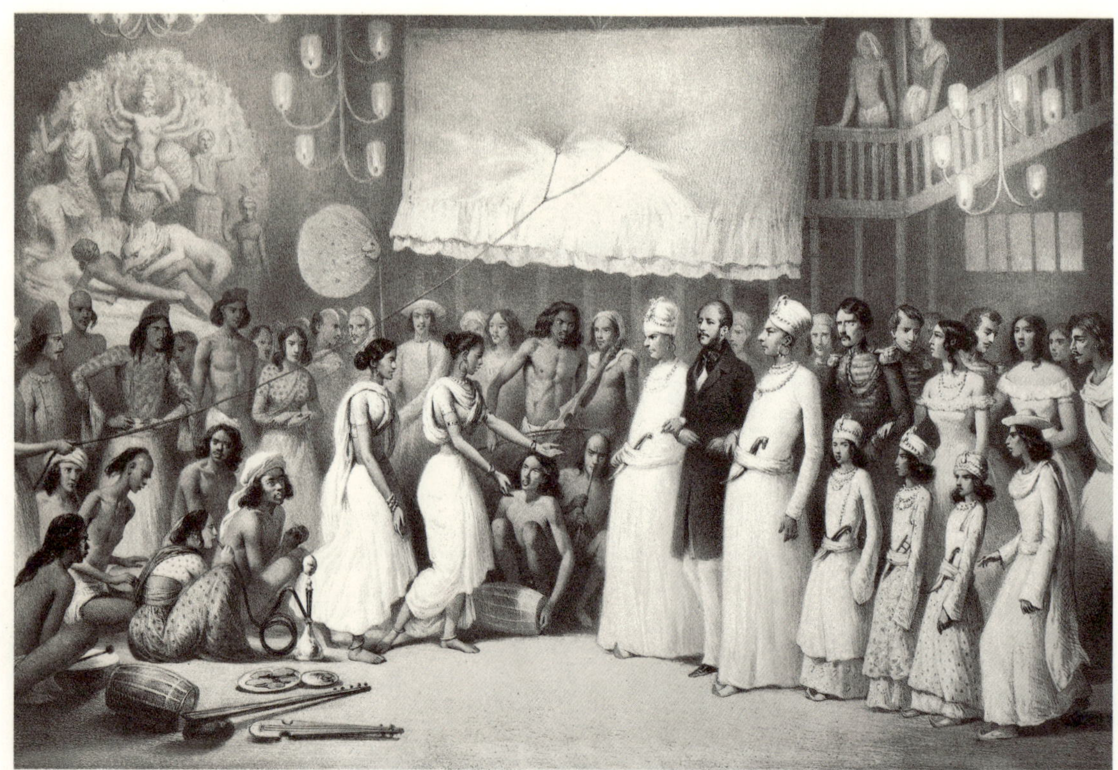

63. Prince Alexis Soltykoff. *Festival of the Goddess Durga at Calcutta* from *Indian Scenes and Characters*. 1858. Lithograph. Walter Collection.

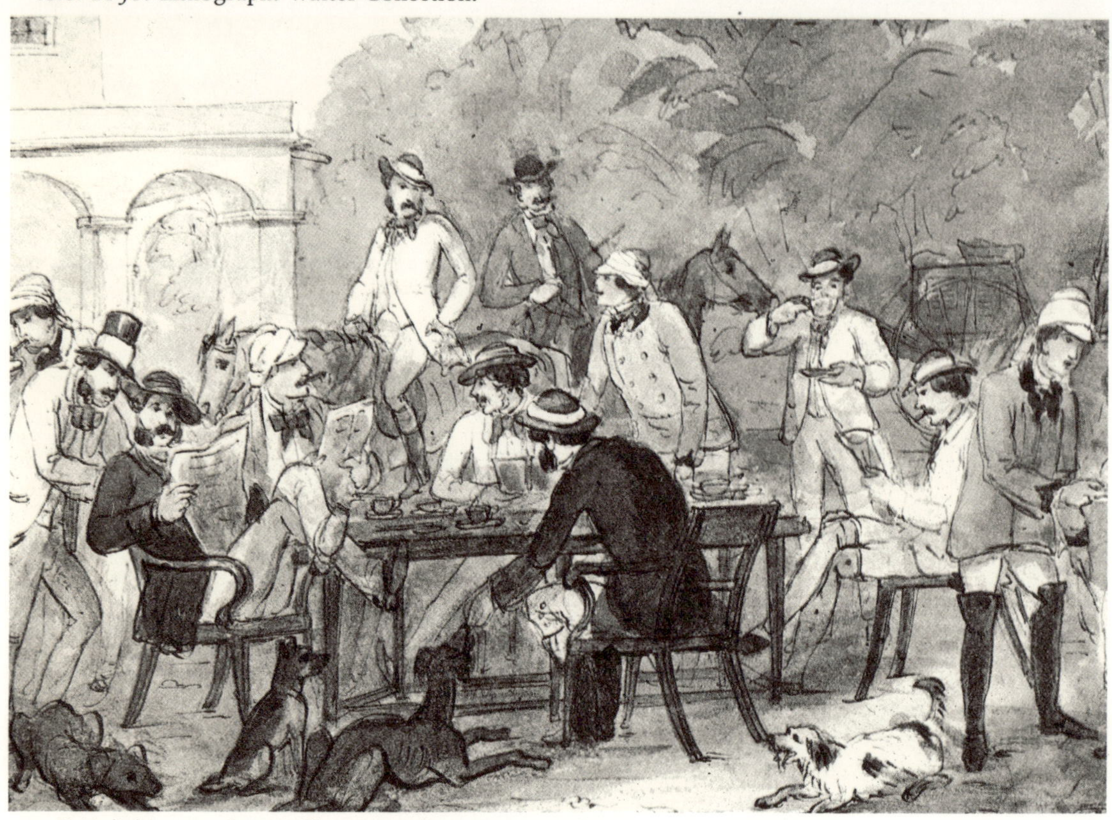

64. G. F. Atkinson. *Our Coffee House* from *Curry and Rice*. 1859. Lithograph.

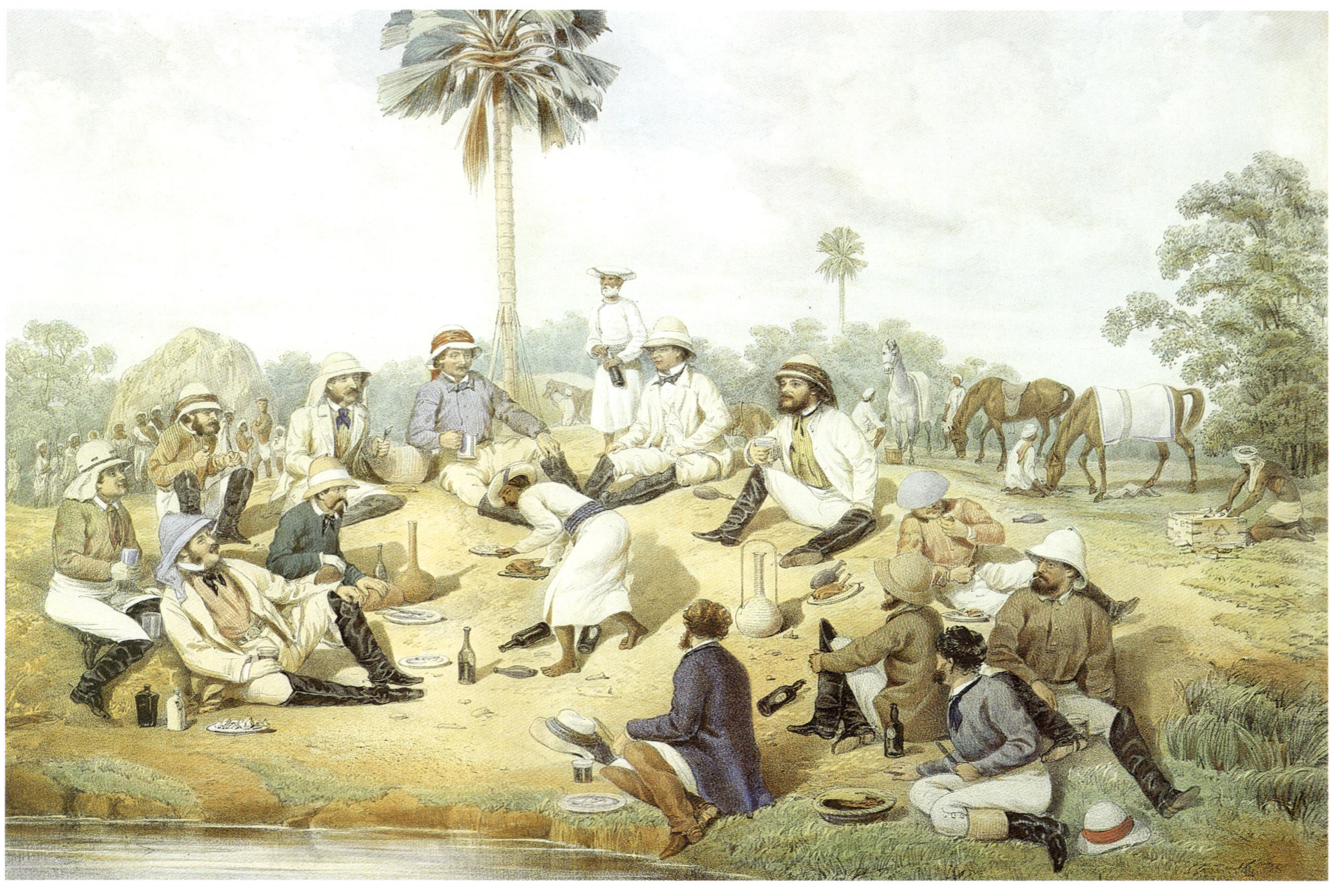

COLORPLATE 5.
Percy Carpenter. *The Tent Club at Tiffin.* 1861. Lithograph.
Walter Collection.

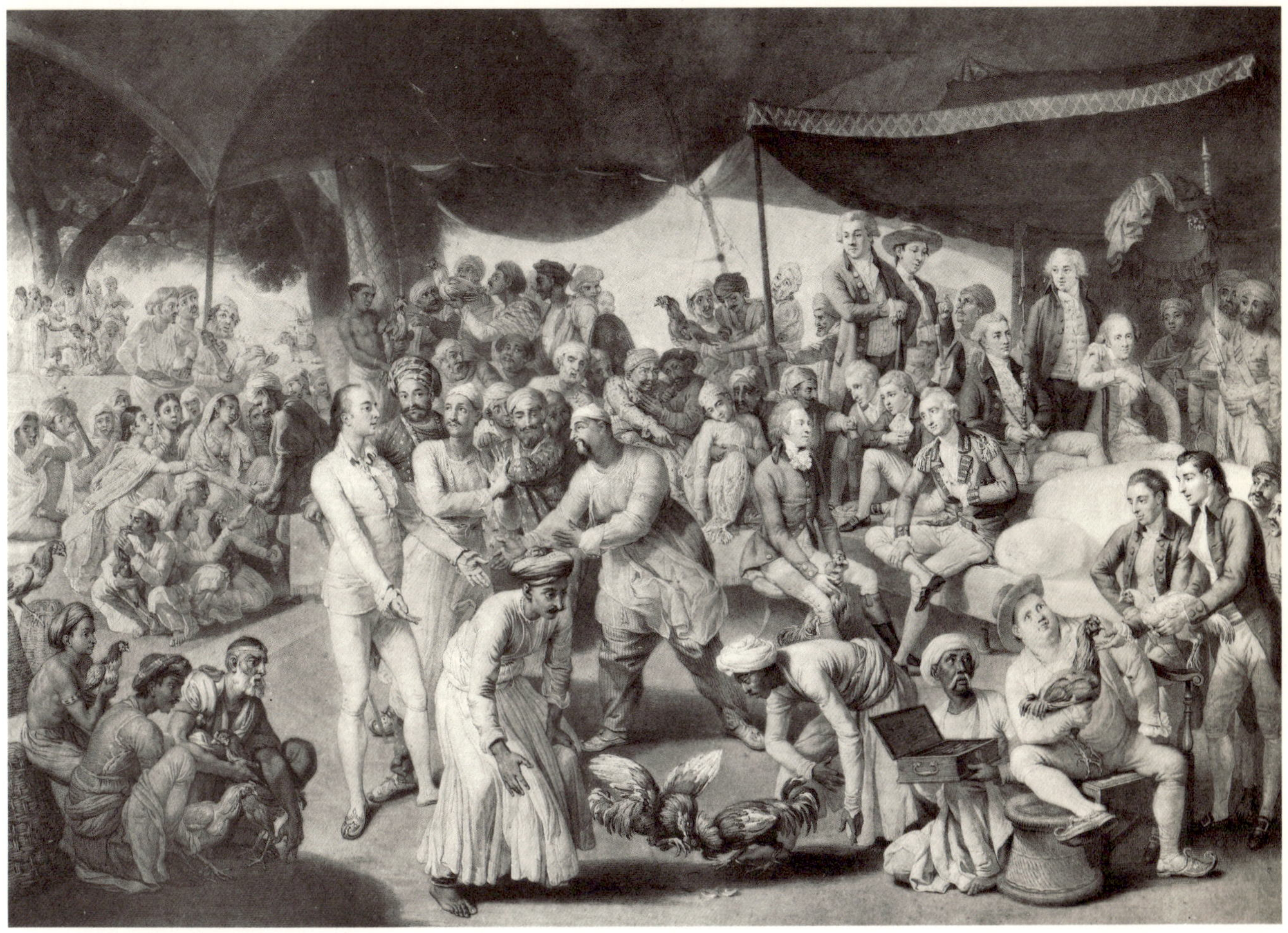

65. Johann Zoffany. *Cockfight*. c. 1784. Lithograph. Walter Collection.

ciety" was abandoned by the British during Hickey's sojourn in Calcutta.

The polished society in Lucknow entertained itself with cockfights, immortalized by Zoffany in his masterly composition (fig. 65). The representation remains a testament to the freer social interaction between Europeans and Indians that prevailed in the age of the nabob. Cockfights, however, were not to everyone's taste. "This barbarous amusement is a particular favourite with the people of Lucknow, and is as great a source of demoralisation here, as it is in every country where the custom prevails," wrote a young captain visiting the city in the 1830s.[16]

Hunting was one of the favorite pastimes of the higher echelons of Anglo-Indian society and of the nawabs and maharajas. Indeed, a *shikar*, or shoot, remained one of the few occasions when the rulers and the ruled mixed freely. Throughout the British presence in India, the *shikar* remained the principal diversion of the Raj and was considered an essential means to augment the imperial image. Percy Carpenter's lively picture, *The Tent Club at Tiffin*, does not include Indians or British women, but the latter often accompanied their men on such occasions (colorplate 5). In addition to hunting jackals (instead of the English fox), pigsticking was a particularly favorite sport. For visiting British dignitaries, the maharajas would arrange elaborate tiger hunts or deadly duels between tigers and buffaloes which the distinguished visitors watched from the safety of a high stand beyond the securely palisaded arena. Needless to say, these *shikars* resulted in the large-scale slaughter of countless numbers of animals. In 1912 the

73

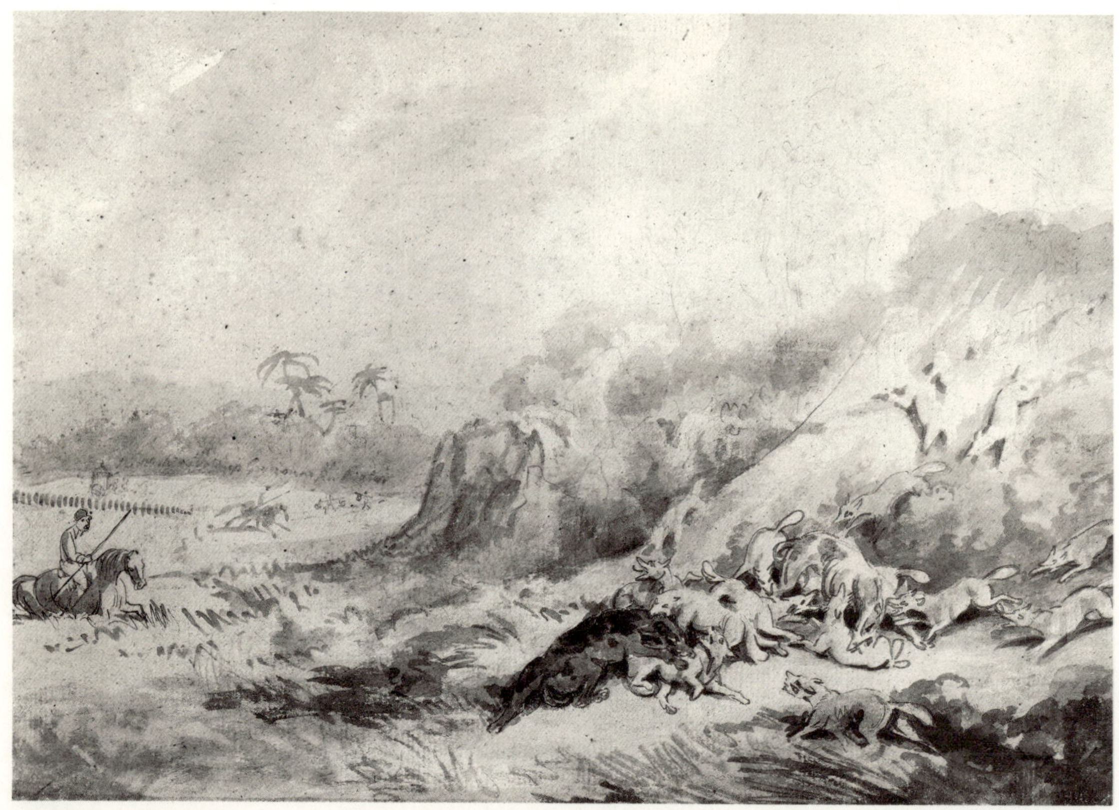

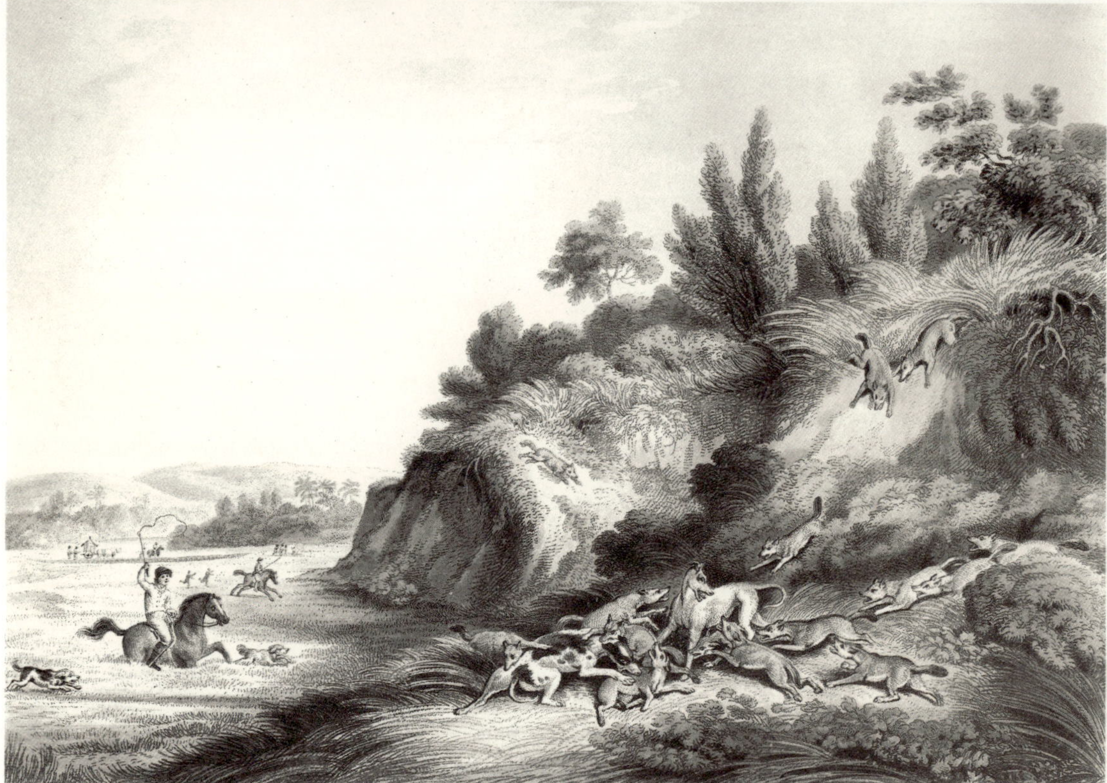

66 a, b. Captain Thomas Williamson. *Hunting Jackals*. 1806 Original watercolor sketch and colored lithograph. Walter Collection.

74

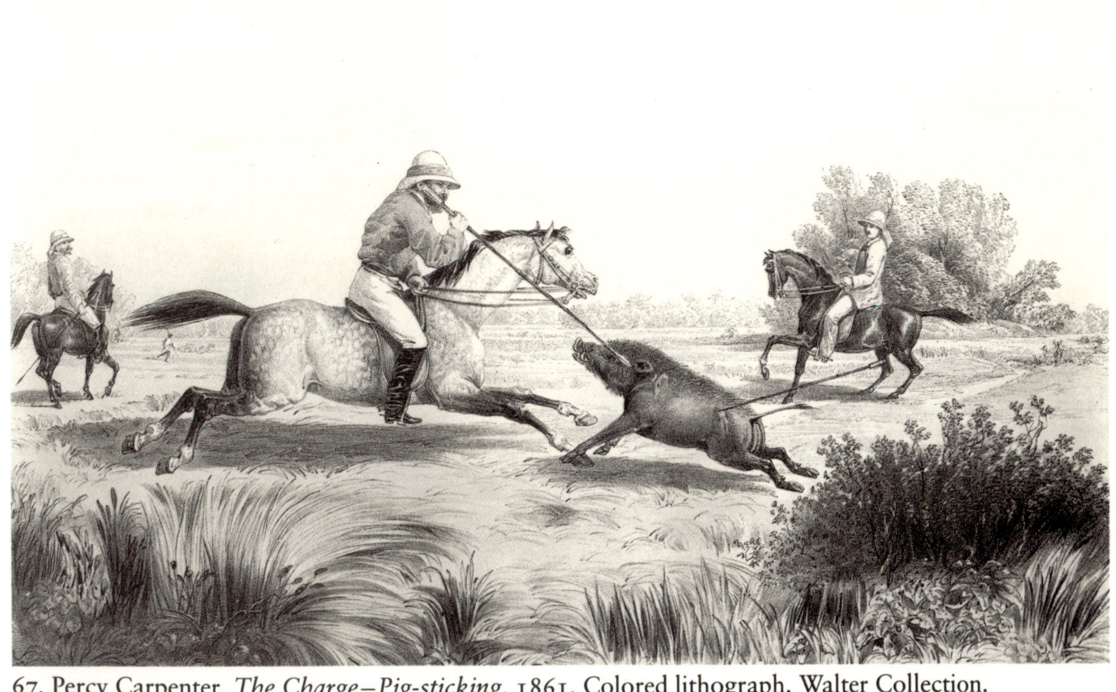

67. Percy Carpenter. *The Charge—Pig-sticking*. 1861. Colored lithograph. Walter Collection.

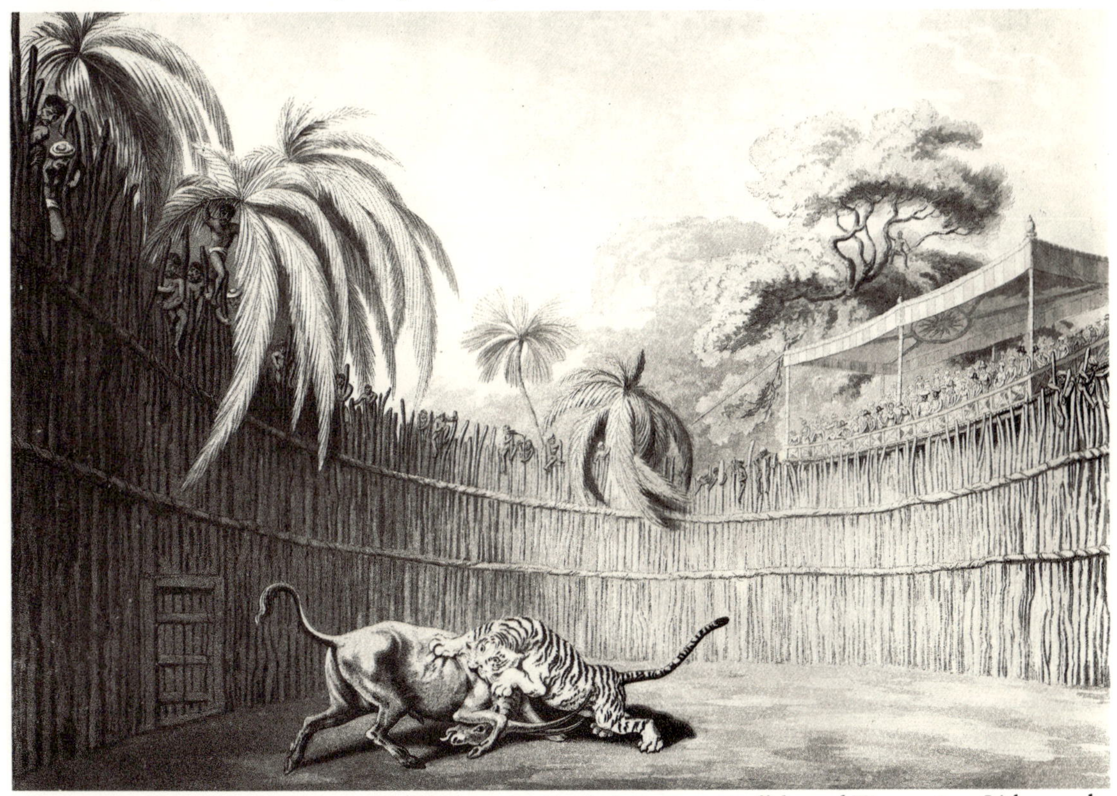

68. Captain Thomas Williamson. *Exhibition of a Battle between a Buffalo and Tiger*. 1807. Lithograph. Walter Collection.

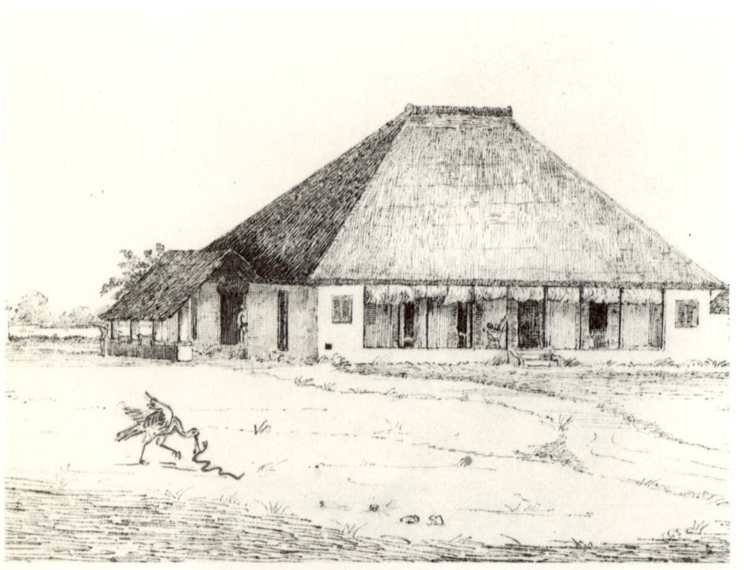

69. P. C. French. Detail from *Desolation Hall, Futtehpore*. 1844. Pen and ink. Walter Collection.

Delhi Tent Club alone was responsible for 385 boars. In his memoirs, Sir Basil Gould, whose distinguished career in the Indian Civil Service spanned almost the entire period of the British Raj in the twentieth century, wrote:

Whatever may have been the political pros and cons of moving the capital to Delhi, it was a splendid place in those days for sport. From my bed in the early morning I could hear black and grey partridge calling, the Ridge between Viceregal Lodge and the City was full of hares, there were wild pig within a mile, and the country all round teemed with game—blackbuck, chinkera, duck, teal, snipe, partridge, peacock, geese, quail, and a lot more.[17]

There is ample evidence to disprove Charles Allen's recent statement that the average British hunter "generally shot 'for the pot'" and that the practice of slaughtering large numbers of animals and birds "was confined to the Native States. . . ."[18]

The *shikars* also affected the lives of the poor peasants whose crops were thoughtlessly damaged. In 1914, the master of the Madras hunt sent the following memorandum to his subscribers: "to refrain, as much as possible, from riding over crops. . . . Remember that even a few annas worth of damage is of material conse-

quence to the small cultivator and that his good will is essential for the sport."

VI

THE picture of Anglo-India that the British artists, whether professional or amateur, left behind is essentially incomplete. Kettle, Zoffany, and others only painted portraits of the upperclass Anglo-Indians who could afford their fees. Most of their clients lived in the larger cities and towns in palatial mansions; in Calcutta, most owned both townhouses and large garden houses. There was, however, a large population of Europeans that were less affluent but literature and the visual arts provide us with little insight into their lives. The generals had their memorials and monuments but the ordinary British soldier, who first helped expand and then preserve the empire, remains a shadowy figure.

As George Orwell wrote in 1935, "The life of the 'Anglo-Indian' officials is not all jam. In comfortless camps, in sweltering offices, in gloomy *dak* bungalows smelling of dust and earth-oil, they earn, perhaps, the right to be a little disagreeable."[19] P. C. French was a witty and competent amateur in the D'Oyly tradition and his title for his sketch, *Desolation Hall, Futtehpore*, speaks a volume (fig. 69). This sort of bungalow was the typical home of an officer. French's drawing is evidently accurate from the description of such a bungalow given by a civil servant:

With most bungalows you got a thatched roof and then the ceiling of each room was a hessian cloth painted with white-wash. Between the hessian cloth ceiling and the thatch roof was a space which was usually inhabited by bats and often by snakes—you could look up and sometimes see a snake wriggling along the other side of the cloth.[20]

It is not surprising that a civil servant waited years before bringing home a bride—not before he had moved on to the *pukka* (solid) bungalow in one of the larger stations, a more modest version of the two-storied, flat-roofed structure with pillars and pediment shown in colorplate 4.

76

VII

IN 1858, John Company ceased to exist and the British Crown assumed direct responsibility for the fate of its most important possession. The events that precipitated the demise of the Company's rule are variously referred to as the Mutiny, the Revolt, the Rebellion of 1857, the Sepoy Rebellion, or the First War of Independence. A general war of independence it was not, but it did brutally express the hatred of British authority felt among certain segments of Indian society. It was not a mass uprising, and it did not have a nationalistic or an intellectual basis. By and large, it began as a revolt of sepoys, both Hindu and Moslem, in the Company's armies and gained momentum from disgruntled landowners and some native princes in what was then known as the upcountry (areas in what are today Uttar and Madhya Pradesh).

There was genuine discontent among the native regiments whose pay and quarters were far inferior to those of their British counterparts. In addition, there were various complications as a result of their religious sensibilities; Hindu sepoys, for example, did not want to go abroad for fear of losing their caste status. In the eighteenth century, missionaries had not been allowed to work in India but this policy had changed by 1830 and great numbers of them flocked to India to spread the gospel and "civilize" the natives. Often with the approval of both civilian and military authorities, they set about to convert the Indians, especially the soldiers. Their disregard for the sepoys' religious convictions was one of the sparks that ignited the fuse. Another provocation concerned the rifle cartridges that the British had supplied which were wrapped in paper heavily greased with tallow. The ends of these cartridges had to

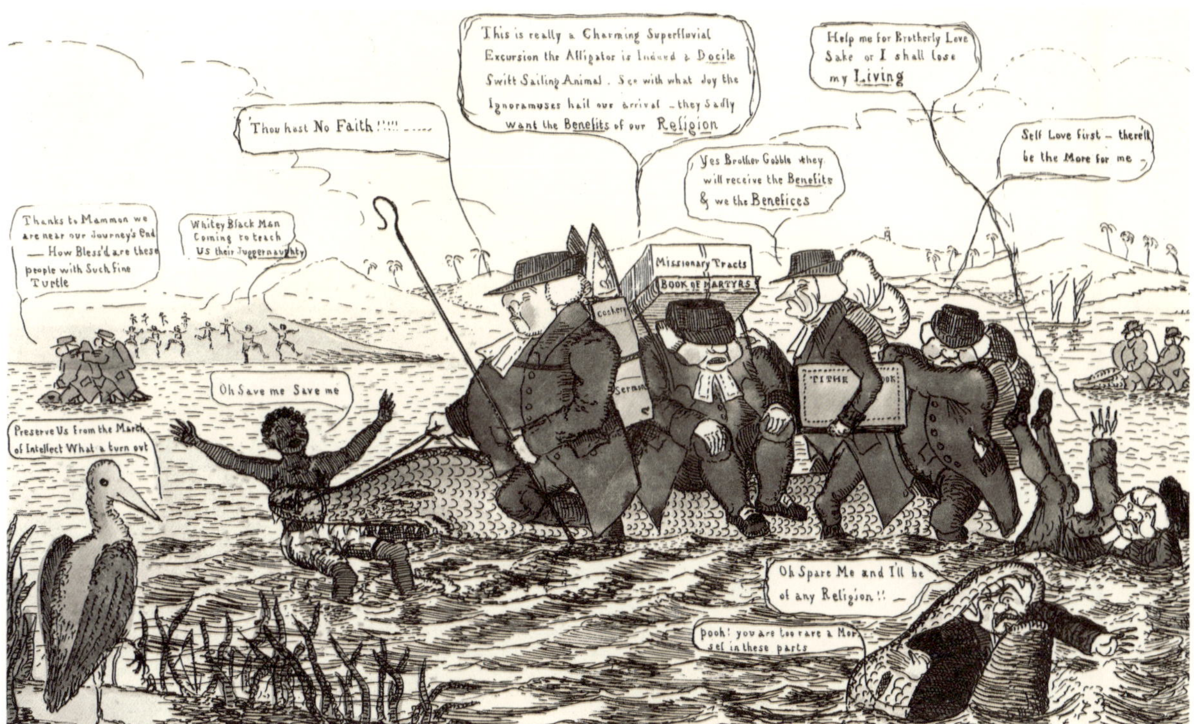

70. Anonymous. *Emigration of the Clergy, or a Translation to India to Convert the Innocent Indoos.* 1830. Colored engraving. Walter Collection.

be bitten off before they could be loaded into the guns. As these cartridges had been manufactured in England, it was uncertain whether the tallow was made from beef or pork fat, both of which were offensive to the Hindus and the latter to the Moslems. Though the British made an effort to replace the cartridges, suspicions had become deeply rooted and the damage was done.

The major cause of disaffection among the landholders and some of the Indian rulers was the aggressive policy of annexation adopted by Lord Dalhousie who arrived in 1848 as the new governor-general. Dalhousie was ruthless in dis-

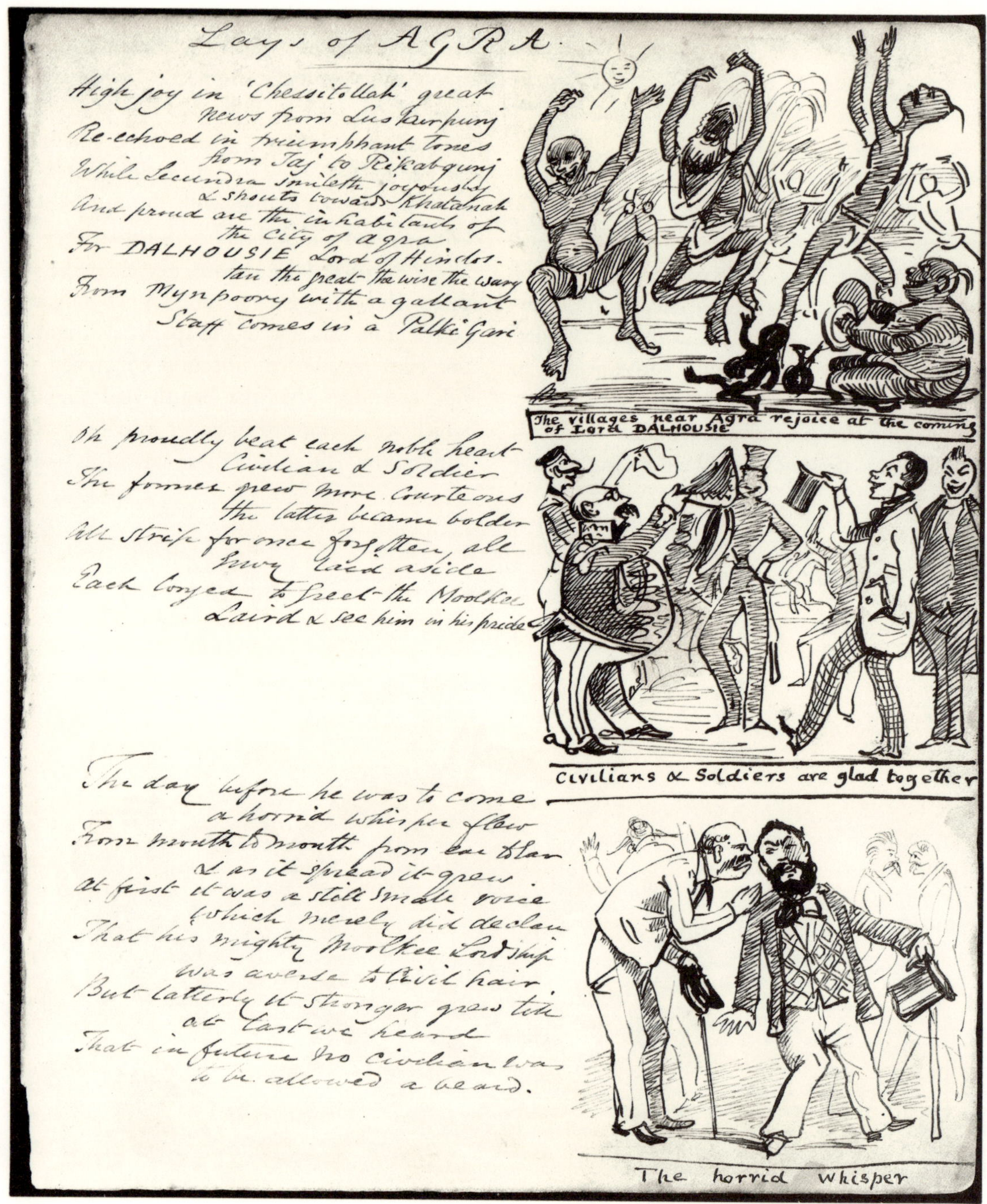

71. P. C. French. *Lays of Agra—Poems and Sketches.* 1844. Pen and ink. Walter Collection.

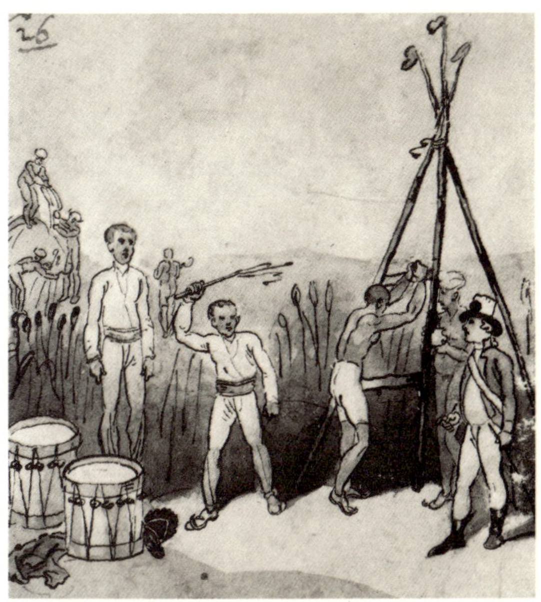

72. Robert Mabon. *Sepoy Punishment*. c. 1792. Watercolor over pencil. Yale Center for British Art, Paul Mellon Collection.

possessing major landholders of large portions of their estates, while thousands of lesser landlords lost their land altogether. As Hibbert points out, "Many, relatively poor, who let out small parcels of land while ploughing other pieces themselves—the kind of men from amongst whom most sepoys were recruited—had also been deprived of the lands which they inherited. So they, too, felt deeply aggrieved by the Governments' reforms, apprehensive as to what further deprivations their British rulers [had] in mind."[21] Dalhousie was equally high-handed and tyrannical in annexing territories of Indian rulers on the slightest pretext of misgovernance and refused to recognize the ancient Hindu custom of adopted heirs. All this angered Hindus and Moslems alike and shook their faith in the British system.

The situation was further exacerbated by the drastically altered attitude of the British officers by the mid-nineteenth century. As Hibbert notes, "All the sepoys' fears, suspicions and grievances might even so have been overcome, had there remained the same sympathy and understanding between them and their officers as had existed in the earlier years of the century and in the century before."[22] Sita Ram Pande, a sepoy in the Twenty-sixth Bengal Native Infantry, recalled that era:

In those days the sahibs could speak our language much better than they do now, and they mixed more with us. Although officers today have to pass the language examination, and have to read books, they do not understand our language . . . . The only language they learn is that of the lower orders, which they pick up from their servants, and which is unsuitable to be used in polite conversation. The sahibs often used to give nautches for the regiment, and they attended all the men's games. They also took us with them when they went out hunting, or at least all those of us who wanted to go . . . . Nowadays they seldom attend nautches because their padre sahibs have told them it is wrong. These padre sahibs have done, and are still doing, many things to estrange the British officers from the sepoy.[23]

An unknown British resident who wrote about the rebellion was less circumspect than Pande regarding the prevailing attitude of the officers:

The sepoy is [regarded as] an inferior creature. He is sworn at. He is treated roughly. He is spoken of as a "nigger." He is addressed as "suar" or pig, an epithet most opprobrious to a respectable native, especially the Mussulman, and which cuts him to the quick. The old [officers] are less guilty . . . but the younger men seem to regard it as an excellent joke, as an evidence of spirit and a praiseworthy sense of superiority over the sepoy to treat him as an inferior animal.[24]

VIII

It is often said the Mutiny began with the capture and execution of a sepoy called Mangal Pande in Barrackpore near Calcutta in March 1857. A serious outbreak erupted in Meerut on May 10 and the following day Europeans in Delhi were massacred. By May 30, the regiments at Lucknow had rebelled and a week later the sepoys of the Second Cavalry at Cawnpore had joined the fray. Lucknow and Cawnpore witnessed some of the most savage action of the war which was brought to a close on June 19, 1858 at Gwalior in central India; it is not surprising they feature more prominently in literature and art than any of the other sites of the year-long war.

79

The Swedish artist Lundgren, who had settled in London in 1853 and quickly become a well-known figure in the English art world, was sent to cover the Mutiny as vividly and as authentically as the Crimean War of 1854–56 had been reported on by Fenton, Simpson, and others.[25] However, by the time Lundgren journeyed by boat up the river from Calcutta to the sites of the battle, the war was almost over. He did catch up with Sir Colin Cambell, Commander-in-Chief, and witnessed some of the residual, mopping up action that continued throughout the year. He met the photographer Felice Beato and decided to leave the reportage to him. Lundgren's memoirs are a far better indication of his reaction to the cruelty that he witnessed than are his drawings and sketches. However, even if limited in his vision and less forthright than the reports sent to *The Times* by the journalist William Howard Russell, Lundgren's depictions remain among the most aesthetically satisfying of all works inspired by the unfortunate events.

Wars have a way of obliterating the distinction between the civilized and the uncivilized. The Indian sepoys and rebels were no less savage than the British. At Satichura Ghat in Cawnpore, a group of British men, most of whom were wounded, women, and children attempted to evacuate the city by boats, having been assured of safe conduct by the rebels, and were savagely attacked as they set sail. According to one survivor, "The air resounded with the shrieks of the women and children, and agonized prayers to God for mercy. The water was red with blood, and the smoke from the heavy firing of the cannon and muskets and the fire from the burning boats lay like dense clouds all around us."[26] A woman whose son had been killed before her eyes, later wrote, "Children were stabbed and thrown into the river. The schoolgirls were burnt to death. I saw their clothes and hair catch fire. In the water, a few paces off, by the next boat, we saw the youngest daughter of Colonel Williams. A sepoy was going to kill her with his bayonet. She said, 'My father was always kind to sepoys.' He turned away, and just then a villager struck her

on the head with his club and she fell into the water."[27]

The carnage that the British soldiers, along with their faithful Indian comrades, perpetrated in retribution was no less grisly. In the words of a lieutenant of the Ninety-third Highlanders who, joined by the Sikhs, attacked the Sikander Bagh in Lucknow:

But at the same time it gave a feeling of gratified revenge. You may think me savage but I gloated over the sights of this charnel house. Who did not who saw the slaughter at Cawnpore? . . . Among the corpses were those of several women . . . I saw the body of a woman lying with a cross-belt upon her and by her a dead baby also shot with two bullet wounds in it. The poor mother had tied the wounds round with a rag. . . .[28]

Felice Beato's dramatic photograph of Sikander Bagh in Lucknow with its front yard littered with the skeletons of the 1700 slaughtered rebels is a gruesome reminder (fig. 73).

Expressions such as "Cawnpore! You bloody murderers" or "Cawnpore! God forgive us" became the battle cries of the British soldiers. Indeed, the bayonet came to be known as the "Cawnpore dinner." Cawnpore was chosen as the site for the major memorial of the Mutiny (fig. 74). It was built over a well into which a number of English women and children had been thrown by the rebels. The marble angel with folded arms was designed by Sir Henry Yule and carved by Charles Marochetti (1805–67). It was paid for by a fine levied on the Indian citizens of the city, but no Indians were ever allowed to enter the memorial.

Cawnpore and Lucknow were devastated during the Mutiny but the latter was hardest hit. Except for the British cantonments stretching for six miles along the Ganges, Cawnpore was not a historically important city, though it had some fine examples of Anglo-Indian architecture. Lucknow, as the capital of Oudh, had been lavishly decorated by the royalty with beautiful palaces and gardens, many of which contained vast quantities of Indian and European art and artifacts. As one British officer

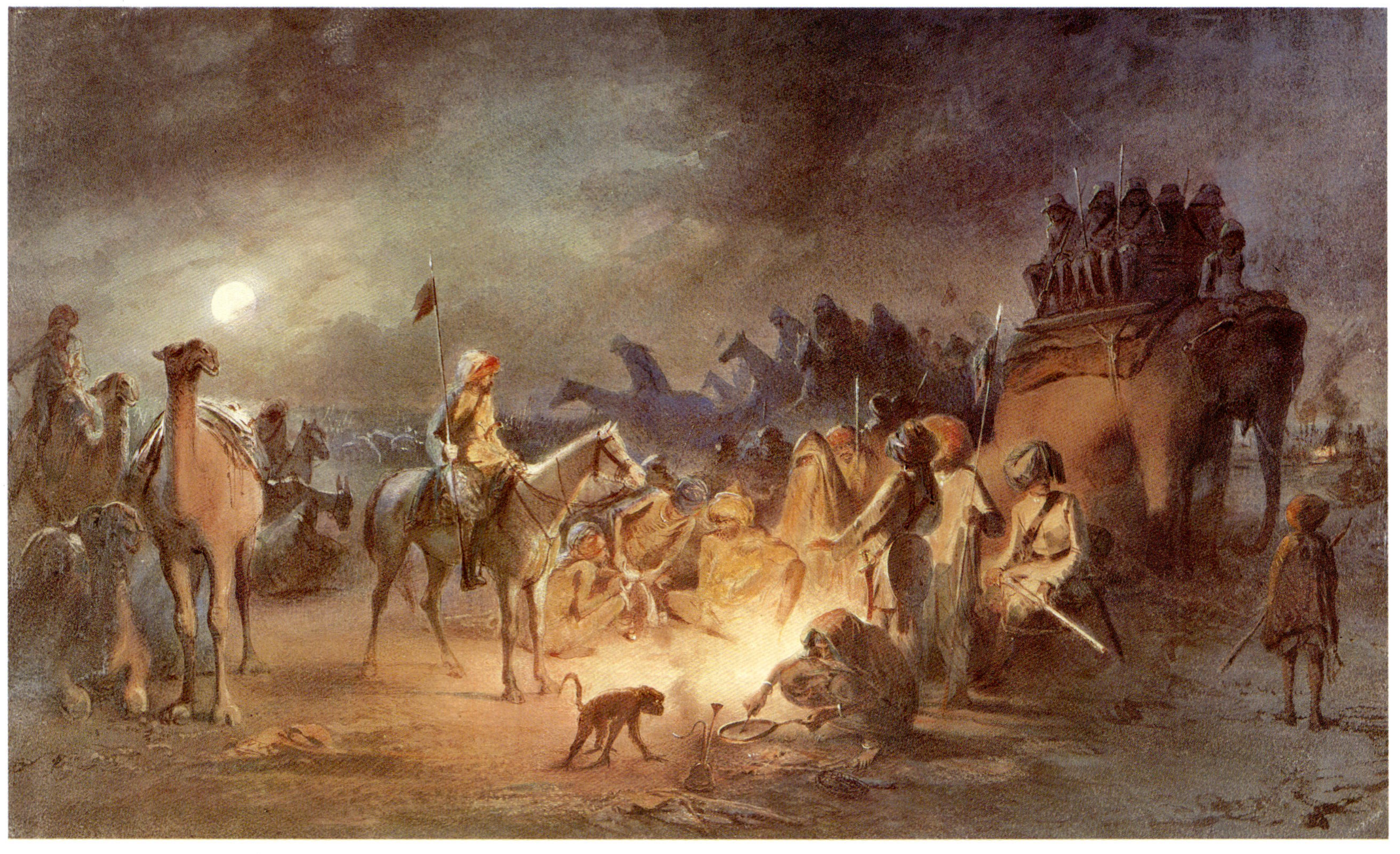

COLORPLATE 6.
Egron Sillif Lundgren. *Dawn at Beylah*. 1858. Watercolor.
Walter Collection.

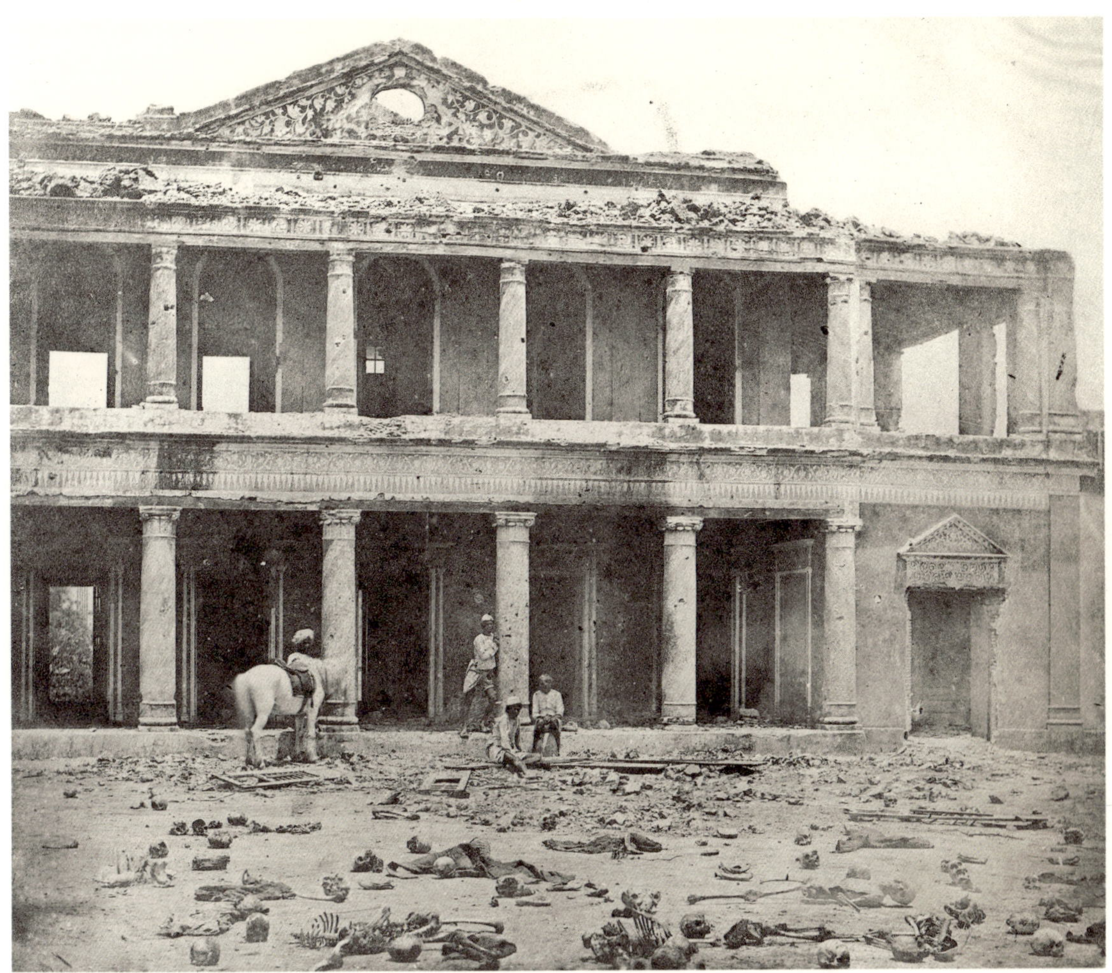

73. Felice Beato. *The Interior of the Secundra Bagh, the Spot where 1700 Rebels were Killed by H. M.'s and Greens' 4th Punjab Infantry.* 1858. Albumen print. Walter Collection.

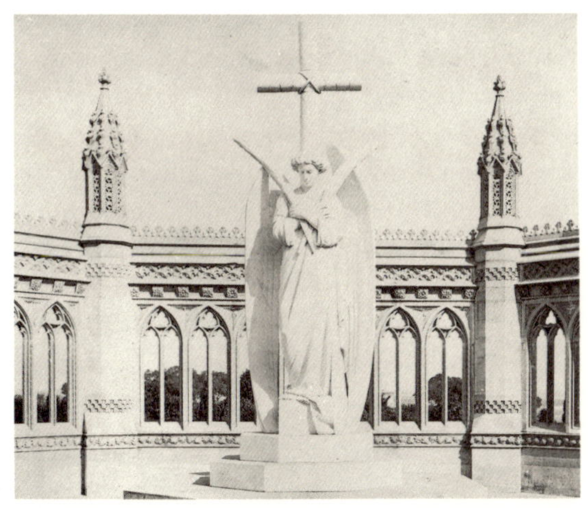

74. Samuel Bourne. Detail from *The Memorial Well, Cawnpore.* Mid-1860s. Albumen print. Walter Collection.

commented after the Mutiny, "Lucknow used to be the finest city in India and beat Delhi into fits. Some of the buildings are the finest I saw in any part of the world . . . but it is a most miserable looking city now."[29]

Once the hospitable, cosmopolitan, cultured host to the British who visited India during the Georgian and early Victorian eras, Lucknow lay in ruins. One of the most damaged buildings was the British Residency; it was never rebuilt and the remains were maintained until 1947 as that city's memorial to the horrors of 1857 (fig. 76).

IX

No other event in the history of British India

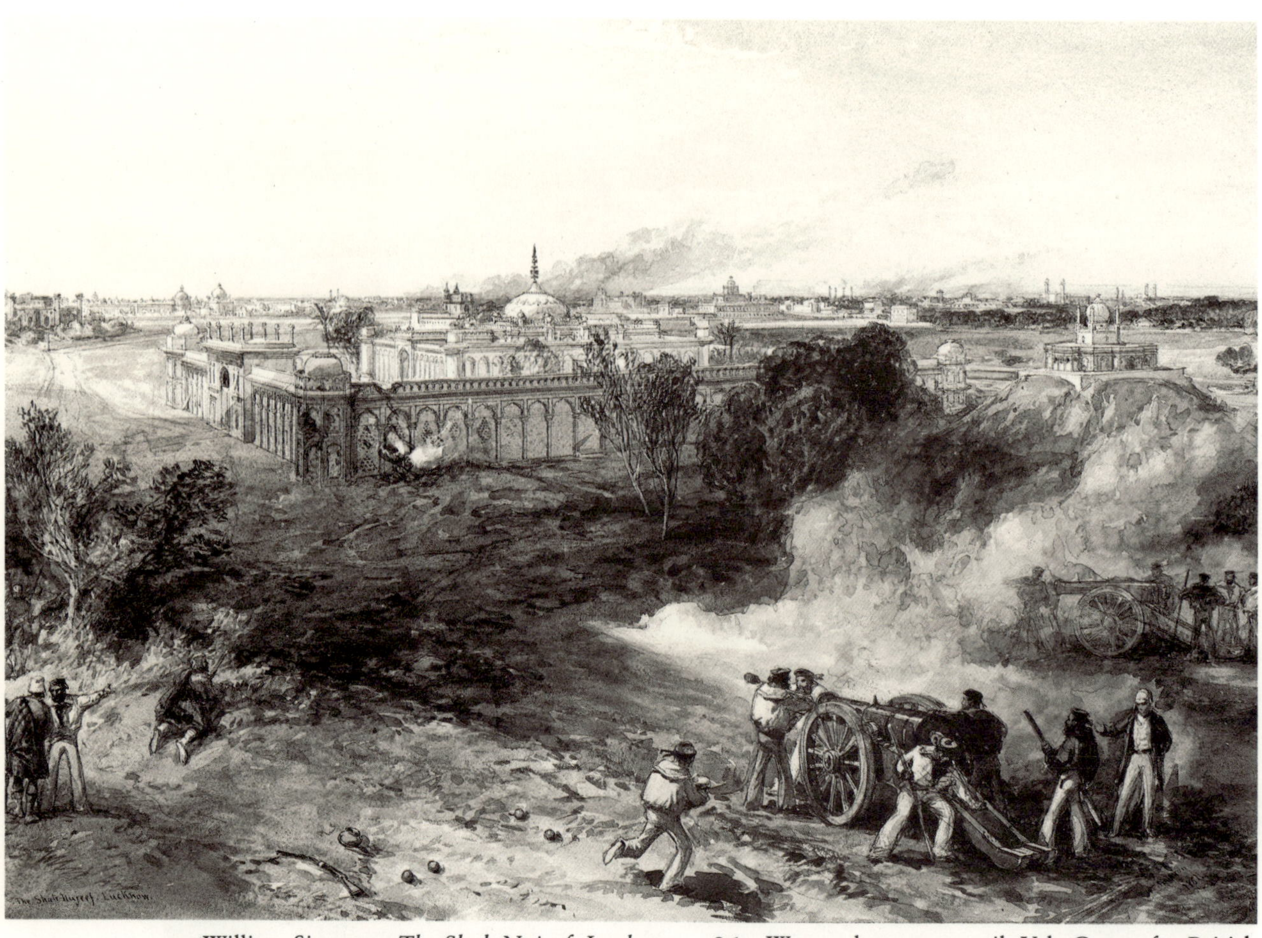

75. William Simpson. *The Shah Nujeef, Lucknow*. 1861. Watercolor over pencil. Yale Center for British Art, Paul Mellon Collection.

has aroused as much passion or inspired as much literature as the Mutiny. It became a far greater obsession than either the myth of the Black Hole of Calcutta or the Anglo-Mysore wars and Tipu Sultan. It certainly shook the self-confidence of the British and their complacent feelings of superiority and undermined their trust of Indians. The latter realized that the British were mortal and vulnerable, instead of the invincible Olympians they had come to represent. If the miserable events of 1857 must be characterized as a "war of independence," as some Indian historians are inclined to do, then all it gained the rebels was a more rigid state of bondage under a foreign queen. Indeed, Victoria remained the queen and after 1877 the empress of India for almost half of the ninety years of British rule.

Although Victoria may have wanted her Indian subjects to be treated fairly and to lead fulfilling, happy lives, and although her first viceroy, Lord Canning, who had witnessed the atrocities of 1857-58 and was remarkably lenient and conciliatory (so much so that to the sepoy-hating Anglo-Indian community he was known as "Clemency Canning"), the wounds really did not heal until the British left a divided India in 1947. If anything, the British became even more uncompromising in their contemptuous and disdainful attitude toward the Indians. Even as Canning was reading out the royal proclamation transferring power to the Crown and promising, among other things, justice, the journalist William Howard Russell overheard a sergeant who was on duty at the foot of the platform staircase call to one of the

82

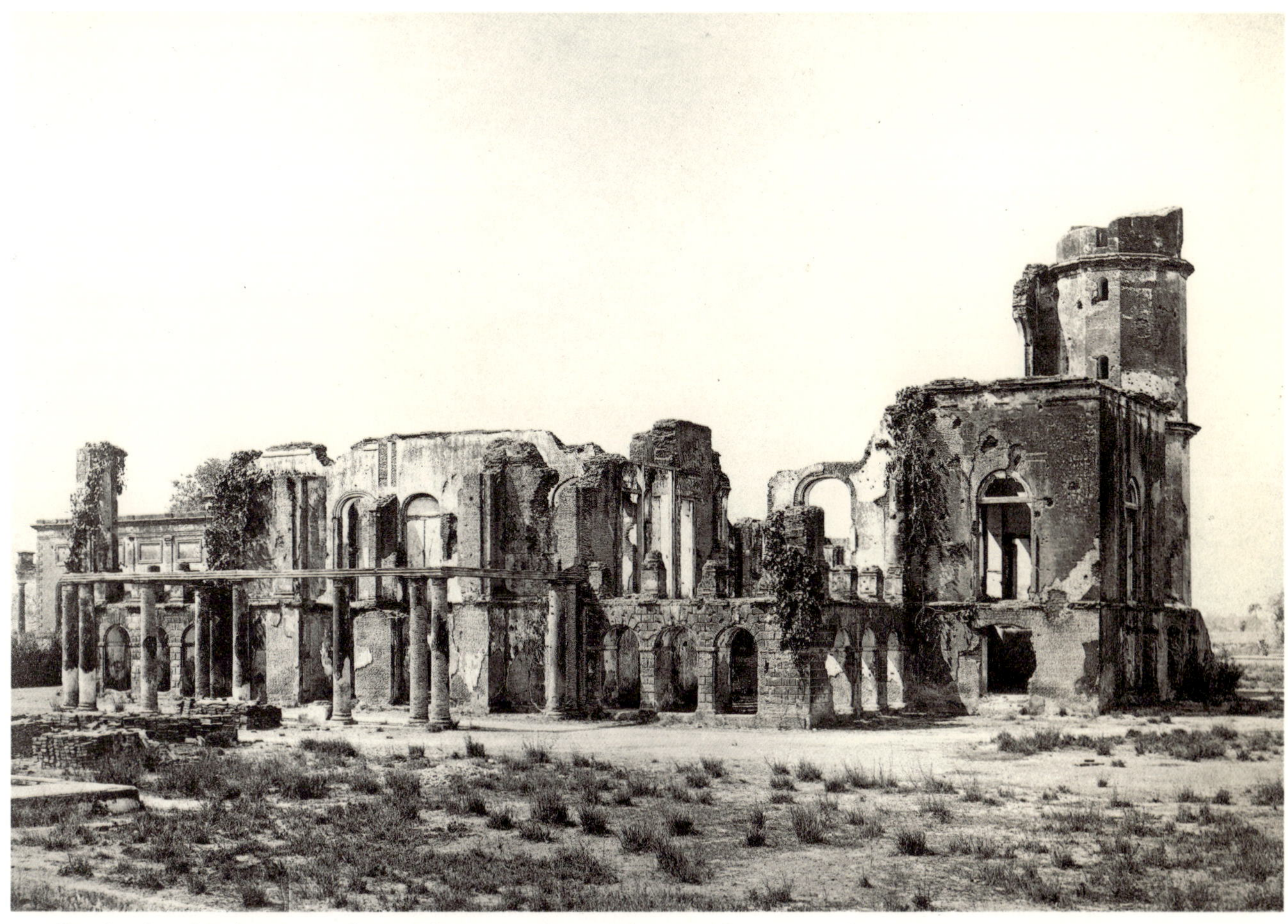

76. Shepherd and Robertson. *The Residency, Lucknow, Showing the Room where Sir Henry Lawrence was Mortally Wounded.* 1864. Albumen print. Walter Collection.

men, "I am going away for a moment. Do you stay here and take care that no nigger goes up."

Although the word nigger is found occasionally in earlier Anglo-Indian literature, it became commonplace after 1857. In 1875, during his visit to India as Prince of Wales, Edward VII was shocked by his British subjects' treatment of the Indians. He strongly protested to Lord Salisbury, the secretary of state for India, about the "disgraceful habit of officers speaking of the inhabitants of India, many of them spring from the great races, as 'niggers'. . . ."[30] "Because a man has a black face and a different religion from our own," he wrote to Lord Granville, "there is no reason why he should be treated as a brute."[31] Nevertheless, racial prejudice remained a fact of life for the Indians. It probably did not affect the masses as much, especially those in village

India, most of whom rarely saw an Englishman. But for educated Indians, racial discrimination was a virulent pestilence. Before 1918, Indian members of the Indian Civil Service could not travel in the same railway carriage with a European or drink at the same bar in a club, or bathe in the same pool, even though many of them employed English governesses for their children. Some of these attitudes prevailed until the very end of the British imperial adventure in India, as is evident from the writings of visitors such as E. M. Forster and Ackerley in the 1920s and 1930s (see introduction).

X

PRESERVATION of structures of power and of British superiority was what the Raj was about. Any attempt to bridge the gulf between Euro-

83

peans and Indians was regarded as a threat to that power and authority which were nowhere more ostentatiously manifest than in the durbars and levees, whether held locally or on an imperial scale.

The durbar was a typically Indian institution that the Company adopted in the late eighteenth century and turned into an effective instrument for the public display of imperial might used throughout the duration of the Raj. Durbar literally means a royal court; while the court was held daily by the Indian rulers, more elaborate affairs were organized on special occasions. Since 1600, representatives of the Company had been humbly attending such durbars at the Mogul courts in Agra and Delhi and at Murshidabad. By 1800, the practice had become an essential part of the governor-general's duties, even though he was not a king and did not have a court. Small durbars were frequently held at the magnificent palace built by Wellesley around the turn of the century in Calcutta. Native gentlemen and maharajas were presented and received the traditional *khelat* that included an article of clothing, a betel leaf, and a nut, given by a superior authority to an inferior as a mark of distinction. Similarly, according to Indian custom, *attar* of roses was sprayed upon the guests, who were expected to bring an appropriate gift, or tribute, known as *nazrana*, or a gold or silver plate, to the burra sahib who indicated his pleasure by simply touching the plate.

The British had adopted the trappings of Indian royalty before their imperial venture was really under way. As early as 1818, a governor-general apparently fancied himself deserving of royal treatment, as an eyewitness recalled that he sat, "In a state chair covered with crimson velvet and richly gilt, with a group of aides-de-camp and secretaries standing behind him. . . . Two servants with state punkahs of crimson silk were fanning him, and behind them again were several native servants bearing silver staffs."[32]

Lord Auckland is shown in a similarly royal setting as he prepared to receive the raja of Nahun in a painting by Emily Eden (color-plate 7). The governor-general sits on a lion throne with a ceremonial footstool at his feet; *morchas* and *punkahs* are held by servants behind him. These durbars were similar to the investiture ceremonies of the maharajas, as seen in an 1871 photograph of the Udaipur Durbar (fig. 78). The representative of the Raj is equally ostentatious in displaying the symbols of regality.

Although the official decision to transfer the capital from Calcutta to Delhi was not made until 1911, soon after 1857 it must have become apparent that Delhi was more suitable, for the last Mogul ruler of the city was quickly dethroned and dispatched to Burma with imperial disdain. It is not surprising therefore that Queen Victoria was proclaimed Kaiser-i-Hind in Delhi. A magnificent durbar was organized for the occasion and the artist Valentine Prinsep (1836–1904) was personally selected by the Queen to record the events. Each subsequent durbar held in Delhi was grander than the one before, and countless smaller durbars were organized in every city and princely state visited by the viceroy. "The main task of the Prince of Wales in India [in 1875]," writes his biographer Philip Magnus, "was to show himself to princes, soldiers, peasants and workers as the incarnation of the British Raj, which had previously been no more than a remote and abstract symbol. . . ."[33] Thanks to photography, the emperor and his viceroy were familiar faces to a large number of their subjects in a way that the Mogul emperors never were. Framed photographs of both the royal and viceregal couples hung on the walls of every government office whether in the capital or in the mofussil, and even in most princely states.

If any viceroy can be regarded as the very embodiment of the Raj, it was Lord Curzon of Kedleston (1899–1904) who had, even as a student, made clear his dedication to the imperial cause: "There has never been anything so great in the world's history as the British Empire; so great an instrument for the good of humanity. We must devote all our energies and our lives to it."[34] Although the most imperious viceroy ever to govern India, Curzon was not insensitive to

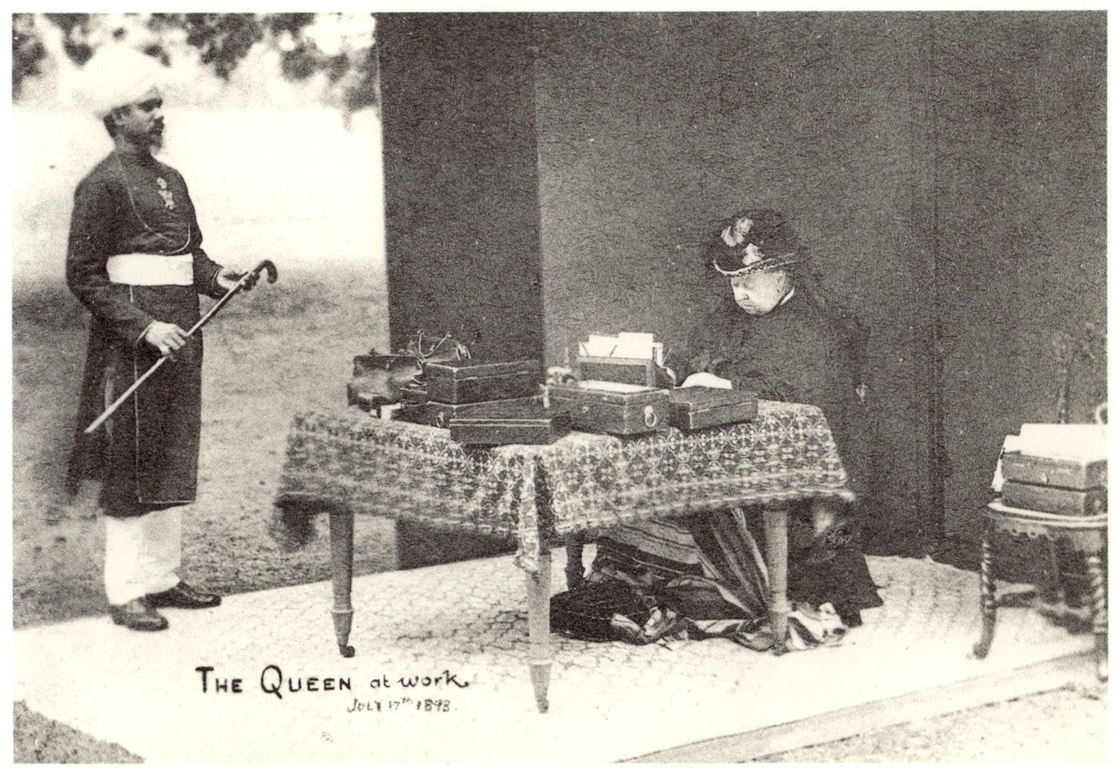

77. Anonymous. *The Queen at Work*. 1893. Albumen print. Walter Collection.

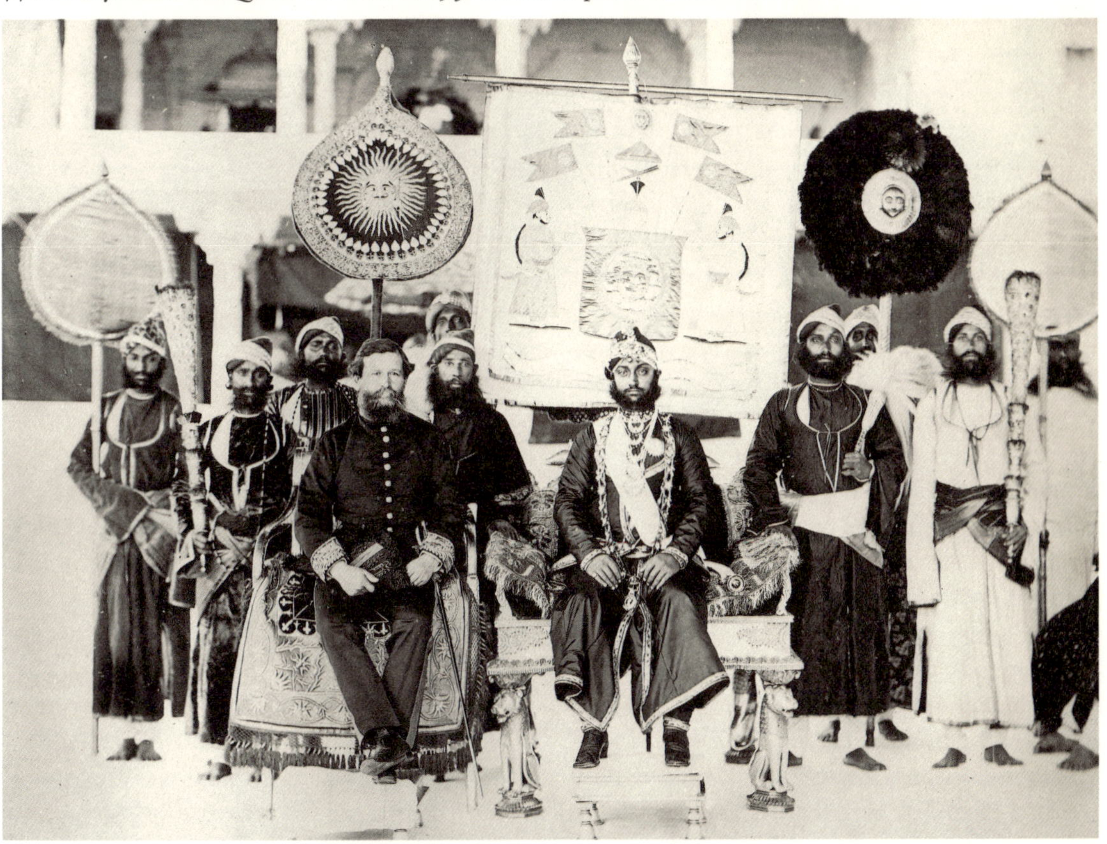

78. Anonymous. *Investiture of the Raja of Oodeypore*. 1871. Albumen print. Walter Collection.

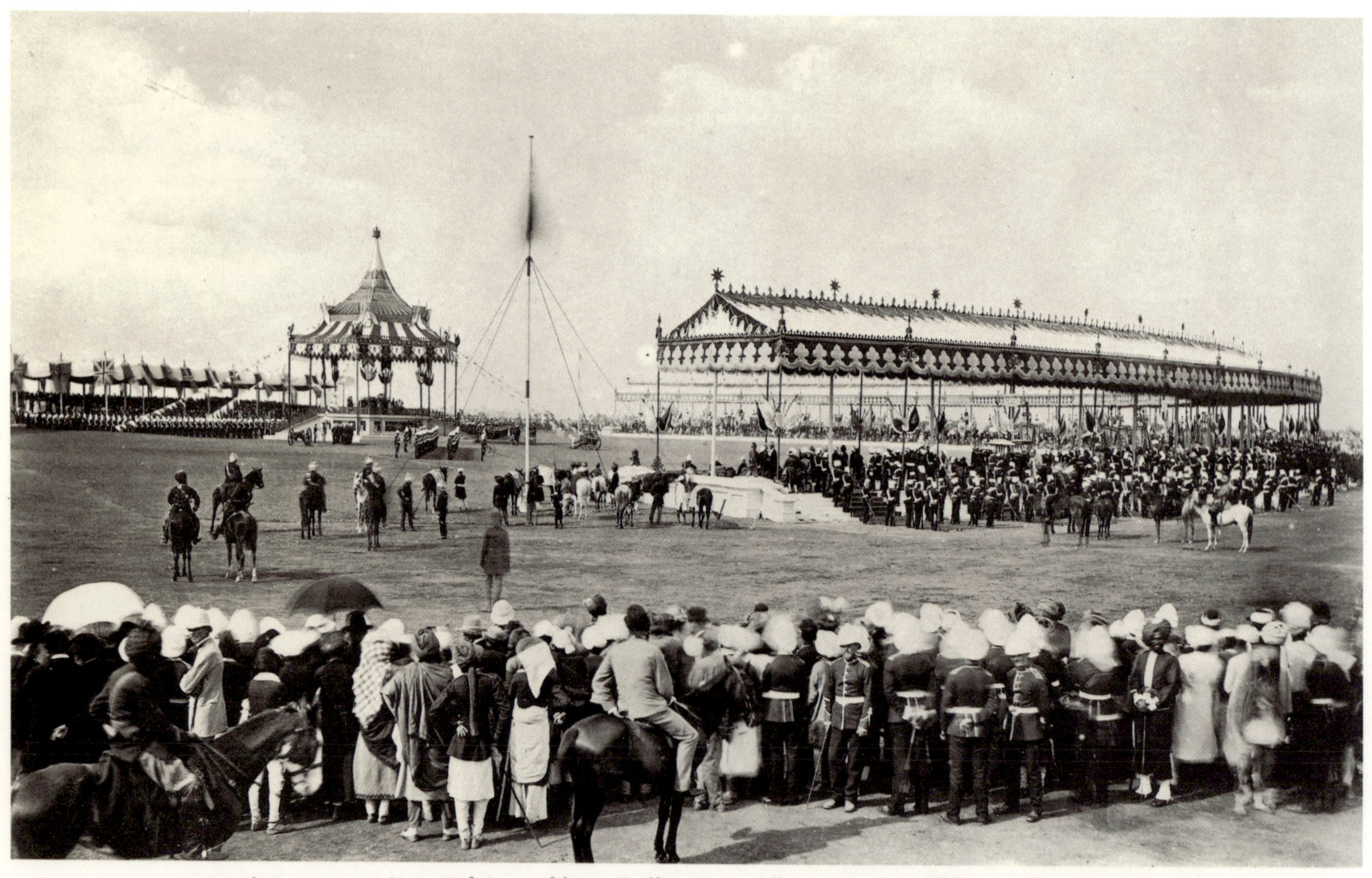

79. Anonymous. *Imperial Assemblage, Delhi.* 1877. Albumen print. Walter Collection.

Indian interests, and among the more lasting legacies of his administration are the measures he adopted to save the Indian temples and monuments which otherwise would probably not be standing today.

It was inevitable that Curzon's imperial design would include the ultimate durbar and the occasion presented itself with the accession of Edward VII in 1901. It was organized in Delhi during the winter of 1902-3. Although officially called the Coronation Durbar, unofficially the occasion was known as the Curzon Durbar. The king was represented by his brother, the duke of Connaught, and his sister-in-law, but it was they who took their places before Curzon made his triumphal entry atop an elephant. Appropriately, the investiture ceremony of the durbar was held in the Dewan-i-Am, or the audience chamber, of the Red Fort in Delhi, where the imperial Moguls held their durbars. Interestingly, as we

see in Melton Prior's (1845–1910) sketch of the occasion, Curzon himself, seated on a lion throne, does the investiture while the duke merely watches from an ordinary chair (fig. 81). The sight was no less splendid than a procession of the grand Moguls of the sixteenth or seventeenth centuries, witnessed by a handful of English merchants struggling to receive imperial favors.

An even more grandiose and lavish durbar was held nine years later in Delhi when George V was crowned in person in 1911. This was also the occasion for the formal announcement of the transfer of the capital from Calcutta to Delhi. If Curzon had thought in 1902 that building a five-mile-long railway in the durbar area to transport people around its various sections was applaudable, the logistics of the Coronation Durbar of 1911 were awesome. An entirely new "city" of tents was created that in-

86

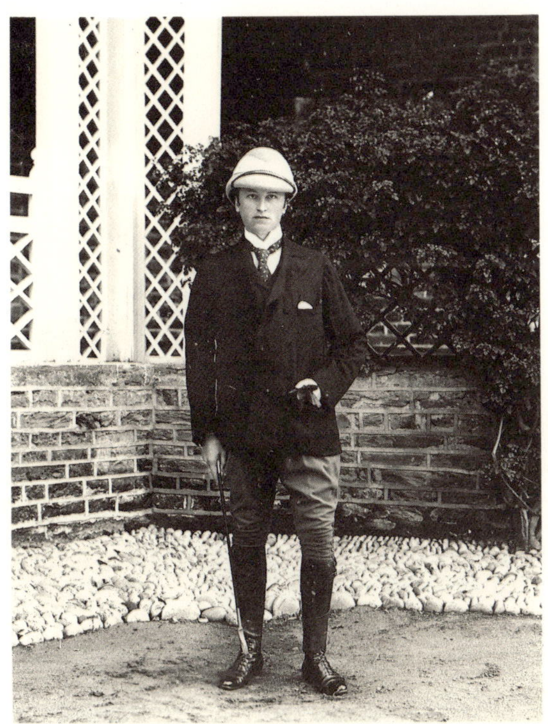

80. Anonymous. *H. E. Lord Curzon, taken at Chamba.* 1900. Gelatin-silver print. Walter Collection.

volved 233 camps covering twenty-five square miles with ten square miles of canvas, sixty miles of new roads, twenty-six and a half miles of broad-gauge and nine miles of narrow-gauge railway with twenty-four new stations, fifty miles of water mains, and thirty miles of water pipes. Two weeks after the durbar, Lord Hardinge, the viceroy who organized the whole affair, had good reason to congratulate himself as he wrote in a letter to Lord Morley:

It is now nearly a fortnight ago that the Durbar festivities were concluded. I think it all went off extremely well and that history will describe it as a success. I should say that dignity and grandeur were its chief characteristics rather than a Barnum's show as in 1903.[35]

If the British overlords brought dignity to the durbars, the grandeur and color were provided by the maharajas. Most Indian rulers had remained loyal to the British during the Mutiny yet by the same 1858 proclamation that transferred the Company's power to the Crown, they

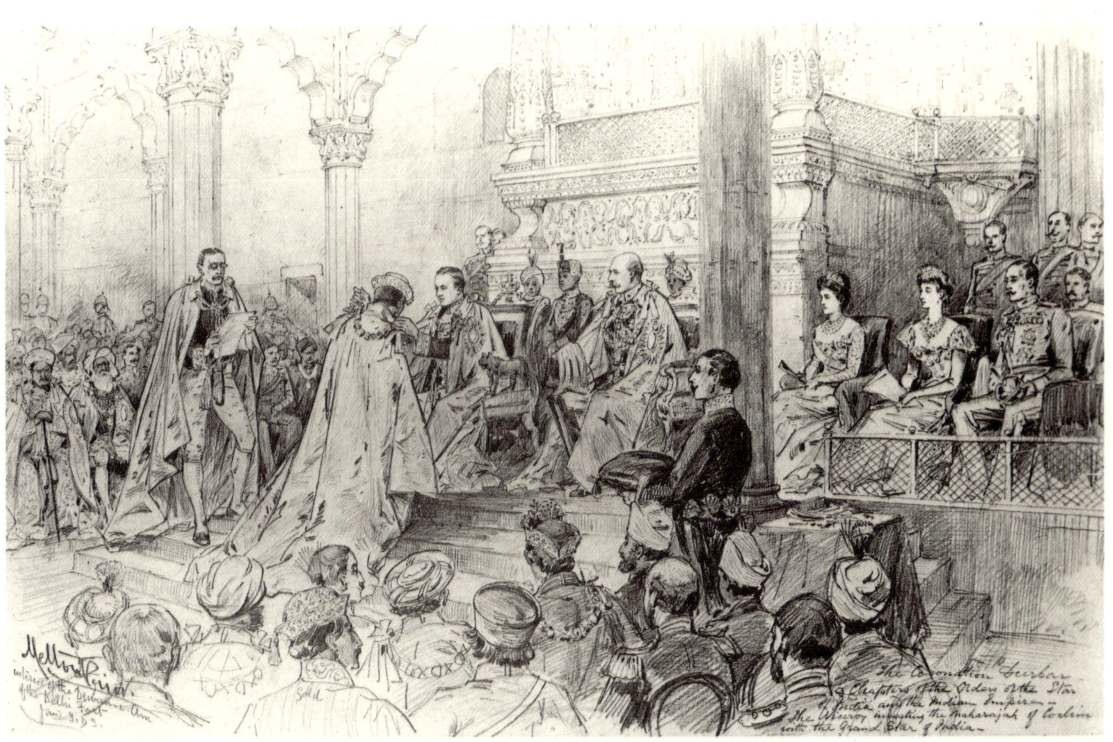

81. Melton Prior. *Curzon Investing the Maharaja of Cochin at the Coronation Durbar, Delhi.* 1903. Pencil. Reproduced by permission of the India Office Library and Records (British Library).

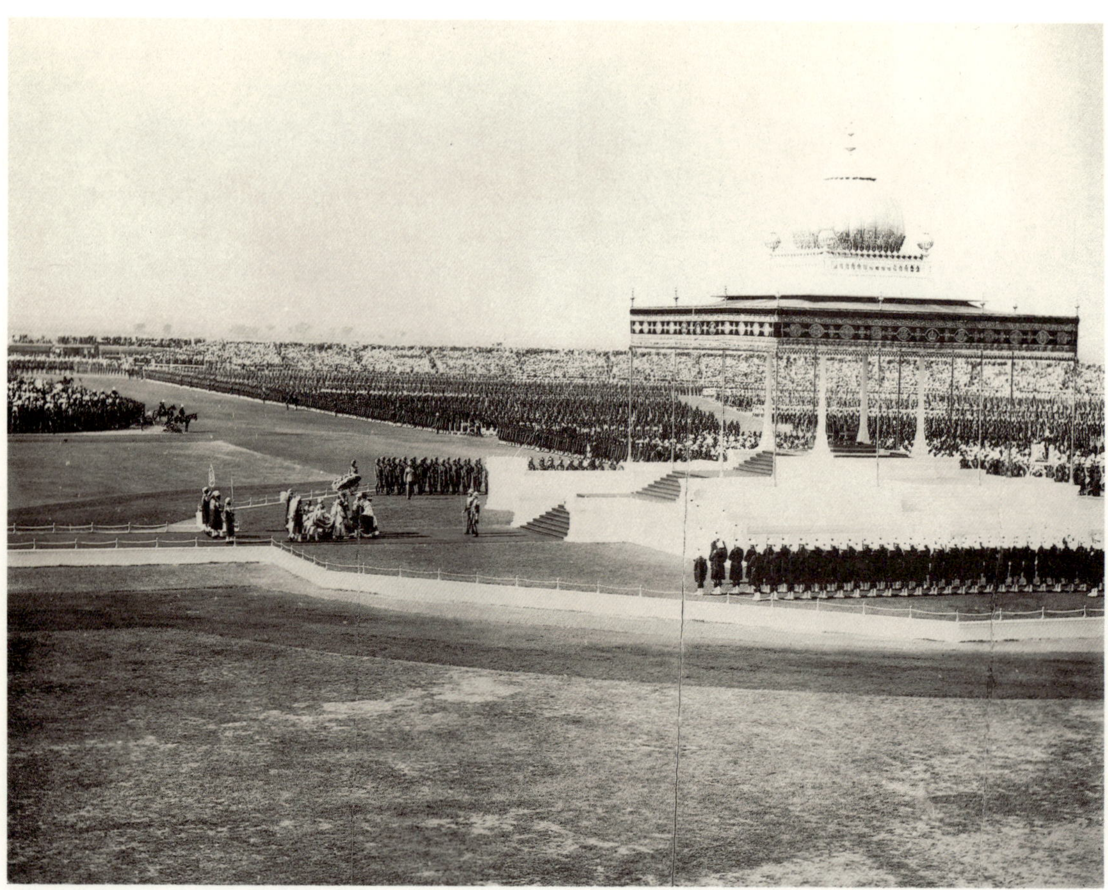

82. Anonymous. *View of the Imperial Assemblage.* 1911. Gelatin-silver print. Walter Collection.

were demoted from kings to princes. No longer were the rulers answerable to their subjects but to the British queen through her viceroy. On paper they were sovereigns in their states, but in reality, they only enjoyed the illusion of power. A resident or political officer was always present and one move that displeased him could have disastrous consequences for a prince. Indeed, the arrogant and authoritarian attitude of the political officers did not escape the Prince of Wales during his 1875 visit. In one of his letters to his mother, written from Poona, he complained about "the rude and rough manner with which the English political officers . . . treat the princes and chiefs upon whom they were appointed to attend." [36]

Nevertheless, although politically powerless, the maharajas were spoiled and pampered by the British with meaningless titles, honors, and gun salutes. In exchange for all these dubious honors and privileges, the princes remained faithful allies of the British and were the most glittering adornments in imperial Britain's political structure. The image of the Raj would hardly have been as glamorous as it seems today without the flamboyant spectacle of the maharajas, whether in Delhi or in London, at the horse races or the polo grounds, at tiger shoots or New Year's dances, at jubilees or durbars. So inseparable a part of the imperial image had the maharajas become that a special Chamber of Princes formed an integral part of the new Assembly House, while their palaces surrounded the new mall in Lutyen's New Delhi, inaugurated in 1931.

XI

THE separateness, or in Kipling's words, the "shut-upness" that characterized the British stance in India, especially after 1857, also

88

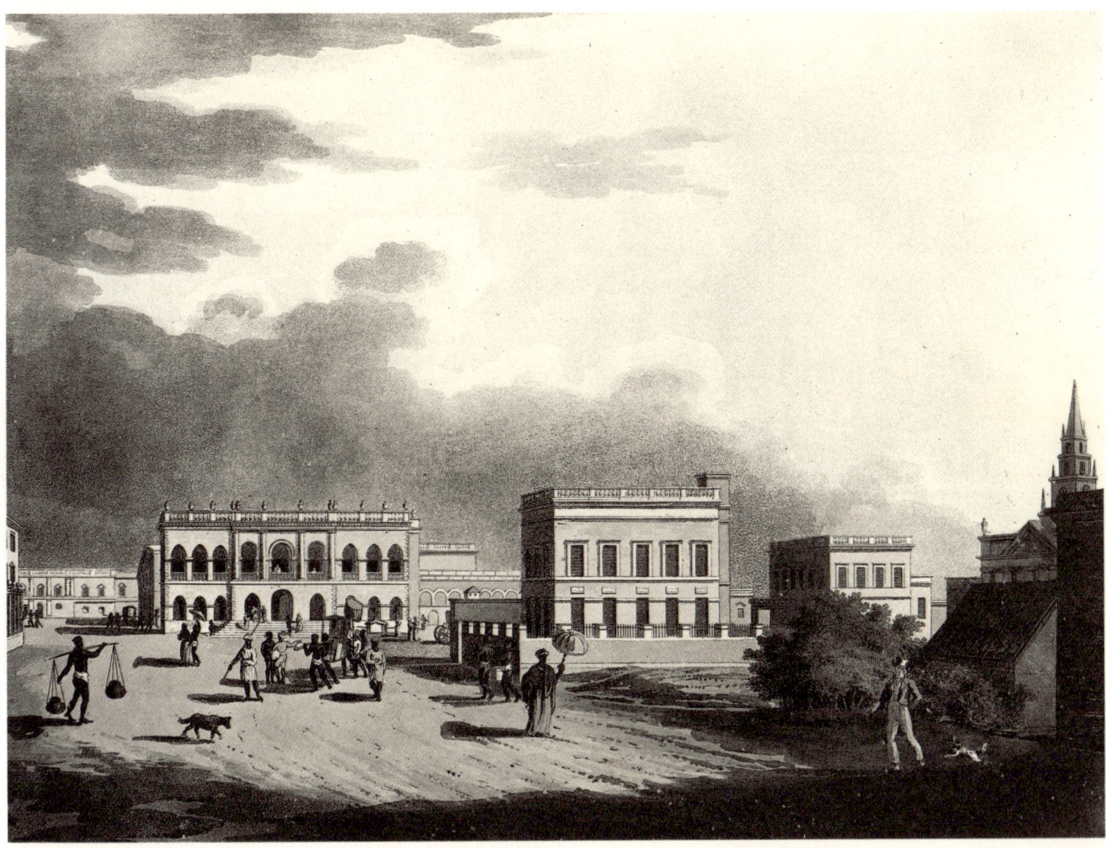

83. Edward Orme. *The Old Courthouse, Calcutta* from *A Brief History of Ancient and Modern India.* 1805. Engraving. The Thomas John Willis Collection.

permeated their settlements and architecture, whether domestic or official. In every city and town, the European and native communities were clearly demarcated, both socially and physically. While this distinction was the least obvious in Bombay, Madras and Calcutta were known in the eighteenth century for their "Black Towns." As the empire expanded throughout the nineteenth century, most towns had separate cantonments and civil lines: in the former, the native and the British soldiers lived in segregated barracks; the latter was the exclusive preserve of the European civilians. Physical unapproachability in turn augmented the British feelings of domination and authority. As Jan Morris observes:

They ruled in enclave, and their buildings almost always, even when ostentatiously Indianified, spoke of an alien and exclusive presence. . . . Even the smallest bungalows tried, with grand gates, wide compounds and ramparts of potted plants, to shut themselves up against the kaleidoscopic life of India all around: and at the other end of the scale, whole cities were arranged so that British communities could shut themselves away from the Indians.[37]

It is not surprising therefore that the style that the early architects, none of whom were professionals like the early British artists, chose was severely classical with imposing Doric or Ionic columns that were intended to be overwhelming. In all three Presidency towns—Calcutta, Madras, and Bombay—there was no competition from any native architectural styles, Hindu or Moslem. This, along with the conscious desire to be distinctive, and perhaps a nostalgic longing for home, may have contributed to the wholesale transplantation of the prevailing Neoclassicism of Georgian England. The style suited the changing mood of the times as merchants were rapidly and inexorably becoming

89

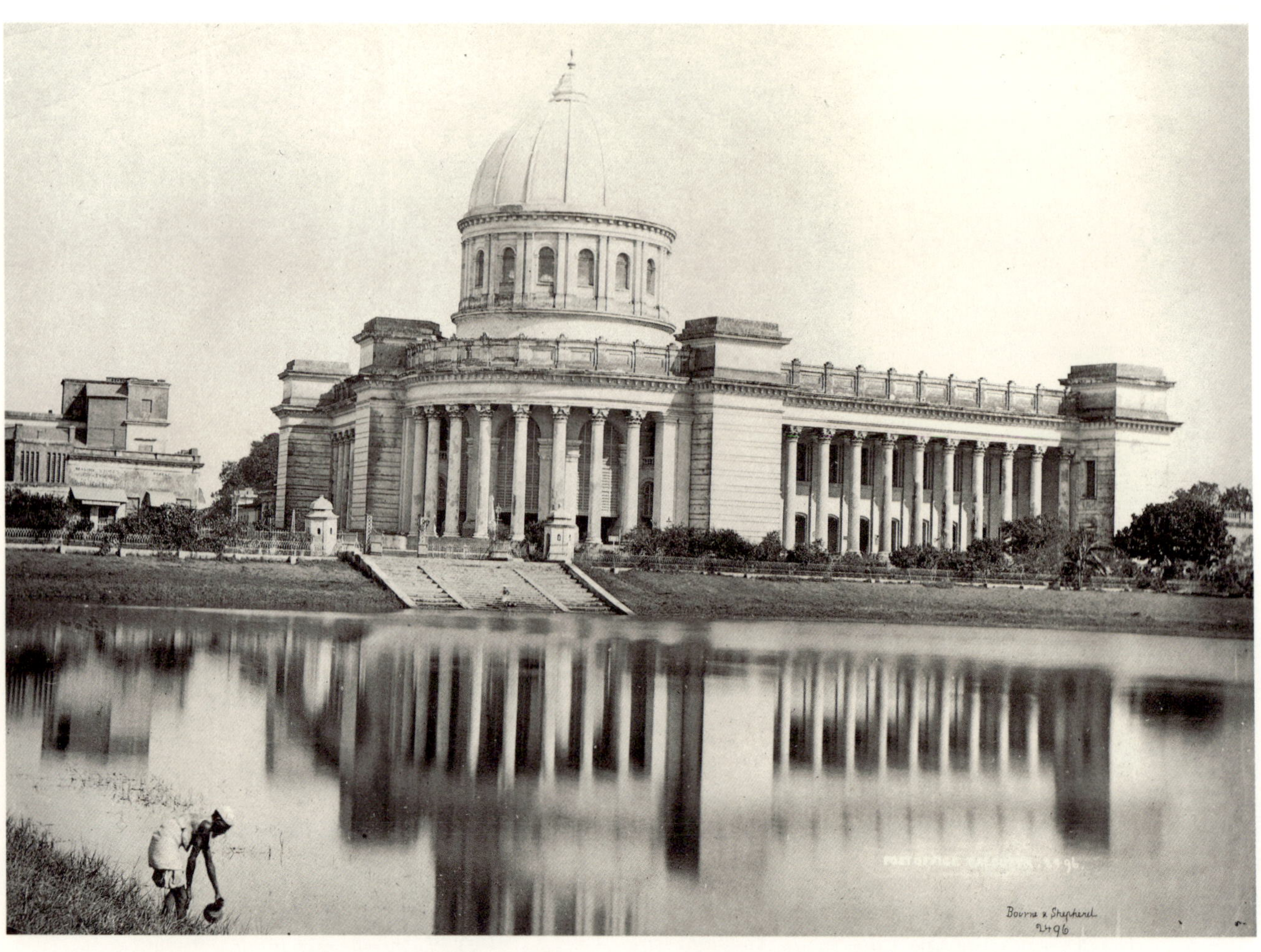

84. Bourne and Shepherd. *Post Office Calcutta*. 1870. Albumen print. Walter Collection.

empire builders. William Hodges was moved to compare Madras with "what we may conceive of a Grecian city in the age of Alexander." In the days before Plassey, the traders had not been interested in settling in India, but the nabobs and merchant princes of Cornwallis's and Wellesley's India savored the illusion of permanence that accompanied their imperialistic dreams. As Thomas Daniell observed in 1810, "the bamboo roof suddenly vanished" and "the marble column took the place of brick walls."

Walter Granville's design for the General Post Office in Calcutta, 1870, is a splendid example of the classicizing Georgian style, with its green copper dome atop a Greek colonnade (fig. 84). Granville was the official government architect. However Indianized with Buddhist stupas and Moslem turrets, Lutyens's and Baker's buildings in New Delhi are also essentially classical. Indeed, the Assembly House, now the Parlia-

ment building, was designed after the Roman Forum (fig. 85).

The Victorian Gothic style was introduced to India as early as the 1780s but remained confined mostly to churches. St. Paul's Cathedral in Calcutta, begun in 1839 and consecrated in 1847, remains one of the finest examples of Gothic architecture on the subcontinent. Espoused by Ruskin, Pugin, and others in England, the Gothic was considered the ideal style for the Victorian empire builders. It suited the aims of the church fathers who considered it more Christian than pagan Neoclassicism, it was less costly to build, and "with its natural profusion of ornament, its pointed arches and vaulted roofs," it was a much more suitable vehicle for the delicate and intricate ornamentation that was especially admired by the Indians, Hindus, and Moslems. The authorities probably felt that some concessions could therefore

90

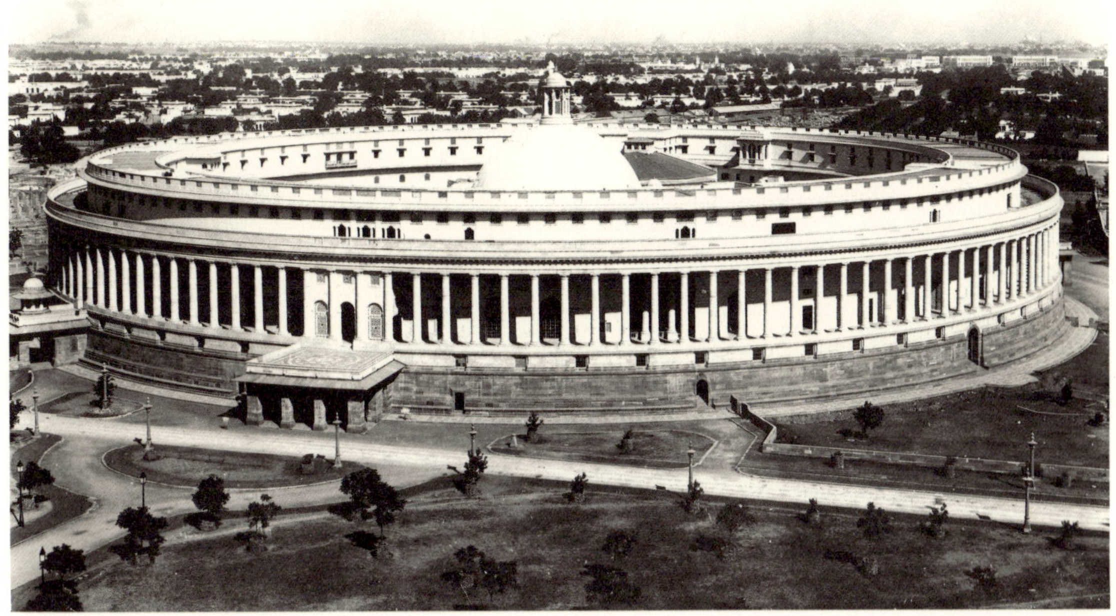

85. Anonymous. *Parliament House, New Delhi.* c. 1930. Gelatin-silver print. Walter Collection.

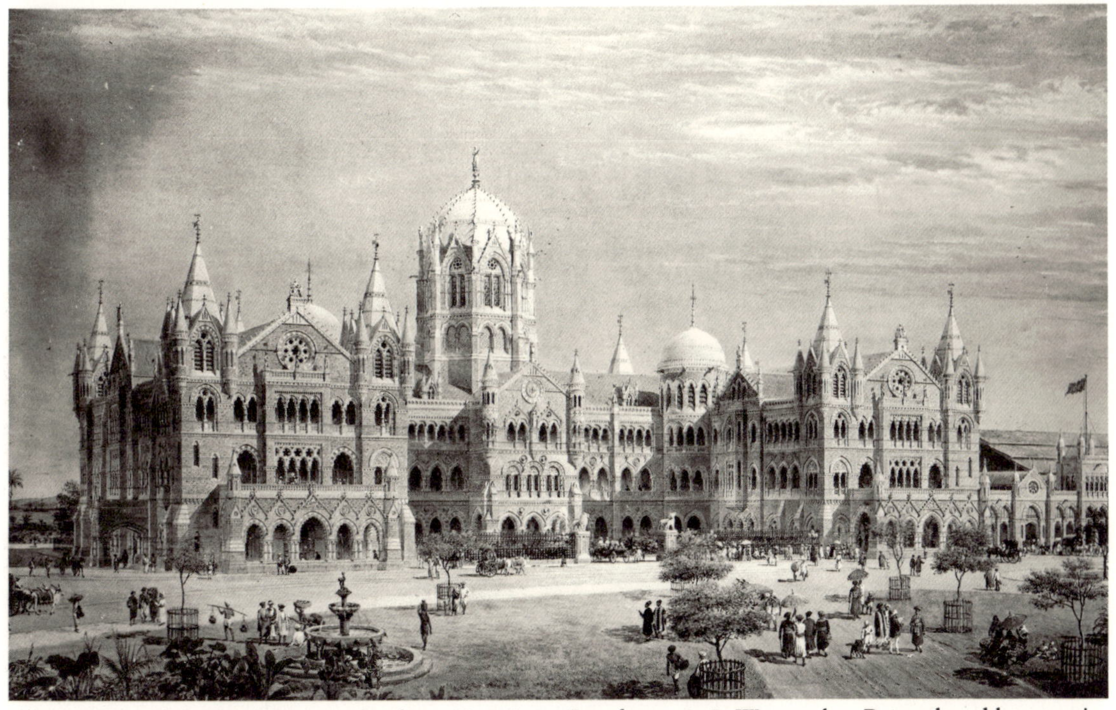

86. Axel Herman Haig. *Victoria Railway Terminus, Bombay.* 1878. Watercolor. Reproduced by permission of the India Office Library and Records (British Library).

be made to native tastes without threatening their position. Thus a hybrid style of architecture was developed in the late nineteenth century, as a conscious effort to incorporate Indian elements in official British architecture as the rising tide of Indian nationalism began to gather momentum. Bombay's Victoria Terminus is a good example of this hybrid style (fig. 86) as is Lord Curzon's Victoria Memorial in Calcutta, designed by William Emerson with the Taj Mahal in mind (fig. 87), and the Kaiser Pasund in Lucknow (fig. 88).

In the eighteenth century the nabobs lived in Palladian mansions surrounded by enormous gardens which were meant to remind them of country estates in England. Trim lawns and potted flowers surrounded the bungalows in the civil lines and cantonments, decorated entirely in European modes, however outdated. It became customary for architects to copy the designs of European buildings for public structures as well. When Wellesley decided to rule India from a palace and flaunt the majesty of the burgeoning empire, he simply commissioned a slightly modified version of Kedleston Hall, one of the most admired country houses in England (fig. 89). Access to the government house was through imposing arches that were inspired by those at Sion House in Middlesex. (Less than a century after it was inaugurated with a magnificent ball in 1803, it was occupied by George Nathaniel Curzon, a scion of the family that owned Kedleston Hall.)

St. John's Church in Calcutta, consecrated in 1787, was designed to look like Gibbs's St. Martin-in-the-Fields and Wren's St. Stephen's in London. Bombay's arcaded commercial plaza, once known as Elphinstone Circle and now renamed Horniman Circle, was built in the 1860s, following the style of Tunbridge Wells, or Leamington Spa; the city's other landmark, the Flora Fountain, could easily have been transplanted

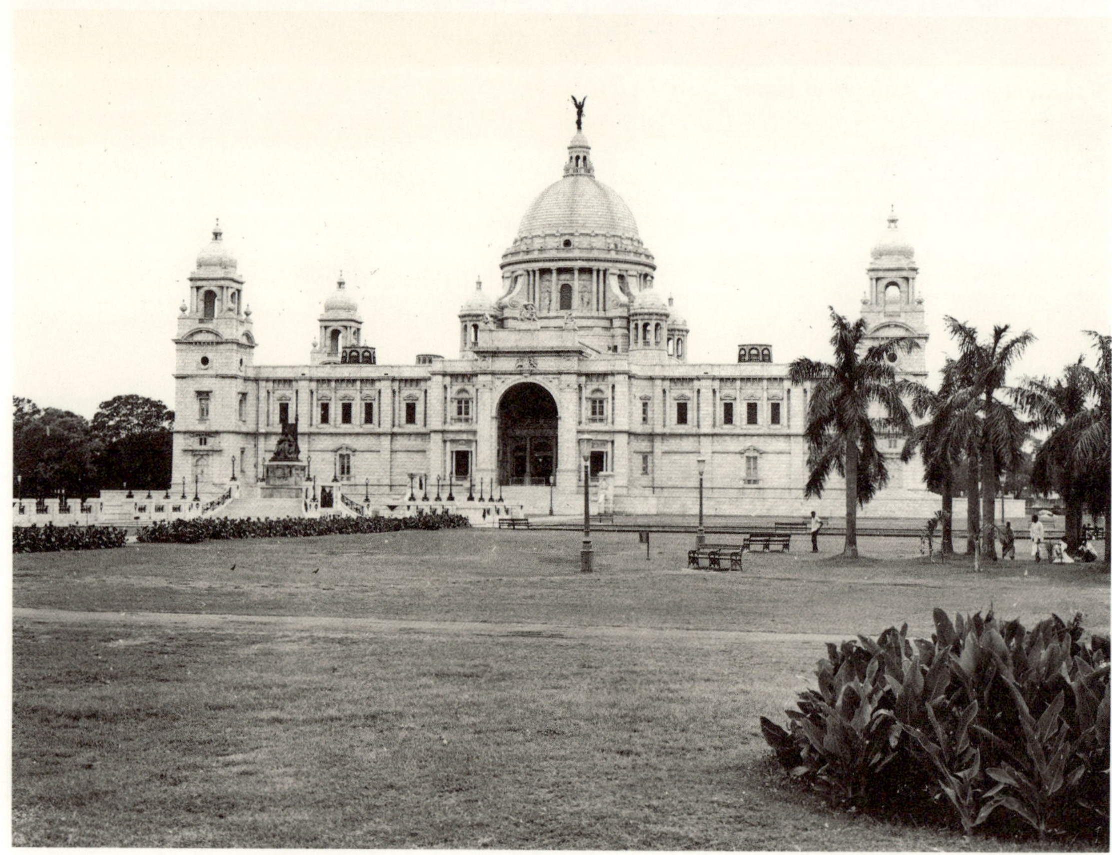

87. *Victoria Memorial, Calcutta.* Built 1906–1921. Photograph courtesy of Amari AP/Leo deWys Inc.

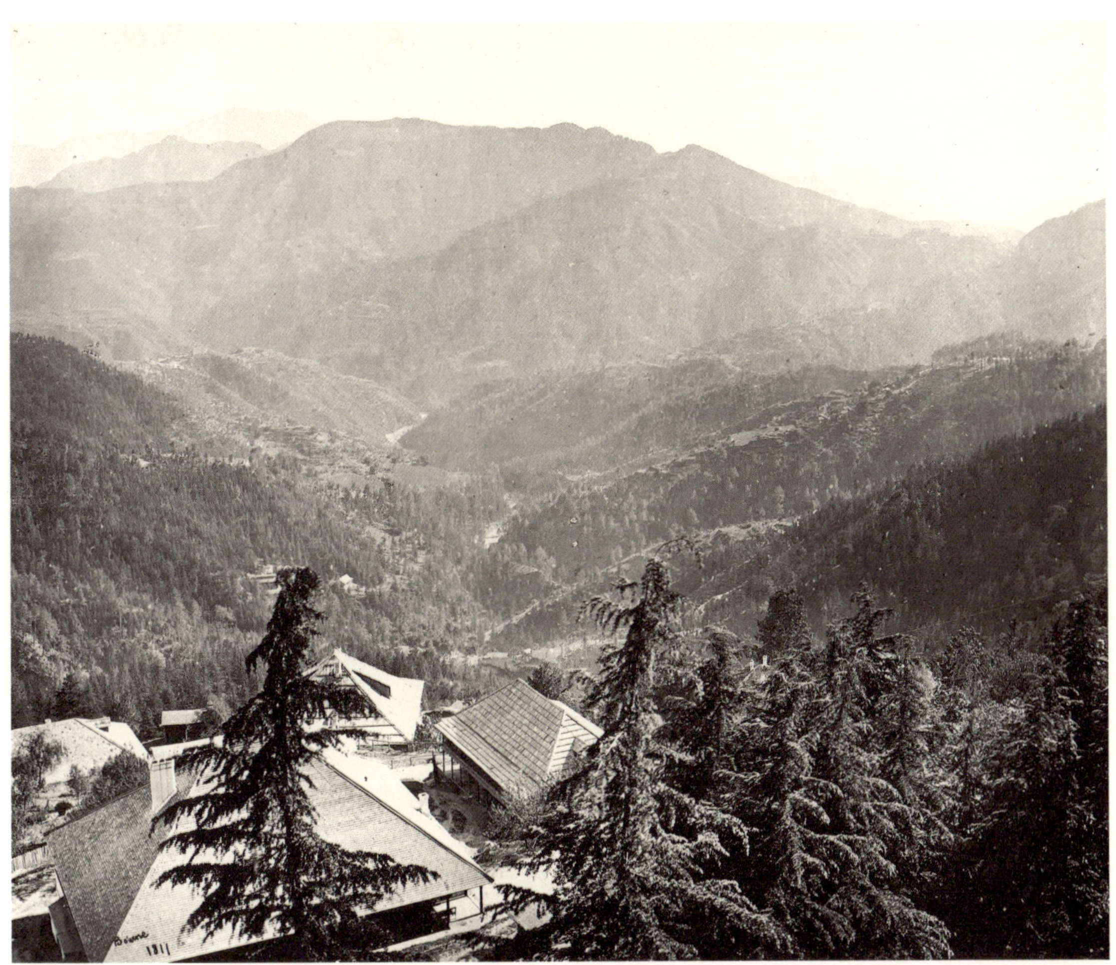

88. Samuel Bourne. *The Kaiser Pasund, Lucknow.* Mid-1860s. Albumen print. Walter Collection.

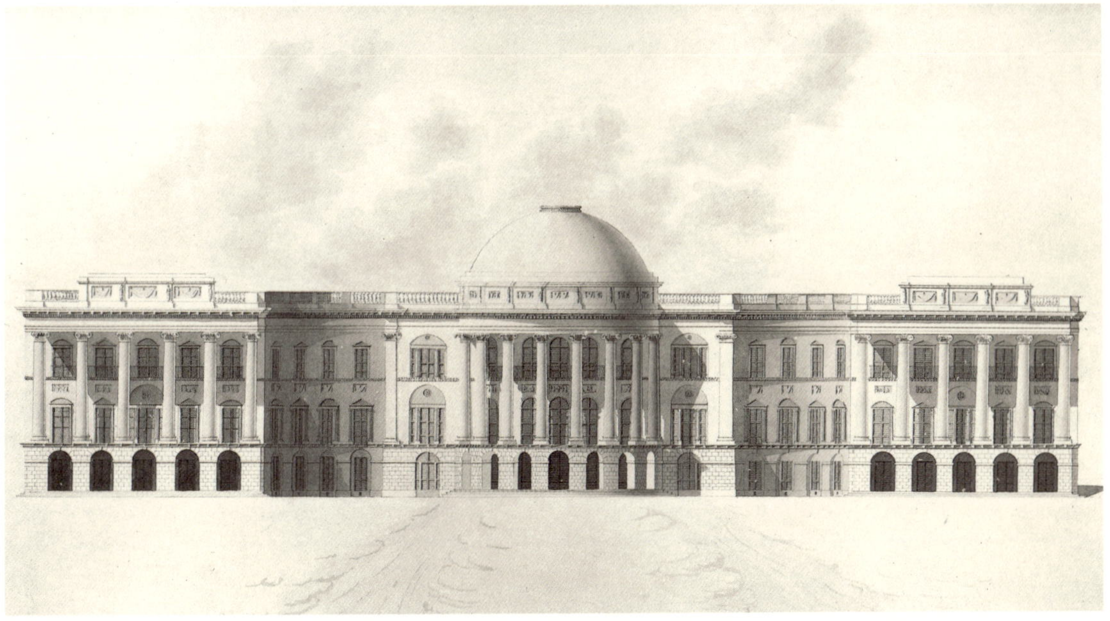

89. J. F. Bordwine. *Southeast Front of the New Government House.* c. 1798. Pen and ink and wash. Walter Collection.

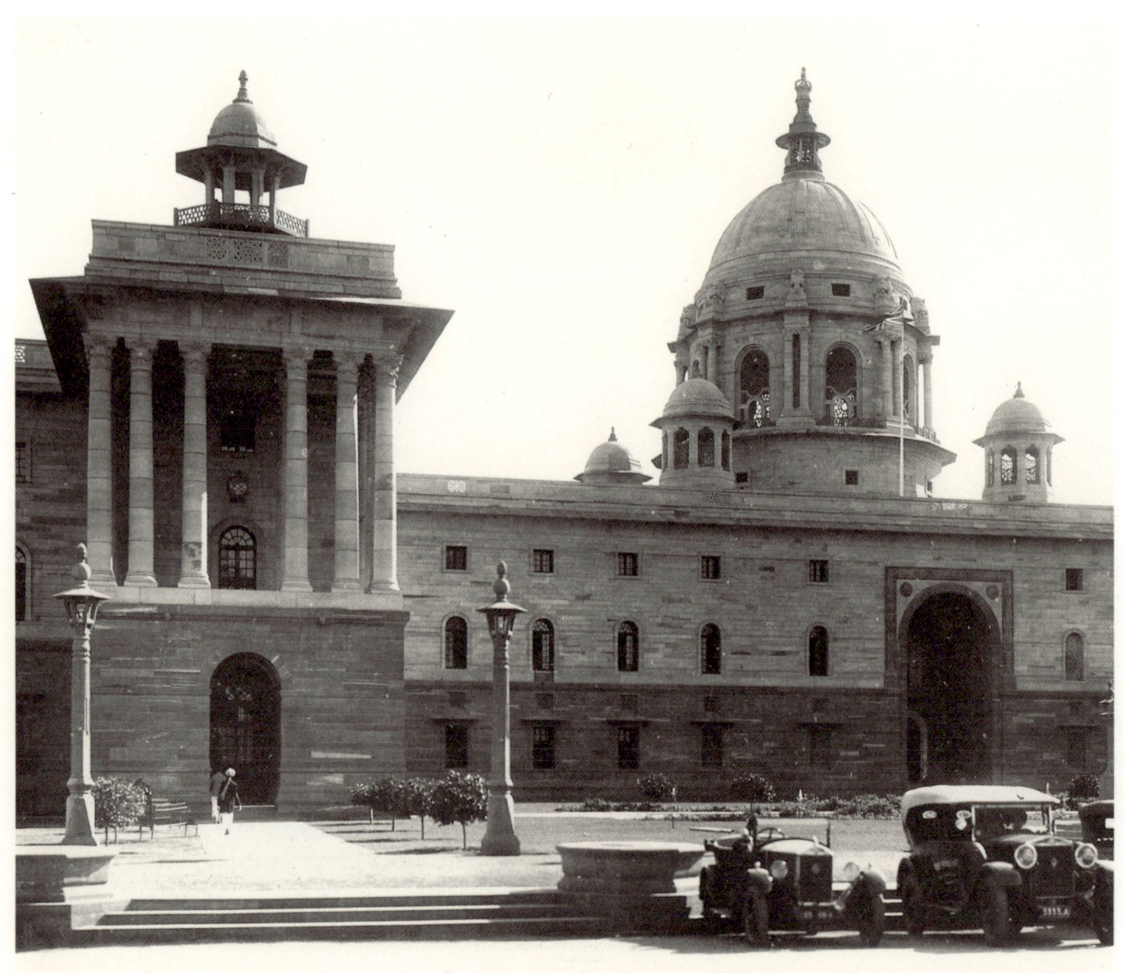

90. Anonymous. *View of the Secretariat, New Delhi.* c. 1930. Gelatin-silver print. Walter Collection.

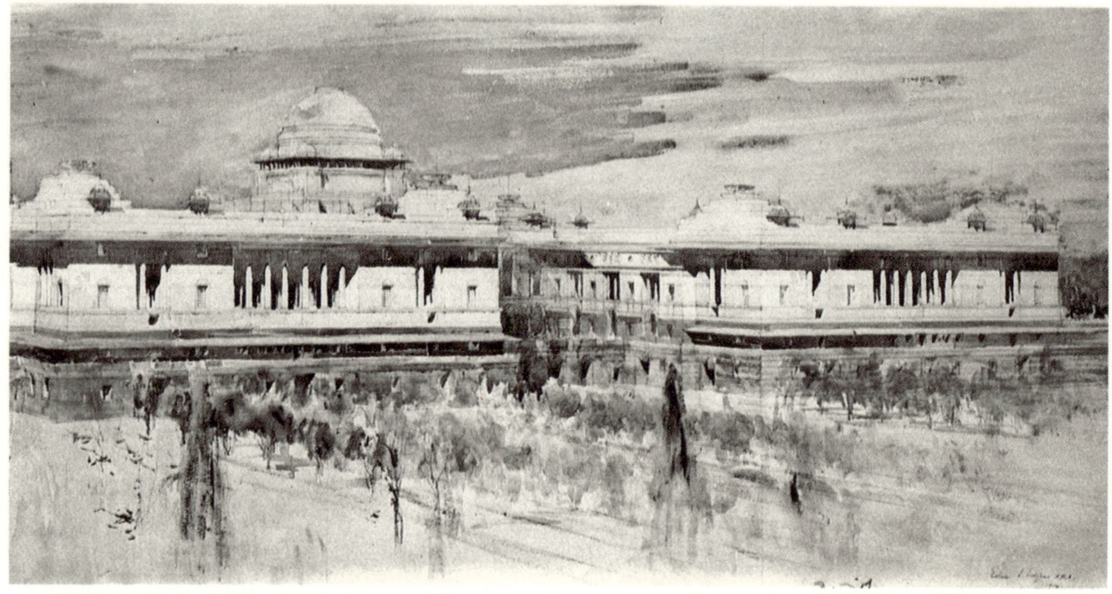

91. William Walcot. *The South Front of Viceroy's House.* 1913. Watercolor. Collection of Lord Romsey.

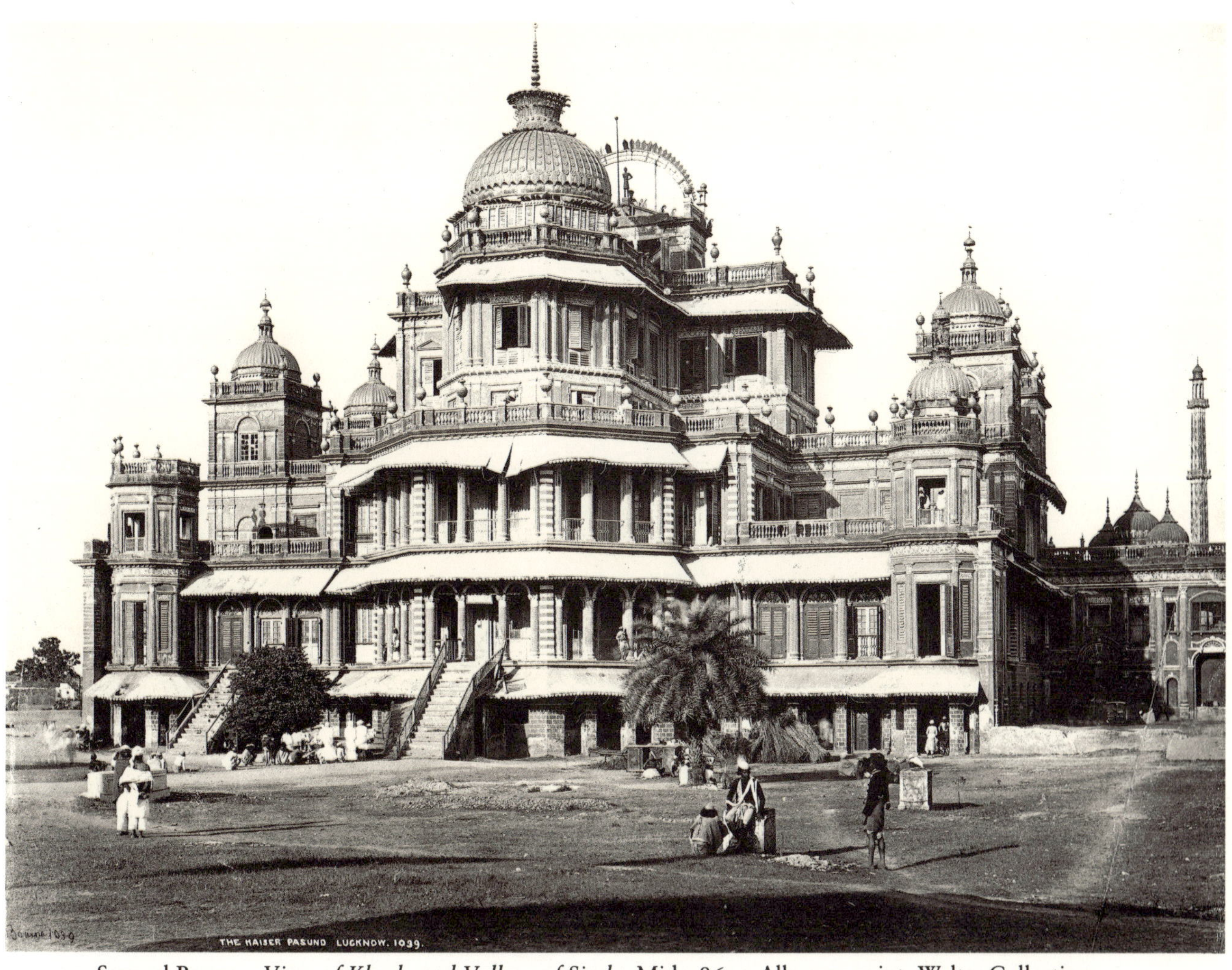

92. Samuel Bourne. *View of Khuds and Valleys of Simla*. Mid-1860s. Albumen print. Walter Collection.

from Paris or Rome. Valentine Prinsep remarked after a visit to Simla in 1876, "Everything is so English and unpicturesque here that except the people one meets are those who rule and make history—a fact one can hardly realize—one would fancy oneself at Margate."[38]

The mammoth project of designing and building the new capital at New Delhi was the last gasp of the empire, even though those who built it thought that the Raj was eternal. Although Lord Hardinge, who initiated the project, wanted to see "buildings of a bold and plain character with oriental adaptation . . . call it bastard or what you like" and although the architect Lutyens did not care for the indiscriminate use of Indian effects, he indeed did combine the simplicity of classicism with Indian ele-

ments for the palace, while the legislative building is almost purely classical (fig. 90). As Jan Morris has written, "he built the palace in a style that defied easy classification, either political or aesthetic, being classical in form, country English in manner, and recognizably influenced in the end not only by Muslim forms, but by an Indian cultural heritage hitherto neglected by Anglo-Indian architects, Buddhism."[39] The impressive, 180-foot copper dome was apparently inspired by the Buddhist stupa of Sanchi near Bhopal.

Befitting the imperial image, the new palace in New Delhi is 600 feet long and is situated on four and a half acres of exquisitely landscaped formal gardens inspired by those of Kashmir and Sussex (fig. 91). It took three million cubic

95

feet of stone to build it and a staff of 6,000 for its upkeep. Awed by the incongruity of its scale and grandeur in a land where most of the Crown's subjects lived in mud huts with thatched roofs, it is not surprising that in 1931, its rising dome above the new city struck Robert Byron as "the shout of the imperial suggestion—a slap in the face of the moderate average-man with his second-hand ideals."[40] The last British occupant of this glaring symbol of imperialism was the emperor's cousin Lord Mountbatten who left in 1948; today it is occupied by a democratically elected Indian president in a country whose citizens continue to live in huts of thatch and rubble.

Nothing, however, so effectively symbolized the British emphasis on isolation and mitigated their feelings of homesickness as that quintessentially English creation, the hillstation. Built mostly in the Himalayan foothills at altitudes of three to seven thousand feet, these hillstations were havens from the heat and turmoil of the plains, and were in many ways a bit of Scotland or England. Across the Himalayas from Punjab to Bengal, a string of them sprang up mostly in the second half of the nineteenth century. Muree, Mussoorie, Dalhousie, Simla, Nainital, Almora, Darjeeling, and Kalimpong are some of the better known names of the Himalayan chain. Simla was the star among them as it was the summer capital of the viceroy (fig. 92). It, like all of the other hillstations, was thoroughly British save the rickshaws, coolies, and servants; one could easily have imagined oneself in a small Scottish or English town. The most famous non-Himalayan hillstation was beautiful Ootacamund, nestled in the blue hills of the Nilgiris in southern India.

An anonymous bard of Anglo-India wrote of the allure of the hills:

> Give me but five months of Simla;
>   Let me see it ere I die;
> Fresher are its mountain breezes,
>   Than this hateful burning sky.
> Oh! my heart is sick and heavy,
>   Agra gales are not for me;
> Though the khuds [ravines] be tempest riven,
>   Place me there and set me free.[41]

3. In Search of Romantic India

The rage for making tours which has so long distinguished the British people has increased for several years until it has become the prevailing taste of the higher families to explore the country in search of the picturesque. Numerous portfolios are filled every summer with topographical studies made by amateurs, as well as artists during these excursions.

W. H. PYNE — 1815[1]

The Lure of the Picturesque

I

THE British artists' response to the Indian panorama was immediate and spontaneous. The imagination of both the amateur and the professional was captivated by the varied landscapes of the country as much as by its exotic temples and ruins. However, the dominant factor that molded the British artistic perception of the Indian landscape was the concept of the "picturesque." In eighteenth-century Britain, where the cult of the picturesque had been established in the sphere of landscape painting, the word "picturesque" implied the avoidance of anything precise, trim, or tame; its keynote was the presence of ruggedness, of wild or unkempt beauty. In his famous essay on the picturesque, William Gilpin specified that "ideas of neat and smooth . . . strip the object . . . of picturesque beauty."[2] Elaborating on the objects that may be included in a picturesque landscape, he wrote, "The cottage offends. It should

be a castle, a bridge, an aqueduct, or some other object that suits its dignity."[3]

Motifs had to be selected from nature and juxtaposed in a harmonious manner so as to present an acceptable, picturesque landscape; this usually involved the creation of imaginary scenes. Gilpin, for instance, painted the English Lake District, but it is completely unrecognizable, for the landscape has been transformed into a wild, rocky terrain filled with precipices and stormy rivers.[4] The need to create a picturesque view from the material afforded by nature forced artists to take liberties with the landscape, often making it more rugged than it actually was.

India, on the other hand, unfolded before the artist's eye all of the elements that he formerly had to conjure up from imagination at home. The vast subcontinent, with its great rivers, wild desolate plains, mountain ranges, and rocky outcrops was superb raw material which the artists could transmute into picturesque landscapes. The profusion of architectural monuments, temples, mosques, bridges, and ruins were indeed objects that suited the cult of the picturesque. If human figures were needed to enhance a landscape, India again afforded picturesque material that would have met with the approval of Gilpin, who pleaded with his artists to avoid ladies with parasols and concentrate on bandits with flowing cloaks![5] The people of India, with their deep olive complexion and exotic costumes, provided ideal accents for any landscape.

The dramatic use of light and shadow, also a sine qua non of the picturesque, called for considerable ingenuity on the part of artists painting in the dull light of Britain. In India, on the other hand, there is always a contrast between bright sunlight and the deep shadows, except around noon.

During this period, there also arose an obsession with the romantic, an infatuation with the new, the unknown, the remote, the exotic. Again, India supplied the perfect answer for the combined expression of picturesque and romantic beauty.

By the early nineteenth century the word picturesque began to appear with great regularity in Anglo-Indian literature of the period. For instance, Fanny Parks, an enthusiastic amateur artist who traveled extensively in India, entitled her volume *Wanderings of a Pilgrim in Search of the Picturesque* (1850), while army officer and amateur painter Lieutenant Colonel Forrest called his book *A Picturesque Tour along the Rivers Ganges and Jumna* (1824). One writer after another commented on the picturesque landscape, the picturesque river boats, and the picturesque natives of India. Bishop Heber, for instance, describes the Ganges as a "broad river, with a very rapid current, swarming with picturesque canoes, and no less picturesque fishermen,"[6] while Honoria Lawrence writes of the native fishermen, "The strong red glare of the fire, falling upon their bronzed figures, and lighting up their bright black faces looking very

picturesque."[7] The overuse of the expression "picturesque" continued in the present century; a correspondent for *The Daily Telegraph* reporting on the march of the maharajas at Curzon's durbar in 1902–3 writes, "for sheer bizarre picturesqueness and vivid tumult of barbaric arms and colour, nothing compared with it."

Certain recurrent themes held a great fascination for both artist and writer, and the most important of these was the river Ganges. Being accustomed to the smaller rivers of Europe, its immensity awed the British who frequently commented on the amazing fact that they were often unable to view its other bank. Colonel Forrest described it as

an immense and grand expanse of water, rather resembling an inland sea than a river. The opposite shore, being very low and flat, was scarcely to be distinguished; and looking up the stream, it had apparently no bounds.[8]

The Ganges was also the lifeline of northern India, its main avenue of transportation; every British artist to visit India traveled up the Ganges sketching the river with its country craft, strange rock formations, and numerous bathing ghats lining its banks. Emma Roberts tells us that even the smallest villages on the banks of the Ganges have their own ghats and that

Nothing can be more animated than an Indian ghaut; at scarcely any period of the day is it destitute of groupes of bathers, while graceful female forms are continually passing and repassing, loaded with waterpots, which are balanced with the nicest precision on their heads.[9]

The town of Benares along the Ganges attracted many British visitors and almost every British artist in India depicted the holy city. Captain Robert Elliot writes of the ghats of Benares:

The immense flight of steps called the Ghauts of Benares, form a great ornament to the river face of the city. . . . Crowds of people come down to wash in, and also to worship, the Ganges. . . . The gracefulness of many of the washing figures, the various colours of their dresses, the easy and elegant attitudes in which they stand, and the admirable groups into which they occasionally fall, would form excellent subjects for a painter.[10]

The vibrant life along the river moved Emma Roberts to write:

The ghauts are literally swarming with life at all hours of the day and every creek and jetty are crowded with craft of various descriptions, all truly picturesque in their form and effect. . . . No written description, however elaborate, can convey even a faint idea of the extraordinary peculiarities of a place which has no prototype in the East. . . . It is only by pictorial representations that any adequate notion can be formed of the mixture of the beautiful and the grotesque, which, piled confusedly together, form that stupendous wall which spreads along the bank of the Ganges at Benares.[11]

The source of the holy Ganges was another subject that intrigued the British, and in 1815,

James Baillie Fraser located and sketched the small snowbound hollow at Gangotri from which the Ganges emerges. Several artists after him succumbed to the lure of the source of the mighty river, including painter William Simpson and photographer Samuel Bourne.

One monument in India, which remains to-day a more familiar symbol of the country than any other—the Taj Mahal—attracted every British artist. Although sketched and painted by generations of them—and not always that successfully—it was left to the photographer to make the monument known the world over.

The banyan tree, which grows all over India, was another subject portrayed by every artist from Hodges in the 1780s to Bourne a hundred years later. Describing one extraordinary banyan, artist James Forbes wrote that it was "near two thousand feet in circumference, measured round the principal stems. . . . The large trunks

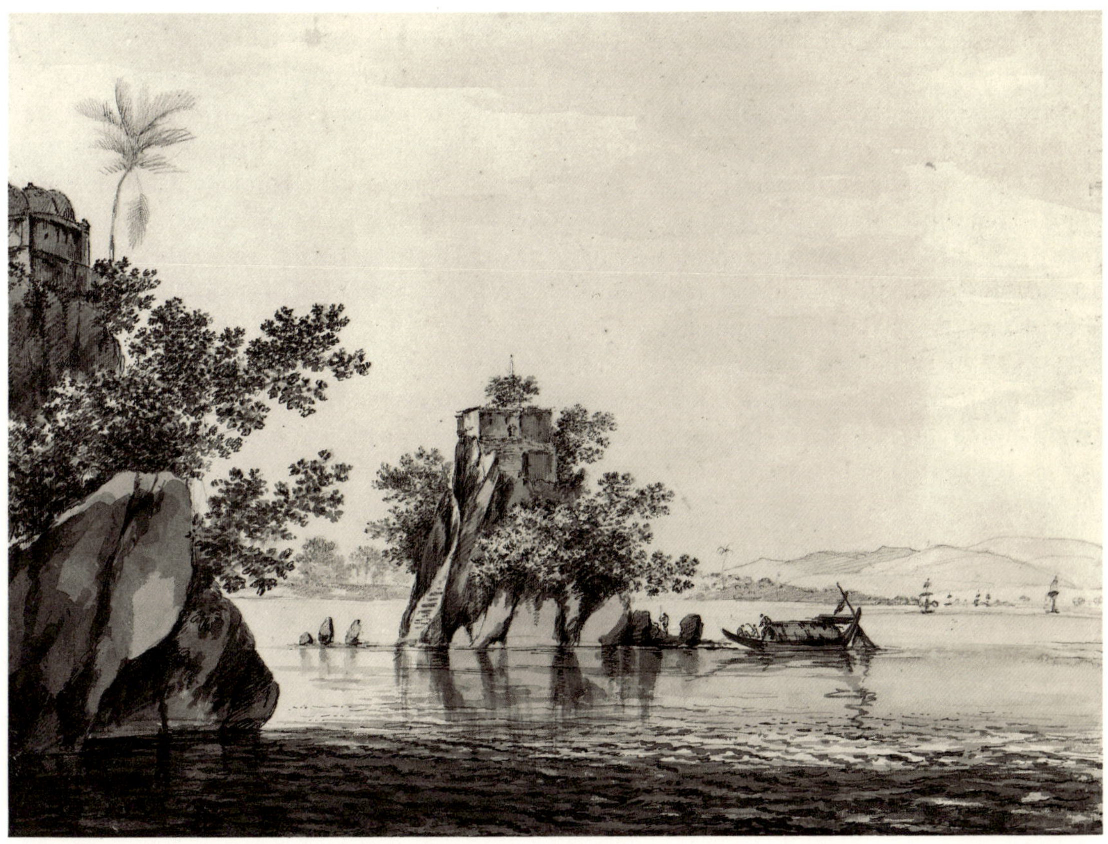

93. William Hodges. *A View of an Insulated Rock in the River Ganges at Jangerah*. c. 1780. Pen and gray wash over pencil. Yale Center for British Art, Paul Mellon Collection.

of this single tree amount to three hundred and fifty, and the smaller ones exceed three thousand: each of these is constantly sending forth branches and roots, to form other trunks, and become the parents of future progeny." Forbes proceeds to tell us of a chieftain who camped beneath this celebrated tree in magnificent style, "having a saloon, dining room, drawing room, bed-chambers, bath, kitchen, and every other accommodation, all in separate tents; yet did this noble tree cover the whole; together with his carriages, horses, camels, guards, and attendants."[12] It is little wonder that artists were drawn to this amazing creation of nature.

The exotic customs of the Hindus were another subject that captivated the British artists. The annual fairs along the rivers, especially those at Allahabad and Hardwar, where millions gathered for the festivities, could scarcely be believed. Lieutenant White tells us that while it was difficult enough to convey an idea of the grandeur of the monuments at these sites, it was "still more so to convey even a faint notion of the swarms of living creatures, men and beasts of every description, which occupy every foot of ground during the time of the fair . . . The noise," he commented, "baffles all description."[13] The Hindu practice of *suttee*, in which a widow burned herself on the funeral pyre of her husband, exercised a morbid fascination upon the artists who generally romanticized it. Jugglers, sword swallowers, and snake charmers mesmerized the British, while the many religious mendicants of India—the sages and *sadhu*s, the *fakir*s and *sunyasee*s—were equally captivating.

II

THE first of the professional landscape artists to visit India was William Hodges who traveled across much of the northern part of the country between 1780 and 1783, and made numerous sketches of the land, its monuments, and its ruins. A devoted practitioner of the picturesque, Hodges occasionally rearranged the elements of a scene to make it more evocative, for which he was sharply criticized by some, particularly the

uncle and nephew team of the Daniells, who favored topographic accuracy. A remarkable feature of Hodges's work is his mastery of light and shadow; with apparent facility, he portrayed the shimmering sunlight of India, the clear colors of her morning sky, the opacity of clouds, and the reflection of monuments in her waters. He was fascinated by atmospheric conditions and frequently commented on them in his writings.

Traveling up the Ganges, Hodges, enchanted by the river, the atmospheric light, the shapes of the boats, and the scenery along the banks, wrote, "The rivers I have seen in Europe, even the Rhine, appear as rivulets in comparison with this enormous mass of water."[14] His drawing, *A View of an Insulated Rock in the River Ganges at Jangerah*, captures the early morning light on the rippling waters of the mighty river (fig. 93). He has juxtaposed the strange rock formations with the broad expanse of water to build a striking composition, ebullient with the light of India. There are two large granite rocks at Sultanganj, one of which projects into the river and is cut off from the bank when the water rises. Hodges tells us, "This rock, opposite the little village of Jangerah . . . is made famous amongst the Hindoos from its having on the top of it a small hermitage for a Hindoo fakir. The situation this holy father has chosen is certainly a proof of his taste as well as of his judgement; for, from the top he has a most extensive view of all the neighbouring country, and in the summer heats is much cooler than any other situation in the country. This rock is always considered as a place of sanctity, having upon it a small temple of the Hindoos, and on many parts of the rock an imperfect representation in sculpture of some of the Hindoo deities."[15]

Hodges made several sketches of the island rock before he came up with the final drawing from which the aquatint was made for his *Select Views of India*. One drawing gives us a close-up of the island, highlighting its ragged rock formations and showing the rock-cut sculptures on the cliff face; this sketch is remarkably akin to the version produced later by the Daniells.[16] In

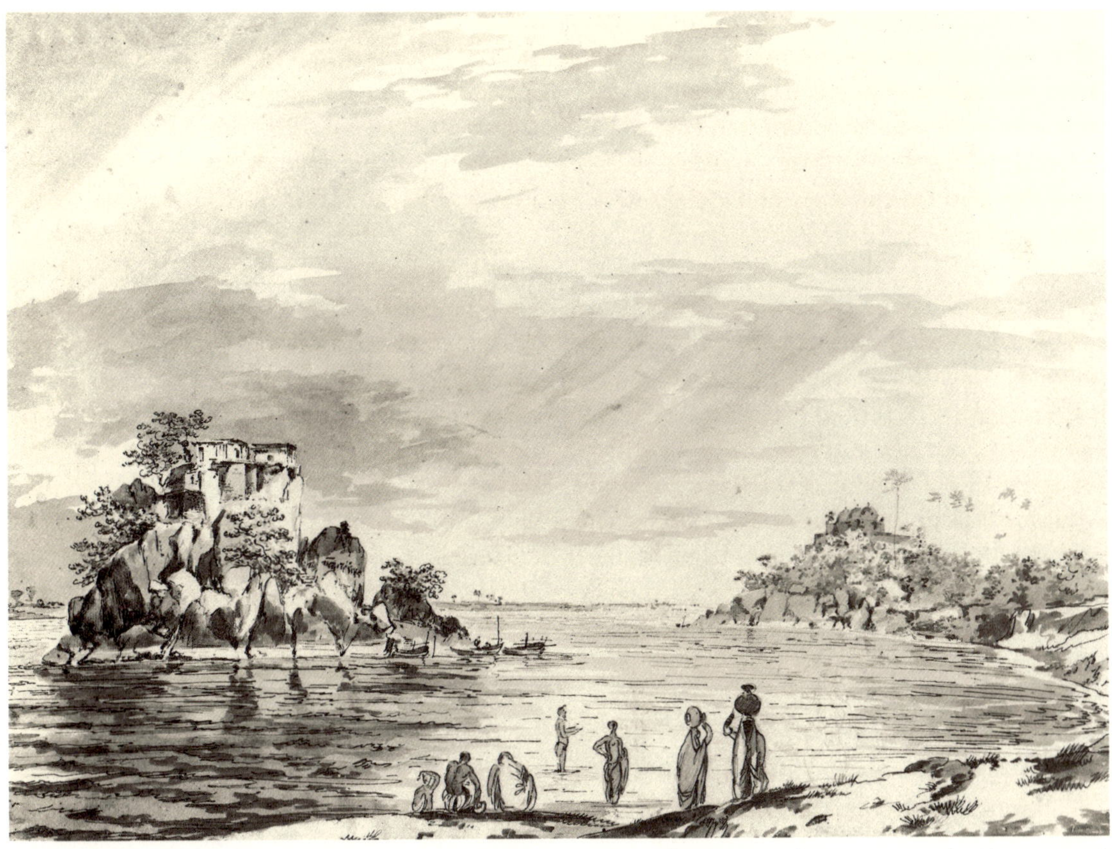

94. William Hodges. *View of the Island of Jangerah at Sultanganj with Figures in the Foreground.*
c. 1780. Pen and gray wash over pencil. Yale Center for British Art, Paul Mellon Collection.

two other drawings, Hodges experimented with placing colorful local figures in the foreground, primarily village women, who had come to bathe and collect water, and are shown with waterpots elegantly balanced on their heads (fig. 94). His final picture is a finely balanced composition that omits the human figures and ignores the sculptured images on the island rock, but gives prominence to a simple sailboat anchored near the island. Hodges's accounts tell us of his fascination for the varied roughly built craft seen on the rivers, and in addition to boats in all of his Jangerah views he made at least one independent drawing of an Indian sailing vessel.

Hodges's artistic background and training are interesting; it seems that he became a painter almost by accident. The son of a blacksmith, he learned to draw when he was working as an errand boy in Shipley's drawing school. He must have exhibited considerable talent, since we

find the established classical landscape painter Richard Wilson (1714–82) taking on Hodges as his pupil. Wilson's reputation was such that when the Royal Academy was founded in 1768, he was invited to be one of its first members. Well known for his Italian landscapes, Wilson took liberties with the scenery, rearranging elements and presenting his viewers with a feel for the scene rather than with exact topographical details. Hodges was one of his best pupils and became his assistant. He was able to copy a Wilson so exactly that there is sometimes doubt as to whether a late Wilson is, in fact, actually a Hodges. If his seven years of apprenticeship with Wilson laid the foundation of Hodges's style, almost as important was the influence of his three-year appointment as official draftsman on Captain Cook's South Pacific expedition, 1772 to 1775. Long hours of observation from the deck of the *Resolution* made him increasingly aware of meteorological conditions, the effect of moonlight and sunshine on water, shorelines and icebergs, and he began to experiment with paint and novel compositions.

Hodges brought his interest in atmospheric conditions and fascination with strange, stark shapes to India, and they are apparent in his first drawings and written accounts of the subcontinent. On landing in Madras, he noted in his journal, "The clear blue cloudless sky, the polished white buildings, the bright sandy beach, the dark green sea, present a combination totally new to the eye of the Englishman just arrived from London, who accustomed to the sight of rolling masses of clouds floating in a damp atmosphere, cannot but contemplate the difference with delight." [17]

To appreciate the artist's preoccupation with light, one has but to see his drawing *View of Part of the City of Benares* (fig. 95). The shimmering quality of Hodges's drawing is quite spectacular. Of the ninety Hodges drawings at Yale, this is the only one "squared" for transfer to canvas and it is clearly the composition that served as the basis for the large (59 × 89 in.) oil painting executed for Warren Hastings and exhibited at the Diploma Gallery of the Royal Academy in 1787. In many ways, Hodges was a forerunner of Turner, that great master of light and color.

Influenced by the classical tradition of Wilson, Hodges had acquired an interest in monuments, for the indulgence of which he found ample material in India. He depicted numerous architectural monuments, often with a dramatic use of foreshortening; *View of the Masjid, or the Tomb at Jaunpur* demonstrates his successful use of this technique (fig. 96).

Hodges's greatest patron and keenest supporter was Warren Hastings who commissioned all of the major oils that the artist produced. Among the paintings Hodges did for Hastings after his return to England was *Storm on the Ganges with Mrs. Hastings Braving the Eddies Near the Col-Gon Rocks* (fig. 97). The work commemorates the dangerous three-day journey undertaken by Mrs. Hastings on the stormy turbulent waters of the Ganges during the rainy season to return to the bedside of her ailing husband. Its evocative storm clouds and dark swirling waters contrast with the rainbow and sharp, clear light. Hodges was most impressed by the area and wrote, "The country about Colgong is, I think, the most beautiful I have seen in India. The waving appearance of the land, its fine turf and detached woods, backed by the extensive forests on the hills, brought to my mind many of the fine parks in England; and its overlooking the Ganges, which has more the appearance of an ocean at this place than of a river, gives the prospect inexpressible grandeur." [18]

Hodges had no specific itinerary for his travels in northern India. More than once he accompanied the party of Governor-General Warren Hastings. On one such trip to Benares, he arrived at Chunar and Bhagalpur, where he decided to stay for four months, having made friends with Company official Augustus Cleveland. Later, he accompanied a mission dispatched by Hastings to Delhi, spending much time sketching and exploring in the Agra region. His basic route was followed by the Daniells who often made sketches from the identical spots Hodges had chosen. The artist adapted easily to India and tells us in his journal of how he ate and enjoyed curries and pillaws.[19] His appreciation of Indians is also evident in his writings (see introduction).[20] On his visits to villages where no Europeans had ever been seen, he was impressed by the hospitality of the people and mixed freely with them. He must have been a man of considerable personal charm judging from the ease with which he made friends, generally with influential persons who frequently gave him commissions.

After spending three years in India, Hodges returned to England and began work on his aquatints for *Select Views of India*, a series that he dedicated to the East India Company. The project was well received, but over the three years that it took to get the aquatints ready for publication, Hodges found himself in severe financial trouble and died a debtor. Though he

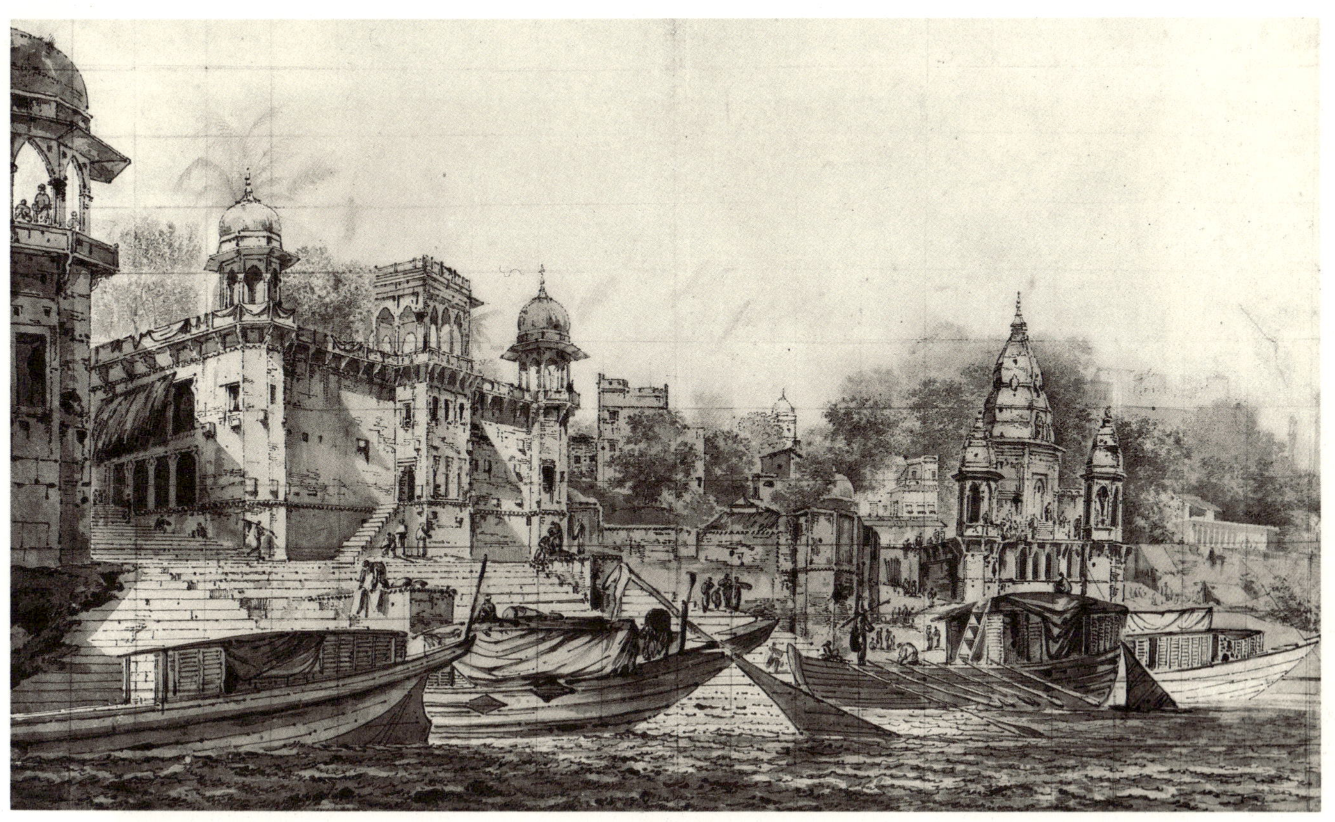

95. William Hodges. *View of Part of the City of Benares*. c. 1780. Gray wash with brush and brown ink over pencil. Yale Center for British Art, Paul Mellon Collection.

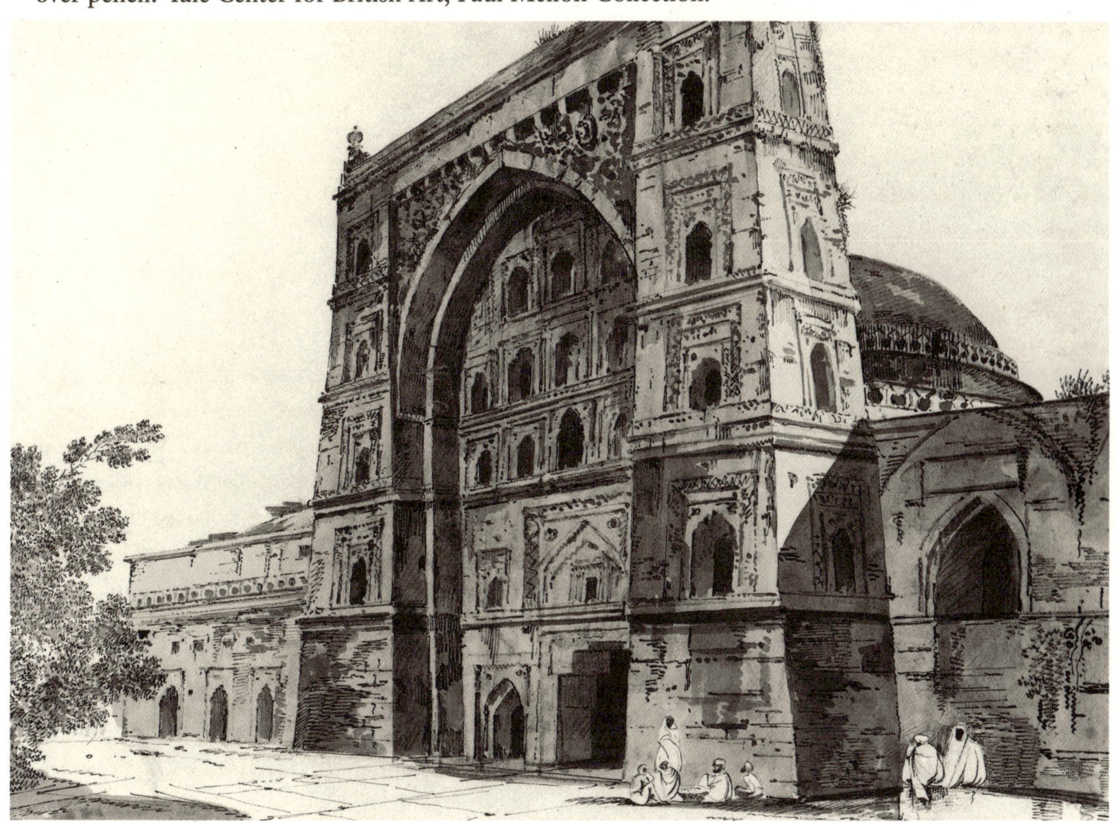

96. William Hodges. *View of Musjid, or the Tomb at Jaunpur* from *Select Views of India*. c. 1786. Gray wash with pen and gray ink over pencil. Yale Center for British Art, Paul Mellon Collection.

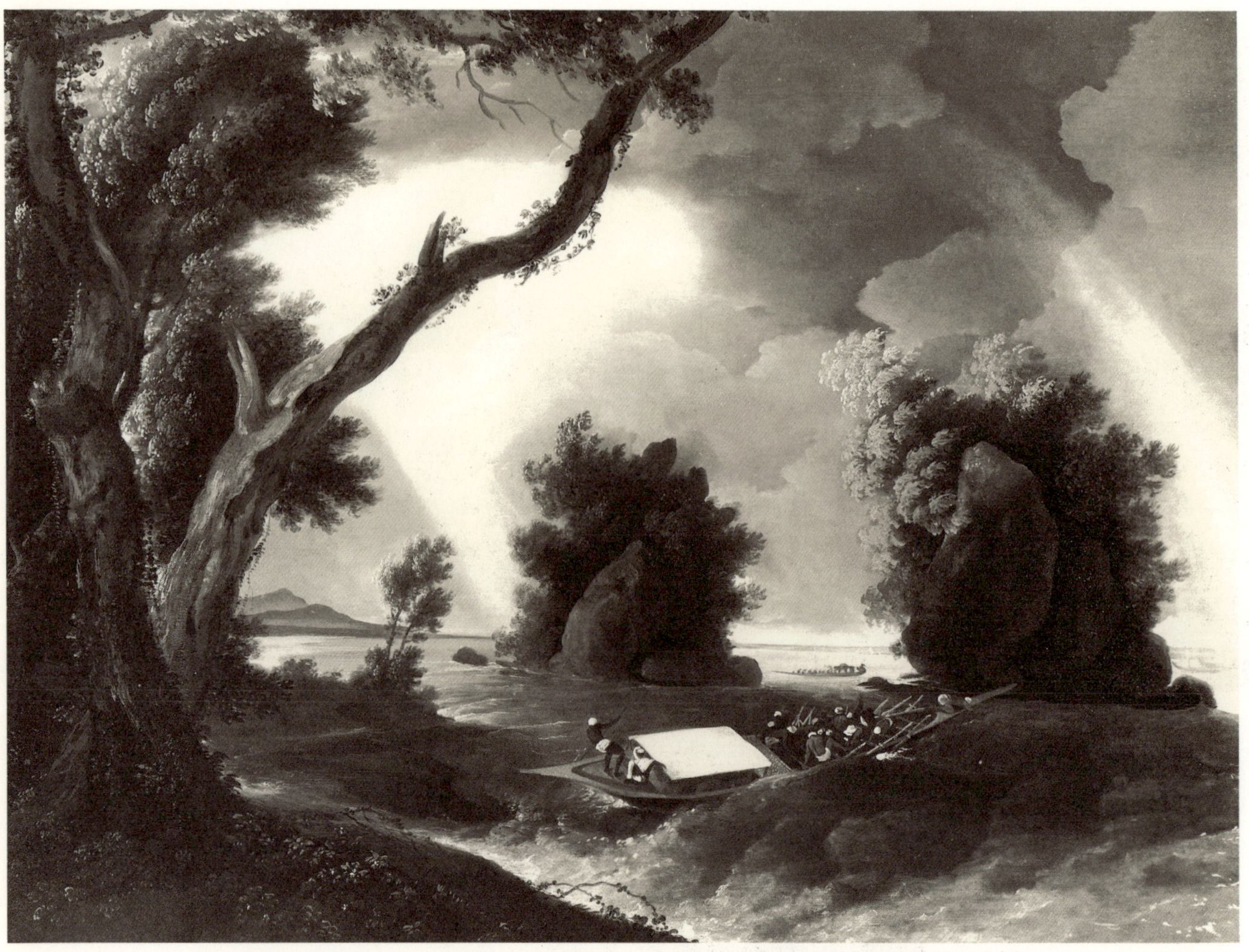

97. William Hodges. *Storm on the Ganges with Mrs. Hastings Braving the Eddies near the Col-Gon Rocks.* 1790. Oil on canvas. Yale Center for British Art, Paul Mellon Collection.

exhibited several times at the Royal Academy, Hodges was never recognized as a landscape painter of any note, despite Sir Joshua Reynolds's commendation of him as an ingenious artist and a landscapist of considerable merit.[21] A reappraisal of Hodges's talent and a reevaluation of his picturesque, light-filled landscapes reveals a man who was ahead of his times. In that sense, his Indian experience may have contributed more to British landscape painting than has hitherto been recognized.

III

ALTHOUGH a more sensitive landscape painter, Hodges was overshadowed by the Daniells, who were highly talented topographical artists. The Daniells, who spent seven years in India, from 1786 to 1793, were enthusiastic and inveterate travelers who wandered all over the country visiting several uncharted regions. They were painstaking in their sketches, making drawings of people, animals, trees, sculpture, architectural details, and the like. Several drawings contain notations for color and enlarged details of ornament. They amassed a vast stock of sketches which were carefully preserved by both uncle and nephew who continued to use them for the rest of their lives. When they returned to England, they published six volumes entitled *Oriental Scenery*, containing 144 aquatints of India; so great was the success of the series that the famous J. M. W. Turner remarked that he

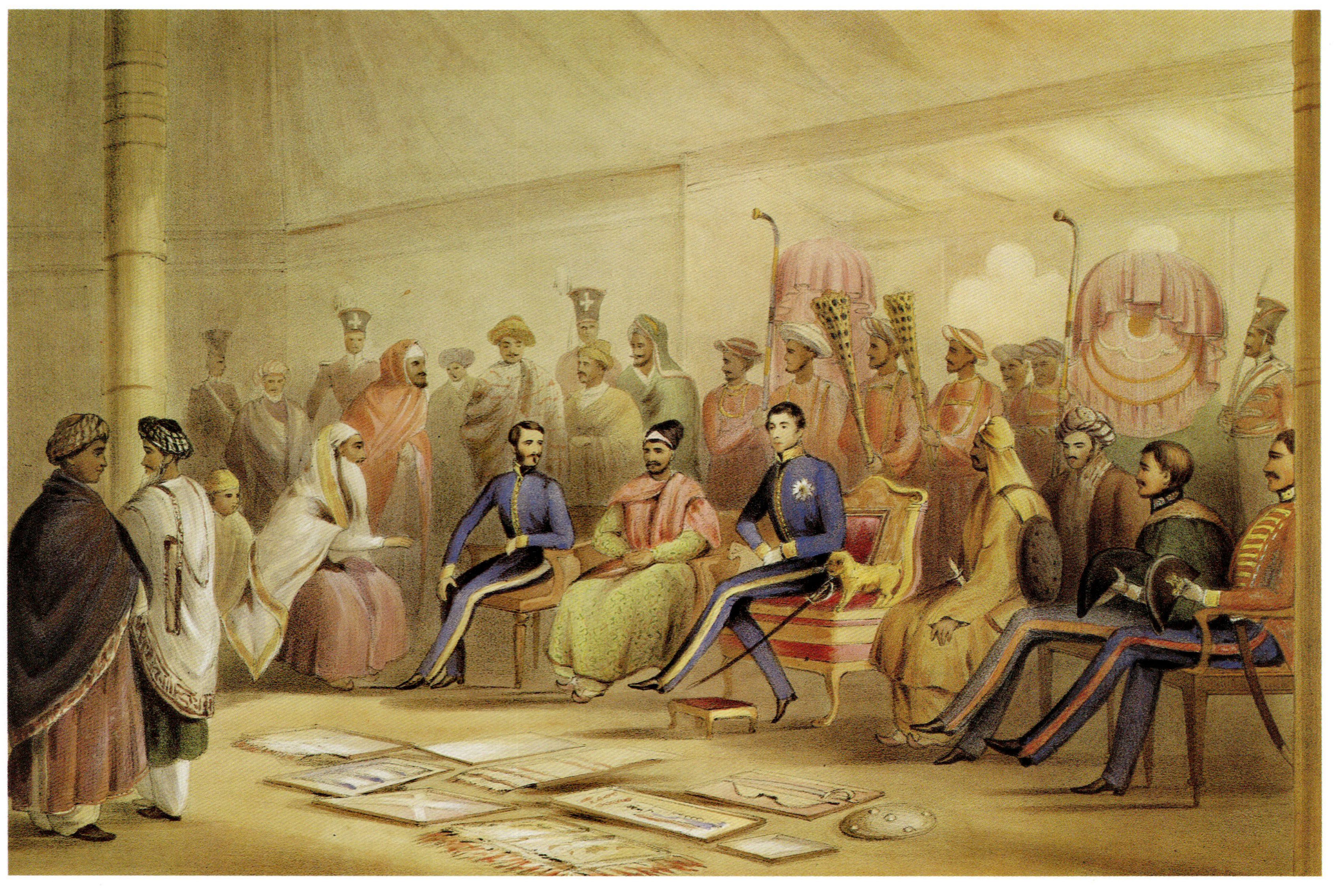

COLORPLATE 7.
Emily Eden. *Lord Auckland Receiving the Raja of Nahun in Durbar.* 1844. Watercolor.
Walter Collection.

would like to have the plates for his work, *Liber Studiorum*, "engraved like Mr. Daniell's."[22] As the Daniells were primarily topographical artists, the renown they achieved in their own lifetime is unusual. They seem to have been able to command a high price from their customers; diarist Farington relates that in September 1804, "Turner was to have painted two pictures for Mrs. Barnard at a certain price, but on hearing Daniell had that price demanded double. . . ."[23] Both Thomas and William were elected to the Royal Academy; a later critic who remarked that this honor, "will always remain one of the enigmas of the early days of the Institution,"[24] seems to have been more reserved in his appraisal of their work.

Thomas Daniell, like William Hodges, came from simple beginnings, starting life as a bricklayer, and then apprenticing with a coach builder, where he learned the rudiments of painting. He soon began painting on a wider scale—first flowers, then portraits, and finally landscapes. Finding that commissions in Britain were increasingly difficult to secure, and more so for artists of middling caliber, Thomas Daniell obtained permission to go to India together with his fifteen-year-old nephew William; they arrived in Calcutta in 1786 after a long journey via China. Their first project was the publication *Views of Calcutta*, a set of twelve aquatints, in which they were aided by Indian engravers. The results were disappointing, probably due to the inexperience of the Indian collaborators. While they were in Calcutta, between 1786 and 1788, volumes of Hodges's *Select Views* arrived in India, giving the Daniells an indication of what could be achieved in the genre of illustrated travel books. They decided thenceforth to concentrate on sketching, drawing, and painting and to abandon engraving and publishing until they got back to Britain. Hodges's volumes also gave them an idea of the places they could visit, and accordingly, they planned an extensive tour of northern India, basically following Hodges's route. A journey up the Ganges, with a trip to Delhi and Agra, was obligatory. The Daniells were displeased with *Select Views* for several

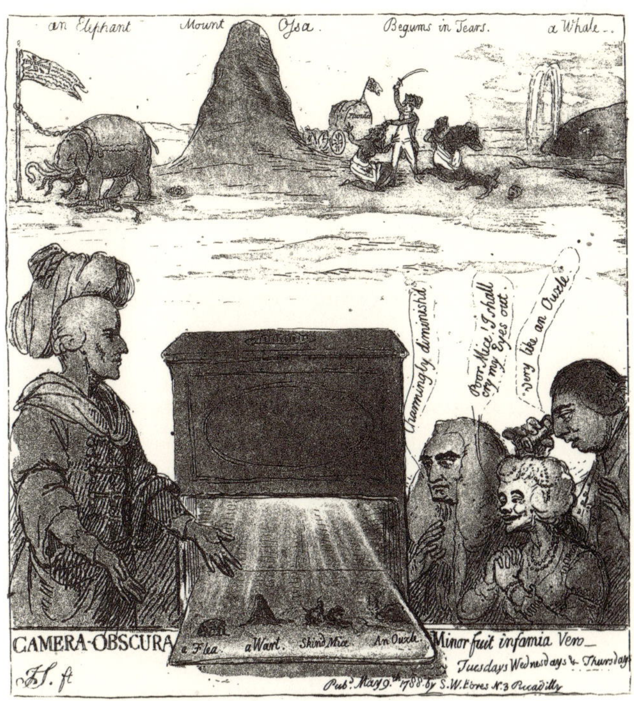

98. Anonymous. *Camera-Obscura*. 1788. Engraving. Walter Collection.

reasons and William, in particular, was outspoken in his criticism. Ardent topographers, they made their sketches with the aid of the camera obscura, and totally disapproved of the "inaccuracies"—the picturesque renderings—that were Hodges's specialty.[25] Occasionally, as in the instance of the tomb at Jaunpur, the Daniells made a drawing of an identical view, correcting in their version, what they deemed Hodges's inaccuracies. They clearly wished to compile a more impressive and accurate record of India, and outdo Hodges, which they did achieve inasmuch as they visited and made drawings of a number of sites unknown to him. From the great Sanskrit scholar Wilkins, they learned of several spectacular Hindu monuments; from Samuel Davis, amateur artist and officer of the East India Company, who had been on an embassy to Tibet, they learned of the Himalayan ranges. Encouraged by several well-wishers in Calcutta, the Daniells set off on an extensive trip through northern India, traversing in a period of three years a much wider area than Hodges. They traveled up into the lower Himalayas and discovered that they were the first Europeans to set foot in the Garhwal city of

Srinagar. Their second major expedition was a tour of southern India, an area less known to the British and penetrated by fewer travelers, where they sketched the countryside and its monuments. Their third trip took them to Bombay, where artist James Wales introduced them to the riches of the cave architecture of the region. Having spent over seven years in India, the Daniells returned to England.

Hindoo Temples at Bindrabund on the River Jumna, engraved by Thomas Daniell in 1795 from his own earlier drawing made in 1789, is one of their less successful works (colorplate 8). Brindaban, the sacred land of Krishna, was one of the Hindu sites the Daniells had heard of from Wilkins. They were most impressed by these "beautiful and singular Pagodas. They are more elegantly sculptured; certain carved ribs go equidistant into small figures prettily filled with rosettes."[26] The aquatint is executed in very somber hues, and these dark colors, better suited to the depictions of dense Italian woods in the classical style, are indeed characteristic of a number of Daniell productions. Although this drawing has been described by one critic as "one of the dullest" and "more gloomy" of his works,[27] the temples made such an impression on Thomas Daniell that, back in England, he painted the subject in oil in 1797 as his diploma work for the Royal Academy. The influence of the subject was far in excess of the quality of the renderings. For instance, the Brindaban pagodas were used by Humphrey Repton as his model for the aviary at the Brighton Pavilion, and in his proposed but never executed drawing he transformed the solid temple into an open, airy structure.[28] A Brindaban pagoda featured prominently in a Dufour wallpaper titled "Paysage Indien."[29]

Often the coloring used by the Daniells gives

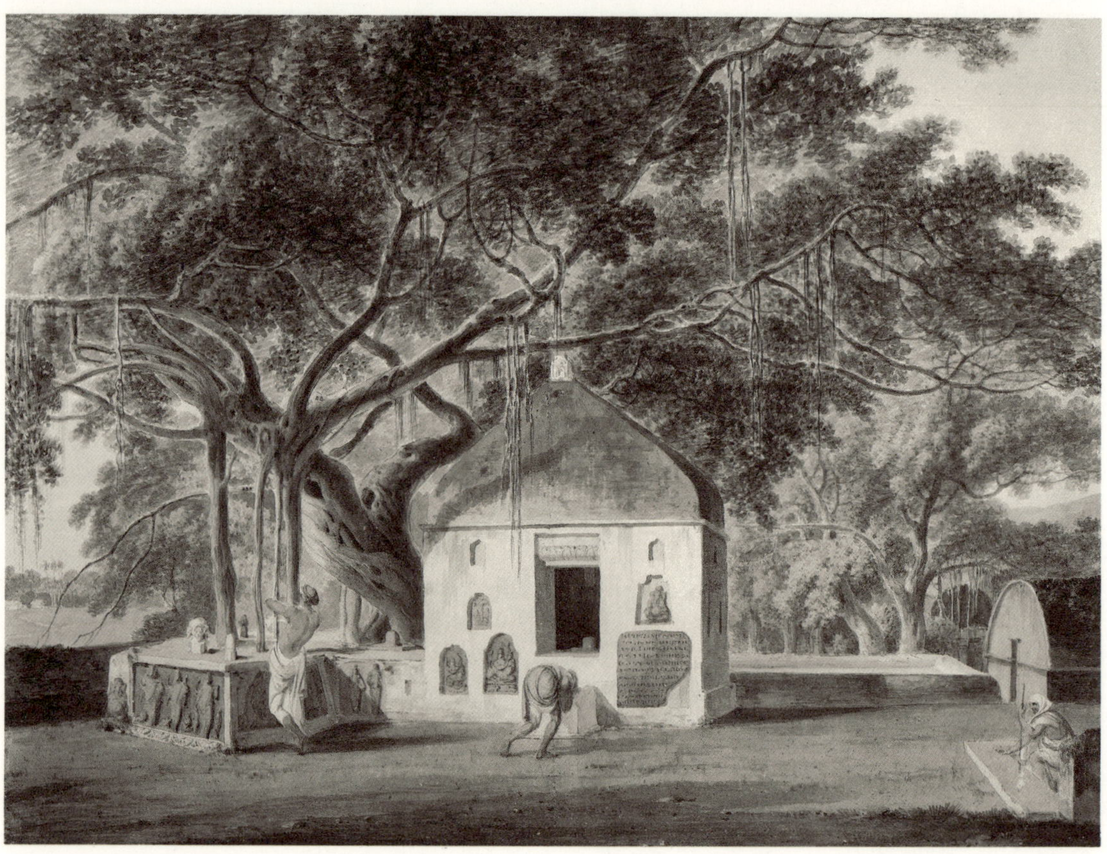

99. Thomas and William Daniell. *The Sacred Tree of the Hindoos at Gyah.* 1796. Aquatint. The Pierpont Morgan Library.

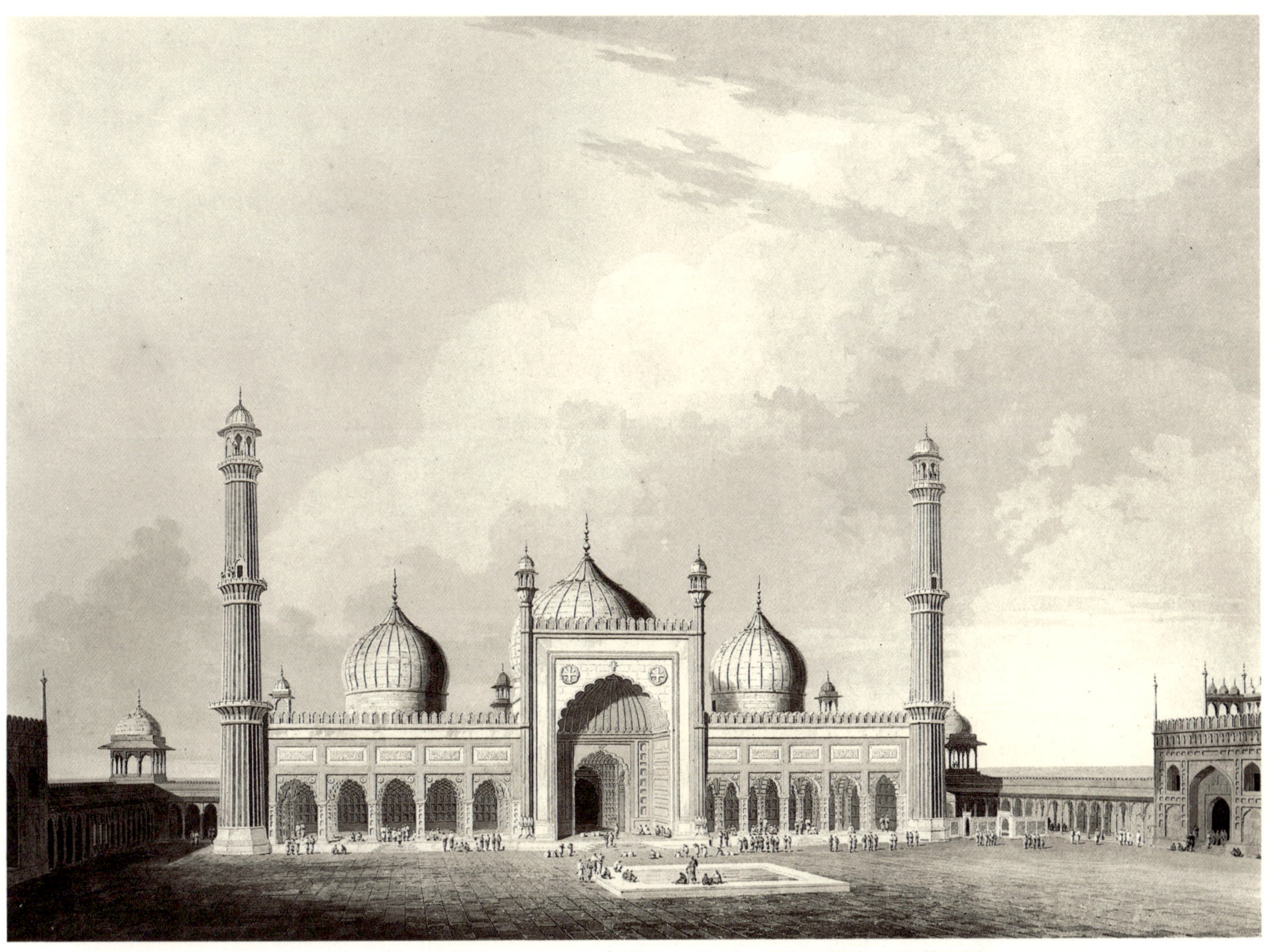

100. Thomas and William Daniell. *The Jama Masjid, Delhi.* 1797. Aquatint. Walter Collection.

the impression of a shaded country where the sun scarcely penetrated through a blanket of clouds. For example, their aquatints of Benares are in neutral tones of tan and blue that scarcely convey the feel of the sun-drenched crowded bathing ghats, with their kaleidoscope of colors. But, the Daniells were certainly impressed by the town: "The general view of Benares . . . was so very grand that I staid on Board the whole day to draw it, fearing if we let slip the present opportunity that we might never see it in a better point-of-view." [30] On their return journey they explored it further and made numerous sketches. While they were able to accurately record what they saw, they failed to capture the spirit of the city. Dramatic color effects

and mood were sacrificed in favor of structural accuracy. Edward Lear (in India 1873–75), who visited Benares almost a hundred years after the Daniells and was equally charmed by the city, remarked, "How well I remember the views of Benares by Daniell R.A.!–pallid,– gray,–sad,–solemn. I had always supposed this place a melancholy, or at least a 'staid' and soberly, coloured spot, a gray record of bygone days! Instead, I find it one of the most abundantly bruyant and startlingly radiant places of infinite bustle and movement!!! Constantinople, or Naples, are simply dull and quiet in comparison!!!" [31]

The Daniells, like many artists after them, succumbed to the fascination of the banyan tree

107

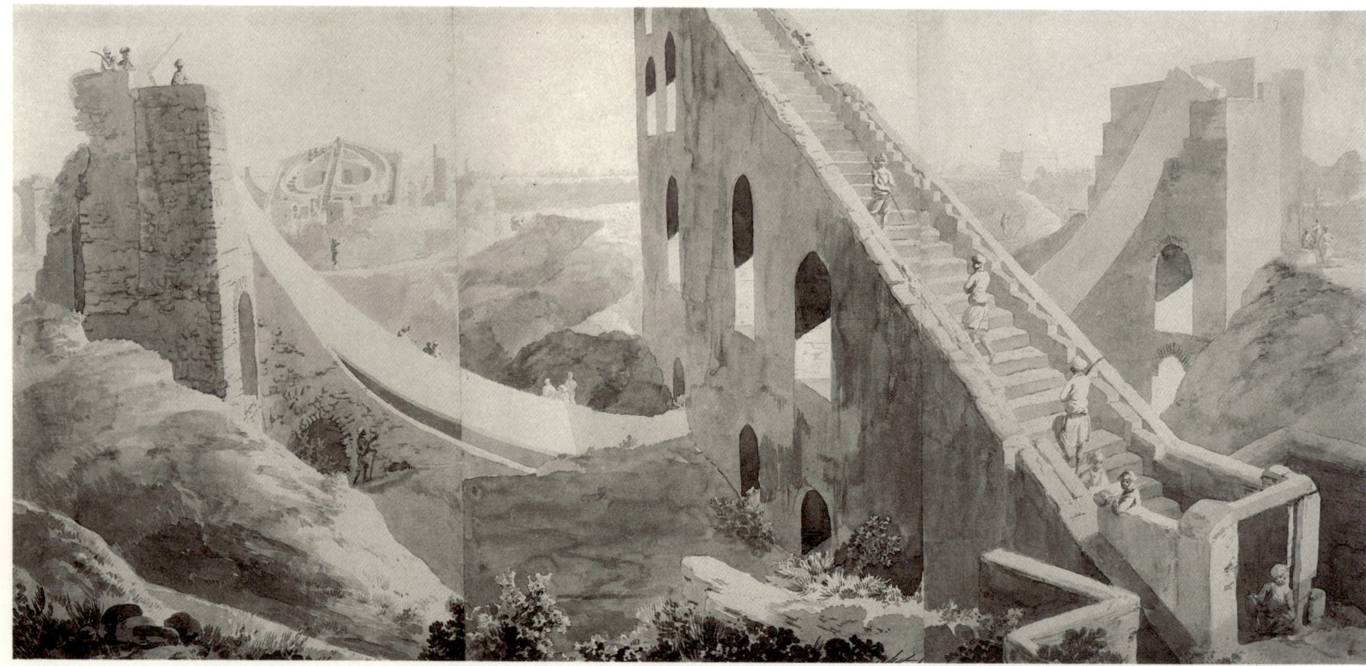

101. Thomas and William Daniell. *Jai Singh's Observatory, Delhi.* 1790. Pencil and wash. Walter Collection.

and made several sketches and paintings of this natural wonder. Their *Sacred Tree of the Hindoos at Gyah* is a somber vision, but in this instance, justifiably so (fig. 99). The great banyan tree with its drooping roots casts a shadow over everything and dominates the picture. Idols of various types stand beneath it, with a small shrine to one side, and Hindus are shown paying obeisance to the sacred tree. This print and the drawing that preceded it are almost entirely in varying deep shades of green and blue.

Among the light and airy compositions of the Daniells, one of the finest is of the Jama Masjid in Delhi (fig. 100). This magnificent structure, described by E.M. Forster as "one of the noblest buildings in India and the world,"[32] is indeed awesome. While the accuracy of the Daniells as draftsmen is unsurpassed, in their depiction of the Jama Masjid, they have also managed to capture the aura of the sublime. The pale clouded sky occupying half of the picture echoes the colors of the mosque—of translucent marble domes and pale pink sandstone—and the entire aquatint is executed in shades of tan, pale coral, white, gray, and blue.

Equally spectacular is their enormous sketch (28 x 51 in.) of the observatory at Delhi known as Jantar Mantar, executed on three sheets of paper, pasted together (fig. 101). The extraordinary shapes of these gigantic observatory instruments intrigued the Daniells who used the word "singular" to describe them. Their pencil drawing with a light wash of gray and tan is effective in conveying the immensity and complexity of the structure. Much enthusiasm was exhibited for this great astronomical complex, built by Maharaja Jai Singh II of Jaipur around 1724. "It is not possible to convey any idea by description of these enormous instruments," wrote Emma Roberts in 1837, "but persons desirous to make themselves acquainted with them have only to consult the splendid and accurate views taken by Mr. Daniell."[33] Certainly, it must have been Samuel Davis, their East India Company officer friend, who inspired the Daniells to visit and sketch this site. Davis wrote an article entitled: "On the astronomical computations of the Hindoos," which was published in *Asiatick Researches* in 1799, but which he must have been preparing when the

108

Daniells stayed with him ten years earlier.

The Daniells made several sketches of the Great Rock at Trichinopoly in southern India and four aquatints of varying views of the site for inclusion in *Oriental Scenery* (fig. 102). This disproportionate amount of attention given to Trichinopoly is explained partly by its dramatic "picturesqueness" and partly because the site had become a popular symbol of British military prowess in India. The temple on the rock—the Great Pagoda of the Daniell picture—was built in the seventeenth century and the high surrounding walls give it a fortlike appearance. This picture is a dramatic view of the walled "pagoda" and the craggy, barren hill upon which it sits. The view is taken from half-way up the rock where most of the Brahman priests reside. Once again, we see the typical Daniell sober hues of brown, tan, and gray with only the terracotta-colored roof tiles enlivening the picture.

All of the Daniells' pictures have an atmo-sphere of quiet composure, primarily due to the extensive use of gray, tan, brown, and deep green. Using sepia, blue, and gray for the printing, they then "stained" the prints to reproduce with fastidious accuracy the exact tonal effects of the original watercolors. The superb quality of the aquatinting technique adopted by the Daniells was much admired and reviews were full of appreciation.[34] However, the vibrant atmosphere of India never emerges; instead one is presented with gray skies, so reminiscent of England. While the subject matter was novel and exotic, the manner of presentation was familiar and acceptable, and this no doubt was responsible for the popularity of the Daniell volumes. Their work accorded with the requirements of classical landscape painting, being generally meticulous and precise. There is none of the air of restlessness or unkempt grandeur that permeates Hodges's work. The Daniell views became so popular that they inspired an entire range of Staffordshire blue-and-white porcelain devoted

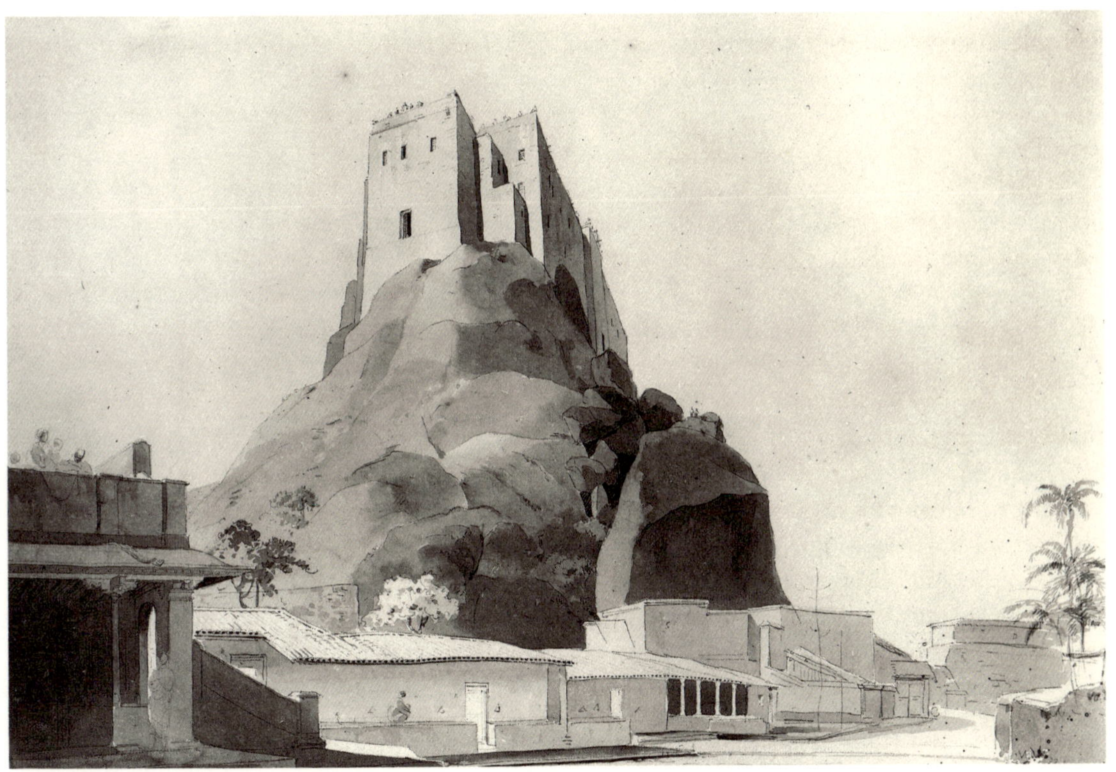

102. Thomas and William Daniell. *The Great Pagoda, Trichinopoly.* 1797. Aquatint. The Pierpont Morgan Library.

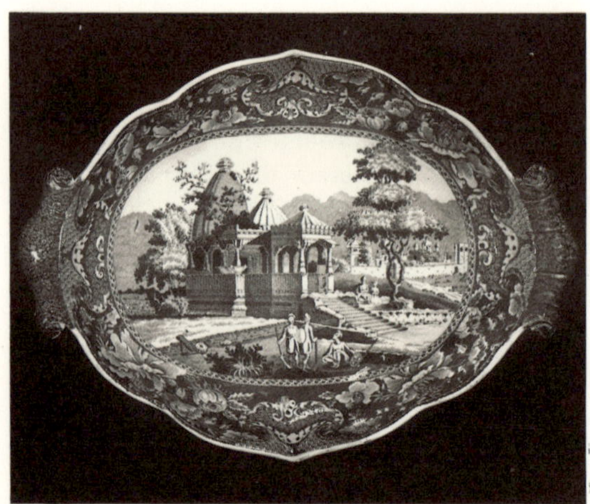

103. Anonymous. English Staffordshire earthenware compote with the Daniells' *Hindoo Temple in the Fort at Rohtas, Bihar*. 19th century. Walter Collection.

to Indian scenes; plates depicted Chitpore Road, meat dishes displayed Delhi monuments, and an elegant bowl portrayed in its entirety Daniells' *Hindoo Temple in the Fort at Rohtas, Bihar* (fig. 103). Their continued popularity is evident from the demand for their works among collectors, and from the fact that more has been written about them than about any other British artists who worked in India.

IV

ONE of the greatest British artists who visited India was Zoffany, who is generally admired for his portraits which constitute the majority of his surviving works.[35] In all of his portraits, Zoffany invariably included a reference to Indian life: his large painting of Mr. and Mrs. Warren Hastings introduces the figure of an Indian maid; the Elijah Impey family is portrayed listening to Indian musicians who occupy over half the canvas. Even simple portraits, such as the one of General Macleod or of his wife Sarah, emphasize the local setting: the general's portrait shows us a backdrop of an army camp with elephants, camels, horses, and palanquin, while Sarah is portrayed against a setting of trees and a Mogul tomb.

One suspects that Zoffany was a landscape painter at heart. In his large oil painting, *Colo-nel Antoine Polier with his Friends Claud Martin, John Wombwell, and the Artist*, Zoffany made himself the focus of the picture, seated before an easel upon which is a landscape depicting a banyan tree with two ascetics and a nude female beneath it (fig. 21). The five other pictures, all in Zoffany's style, which are hanging on the wall, are of Indian scenes: a waterfall with elephants bathing in the stream; pilgrims bathing along the ghats; a suttee, with the funeral pyre just about to be lit; a dying Hindu lying beside a river; a scuffle between Indian and British soldiers. Zoffany's love of landscape painting is further borne out by the diaries of William Daniell in which he speaks of several landscape drawings by Zoffany in the collection of Colonel Martin in Lucknow. He tells us that his uncle Thomas looked over these Zoffany sketches and even "put in the background to the sketch of a fakir."[36] Another large oil, *The Blair Conversation Piece* of 1786, also shows evidence of Zoffany's skill as a landscapist (fig. 104).[37] Three landscapes hang on the wall behind the Blair family and their native servant girl: a scene of a hill crowned with a tomb and a native encampment in the foreground, and two smaller scenes that show a suttee and hook-swinging.

Zoffany made a number of pen-and-ink landscape sketches, probably during his last year in India, primarily in the Lucknow region. Spending a considerable amount of time in boats, he sketched several riverside scenes (fig. 105). This annotated drawing is dated 29 November 1788, two months before Zoffany left India on his voyage back to England. We hear later from Forster, the naturalist on Captain Cook's second voyage, who visited the artist in London, that, "Mr. Zoffany . . . has in particular portraits of Indians, men and women, from different castes and tribes. . . ."[38] There is today no evidence of the drawings and they, along with several other sketches of landscapes, buildings, and ruins, may have been among those burned in 1832, "for health reasons,"[39] when his wife and daughter died of cholera.

Like Zoffany, George Chinnery (in India

110

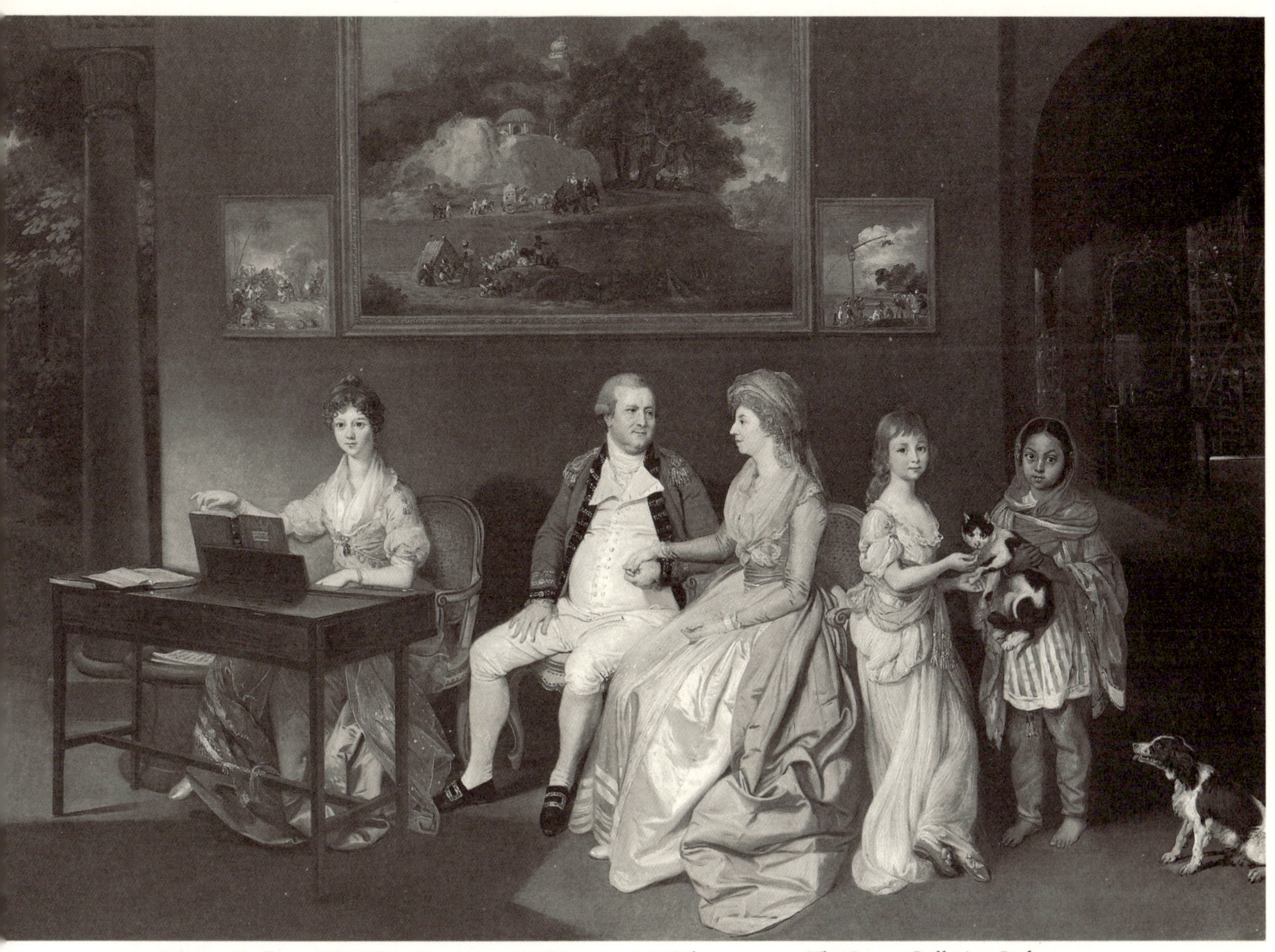

104. Johann Zoffany. *The Blair Conversation Piece*. 1786. Oil on canvas. The Leger Galleries, Ltd.

1802–25) made a name for himself in British social circles in Calcutta as a portrait painter; yet he, too, had an abiding interest in landscape. His influence on amateur British artists in India was profound and enduring. Chinnery taught Sir Charles D'Oyly the art of landscape painting and D'Oyly passed on the basics of Chinnery's style to an entire generation of young aspiring artists. While in his teens, George Chinnery had enrolled for classes at London's Royal Academy where he studied art under Britain's renowned Sir Joshua Reynolds. His classmates included J. M. W. Turner, who later became one of England's most celebrated artists. Traveling to Madras in 1802, Chinnery moved on to Calcutta, where he settled in 1807. He was known primarily as a portrait painter, working in oils, watercolor, and miniatures on ivory. Such was his fame that everyone of impor-

tance in Calcutta wished to have their portrait painted by Chinnery. We hear from several accounts that the artist was an eccentric but likeable man, whose moods swung sharply between euphoria and depression. Chinnery spent twenty-three years of his life in India, moving from there to China and then to Macao, where he died.

While portraiture provided him with a living and fame, landscapes were his true interest. Sir Edward Paget, a friend and patron, wrote, "He likes landscape painting a thousand to one better than portrait painting. . . ."[40] Chinnery's numerous sketchbooks, recording the most casual incidents of street and village life in Bengal, often dated, signed, and even annotated, reveal an inveterate walker with a passion for the Indian countryside. He enjoyed sketching peaceful village scenes: mud huts with thatched roofs,

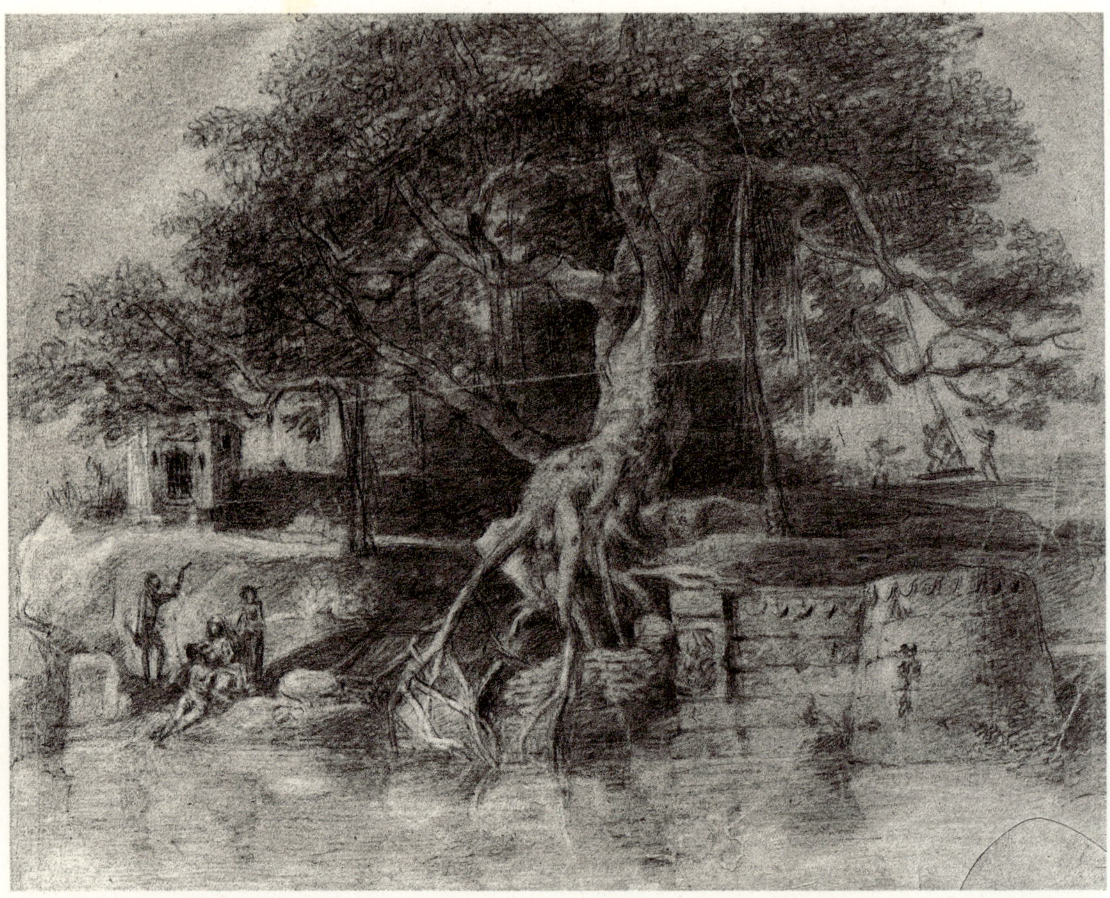

105. Johann Zoffany. *Dying Hindoo Brought to the Ganges.* 1788. Chalk. Yale Center for British Art, Paul Mellon Collection.

chickens scratching for food, cows and goats grazing in the fields, bulls asleep by their carts, dogs lazing in the sun, village women cradling babies, or carrying water pots on their heads. River scenes were also a favorite, with the strange shapes of the sailboats and canoes often juxtaposed against ruins. It has been suggested that some of these sketches were designs for a title page as they are often inscribed "Scenery in Bengal" at appropriate places in the design: on a piece of rock, a fallen tree, a plinth. Many such "title pages" exist, but if Chinnery planned a Bengal series in several volumes, it certainly did not come to fruition.

Chinnery's sketches were often bound into albums, and from one of his letters we learn that he placed great value on these:

The vol in question is one of my best I am happy to say; and there are many filled in fully, excellently, but they must be *all* so filled in before you get it, and altho I say it that should not, it will be the Sketch Book of a Painter and some 50 years hence may be interesting—here and there I'll leave one in a un-finished state that G. C. may be seen more clearly, when it may come under the eye of a Brother of the Pencil.[41]

Some of these albums, carefully designed with title pages, were presented to the artist's friends and pupils.

Figure 107 shows a typical Chinnery water-color of a river scene, done in shades of brown, tan, and gray, with a fishing boat and native fig-ures in front of ruins. The exposed brickwork of the ruins stands out dramatically against the pale blue sky and the dark green foliage. *Ruins of a Temple, Sunset* is painted in somber shades, and shows the remains of a temple with the

112

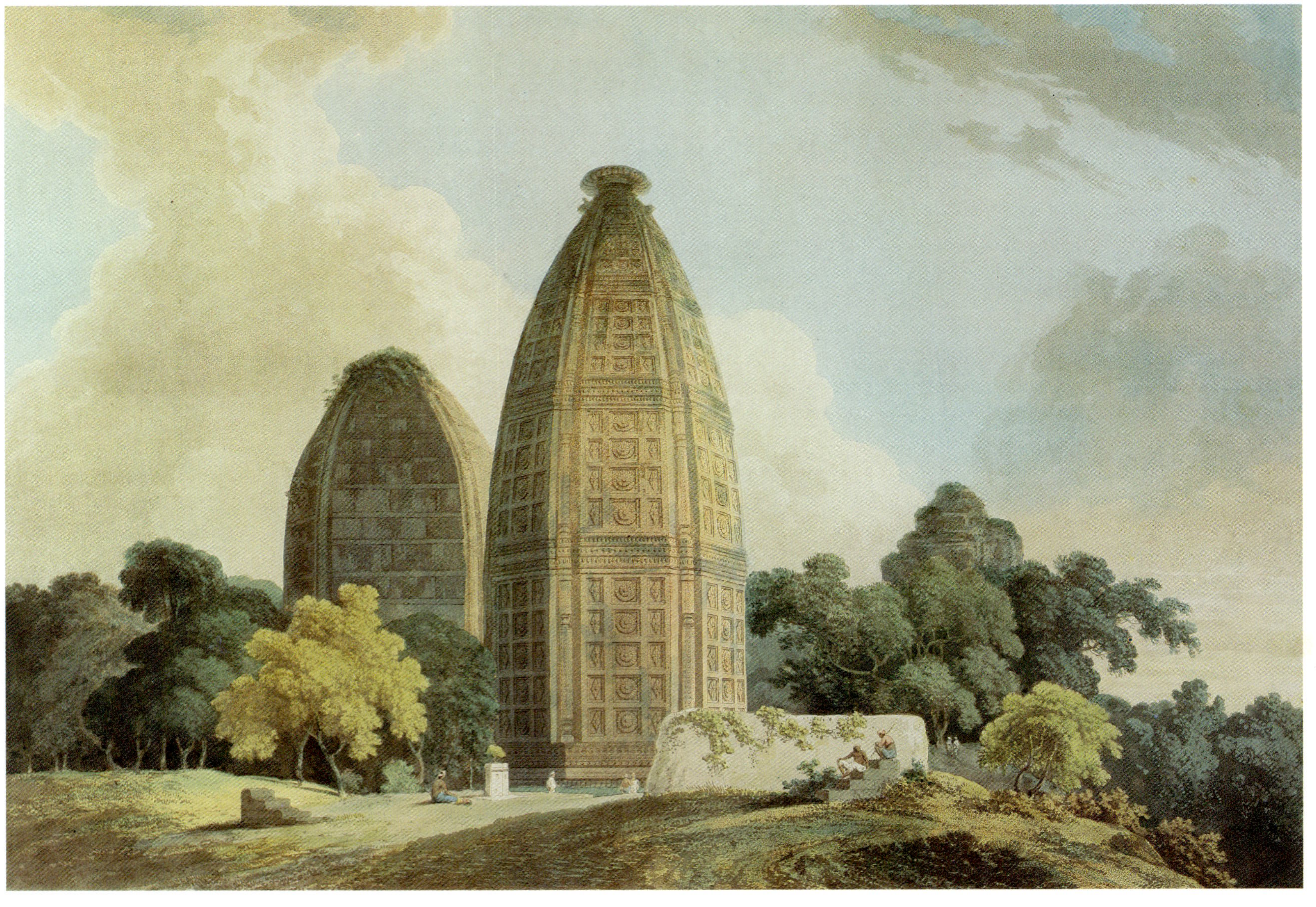

COLORPLATE 8.
Thomas Daniell. *Hindoo Temples at Bindrabund on the River Jumna*. 1795. Aquatint.
Walter Collection.

purple gloaming beyond; the only spot of color is the clear blue of a distant lake (fig. 108). Chinnery occasionally painted landscapes in oil but few have survived.

Chinnery, like Zoffany, chose a subtle way to assert that, although famed as a portraitist, he was also a painter of landscapes. His self-portrait in the National Portrait Gallery in London depicts the artist standing with brush in hand in front of his easel. An Indian land-scape—a rural scene with the ruins of a tomb and villagers bathing in a stream—sits upon the easel, while a Macao street scene hangs on the wall behind him.

Among other professional artists who visited India in the pre-Mutiny period, Henry Salt (1780–1827) had an unsuccessful career in London as a portraitist, and finally found his true calling as a painter of landscapes in India. When his friend Lord Valentia decided to make a trip to the subcontinent, Salt accompanied him in the dual role of secretary and draftsman. The two traveled extensively in India between 1802 and 1804, making a trip up the Ganges from Calcutta to Lucknow, touring southern India, and spending time in the rock-cut cave temples of the Bombay region. Salt made numerous watercolors during the tour and kept a journal. His work closely resembles that of the Daniells; his colors are the familiar restrained grays and browns, dull blue and green. Back in England in 1807 and 1808, Salt prepared his drawings for engraving and supervised their execution. Among Salt's finest works are his views of the cave temples of the western coast of India (fig. 109).

V

BY the start of the nineteenth century, it had become evident to the British artist that great for-

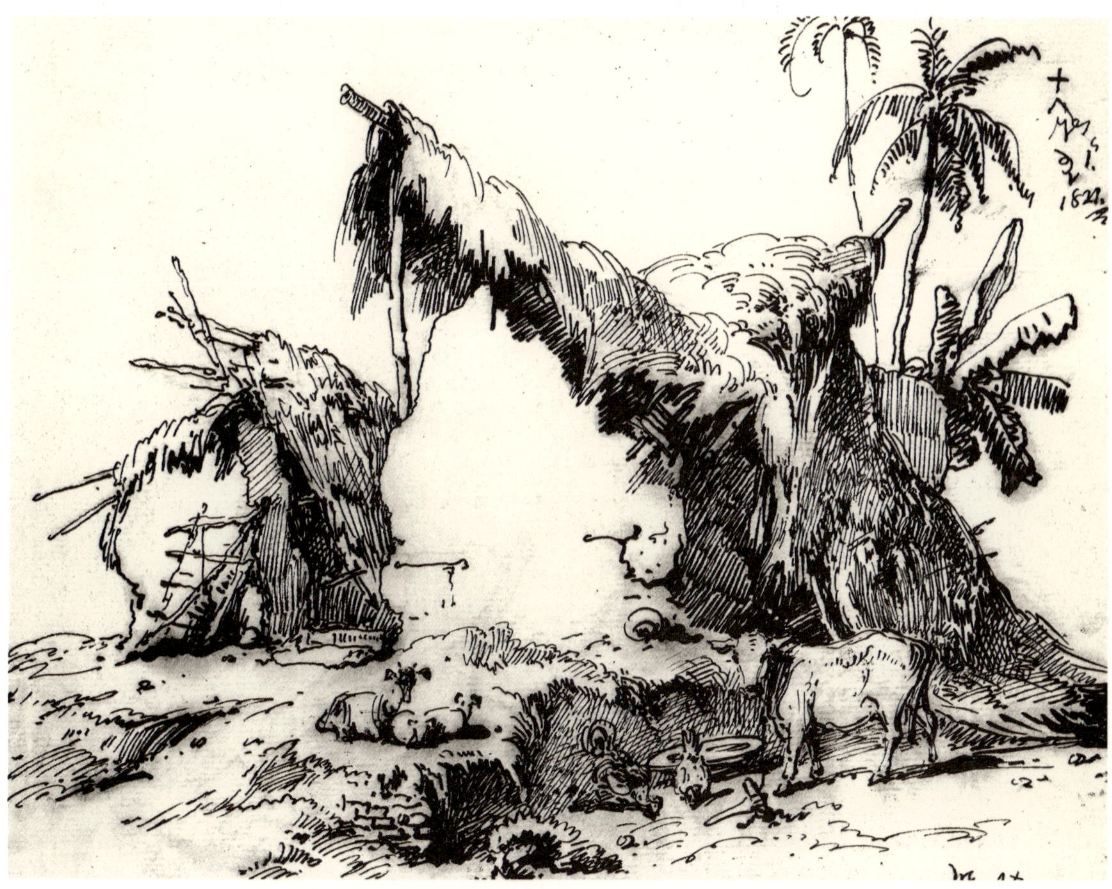

106. George Chinnery. *Two Thatched Indian Huts*. 1821. Pen and ink. The Pierpont Morgan Library.

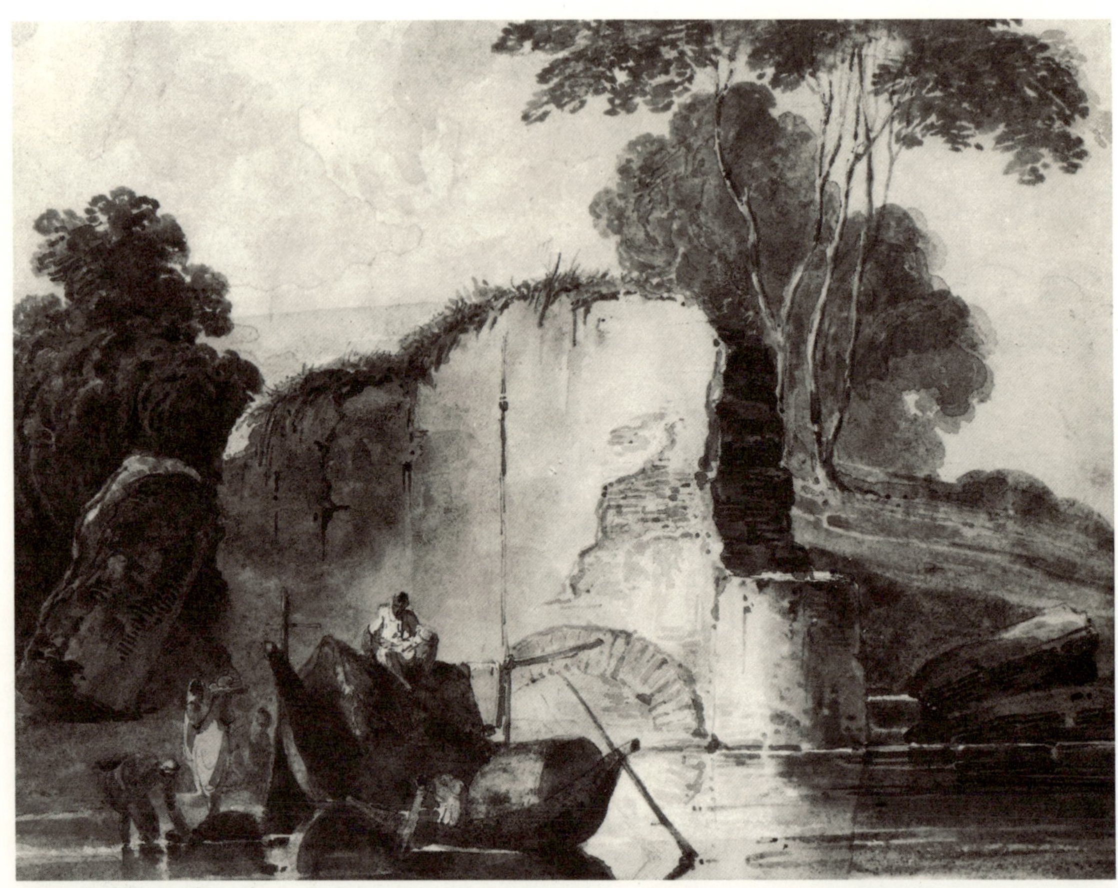

107. George Chinnery. *A River Scene with Figures and a Fishing Boat Moored Beside Ruins.* c. 1800. Watercolor. Yale Center for British Art, Paul Mellon Collection.

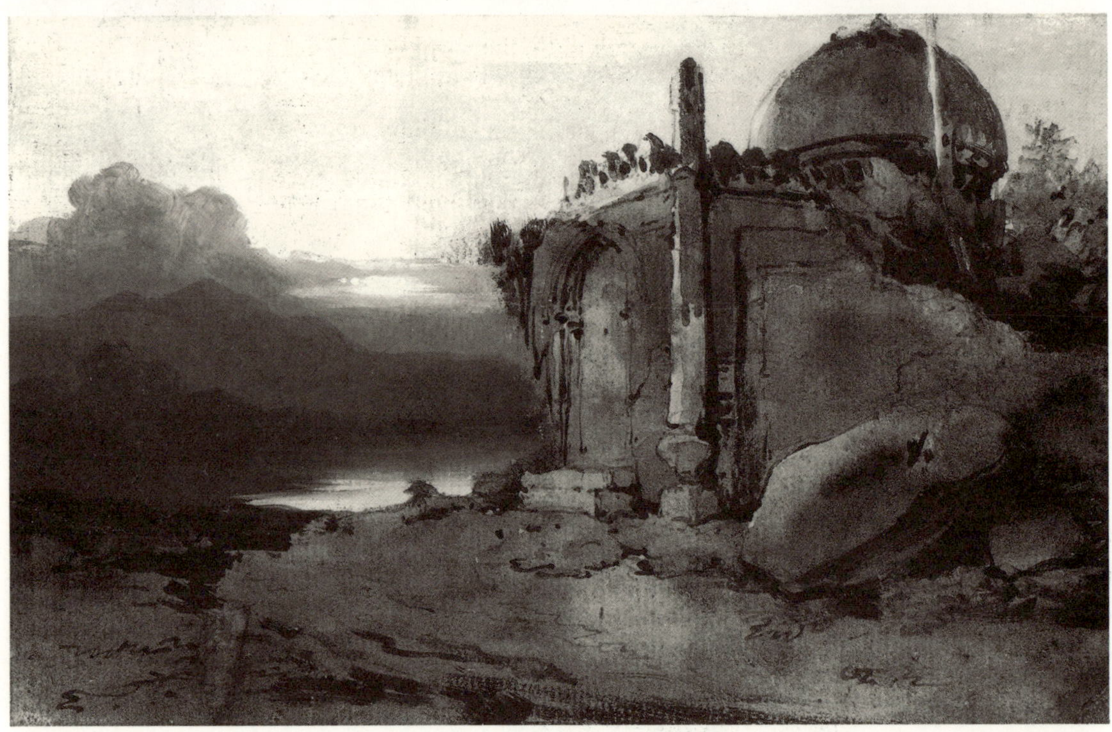

108. George Chinnery. *Ruins of a Temple, Sunset.* c. 1800. Watercolor and gouache. Yale Center for British Art, Paul Mellon Collection.

114

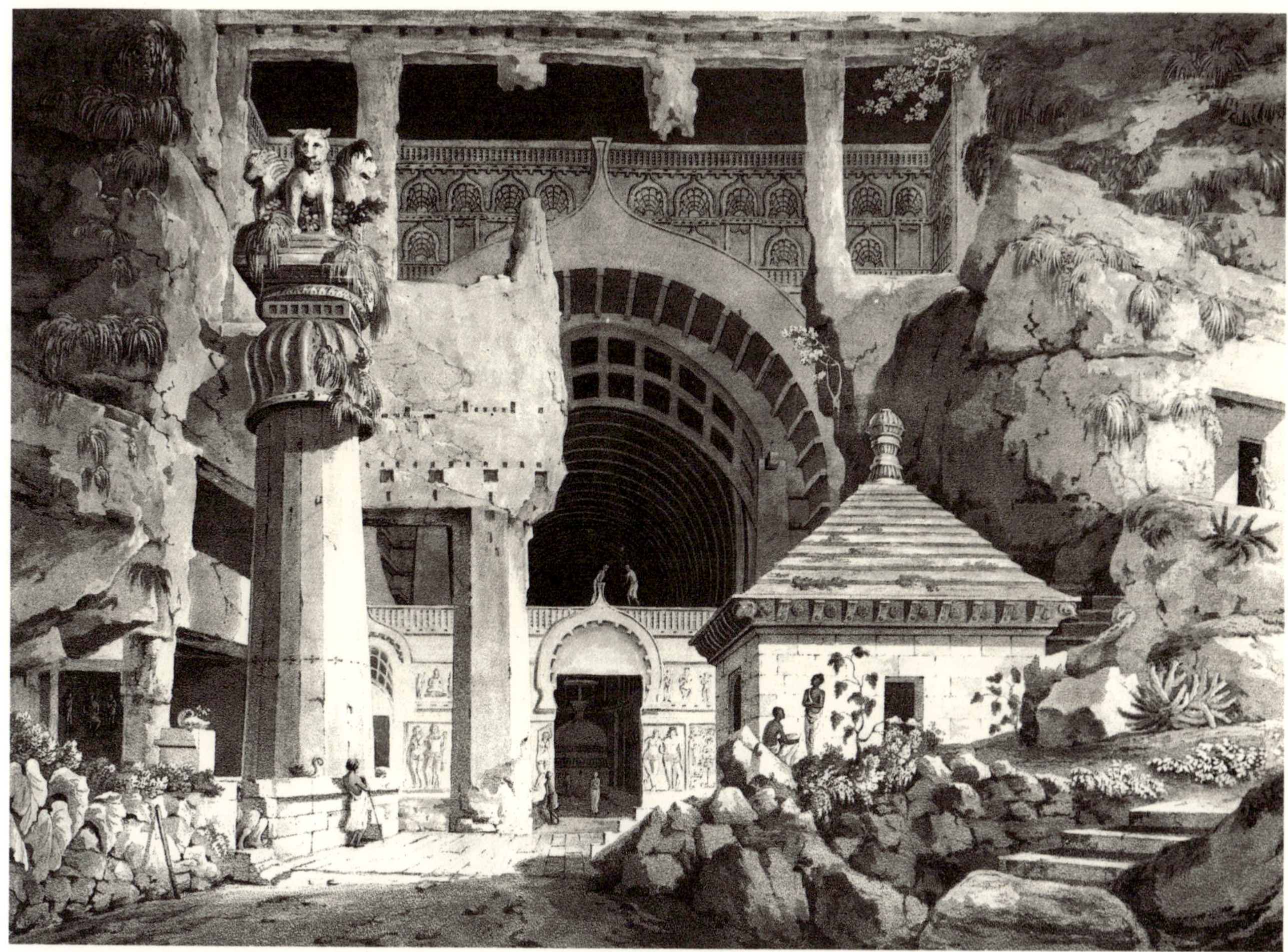

109. H. Salt. *Ancient Excavations at Carli.* 1809. Aquatint. Reproduced by permission of the India Office Library and Records (British Library).

tunes were no longer to be made in India. Fewer professionals undertook the long, arduous journey, but the subcontinent continued to provide the amateur artist with ample material for his picturesque sketches. Painting and sketching were considered essential elements of a liberal education in eighteenth-century Britain, and it was customary for young men and women of any social position to take lessons from a drawing master who would visit their homes weekly.

By the end of the eighteenth century, books containing etchings, aquatints, or lithographs were available for study. In these books a series of pages would be devoted to the sketching of cloud formations, for instance, and the pages were arranged in the order of the complexity of the task. In watercolor drawing, which was the term for amateur sketching, the subject was drawn in pencil at the site and reinforced in ink; later, the shadows were laid on in sepia and the whole was treated with washes of transparent color. Drawing was also considered an important part of the curriculum at military academies, and General Jarry, the inspector-general of instruction at Sandhurst, maintained that a sketch was always superior to a report.[42] With such emphasis placed on the acquisition of drawing and painting skills, it is not surprising that a large number of sketches and watercolors of Indian scenes were prepared by amateur artists, often in the service of the East India Company, or by officers of the British army.

Many of the amateur artists in India were extraordinarily gifted and it is frequently a fine line

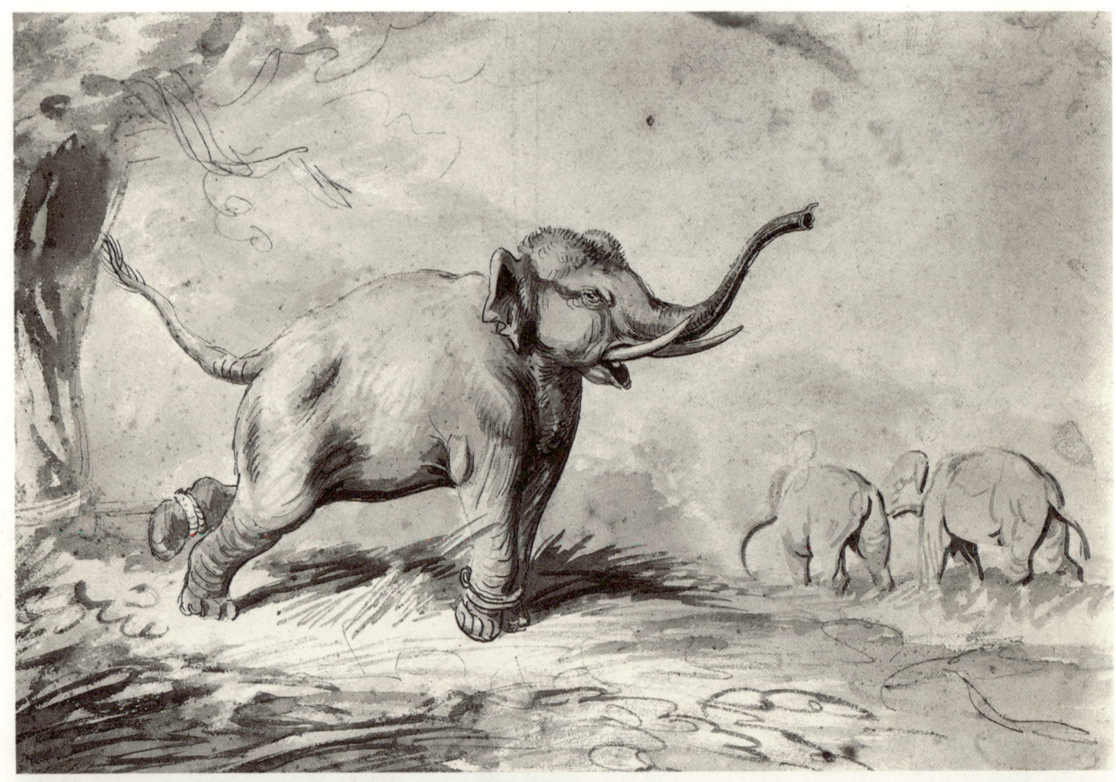

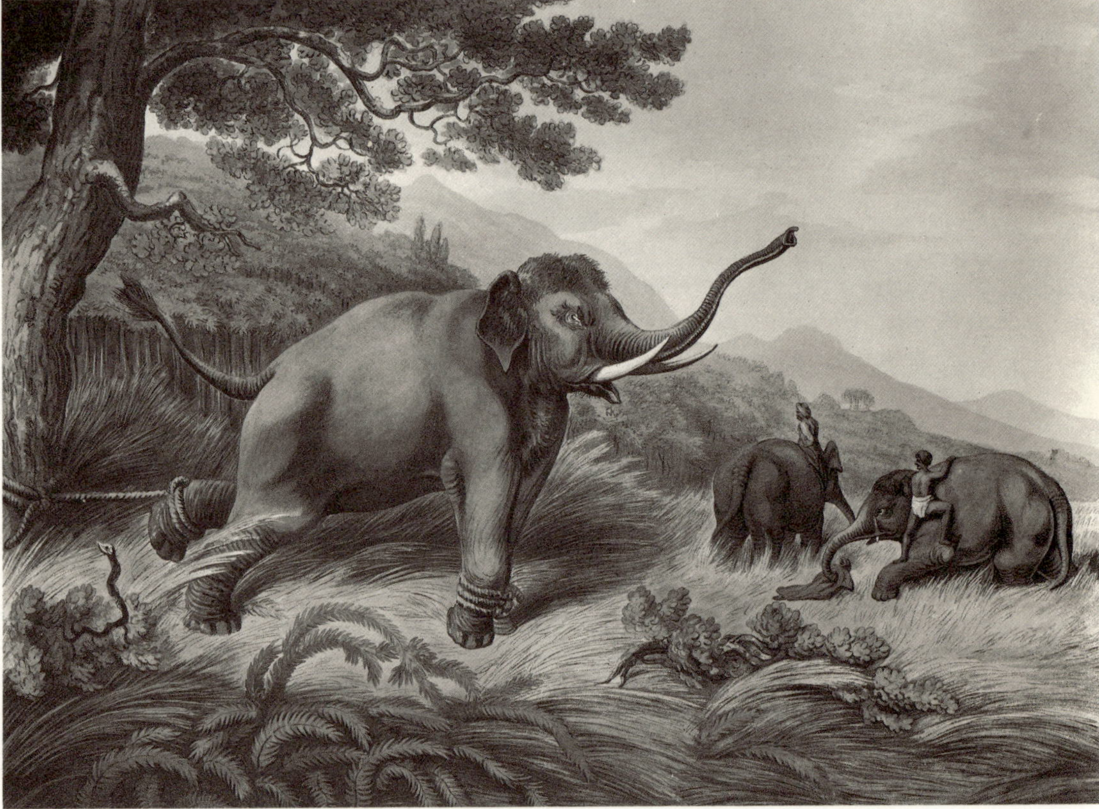

110 a, b. Captain Thomas Williamson. *Decoyed Elephants Leaving the Male Fastened to a Tree.* 1805. Original sketch and colored lithograph. Walter Collection.

116

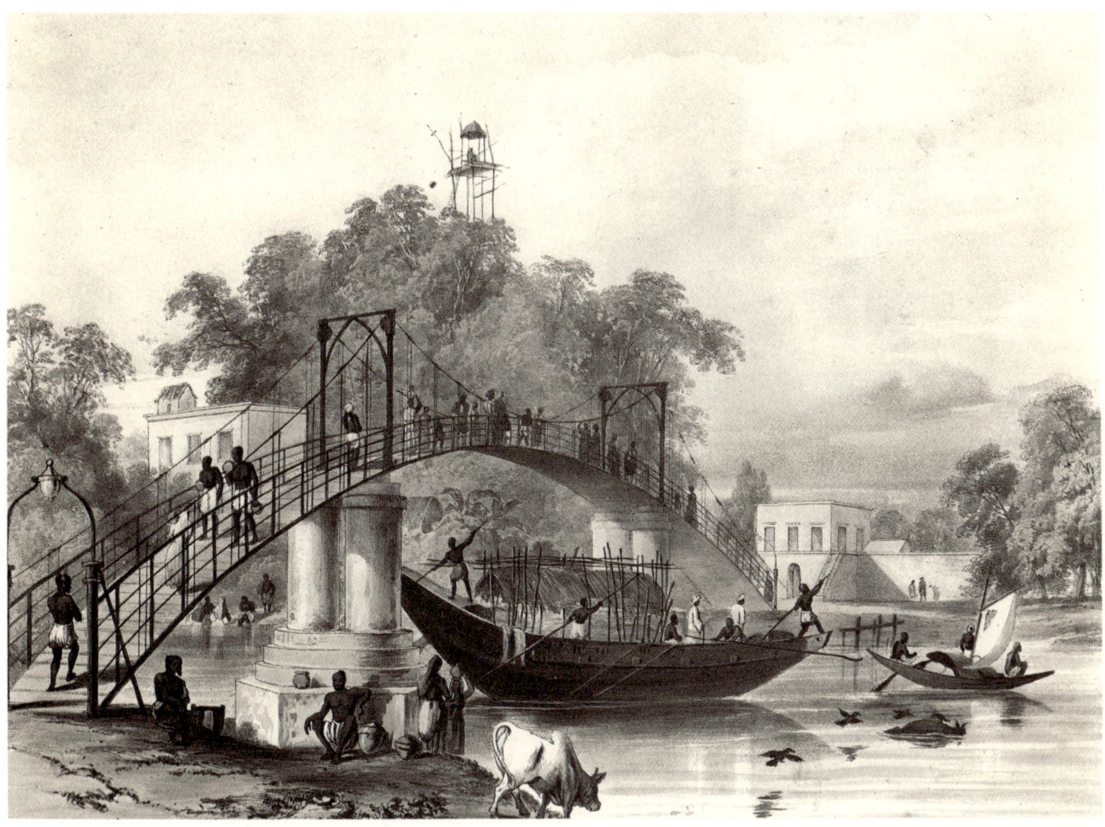

111. After Sir Charles D'Oyly (1833–38). *Suspension Bridge at Alipore Over Tolly's Nulla.* 1848. Lithograph. Private Collection.

that separates their work from that of merely adequate professionals. It became accepted practice for the amateur who had built up a fine collection of sketches to have his pictures converted into aquatints or lithographs. This was the case with Captain Thomas Williamson's sketch *Hunting Jackals* which was worked up by Samuell Howitt and then done as a color lithograph (fig. 68 a, b); his drawing *Decoyed Elephants Leaving the Male Fastened to a Tree* underwent the same procedure (figs. 110 a, b). They graphically demonstrate the degree of transformation between the original sketch and the final lithograph. While the prints have lost some of the spontaneous vivacity of the sketches, they have gained sharper detailing, a more focused composition, and a "finished" look in the hands of the professional.

One of the finest amateur artists was Sir Charles D'Oyly. Born in Calcutta, the son of a nabob, he was educated in England and returned to his home in 1798 as an officer of the East India Company. It was while he was collector at Dacca from 1808 to 1818 that he and his wife took drawing lessons from Chinnery. The older artist taught D'Oyly to appreciate Indian village scenes, to observe the picturesqueness of dilapidated shops and ruined temples, to seek an unusual scene such as the *Suspension Bridge at Alipore over Tolly's Nulla* (fig. 111). The busy composition, with the bridge, trees, buildings, boat, and animals, is typical of D'Oyly, and even if somewhat overcrowded in comparison to Chinnery, his pictures invariably capture the appropriate mood of the scene.

D'Oyly was a prolific artist whose work was much admired by the local European community. During his years in Patna, when boats moored for the night on the river Ganges, Europeans would disembark just to visit D'Oyly's studio and view his drawings. Bishop Heber, who was greatly interested in the artist's sketches, remarked:

He is the best gentleman-artist I ever met with. . . . He says India is full of beautiful and picturesque country, if people would but stir a little way from the banks of the Ganges, and his own drawings and paintings certainly make good this assertion.[43]

D'Oyly, who founded an art society in Patna, exercised considerable sway over British amateur artists. He also influenced several Indian artists who worked with him in Patna and who learned to alter their style to suit British taste. In addition, D'Oyly imported a lithographic press which he ran with the help of local Indian talent.

Two other amateur artists, both army officers who worked in southern India almost contemporaneously (1780–90), were Robert Colebrooke (1762–1808) and Alexander Allan (1764–1820). Colebrooke made an extensive series of drawings of southern India while serving in the Mysore wars of 1781–85. Figure 112 is a typical pencil sketch of the southern countryside with scattered palm trees and a hill in the far distance, upon which is a barely discernible temple. These drawings were later engraved and published in 1794 as *Twelve Views of Places in the Kingdom of Mysore*. The area of Mysore, still under the rule of Tipu Sultan, was largely unknown to the British in the late eighteenth century.

Sir Alexander Allan took part in the third and fourth Mysore wars and it was during the earlier of these engagements that he made a series of sketches of the region, also published in 1794 as *Views in the Mysore Country*. Allan continued to serve in the Madras Infantry, reaching the rank of major before retiring in 1804. His evocative watercolor of *Tritteny Pagoda* is probably from this later period (fig. 113). It depicts the Tiruttani temple in restrained hues of

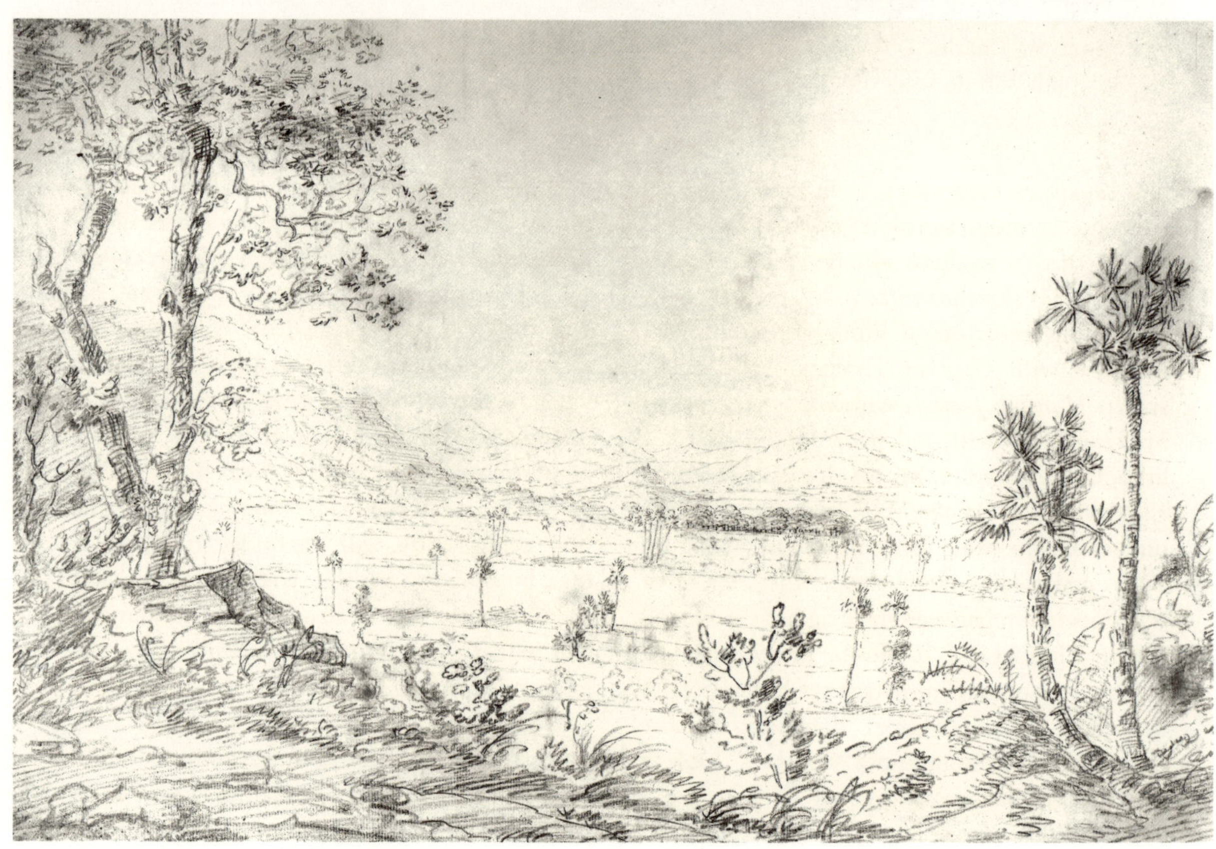

112. Robert Colebrooke. *Southern Countryside*. c. 1782. Pencil. Walter Collection.

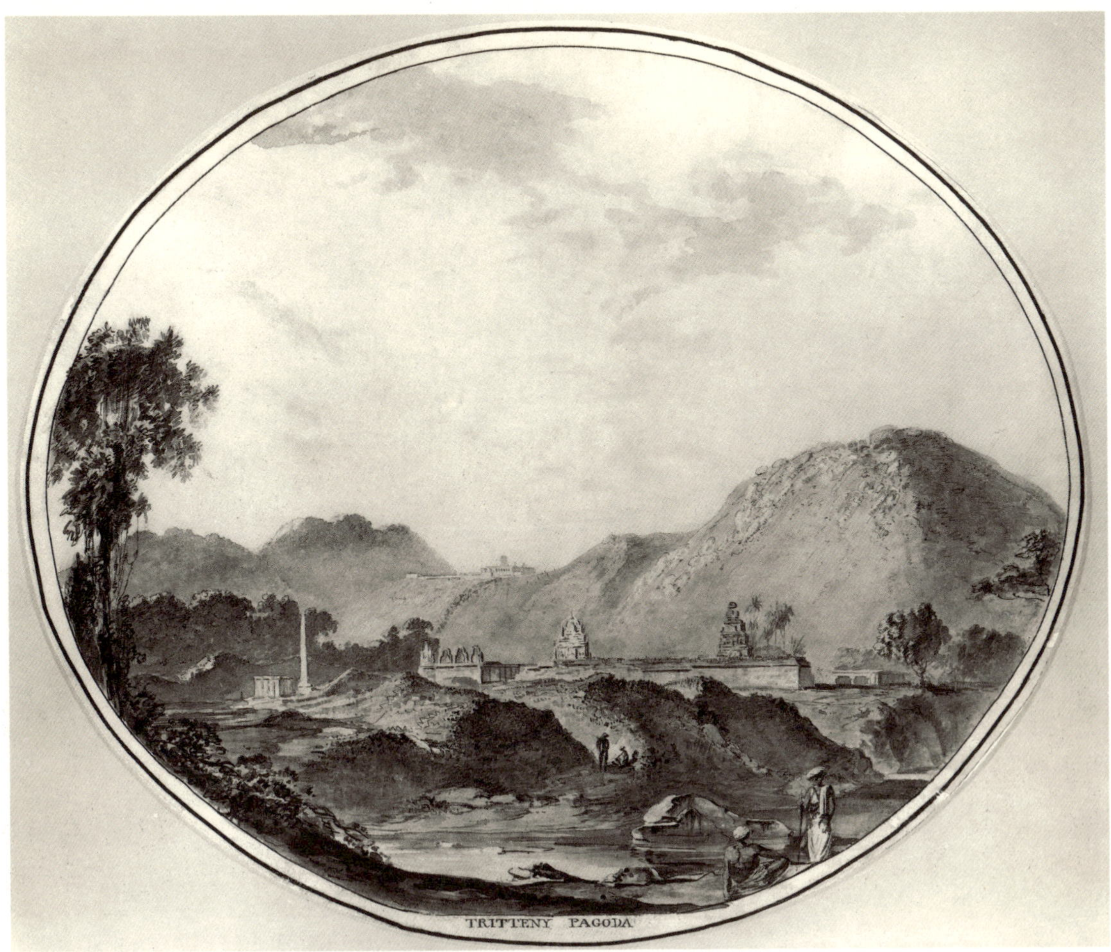

113. Sir Alexander Allan. *Tritteny Pagoda*. c. 1800. Watercolor. Walter Collection.

green, gray, and tan, with a mere hint of blue in the foreground stream; the gray hills in the background almost merge into the pale white-gray sky which occupies half of the tranquil scene.

Charles Stewart Hardinge (1822–94) was an amateur artist who traveled in India between 1844 and 1848 as an aide-de-camp to his father Lord Hardinge who served as governor-general during those years. His sketchbook seems to have been with him constantly during his travels and his drawings were lithographed and published in 1847 under the title *Recollections of India*. The striking view of *Kote Kangra* comes from volume one of this work, *British India and the Punjab* (fig. 114). Hardinge has effectively portrayed the almost impregnable nature of the Kangra fort, built as it is upon a mountainous, rocky outcrop that is encircled by the Beas and the Ban Ganga rivers. A group of British soldiers are lounging in the foreground, with their horses and canons. The picture was clearly made after Kangra became the property of the British in 1846, after considerable resistance by the local raja and his subjects.

Cavalry officer Captain Melville Clark was one of those rare artists who was a watercolorist and a photographer. His military duties took him across much of northern India right up to the borders of Tibet, and the many photographs taken during his travels were subsequently published in 1862 in a volume entitled *From Simla through Ladac and Cashmere*. The photographs have been pasted into the book which contains a number of striking views of Simla, Leh, Srinagar, and of the mountainous terrain.

Clark also did a number of watercolor landscapes, all of which reveal the hand of a skillful

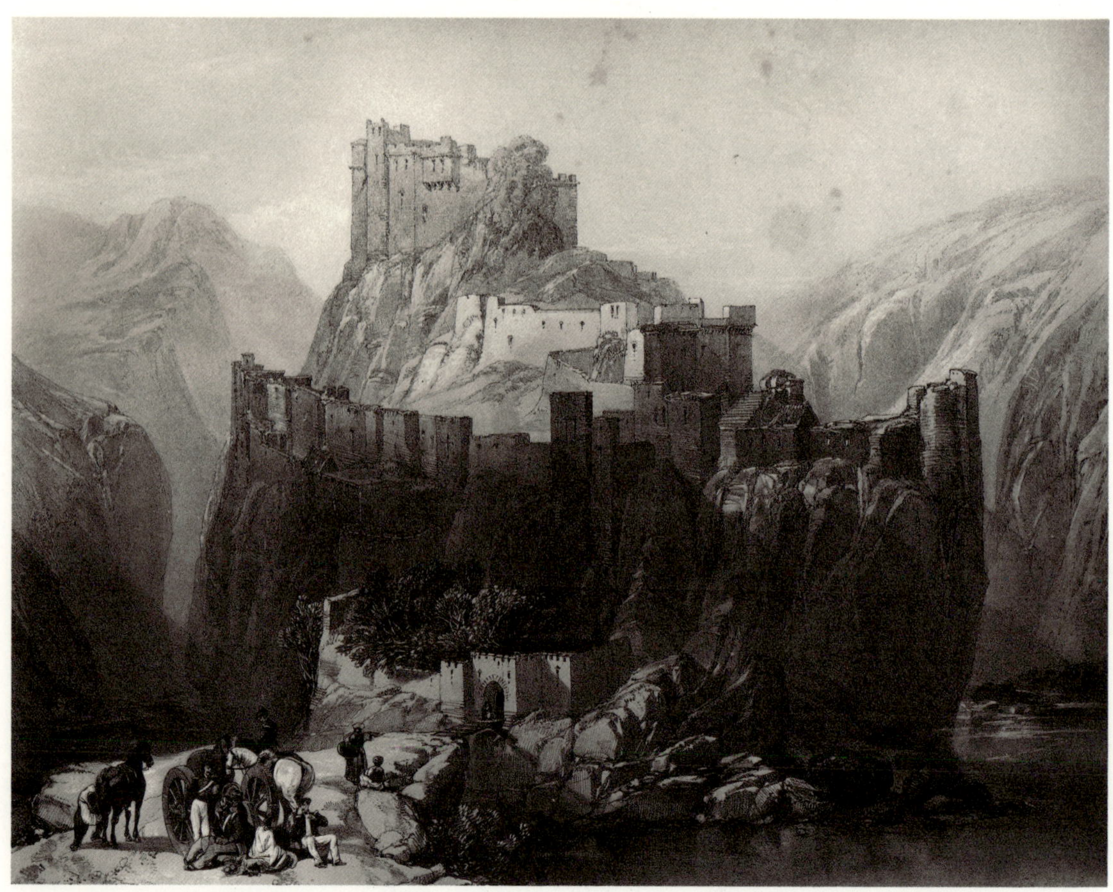

114. Honorable Charles Stewart Hardinge. *Kote Kangra*. 1847. Lithograph. Walter Collection.

colorist. In his *Bridge at Poona*, the warm pink glow of the setting sun competes with the purple of twilight, while his *Banyan Tree* is set in the morning light, with the haze having just lifted over the mountains in the distance (fig. 115). His facility with pen and brush and his expertise with the camera brings to mind the words of an artist who stated, "I photograph what I do not wish to paint and I paint what I cannot photograph!"[44]

VI

THE year 1857, which witnessed the Indian Mutiny, was the beginning of the decline of British artistic expression in India. Fewer artists made the journey and even more importantly, perhaps, this period also coincided with the introduction of the camera. However, artists like William Simpson, Edward Lear (1812–88), Mortimer Menpes (1860–1938), Ernest S.

Lumsden (1883–1948), and John Griffiths were working in India during the Victorian age.

In sharp contrast to the first hundred years of the British artist in India, on which several volumes have been written, little work has been done on the artists of this later period. Some individuals like Mortimer Menpes and E. S. Lumsden remain vague and shadowy figures and only a few of their works are yet known; others like William Simpson and Edward Lear have left us their journals and autobiographies and a large corpus of works. In general, during this period there was a slackening in depictions of conventional landscapes and standard architectural monuments. One must assume that the paintings of the previous hundred years had satisfied the curiosity of the British back home about the exotic colony. Artists like William Simpson looked for new and more challenging subjects that had not been portrayed before.

120

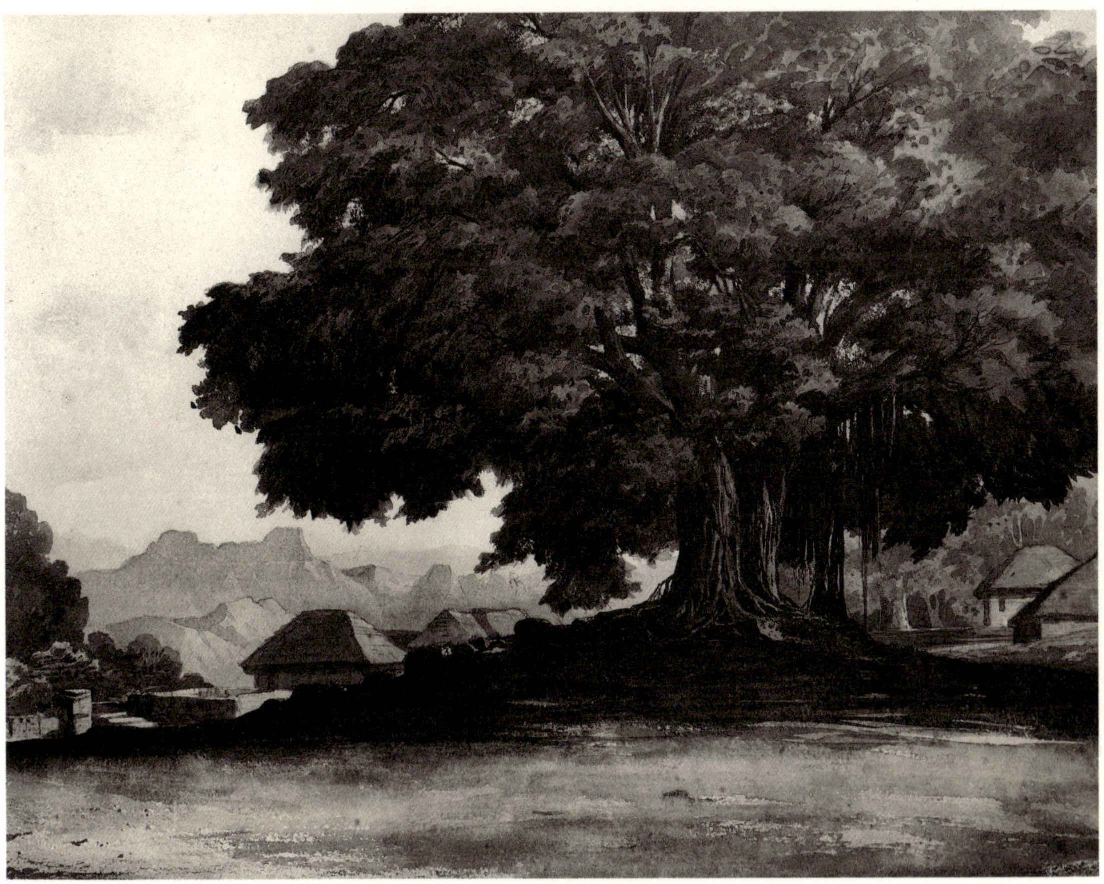

115. Captain Melville Clark. *Banyan Tree*. c. 1870–80. Watercolor. Walter Collection.

There are, however, several parallels with the work of earlier artists. Benares and the Ganges, for instance, continued to exercise an irresistible attraction. While the Ganges was no longer the lifeline of the country, the newly introduced railway ran along the course of the river, so artists now traveling by train came across many of the same sites sketched by the earlier artists who had gone by boat. The introduction of the railway facilitated travel so tremendously that Edward Lear could cover in a period of fourteen months the same territory that a hundred years earlier had taken the Daniells seven years to traverse.

Painter and lithographer William Simpson went to India immediately after the Mutiny. He was employed by the well-known London lithographers Day and Son, for whom he had successfully completed a series of lithographs on the Crimean War. With the upsurge of inter-est in India that followed the Mutiny, Simpson was commissioned to go to India to make a series of drawings for a proposed work of 250 lithographs, which would faithfully reproduce the originals in color. Before Simpson embarked on his journey, he spent a considerable amount of time researching in the India Office Library, and later recalled in his autobiography that he studied the Daniell volumes "to see what had been already done, and to get hints as to places I ought to visit." [45] Having procured the queen's permission to dedicate his work to her, Simpson arrived in India in 1859 and spent three years touring the country. He did several watercolors of Lucknow that documented the aftermath of the Mutiny. These include views of the ruins of the Residency, the Dilkoosha, and the Shah Nujeef palace. His eye for the newsworthy picture landed several of these in *The Illustrated London News*.

121

Simpson was a highly imaginative painter and he chose unprecedented subjects. He painted the extraordinary dust storms, so prevalent in the plains of northern India in the summer months preceding the onset of the monsoon. An entire cloud of dust whirls across the countryside, temporarily blotting out the sun and sweeping aside everything in its path. Man, beast, and bird seek shelter and no sign of life is evident outdoors until the storm, with its climactic cool, moist breeze, has passed. Obviously, Simpson must have witnessed more than one of these sweeping storms and the effect of lulled desolation that followed. Using deep contrasts, he captured the onset of a swirling storm near Jaipur in Rajasthan, on the borders of sandy desert country, and the startled men and animals dashing for shelter (fig. 116). The vibrant blue of the foreground sky is about to be obliterated by the deep purplish dust that is spreading rapidly. The theme demanded not only the skill of a topographer, but the creative imagination of the artist as well. Simpson's ink-and-wash sketch of the 1866 famine shows the huddled figures of the starving along the Benares ghats and a number of others praying for divine intervention in front of Siva's sacred bull (fig. 117).

Simpson's haunting watercolor of the Ganges captures the early morning haze over the river, when the crocodiles emerge onto the mud flats (fig. 118). The British were fascinated by these creatures which they frequently saw along the rivers and were astounded at the casual manner in which the natives disregarded them. A contemporary account tells us:

They seem to excite neither fear nor apprehension . . . . They sometimes wallow in the shallows with their heads turned towards the sun in all the indolent repose of familiar luxury, regardless of any thing but the stronger of their own species.[46]

Simpson accents the white smoke of a funeral pyre on the ghats to the left, and the vultures that swoop down over the water—presumably over the remains of the bodies consigned to the

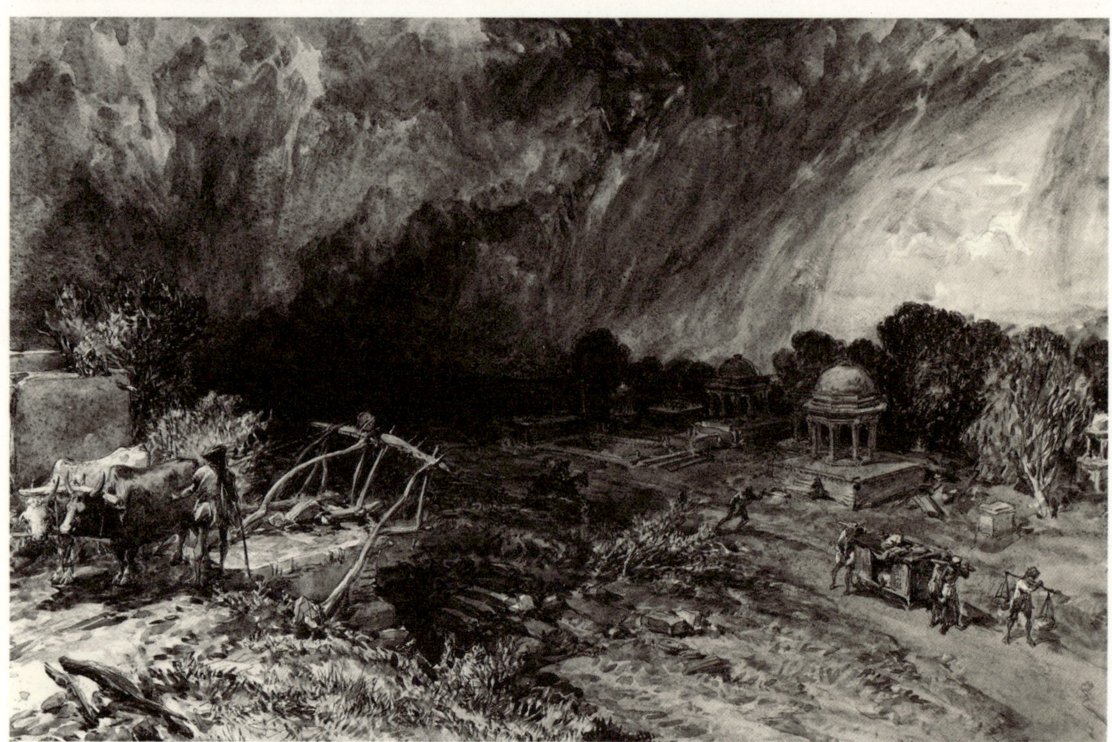

116. William Simpson. *Dust Storm Coming On, near Jeypore Rajportana.* 1863. Watercolor over pencil. Yale Center for British Art, Paul Mellon Collection.

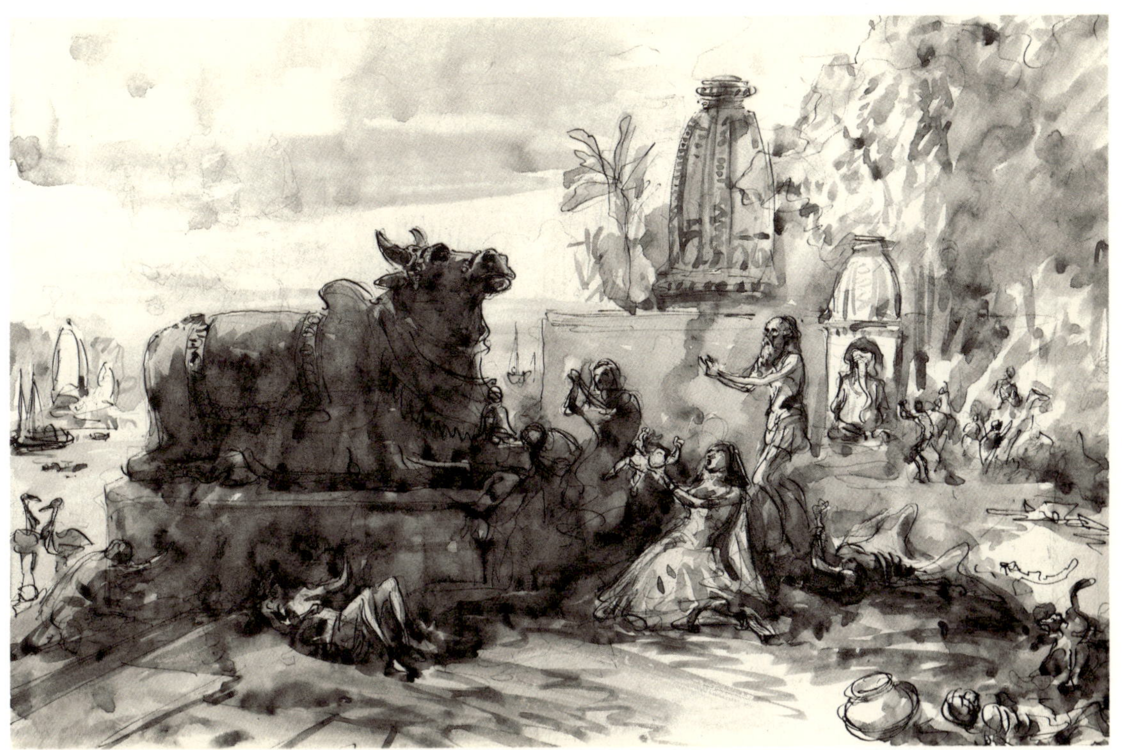

117. William Simpson. *The Famine in India.* 1866. Ink and sepia wash. Walter Collection.

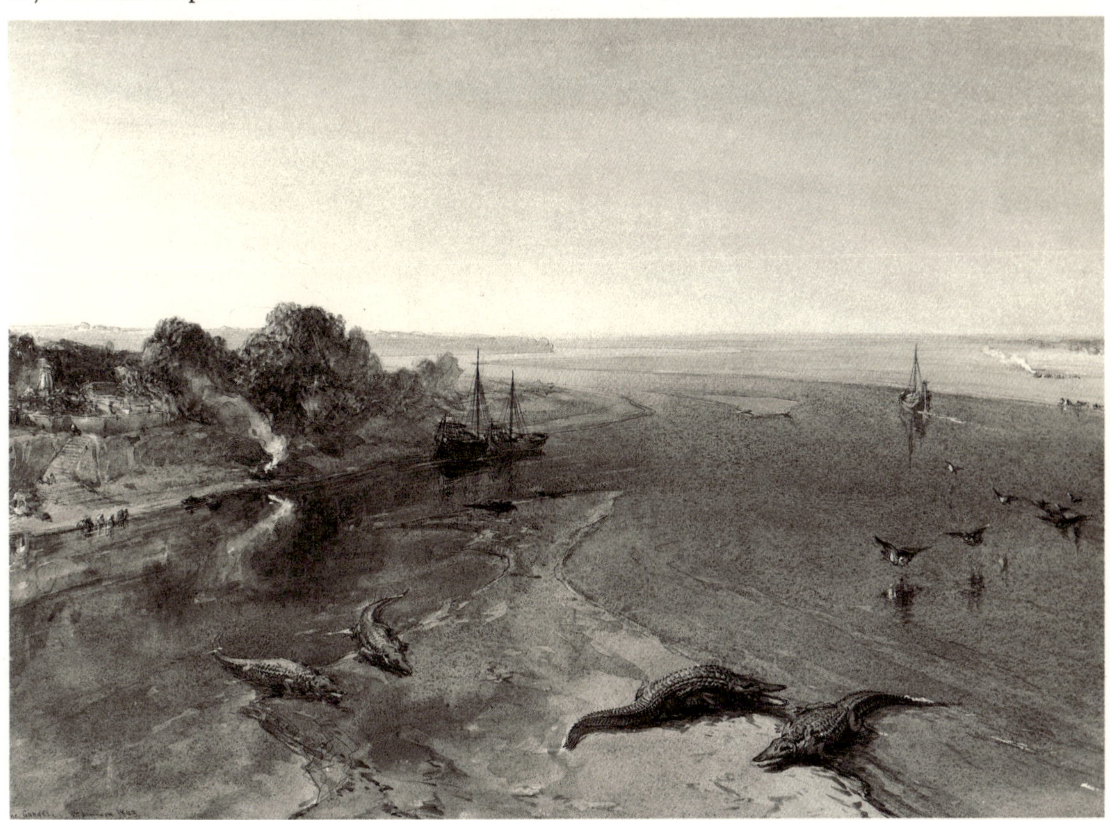

118. William Simpson. *The Ganges.* 1863. Watercolor over pencil. Yale Center for British Art, Paul Mellon Collection.

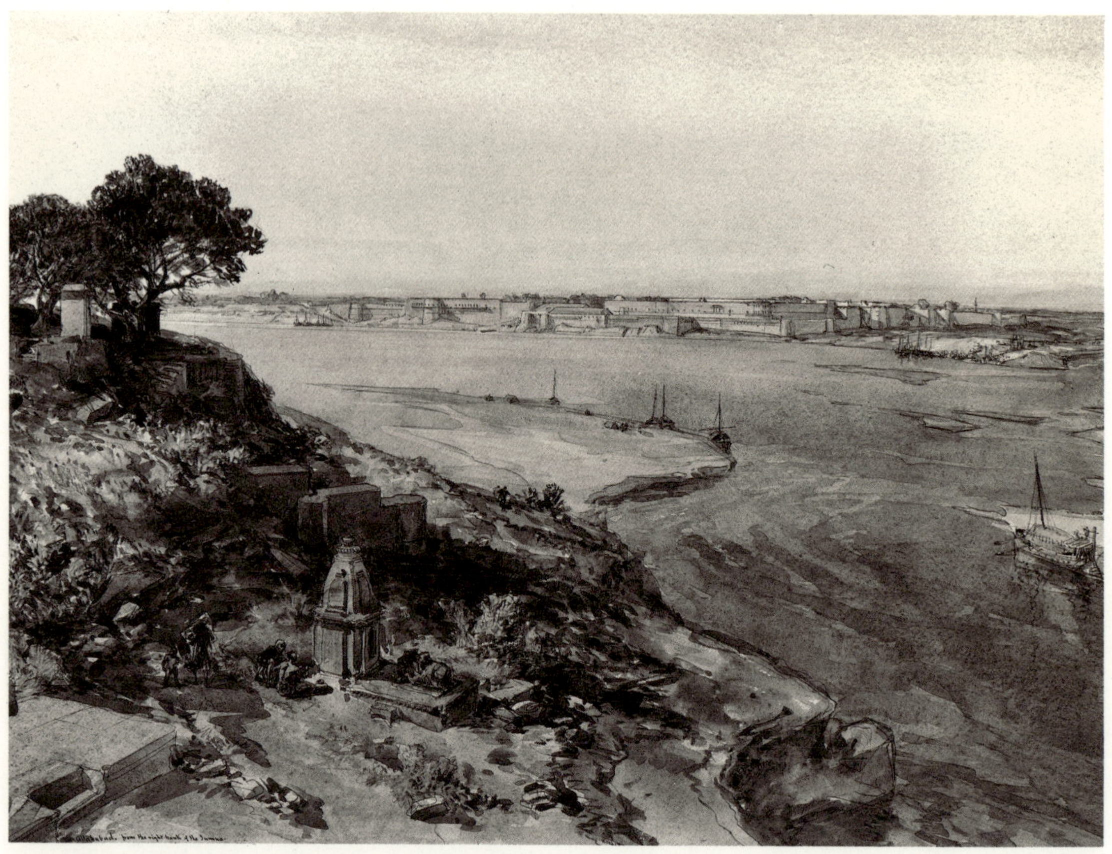

119. William Simpson. *Allahabad, from the Right Bank of the Jumna.* 1864. Watercolor over pencil. Yale Center for British Art, Paul Mellon Collection.

river after partial burning. Contrasting in mood and color is his view of Allahabad (fig. 119). Once again, it is a river scene, but instead of the gray, white, and blue color scheme of the previous work, this is in vibrant mustard, brown, and tan, with inspired touches of lavender in the distant town. A peach-orange sunset, pale blue water, and a small temple with a Siva's sacred bull complete the picture.

When Simpson returned to Southampton after three years in the vivid sunshine of India he remarked, "To my eye, after the bright colours of India, the contrast was great, and it seemed to me that the people went about with the appearance of black beetles."[47] Day and Son of London reproduced Simpson's views of India in 1867 in a volume entitled *India, Ancient and Modern.* Simpson, who had enjoyed his travels, returned to India in 1875 as the correspondent for *The Illustrated London News,* to follow

the tour of the Prince of Wales in India. He made some two hundred sketches on this second tour which were exhibited in Picadilly and sold quite well.

VII

EDWARD LEAR was the second major artist to visit India after the Mutiny. In the brief period of fourteen months that he spent in India, from November 1873 to January 1875, he was constantly on the move, traveling over the entire country, sketching extensively and keeping a diary of his journey. He made around 3,000 drawings of India, ranging from small sketches to large watercolors. Detailed marginal notes tell us the exact date and even the time of day at which a particular sketch was made. The image of a fascinating voyage emerges, recorded vividly and with great enthusiasm.

Edward Lear is best known as the author of

124

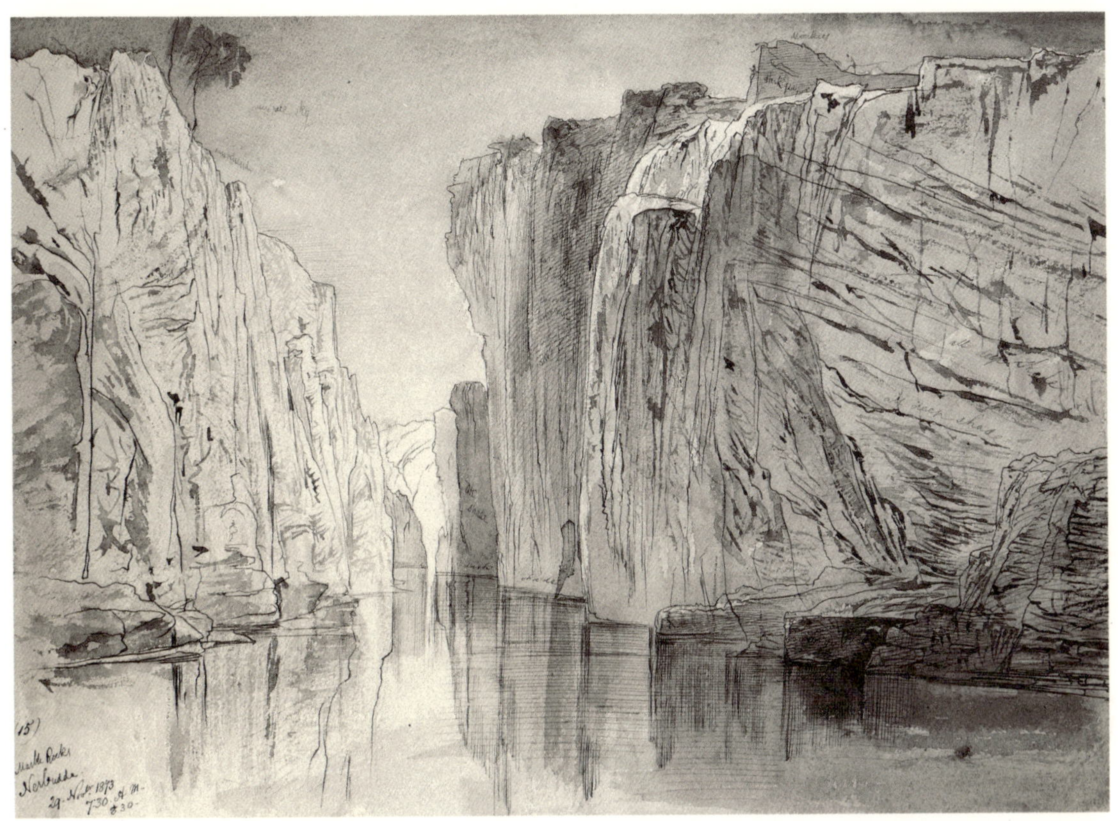

120. Edward Lear. *Marble Rocks, Nerbudda.* 1873. Watercolor. Houghton Library, Harvard University.

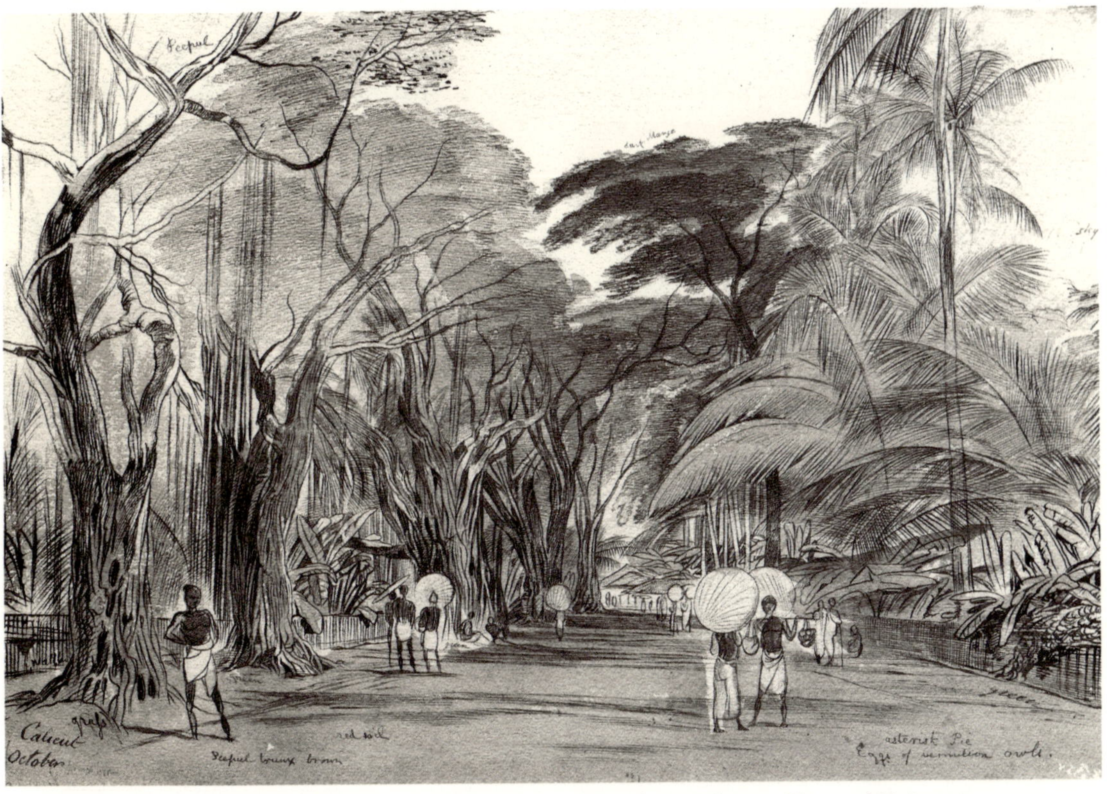

121. Edward Lear. *View of Calicut.* 1873. Watercolor. Houghton Library, Harvard University.

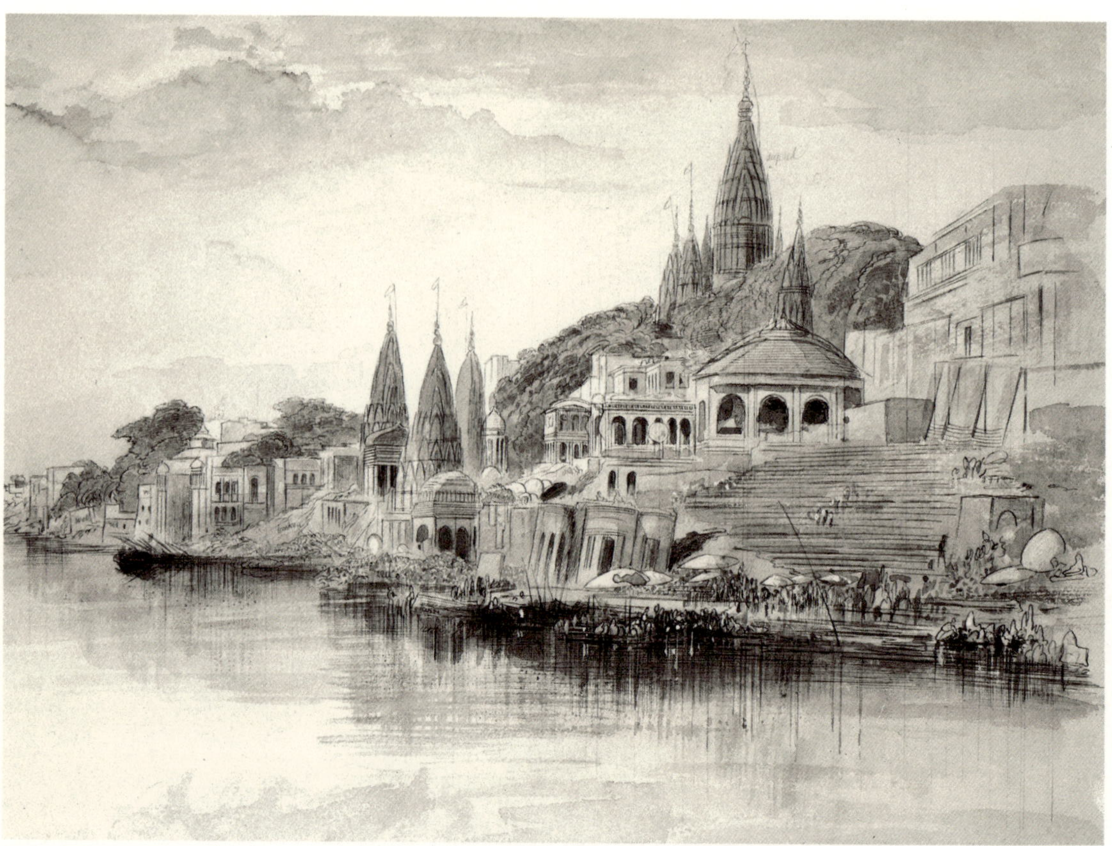

122. Edward Lear. *Benares*. 1873. Watercolor. Houghton Library, Harvard University.

an endearing series of nonsense poems and limericks. He became so famous for these that even in faraway India, he personally encountered children reciting his verses. Lear was the youngest of a family of fifteen children; he began life as a commercial artist, and later became a draftsman at the Zoological Society. It was only at a much later date that he turned his attention to landscapes.

While Lear's drawings are more in the tradition of the topographical draftsman, he never used the camera obscura as the Daniells did and was generally more talented. He would make a quick pen or pencil sketch while he was out in the field, with careful notations on time of day and occasionally on color. His artist friend Congreve, who accompanied him on his tours of England and Wales, described the process:

Lear would sit down and taking his block [of papers] from George, would lift his spectacles, and gaze for several minutes at the scene through the monocular glass he always carried; then laying down the glass, and adjusting his spectacles, he would put on paper the view before us, mountain range, villages and foreground, with a rapidity and accuracy that inspired me with awestruck admiration.[48]

Sometimes, as with *Marble Rocks, Nerbudda*, he made half a dozen small sketches at varying times of the day between seven and three, as well as three large versions of the scene that differed marginally in the intensity of the light (fig. 120). The larger versions were probably finished later in his studio. Coloring was generally sparing, sober, and subtle, as in the *Marble Rocks*, which is done entirely in white, grays, blues, and tan with the faintest touch of pink. Lear always attempted to make his drawings reflect the time of day and his efforts in this direction were usually successful. Of the *Marble Rocks* he notes in his diary: "River like 1st Cataract of Nile, but valley very close and narrow. Fine bit of waterfall. Rocks, foam, - sketch."[49]

126

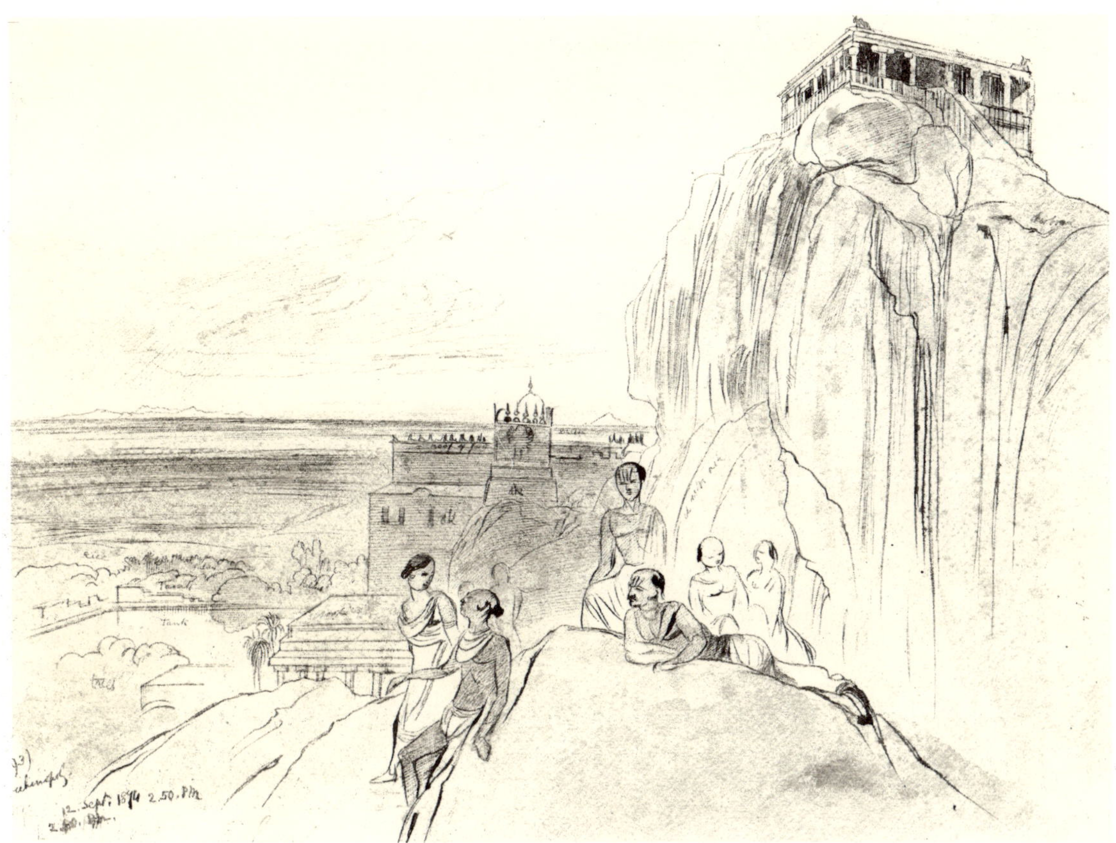

123. Edward Lear. *Trichinopoly.* 1874. Watercolor. Houghton Library, Harvard University.

He occasionally worked indoors on his drawings—"penning out"—as he calls it, and relied on photographs for architectural subjects. After reworking the outdoor pencil sketches with pen, he freely added color washes to the composition. This had become standard procedure in England by 1850. Lear selected from his notations those that seemed appropriate and added these, too, to the finished sketches, and on such occasions he generally re-signed and re-dated the pages. In a view of Calicut, for instance, he seems to have been rather pleased with his depiction of the local crows and neatly wrote in, "O, ye crows of Malabar / What a qualified bore you are!"

Reared on the British tradition of the picturesque, Lear did not develop a distinctive style, but became instead a master of picturesque topography. His sketches are generally serene and composed; rarely did he depict turbulence. His introduction to India, via Bombay, left him ex-claiming at the "impossible picturesqueness of the countryside." [50] He waxed eloquent on the scenery, "Right, long lines of flat, with lovely green hills—left, great granite like piles of rocks, with endless green woods." [51] He was struck by the varying beauty of the Cawnpore region: "December 10: I returned to where the whole scene was like a beautiful Home English Park in a dry late summer; no fern—it is true—but big trees exactly like Oak and Ash (Neem, Banyan, etc.) and altogether unlike my previous 'ideas' of India as possible . . . . The beauty of this Cawnpore scene, with its Campagna-like levels, and its broken hollows and banks, ain't to be told . . . ." [52] Many of his Cawnpore compositions could indeed be mistaken for the Italian countryside, but for the occasional inclusion of an Indian figure.

The city of Benares made a tremendous impression on Lear. Though he drew several very successful sketches of the city, he wrote:

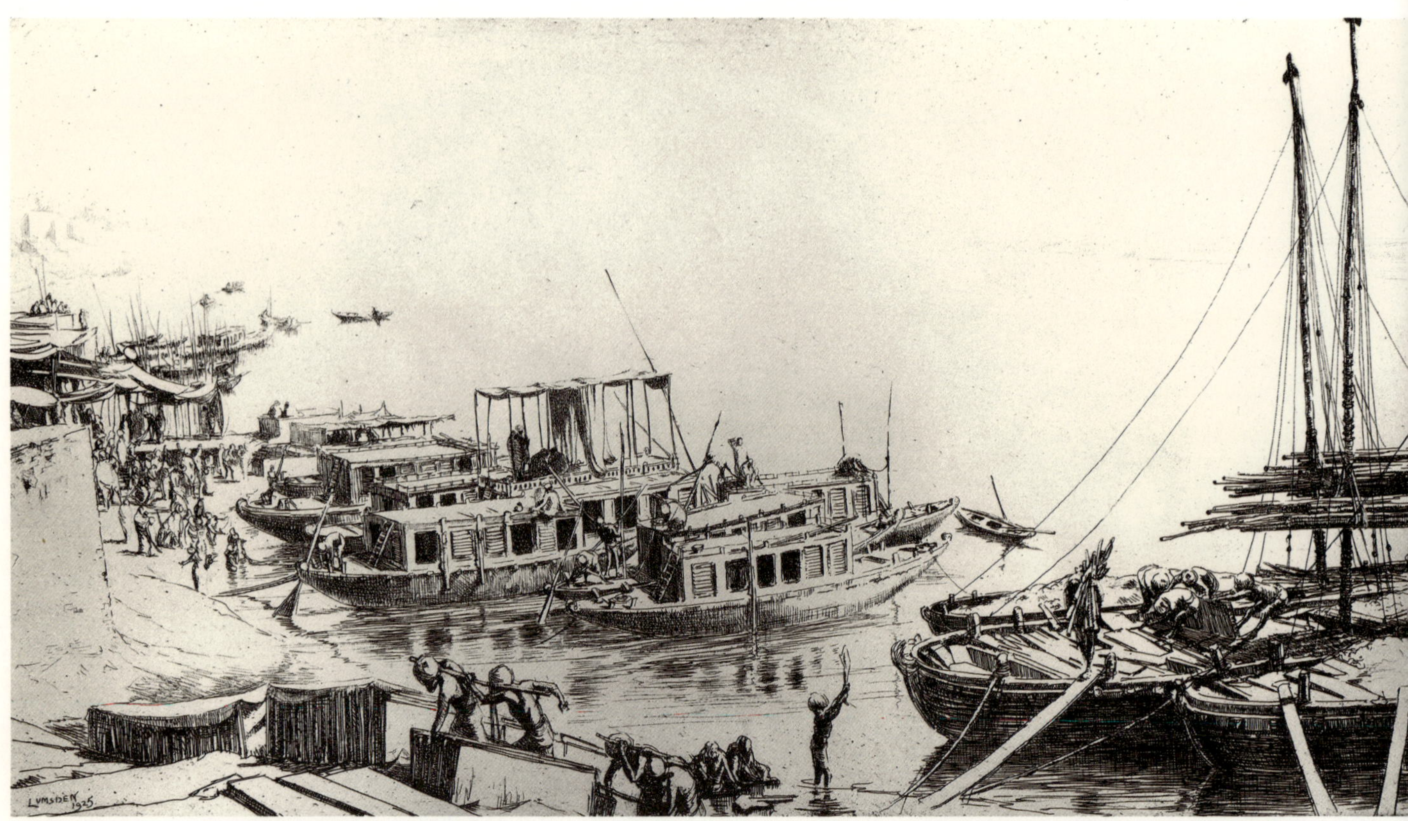

124. Ernest Stephen Lumsden. *River Craft, Benares.* 1925. Etching. Walter Collection.

Nothing, short of a moving opera scene, can give an idea of the intense and wonderful colour and detail of these Benares River Banks! And nothing is more impossible than to represent them by the pencil![53]

The ghats at Hardwar also inspired Lear, who drew them in an almost impressionistic style which he attempted very rarely, preferring detailed delineation. He wrote of this "wonderfully picturesque Hindoo town": "The tall, slender gray temples . . . the variety of costumes! new every moment . . . . The great multitude of bathers . . . . The colours of dresses . . . . It is certainly a most remarkable sight!"[54]

His pictures of Allepee and Calicut seem to overflow with the verdure of the southern coastal region. Of Calicut, Lear wrote with "poetic" eloquence, his phraseology seemingly incomplete without a series of exclamation marks:

Roads of such redundant beauty one could scarcely dream of! India Indiaissimo! . . . The plenitude of palmery here is overwhelming! Those deep gray green misty hollows full of endless vistas and series of Palm leaves and stems.[55]

The Kerala coastline embodied the picturesque:

All at once . . . we turned into a very narrow canal, overhung with Palms, full of boats moving and stationary, and more exquisitely beautifully picturesque than any canal I ever saw![56]

As the figure played a subordinate role in his work, his sketch of Trichinopoly is unusual in that it shows a couple of lounging Brahman priests featured prominently in the foreground (fig. 123). Strangely enough, he does not mention them in his diary:

The view from that height is over noble, and the summit of the Rock with its Temple above all make a great foreground to the wide expanse of foliage-covered plain, the broad River Cauvery and the Srirangam Island with its temples, and the line of hills beyond.[57]

128

Lear has left us with a remarkable series of drawings of India, which should help establish his reputation as an artist, even though "it is on the Himalaya of Nonsense that Edward Lear sits enthroned."

Few landscape artists seem to have traveled to India in the forty years that separated Edward Lear from Ernest Stephen Lumsden who was a master etcher. The medium was well suited for the exhaustive detail that Lumsden favored, and his technical virtuosity is apparent in a volume he published in 1924, *The Art of Etching*, which is illustrated with 336 of his etchings. Lumsden was a keen traveler who made three trips to India between 1913 and 1919 accompanied by his wife Mabel Royds, an artist who worked with woodcuts. Lumsden seems to have been fascinated by the Ganges, the craft moored along its banks, and the ghats at the town of Benares, and he recorded them with remarkable accuracy and perception. His *River Craft, Benares* (fig. 124), with coolies carrying slabs of stone in the foreground and boats of various types moored along the ghats, recalls Lumsden's vivid description of the river after sunset:

Dotted over her surface will be many small boats, while upstream, beyond the drifting wood smoke from the funeral pyres on the *Manikarnika ghat* are always two or three lumbering high-sterned craft which bring down wood for the burning and stone for building, from near Chunar, swinging slowly at their moorings. These vessels lie off the central or *Dasaswamedh ghat*, the only one fed by a road wide enough for wheeled traffic; and from early morning till late evening gangs of coolies toil up the steep ascent carrying the huge blocks of stone in slings, which, stacked in rows, are taken away as required in ox-carts.

The critic M. C. Salaman, writing in 1925, highly commended Lumsden's work and commented "whether with etching-needle or descriptive pen," Lumsden communicates his experience of the mystery and beauty of Benares "with the imaginative touch of a master."[58]

Like other artists before him, Lumsden did several etchings of the sacred banyan tree; his many striking views of monasteries perched on barren mountainous outcrops were inspired by his adventurous trek into the Himalayas. His etchings are in the tradition of picturesque topography; they are accurate and almost sedate in comparison to the works by some of his contemporaries who tended to dramatize the subject and indulge in flights of fancy. Lumsden's wife Mabel Royds did several color woodblock prints of scenes along the Ganges and in the Himalayas in which she focused on the natives, using the landscape only as backdrop. Although she exhibited regularly in galleries in the United Kingdom, she did not receive the acclaim achieved by her husband.

All Creatures Great and Small

VIII

THE varied landscape of India with its many monuments and architectural ruins furnished British landscape painters with an inexhaustible supply of subjects. Equally compelling for artists of another bent were the exotic peoples of India. Just as the British concept of "picturesque" colored their representations of the land and dictated the choice of subjects, the Western concept of beauty influenced British portrayals of the native peoples. William Hodges openly acknowledged that his portraits of Indians were indeed based on ideas of classical beauty. Referring to the women at the Benares ghats, he wrote:

To a painter's mind, the fine antique figures never fail to present themselves, when he observes a beautiful female form ascending these steps from the river with wet drapery, which perfectly displays the whole person, and with vases on their heads, carrying water to the temples.[59]

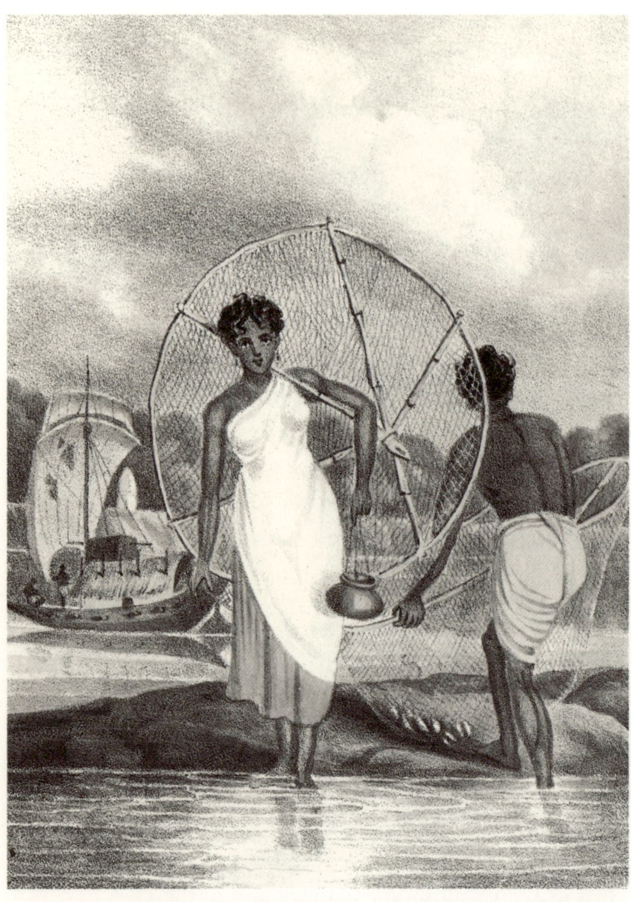

125. Sir Charles D'Oyly after George Chinnery. *Fishers of Small Fry* from *Costumes of India*. 1830. Colored lithograph. Walter Collection.

Such descriptions of women at the wells and rivers are, like the banyan tree and the nautch girl, a recurring theme in Anglo-Indian literature. James Forbes also perceived the Indian women in terms of his image of the women of antiquity. He was charmed by the women of Gujarat villages:

The women are modest and delicate; their drapery, however coarse, is rendered becoming by an elegant carelessness of the folds, and their attitudes are peculiarly graceful. Greatly resembling the pastoral manners of the Mesopotamian damsels in the patriarchal days, the young women of Guzerat draw water from the public wells, and sometimes carry two or three earthen jars, placed over each other, upon the head; which requiring perfect steadiness, gives them an erect and stately air.[60]

Elsewhere, Forbes observed that young women

washing clothes reminded him of "Homer's picture of Nausicaa."[61]

Charles D'Oyly's statuesque fisherwoman (after a Chinnery drawing) reveals a romantic conception based on the classical proportions of those "fine antique figures" and "Mesopotamian damsels" (fig. 125). This perception was perhaps unavoidable considering the training the British artists received. It permeated their

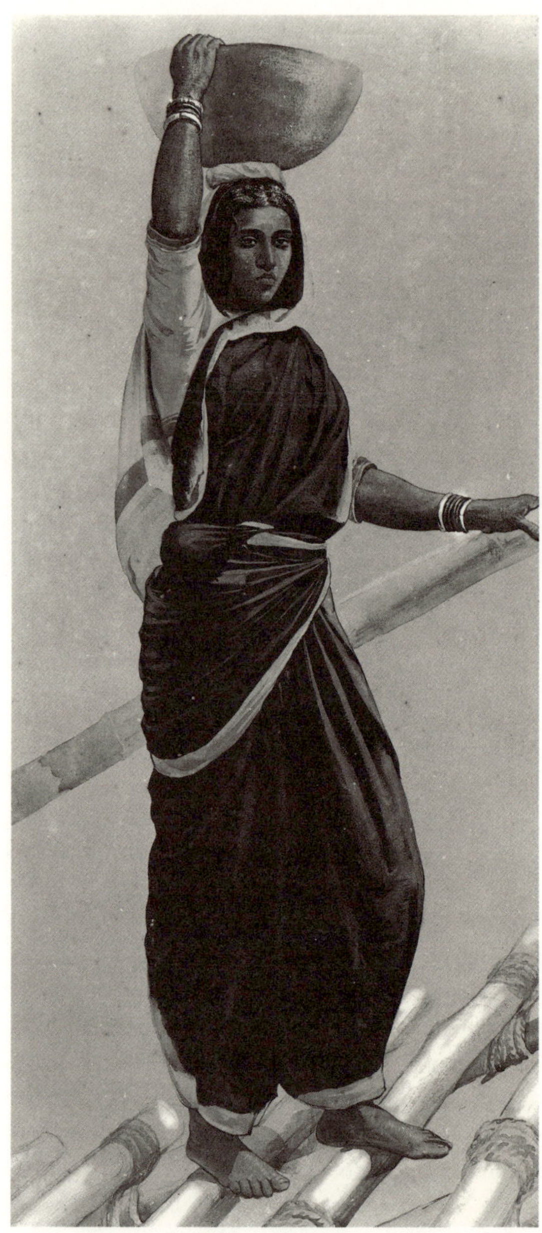

126. John Griffiths. *Woman Labourer*. c. 1870–80. Watercolor. By courtesy of the Board of Trustees of the Victoria and Albert Museum.

portrayals of Indian men, too, whether D'Oyly's muscular fisherman or Devis's fakir.

Another aspect of this romanticization is that all Indians are immaculately dressed. Much as in a Hollywood movie, one never sees even the lowliest native in dirty or torn clothes. This tendency continues with John Griffiths (in India, 1865–95); it is blatantly evident in the classicizing dignity, aristocratic stance, and immaculate clothing of his female laborer (fig. 126).

British artists produced a wide range of depictions of various aspects of Indians and Indian life. There were formal portraits of nawabs and princes, and also of servants and villagers. Some documented the tribes and castes of India, producing works of ethnographic interest, while others focused on the exotic customs and festivals of the natives. There is an entire range of cityscapes, from the busy streets of Calcutta and Madras to rural village scenes. Still others concentrated on the Oriental plants, birds, insects, and animals that surrounded the British in their new environment.

Early British artists who specialized in portraiture also produced formal pictures of Indian rulers that are closely akin in style to their portraits of the British. John Dixon's (1740–1811) portrait of the nawab of Arcot, painted in 1772, is an imposing figure, striking a regal stance and giving off an air of authority and arrogance like a British judge or general (fig. 127). Only his exotic clothing sets him apart.

From the upper classes of Indian society, whether maharaja or well-to-do merchant, the British artists found themselves restricted to portraying men. Social rules did not permit the women to be painted by men, which remained the case until 1900, when the demand for photographs among the women prompted the opening of studios run by women. The few perceptive portraits of women that we find from the hands of artists like Tilly Kettle or Francesco Renaldi are of the *bibis*, the unofficial wives of British officers. Several *bibis* were faithful companions whom the British officers never formally married, but who produced children and were recognized by society. As William Hickey

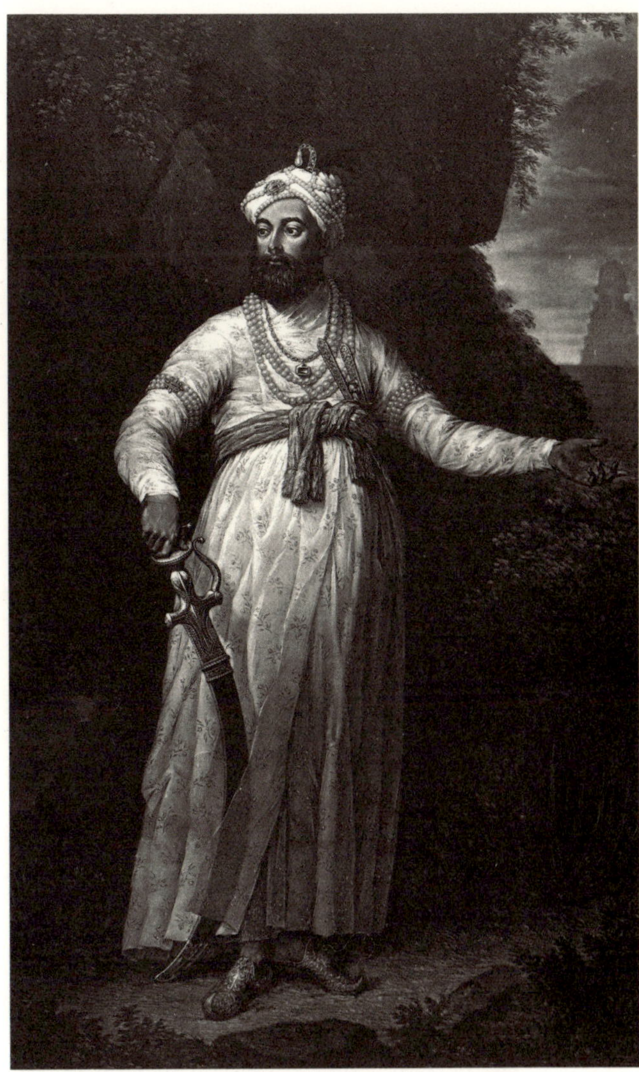

127. John Dixon. *Omdut-ul-Mulk, Nawab of Arcot.* 1772. Mezzotint. Los Angeles County Museum of Art. Gift of Dr. and Mrs. Pratapaditya Pal.

noted regarding such a relationship, "A beautiful Hindostanee woman to whom he was greatly attached, and who returned his kindness by every degree of respectful attention in her power to bestow. . . ."[62]

One such *bibi* painted by Renaldi, the most romantic of portrait painters to travel to India, is a slender girl clad in gauze and silken garments, relaxing against a bolster cushion upon a carpet, holding the mouthpiece of a hookah in one hand (fig. 30). Many British in India in the eighteenth century happily settled down with

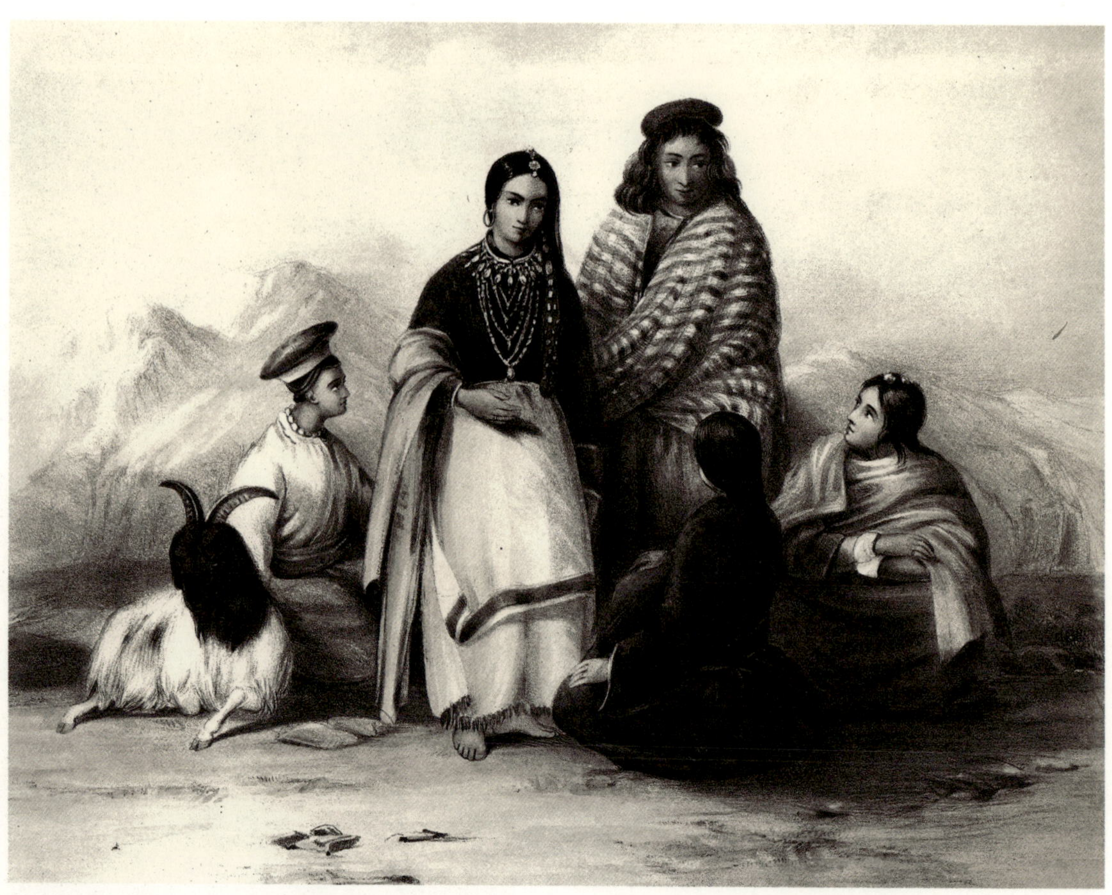

128. Emily Eden. *Group of Tibet Tatars*. 1844. Colored lithograph. Walter Collection.

these women and had families, although many were left behind when the sahib returned to England. The pathos of such a parting is poignantly expressed in a ballad sung by an abandoned Indian woman:

'Tis thy will and I must leave thee,
O thou best beloved farewell
I forbear lest I should grieve thee,
Half my heart felt pangs to tell.
Soon a British fair will charm thee,
Thou alas her smiles must woo,
But tho' she to rapture warm thee
Don't forget thy poor Hindoo.[63]

Apart from the *bibi*s, and far more accessible, were the courtesans and nautch girls who had no inhibitions about modeling for the sahib artists. This did not change until after World War I. In 1877, Valentine Prinsep wistfully remarked about the *zenana*, "Fancy what a world of intrigue it must be, and a world into which no men able to record its life, with its passions, joys, and tears, has ever been able to faithfully penetrate."[64]

Among the artists who portrayed both princes and commoners was Emily Eden, who went to India to join her brother Lord Auckland when he became governor-general. She spent the years between 1836 and 1842 traveling extensively and writing long letters to her sister which were published in London in 1866 under the title *Up the Country*. These letters afford fascinating glimpses of the India of her times. Like many an accomplished young lady of a certain social status, Emily Eden had taken lessons in England from the best drawing masters of the day and became a talented amateur artist.

Eden's artistic endeavors were her first priority; she would even go out on an elephant "in search of a sketch."[65] While scouting for an exotic subject she wrote, "I found my idol, made a

132

lovely coloured sketch with quantities of Venetian red, and got back just as it grew dark." [66] She frequently searched for ruins, but figures were her primary interest. As sister of the governor-general, she was particularly well situated to paint portraits of important people, and her studies of the Sikh ruler Ranjit Singh and his entourage are of great historical interest. She was especially sympathetic to the Sikh nobility; Sher Singh at the Sikh court of Ranjit was "a gorgeous figure all over diamonds and emeralds." [67] Curiously, although she was a woman, she does not appear to have had access to the *zenana*.

Eden sketched the common Indians with equal zeal. An unusually fine study shows a charming group of Tibetan Tatars accompanied by one of their typical long-haired mountain goats against the snowy Himalayas (fig. 128).

For a woman who never really enjoyed her six-year stay in India or got over the feeling of exile, Eden was remarkably active and perceptive. Apparently, like James Forbes, she found solace in drawing. Although she complained constantly about the climate, the discomforts of camp life, the vapid conversations that took place in the Anglo-Indian community, the long days spent in dark, shuttered rooms, and the boredom of countless balls and durbars, she admitted that "the setting provided prodigal examples of the picturesque." [68] So, she occupied herself drawing the servants: "Every servant in the Government House is a picture by himself . . . . I keep up my drawing, but entirely in the figure live, as there is no landscape in Bengal, and also the glare is so great that nobody could draw it if there were. . . ." [69]

IX

SEVERAL artists portrayed the Indians as subjects of ethnographic relevance. Some, like Solvyns, made a complete record of the castes and tribes, while others, like Devis, focused on their occupations. Frans Balthazar Solvyns, who trained in Antwerp as a painter, sketcher, and engraver, went to India in 1790 and was the first to make a comprehensive survey of Indian

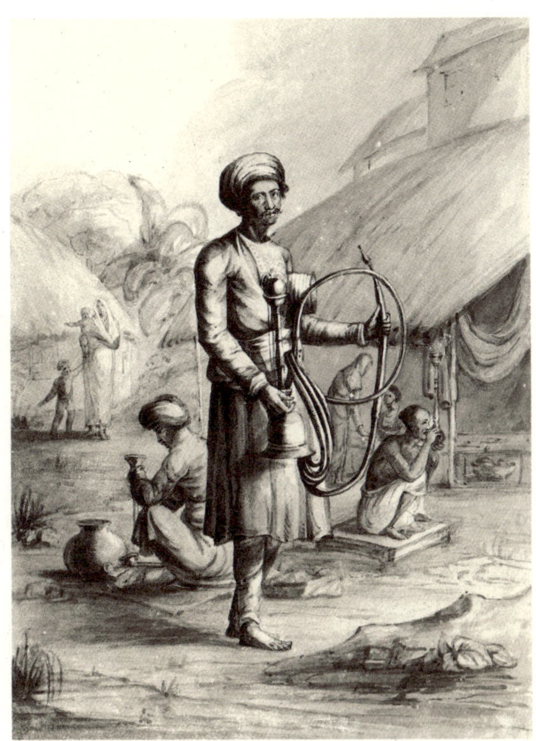

129. Balthazar Solvyns. *Hookah-bearer.* c. 1800. Pen and ink and wash. Walter Collection.

communities, costumes, and customs. Having fallen prey to the fascination of India, he started learning Hindi in Calcutta and made friends with learned pundits and Brahmans. With the encouragement of Sir William Jones, Solvyns announced schemes for a large-scale work, finally producing a collection entitled *Two Hundred and Fifty Coloured Etchings descriptive of the Manners, Customs and Dresses of the Hindoos.* This work, issued in parts in 1793 and completed by 1799, was undertaken partly with the idea that

it would be particularly interesting to those who had resided many years in India, as a help to them, on their retreat to their native Country, to recall to their recollection, occurrences of their youth and scenes formerly familiar to them; at the same time that it would serve to illustrate to their friends in Europe, their observations and descriptions of the character, customs and manners, the persons, and dresses, of the inhabitants of Hindostan, their modes of conveyance by land and water, the various sectaries of religion with their peculiar ceremonies, and the appearance of the face of the Country.[70]

133

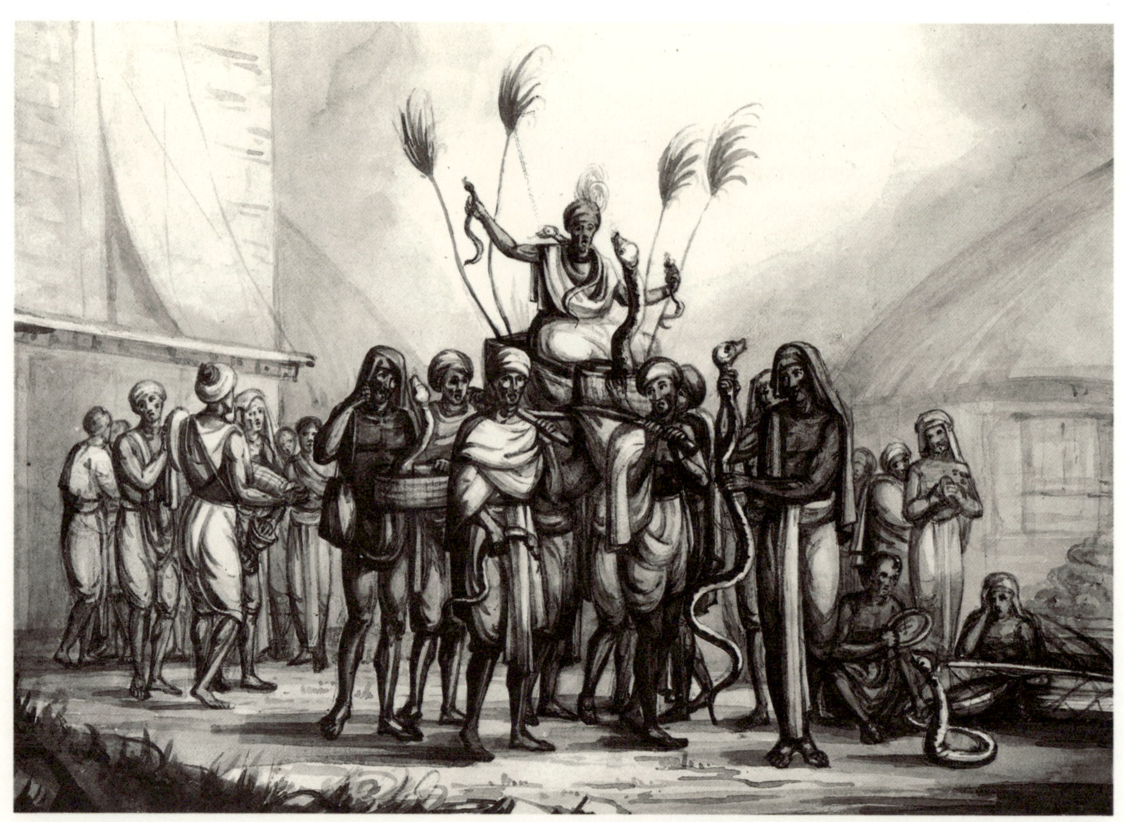

130. Balthazar Solvyns. *Snake Festival.* 1799. Pen and ink and wash. Walter Collection.

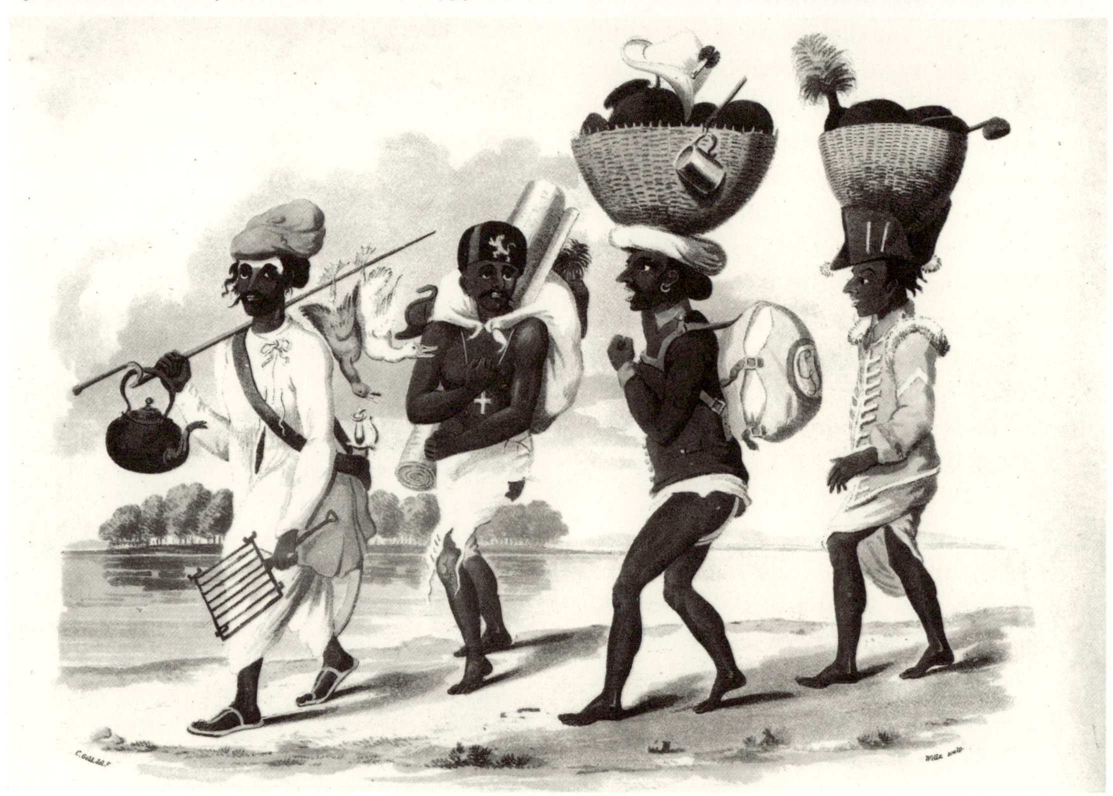

131. Captain Charles Gold. *Itinerant Traders* from *Oriental Drawings*. 1806. Aquatint. Walter Collection.

134

Interest had been aroused in the lifestyles of the Indians, and the time seemed ideal for a venture that was the first of its kind. Initial reaction must have brought in sufficient subscriptions, since Solvyns set to work immediately, wandering all over Calcutta and sketching with relentless energy men and women of all possible types: the milkman and the painter of festival images, the drummer and the sitar player, the fisherman and the hunter. He sketched the servants employed in a British household, drew pictures of bullock and horse carts, depicted snake charmers, and lingered upon the colorful festivals of the Indians. Having completed the drawings, he made etchings and colored them by hand.

Solvyns was earlier a purely maritime painter which might account for the strange melancholy that surrounds his human figures, a melancholy emphasized by their tall slenderness and long sad faces. His drawings for the drummer and the hookah bearer testify to his unusual manner. As a contemporary notice states:

His sketches, though not very picturesque, are very faithful delineations, and he must have been a man of very labourious and observant research. The engravings, executed by himself and published in Calcutta, are very rude.[71]

Apart from the exceedingly serious, almost depressive attitude of the figures in his drawings, he had a problem with the quality of his engravings. Skilled engravers were not available in Calcutta and we have seen how Thomas Daniell, who attempted a twelve-plate *Views of Calcutta* in 1786, postponed the idea of further engraving until he returned to England. Solvyns's elongated figures, rough hatching, and fuzzy shading added to the somber coloring did not make for success. His drawing for a festival of snake charmers is reproduced almost exactly in the engraving; only minor changes are evident, as in the replacement of the seated figures to the right by a standing group, and in the elaboration of the thatched hut behind them into a building with elegant architectural details (fig. 130). The snake charmer group comes from Section 12 of

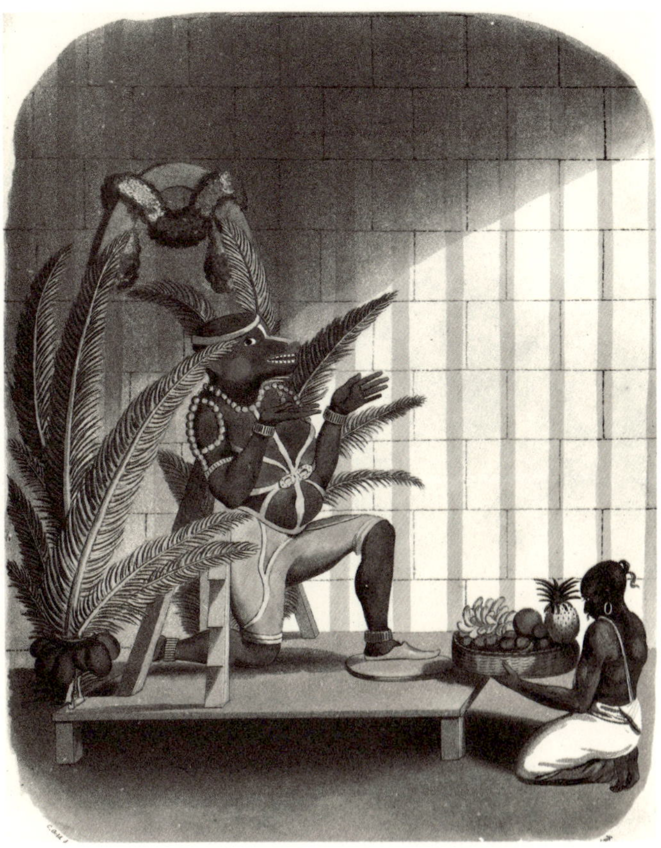

132. Captain Charles Gold. *Hanuman King of Apes, an Indian Deity* from *Oriental Drawings*. 1806. Aquatint. Walter Collection.

his book which is subtitled "22 Public Festivals." From Section 7, "12 Prints of Faquirs," is the holy man called a "Soonassey," a striking portrayal of a loincloth-clad ascetic with a backdrop of a palm tree slanting diagonally across the page.

In Europe between 1808 and 1812, Solvyns brought out a French edition of this work; this too was not a financial success and if not for support from his wealthy British wife, the artist would have been in dire financial straits. His work is of interest despite its shortcomings and meager artistic qualities because it is a unique survey of the people, costumes, and customs of Bengal.

Charles Gold, an officer who joined the army as a captain in 1776 and rose to the rank of colonel in 1825, was an amateur artist who concentrated on portrayals of Indian costumes

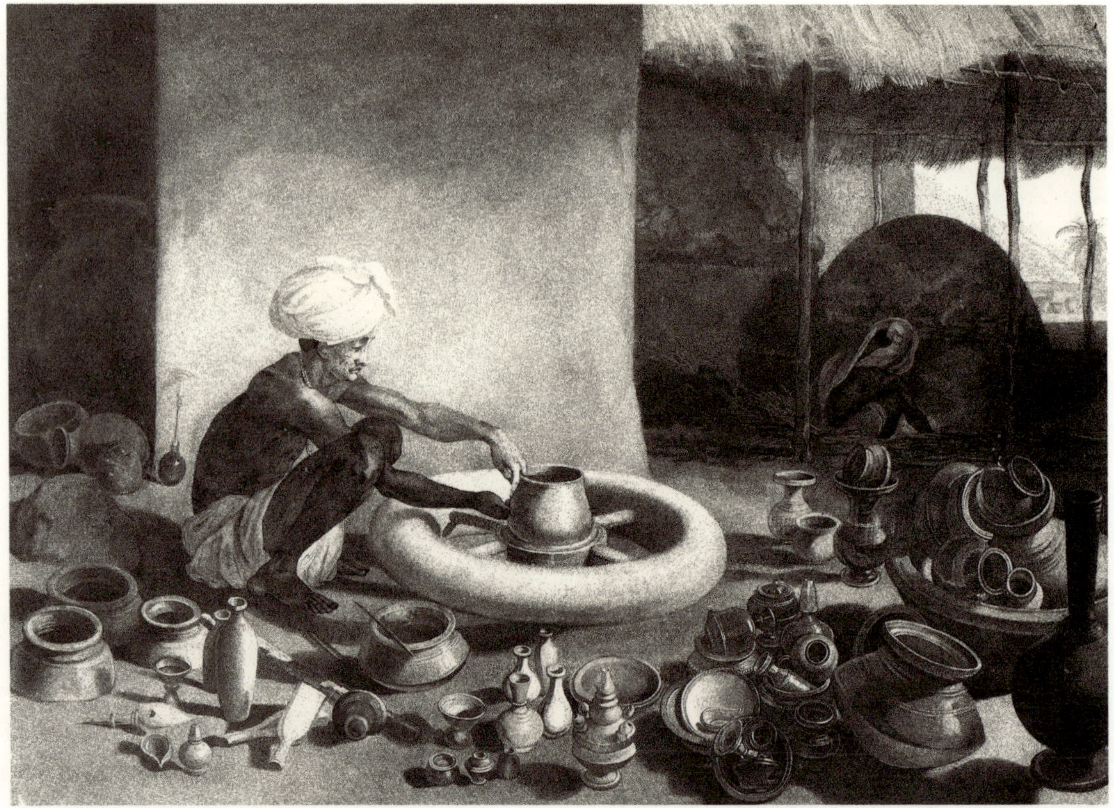

133. Arthur William Devis. *A Pottery with Various Utensils in General Use*. c. 1800. Colored engraving. Walter Collection.

and occupations. We are told that, "not being enabled, from his professional duties, to go in search of the extraordinary subjects, with which it [India] so eminently abounds, he was necessitated to take them as they occurred."[72] While stationed in southern India, he drew the people of the Coromandel coast and the Mysore region. We read that Gold allowed "none to pass his quarter, without an invitation to walk in, which they always accepted and most readily permitted him to draw their portraits . . . . [Subscribers] may be assured that the dresses are minutely attended to, and characters strictly preserved. . . ."[73]

Gold's lively and spontaneous drawings range from a view of a dramatic dust storm to a group of itinerant traders to an ascetic wandering minstrel or a pious Brahman making offerings to the monkey god Hanuman in a temple in Madras (figs. 131, 132). *Hanuman King of Apes* is vivid, if somewhat flamboyant, with Hanuman's deep green body clothed in pink. Gold noted:

I had only time to sketch the one [idol] nearest the door, which was in the best light, and from his apish countenance appears to be *Hanuman*, immortalised for the services he performed under the God Rama at the conquest of Ceylon. He is on a stage, in the exact attitudes of the original, and represented as accepting an offering of fruits.[74]

Gold's drawings were reproduced as aquatints in a series of volumes entitled *Oriental Drawings* published in 1806.

Arthur William Devis, though primarily a portraitist, also produced a series called "Occupations in India." Having been shipwrecked near Borneo, Devis arrived in India by chance, reaching Calcutta via Macao. He belonged to a family of portraitists, and was tutored by his father before training at the Royal Academy. During his eleven-year sojourn in India (1784–95), Devis painted the British in the setting of their own homes, and acquired an enviable reputa-

136

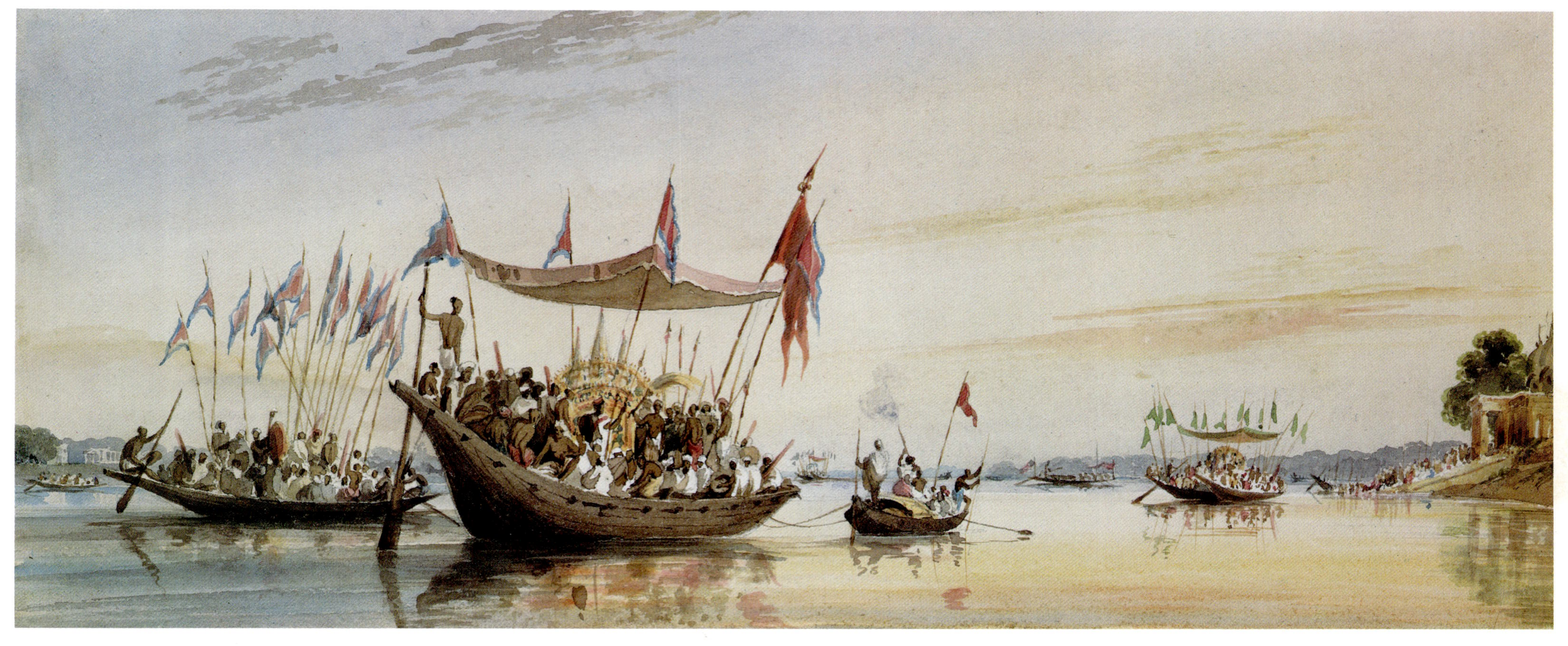

COLORPLATE 9.
William Prinsep. *Isherah—Water Procession of the Image of Doorga Previous to her Immersion at Sunset.*
1825. Pencil and watercolor.
Formerly in the collection of Spink & Son, Ltd.

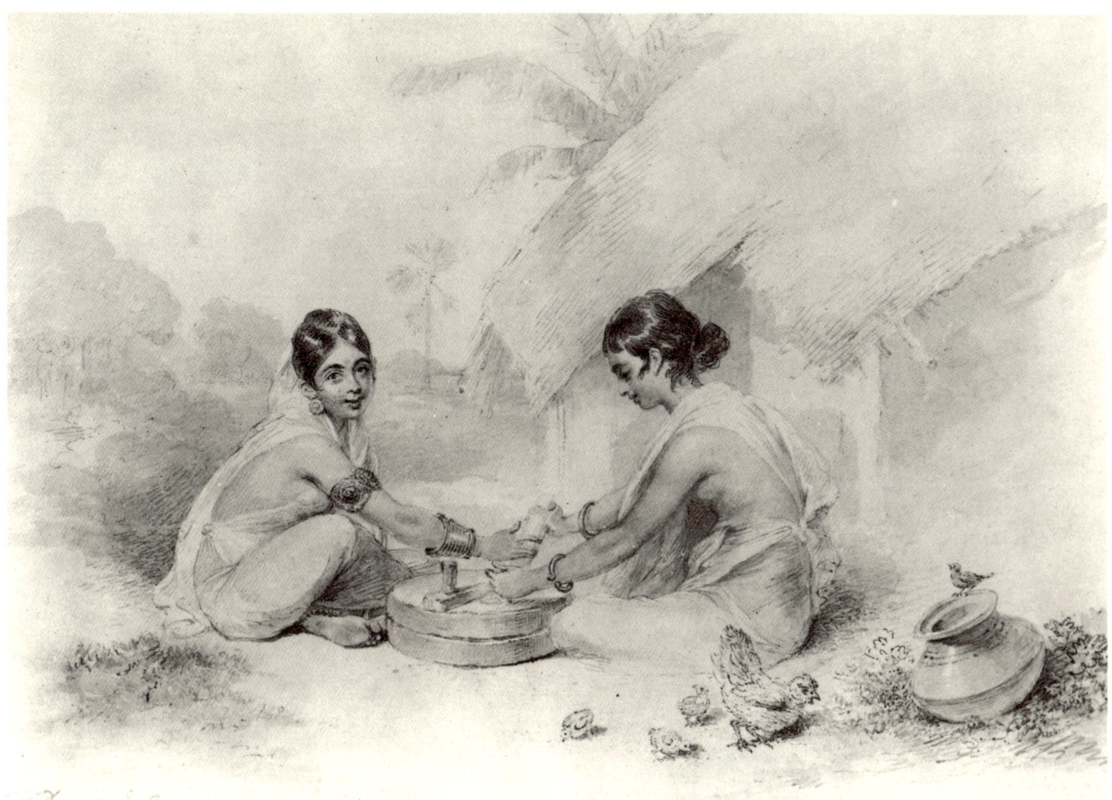

134. Arthur William Devis. *Native Women from Bengal Grinding Flour Outside a Hut.* c. 1800. Watercolor. Yale Center for British Art, Paul Mellon Collection.

tion as a portraitist; he was a popular figure in Calcutta society, and regarded as amiable and very clever.

In 1792, finding that portrait commissions were slackening, Devis decided to paint a series recording rural occupations. He moved to the village of Santipur, sixty miles north of Calcutta, and sketched the people grinding corn, making paper, weaving cloth, manufacturing salt, throwing pottery, and smithing. Devis proposed to publish a series of thirty prints, to be engraved under his supervision in England. The project was never realized, however, and by 1803 only *The Weaver* and *The Potter* are known with certainty to have been engraved and delivered to subscribers in India. The seven-by-ten-inch drawing of *The Potter* in the Yale Center for British Art is probably the original sketch, which Devis must have enlarged and colored for the engraving (fig. 133). The scene is a fine rendering of a potter working at his

wheel, with the kiln at the rear of his open hut; several finished pots of various shapes and sizes are lying around him drying out.

It appears possible, from an inventory made after Devis's bankruptcy, that three other pictures of this series were engraved, including one of women grinding corn. This seven-by-ten-inch watercolor is a charming, though rather overly sentimental, scene of two young village girls sitting outside a hut, jointly working a grindstone placed between them (fig. 134). A light wash of blue-gray has been added and a few touches of tan for their bodies and for the mud pot. While the picture captures the tranquility of a Bengal village, only the girls' faces are at all Bengali; their bodies are strictly classically sculptural.

X

THE appeal of the exotic inspired paintings of bizarre customs like *suttee*, some of the more unusual festivals, and the many *fakir*s and

137

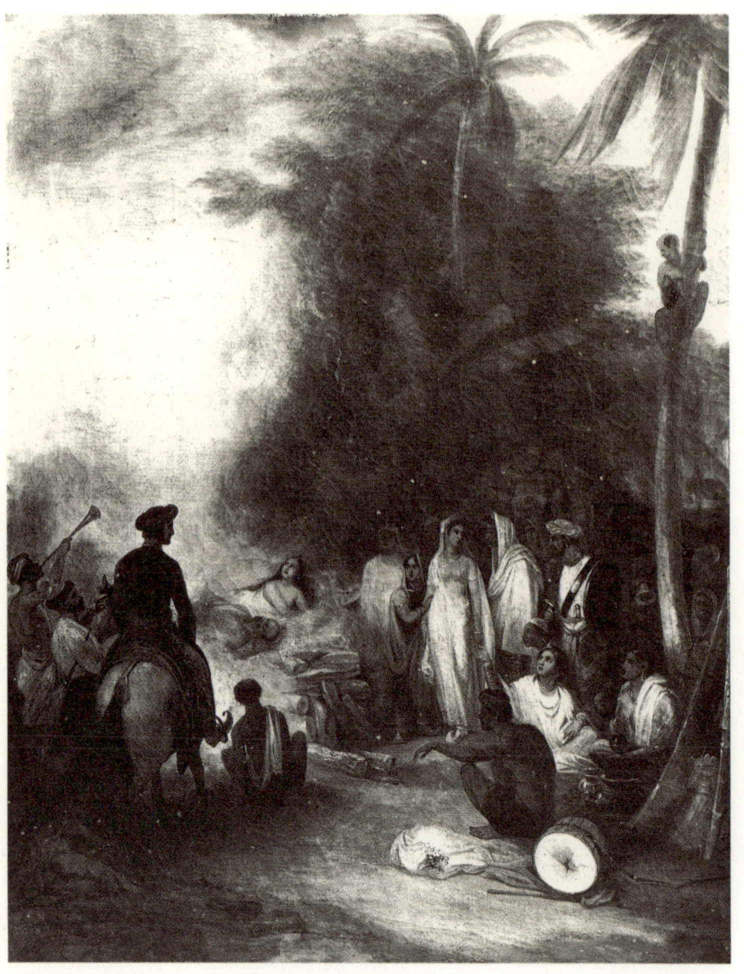

135. James Atkinson. *The Suttee*. 1831. Oil on canvas. Reproduced by permission of the India Office Library and Records (British Library).

*sadhu*s. One of the more dramatic, yet highly romanticized portrayals of a *suttee*, a Hindu religious practice in which a newly widowed woman burned herself on the funeral pyre of her husband, was painted by the amateur James Atkinson (in India, 1805–45), who was a medical doctor in the employ of the Company. Like the D'Oylys, both Atkinson and his wife took drawing lessons from Chinnery while in Calcutta. *The Suttee*, painted in 1831, is so idealized that it is fairly certain Atkinson never actually witnessed one (fig. 135). The first wife is already on the pyre next to her dead husband, while the second wife is being led in. Both women are classically proportioned, elegant, statuesque beauties.

Occasionally, we read that such willing acquiescence actually occurred. Sir William Sleeman left an eyewitness account of a *suttee* that took place in November 1829:

She came on with a calm and cheerful countenance, stopped once, and, casting her eyes upward, said: "Why have they kept me five days from thee, my husband? . . ." She then walked up deliberately and steadily to the brink, stepped into the center of the flame, sat down, and leaning back in the midst, as if reposing upon a couch, was consumed without uttering a shriek or betraying one sign of agony.[75]

However, considerable evidence exists which indicates that it was social and familial pressure that forced most women to undergo the ritual. The practice was one of the most controversial and emotional issues of the day. There was a long Indian tradition behind it and the more orthodox did not wish to see the practice abolished. Hindu society itself was split over the matter, with the more enlightened supporting the British who abhorred the practice and were working toward banning it. Finally, in 1832, Lord Bentinck succeeded in having a bill passed that outlawed *suttee*.

An anonymous watercolor of a *suttee* vividly conveys the confusion of the scene, and is considerably more realistic than Atkinson's romanticized version (fig. 136). The widow, seen in the midst of high flames, raises one hand despairingly to the heavens; in a menacing circle around her are men brandishing swords while others are bringing in more firewood and torching the already blazing pyre, as if to insure the success of the project. A band playing drums and trumpets adds to the tumult.

The numerous colorful fairs and festivals of India, many of which took place on the banks of the Ganges, were perfect subjects for the artist. George Farington (in India, 1783–88) was particularly interested in Hindu ceremonies, and his premature death was, in fact, due to his having "imprudently exposed himself to the night air, to observe some ceremonies of the natives, in order to complete a series of drawings begun for that purpose."[76] Others, like James Prinsep (1799–1840), drew the massive annual

138

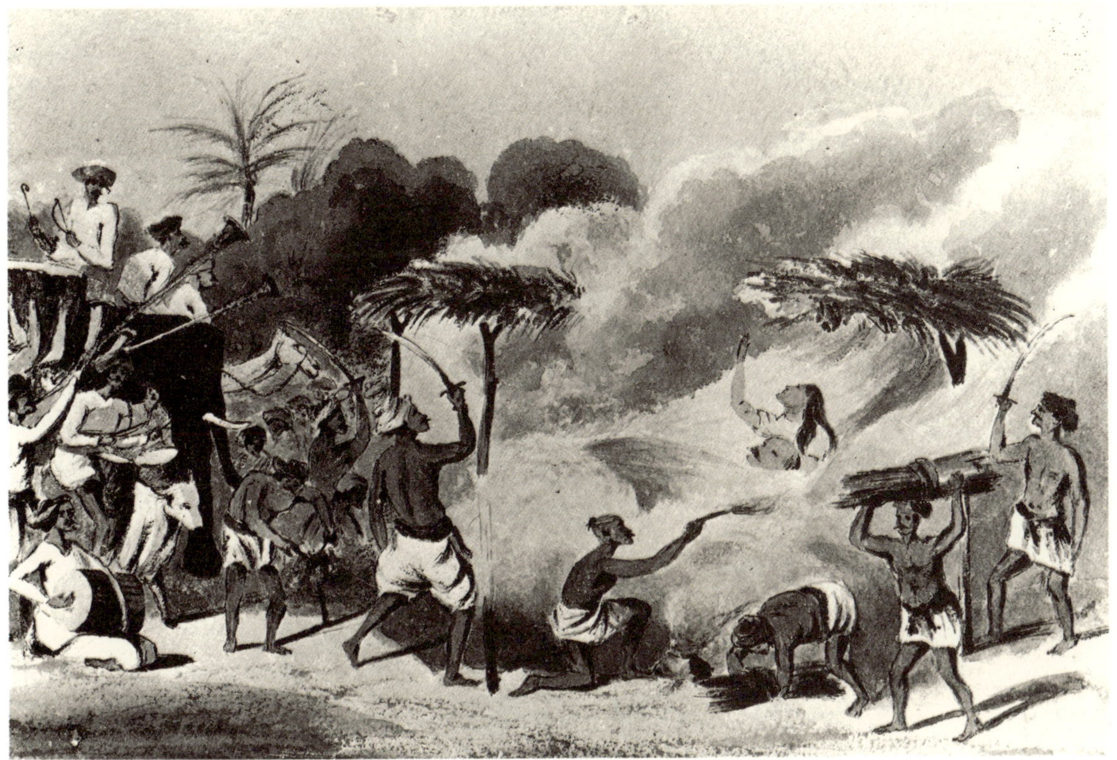

136. Anonymous. *The Suttee*. c. 1830? Watercolor. Reproduced by permission of the India Office Library and Records (British Library).

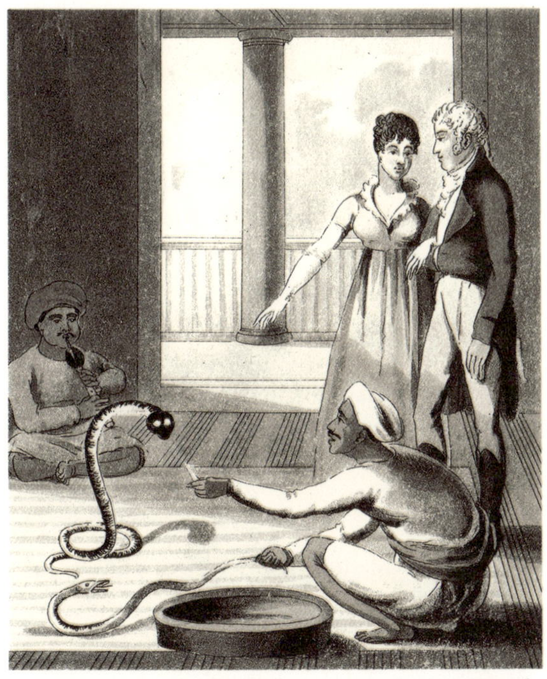

137. Sir Charles D'Oyly. *A European Couple Watching Snakecharmer* from *The European in India*. 1813. Colored lithograph. Walter Collection.

pilgrimages to holy cities like Benares, Hurdwar, and Allahabad, and the Dussehra festival where the image of Ravana is burned. Lieutenant-Colonel George Francis White, a talented amateur artist, witnessed such a festival and remarked:

The noise baffles all description; the shouts and cries of men come mingled with the neighing of horses, the trumpeting of elephants, the grunts of camels, the lowing of cattle, the bellowing of bulls, the screams of birds, and the loud sharp roars of the wild beasts; and, as if these were not enough, there are gongs and drums beating, trumpets blaring, conch-shells blowing, and bells ringing, which never cease for a single instant. In the midst of all this discord, regular musicians perform to groups assembled in different parts of the city or fair . . . and amid the more melodious snatches which are caught here and there, the bugles of the British battalion may be heard, playing some well-remembered air. . . .[77]

William Prinsep, though not an Indologist like his brother James, was also a talented amateur artist, who did some watercolors of Indian

139

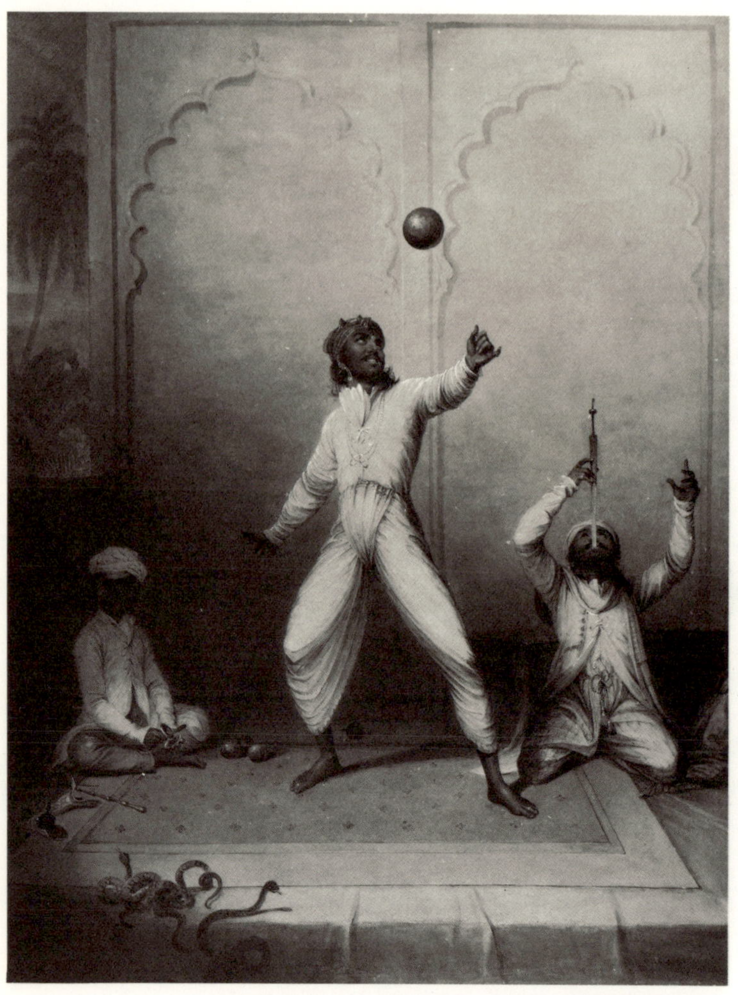

138. James Green. *The Indian Jugglers*. 1814.
Watercolor. Collection of Mr. Kenneth Lane.

ceremonies. *Water Procession of the Image of Doorga*, painted in 1825, shows the moments before the ceremony of the immersion of the image on the last day of the Bengali Durga festival (colorplate 9). The river is crowded with decorated canopied boats filled with worshippers; each boat carries the painted clay images which are produced anew for the festival each year. This theme was treated by lesser artists like Solvyns, whose views are important as an ethnographic record, but lack the artistic value of Prinsep's picture, with its evocative use of color.

Jugglers and snake charmers were quite a novelty for the British; Emma Roberts speaks of the famous Madras jugglers whose bodies "are so lithe and supple, as to resemble those of ser-

pents rather than men. . . . Swallowing the sword is a common operation, even by those who are not considered to be the most expert; and they have various other exploits with naked weapons of a most frightful nature." [78] The professional artist James Green's (1771–1834) watercolor of a group of jugglers is probably one of the finest of its kind (fig. 138). The focus is on the extraordinarily elegant standing figure of the juggler whose companions are a sword swallower, a young boy, and group of wriggling snakes. The painting was exhibited at the Royal Academy in London in 1814. From Emma Roberts's narration of the success of the London performance of Ramoo Samee, it is apparent that groups of Indian jugglers frequently traveled to England. James Green himself never visited India and one may conclude that his extremely successful watercolor was inspired by one such traveling troupe, perhaps the very one referred to by Emma Roberts.

Another exotic subject that attracted the British artists was the *fakir*. Solvyns drew as many as twelve categories of these ascetic mendicants, each with a different title and of a distinct affiliation. Emily Eden portrayed a *fakir* with knee-length hair standing in a mountainous setting with a waterfall. Arthur William Devis's ascetic mendicant is holding a string of *rudraksha* beads in one hand and his ankle-length hair in the other; he is clad in only a loincloth and is seated beneath a great banyan tree next to a sculpture of Vishnu and two attendants (fig. 139). This work seems to have been one of three paintings of ascetics by Devis and was intended as the frontispiece for a book on Indian occupations entitled *The Economy of Human Life* which was never published. [79]

XI

WHILE the human interest pictures of the British were often highly romanticized and classical, natural history subjects were rendered with much greater—almost clinical—accuracy. Some were done purely as artistic endeavors while others were meant as scientific studies. This genre seemed to appeal more to the amateur

140

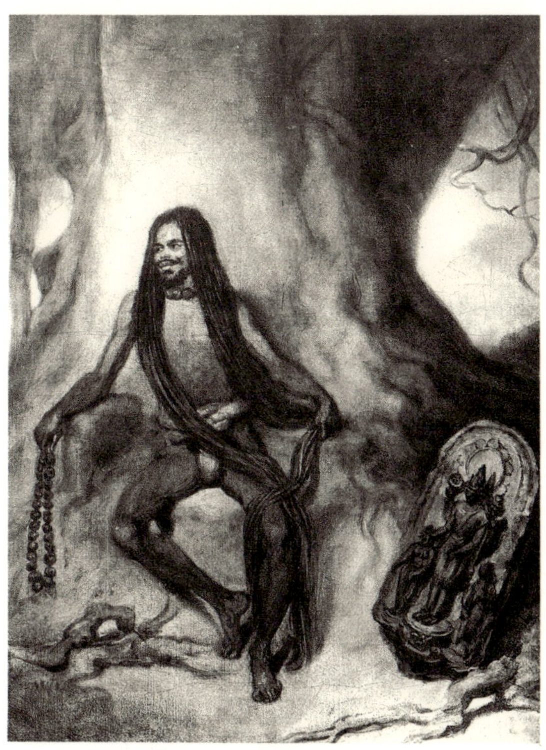

139. Arthur William Devis. *Portrait of a Holy Man Seated Under a Tree.* 1792. Oil on canvas. Private Collection. Photograph courtesy of Hobhouse Ltd.

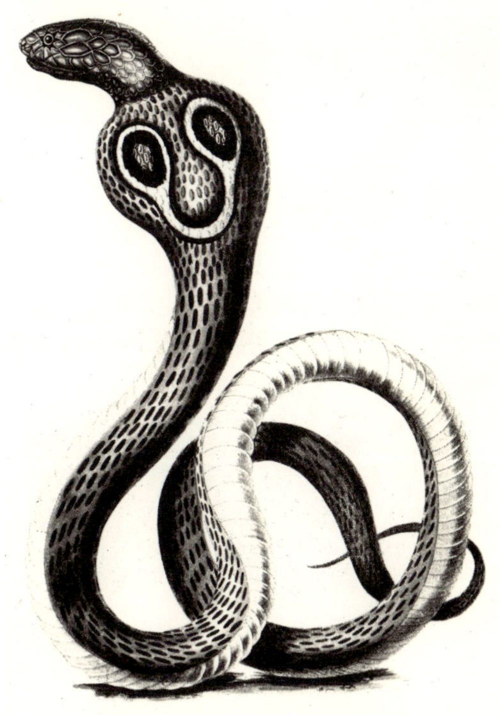

140. William Hooker after James Forbes (1773). *Cobra de Capello, or the Spectacle-snake* from *Oriental Memoirs.* 1813. Colored engraving. Avery Library, Columbia University.

artists; while many of the professionals were keen landscapists, few displayed either the scientific curiosity or the infinite patience that are necessary for detailed scientific drawing.

One of the earliest and finest amateur artists who chose natural history subjects was James Forbes. A civil servant in the Bombay Presidency from 1765 to 1784, he enjoyed his years in India and produced lively drawings of the countryside, emphasizing its flora and fauna. These drawings were engraved and published in 1813 in four volumes entitled *Oriental Memoirs*, which contain vivid accounts of Forbes's sojourn in India. The work contains five of the earliest of all English lithographs, three of them colored and produced by the artist himself who had become keenly interested in this new technique. These lithographs are signed by Forbes with a note to the effect that they were copied on stone in the year 1811.

Forbes took great pride in the colored draw-

ings he executed "of the beasts, birds, fishes, insects, fruits, flowers and vegetables, produced in such variety in those climates." [80] He told of the cooperation and encouragement he received:

In my secluded situation in Guzerat, I seemed to be blest with another sense. My friends in India were happy to enlarge my collection; the sportsman suspended his career after royal game to procure me a curiosity; the Hindoo often brought a bird or an insect for delineation, knowing it would then regain its liberty; and the brahmin supplied specimens of fruit and flowers from his sacred enclosures. [81]

The highlights of the book are the superb colored plates, aquatinted by William Hooker, a well-known professional artist. Especially striking is the study of the cobra de capello, that "large but beautiful serpent . . . . It is called the hooded snake, from having a curious hood near the head, which it contracts or enlarges at pleasure; the center of this hood is marked in black

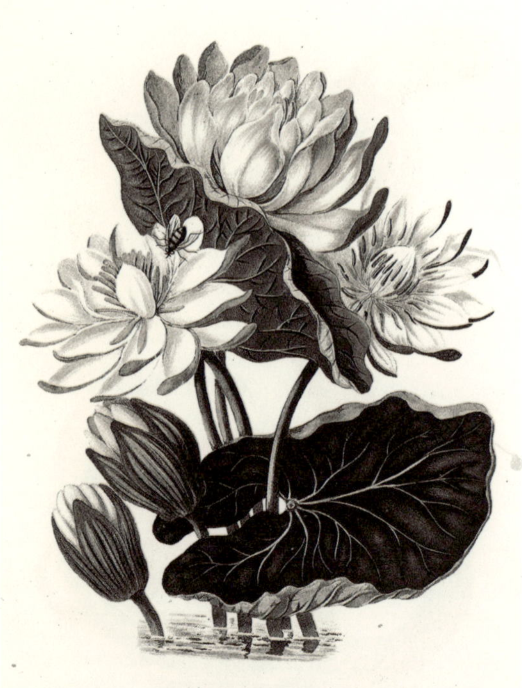

141. William Hooker after James Forbes (1781). *Red, Blue and White Lotuses of Hindostan* from *Oriental Memoirs.* 1813. Colored engraving. The Thomas John Willis Collection.

and white like a pair of spectacles from whence it is also named the spectacle-snake" (fig. 140).[82] Forbes discourses on how the dancing snakes of India are of this type and of the snake charmers,

who play a few simple notes on the flute, with which the snakes seem much delighted, and keep time by a graceful motion of the head; erecting about half their length from the ground, and following the music with gentle curves, like the undulating lines of a swan's neck.

His drawing of the cobra, in various shades of brown, was made while it

danced for an hour on the table while I painted it, during which I frequently handled it, to observe the beauty of the spots, and especially the spectacles on the hood, not doubting but that its venomous fangs had been previously extracted.[83]

His tale has a dramatic ending: the next morning his servant Mahomet rushed in to ask Forbes to immediately give thanks to God, for he had just witnessed the same snake attacking a young woman who had died a half hour later!

142

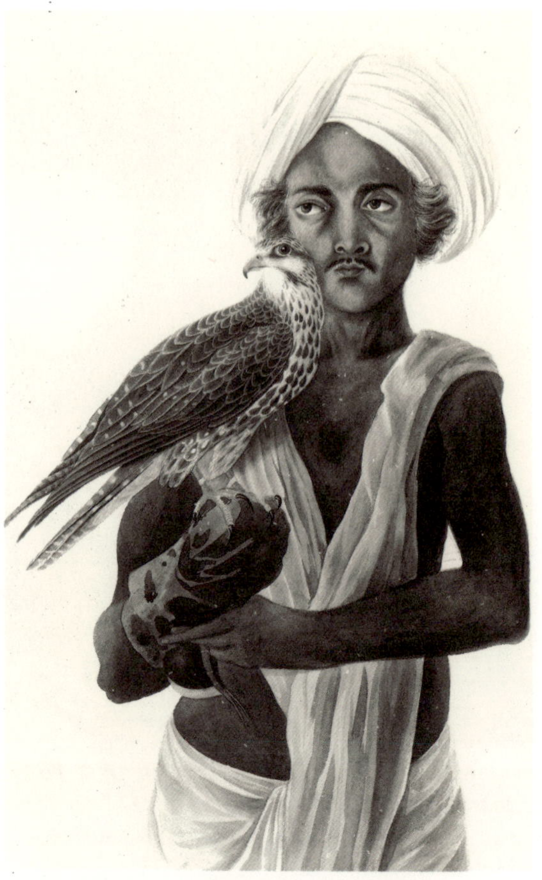

142. Christopher Webb-Smith. *Luggar Falcon.* c. 1825–30. Watercolor. Balfour and Newton Library, University of Cambridge.

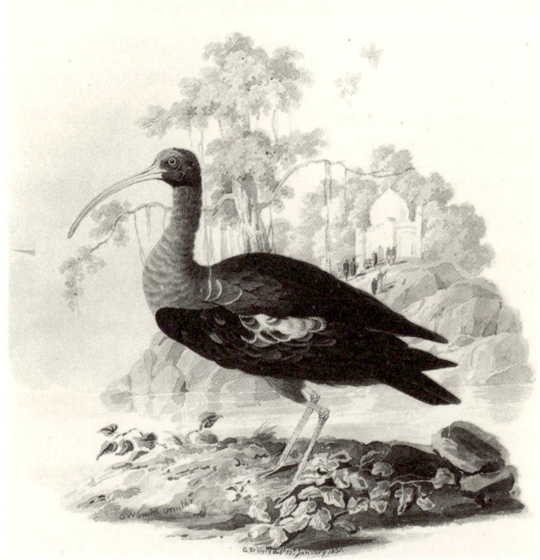

143. Christopher Webb-Smith and Sir Charles D'Oyly. *Ibis.* 1831. Watercolor. Balfour and Newton Library, University of Cambridge.

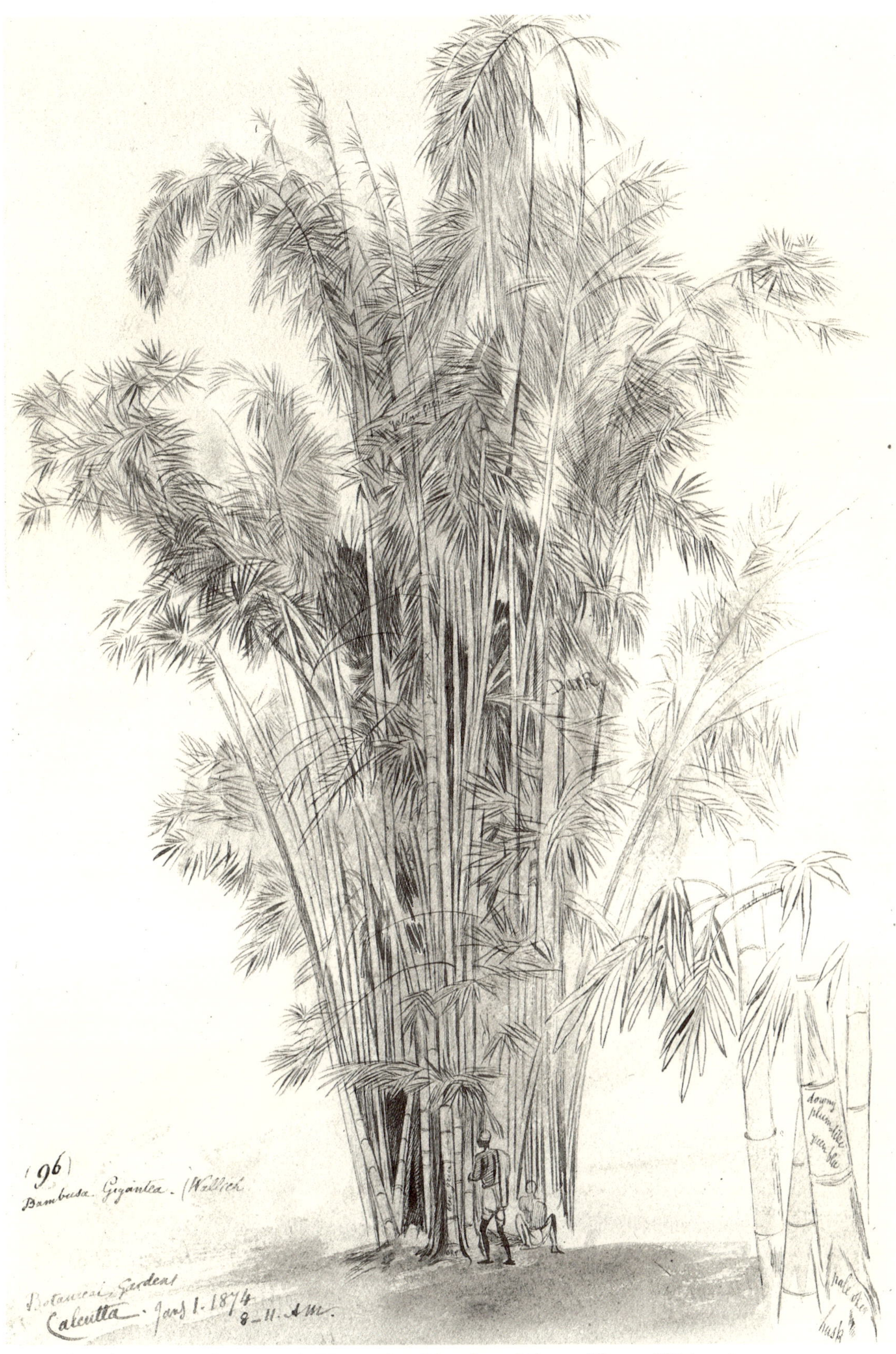

144. Edward Lear. *Bamboos*. 1874. Watercolor. Houghton Library, Harvard University.

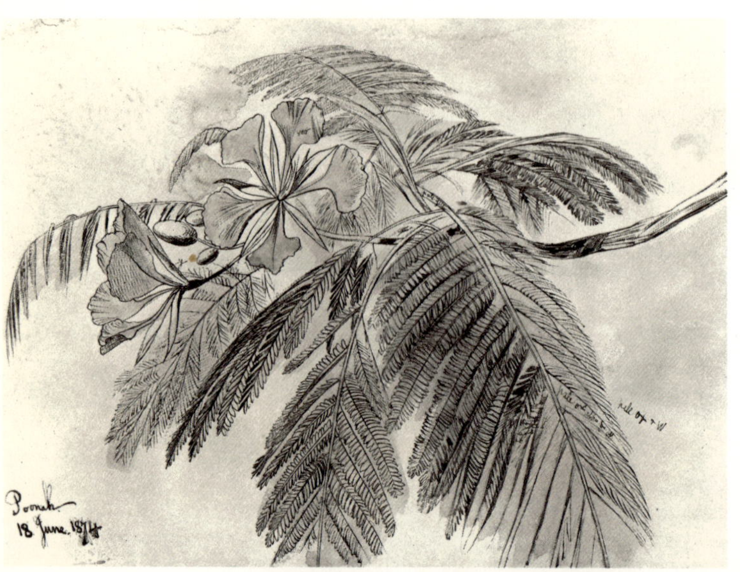

145. Edward Lear. *Branch of a Gul-mohr Tree.* 1874. Watercolor. Houghton Library, Harvard University.

A superb example of Forbes's style is his vivid picture of the Taylor bird (colorplate 10) which is named thus because of

its instinctive ingenuity in forming its nest; it first selects a plant with large leaves, and then gathers cotton from the shrub, spins it to a thread by means of its long bill and slender feet, and then, as with a needle, sews the leaves neatly together to conceal its nest . . . the hen is clothed in brown; but the plumage of the cock displays the varied tints of azure, purple, green and gold. . . . [84]

The superbly colored engraving shows the brilliant male bird perched by its ingenious nest upon a branch of convolvulus, with its bright blue trumpet-shaped blossoms and red fruit. The brown and yellow female swoops down with a piece of thread in its beak to finish the nest, which holds two eggs. The original drawing was made in 1768.

Another magnificent plate shows the lotus, the great symbolic plant of India, which has featured prominently in Indian art since pre-Christian times (fig. 141). Forbes writes that "the sweet variety of the red, white and blue lotos, gently agitated by the breeze, or moved by the spotted halcyon alighting on the stalks . . . are altogether lovely." [85]

Forbes's delicately colored drawing of a humble-looking mango is of interest. [86] He praises the Alphonso mango of Goa, describing it as one of the greatest blessings of the country and undoubtedly superior to every other variety of mango. Viscountess Falkland (Lord Falkland was governor of Bombay in the 1840s) seemingly concurred:

The flavour combines that of the melon, apricot and strawberry. The blossom is beautiful, the rind has tints of green, red and orange. It must have been the fruit which tempted Eve and that weak man Adam, who afterwards threw all the blame on his poor wife. [87]

Christopher Webb-Smith (b. 1793) was an amateur artist who was a lover of bird life. He was a judge and magistrate in the service of the East India Company from 1814 to 1842, and was one of the first to codify the ornithology of India. Fascinated by the new species and stationed in the remote upcountry which afforded plenty of leisure time, Webb-Smith wandered the low-lying paddy fields, gun in hand, watching birds. As often as not, he would shoot one and bring it back for detailed study. His manuscript volume *Notes on the Birds of India* contains 295 watercolors with methodical annotations. The striking watercolor of a luggar falcon seated on the protected hand of a young turbaned Indian is accompanied by notes on the varieties of hawks and falcons and the habitat of each, training and food, and their price (fig. 142). Apparently a fine falcon, untrained, could cost as much as 120 rupees! [88] His admiration for the falcon emerges from his drawing and the appended remarks: "There is something peculiarly erect and noble in the appearance of this bird, the eye is brilliant and the brow prominent."

In 1824, Webb-Smith was posted to Patna where he met and befriended Sir Charles D'Oyly. Webb-Smith was named vice-president of the art society of which D'Oyly was president. A manuscript volume of 191 watercolor plates, which measured 25 by 19 inches, resulted from a collaboration between the two friends. Webb-Smith drew the birds in isolation, with notes on

144

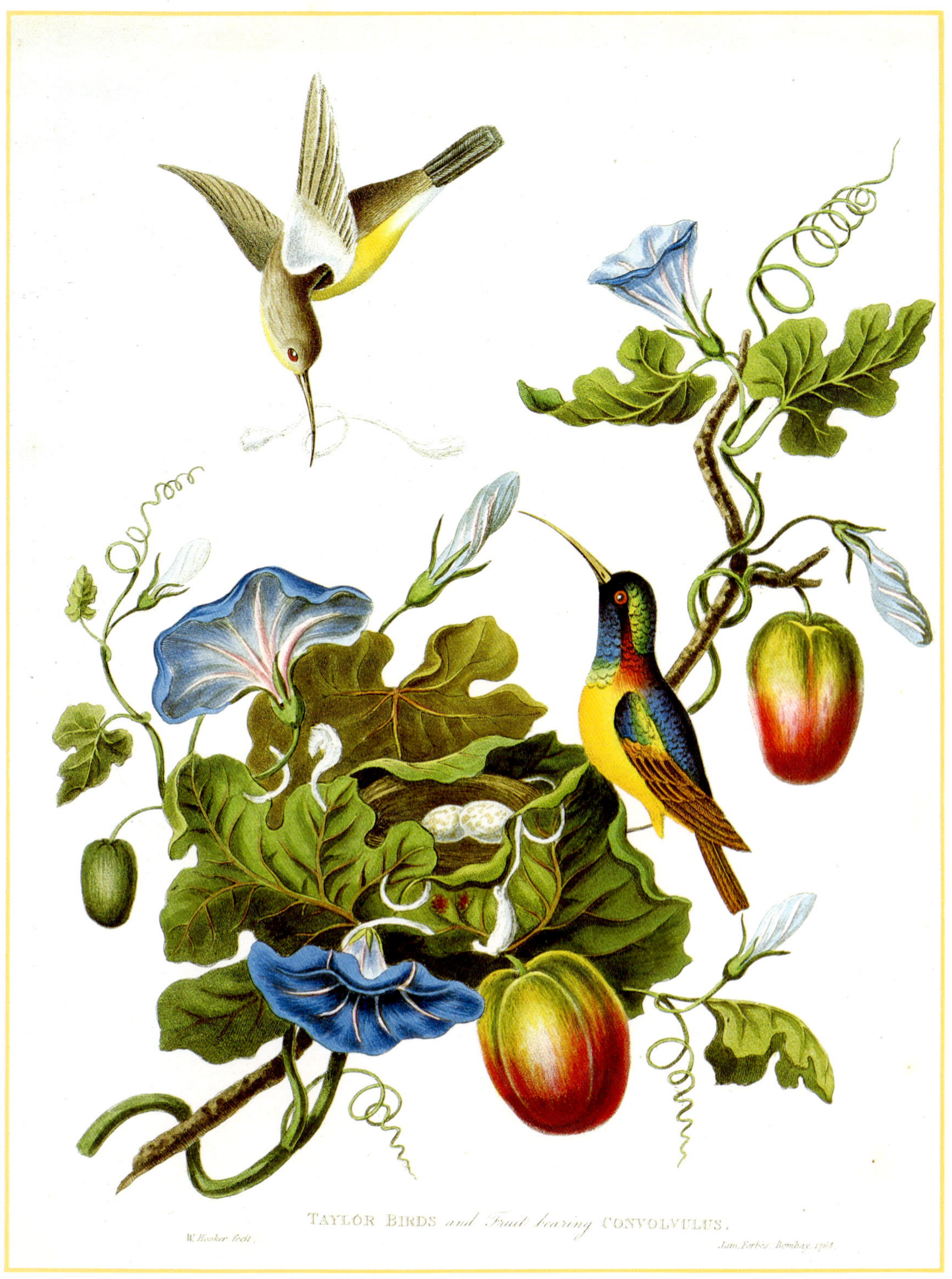

COLORPLATE 10.
William Hooker after James Forbes (1768). *Taylor Birds and Fruit-Bearing Convolvulus* from *Oriental Memoirs*. 1813. Colored engraving. The Thomas John Willis Collection.

their habitat and suggestions for the settings in which they should be placed; the adequate setting and landscape, usually with ruins, were then added by D'Oyly. Figure 143 shows the black ibis with a typical charming D'Oyly landscape in the background. The names of both artists and the date of completion are at the bottom. Although the ambitious volume was never published, both Webb-Smith and D'Oyly found the project most rewarding.

Although Edward Lear was primarily a dedicated landscapist, he was extremely interested in the plants and flowers of the Indian countryside and several of his sketches are devoted to this subject. While his depictions are not as detailed as those of Forbes and other artists who specialized in scientific accuracy, his drawings are quite sensitive. Lear did start out as a natural history artist, working at the Zoological Society in London, and many think of him as the famous painter of parrots. This may explain his continued interest in plant life once in India.

Lear's trees are always spectacular, particularly the palms. In a morning spent in Calcutta's botanical gardens, Lear made an extensive series of sketches of trees, including a delicate rendering of a clump of bamboos (fig. 144), some swaying palms, that perennial favorite the banyan, and the white-barked papaya trees with their shapely cut-out leaves. In Simla, the splendor of the flowering rhododendron caught his attention; in Sholapur, the lotus. He was similarly interested in the tall flowering gul-mohr trees of Poona: "The wonderful orange blossomed Gold-mohr tree is now a sight here, as every compound has one or two in it . . . . Went out and got a branch of the exquisite Gohl-mohr tree (*Poinciana regia*) and made drawings of it"[89] (fig. 145).

Lear's journals suggest that he made drawings of Indian birds, but so far none of these have been found; "Walked a long way to find Adjutant cranes; too late." But the next morning, he was happy to find them across the wide maidan, all in a row.[90] Another entry reveals both his knowledge of bird life and his abiding interest in it:

Several small, green bee-eaters, and at Tollygunge, a largish green bird with red and blue about head, on top of a tree; seemed a big woodpecker, only sate still on the very top of the tree, a habit non-woodpeckerish, and making an odd noise.[91]

Lear made some detailed sketches of some of the animals of the Indian countryside, including the monkeys and the humped bull. He also made detailed studies of boats that were used later in his large landscape compositions. All of his meticulous sketches are done in pen and ink and wash and reveal a high degree of finish.

Lear appears to have been one of the last of the naturalist artists to visit India. The era of the camera was beginning and the fauna and flora of the country seem to have been of little interest to the photographer.

XII

CITYSCAPES were another popular genre; they include vivid depictions of small towns, of Calcutta and Patna, of Bombay and Jaipur. As early as 1765, Forbes had sketched several views of Surat and Bombay—rare engravings which are more of documentary than aesthetic interest. They do, however, provide some of the earliest views of these two early British settlements. But for the coconut trees and the natives in the foreground, Forbes's engraving of Bombay Green of the 1790s could well have been a quiet English village with its characteristic green (fig. 147). The *maidan*, or open ground, was where, after their afternoon siesta, the sahibs and memsahibs strolled or rode in the early evening to enjoy the fresh air when the setting sun created the illusion of coolness. Solvyns drew a number of scenes of Calcutta which are of considerable historical interest, particularly his views of the Kalighat temple area and the "Black Town" of Calcutta (figs. 178, 26). Edward Orme painted many views of Madras, and because of the Mutiny, several artists, including William Simpson, have left us very graphic and vivid representations of Lucknow.

The Daniells made several sketches of "native" areas of Calcutta. *Chitpore Road* shows the house of a Bengali merchant, part of an

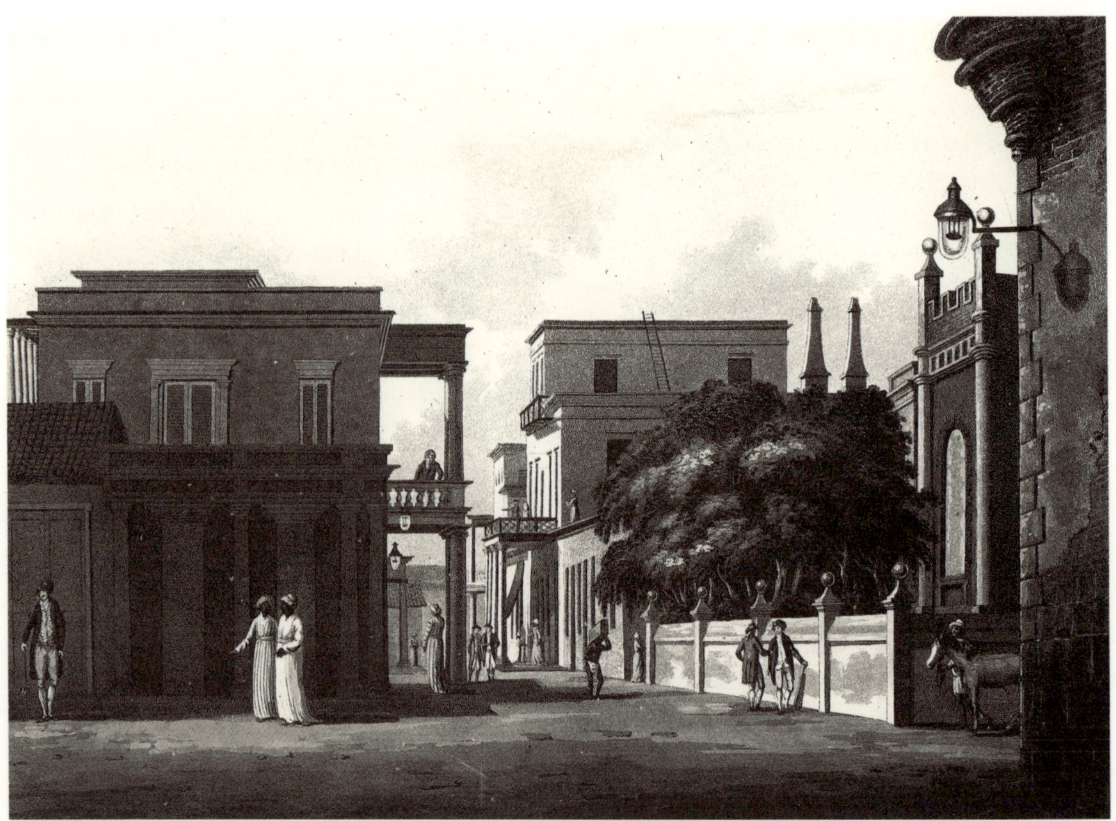

146. Edward Orme. *A View of Part of St. Thome Street, Fort St. George* from *A Brief History of Ancient and Modern India*. 1805. Engraving. The Thomas John Willis Collection.

adjoining market area, and a modern Hindu temple, all in restrained shades of gray and tan (fig. 148). A very different view of British Calcutta was produced by Sir Charles D'Oyly as part of a series of drawings lithographed by Dickinson and published in 1848, after D'Oyly's death, under the title *Views of Calcutta Environs. Fort and Town of Calcutta* is typical of D'Oyly's more formal landscapes (fig. 149). When the British visitor to India first set eyes on Calcutta, he was invariably struck with wonder:

I have seen few sights in my wanderings more beautiful and imposing than the approach to this Petersburgh of the East, this magnificent capital of our Eastern empire . . . . Numerous boats glided up and down the river . . . all, in fact, bespoke the close vicinity of a great capital.[92]

Seen through D'Oyly's eyes and through some of the flattering descriptions provided by early Victorian visitors, one can hardly believe that Calcutta is the same city that so disgusted Rudyard Kipling who characterized it during the later Victorian era as "a packed and pestilential town."

An admirable pen-and-ink composition by D'Oyly, now in the India Office Library, is the view of a street in Patna which shows very realistically the thatched roofs of the houses sloping down toward a busy street and the cupolas of the fort gateway in the distance. D'Oyly seems to have then done the same scene in oil on canvas, repeating almost exactly the details of his pen-and-ink sketch (fig. 150). The oil is basically in shades of tan and brown, with a terracotta-pink for the tiled roofs contrasting with the somber green trees. White clouded skies contain just a hint of blue. While most of the natives on the street are dressed in white, occasional specks of blue and red distinguish the women, with deep brown for the horses and black for the elephant. D'Oyly also did a view of the east-

146

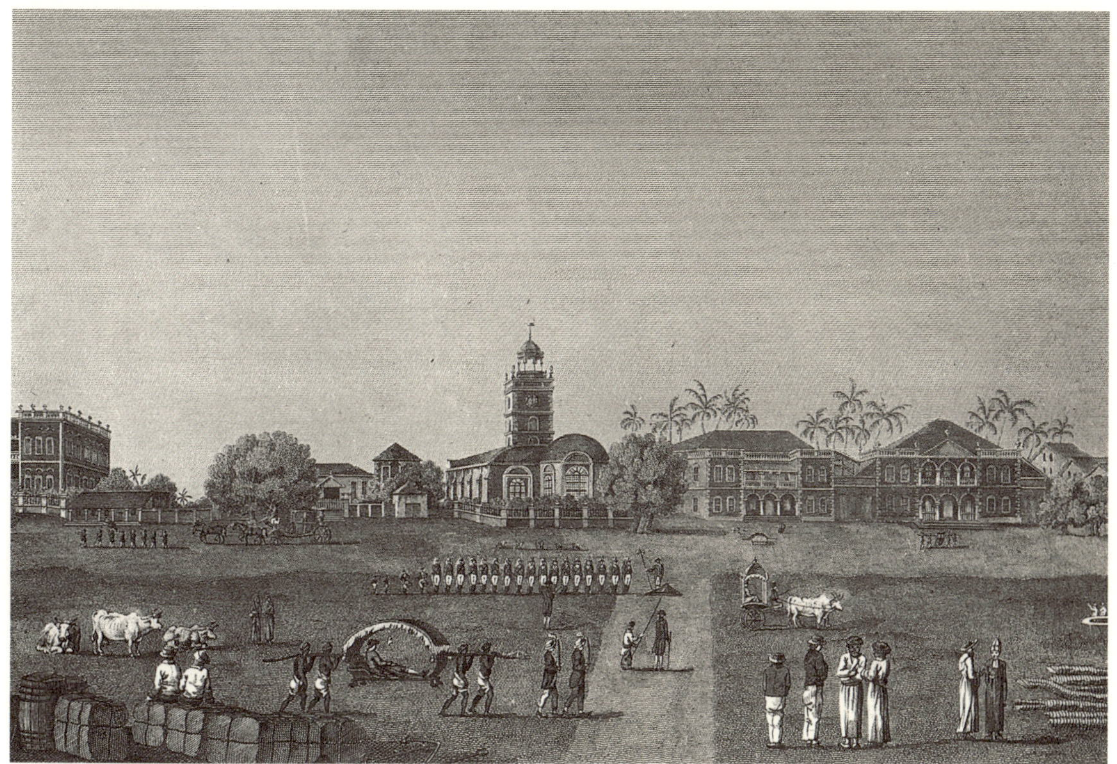

147. Charles Heath after James Forbes (1795). *View of Bombay Green* from *Oriental Memoirs*. 1813. Engraving. The Thomas John Willis Collection.

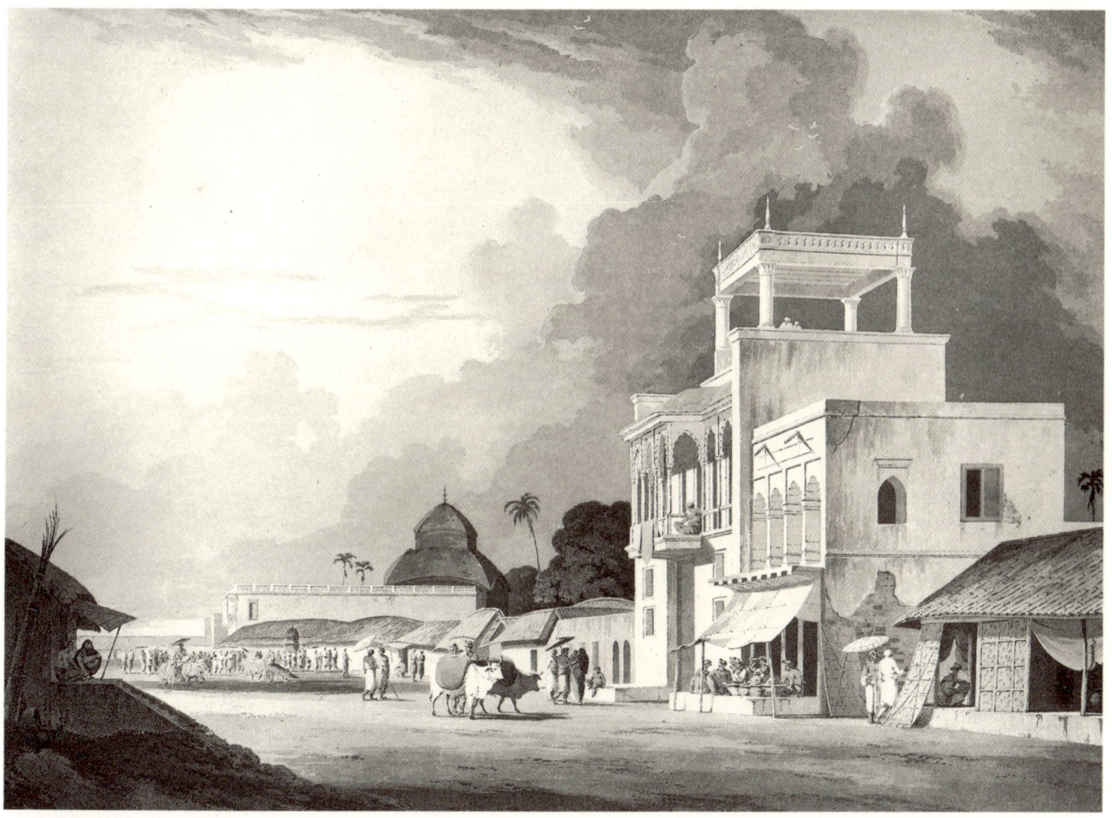

148. Thomas and William Daniell. *Chitpore Road*. 1797. Aquatint. Walter Collection.

147

ern gateway into Patna, which includes the tangled roots of the tree growing out of the brickwork of the gateway, and an elephant, horses, and foot soldiers in the foreground.

Apart from his Lucknow views, Simpson painted several cityscapes which artists before him had not thought worthy of their attention. His *Street Scene in Bombay* depicts the native

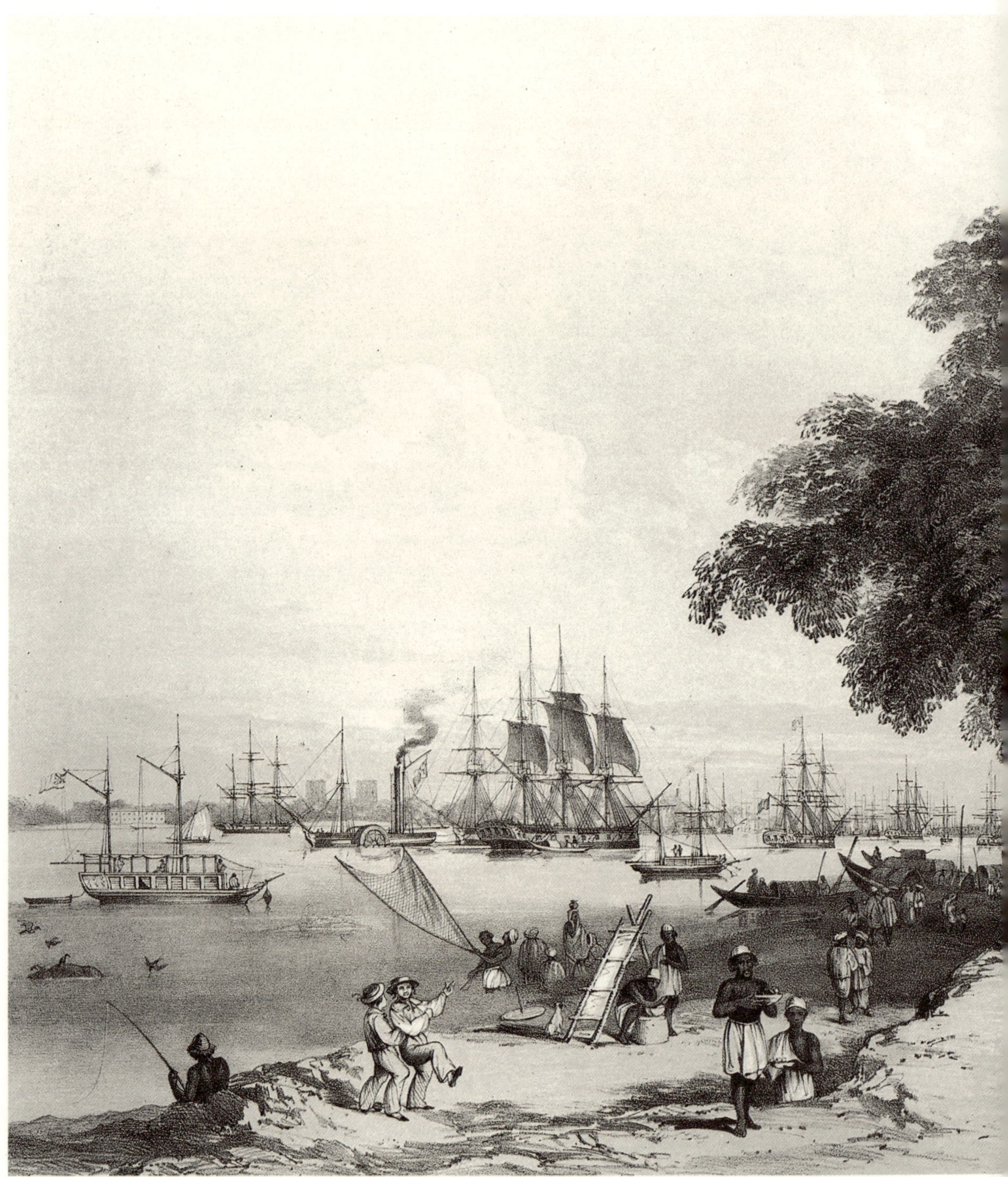

houses with their sloping eaves, shuttered windows, and intricately carved wooden brackets of terracotta-pink (colorplate 1). Horsedriven carriages and Parsi gentlemen in traditional garb are included in the throng. His watercolor of the *Village Well* (*Rajasthan*) shows the pink tiled roofs and white mosque as a backdrop for the village women in their colorful clothes standing

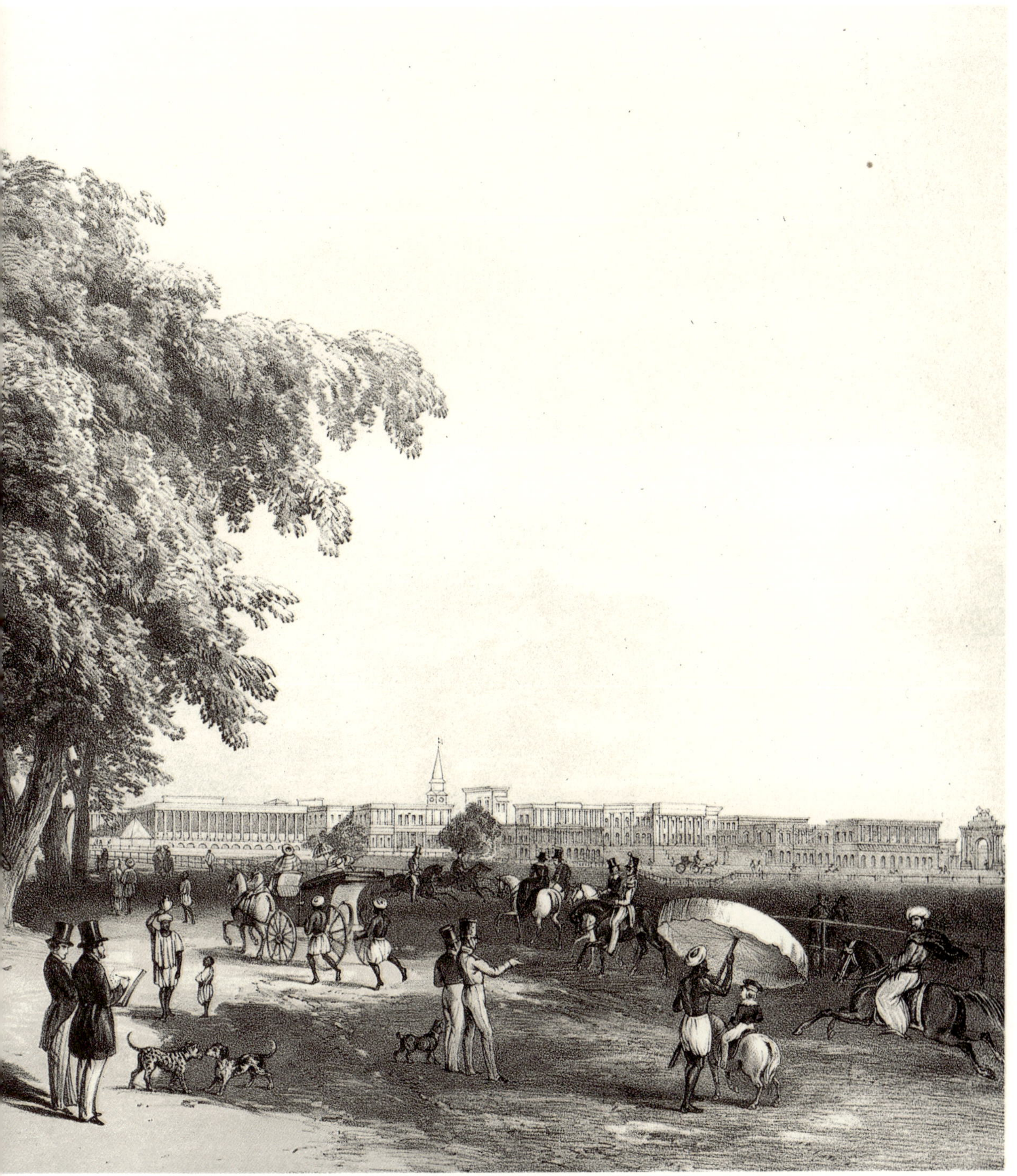

149. Sir Charles D'Oyly. *Fort and Town of Calcutta* from *Views of Calcutta Environs*. 1848. Lithograph. Walter Collection.

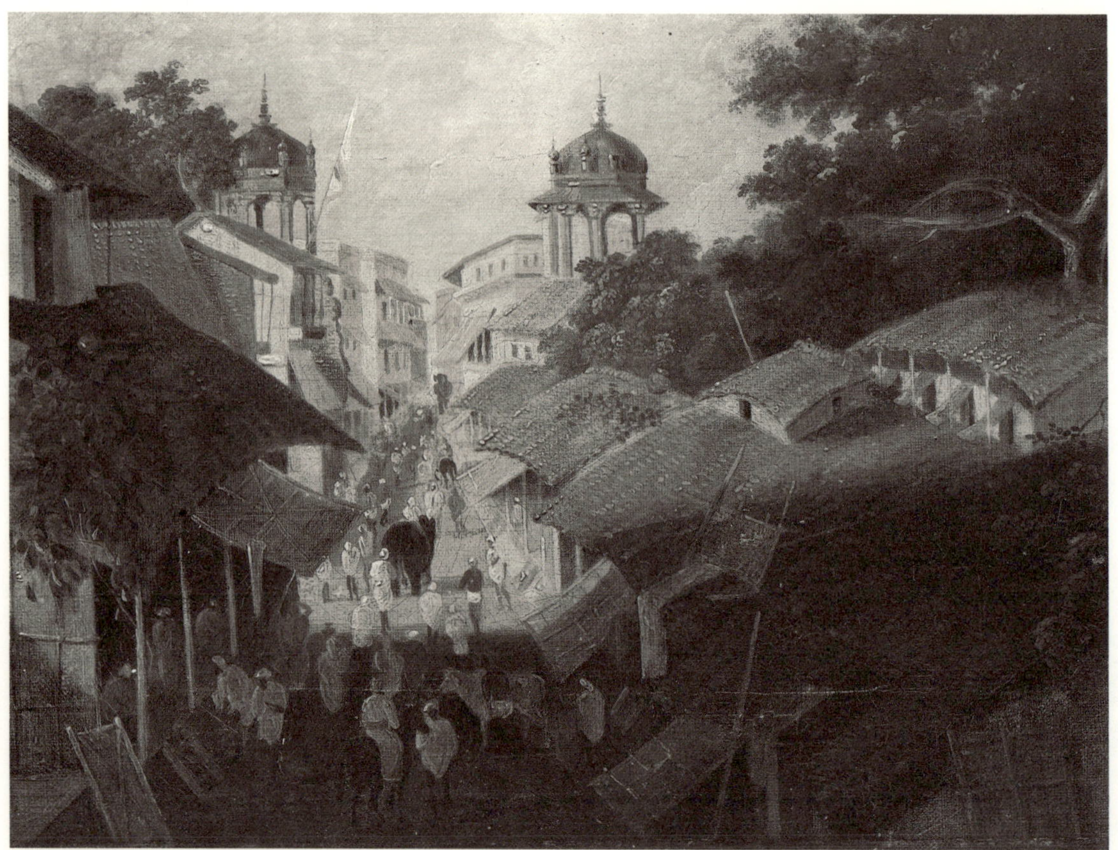

150. Sir Charles D'Oyly. *View of a Street in the City of Patna*. c. 1825. Oil on canvas. Yale Center for British Art, Paul Mellon Collection.

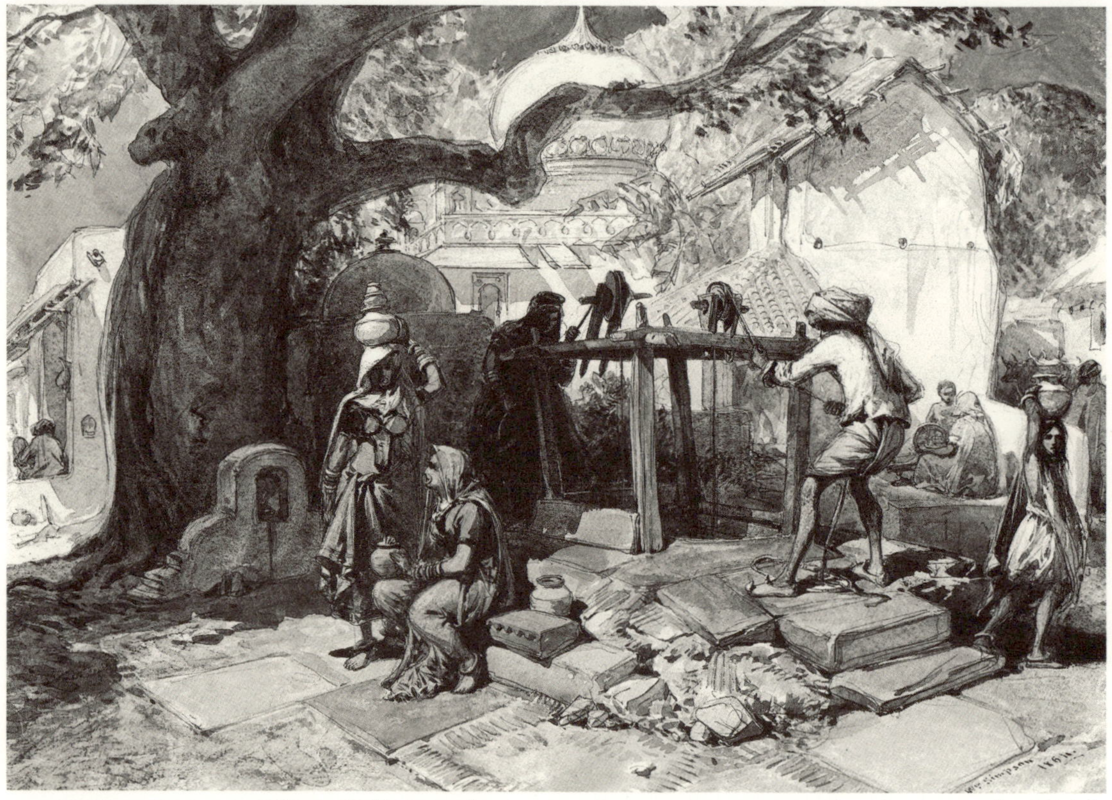

151. William Simpson. *Village Well (Rajasthan)*. 1864. Watercolor over pencil. Yale Center for British Art, Paul Mellon Collection.

150

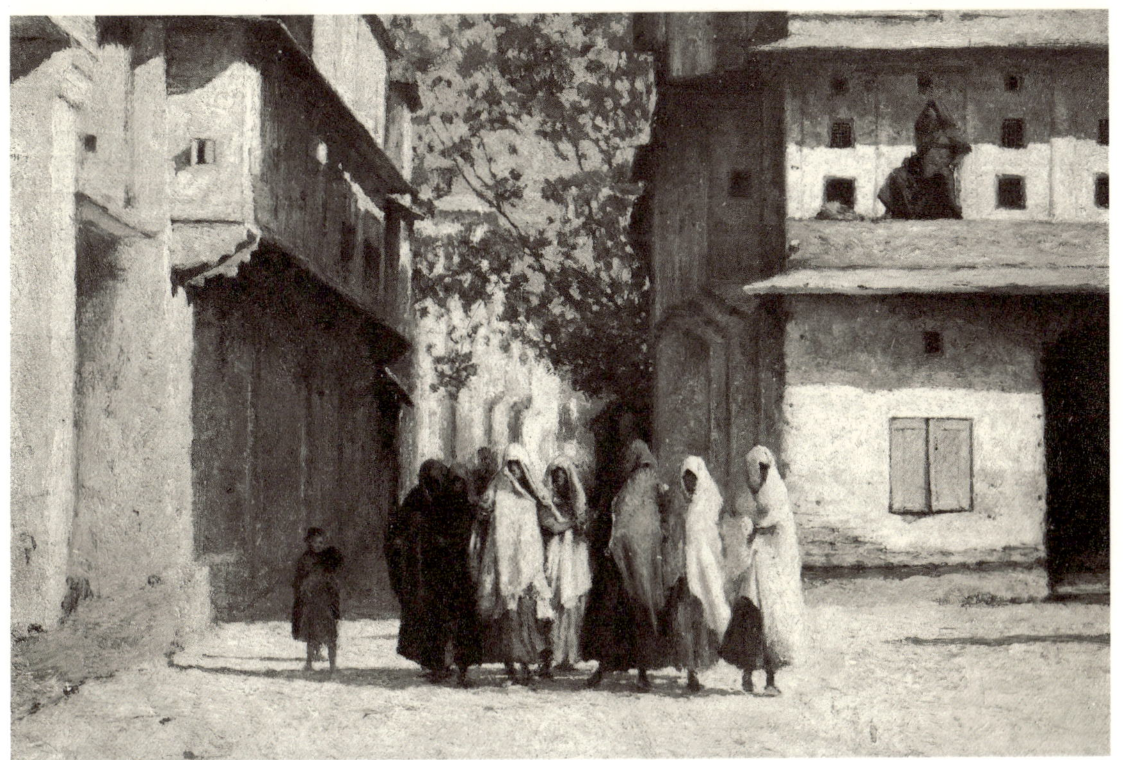

152. Mortimer Menpes. *Jaipur*. c. 1900. Oil on canvas. Walter Collection.

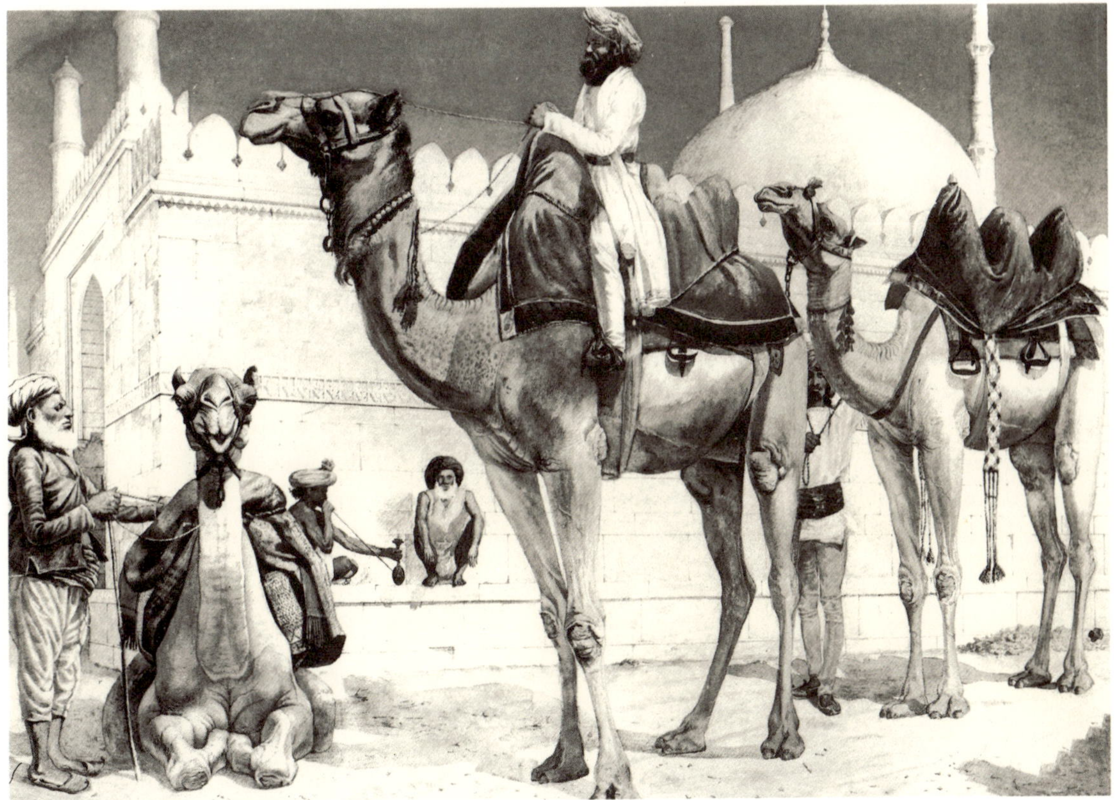

153. John Griffiths. *The Mid-day Sun—Camels Before a Shrine in Western India*. 1868. Watercolor. Photograph courtesy of Hobhouse Ltd.

around the well (fig. 151). In this charming picture, and in the view of Jaipur by Menpes (fig. 152), there is an element of the texture and flavor of nineteenth-century "Orientalist" paintings of street or village scenes of Egypt or the Holy Land, which fascinated the European artists of the period.

Mortimer Menpes was a professional artist who was commissioned by journals in London, including the *Pell Mell Gazette*, *The Illustrated London News*, and *Punch* to cover the grand Curzon Durbar in 1902 / 1903. This commission produced a hundred paintings which were reproduced in a volume entitled *Durbar*. Menpes, who appears to have traveled extensively in northern India after completing his assignment, favored the cityscape. His oils, while usually fairly small in format, are meticulously detailed. Menpes painted the monuments and the busy native quarters of Delhi, Agra, Mathura, Amritsar, Jaipur, and Ajmer. Jaipur appears to have been of particular interest; eleven views of the city are included in a volume entitled *India*, published in London in 1905. In an oil of Jaipur from circa 1900, Menpes emphasized the clear blue of the skies, the green shuttered windows of the native houses seen all over northern India, and the bright colors of the skirts and long scarflike *odhnis* worn by the Rajasthani women to partly cover their faces (fig. 152). *India*, with a text by Flora Annie Steel, is enlivened with seventy-five reproductions of Menpes's cityscapes. A companion volume, *The People of India*, contains thirty-two works by Menpes. The artist seems to have been both a prolific painter and an inveterate traveler; he produced other volumes on areas as diverse as China, Japan, Paris, Venice, and Brittany.

John Griffiths's vivid street scene of camels in front of a gleaming white mosque in a town in western India is unusual in that it was done at midday (fig. 153). Whether painters or photographers, artists generally worked early in the morning or in the evening because of the glare and the white haze that descended over everything once the sun was at its peak. Griffiths's *The Mid-day Sun—Camels Before a Shrine in Western India* is a superbly composed and crafted picture which remains one of the most evocative and aesthetically satisfying Indian scenes by a Victorian artist.

———

THERE is no doubt that the heyday of the British artist painting in India was the century prior to the invention of the camera. Professionals like Hodges, Thomas and William Daniell, Tilly Kettle, and Renaldi, as much as amateur artists like D'Oyly, Forbes, or Webb-Smith, all belonged to the pre-photography era (which coincided also with the pre-Mutiny era). These artists provided a valuable record of the landscape and monuments of India, her variegated flora and fauna, and her various native peoples with their colorful costumes and customs. For those back in England who would never have the opportunity to visit the faraway land, the volumes of aquatints and lithographs prepared in England from the paintings of these artists provided their only knowledge of this distant part of the British empire. While a few artists like William Simpson and Edward Lear continued to produce watercolors after the introduction of the camera, the days of the British landscapes and genre scenes of India were clearly numbered.

4. Native Artists and Exotic Art

Today, Company painting must be regarded from
two distinct angles—Indian and British. In terms of
Indian painting, it is the last original contribution
by Indian artists before the modern deluge. Its use
of water-colour as a technique, its adoption of
Western-style perspective, its cult of realism and its
concentration on the common people as prime subjects for painting broke sharply with prevailing
conventions. In this respect, it is a clear precursor
of modern trends and the first step towards the
Westernization of style which is now a commonplace of contemporary Indian art. For the British,
its appeal is more sentimental. It's a panorama of
the India in which their ancestors found delight,
comfort, and fulfillment; it evokes nostalgia for a
charmed era.

MILDRED ARCHER — 1972[1]

I

THERE are probably very few Britons or Indians who are familiar with the works of
the Company school. Nevertheless, this school,
which developed in the last quarter of the eighteenth century as a result of the interaction between British art and Indian artists, "is the last
original contribution by the Indian artists before the modern deluge."[2] The term Company
school usually refers to paintings that were done
by Indians, generally for British patrons, in
a hybrid Indo-British or Indo-European style
in various parts of the country between 1775
and 1900.

Indian artists had been introduced to European art almost two centuries before they were
exposed to the works of the first British artists
in Lucknow. Artists at the court of the Mogul
emperor Akbar, and at the courts of the contemporary rulers of Bijapur and Golconda,
knew European religious art as it had been
brought by missionaries and merchants in the
sixteenth century. European prints were copied
with admirable precision by many of the Mogul
artists to increase their own skill in drawing,
as well as to display their technical virtuosity
for their appreciative masters. The marvelous

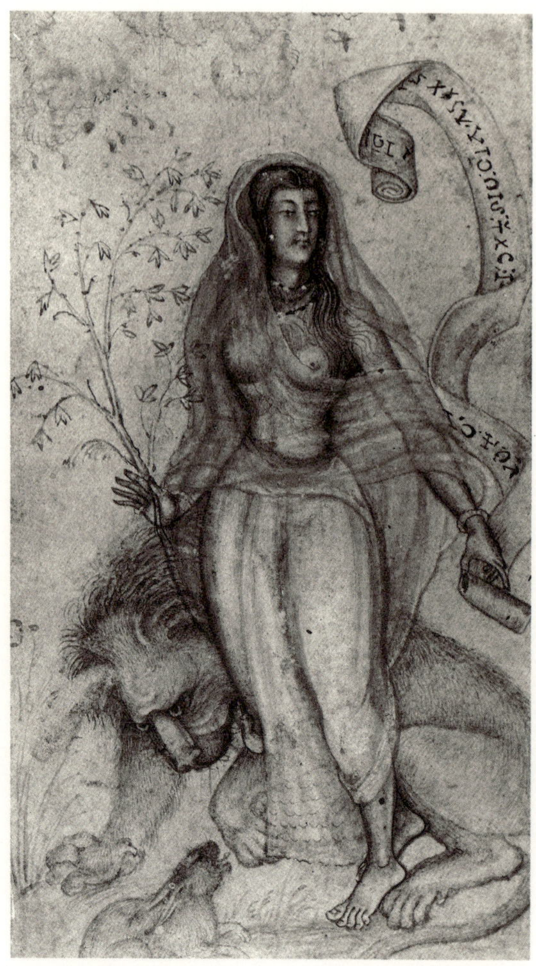

154. Attributed to Basawan. *Allegorical Picture of Fortitude*. c. 1600. Watercolor and gold. Los Angeles County Museum of Art. Nasli M. Heeramaneck Collection.

watercolor of Fortitude may well have been done by the greatest of Mogul masters, Basawan, for either Akbar or his aesthete son Jahangir (fig. 154). When Sir Thomas Roe, the British ambassador, visited the imperial court between 1615 and 1619, he was astute enough to present Jahangir with an English miniature. So impressed was the emperor that he ordered his artists to make copies, and was delighted when the ambassador could not distinguish the copies from the original.

Indian artists were highly selective in borrowing from the European works available to them. They adopted elements of landscape designs by introducing distant views of towns and hills and winding roads almost like stage props. They manipulated their brushstrokes to create volume and employed overlapping forms to suggest depth. The hazy blue they used for hills and fields effectively imparted a sense of space to their pictures. Generally, however, even the great Mogul artists seem to have been unable or uninterested in mastering the techniques involved in showing accurate perspective. The Mogul artists did possess a keen sense of naturalism which served their descendants well when they were employed by British patrons.

Eighteenth-century British patrons were consistently critical of Indian artists for their inability to master the rules of perspective. While ungrudgingly admiring the native artists' extraordinary ability to copy faithfully and to render details with both finesse and patience, they invariably remarked about their lack of understanding of space. Michael Symes, who had been sent to Burma in 1795, regretted that his Indian draftsman, "though skilful in copying figures and making botanical drawings, was unacquainted with landscape painting and perspective."[3] Decades later, when Valentine Prinsep was sent to India by Queen Victoria to record the historical occasion of the Proclamation Durbar, he, too, noted how deficient the Indian artist was in the serious matter of perspective:

Today I have received visits from the artists of Delhi: they are three in number, and each appears to have an *atelier* of pupils. The best is one Ismael Khan. Their manual dexterity is most surprising. Of course, what they do is entirely traditional. They work from photographs, and never by any chance from nature. Ismael then showed me what his father had done before photographing came into vogue, and really a portrait of Sir C. Napier was wonderfully like, though without an atom of *chic*, or artistic rendering. I pointed out to the old man certain faults—and glaring ones—of perspective, and he has promised to do me a view of the Golden Temple without any faults.[4]

The portrait of Sir Charles Metcalfe (resident in Delhi, 1811–14) done by an unknown Delhi artist circa 1830 is typical of the type Prinsep

154

probably saw (fig. 155). It is certainly a tolerable likeness; the three-quarter view of the face, instead of the invariable profile preferred by the Mogul artists, as well as the naturalistic pose, are due largely to British influences.

II

By the 1750s, the Moguls in Delhi were only nominal emperors and enjoyed neither the power nor the wealth for which their forebearers have remained legendary. Inevitably, painters from the capital had moved out to the provinces where local nawabs and maharajas had set up courts that only paid lip service to the emperor in Delhi. The most important of such provincial courts was that of Oudh, with its capital first at Faizabad and then at Lucknow. While the nawabs embraced European culture, they remained generous patrons of Indian artists, many of whom had probably migrated from Delhi and Agra. Those in Lucknow

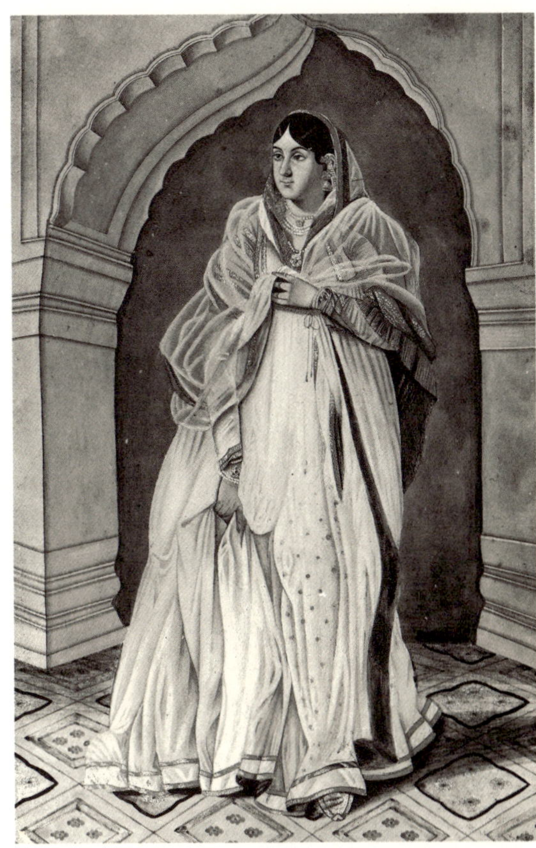

156. Anonymous (Lucknow). *Portrait of a Lady* (presumably after a painting by Tilly Kettle). c. 1780. Watercolor. Walter Collection.

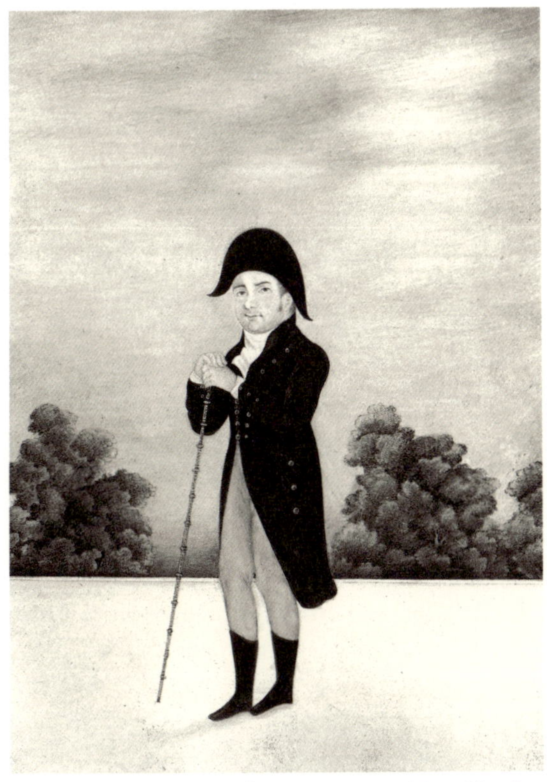

155. Anonymous (Delhi). *Portrait of Sir Charles Metcalfe.* c. 1830–40. Watercolor. Walter Collection.

were probably among the first to be exposed to British art. The majority of British artists, beginning with Tilly Kettle, went to Oudh at the end of the eighteenth century seeking their fortunes. Kettle was in Faizabad from 1772 to 1773, and Zoffany visited Lucknow between 1783 and 1789. Ozias Humphry, Charles Smith, the Daniells, Francesco Renaldi, George Place, Robert Home, and George Beechy were there as well. Home and Beechy were even court artists. Thus, Lucknow was continuously occupied by British artists from 1772 almost until 1857.

The Indian artists of Lucknow, therefore, directly observed British artists at work for at least two or three generations; they had to copy their paintings for almost as long, as many of the European patrons, such as Martin Gentil and Polier, wanted smaller versions for their own collections. Kettle's paintings appear to have been especially popular, though copies of other artists' works also exist. A large number were probably destroyed during the Mutiny. Figure 156 is a typical example of an Indian copy of a British painting, in this case one by Kettle. The identity of neither the subject nor the artist is known, but Kettle's characteristic style is evident in the background, the statuesque posture of the figure, and the treatment of her voluminous dress.

Among the most fascinating of such copies is a gouache done around 1815 by an unknown artist (fig. 157). A formal portrait, one of several that Kettle did of Nawab Shuja-ud-daula and his ten sons, it includes a self-portrait of the artist painting this very picture. From the way the artist has turned his head toward the viewer, it would seem as if he were following the instructions of a photographer. Even though the original is lost, there is no doubt about the "Indianness" of the copy. Wonderfully adroit at rendering details of architecture, jewelry, and dresses, the artist was not as skillful when it came to faces, which are almost expressionless. Very likely, also, the artist did not succeed in capturing the nuances of light and shade, or of the subtle tones of color. However, Kettle's paintings were oils, whereas this, as well as the majority of copies, was done in gouache; hence, the significant differences in texture which make the copies easily distinguishable.

In 1872, B. H. Baden-Powell, a civil servant and admirer of Indian handicrafts, made the following comments about Indian artists he observed while on duty in the Punjab:

[He] has an instinctive appreciation of colour, and, though without any knowledge of the principles which should regulate its use, is often more happy in his combinations than the educated workman of Europe. His colour is often exaggerated, but it is always warm, and rich and fearless. The native artist is also patient: for weeks and months he will work at his design, painfully elaborating the most minute details; no time is considered too long, no labour too intense to secure perfection in imitation or delicacy in execution. The greatest failing in native artists is their ignorance of perspective and drawing, and it is fortunate that this want is the most easily supplied.[5]

An anonymous artist's portrait of an unknown but beautiful Englishwoman, done around 1800 in the Kangra Valley which was then part of the Punjab, certainly lives up to Powell's appraisal (fig. 158). The work is not much larger than the miniatures on ivory by a talented British miniaturist like John Smart, and no less elegant. The oval frame is very likely copied from a miniature, and although the Kangra artist has selected a profile view in the customary manner, he has vividly captured the lady's delicate features and the tonality of her pale, white skin, almost as if he were copying an ivory. It is the kind of miniature that could easily have been, in the words of Sir Charles D'Oyly:

. . . chief to absent lovers dear, who gaze
Hours, days, and years, on imitative charms,
Press the cold ivory to their hearts, and raise
The image of their lost one to their arms.[6]

The ability of an Indian artist to master the Western techniques of realistic portraiture depended not only upon his own innate talent, but his opportunity to learn directly either from a British artist or from repeated copying of European works. The artist responsible for a stately and symbolic portrait of Nawab Ghazi-ud-din Haidar of Oudh was eminently successful in this (fig. 159). The rich use of shading in the nawab's garments and face, shown in three-quarter profile, reveals the artist's complete assimilation of European techniques. The details of the garments and ornaments are not as painstakingly rendered as was the practice in Mogul painting, but are suggested by more impressionistic brushstrokes. The cherubic angels holding the parasol above are obviously European, but the docile tiger and complacent goat in the foreground are symbols drawn from the Mogul artist's own repertoire. Their peaceful coexistence signifies the unflinching authority of the monarch in his kingdom.

It is very likely that the artist responsible for this watercolor was either copying a portrait by Robert Home, or had been trained by the Brit-

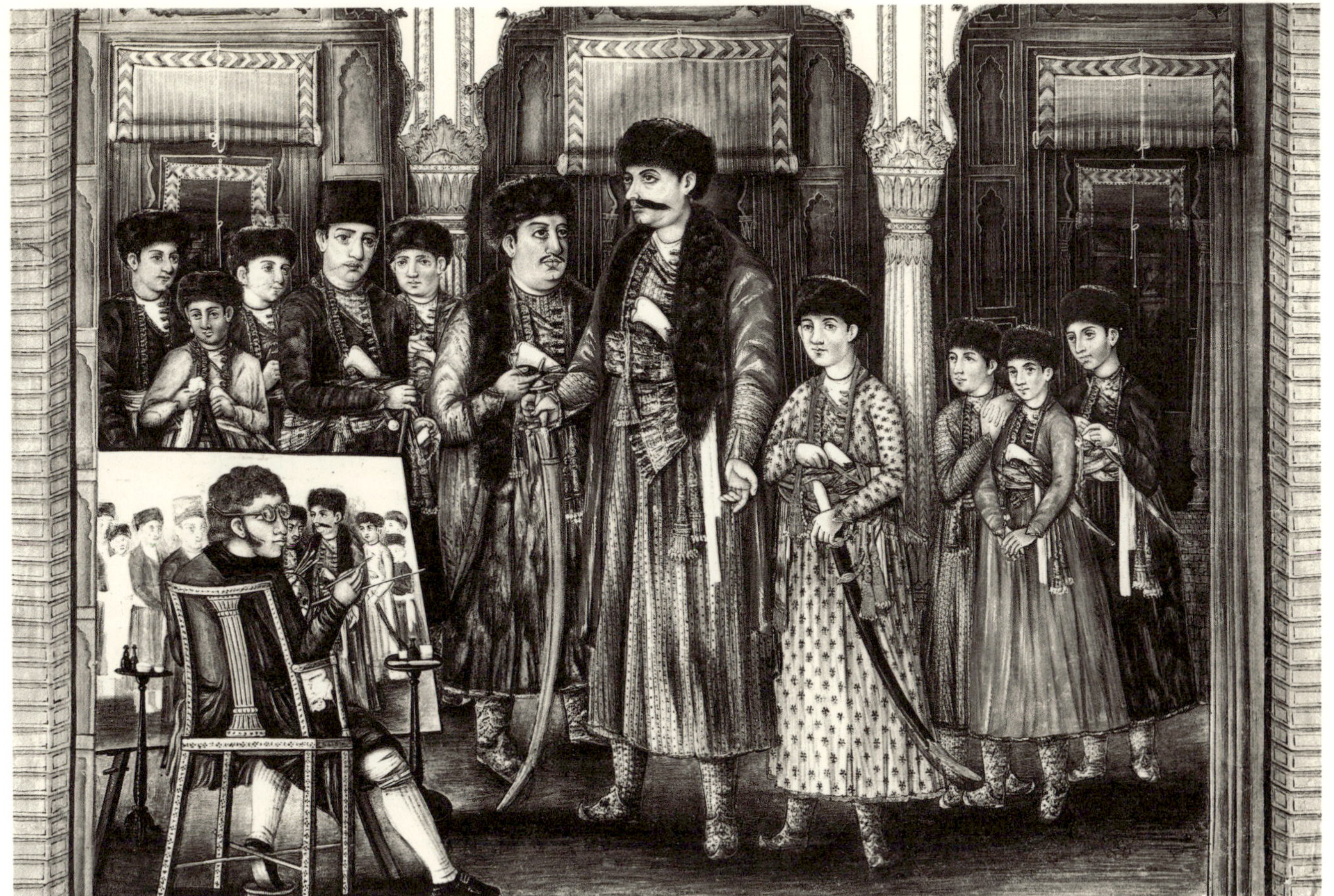

157. Anonymous (Lucknow). *Tilly Kettle Painting a Portrait of Shuja-ud-daula, Nawab of Oudh, with Ten Sons* after a painting by Tilly Kettle (1772). c. 1815. Gouache. By courtesy of the Board of Trustees of the Victoria and Albert Museum.

ish artist. Home was the court artist of Oudh for thirteen years beginning in August 1814. Ghazi-ud-din loved to have his own portrait drawn for presentation to visiting dignitaries, and this may have been intended for that purpose. The monarch's crown was designed by Robert Home after Ghazi-ud-din was formally crowned King of Oudh in 1819. In a durbar scene painted by Home at about the time this watercolor was done, the monarch is shown wearing the same robe and crown.[7] The date given at the bottom of the anonymous work may have some bearing on the precise dating of Home's formal portraits.

A less formal Lucknow portrait done around 1850 better demonstrates the degree of synthesis of the two pictorial traditions achieved by the Indian artists (fig. 160). The inscription identifies the figure as Mirza Bidar Bakht Sandhar Khan, who is shown seated on a couch with a lady, probably his *begum*. Both have their own hookahs and are being fanned by an attendant.

The lady seems to be more comfortable than the male whose posture is somewhat awkward. Interestingly, the artist has drawn the three faces in three different views—frontal, three-quarters, and full profile—almost as if he were eager to demonstrate his skill in this regard. He has successfully captured the character of his sitters. The background of pillars, lamps, looped curtains, and a view of the garden beyond is clearly derived from British painting. If the lady is indeed the gentleman's *begum*, then this must be regarded as a rare portrait of an upper-class Indian couple, for most such women would not have sat for even an Indian artist at that time.

III

THE British patrons of the Indian artists included the East India Company as well as individuals. The earliest examples of Company painting appear to have been produced in the south where Tanjore was the principal center; others included Madras, Trichinopoly, and

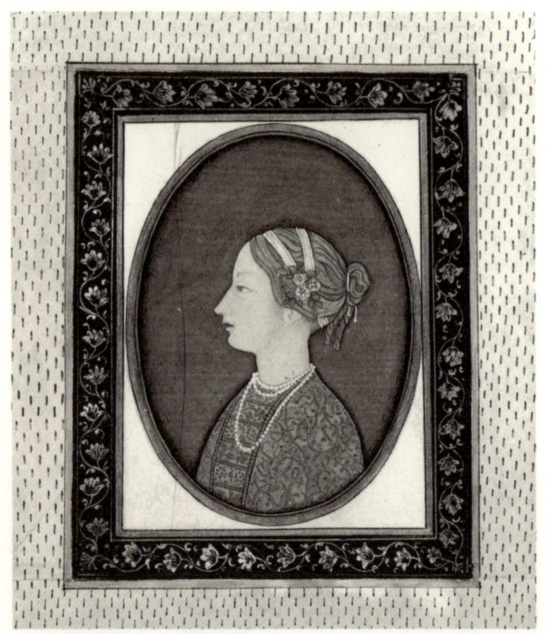

158. Anonymous (Kangra). *Portrait of an English-woman.* c. 1800. Watercolor and gold. Walter Collection.

Pudukkottai. In the north and east, the artists found patronage in most important British settlements like Calcutta, Patna, and Benares, but also in Murshidabad and Lucknow, as well as in places like Cuttack and Chapra. Artists in Delhi and Agra, and in the Punjab, adopted the style early in the nineteenth century. Western Indian artists appear to have been slow in accepting the new trends, for most Company school paintings in that region were done after 1850. Although regional differences are discernible, especially between the north and the south, due largely to ethnic distinctions as well as various local styles, most Company paintings reflect a stylistic unity that can be attributed both to the uniform taste of the patrons as well as the subject matter.

Most paintings, whether in the north or south, depict trades and crafts, flora and fauna, festivals and deities, costumes and conveyances—all subjects of ethnographic interest. The earlier pictures clearly reflect the British curiosity about India, paralleling in many ways the works of a Forbes or an Eden, who recorded the various ethnic groups. Although much of the mate-

rial is of great ethnographic significance, especially as India is changing rapidly today and many of the trades and crafts have been abandoned, the products of the more gifted artists are aesthetically appealing as well. The unknown artist of Malabar, on the southwestern coast, who painted a series of watercolors of ethnographic interest, was obviously a very talented draftsman (fig. 161). He had mastered European techniques—especially the rich use of shading to suggest volume and mood—so well that he seems to have also acquired a classical conceptualization in the execution of the figures. This artist seems to have been exceptionally gifted in comparison to others who concentrated on similar subjects.

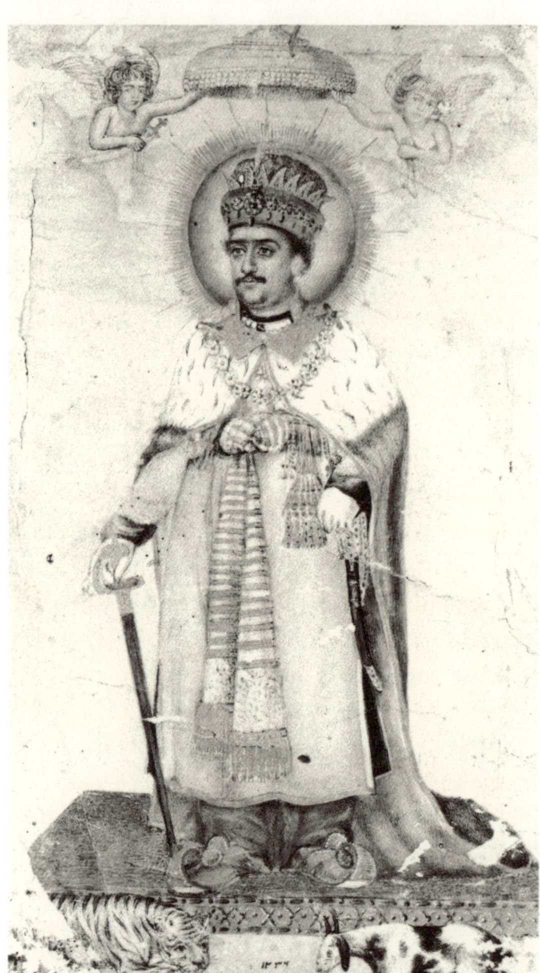

159. Anonymous (Lucknow). *Nawab Ghazi-ud-din Haidar of Oudh.* 1820. Pencil and watercolor. Collection of Edwin Binney, 3rd.

Indian artists were employed to record both historic occasions and the domestic lives of their patrons. The events that were usually recorded were visits to native courts by British dignitaries, scenes of entertainment, and ceremonial processions with British participants. The anonymous watercolor in figure 162 shows Nawab Wajid Ali Shah, King of Oudh (r. 1847–56), embracing the governor-general Lord Hardinge who visited the state in 1847. Such pictures usually depict banquet or durbar scenes, but this one shows the two rulers in an atypical embrace. The Indian artist gave his monarch prominence and emphasized the somewhat stiff, formal postures of the British officers.

After 1857, when India was no longer mysterious and photography had become commonplace, interest in ethnographic subjects seems to have been replaced by a more personal desire to record one's own environment, such as one's bungalows and servants. Not surprisingly, Indian artists were not encouraged to do portraits

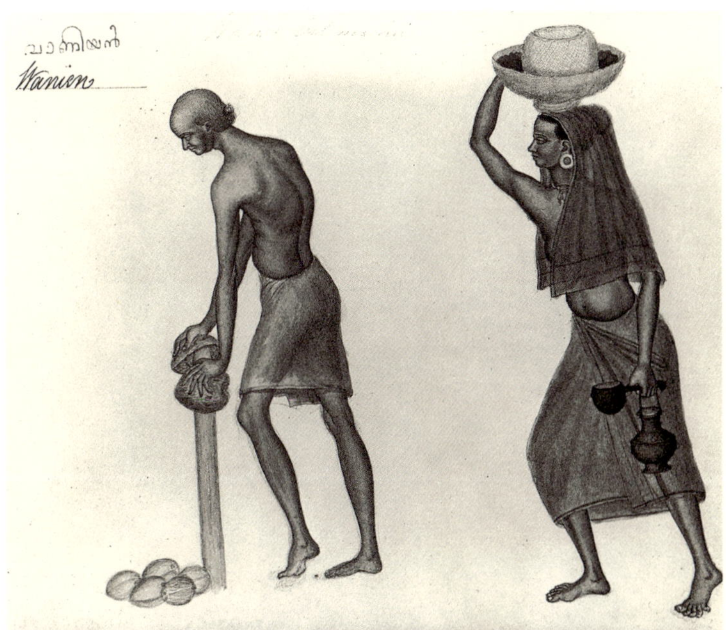

161. Anonymous (Malabar). *Coconut Seller and Woman Vendor*. c. 1820. Watercolor. Los Angeles County Museum of Art. Gift of Edwin Binney, 3rd.

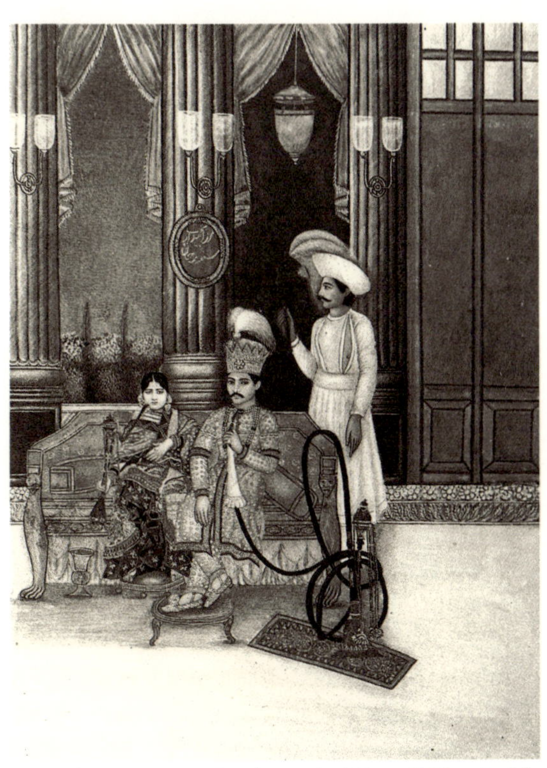

160. Anonymous (Lucknow). *Mirza Bidar Bakht Sandhar Khan and Wife*. c. 1850. Watercolor. Collection of Edwin Binney, 3rd.

or landscapes. In drawing monuments and copying designs of buildings, however, their skill was unquestionable, as evidenced by the exquisitely detailed rendering of the interior of the mausoleum of Itimad-ud-daula in Agra by an unknown artist (colorplate 11). No one could fault this artist for his draftsmanship or his skill in "perspective." Such depictions of the monuments of Delhi and Agra were very likely done for visitors to these places.

Although the Company itself was not interested in art for art's sake, it did employ Indian artists to help its officers make maps and prepare architectural drawings. Official surveys and missions often needed draftsmen and the Indian artists recruited were trained by the officers in Western methods. Drawings for the buildings raised by the British were also often prepared by Indian draftsmen. As Mildred Archer has noted, Markham Kittoe is still remembered in Benares "for the way in which he trained Benares painters to help him with designs for the new Sanskrit College and for his record of local monuments and sculpture."[8]

159

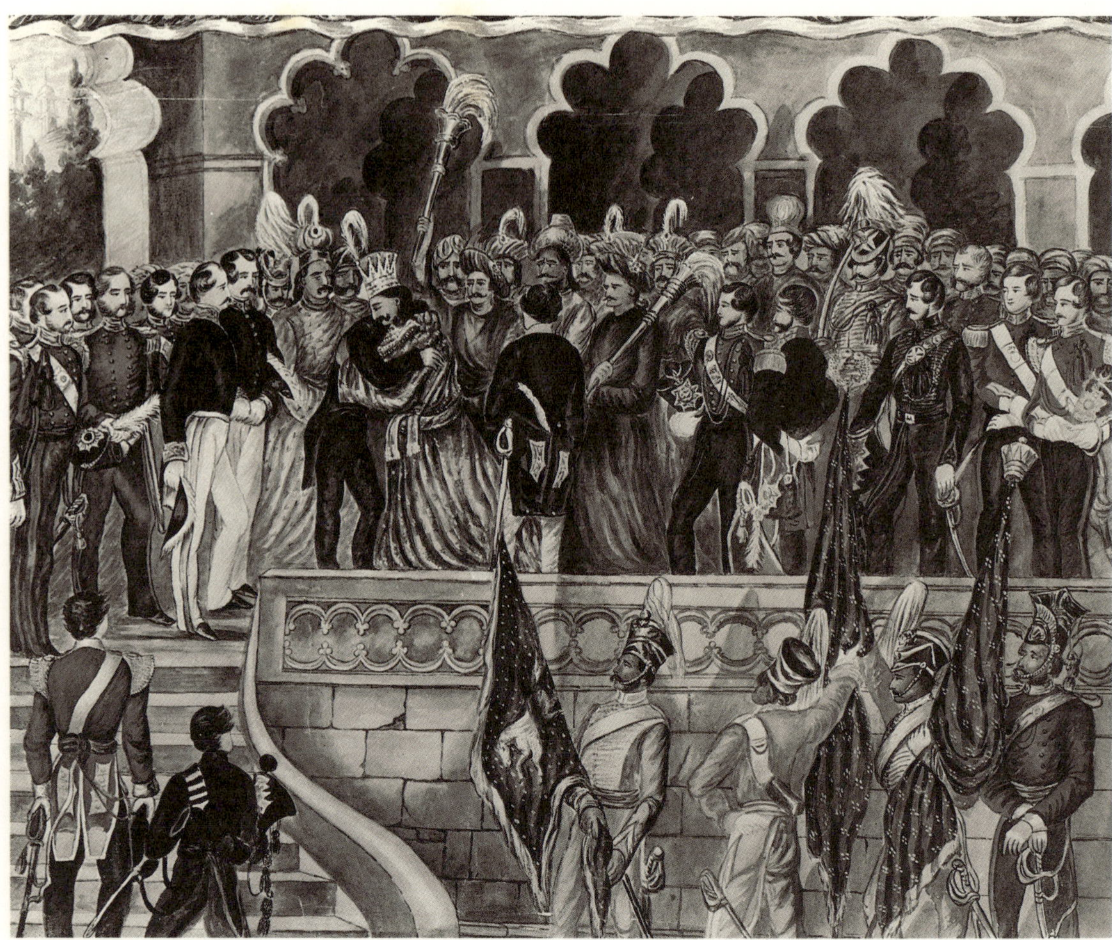

162. Anonymous (Lucknow). *Nawab Wajid Ali Shah Embracing Lord Hardinge*. 1847. Watercolor. Reproduced by permission of the India Office Library and Records (British Library).

Indian artists were also employed by such Company institutions as the Sibpur Botanical Garden near Calcutta and the Barrackpore Menagerie, a favorite of Wellesley. An ardent enthusiast of natural history, Wellesley established the menagerie and aviary between 1800 and 1804, and had the Company hire Indian artists to draw and describe the wildlife.

The British appear to have been primarily interested in pictures accurately depicting the trades and crafts, as well as the processions and festivals, which they probably took home as "photographs" of their days in India. Most could not afford works by professional British artists, who were few in number anyway, and had no access to the works of amateur artists as these were generally not sold. Aquatints and engravings by British artists were available, but in limited quantities and subjects. And, owning a series of engravings of the castes and customs of the Hindus by a British artist was not quite the same as retaining or commissioning a competent Indian artist to do a series of pictures according to the owner's precise needs. Moreover, Indian artists must have been relatively inexpensive. We do not know what they were paid, but an individual could not have received much more than a hundred rupees a year, which is the sum the Company paid an artist who accompanied Francis Buchanan on his statistical survey of the Bengal Presidency in the early 1800s. It is also known that there were talented freelance artists like Muhammad Amir of Karraya who went from door to door seeking work.

Many of the so-called ethnographic or human interest pictures are fairly straightforward

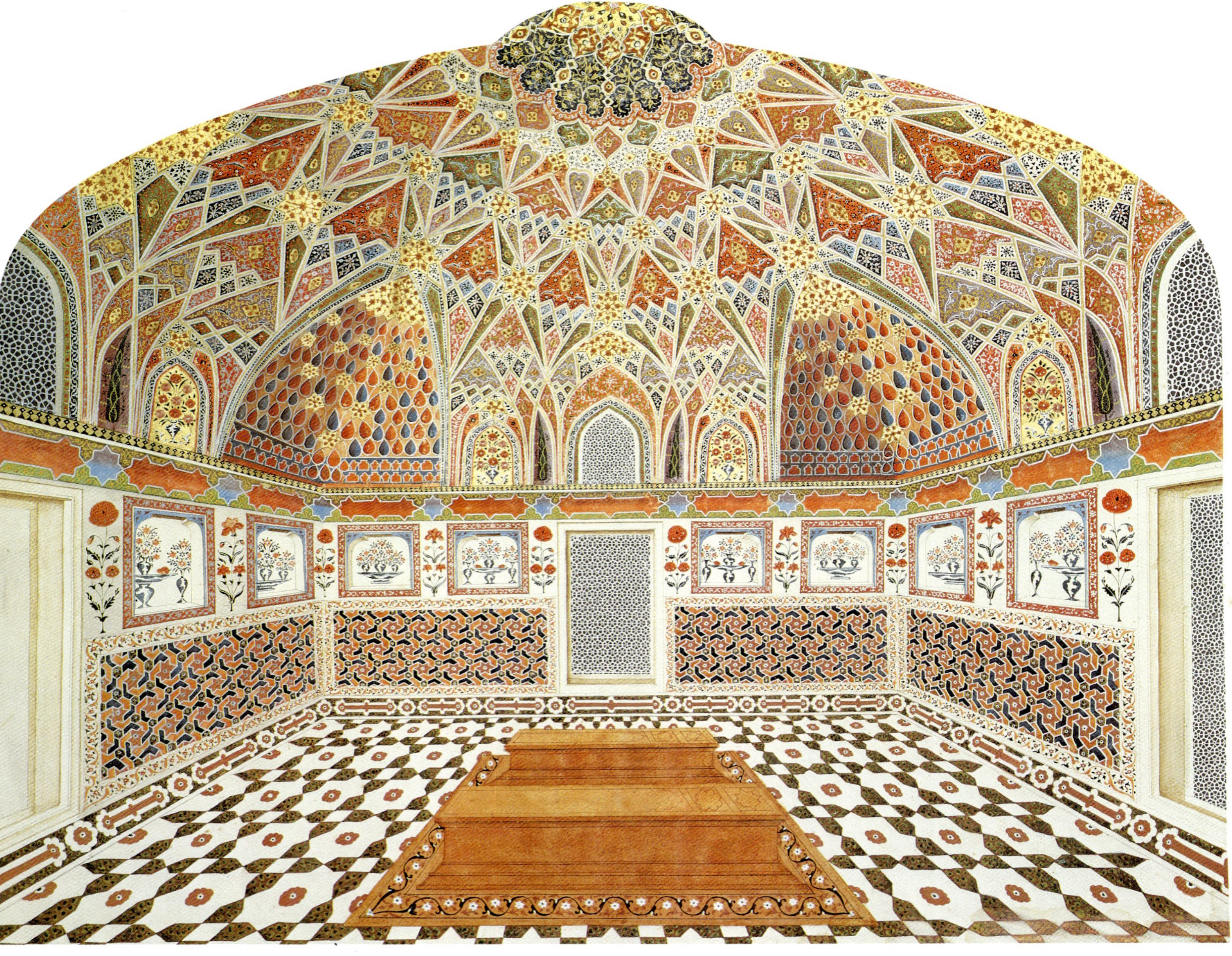

COLORPLATE 11.
Anonymous (Agra). *Interior of the Tomb of Itimad-ud-daula.* c. 1830.
Watercolor heightened with gold. Walter Collection.

representations such as the picture of tumblers in figure 164 by a competent south Indian artist, circa 1850. Their quality probably depended very much upon how discriminating the patron was or how much he was willing to pay. When Valentine Prinsep criticized the Delhi artist Ismael Khan's work, the old man defended himself by saying, "These are done for the *sahibs* who do not understand. I know they are wrong, but what does it matter? No one cares."[9] There must have been a general state of apathy in India, especially in Delhi, toward traditional arts and crafts in the 1870s. Indian patrons had disappeared from the scene, and even the maharajas and nawabs were abandoning their interest in Indian art and were mimicking their imperial overlords by building new Western-style palaces and decorating them with En-

glish furnishings, pictures, and objets d'art. Ismael Khan was stating the truth when he said that all sahibs were not necessarily connoisseurs. The majority of Company school pictures, especially of the trades and professions, are indeed devoid of great artistic merit or ingenuity.

Apart from watercolors on paper, the Company artists painted on both ivory and mica, which became rather popular around 1850. Among the most popular subjects were the Mogul emperors and empresses and the monuments of Delhi and Agra on miniature oval ivories mounted on carved wooden frames. A less conventional subject is the beautifully painted nude on ivory (fig. 165). Two paintings on mica, one of the Moslem festival known as the Mohurrum, and the other of the more bi-

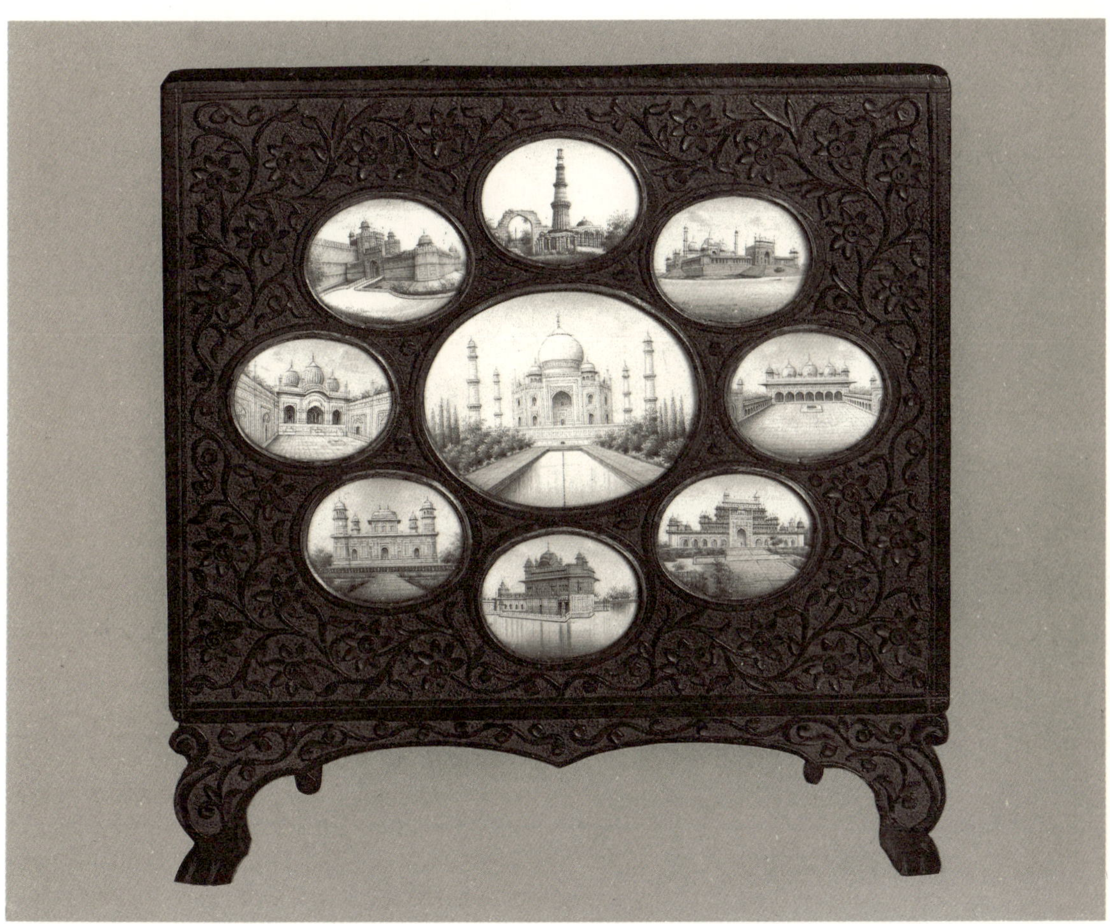

163. Anonymous. *Principal Monuments of India, including the Taj Mahal.* 19th century. Oil on ivory, mounted on ebony frame. Los Angeles County Museum of Art. Gift of Albert G. Wassenich.

zarre Hindu festival of Charak (hook-swinging)
that simultaneously revolted and intrigued the
British, are characteristic examples of the type
of festival pictures that the British patrons took
back home (figs. 166, 167). Sewak Ram of
Patna was a much sought after painter of processions and festivals and many of his pictures
belonged to the first Earl of Minto, governor-
general from 1807 to 1813. His version of the
Mohurrum, when contrasted with the more
commercial painting on mica, reveals how the
same subject can become a visual delight in the
hands of a gifted artist (fig. 168).

Undoubtedly, the *tour de force* among Company genre paintings are the recently dispersed
pictures from what has come to be known as

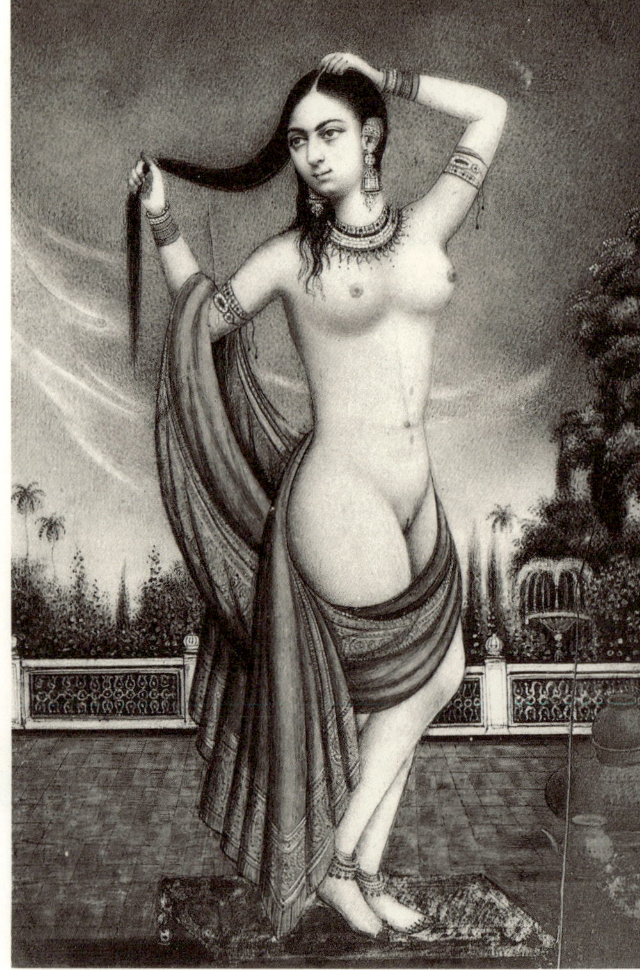

165. Anonymous (Delhi). *Nude*. c. 1830. Ivory.
Walter Collection.

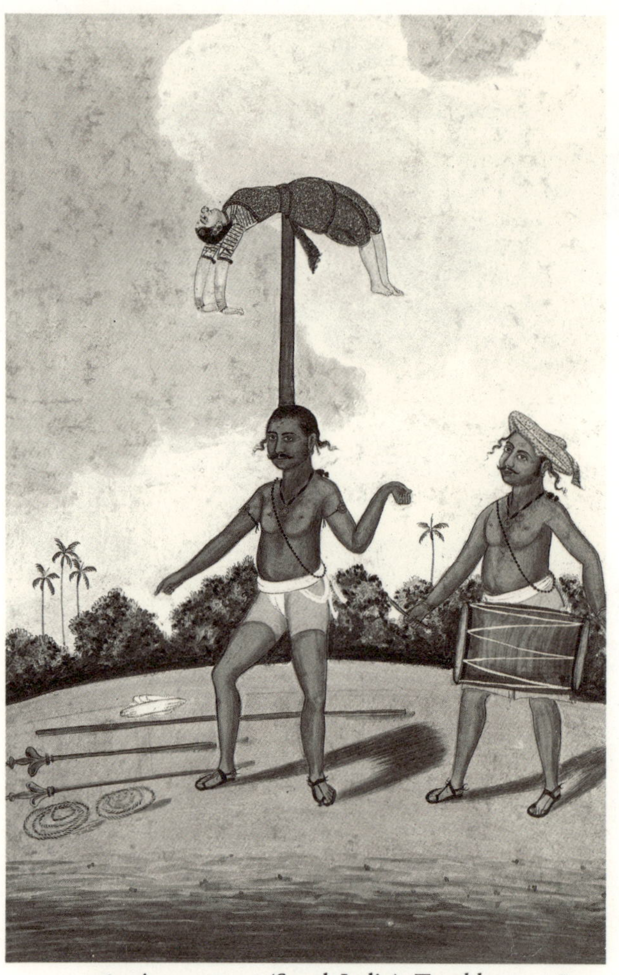

164. Anonymous (South India). *Tumblers*. c. 1850.
Watercolor. Los Angeles County Museum of
Art.

the Fraser Album. Colorplate 12 and figure 169
from this album show a recruit for the famous
Skinner's Horse, a local set of troopers, and a
group of six Afghans. The younger brother of
the amateur artist James Ballie Fraser, William
Fraser (1784–assassinated 1835), who presumably commissioned the album, had an interesting career in India, working with such no-
table personalities as Sir David Ochterlony,
Monstuart Elphinstone, and the colorful Colonel James Skinner, the son of a Scottish officer
and a Rajput woman. He was a close friend of
Skinner, whom he accompanied on a journey to
the Himalayas along with an artist generally
identified as Ghulam 'Ali Khan, although this is
uncertain.

162

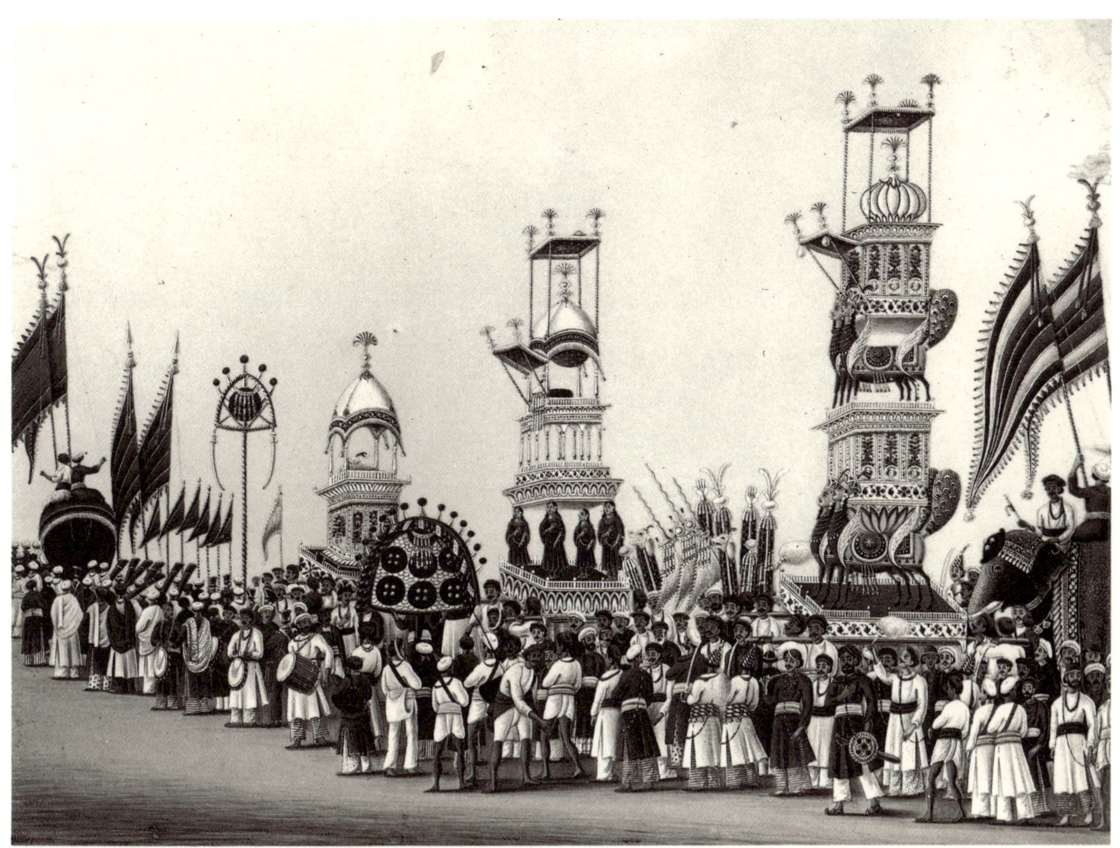

166. Anonymous (Patna). *Mohurrum*. c. 1820. Mica. Walter Collection.

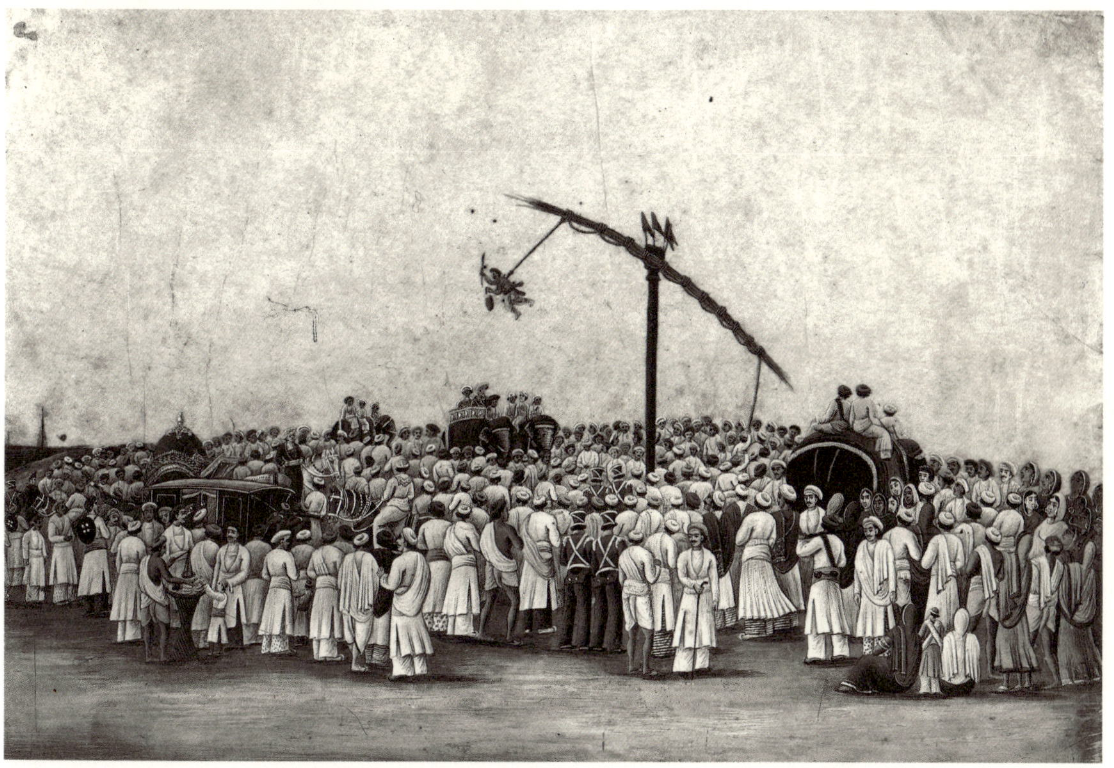

167. Anonymous (Patna). *Hook-Swinging* (Charak). c. 1820. Mica. Walter Collection.

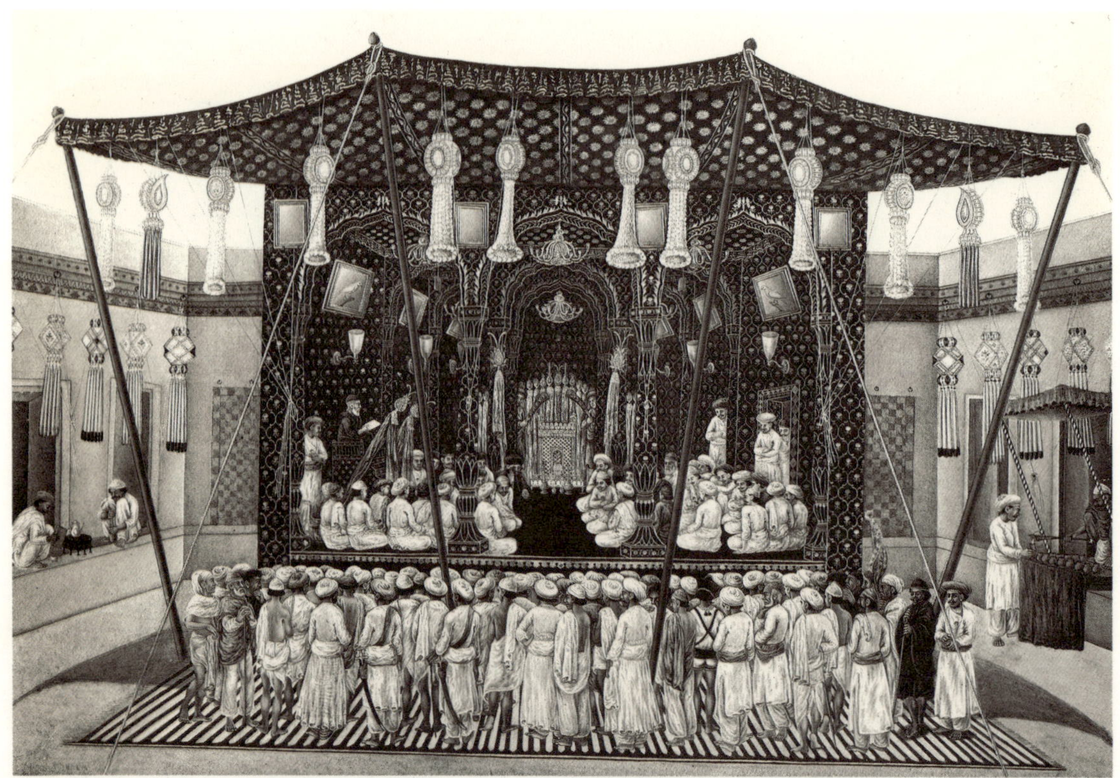

168. Sewak Ram. *Mohurrum*. Before 1819. Watercolor and gold. Walter Collection.

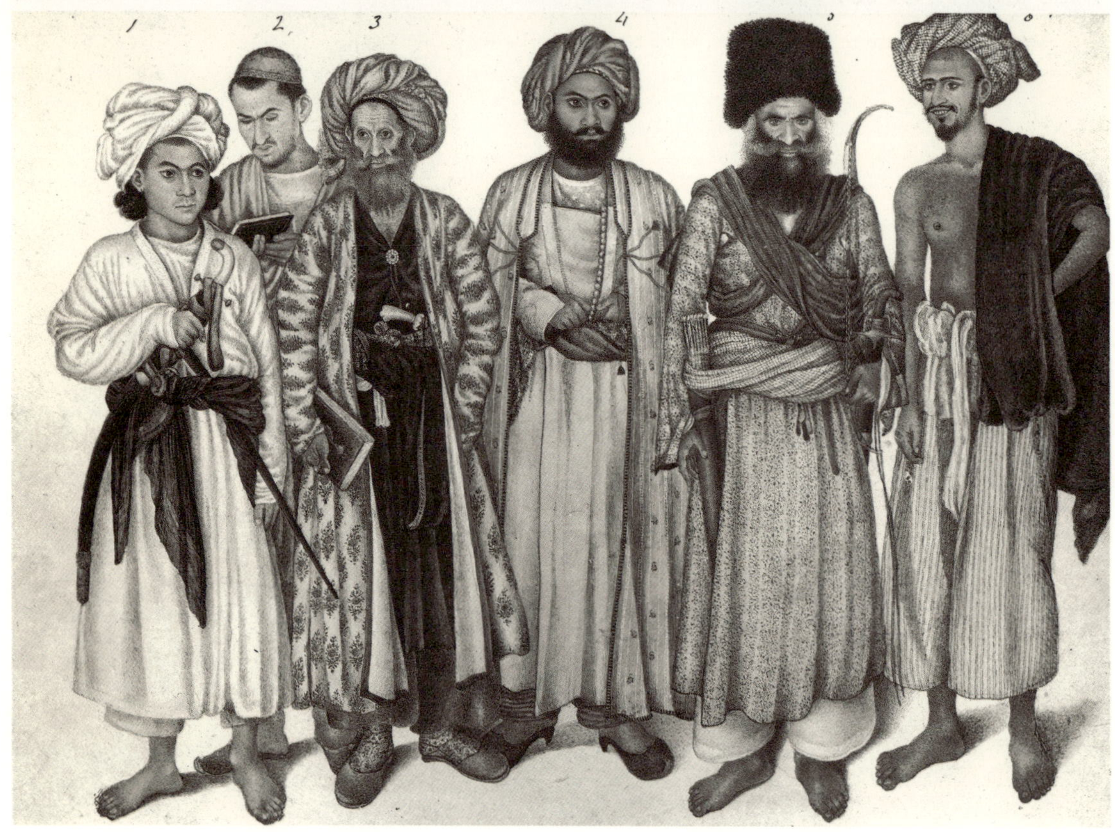

169. Anonymous (Delhi). *Six Afghans*. c. 1820–30. Watercolor. Walter Collection.

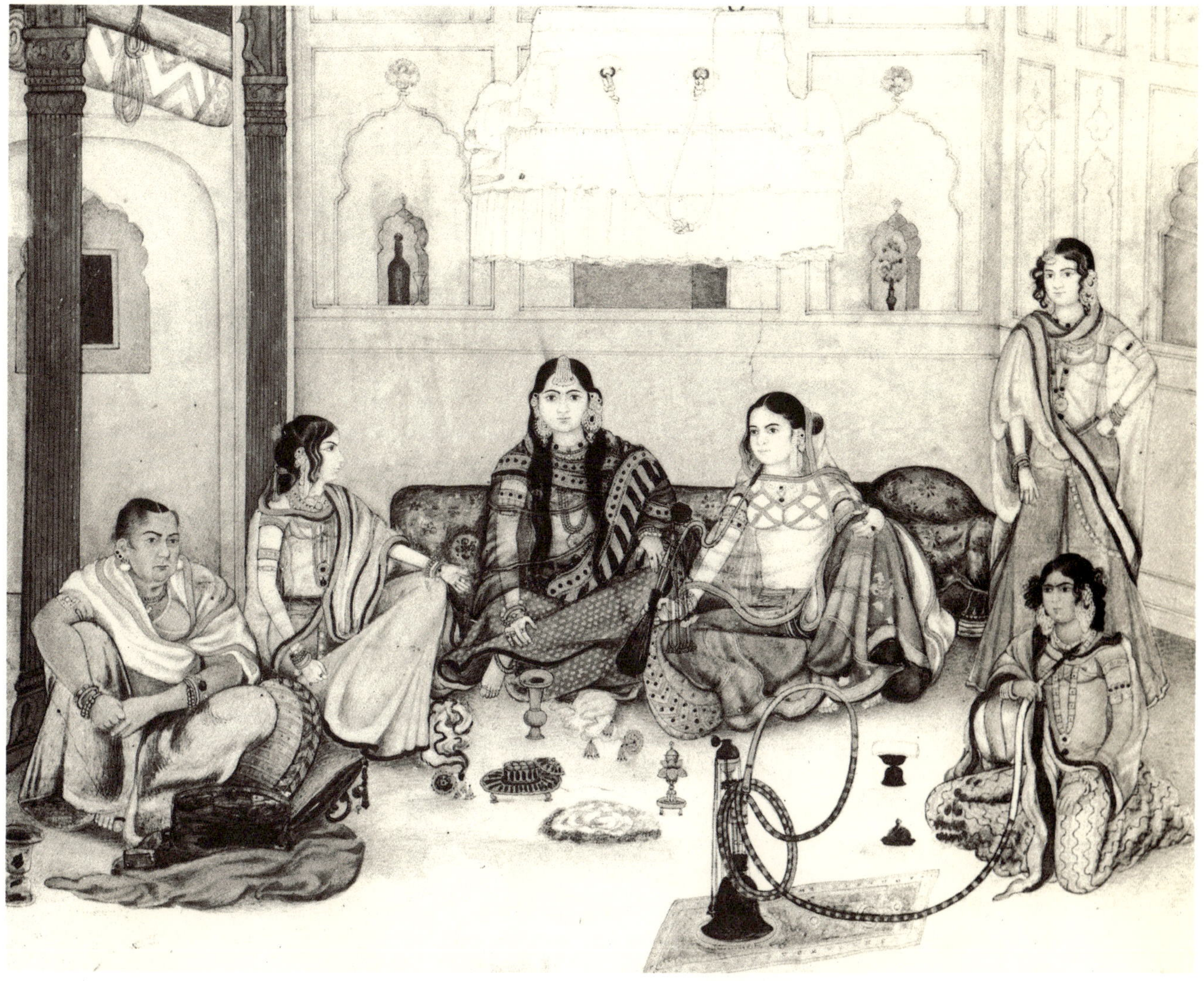

170. Ghulam 'Ali Khan. *Harem Scene*. c. 1820. Watercolor. Collection of Edwin Binney, 3rd.

Ghulam 'Ali Khan was *the* genius among all artists who worked for the Company. In modifying his style for his British patrons, he had sacrificed nothing of his innate sense of color, faultless draftsmanship, complete understanding of human anatomy, and empathy for his sitters. Like the Fraser album pictures, Ghulam 'Ali Khan's harem scene is characterized by technical virtuosity and effortless elegance (fig. 170). If, indeed, this is a harem scene, rather than a group of nautch girls, it is an extremely rare representation. It is unlikely that Ghulam 'Ali Khan had such an intimate glimpse of the *zenana*, but there is little doubt these portraits are drawn from life.

IV

THE first Briton to employ Indian artists to record natural history subjects appears to have been Mary, the wife of Sir Elijah Impey, the first chief justice of the Supreme Court of Calcutta. She maintained a menagerie in Calcutta and loved Indian birds and animals. Three artists, all natives of Patna, worked for her on a series of nature studies which numbered 200 by the time the Impeys returned to England in 1783. The principal artist was Shaikh Zayn-al-din; the other two were Bhawanidas and Ramdas. These three artists from Patna had moved to Calcutta in search of patronage which indicates how the Indian artists moved about from one British

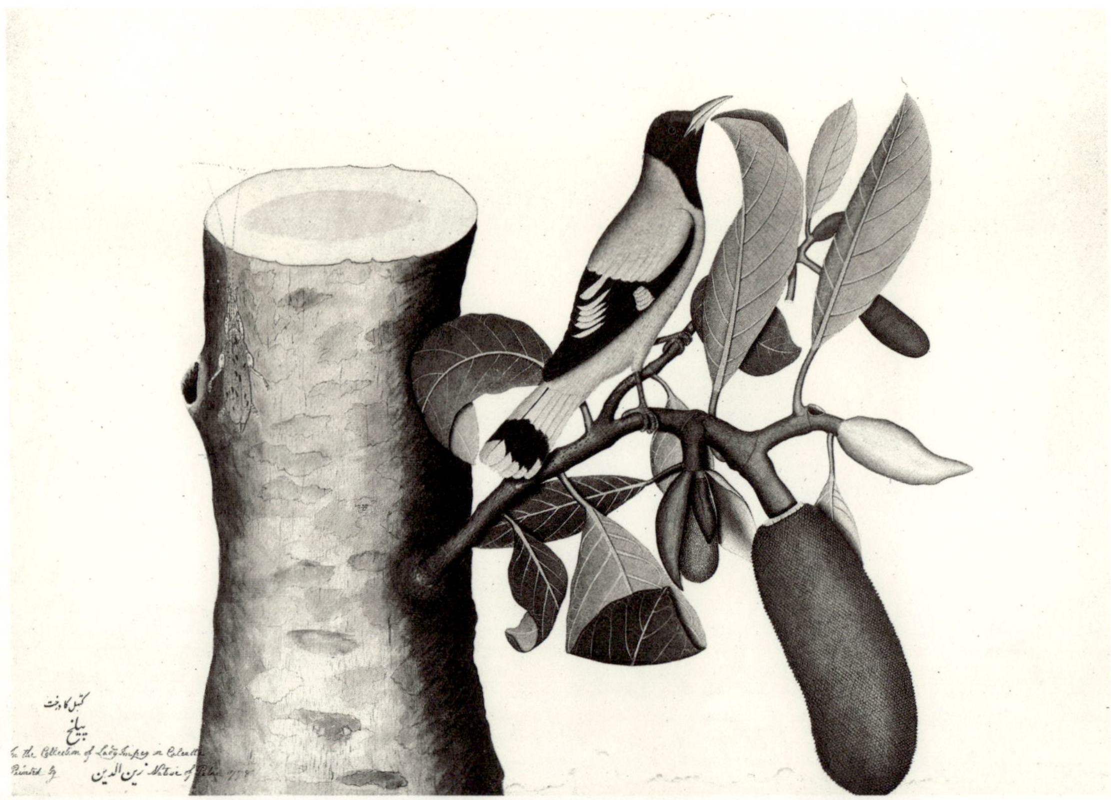

171. Shaikh Zayn-al-din. *Lady Impey's Bird.* 1778. Watercolor. Walter Collection.

settlement to another, just as the professional British artists did in the same period.

Shaikh Zayn-al-din and his colleagues were part of a long tradition; some of their ancestors had worked for the Mogul emperor Jahangir, drawing his animals, birds, and plants from life. The genre continued to appeal to later patrons of Mogul painting as well, and some of the finest surviving paintings were done for the hapless prince Dara Shikoh and are now in the India Office Library in London.[10] The later Indian artists may have had finer technical skills or perhaps a more acute sense of realism gained through consulting such works as Edward's *A Natural History of Birds* (1745–51) or Latham's *A General Synopsis of Birds* (1781–1802), but this was already a firmly established art form in their culture.

Although the best known, Lady Impey was not the only British admirer of Indian flora and fauna. While the three artists from Patna were working for her, an unknown artist in Lucknow produced a monumental and wonderfully perceptive picture of a stork (fig. 173). Note how the artist has not neglected to add the shadow

cast by the bird. Figure 174 is a charming picture of two views of an insect done around 1820 by Seetu Ram, although it is not known exactly where he worked and for whom. The heightened sense of realism or naturalism acquired by Indian artists working for British patrons is evident in a wonderful depiction of a *Horse and Groom* by a noted Calcutta painter, Shaikh Muhammad Amir of Karraya from around 1845 (fig. 175). A comparison with a fine rendering of a horse by one of his forbears clearly demonstrates how easily Muhammad Amir had adapted to the tastes of the new masters. Not only had he completely mastered the techniques of foreshortening and shading to make his representation more naturalistic, he had studied the animal's anatomy and reproduced it as accurately—and attractively—as any Victorian English horse painter.

Shaikh Zayn-al-din also drew plants and again his Mogul inheritance served him well. As with animals and birds, many botanical pictures were by Indian artists trained by British patrons. The tradition seems to have begun with William Rosburgh (1751–1815), who initiated

166

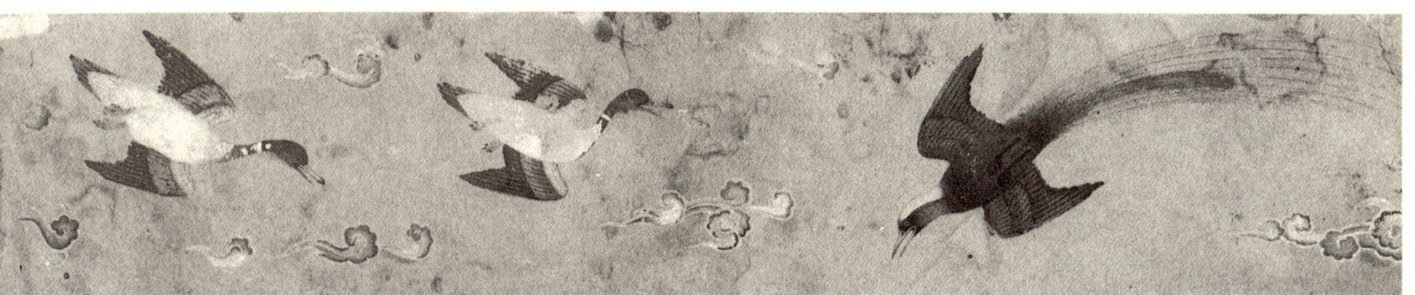

172. Anonymous (Mogul). *Birds* (detail from *Shah Jehan with Two Princes and an Attendant*). c. 1640. Watercolor. Los Angeles County Museum of Art. Nasli and Alice Heeramaneck Collection.

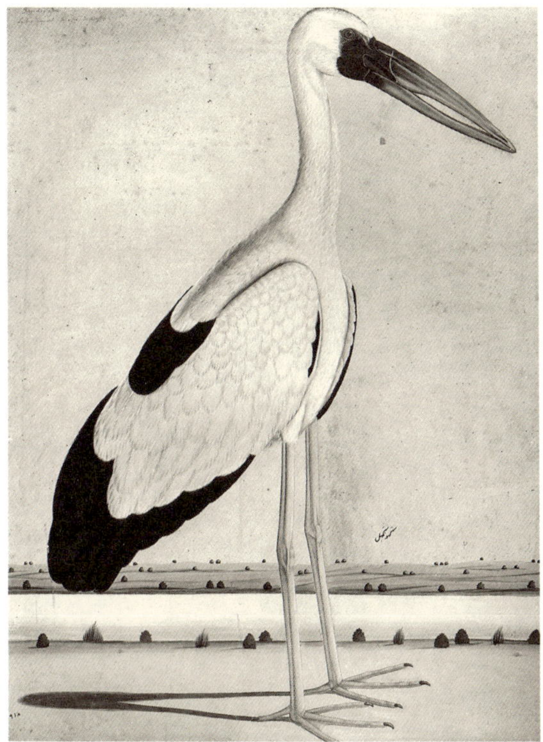

173. Anonymous (Lucknow). *The Stork*. 1780. Watercolor. Walter Collection.

Indian artists in Madras between 1789 and 1793 in making botanical studies. Rosburgh was the Company botanist in Madras. Some three hundred drawings were made by unknown native artists under his direction and were engraved by various English artists for the *Plants of the Coast of Coromandel*, published between 1795 and 1820.

Although much of the material was produced for scientific purposes, it is of artistic merit as well. The paintings are as vibrant and fresh as

nature's originals. The same delicacy, sparkling colors, and exquisite finish that characterize the finest Mogul flower paintings were now combined with a keener sense of observation in the name of greater scientific accuracy to produce series after series of botanical paintings that were among the crowning achievements of the Company school. An unknown artist's meticulously accurate but sensuous study of the lotus, the most admired and sacred of the Indian flowers, was one of the many beautiful botanical studies done for the Marquis of Wellesley (fig. 177). Equally skillful, observant, and imaginative was the south Indian artist Rungia Raju, who was retained for two years by M. E. Grant Duff, governor of Madras between 1881 and 1886, to prepare three botanical albums.

V

WHILE Ghulam 'Ali Khan and Shaikh Muhammad Amir of Karraya were painting in a sophisticated manner that successfully combined Western techniques with Indian vision, a completely different style was developed in Calcutta that has come to be known as the Kalighat school. It is so named because the school originated around the well-known temple of Kali in south Calcutta, although Kalighat-style paintings may have been done in other parts of the city as well. The principal patrons of Kalighat paintings were not the British, but Indian pilgrims who flocked to the temple every day. Nevertheless, the British did collect them and took them back to Britain, as is known from the large extant number of them there and the

167

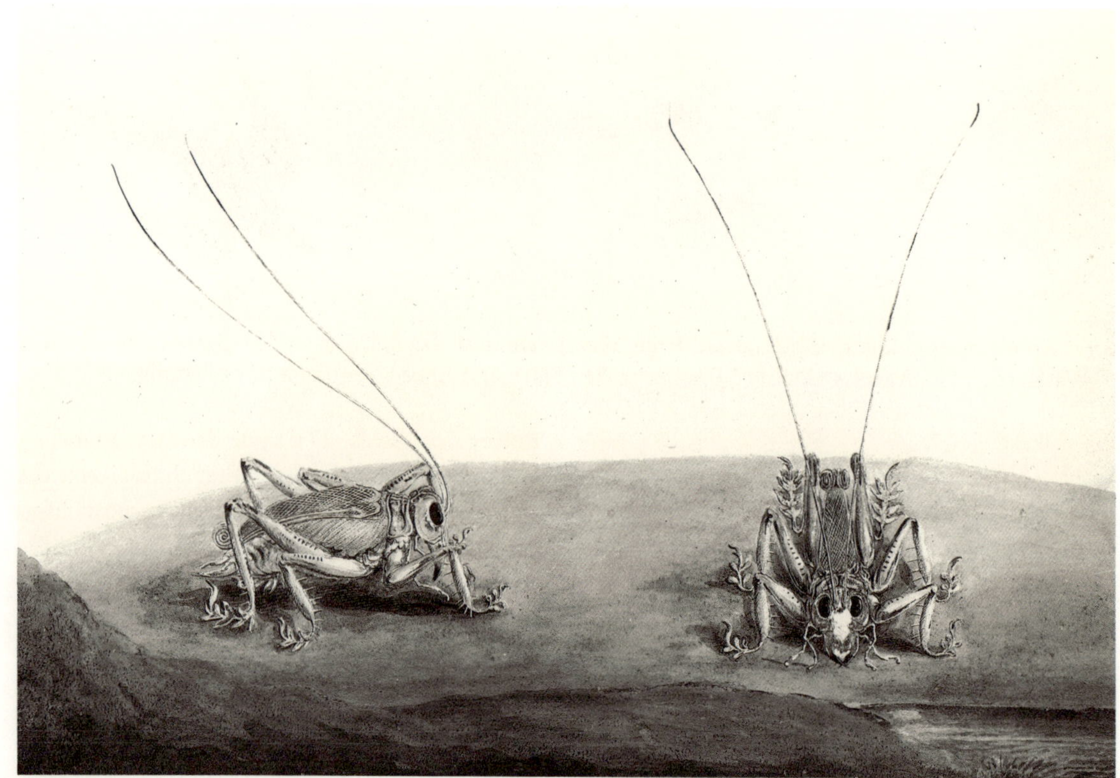

174. Seetu Ram. *Exotic Insect: Two Views.* c. 1820. Watercolor. Walter Collection.

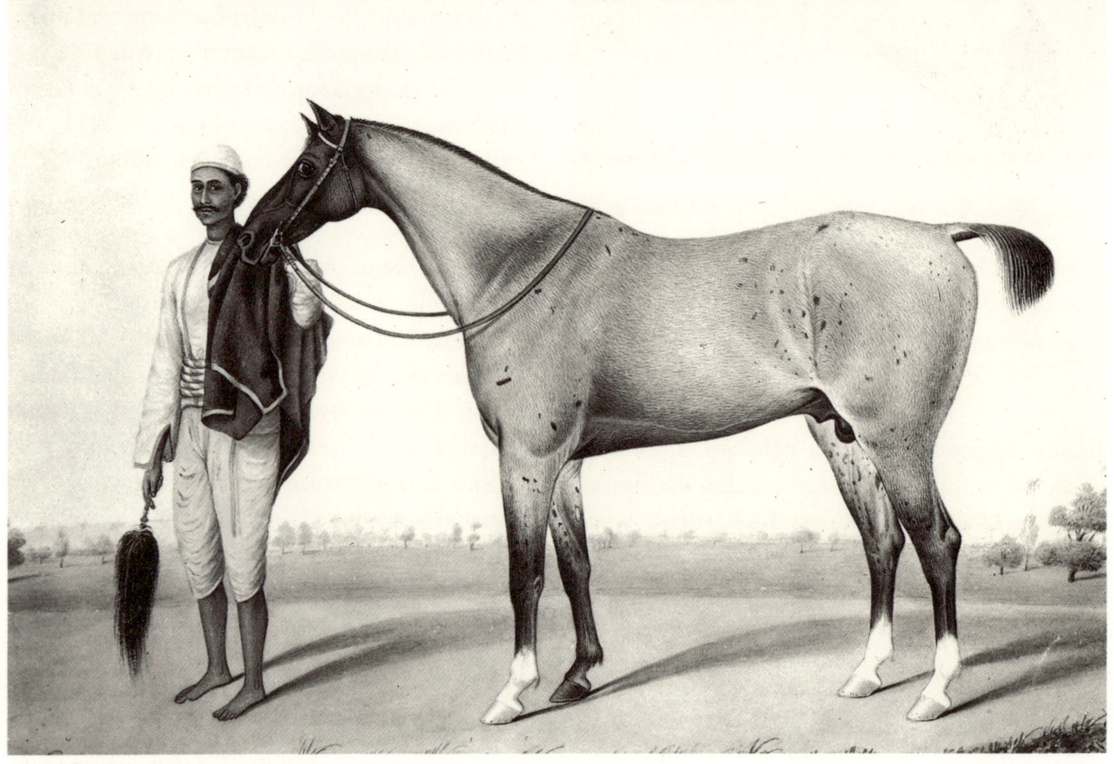

175. Shaikh Muhammad Amir of Karraya. *Horse and Groom.* c. 1845. Watercolor. Reproduced by permission of the India Office Library and Records (British Library).

168

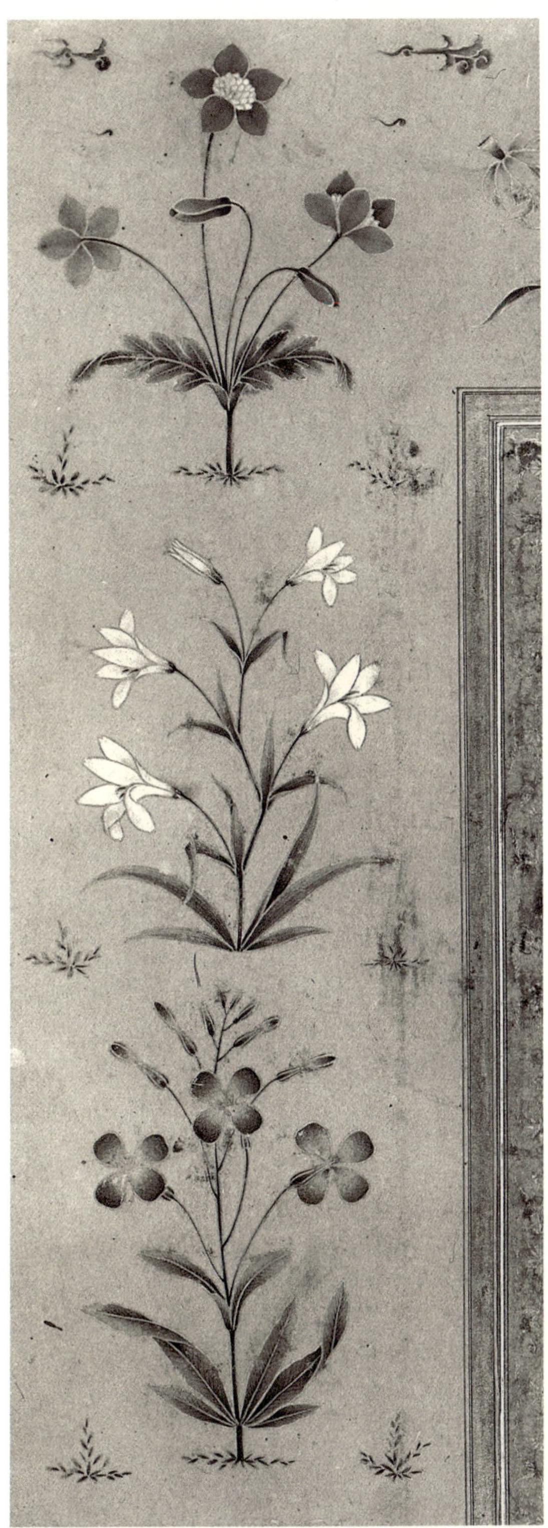

176. Anonymous. *Border with flower studies* (detail from an album assembled for Shah Jehan). 1640–50. Ink, watercolor, and gold. Los Angeles County Museum of Art. Nasli and Alice Heeramaneck Collection.

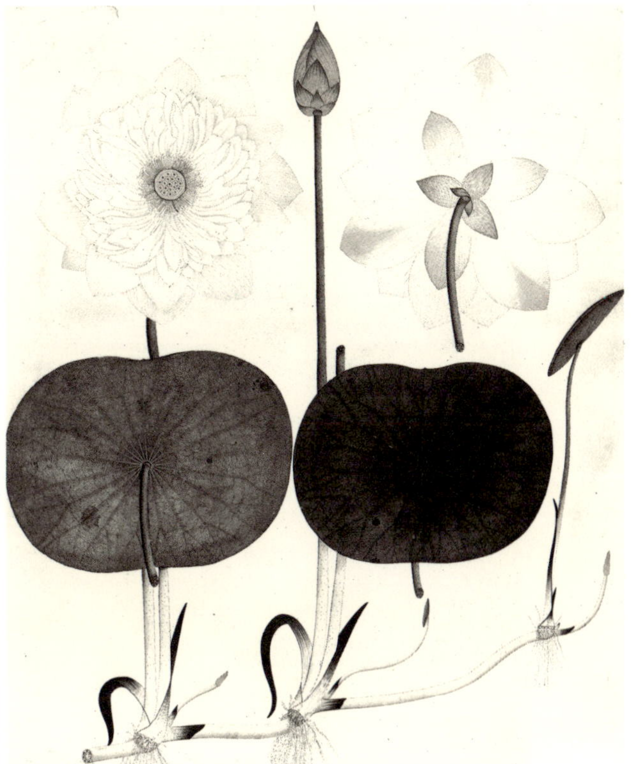

177. Anonymous (Shibpur). *White Lotus.* c. 1800. Fogg Art Museum, Harvard University. Gift of Eric Schroder.

frequent notations in English on the works themselves.

One of the first Europeans who recorded his reactions to Kalighat painting was Egron Lundgren, who had come to India in 1858 to report on the Mutiny. While in Calcutta, he visited a Kali temple to watch the Hindus celebrate the new year and noticed small pictures of gods on sale beneath the trees. "I bought some of these works of art painted with gaudy, bright colours and silver on thin, fine hemp paper." [11] He seems to have found similar paintings in other parts of Calcutta and even visited an artist who showed him more pictures of Hindu mythological subjects: Ganesh, Krishna, and Siva, "hunting gazelles in verdigris-green forests where golden-yellow tigers lurked with silver claws and navy blue tails." Lundgren was mystified by the complex iconography and found the compositions strange, but admired the works nonetheless. Another artist who collected Kalighat paintings

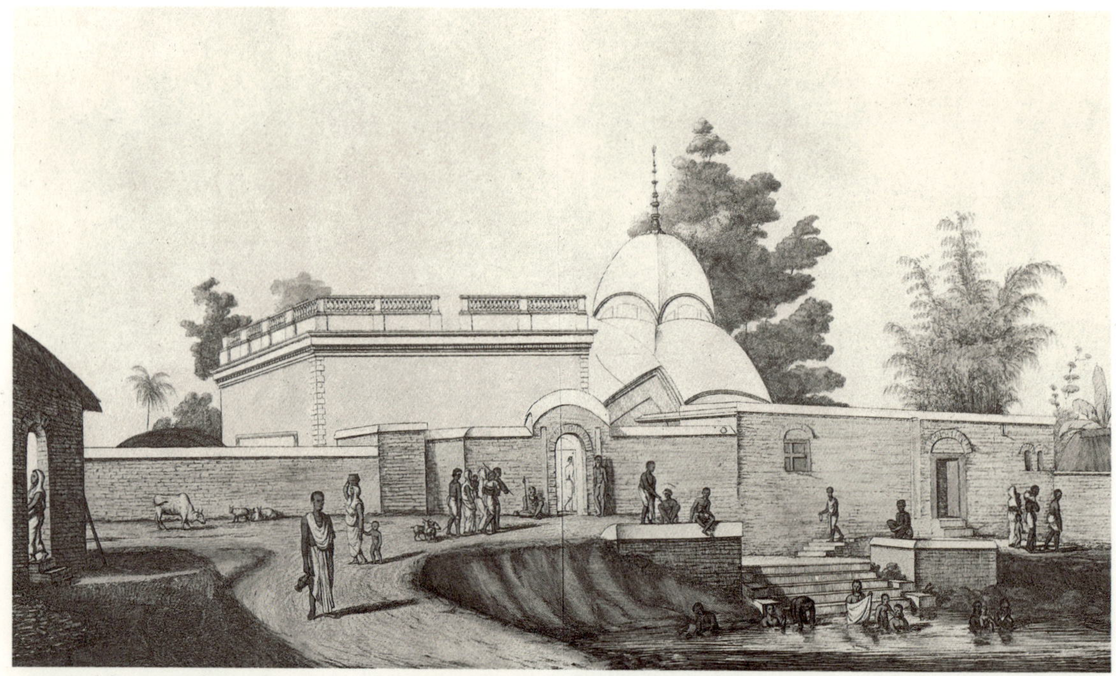

178. Balthazar Solvyns. *A View of the Pagoda of Calleegaut* from *The Hindoos*. 1807. Engraving. The Thomas John Willis Collection.

was J. Lockwood Kipling, who was the principal of Lahore's art school for many years. (His collection was later given to the Victoria & Albert Museum in London by his son Rudyard.) While Kipling may have collected the pictures for aesthetic reasons, most British probably bought them as souvenirs. A large number were bought by missionaries and taken back to Britain to demonstrate how uncivilized the natives were, how grotesque their gods were, and how imperative it was to spread Christianity.

Of all the gods, Kali struck the British as the most gruesome and remained a formidable presence in their imagination. Human sacrifices at Kali temples in Calcutta and elsewhere in Bengal were common, and she was the patron goddess not only of the city but also of the infamous thugs who were a menace to the British and the natives alike until they were suppressed. Almost every Anglo-Indian who kept a journal had something to say about Kali, and although the British artists do not appear to have been too preoccupied with her, Kalighat pictures of the goddess were acquired by many Anglo-Indians during their sojourn in Calcutta. Many

probably visited the temple, and so powerful was her cult, that it is even believed that British merchants and others secretly sent offerings to the goddess for special favors. The Kali temple at Bow Bazar is commonly known as "Firingi Kali" because Indian Christians and Eurasians visited it until recent times, especially during pox and cholera epidemics, the word *firingi* being generally used for Europeans.

A slightly amusing but vivid description of a visit to the Kali temple in Kalighat was included by G. O. Trevelyan in his wry account of his trip to India, published in 1866. He visited the temple on a festival day, and as he proceeded with the crowds, the whole affair reminded him of what a Dionysian festival must have been like in ancient Greece:

During a few minutes I could not believe my eyes; for I seemed to have been transported in a moment over more than twenty centuries, to the Athens of Cratinus and Aristophanes. If it had not been for the colour of the faces around, I should have believed myself to be on the main road to Eleusis in the full tide of one of the Dionysiac festivals. . . . All was headlong licence and drunken frenzy.[12]

When he arrived near the temple, he found it impossible to go any further but as he noted:

Not even religious madness, not even the inspiration of bang and toddy, could overcome the habitual respect paid to a white face and a pith helmet. A couple of policemen cleared a passage for me to within a few feet of the sacred image. It appeared to be a rude block, ornamented with huge glass beads; but I dare say the Palladium, which fell from heaven was not a very elaborate device. . . .

By the time he returned home, "what with the jostling, the hubbub, and stench," Trevelyan was less enthusiastic about the whole experience and penned the following verse in Latin:

Dea, magna domina Tolli, Calie dea domina
Procul a meo sit omnis tuus ore, precor, odor!
Alios age hinc olentes. Alios age putridos.[13]

VI

ALTHOUGH the artists of Kalighat, known as *patuas*, had been painting for over a hundred years beginning in the early years of the nineteenth century, it was not until the 1920s, when the school was on the verge of extinction, that anyone took notice of its prodigious output. In 1926, Ajit Ghose, a prominent Indian collector and critic in Calcutta, wrote:

There is an exquisite freshness and spontaneity of conception and execution in these old brush drawings. They are not drawn with the meticulous perfection which gives such distinction to Mughal portraiture. They have not the studied elegance and striving-after effect of the charmingly sensitive later drawings of the Kangra school with which they are contemporary. But there is a boldness and vigour in the brush line which may be compared to Chinese calligraphy. The drawing is made with one long sweep of the brush in which not the faintest suspicion of even a momentary indecision, not the slightest tremor can be detected.[14]

Ghose went on to compare the Kalighat pictures with certain modern trends and felt that some of them "anticipated by a century or more cubism and impressionism."

William Archer, a member of the Indian Civil Service who came to India in the 1930s, was the first European scholar to write seriously about

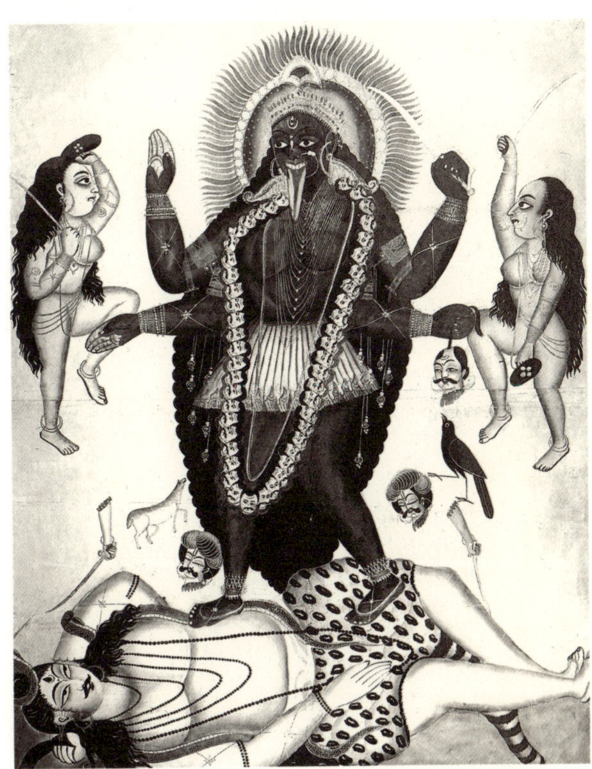

179. Anonymous (Kalighat). *Kali.* c. 1890. Watercolor. Walter Collection.

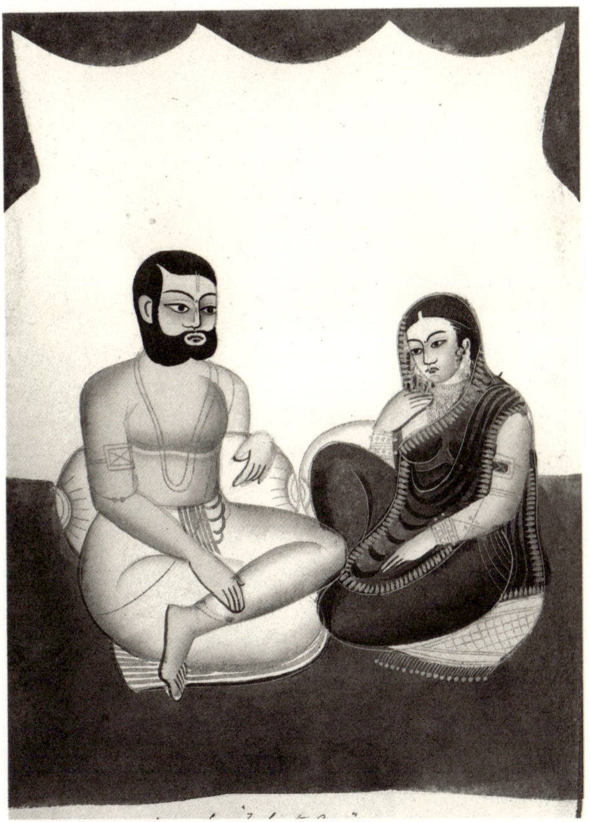

180. Anonymous (Kalighat). *The Mohunt and the Seduced Girl Tête-à-Tête.* c. 1875. Watercolor with silver. Walter Collection.

171

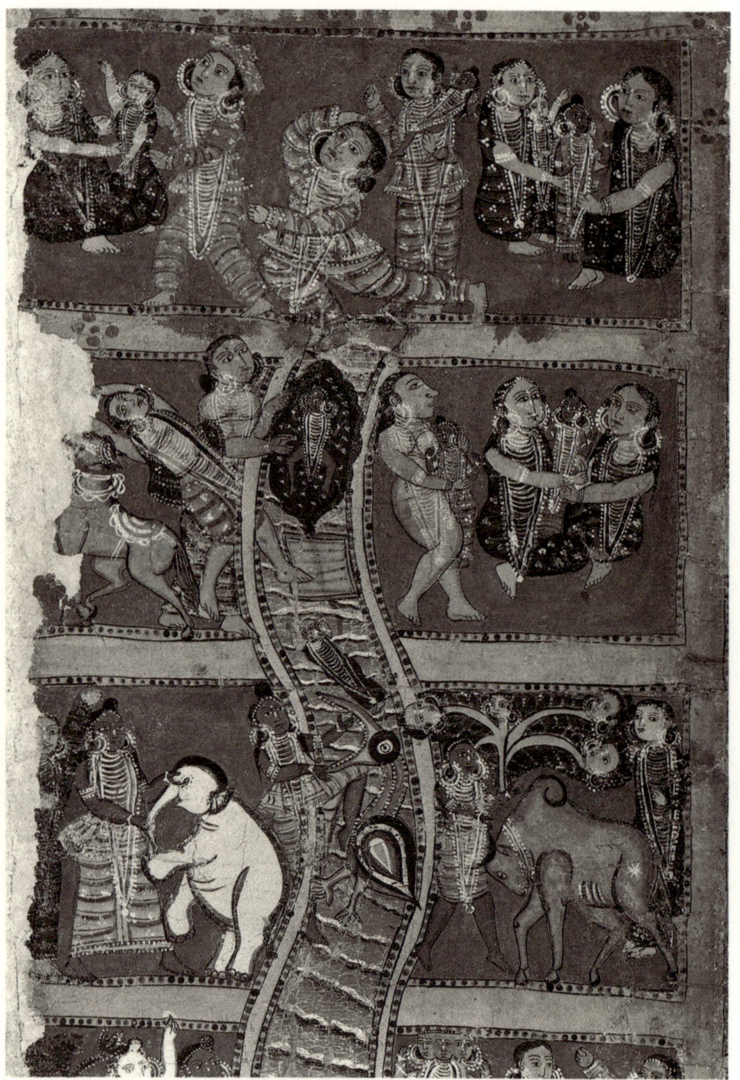

181. Anonymous (Bengal). *Section of a Krishna-lila Scroll*. c. 1800. Gouache, watercolor, and ink. Los Angeles County Museum of Art. Nasli and Alice Heeramaneck Collection.

Kalighat pictures. He found the Kalighat pictures to have "seemingly antedated some of the more audacious inventions of the modern epoch," and further commented:

With their bounding lines and bold rhythms, they were obviously close to the ancient murals of Ajanta and Bagh, while the same qualities of line and rhythm, linked with powerful colour, displayed a surprising affinity with modern art. The work of Fernand Leger was a particularly striking analogy, for here were the same bold simplifications, the same robust tubular forms.[15]

The Kalighat school combined British and Indian traditions to produce a style that was radically different from that of the Company school. As Knizkova has suggested, the Indian antecedents must be sought in the earlier folk styles prevalent in Bengal itself.[16] The village *patuas* had been painting scrolls of mythological subjects long before the Kalighat school came into existence; figure 181 is a typical example. While such paintings, usually done on cloth, frequently did not survive in the climate of Bengal, the style can be observed clearly in the more durable terracotta reliefs in temples going back at least to the seventeenth century.[17] As for the influence of British art, the most important contribution was probably the technique of watercolor and the use of paper, which was cheap and readily available.

The abandonment of traditional careful and meticulous workmanship was probably due to economic reasons. These pictures had to be produced in bulk for no more than a few pennies, and hence the less time it took, the better. The practice of shading the contours and leaving the background blank, again probably dictated by economic necessity, was very likely adopted from Company school studies of crafts and professions. The interest in nonreligious themes probably reflects the taste of the Bengali *babu* and may have been inspired by British preferences. The average, illiterate pilgrims who came to the temple from all over India, and perhaps even from Calcutta, would have wanted to buy subjects of traditional interest such as mythologies and images of deities. But the urbane, educated native of the city would have preferred contemporary themes of more social relevance. Thus, the repertoire of the Kalighat artists was considerably expanded beyond the conventional subjects. Some motifs appear to have been lifted out of illustrations of books on Anglo-Indian life published with some frequency in the first half of the nineteenth century. Others, again following British tastes, depicted natural history subjects but pigeons, crows, muskrats, cats, freshwater prawns, carp (*rui*), and catfish were particularly Bengali subjects.

Subjects that were sexually oriented, such as courtesans or contemporary scandal, essentially catered to the tastes of the nineteenth-century Calcutta *babu*s. The Kalighat artists frequently satirized this group to satisfy the needs of the growing educated middle class who enjoyed ridiculing the idle rich (much as the middle class of Georgian England savored the cartoons and caricatures that brutally exposed the social pretensions and moral depravity of the English upper classes). While it is true that this social consciousness on the part of the humble artists of Kalighat was an indirect result of the British presence in India, it is somewhat remarkable that it was confined almost exclusively to Calcutta.

VII

BOTH caricature and satire are found in the history of Indian art. The repertoire, however, was limited, and almost no attempt was made to mirror in art the social norms and practices, as was done in contemporary Sanskrit literature. Known as *bhan*, the satirist played an important role both in society in general and in the courts in particular, both before and during the British period. Conscious efforts to introduce social satire in art, however, must be attributed to the British fondness for caricatures which were widespread in England in the late eighteenth century. In India, too, British-style caricature and satire were popular in the Anglo-Indian community. Sir Charles D'Oyly was a gifted artist whose depictions of Anglo-Indian life are often mildly satirical, and he wrote a great deal of poetry that is delightfully so. Atkinson's *Curry and Rice* was another example of caustic humor at the cost of the Anglo-Indian. After the appearance of *Punch* in England, an *Indian Punch* was also published in the 1860s, and an Indian version of the French *Charivari* began publication in 1875. The preface to the inaugural album read:

With this number we commence a series of coloured cartoons intended to form a "Charivari Album" in a style of art never before attempted in India. In a comic paper the cartoons must be, to a certain ex-

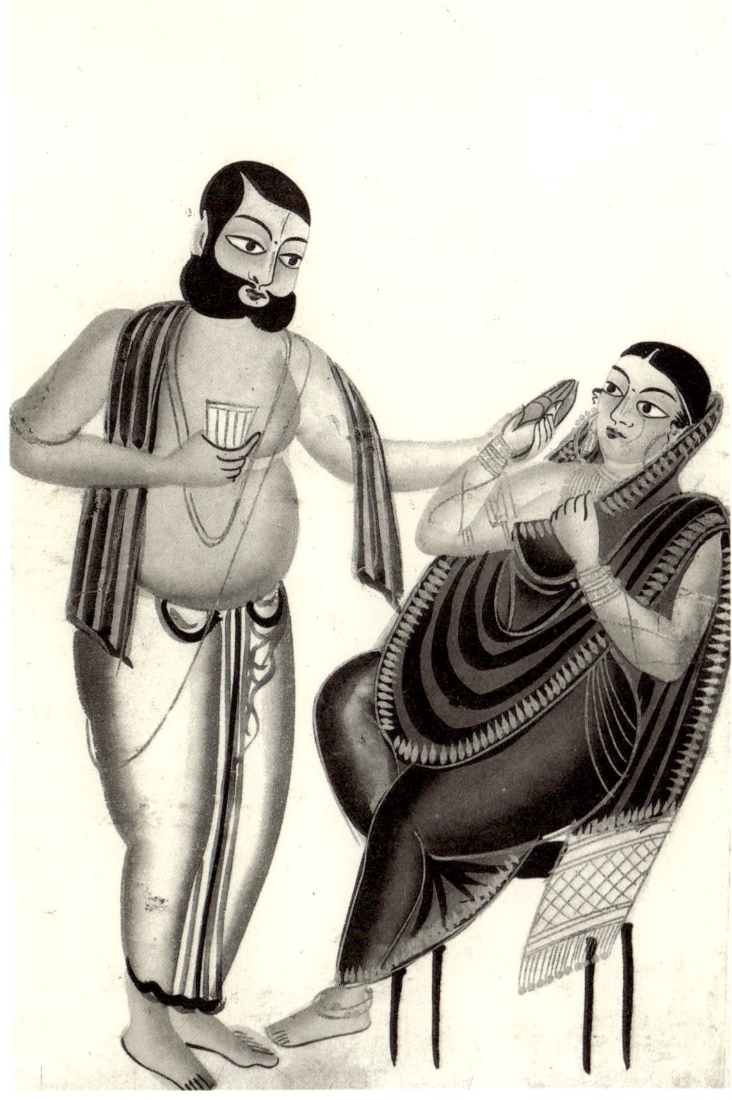

182. Anonymous (Kalighat). *The Mohunt Forcing the Seduced Girl to Drink Some Liquor*. c. 1875. Watercolor with silver. Walter Collection.

tent, caricatures, but we hope to always present such a likeness of the original that our Album may be worth preserving as a gallery of "Men whom India has known." We shall studiously avoid, both in the pictures and in the letter-press, anything that could give offense or be construed into remarks of a personally offensive nature, whilst we hope that both our artist and biographer will be able to "hold the mirror up to nature" in a manner to enable our readers to form a just estimate of the peculiarities and characteristics of their subjects.[18]

One wonders how the Honorable Stuart S.

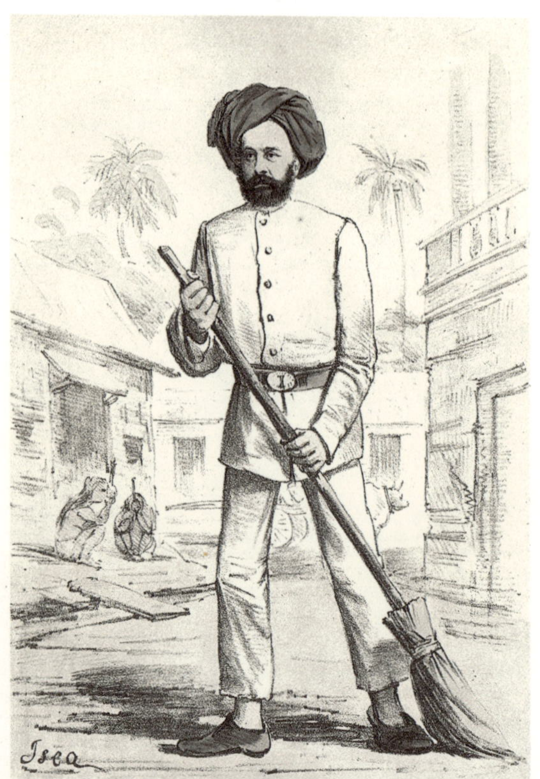

183. *"Misdirected Energy"—The Hon'ble Stuart S. Hogg, Chairman of the Calcutta Municipality* from the *Indian Charivari Album.* 1875. Lithograph. Walter Collection.

Hogg, Chairman of the Calcutta Municipality, reacted upon seeing himself depicted as a sweeper under the caption "misdirected energy" (fig. 183).

Artists of the Company school were introduced to the art of caricature by their British patrons long before the appearance of the Charivari Album. A small anonymous watercolor shows Sir John Burgoyne as a ridiculous bear (fig. 184). Burgoyne was the commander of the Twenty-third Light Dragoons, and Macartney was the governor of Madras (1781–85). The one-legged fiddler is General Stuart and behind him are Admiral Hughes and Mrs. Charles Oakeley, whose scandalous affair that rocked Madras society was no doubt the inspiration behind the caricature. Another contemporary satirical work is an album prepared by an unknown Company artist for a Mr. Adams of the Bengal Civil Service in Calcutta in 1826. Con-

taining 417 folios, each embellished with a rapidly drawn sketch, the album is a remarkably amusing document of Anglo-Indian life and interests. Figure 185 shows the inside of a native school with a pundit seated on the ground teaching Bengali to his students. The exact function of the Englishman seated at the table is not known; he may well represent an inspector. The artist was probably literate as is evident from the Bengali letters and numerals correctly written on the boards hanging from the walls.

Following this tradition, Kalighat artists also indulged in a good deal of graphic satire, mostly about the *babus* and the hypocrisy of the temple priests. A stock motif of the Kalighat artists was a cat holding a fish in its mouth which symbolized the ascetic's hypocritical attitude toward sensual pleasures. The message was also conveyed more directly in a picture of a Vaishnava, whose duplicity was often ridiculed in Bengali literature, at a woman's breast (fig. 186).

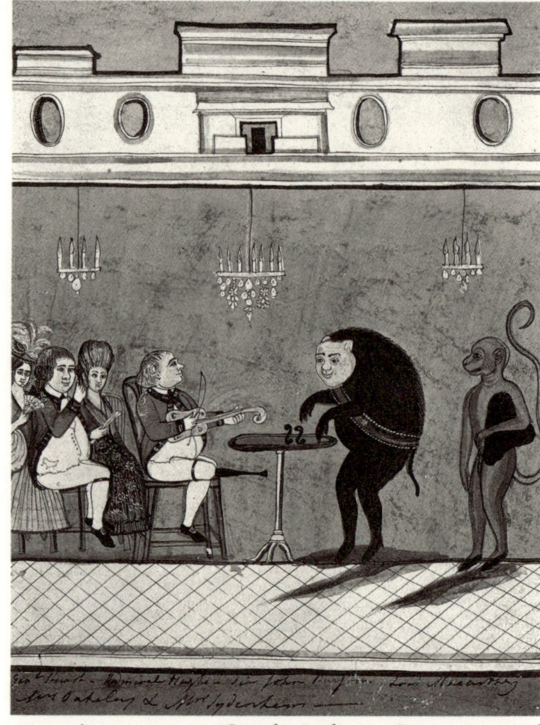

184. Anonymous (South India). *Caricature of General Stuart, the British Governor, Madras.* c. 1783. Watercolor. Collection of Edwin Binney, 3rd.

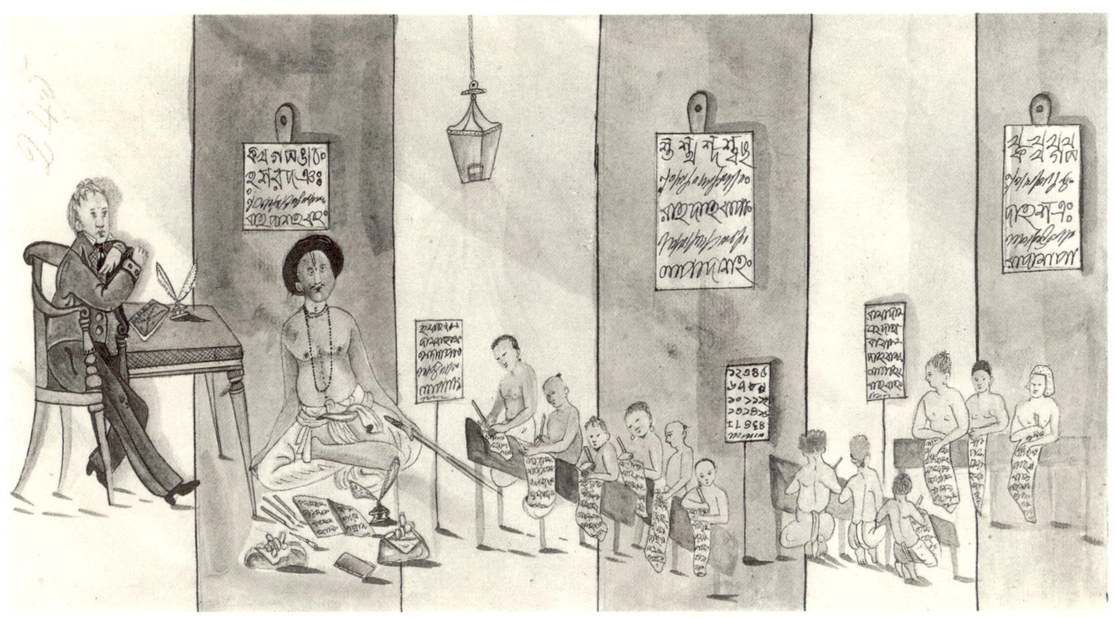

185. Anonymous (Calcutta?). *A School in Calcutta*. c. 1825. Watercolor. Private Collection.

This desire to expose the hypocrisy of the priests and holy men was also no doubt the primary motive behind the popularity of a sensational murder trial of the day. Known as the Tarakeswar Murder, it took place in 1873 and involved both a Brahman family and the *mahant*, or head priest, of the well-known Saiva temple at Tarakeswar in the Hooghly district. The Brahman was Nabin Chandra Banerjee, whose young wife Elokeshi was seduced by the *mahant* of the temple. It appears that the girl's family was privy to the intrigue and even encouraged her to continue the affair and to deceive her husband. On a visit to the village where the girl lived with her parents, Nabin decided to bring his wife to Calcutta where he worked. He had heard of the allegations about his wife's liaison with the *mahant*, but loved her so much he ignored her indiscretions. At this point the *mahant*, who had fallen in love with Elokeshi, complicated matters by attempting to prevent her departure with her husband. This, of course, infuriated Nabin who picked up a fish knife and almost decapitated Elokeshi. Despite public sympathy for Nabin, he was convicted of murder and the *mahant* was incarcerated on the

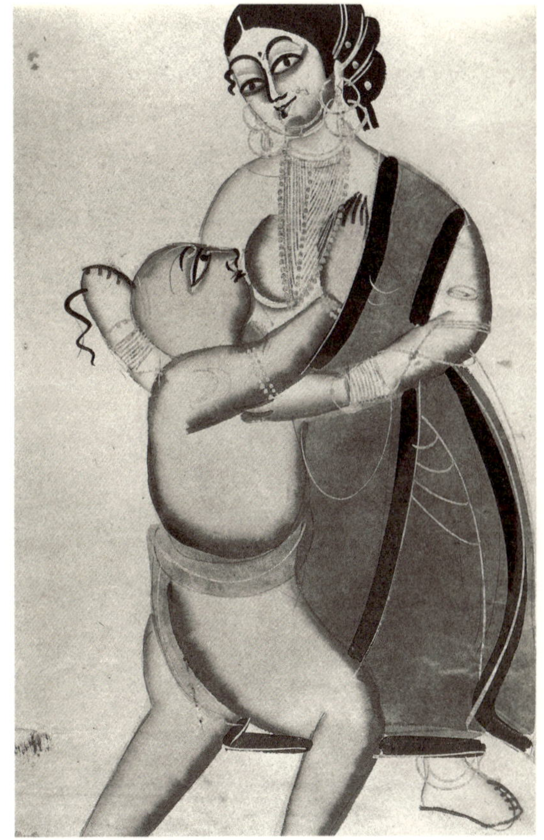

186. Anonymous (Kalighat). *A Vaishnava Priest at a Woman's Breast*. c. 1875. Watercolor. Private Collection.

175

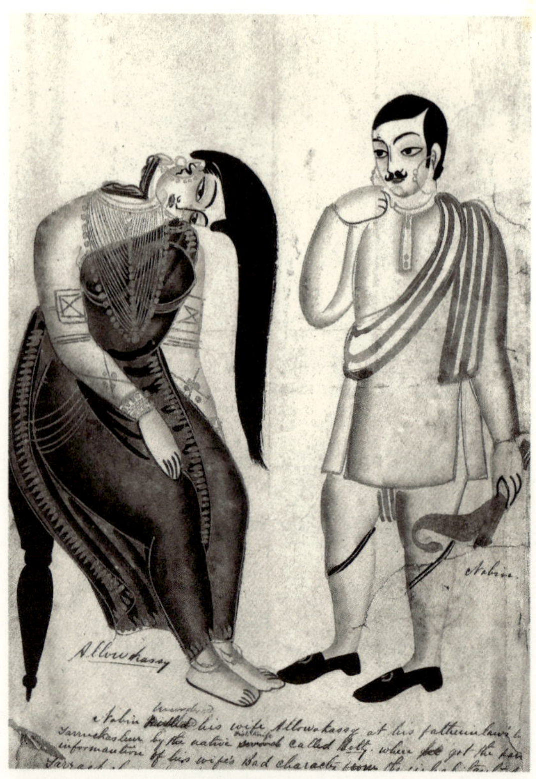

187. Anonymous (Kalighat). *Murder of Elokeshi by Nabin.* c. 1875. Watercolor with silver. Walter Collection.

charge of adultery. In 1878, however, when Edward VII visited India as Prince of Wales, Nabin was released under a general amnesty granted in honor of the royal visit.

Kalighat artists were quick to capitalize on the trial. So many versions of the Tarakeswar murder have survived that it is obvious they sold as fast as they were sketched. The demand for pictures of the episode was so great that prints were also made by other artists in the city who did not belong to the Kalighat school.

VIII

ALTHOUGH woodblock printing on fabric was known in India since ancient times, the technique of reproducing pictures on paper by the processes of metal plate engraving, woodcutting, and lithography was introduced into India by the British. It was a logical development following the arrival of the printing press, which had been introduced on the west coast as early

as 1556 but did not reach the other end of the country until about 1777. Woodcutting, however, was used as early as 1723 in Tranquebar in the south for the title page of *Biblica Damulica*, a Tamil translation of the Bible. By the close of the eighteenth century, Indian craftsmen, working for the European presses in Serampore and Calcutta, appear to have become not only expert in engraving type fonts, but also ornamental designs used to embellish books. The early engravers employed by the presses were drawn mostly from the traditional craftsmen who worked in metal. Early in the nineteeenth century, however, Brahmans became active both in printing and book publishing, and by mid-century, when schools of art were established, caste does not appear to have been a barrier; several Brahmans are listed among the most famous engravers of the day.

Several European printmakers and engravers worked in Calcutta in the late eighteenth and early nineteenth centuries. Among them were Richard Brittridge, Caleb Garlend, John Alefounder, John Brown, Aaron Upjohn, James Moffat, Samuel Davis, Francis Domieux, and Joseph Shepherd. Although some of the British artists and printers claimed that they worked entirely by themselves, this was not the case. In their *Twelve Views of Calcutta* (1786–88), Thomas Daniell states that the going was rough as he himself had to be "Painter, Engraver, Coppersmith, Printer, and Printer's Devil." [19] Yet we learn from William Baillie, writing from Calcutta in 1793, that "The native artists tho' totally incapable of taking advice themselves, can copy extremely well. All Daniells' [views of Calcutta] were stained principally by natives." [20] Another example of collaboration involved Charles Wilkins, who worked with Joseph Shepherd casting type for the Bengali characters for *A Grammar of the Bengali Language* (1778) with the assistance of Panchanan Karmakar, who became a leading engraver of the period. Other well-known books of prints produced in India were William Baillie's *Twelve Views of Calcutta and Fort William* (1794) and *Eight Views of Gour and Rajmahal* (1798), and Robert

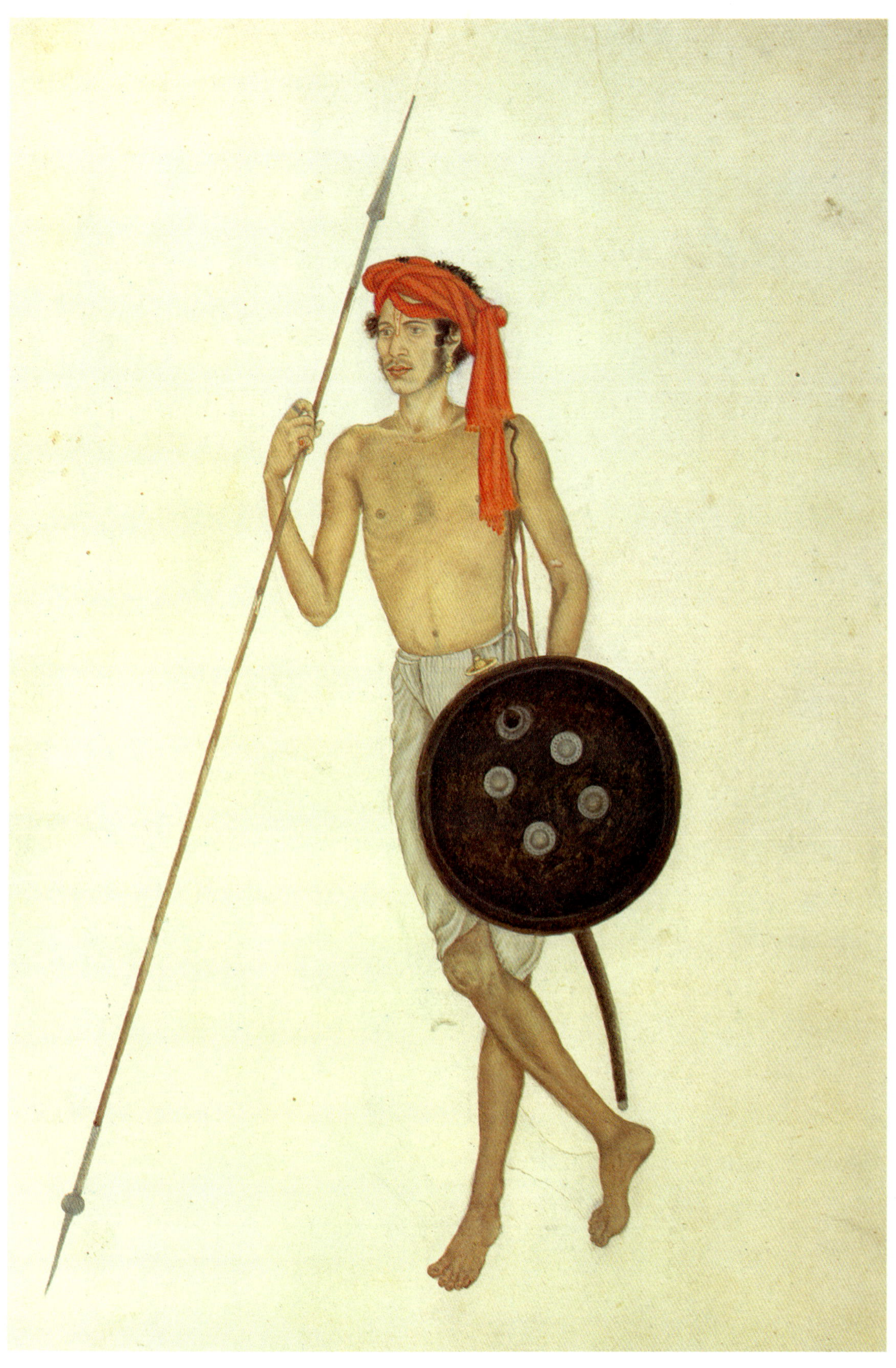

COLORPLATE 12.
Anonymous (Delhi). *Trooper of Skinner's Horse*. c. 1820–30. Watercolor.
Walter Collection.

Mabon's *Twenty Sketches Illustrative of Oriental Manners and Customs* (1797).

There is some disagreement among scholars about whether the early engravers of Calcutta were actually trained by Europeans. Those who had the opportunity to work with the Daniells, or Solvyns, or later in Patna with Sir Charles D'Oyly who had set up a printing shop of his own, must have learned something of the techniques involved. Generally, however, woodcuts, whether done as book illustrations or as individual prints, show very little awareness of British art (fig. 188). The complete lack of perspective, emphasis upon linearity, two-dimensionality, absence of shading, and the hierarchical importance given the figures are all features that were borrowed from earlier traditional styles, not from British art. Unlike the Kalighat artists, the early Indian engravers were not inventive but continued in their traditional flat, decorative style. The illustration from a *Mahabharata*, the great Indian epic, differs little from the slightly earlier pictures of similar battle scenes in classical Rajput paintings (fig. 189). The women in these prints are dressed not in the local fashion, but wear the skirtlike *ghagras*, the mode encountered in Rajput paintings. By the mid-nineteenth century, however, the repertoire was expanded considerably to cater to the secular tastes of the *babu*s. The engravers borrowed heavily from the Kalighat school, taking the most popular themes of the Calcutta dandy and his courtesan, satire and scandal.

By the 1850s, woodcutting was on the wane in India with the growing popularity of lithography. The exact date of the introduction of lithography in Calcutta is uncertain. However, it was probably by one of two French artists, Belros and de Savignac, both of whom were

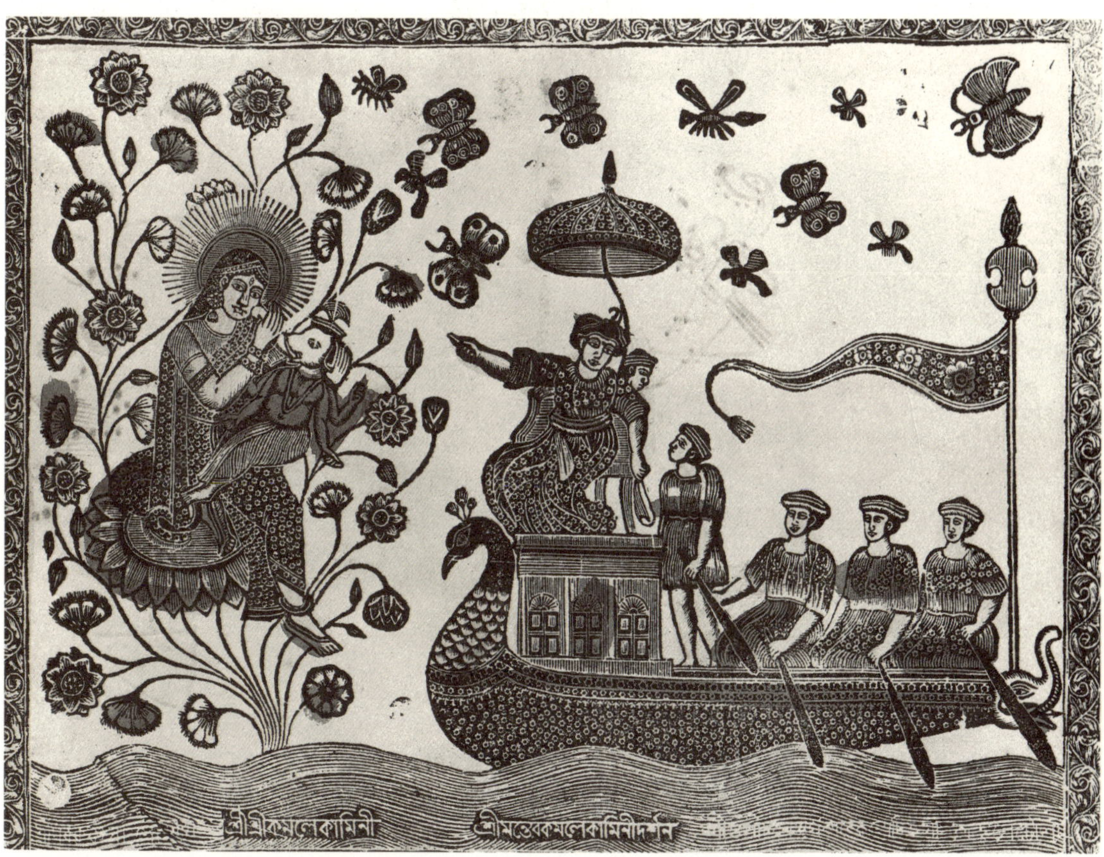

188. Anonymous (Calcutta). *The Merchant Srimanta Sees a Vision of the Goddess.* c. 1850. Woodcut. Collection of Edwin Binney, 3rd.

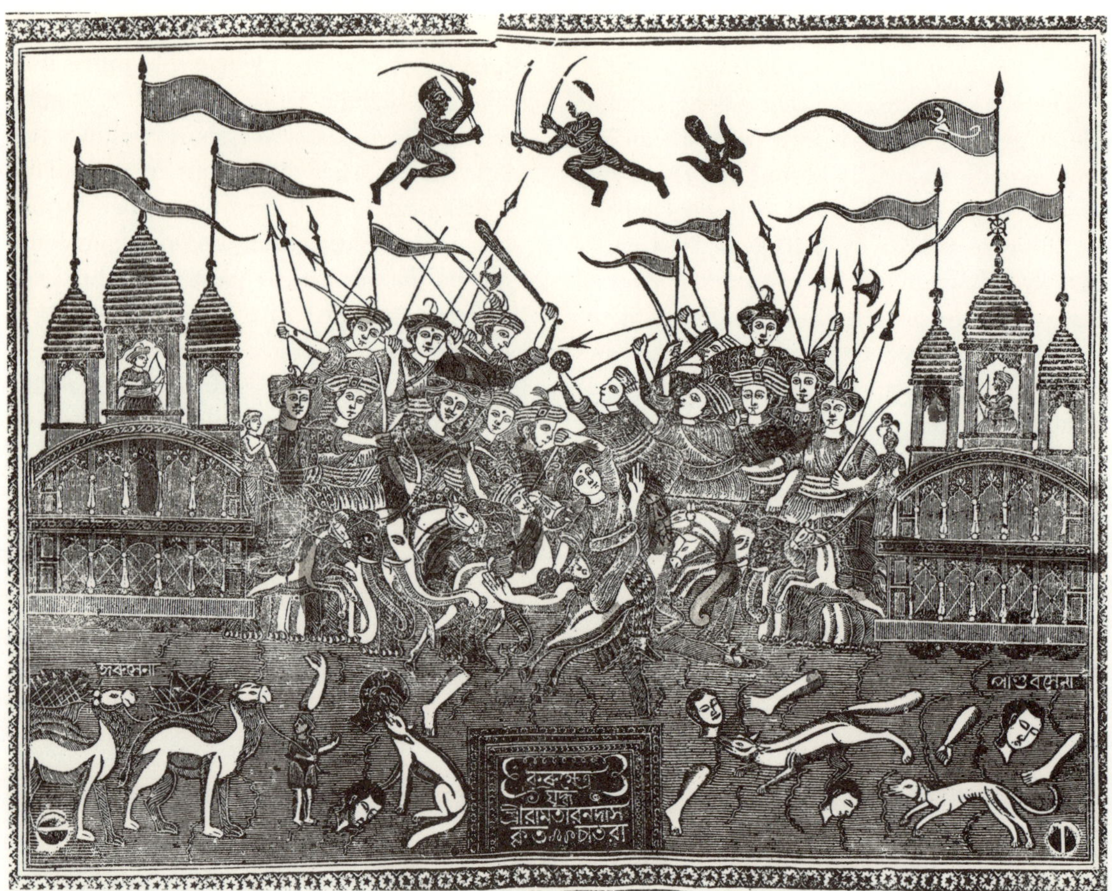

189. Ramtaran Das. *Battle Scene* from the epic *Mahabharata*. c. 1850. Woodcut. Courtesy of the Board of Trustees of the Victoria and Albert Museum.

using lithography by 1822 as reported in the *Calcutta Journal* of that year, or I. N. Hind, Superintendent of the Government Press. In any event, by 1850 a number of lithographic presses were flourishing in Calcutta, all of them owned by Europeans. The Royal Lithographic Press, the first art studio owned by an Indian, was not established until the 1860s. It was run by four artists, all of whom had been trained at the School of Industrial Art.

The effects of the Industrial Revolution in Britain had been disastrous for the Indian economy in general and for the village industries in particular. Rather than impose tariffs to protect Indian manufacturing, the government adopted the questionable policy of establishing art colleges "to maintain, restore, and improve the application of oriental art to industry and manufacture," as well as to "modify existing designs in the light of British taste so as to make them more suitable for export." [21] The first school was founded in Madras in 1850, the second in Calcutta in 1854, and another in Bombay in 1857. The prospectus of the Madras school declared its objective was to "improve the taste of the native people as regards beauty of form and finish in the articles in daily use among them." [22] Artists from Europe were brought to head the newly founded establishments. John Griffiths and Lockwood Kipling went to India in 1865; the former became director of the Bombay school and the latter the first principal of the Mayo School of Arts founded in Lahore in 1875. Among the early teachers at the Calcutta School were the Italian O. Gilhardi and the Englishman Charles Palmer. In 1869, E. B. Havell took over the Calcutta School after having briefly run the one in Madras.

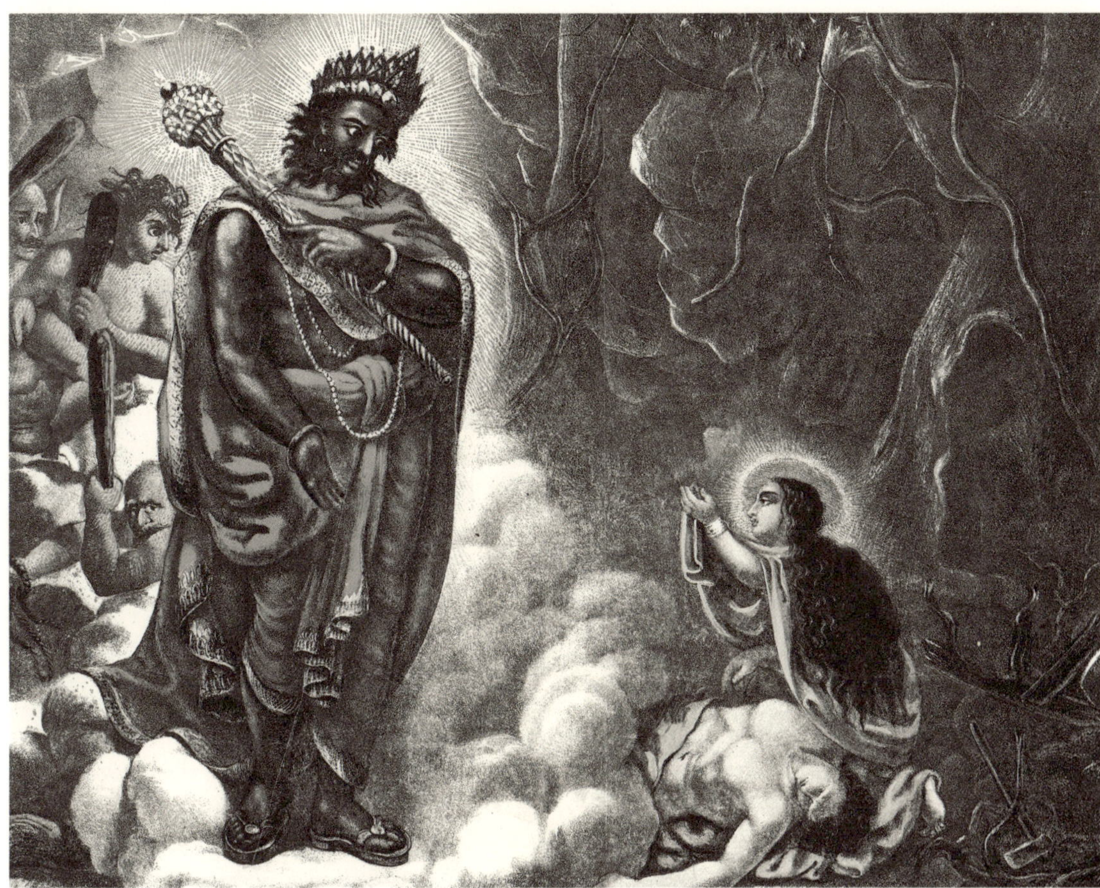

190. Anonymous (Calcutta Art Studio). *Savitri Pleading with Yama, the God of Death, for the Life of her Dead Husband.* 1883. Lithograph. Los Angeles County Museum of Art.

The results of these efforts were discouraging. In 1877, Valentine Prinsep visited Jaipur's art school and wrote, "Of all the feeble institutions here, it is the feeblest. The [drawing] master is an Indian; the things turned out, so many nightmares: large copies of photographs of the Prince of Wales, Lord Northbrook and other Governors-General, with the ghastly stare such things have when done by beginners; drawings done from nature without an atom of art: in fact, a perfect artistic Bedlam."[23] In Madras, when the students were shown Old Master nudes, the school authorities were shocked to discover that, "far from displaying a coldly academic interest, the students regarded them as 'naked English ladies' kindly provided for their delectation by an understanding government."[24] It was extremely difficult for the graduates of these schools to find work; those that did be-

came professional portraitists, lithographers, illustrators, ornamental designers, draftsmen, and photographers.

A few enterprising students from the Calcutta School formed the Calcutta Art Studio and produced rather colorful lithographs of religious subjects that were bought by native and British patrons. Figure 190 shows a typical Art Studio lithograph from the scrapbook *Fifteen Hindu Mythological Pictures.* In 1883, the scrapbook sold for ten rupees. The artist had certainly mastered European technique, but his style is lacking in creativity.

The schools did succeed in breaking down certain social barriers and taboos. Students were admitted from all castes; aspiring artists from Brahman families sat in the same classes as students from the craftsmen castes.

The Indian artist who became famous in the

latter half of the nineteenth century was not a product of any of the art schools, but was the maharaja of Travancore. Ravi Varma (d. 1905) was a self-taught painter but was strongly influenced by European art. He painted in oil and had to reproduce his works in oleograph due to their great demand. In his portraiture, he was certainly influenced by the European painter Theodore Jenson. Ravi Varma's style was very much like that of contemporary Calcutta lithographers; perhaps a touch more sophisticated and subtle, but both, in the words of W. G. Archer, "paralleled British art in its most banal form." As Havell was to write later:

The art which truly reflects . . . the teaching of Anglo-Indian art-schools is exhibited in the paintings of the late Ravi Varma, who is the fashionable artist of modern India for those Indians who do not ignore Indian art altogether. Though not trained in a school of art, all his methods have been based on the academic nostrums of Anglo-Indian schools, fine art societies, and art critics. It is difficult to understand whether the popularity his works have gained is to be attributed more to the common realistic trickery which he has borrowed from European painters or to his choice of Indian subjects. But certain it is that his pictures invariably manifest a most painful lack of the poetic faculty in illustrating the most imaginative poetry and allegory; and this cardinal sin is not atoned for by any kind of technical distinction in the execution.[25]

Havell's criticism of the kind of painting inspired by the "academic nostrums of Anglo-Indian schools" may sound rather harsh, but the simple acquisition of "realistic trickery" without "poetic faculty" was not enough to create original and exciting art. The Mogul painters who worked for the British, or the Kalighat artists, were well aware of this, which is why their works are still admired today. By being critical of the state of art in India when he arrived, and by bemoaning its lack of "Indianness," Havell became the apostle of a revivalist movement. The emergence of the new trend under the direction of Havell and Abanindra Nath Tagore, a graduate of the Calcutta Art School and leader of the contemporary art movement, was an offshoot of the growth of Indian nationalism around the beginning of the twentieth century. The reaction was against British art and modes of perception, but their techniques would remain.

5. India Through the Lens

Painting and photography are not two potentially competitive systems for producing and reproducing images, which simply had to arrive at a proper division of territory to be reconciled. Photography is an enterprise of another order. Photography, though not an art form in itself, has the peculiar capacity to turn all its subjects into works of art.

SUSAN SONTAG—1973[1]

I

For over a hundred years animated debate has continued as to whether photography may be regarded as an art form comparable to, say, painting. In recent years, with photographs taking their place in museum collections, one might have assumed that the debate had been settled once and for all. Yet a certain ambiguity still remains regarding the status of photography, and it appears that this ambiguity is here to stay.

Certainly, the invention of photography created a crisis in art, a crisis greeted by the painter Delaroche in 1839 with the startling proclamation, "From today, painting is dead."[2] Several critics refused to give photography the status of an art form; Baudelaire, for instance, labeled it "a refuge for failed painters."[3] Ingres resented photography and raged:

We do not want this industry . . . let it stay put and not venture near our School, the true Temple of Apollo dedicated to the Art of Greece and Rome.[4]

Yet, even Ingres used photographs in his art classes, before whom he admitted:

Look at this photography, gentlemen! Who amongst you would be capable of such a likeness, of such fidelity of design, of such delicacy of form?[5]

In India, it would appear artists did not regard photography as a threat; on the contrary, they seem to have willingly used photographs as painting aids. Valentine Prinsep, who met the Indian artist Ismael Khan in 1877, noted that "They work from photographs and never by any chance from nature."[6] British artists in India also availed themselves of photographs; Edward Lear, for instance, while drawing the temples of Benares, commented:

I began a drawing of the temples which I had vainly tried yesterday and managed to get what, should photographs be obtainable, may one day prove more or less useful.[7]

Other entries in his journal speak of the purchase of photographs; while in Madras, after having struggled to draw the ruins of Mahabalipuram, he sadly remarked that his sketches would be of no use since he had been unable to find photographs of the architectural remains.

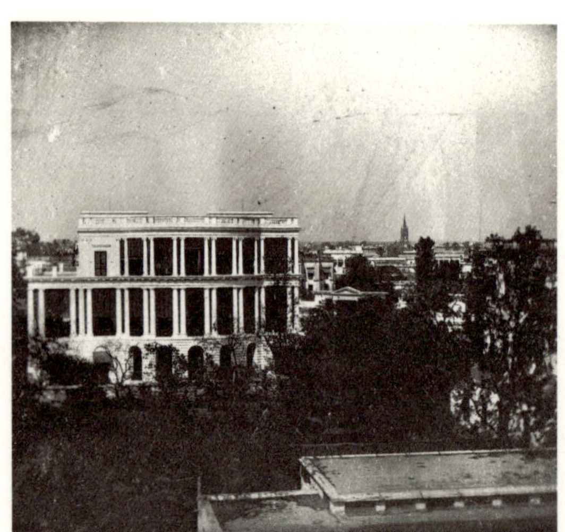

191. Anonymous. *Calcutta with St. Paul's Cathedral in the Background.* c. 1855. Daguerreotype. Walter Collection.

Lear and other British artists appear to have used photographs only for recording architectural structures that were very exotic and unusual, and not for landscapes or genre scenes. The problem with Indian monuments was explained by Valentine Prinsep:

It never rains long together in India at this time of the year, and I had a fine day which I devoted to making a sketch of the Jummah Masjid. . . . My sketch was necessarily slight as Eastern architecture, and Indian in particular, goes into such minute detail, that it is impossible to give anything but the vaguest idea of its colour; but with the help of photos and my own sketches for figures, I think I shall be able to knock up a picture of the mosque.[8]

In a way, photographs were used by artists in India much as the *camera obscura* came to the aid of British artists of the pre-photography era.

While in other inventions, India might have lagged behind Europe, it appears that this was not the case with photography. In 1839, the year of the first daguerreotype, excitement ran high in Paris: would it really be possible to capture "sun pictures"? The invention caught on like wildfire and by November of that year there were two sets of photographers outside Cairo, "daguerreotyping like lions!"[9]

As early as January 1840, Thacker and Company of Calcutta was importing daguerreotype cameras, which it advertised in the daily paper *Friend of India*. The daguerreotype of Calcutta shown in figure 191 with St. Paul's Cathedral in the distance was taken around 1855, and may have come from the earliest daguerreotype studio in Calcutta, the Daguerreian Gallery established by J. W. Newland in 1852. The daguerreotype is produced on the mirrorlike surface of a silvered copperplate; the image is normally reversed, as in a mirror. It is an extraordinarily sharp and exact image; as in the words of an admirer:

Light is that silent artist
Which without the aid of man
Designs on silver bright
Daguerre's immortal plan.[10]

There were commercial photographic establishments that did not do daguerreotypes. In 1849, a professional photographic studio had been set up and the *New Calcutta Directory* for that year lists a certain F. Schranzhofer as the photographer. This studio may have used the calotype process of William Henry Fox Talbot, which employed sensitized paper instead of metal plates. During the summer of 1835, Talbot successfully produced on paper a number of pictures of his country house and exclaimed: "This building I believe to be the first that was ever yet known *to have drawn its own picture.*"[11]

While the *Calcutta Directory*'s 1840 issue listed four professional portrait painters active in Calcutta, the 1849 issue does not list a single painter. Photography seems to have rapidly replaced painting, at least as far as portraiture was concerned, even though sitters had to sit absolutely still for periods of up to ten minutes! By 1850, the earlier term "sun picture" had been replaced by "photograph," a term coined by the astronomer Sir John Herschel from the Greek *photos* (light) and *graphos* (drawing).

The daguerreotype, while capturing details with remarkable clarity, proved to have a number of disadvantages. It could not be duplicated, as it was on a silver plate, and it was fragile and had to be stored under glass, often in a folding case like the one in figure 191. Metalplates were

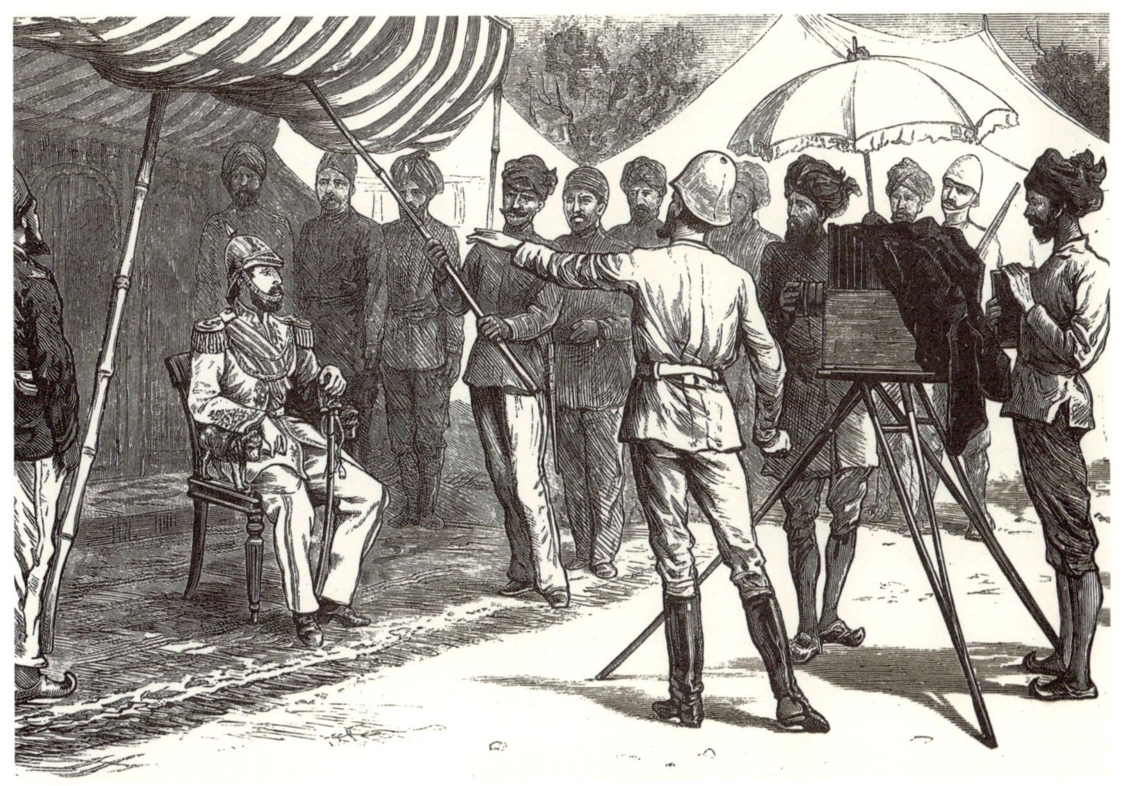

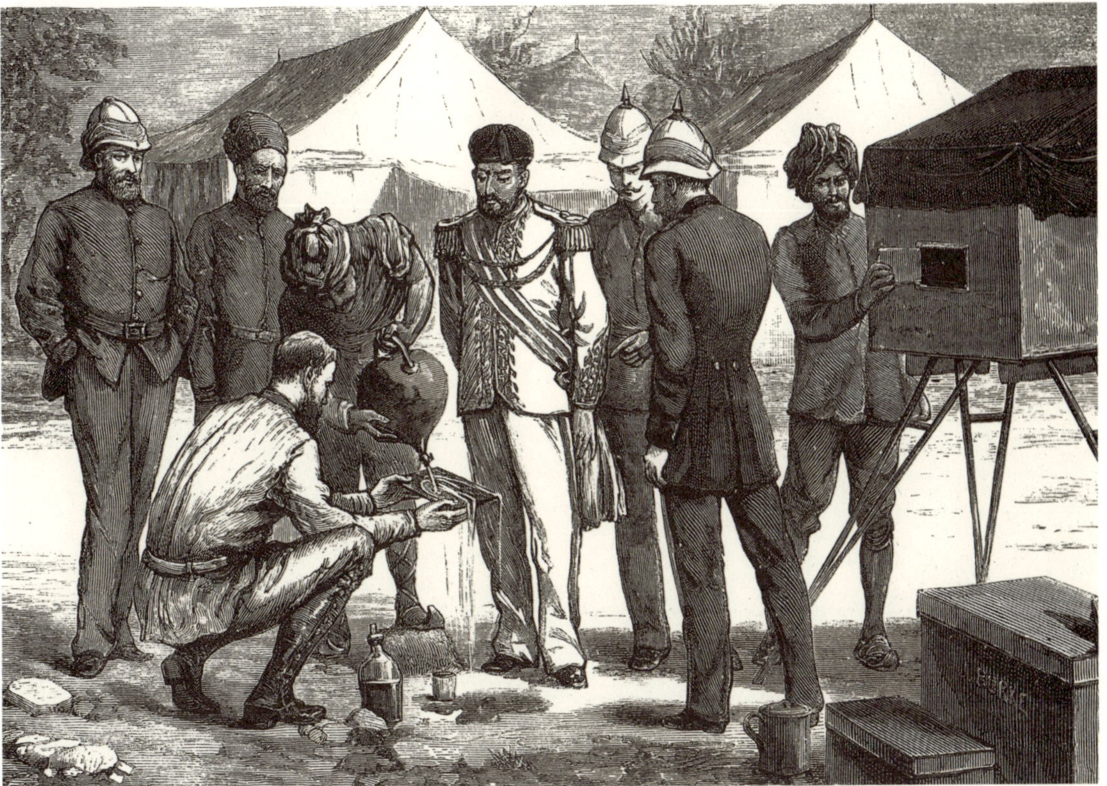

192 a, b. *Burke Photographing the Ameer Yakoob Khan* from *The Graphic*. July 12, 1879. Walter Collection.

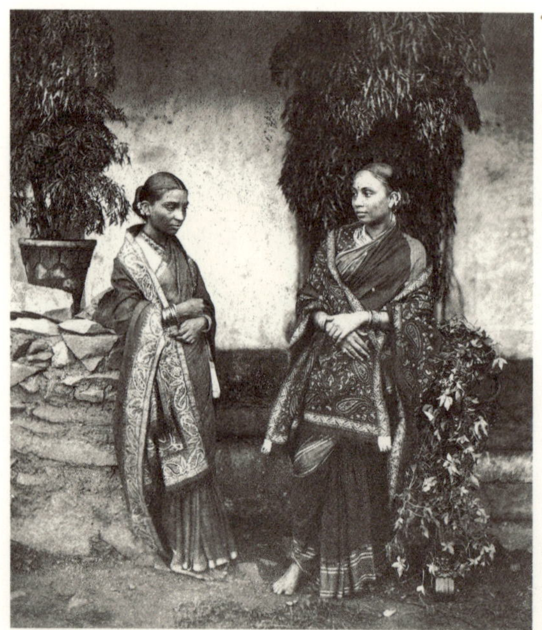

193. Anonymous. *Maharashtrian Women*. Frith publisher. Late 1860s. Albumen print. Walter Collection.

expensive and the fumes from the warmed mercury that was needed to develop the images on the plates were dangerous. When the collodion process was introduced in 1845, it replaced the beautiful silvery daguerreotype.

None of the heated discussions that took place in Europe on the status of photography as art, industry, or science impinged upon photographers in India. The first photographic society was founded in Bombay in 1854, lagging behind London by only one year. By 1855, it boasted over 250 members and had started its own journal. The following year the society organized a photographic exhibition with an opening attended by Lord Canning (then governor-general of India) and his wife. Lord Elphinstone, the governor of Bombay, presented Lady Canning with a leatherbound copy of the society's journal and a similarly bound set of photographs.

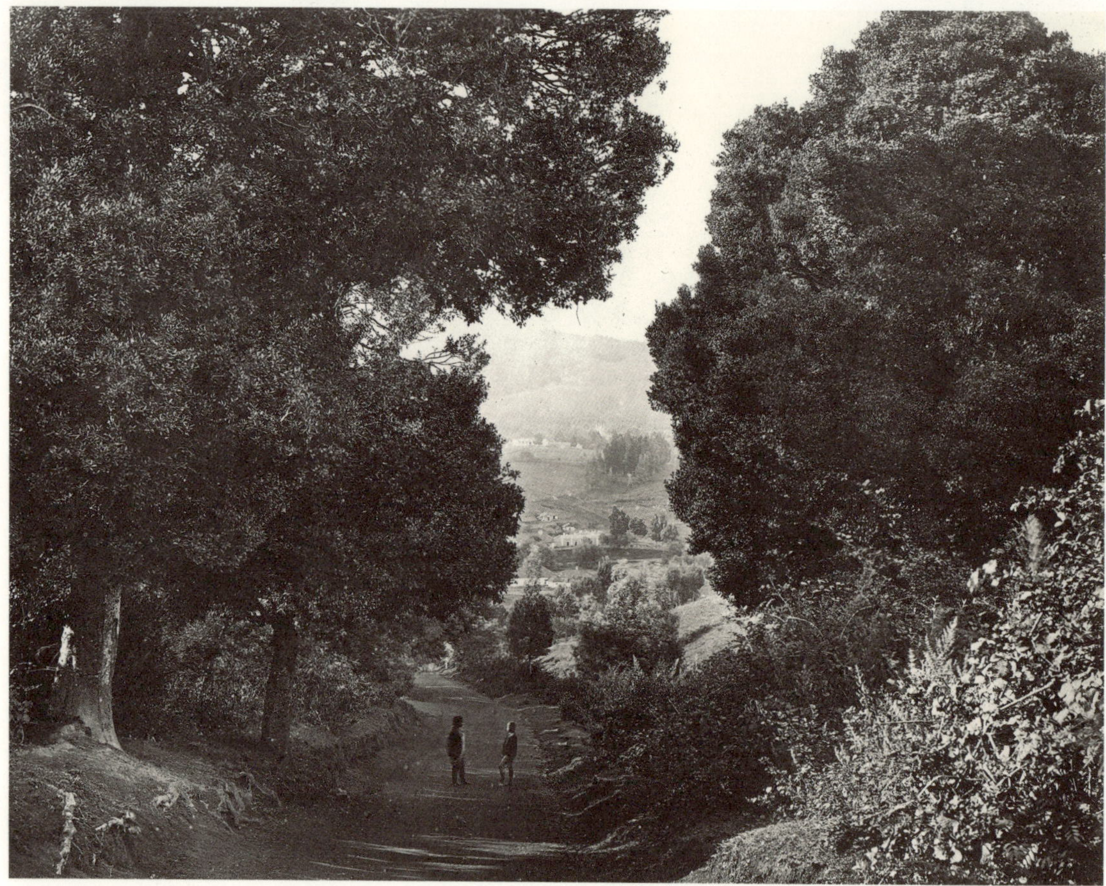

194. Samuel Bourne. *Ootacamund, a Peep from Near Bombay House*. Mid-1860s. Albumen print. Walter Collection.

184

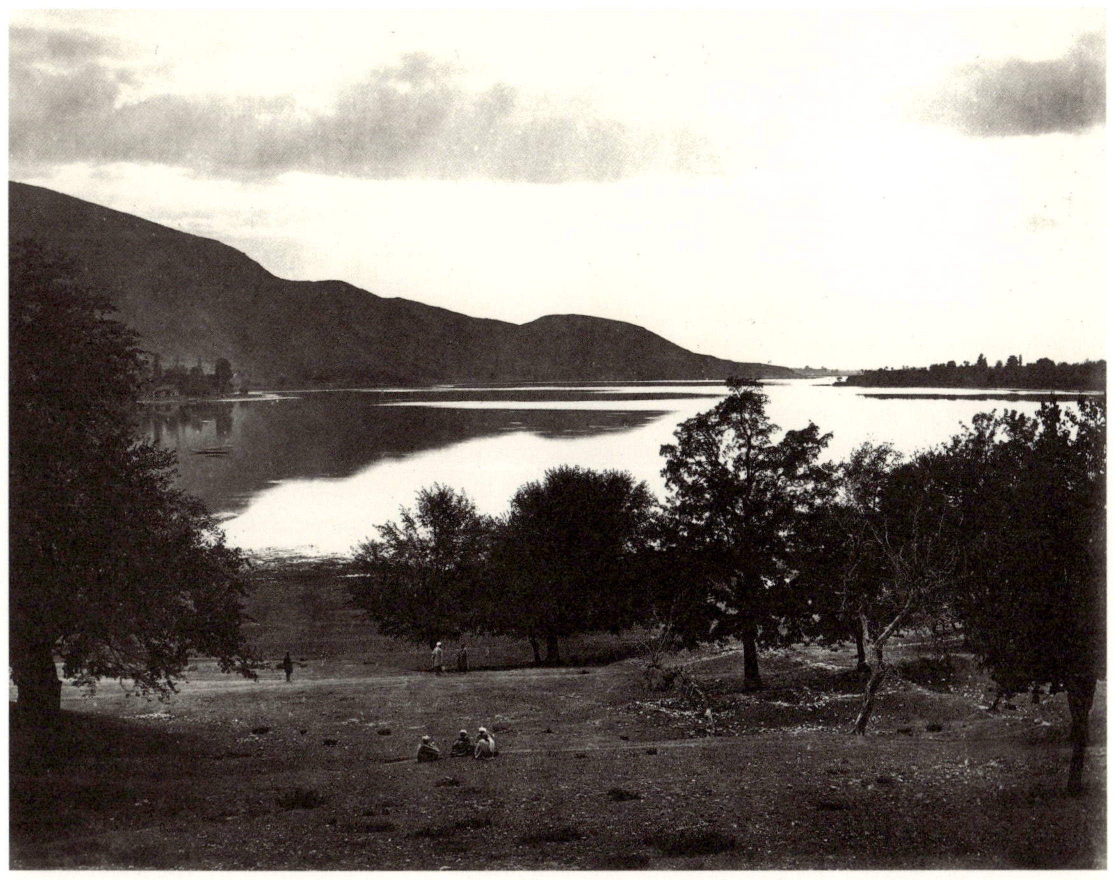

195. Samuel Bourne. *Dal Lake, Kashmir*. Mid-1860s. Albumen print. Walter Collection.

Lady Canning was happy to become the society's patroness, and Lord Canning initiated the production of a set of eight volumes on *The People of India*, a collection of nearly 500 photographs by as many as fifteen amateur photographers, consisting of both civilians and army officers. With such encouragement from the highest quarters, the future of the camera in India was well established. It was Lord Canning who appointed Sir Alexander Cunningham as the first Director-General of Archaeology in India and the camera soon replaced the draftsman in recording the monuments and ruins.

In 1856, photographic societies were formed in both Calcutta and Madras; regular society meetings were held at which papers were presented. Many of these papers gave details of experimental methods to overcome the problems of working in conditions of high heat and humidity. For instance, in March 1858, W. E. Un-derwood told the members the secret of how "to make an iodizing mixture for collodion suited to the climate of Madras."[12] At a Calcutta meeting in October 1856, Mr. Fosberg reported to the members of the Photographic Society of Bengal on his experiments with inexpensive sheets of talc—a soft whitish mineral, much like mica—which he suggested as a replacement for glass "because talc is portable, easily worked with and the collodion film adheres very firmly to it."[13]

By this time, collodion wet plates were in use all over the world, including India, having largely replaced both the daguerreotype and the calotype. This new system offered the clarity of Daguerre's method with the calotype's reproducibility. A glass plate was coated with collodion and sensitized. Exposures could be as brief as two seconds in the open. The main problem facing the photographer was that the plate had to be exposed and developed while the coating was still wet. The photographer thus had to travel with his darkroom, usually a tent. Samuel Bourne's equipment on his expedition to the Himalayas consisted of a ten-foot-high tent, 650 glass plates, two cameras and several lenses, numerous bottles of chemical solutions for coating, sensitizing, developing, and fixing the glass plates, baths in which the plates had to be immersed, funnels and pails and, finally, personal baggage, all of which called for thirty bearers![14] The operation of the cumbersome camera of the day and the need for the immediate development of the wet plate is well documented on the front page of the July 12, 1879 issue of the weekly paper *The Graphic* (fig. 192). The upper illustration depicts the photographer Burke setting up the scene for the picture he intends to take of Ameer Yakoob Khan, while below we see him developing the newly exposed wet plate on the spot and fixing the negative with chemical solutions.

Several photographic studios in India sold "photographic tents," and developing chemicals were much in demand. The minutes of the Madras Photographic Society in 1858 record: "So great is the demand for photographic chemicals that Messrs. Flynn & Co. state that they will have difficulty in supplying it."[15] There were also problems obtaining collodion, the essential ingredient for this type of photography. Officially, there was a virtual ban on importing collodion because it was a basic ingredient in the manufacture of gunpowder. At any rate, the Peninsular and Orient Steamship Line, the only commercial line that sailed to India, refused to transport collodion there and the chemical was smuggled in or manufactured locally.

In 1878, the collodion wet plates that had been used successfully for some twenty years were replaced by gelatin dry plates. The most important result of this innovation was that the photographer no longer had to be close to a darkroom, since the plates were pre-sensitized and could be processed a considerable length of time after exposure. The new technique was heralded:

Onward still, and onward still
it runs its sticky way
And Gelatine you're bound to use
if you mean to make things pay;
Collodion—slow old fogey!—
your palmy days have been
You must give place in future
to plates of Gelatine![16]

Ten years later, George Eastman introduced "film" that was made of paper coated with gelatin, and invented a camera which he named "Kodak." Processing of film was now a task that could be undertaken commercially. "You press the button, we do the rest," was the slogan of the new Kodak cameras of 1888.

II

THE British photographers' perception of India was in many ways remarkably similar to that of the earlier British painters. The realism that was made possible by the camera rarely emerges except in a certain limited category of news photographs. The photographer certainly saw the poverty and squalor of certain parts of India, but he chose not to record them; he was a photographer in search of the picturesque, much like the eighteenth-century landscapists. Writing about his visit to Kashmir, photographer Samuel Bourne remarked, "The first three days after my arrival at Srinugger were spent in 'wanderings in search of the picturesque.'"[17] His comments to the *British Journal of Photography* on the quality of the Indian light recall those of the landscape painter William Hodges:

The more brilliant the sunshine, the more I love to see the image on the ground glass; and, arriving just fresh from England, where the dampness and thickness of the atmosphere so sadly mar the brilliancy and crispness of the picture, and are so unfavourable for producing anything like breadth of effect, I have frequently stood transported at the wonderful brilliancy of the image portrayed on the screen, at the beautiful touches of sunlight amongst the trees, and the fine masses of broad light and shadow everywhere pervading the picture.[18]

Nevertheless, Bourne lamented that "Indian

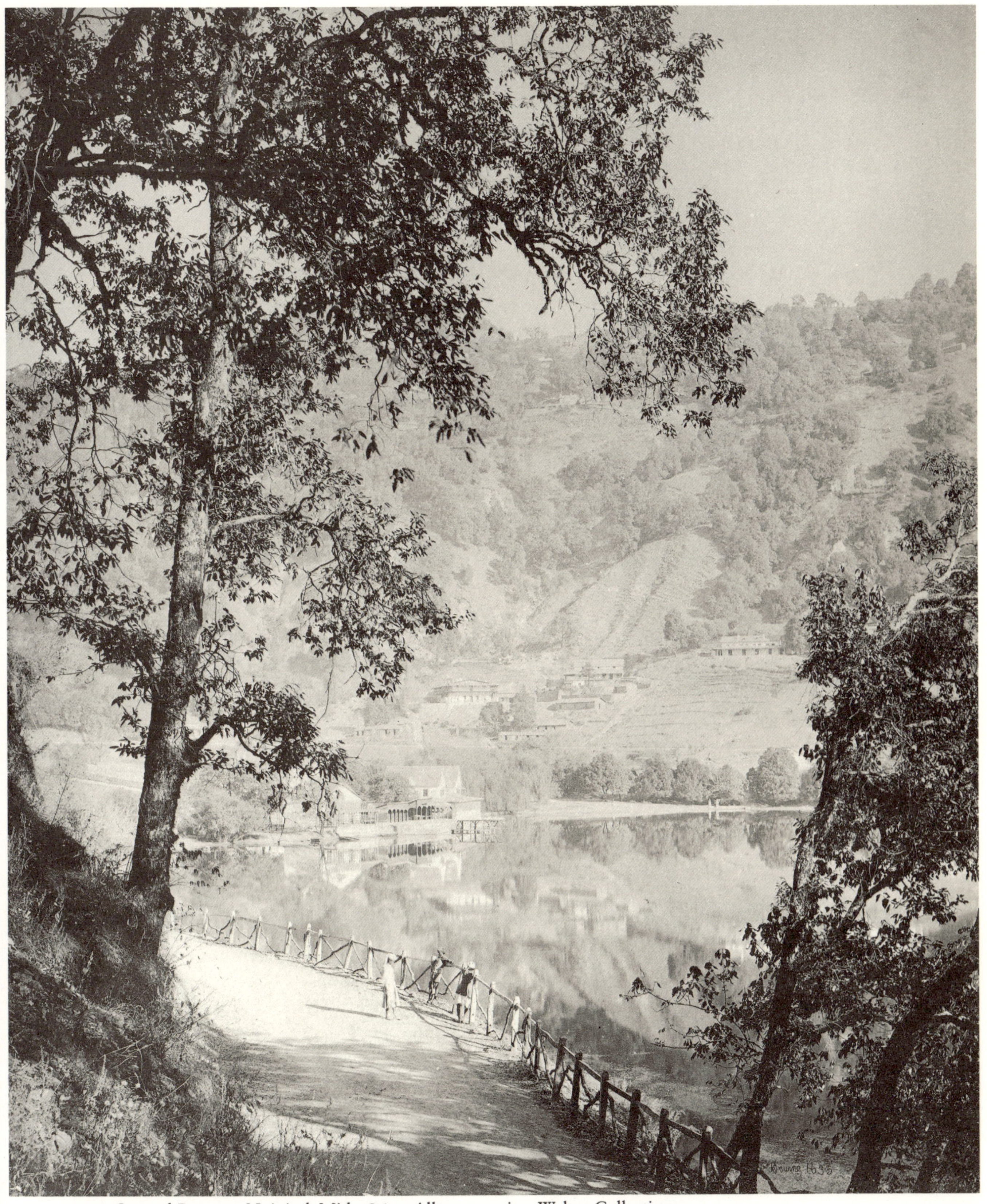

196. Samuel Bourne. *Nainital*. Mid-1860s. Albumen print. Walter Collection.

landscapes I do not think will ever compare with English."[19] He had a set idea of the picturesque which he stated quite clearly:

I am perfectly convinced that no scenery in the world is better, or so well adapted for photography, on the whole, as that of Great Britain. Its mountain cottages, overhung with thickly-foliaged trees, its cascades and waterfalls, its lakes, rivers and verdure, are especially suited for and often so combined as to meet the peculiar requirements of the camera.[20]

Upon visiting Simla, he was disappointed because of the absence of water, which he considered an essential element of the picturesque: "There are no lakes, no rivers, and scarcely anything like a stream in this locality, neither is there a single object of architectural interest, no rustic bridges and no ivy-clad ruins. . . ." He found only mountains and trees and "the beautiful play of light and shade about them are . . . all that the photographer has to compose his pictures."[21]

Architectural photography was preoccupied with famous monuments—the Taj Mahal, the Benares ghats, the Tanjore temple. It was realized early on that the camera could produce a more accurate record of architecture than the artist, and the British soon embarked on a large-scale official documentation of the monuments of India, generally through the services of amateur photographers who were officers in the British army.

The native peoples of India fascinated the photographer. As in the earlier days of Tilly Kettle or Francesco Renaldi, the photographer found himself free to photograph only male subjects, and there are countless pictures of maharajas. When it came to Indian women, the photographer generally had still to depend on courtesans and nautch girls, or on tribal women who did not shy away from the camera. Only on very rare occasions was he able to photograph the upper classes, as in the case of a group of high-caste Maharashtrian women who seem to have posed for an unknown British photographer (fig. 193).

The one field in which photography made a distinct contribution was news reportage. Beato's photographs of the aftermath of the Indian Mutiny communicated the horrors of that war more directly than any drawing. And photographers like Captain Hooper, who did a series of shots of the devastating Madras Famine of 1877, made it startling clear to the viewer what the camera could do.

III

SAMUEL BOURNE (1834–1912) was the most important British photographer in India and certainly the best known. He traveled to the subcontinent in 1863 at a time when photography was enjoying a rather high artistic status, partly because of its novelty. Bourne arrived in Calcutta and joined hands with Charles Shepherd, who had already established a small photographic concern, to form the renowned photographic firm of Bourne and Shepherd which thrives to this day. The work was divided between the partners to the satisfaction of both. Shepherd was content to stay in Calcutta, fixing and printing pictures, acquiring various supplies, especially collodion, and generally handling the business end of the operation. Bourne set off on his more adventurous expeditions and within a few years earned the enviable reputation of India's leading landscape photographer.

It is not mere coincidence that some of Bourne's best landscapes are of places that bear a strong resemblance to the British countryside—the hillstation of Ootacamund, Dal Lake in Kashmir, Nainital. Bourne's *Ootacamund, A Peep from Near Bombay House* is remarkably classical in its composition, and could be mistaken for a view of the English Lake District (fig. 194). It was not merely by coincidence that Ootacamund looked British. Sullivan, the collector of Coimbatore who discovered the hillstation in 1820, sent for a gardener from England, a Mr. Johnson, who arrived with the first seeds for apple and peach trees, strawberries, raspberries, and hollyhocks. Estates with names like Grasmere Lodge, Kenilworth, Woodcock Hall, and Apple Cottage sprung up in Ooty which, at an altitude of over 7,000 feet and only eleven degrees north of the equator, was indeed

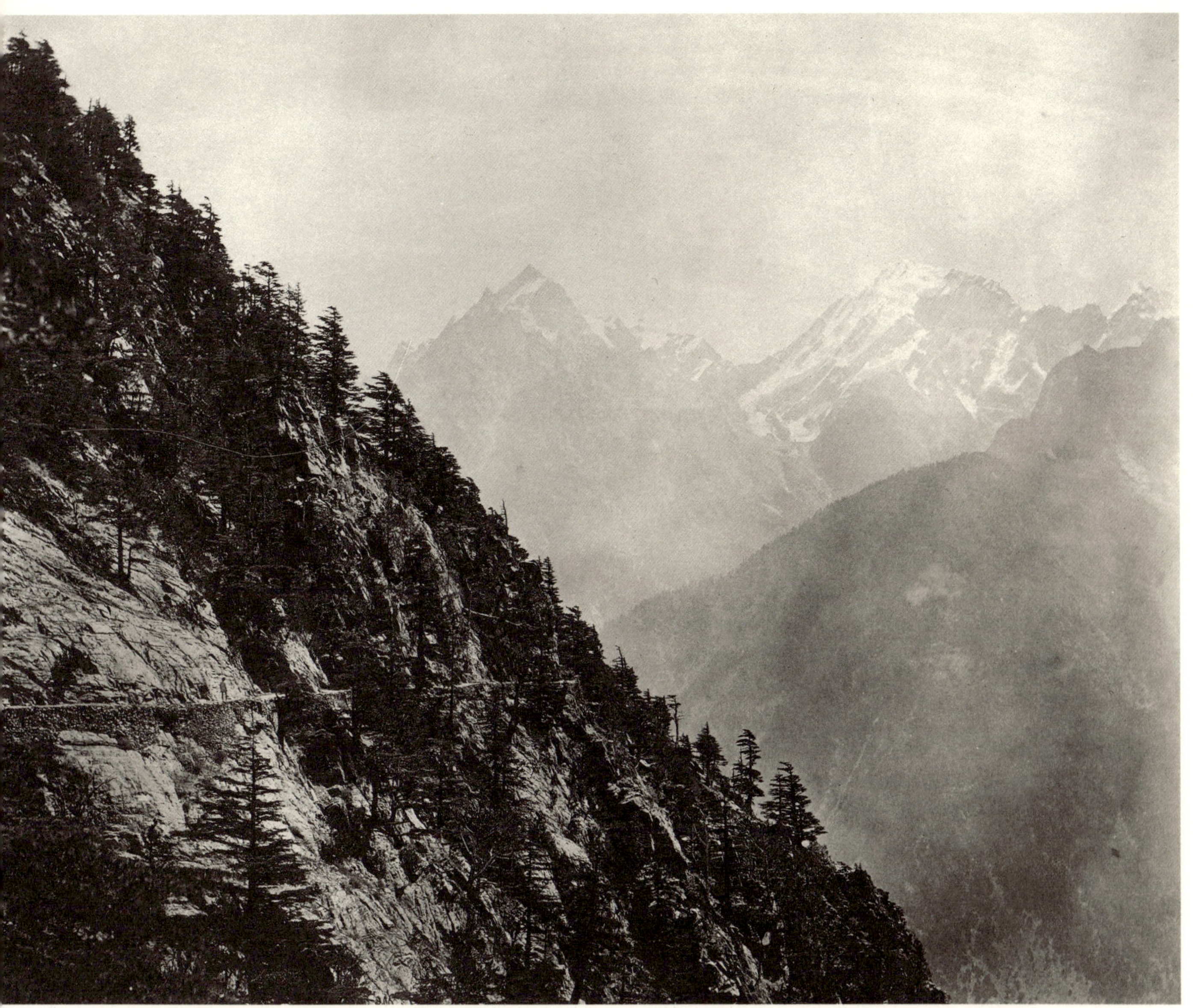

197. Samuel Bourne. *View from New Tibet Road near Cheenee*. Mid-1860s. Albumen print. Walter Collection.

a home away from home. Consider how Lord Lytton, viceroy of India from 1876 to 1880, extolled the glories of Ootacamund in a letter to his wife: "Imagine Hertfordshire lanes, Devonshire downs, Westmoreland lakes, Scotch trout streams . . . ." Even the rainy season did not dampen his enthusiasm, "Such beautiful *English* rain, such delicious *English* mud," he happily wrote.[22] Bourne's pleasing picture of Ootacamund considered alongside Luke Herrmann's description of what constitutes a classi-

cal landscape shows how close the perceptions of the painter and photographer had become:

. . . open foreground like a stage . . . framing trees on one side balanced by an answering motif on the other . . . a circuitous path taking the eye by easy and varied stages to a luminous distance . . . .[23]

In Kashmir, Bourne produced a series of enchanting views of the Dal Lake of Srinagar (fig. 195). There was scarcely a soul who had not heard of the beauties of the Kashmir Valley,

189

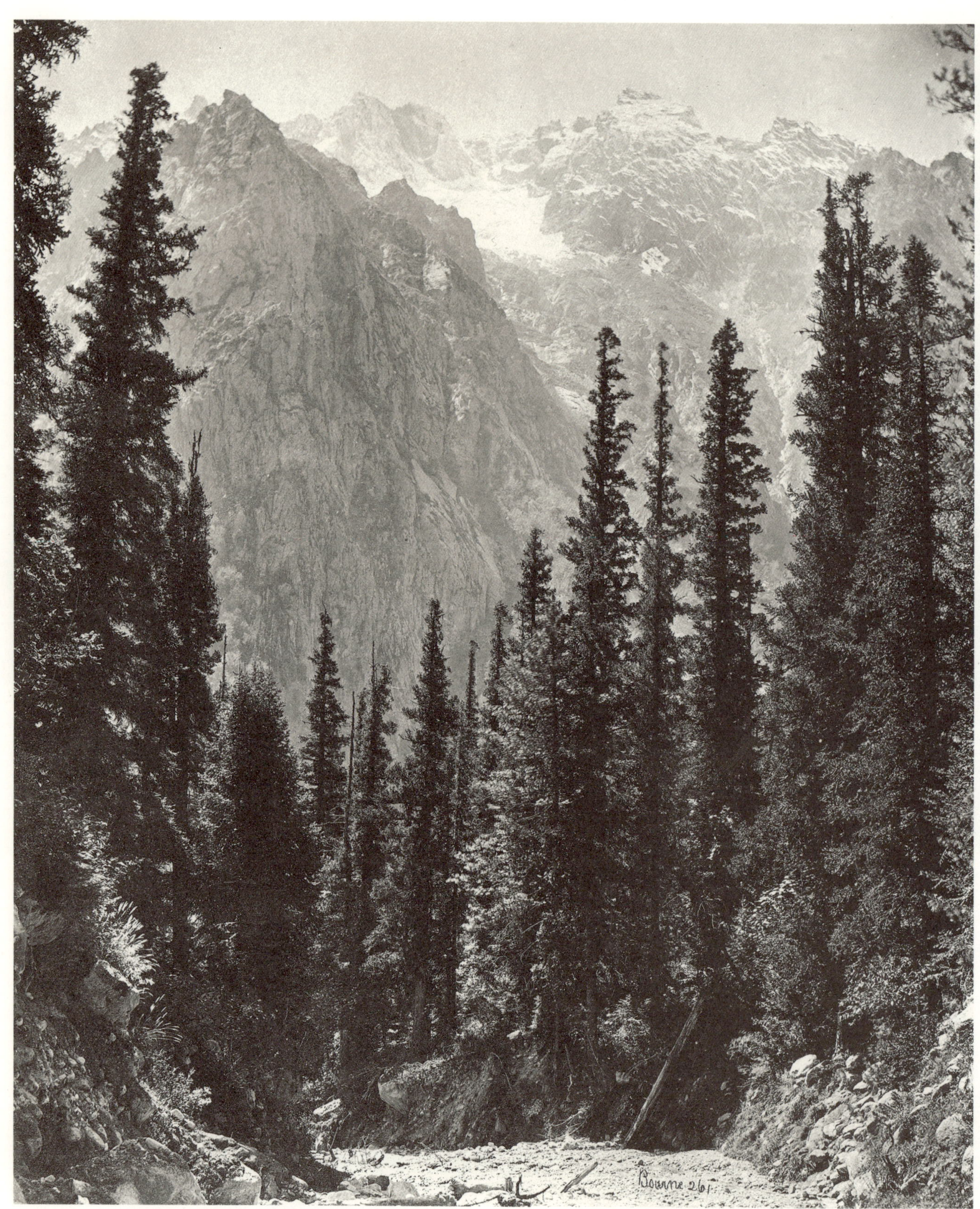

198. Samuel Bourne. *Snowy Heights at Wangtu*. Mid-1860s. Albumen print. Walter Collection.

probably from the poem *Lalla Rookh*, with which Bourne, too, was familiar:

Who has not heard of the Vale of Cashmere,
With its roses the brightest that earth ever gave,
Its temples and grottoes and fountains as clear
As the love-lighted eyes that hang over the wave?[24]

Dal Lake lived up to Bourne's expectations:

Looking up the reach before us the eye is immediately enchanted by the splendour of the overhanging foliage and its reflections in the placid water. Chunars of immense size stretch forward their giant trunks and arms across the stream, as if trying to kiss their fellows on the opposite bank; rows of poplars rise behind, and graceful willows mingle their feathery sprays with masses of denser foliage. Such a scene . . . could not fail to delight the heart of any artist; and when I add that every leaf was still and that not a breath or whisper of a breeze disturbed the image mirrored in the depths of the glassy stream, my readers will understand with what exultation I, as a photographer, feasted my eyes on this scene of unruffled beauty.[25]

Even the weather in Kashmir suited the photographer:

The summer of Kashmir very much resembles that of England, when the latter is what it ought to be—bright and warm . . . . All my chemicals worked satisfactorily . . . . And what a pleasure it was to work on those grassy swards, and in the shadow of those delightful trees.[26]

At Nainital, which Bourne described as a "pretty hill station . . . with a lake shut in by an amphitheatre of mountains,"[27] he shot a set of beautiful, formal photographs (fig. 196). Here, as in Kashmir, he found an abundance of that essential ingredient of his picturesque—water—in the *tal* or lake in Nynee. Again, these photographs of Nynee could be easily mistaken for the English Lake District. Only a naturalist would be able to identify the uniquely Eastern deodar trees framing the picture.

Bourne's excursions into the upper Himalayan regions, with their grand, desolate, and awe-inspiring mountains, left him somewhat disappointed:

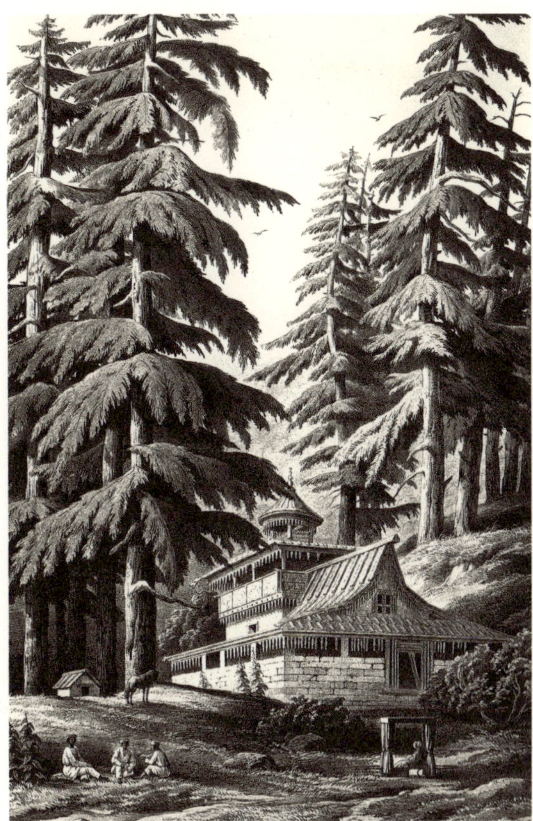

199. Mrs. W. L. L. Scott. *Sunset View of a Temple among Cedars Near Simla*. 1852. Lithograph. Private Collection.

I may here pause for a moment to remark that the character of the Himalayan scenery in general is not picturesque. I have not yet seen Switzerland . . . from the numerous descriptions I have read of it, I should say it is far more pleasing and picturesque than any part I have yet seen of the Himalayas.[28]

Nonetheless, he concluded that the Himalayas "represent a variety of scenery by no means to be despised, if it be not so picturesque and beautiful as some to be found among the Alps of Italy and Switzerland."[29] But, his idea of the romantic picturesque was to find waterfalls dashing through "romantic gorges," or "leaping from rock to rock in many cascades or one impressive fall." The splendid Himalayan scenery was "wanting in variety."[30]

Bourne traveled on the newly constructed Tibet road toward the village of Cheenee and took a stunning photograph of the road on the mountainside, with the lofty snow peaks in the

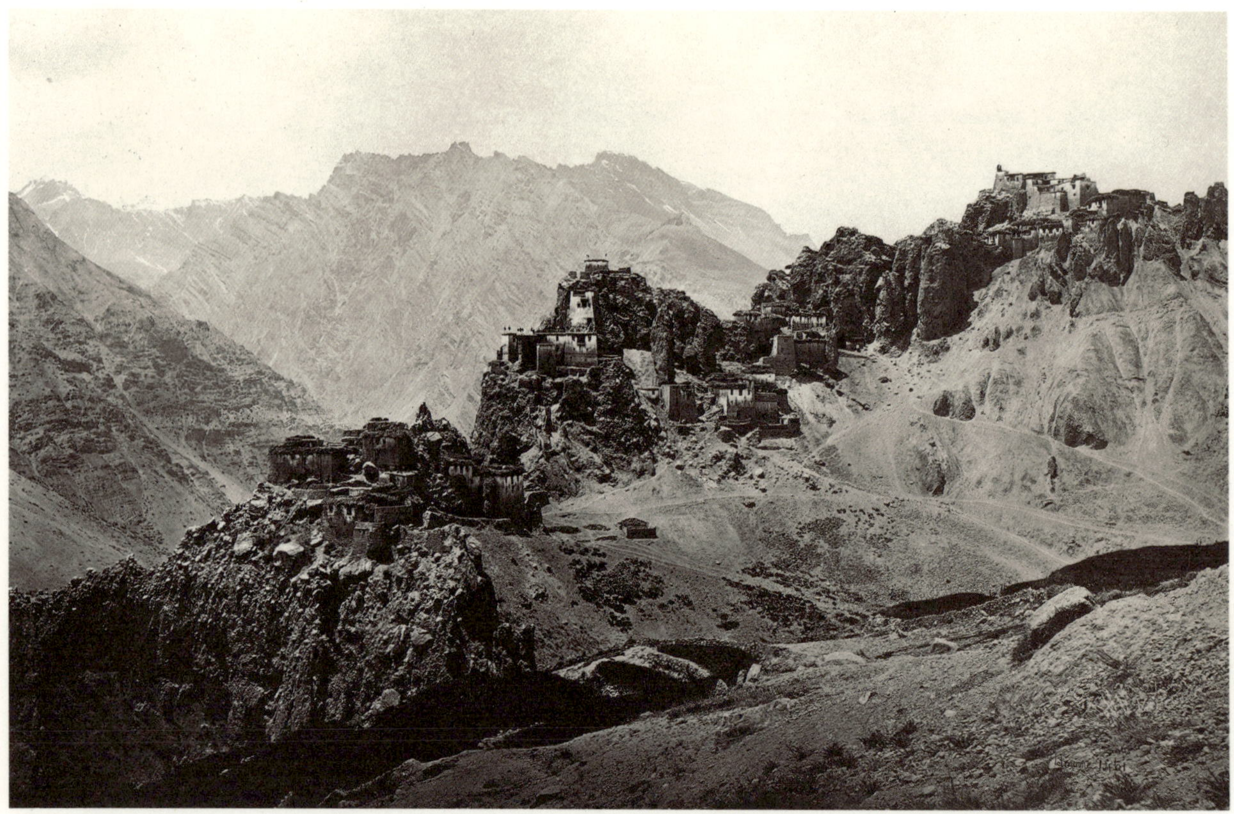

200. Samuel Bourne. *Village of Dunkar, Spiti.* Mid-1860s. Albumen print. Walter Collection.

background (fig. 197). With its opposing diagonals, the photograph is a remarkable document. Bourne spoke enthusiastically about this mountain road:

It winds along successive ranges, following their windings, sometimes at an immense height above the valleys . . . . Here it leads through tremendous forests of noble deodars; there it is carried along the perpendicular face of cliffs hundreds, and in some places thousands of feet in height, making one giddy to glance down to the awful depths below.[31]

Crossing the Taree pass at a height of over 15,000 feet, which, as Bourne remarks, was already 200 feet higher than the Alps, this intrepid photographer descended into the beautiful Wangtu Valley, which answered almost all of his ideas of the picturesque (fig. 198). He wrote, "It has seldom, if ever, been my lot to look upon and photograph a scenery so magnificent and beautiful as that I now met in the Wangtu valley." He spoke with keenness of the trees and tells how, "with the splendid moun-

tain ranges on each side of the valley for backgrounds, these trees combined to form delightful pictures and I lingered amongst them for a week hard at work every day with my camera."[32] Bourne himself felt these pictures ranked "first in my productions."[33] They are well-balanced compositions that accord with the established British principles of classical beauty. It is fascinating to compare the composition of this photograph with a *Sunset View of a Temple among Cedars Near Simla* published in 1852 by Mrs. W. L. L. Scott (fig. 199). The comparison again demonstrates how the perceptions of the artist and the photographer are often very similar.

On Bourne's last Himalayan expedition he traveled into the barren mountain region of Spiti. He wrote of the "curious and picturesque village called Dunkar" (fig. 200):

The houses were built into the sides of the hill, which had been scooped out by nature into holes and caverns; and the way these had been taken advantage of

192

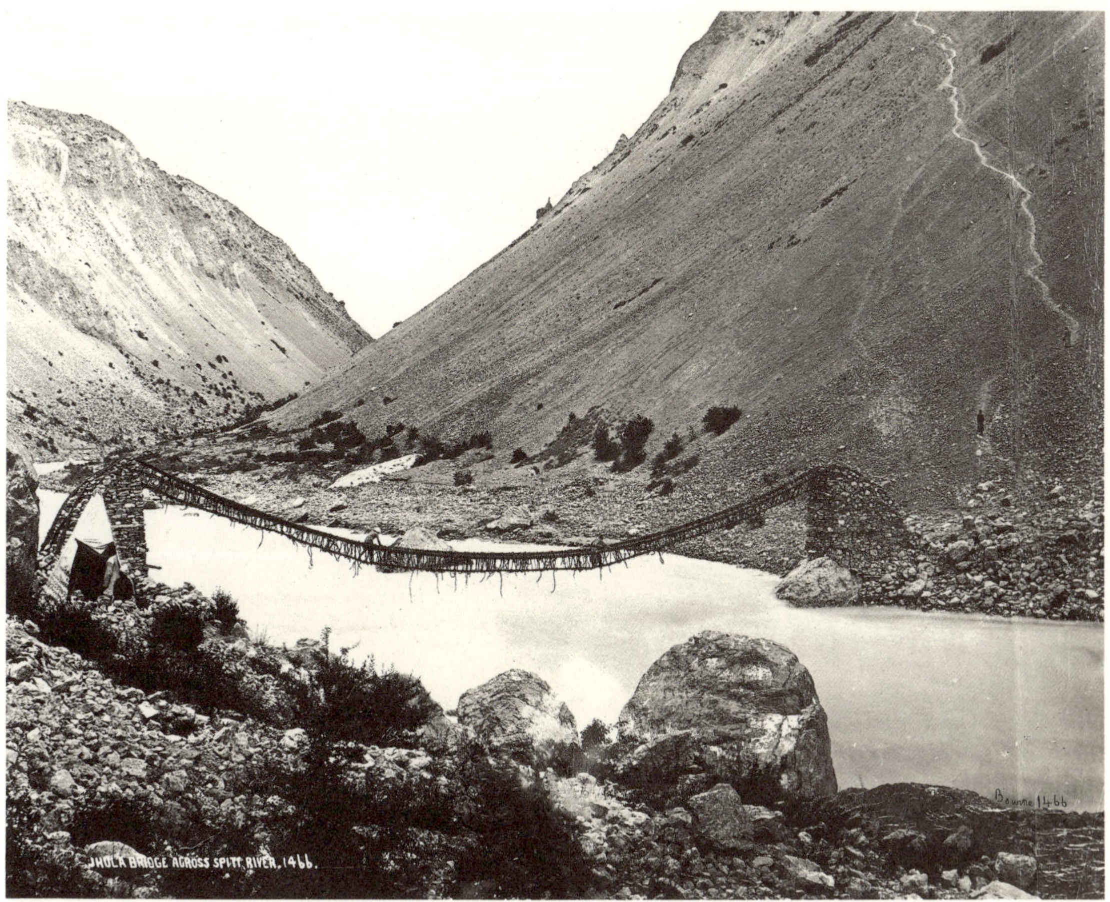

201. Samuel Bourne. *Jhula Bridge at Spiti*. Mid-1860s. Albumen print. Walter Collection.

and built into until the hand of man and the hand of nature seemed to unite, was ingenious and picturesque.[34]

The contrast between the sharp focus on the village houses and the hazy mountains is striking.

Bourne photographed a jhula (swinging) bridge across the Spiti River, "a most villanous bridge, made as usual of twisted twigs" (fig. 201).[35] It is difficult to picture Bourne's party of now forty-two bearers getting across such bridges with all of his precious equipment. Of the precarious bridge at Spiti, he recalled:

I had to scramble over as best I could, experiencing all the time the not very agreeable sensation that I, bridge, and all were being carried down the stream at a furious pace . . . . After getting safely over I could afford to survey it calmly, and took a picture of it with the greatest composure.[36]

On the return journey, he found that this rope "bridge" had indeed been carried away!

Like the early landscape artists in India, Bourne was captivated by the banyan tree. His photograph of a great spreading banyan at Barrackpore is so successful because of the effect of the light streaming through the dense foliage (fig. 202). In the foreground, providing a relative scale, is a seated woman who has been identified as Bourne's wife. This popular photograph appeared time and again in British scrapbooks of India, especially because Shepherd, with his keen sense of business acumen, had issued a catalogue of photographs that could be ordered for purchase. Under the title *A Permanent Record of India*, a choice of nearly three thousand pictures was presented to the Englishman keen on remembering his years in India; as the preface read, "If you want to take a record of the places you have seen, this selection cannot be surpassed."[37]

One of the reasons for the success of Bourne's landscapes is the amount of care and patience he expended on prospecting for views. Hours were spent finding the perfect spot from which

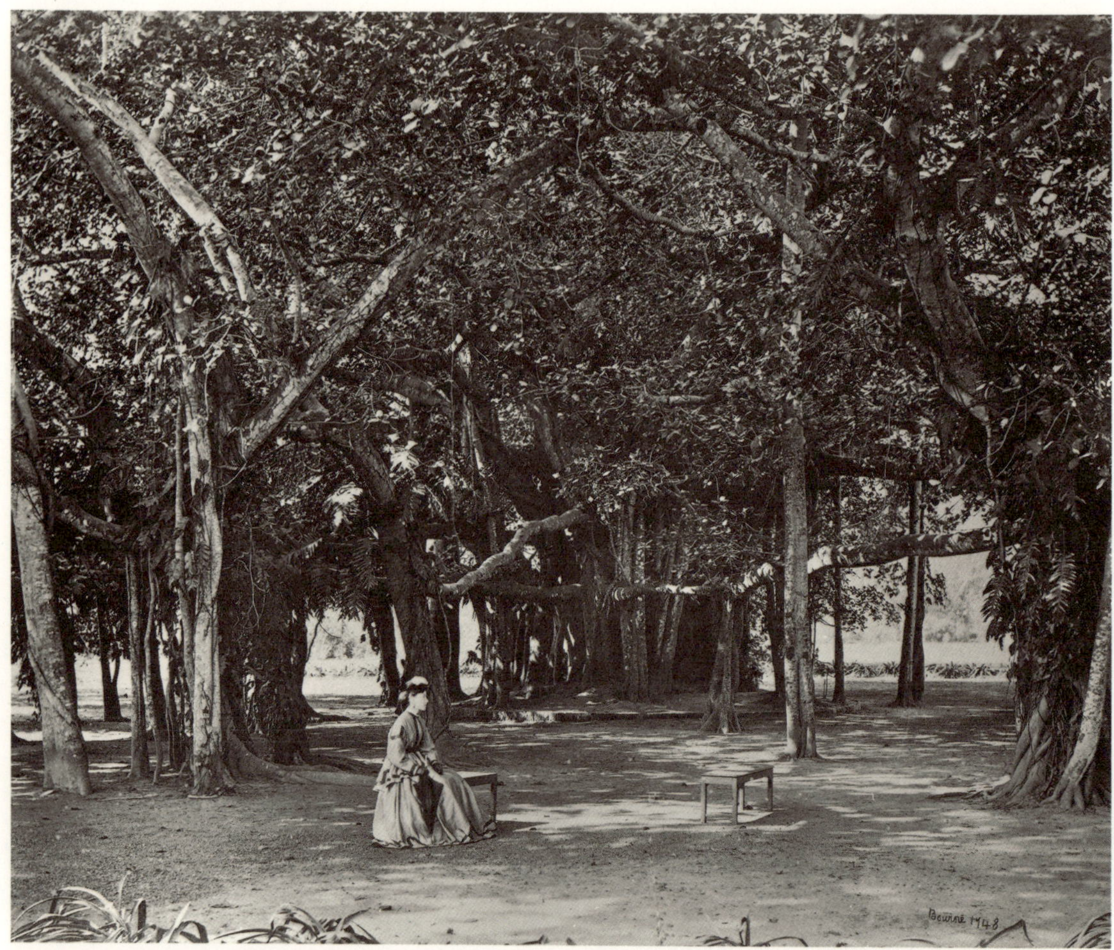

202. Samuel Bourne. *Banyan Tree, Barrackpore*. Mid-1860s. Albumen print. Walter Collection.

to get a photograph. Hours, even days, were spent waiting for the perfect climatic conditions: "On one occasion," Bourne wrote, "I waited six days rather than leave two remarkably fine pictures or take them under unfavourable circumstances." [38] In order to secure the exact view he wanted, he often stationed himself in precarious positions:

My anxiety to get views of some of these fine combinations of rocks and water often induced me to leave the regular track and put myself and instruments in the greatest danger by attempting an abrupt descent to some spot below, indicated by the eye as likely to command a fine picture. [39]

Every exposure was carefully timed and *had* to be successful in view of the difficulties transporting the glass plates and other equipment across the Himalayas.

Bourne's ability to capture cloudy skies and unusual atmospheric conditions is remarkable, and was a technical mystery to his contemporaries who acknowledge this openly in the pages of the *British Journal of Photography*. An editorial in the January 1867 issue read:

We should like to know something more concerning Mr. Bourne's method of operating . . . . We are constrained to admit that the artist is possessed of manipulative or chemical resources shared in common by few . . . .

Bourne returned to England in 1870, having spent seven productive years in India. He went into the family cotton yarn business and devoted his leisure hours to painting watercolors. Photography, however, remained his chief interest. In a lecture to the Nottingham Arts Society, he explained that the instrument used by an art-

194

ist, whether brush or camera or burin, was not of prime importance. He believed that a photographer could stamp his individuality on a photograph just as much as a painter could on a canvas. In all of his public addresses, he stressed the importance of familiarity with photographic materials and chemicals, which he felt were essential to success.[40]

IV

THE camera proved an invaluable aid in the field of architectural documentation. As early as 1855, the East India Company realized the immense potential of photography in this regard and suggested the use of photographers in place of draftsmen in an official dispatch to its officers:

We have recently desired the Government of Bombay to discontinue the employment of draughtsmen in the delineation of antiquities of Western India and to employ photography instead, and it is our desire that this method be generally substituted throughout India . . . . We shall be prepared to forward the necessary apparatus for the use of any of our Governments which may make application for them.[41]

At the same time, the governor of the Company's military academy at Addiscombe in Surrey acknowledged that a familiarity with photography would be useful for his officers and recommended "that some instruction should be imparted to the Gentlemen Cadets in the Art of Photography."[42] The suggestion was accepted and lessons were instituted; the following year, an elementary manual on photography was issued to each cadet. In India, photographic materials were allocated as part of the scientific equipment issued to army personnel.

One of the earliest architectural photographers was Dr. John Murray (1809–98), principal of the medical school in Agra. An amateur photographer, Murray used the calotype process for his photographs taken in and around

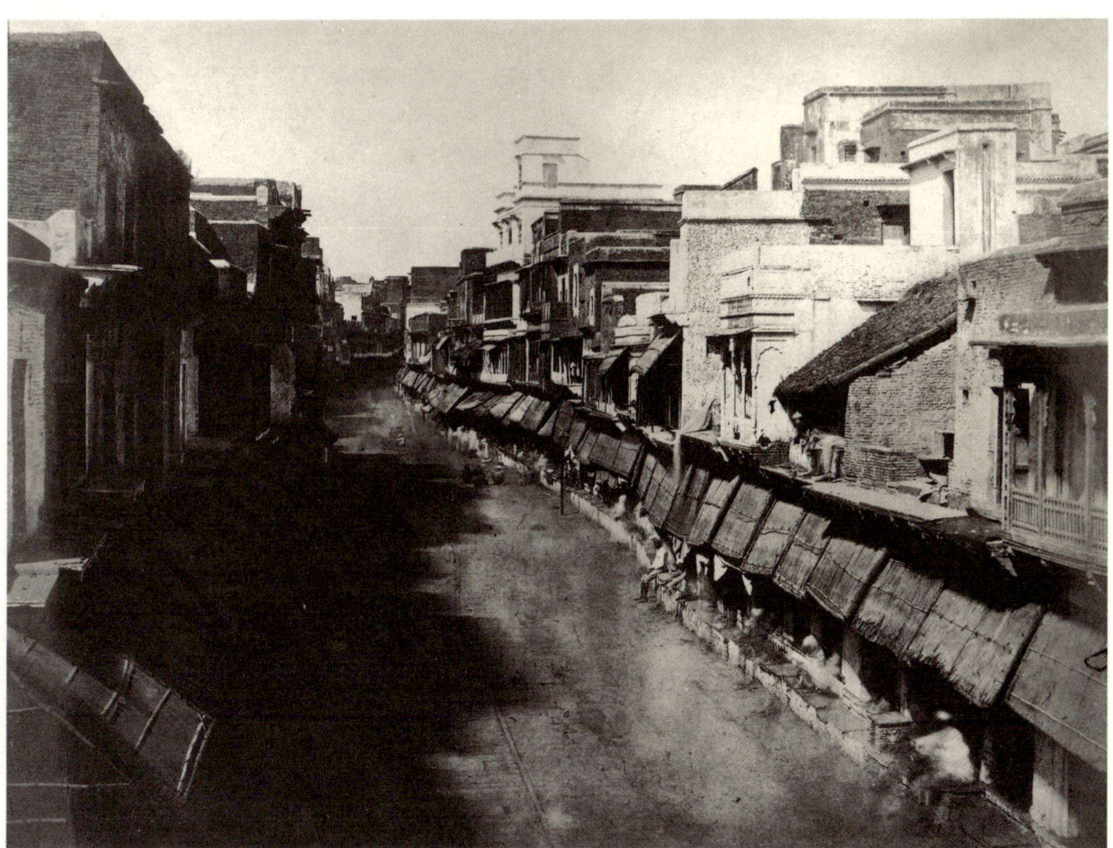

203. Dr. John Murray. *Principal Street, Agra.* 1857. Calotype print. Walter Collection.

Agra in the 1850s. In 1858, the London publisher Hogarth issued a set of thirty of Murray's large prints of Agra (17 x 13 in.), including a view of Agra's main street (fig. 203). Murray obtained the paper for his pictures from England and the name of his supplier, Turner of Chafford Mills in Kent, is on many of his paper negatives. Considering the limitations of calotype, Murray's photographs are remarkably sharp and clear.

Another amateur photographer who specialized in architectural subjects was Captain Linneaus Tripe (1822–1902), who began his career in 1855 as photographer to the British Mission in Burma, taking pictures of a variety of buildings and temples as well as general views of the capital of Ava. In the following year, Tripe was appointed official photographer to the Madras Presidency; his valuable survey of the monuments of Madras was published in a series of six volumes, each devoted to an individual district and containing some thirty photographs. Like Murray, Tripe worked with the calotype and achieved great success with the technique. He often blacked out the skies on his negatives which resulted in a strange unreal whiteness on the finished prints. In 1860, after Sir Charles Trevelyan became governor of Madras, he eliminated the position of official photographer, and the Company was deprived of Tripe's services. While Tripe continued to serve in the Indian army, retiring finally as Honorary Major General, he seems to have totally abandoned photography.

Barely five years after having abolished the post of official photographer, the Madras government changed its policies and commissioned Captain E. D. Lyon to photograph the monuments in the Presidency. Lyon (in India 1865– 71) took nearly 300 photographs, all of very high quality. Some of these were displayed at the 1869 exhibition of the Photographic Society in London where they were much admired:

What painting could record the multitudinous detail of the figure friezes and ornaments of the Buddhist

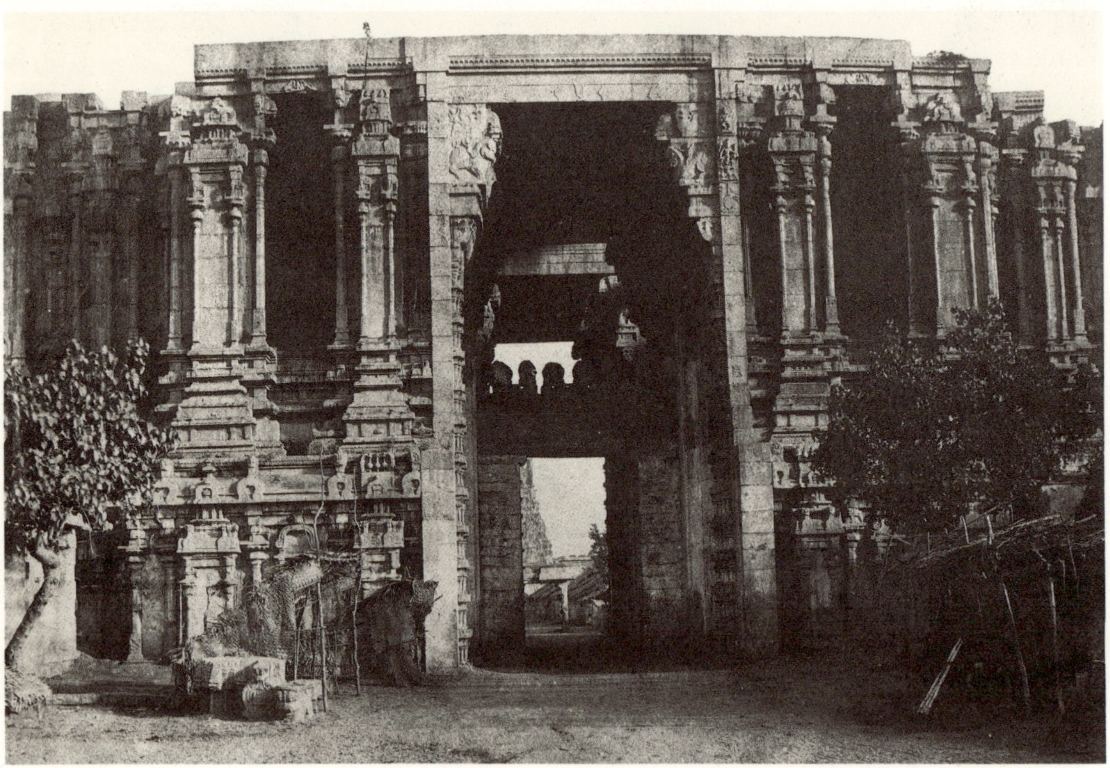

204. Captain Linneaus Tripe. *Unfinished Gopuram*. c. 1858. Calotype print. Walter Collection.

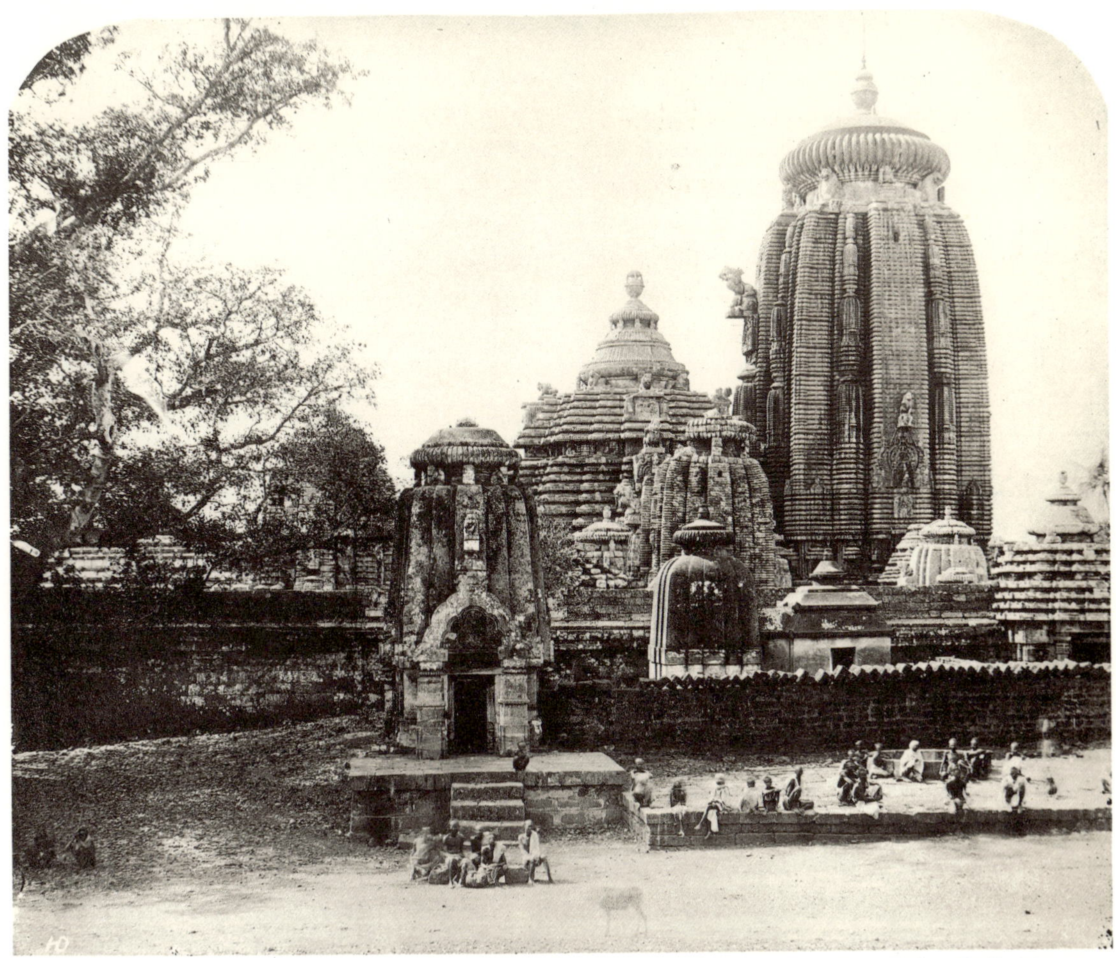

205. Captain Dixon. *The Great Temple at Bhubanesvar.* c. 1858. Albumen print. Walter Collection.

temples of Southern India like these admirable photos of Captain Lyon's?[43]

Comments were made on the "photographic excellence" of his collodiotypes, and "tenderness and delicacy" were the qualities that critics saw in his works. Captain Lyon had exceptional success photographing the impressive but unlit corridors of the Ramesvaram temple, which is some 700 feet long. He tells us of the method he used whereby "light had to be turned on by means of natives stationed at certain points with reflectors."[44] *The London Times* spoke highly of his achievement:

No means except the camera can give any idea of the amazing richness and variety of detail lavished on their sculptured decorations. The scenes of Captain Lyon's is the revelation of a new world of architectural form and ornamentation.[45]

During the same years that Tripe worked in Madras (c. 1855–60) Captain Dixon made a survey of the rock-cut caves and temples of Orissa. A *Times* review of an exhibition of his photographs in London praised them as

a really valuable contribution to Indian archaeology and architecture . . . which will embrace the whole of the singular relics which have as yet been known to us only through imperfect sketches and still more imperfect descriptions.[46]

Samuel Bourne, though primarily a landscape photographer, took several pictures of the monuments of India. He was drawn to Benares and shot views of the temples and ghats (fig. 206). He also photographed the palace known as the Kaiser Pasund in Lucknow (fig. 88). Bourne's photograph is so sharp that it captures the smallest details.

The panoramic photograph, used very effectively with architecture, was part of a search

197

for something new and astounding, for un-precedented effects. It was also an outgrowth of the new emphasis on verisimilitude which had become "a basic principle of nineteenth century English aesthetic doctrine."[47] Using the pan-oramic shot, the photographer found he could dramatize a scene and subtly manipulate its scale. Two successful, if not theatrical, pan-oramas, one of the Taj Mahal and the other of Elphinstone Circle in Bombay, are by anony-mous photographers and were taken sometime in the 1870s (figs. 207, 208). Both were done using the earliest and simplest method of pro-ducing a panorama with a regular box camera; once the first plate had been exposed, the cam-era was revolved so that the next view would partially overlap the previous one. The views were then pasted together to produce the final panorama. Both of these photographs were composed of carefully matched prints: three in the Taj shot and four in the Elphinstone pan-orama. The latter appear to have been trimmed before pasting. Not only did the images have to line up exactly but the tones of the prints had to match from one exposure to the next. Consider-able labor was involved in the production of such views; in the case of the Taj panorama, the photographer must have perched himself and his heavy equipment in a very precarious loca-tion—probably high up on the formal gateway leading to the Taj enclosure—for the consider-able amount of time required for the three exposures.

The Taj Mahal was the subject of paintings and photographs by every artist, amateur and professional, who visited India. The majority of these views were not very successful in captur-ing the spirit of the monument. Bourne wrote of the impact of the building:

Looking down a walk, straight as an arrow, bordered by a double row of cypress trees, with a row of foun-tain jets in the centre, your eye rests on a huge white dome at the other end. Lofty trees intervening hide the other parts of the building, which is shortly to burst on your enraptured gaze, and you saunter through a glorious garden of flowers and foliage un-conscious of what awaits you . . . . Arrived at the top,

why do you stand in breathless astonishment, your feet rivetted to the spot? Ah, why indeed? To that question I can give no satisfactory answer: I can only say the Taj stands before you![48]

A more romantic description of the Taj comes from a letter written by the young Olivia Doug-las to her fiancé in England when on a visit to her brother who was an officer of the East India Company:

From a chapter in the *Arabian Nights*; from the middle of the most gorgeous fairy-tale the mind of man could invent, I write to you tonight.

Often have I heard of the Taj Mahal, read of its beauty, dreamed of its magic, but never in my dreams did I imagine anything so exquisite, so perfect. . . . I am no more capable of describing it than I would have been of building it; you must see it for yourself. It alone is worth coming to India to see.[49]

Elphinstone Circle is one of the most gracious parts of Bombay. In the very heart of the Fort area, and forming its hub, is this circular public garden surrounded by a ring of classical build-ings. The ornate railings of the central garden were imported from England and painted the typical British green. It was built in the 1860s by Forjett, Bombay's municipal commissioner, and named after the previous governor, Lord Elphinstone. The surrounding ring of buildings, with their elegant arched facades, are seen in the panorama from the steps of that most classi-cal of Bombay monuments, the Town Hall, built some forty years earlier. The panorama is extra-ordinarily successful in its presentation of the wide sweep of the circle of buildings and the broad street that surrounds the central garden. The clarity of the production is amazing—every detail of the trellis work on the buildings of the circle is discernable.

V

THE native people of India intrigued the British photographer as much as they had fascinated the earlier British painter. In the 1870s, Lieu-tenant Churchill photographed a group of snake charmers from Gujarat (fig. 209). With their ex-otic costumes, round flat baskets, flutes, and snakes, the three snake charmers form a strik-

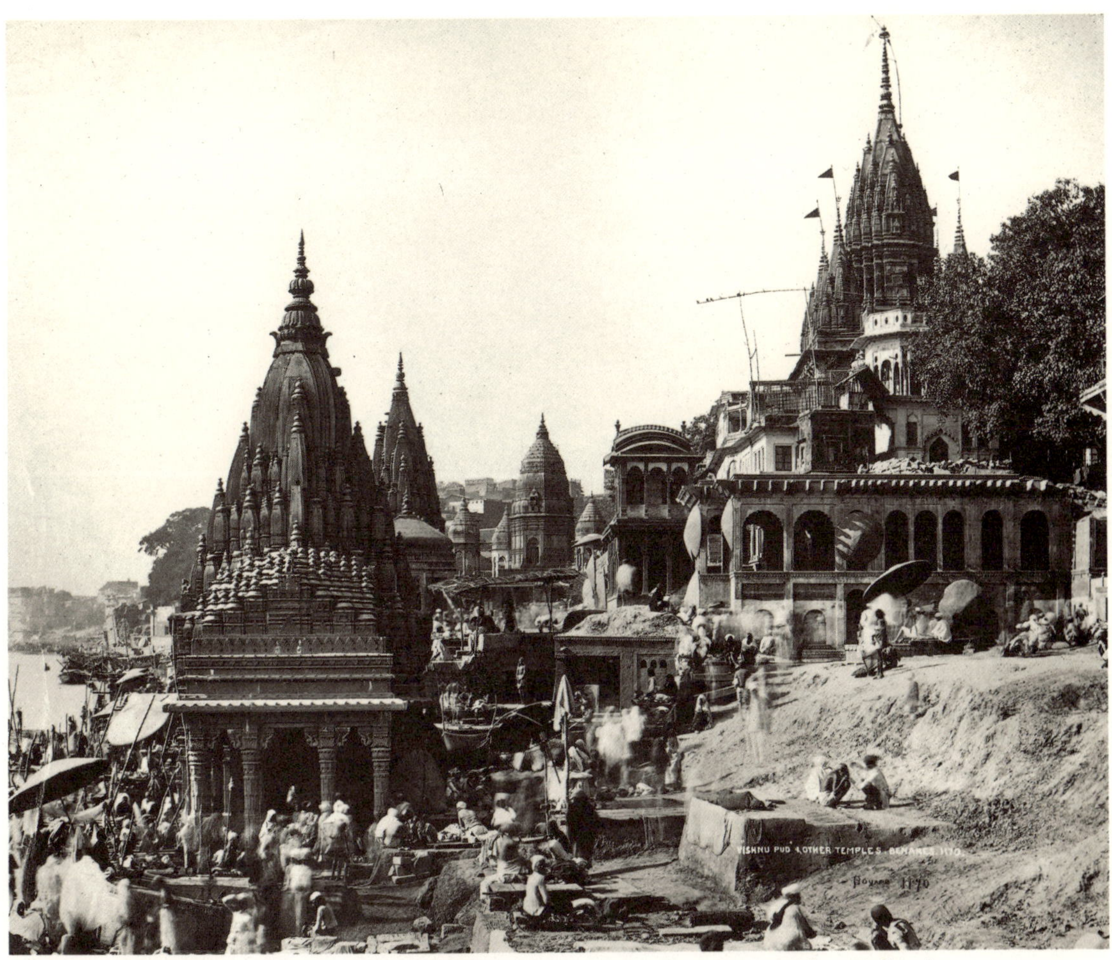

206. Samuel Bourne. *Benares, Vishnu Pud.* Mid-1860s. Albumen print. Walter Collection.

ing composition. The Belgian Sache also photographed the natives; figure 210 is of a *bhisti* (water carrier) holding the leather sack in which water was transported. A comparison with an early sketch of the same subject (fig. 211) shows that the two compositions are strikingly similar, leading one to speculate whether Sache had this sketch in mind when he posed his subject.

Maharajas were another popular subject. From a group of unidentified photographers of circa 1890 comes a series of albumen portraits of maharajas dressed in their complete formal regalia. Among these is a picture of the young maharaja of Kolhapur in western India, taken perhaps a few years after his accession to the throne as a ten-year-old in 1884 (fig. 212). Another photograph portrays the rakish maharaja of Bhawalpur posed in front of a landscape painting (fig. 213). The portrait of the ruler of the small principality of Shahpura dates from the 1890s (fig. 214). Note the prominence given to the volumes of *The Life and Times of Queen Victoria* in an effort to display loyalty to the Crown. The firm of Bourne and Shepherd put out a very similar large series of portraits of princes. The photographs may have been taken by Colin Murray who took over from Bourne who had returned to England in 1871.

An exceedingly fine portrait of Pratap Singh, the maharaja of Idar, processed around 1900 by the photographic firm of Johnston and Hoffman, was probably taken by P. A. Johnston (fig. 215). The crispness of the earlier portraits has been replaced by gentle lines that melt into the background as a result of the new gelatin silver process. The maharaja of Idar was far more

199

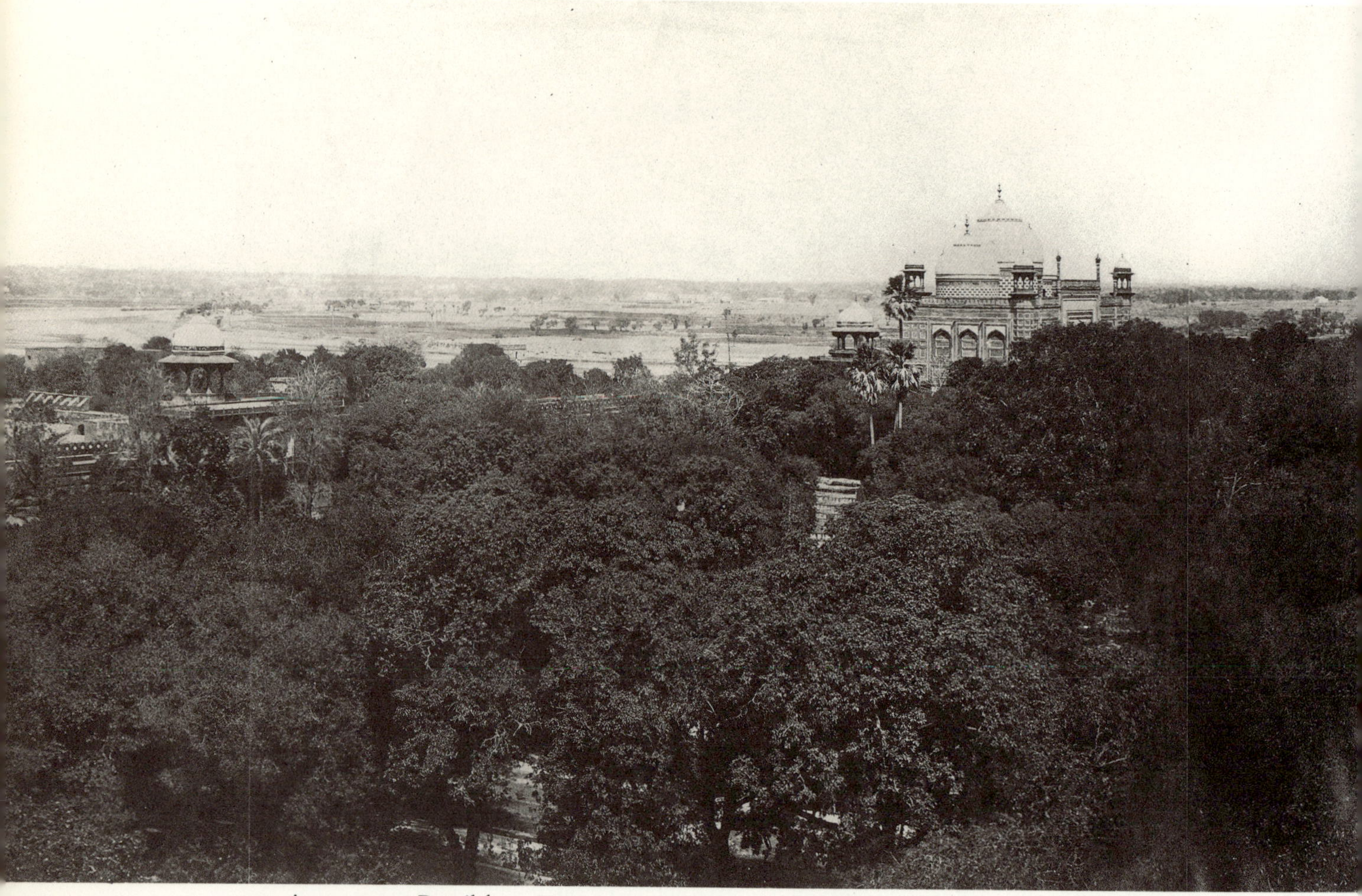

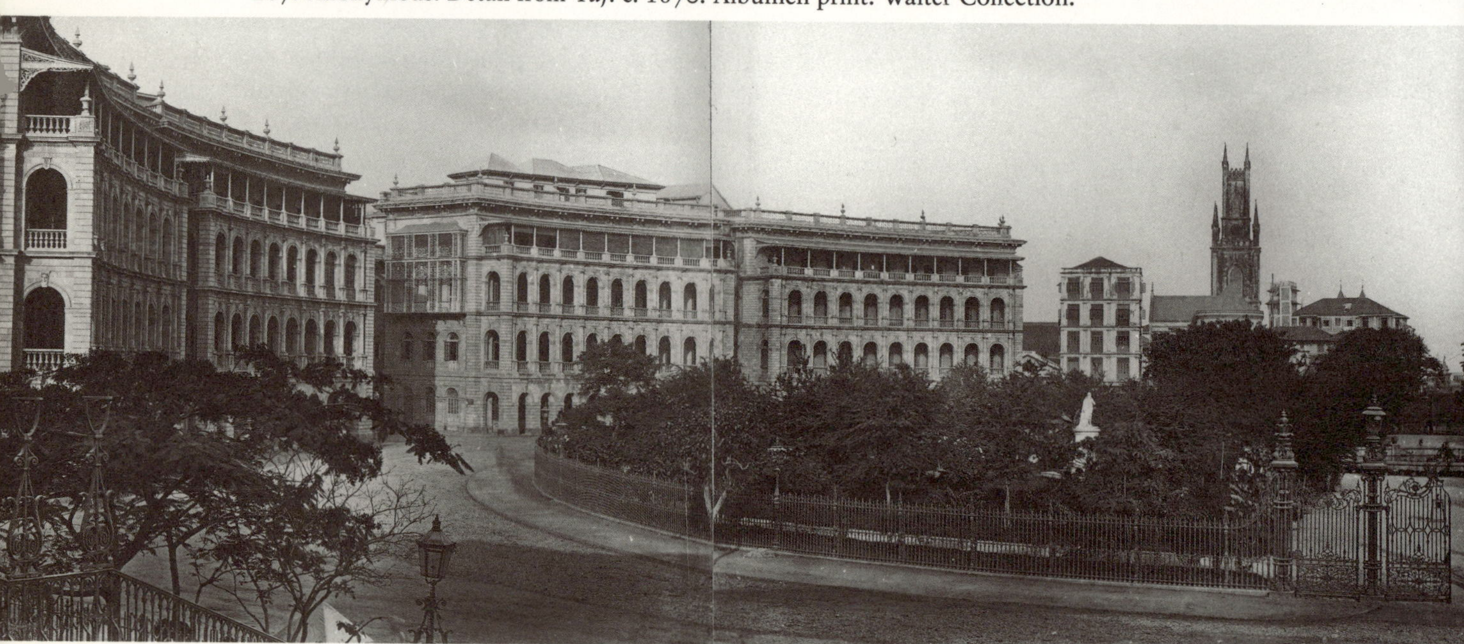

207. Anonymous. Detail from *Taj*. c. 1870. Albumen print. Walter Collection.

208. Anonymous. *Elphinstone Circle, Bombay*. c. 1870. Albumen print. Walter Collection.

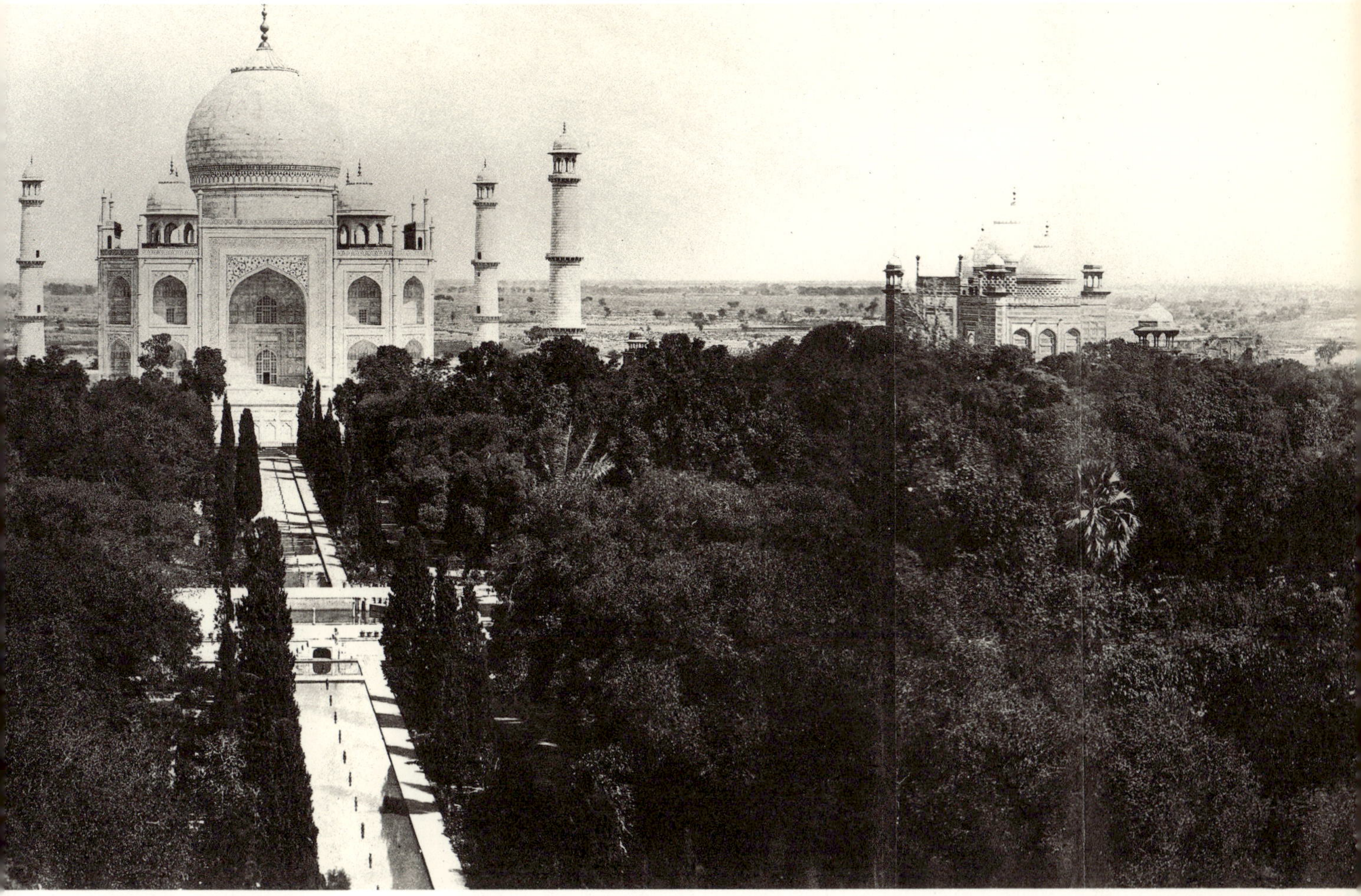

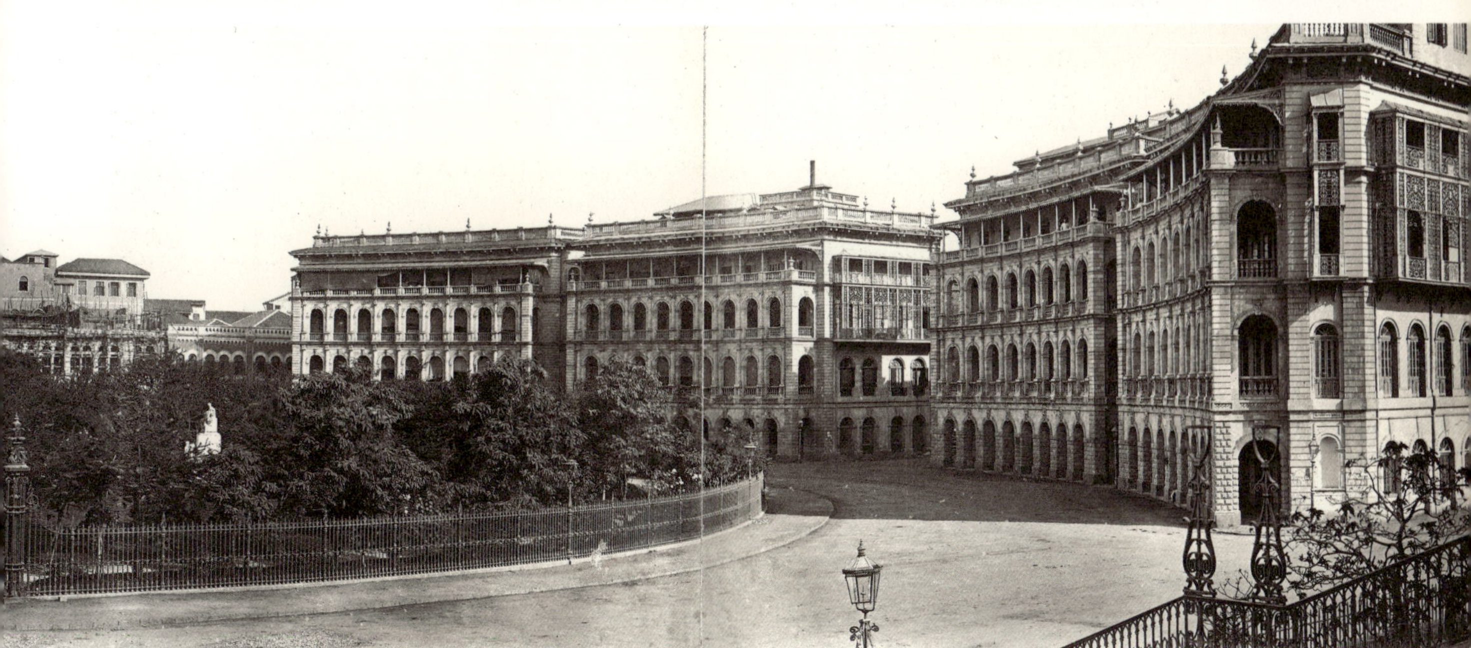

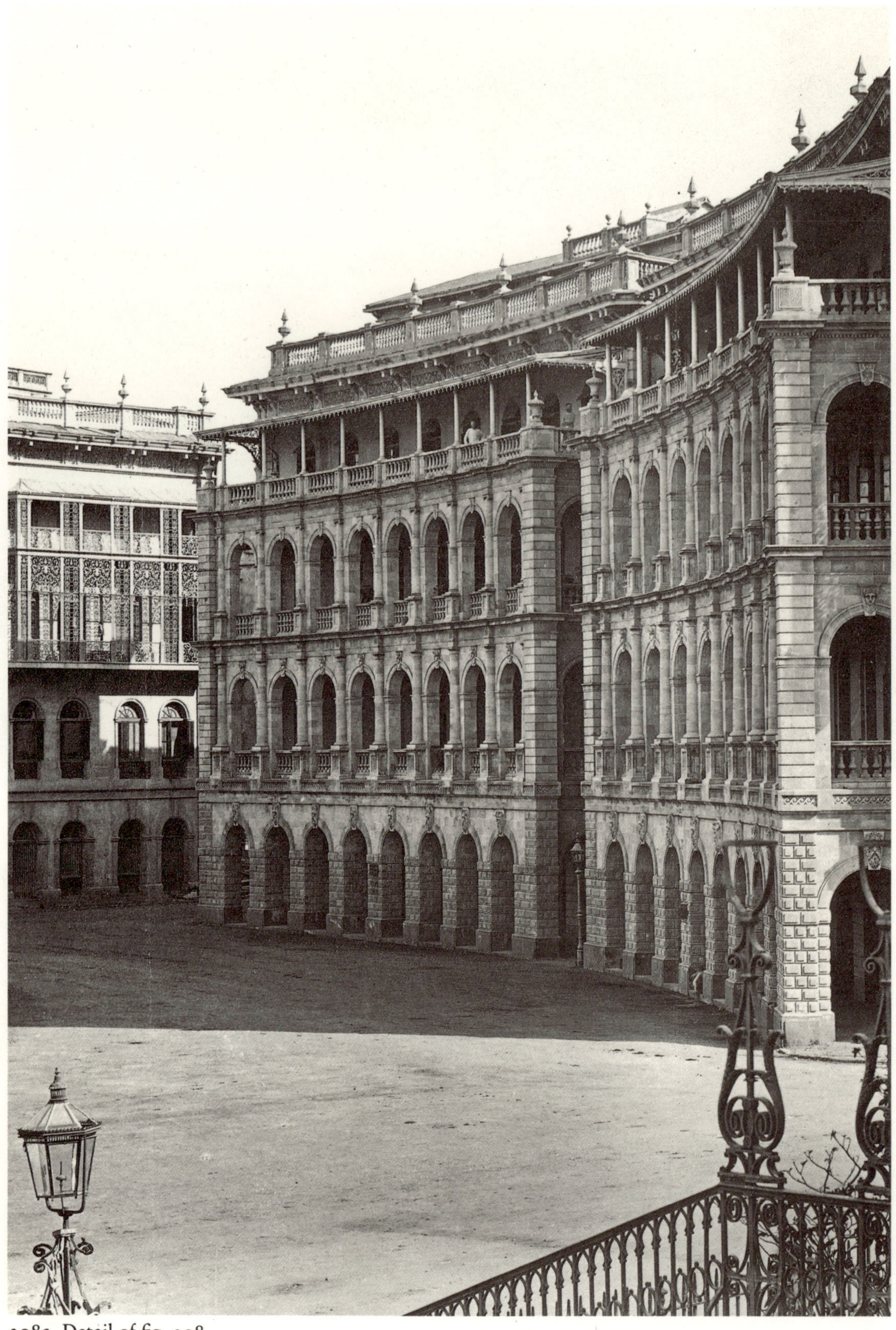

208a. Detail of fig. 208.

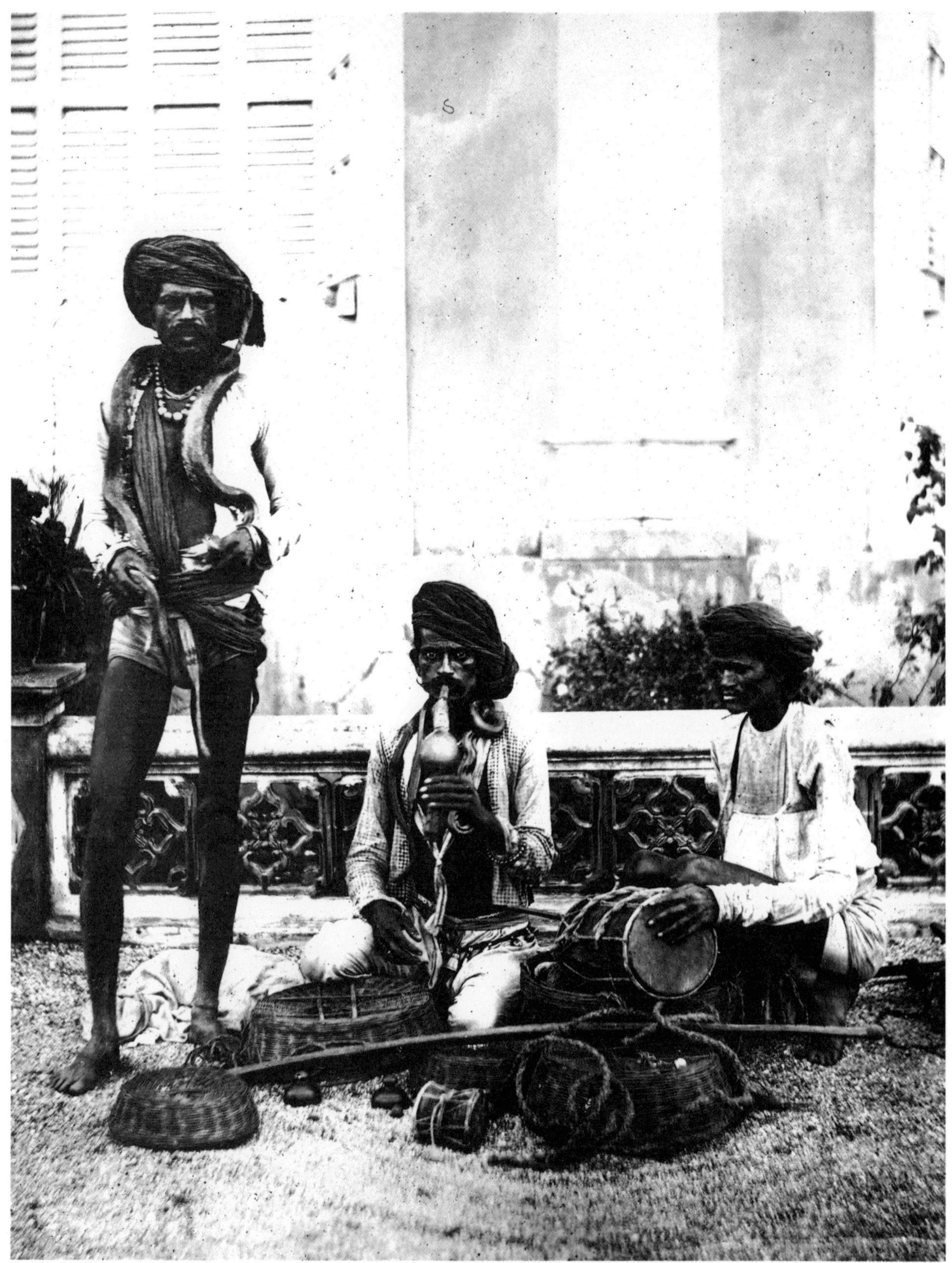

209. L. T. Churchill. *Snake Charmers*. c. 1875. Albumen print. Walter Collection.

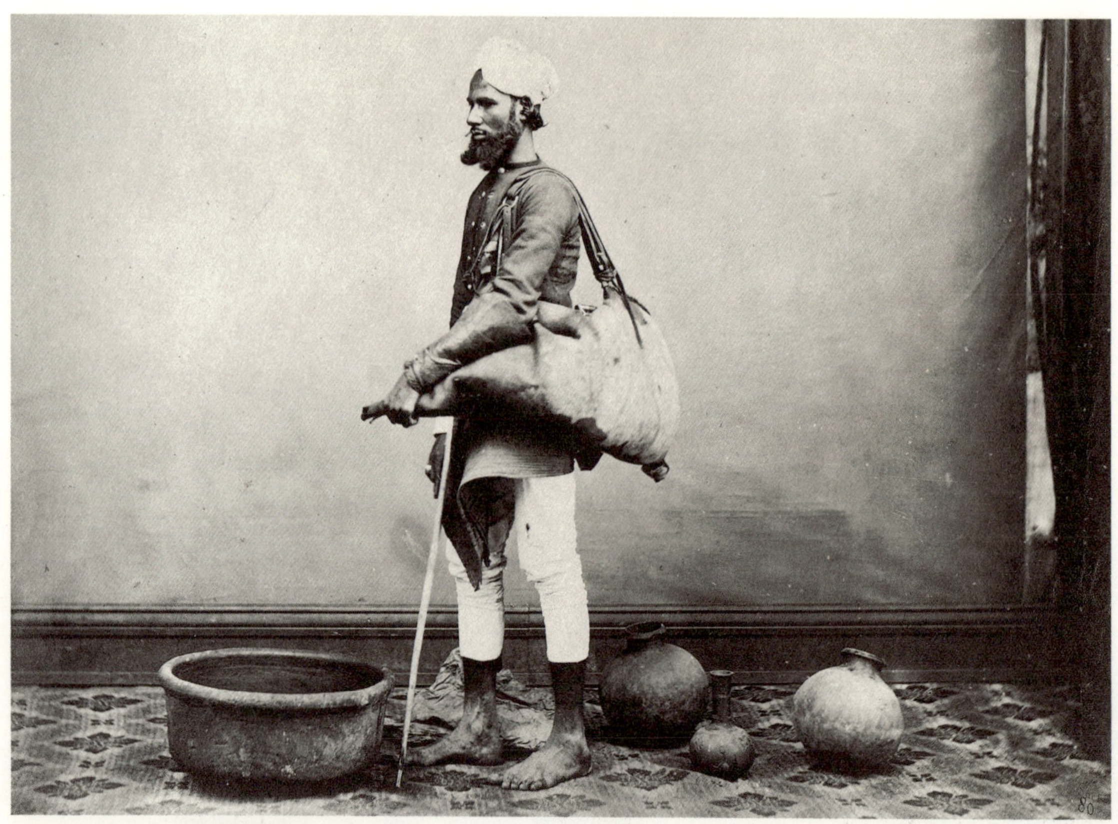

210. Sache. *Calcutta Bhisti*. c. 1870. Albumen print. Walter Collection.

brazen and ostentatious about his display of loyalty than the ruler of Shahpura. His turban is adorned with a miniature portrait of the queen set in a wreath of gold and pearls leaving no doubt as to his affiliation.

Nineteenth-century photographs of well-placed, respectable Indian women are rare, as it was considered improper for women to sit before a camera wielded by a man. Capitalizing on this, a certain Mrs. Garrick decided to specialize in photographing women. The photograph of a courtesan and her maid could have been taken by a European male photographer because they were lower caste women who did not have a status and position to preserve (fig. 216). This powerful and provocative photograph was one of a series taken by an unidentified photographer sometime in the 1860s. Another striking picture taken in the 1870s shows a youthful Benares nautch girl, sitting timidly in a studio (fig. 217).

The firm of Francis Frith published a series

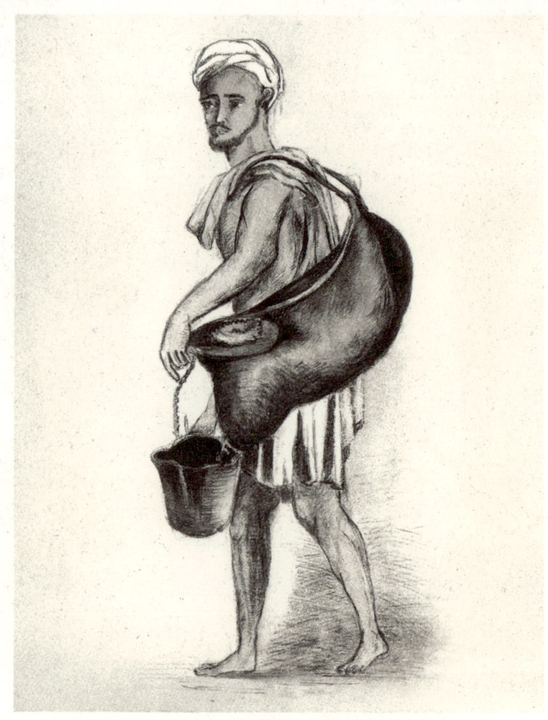

211. B. H. Baden-Powell. *Our Bhisti, Waterman, Calcutta*. 1861. Charcoal. Walter Collection.

204

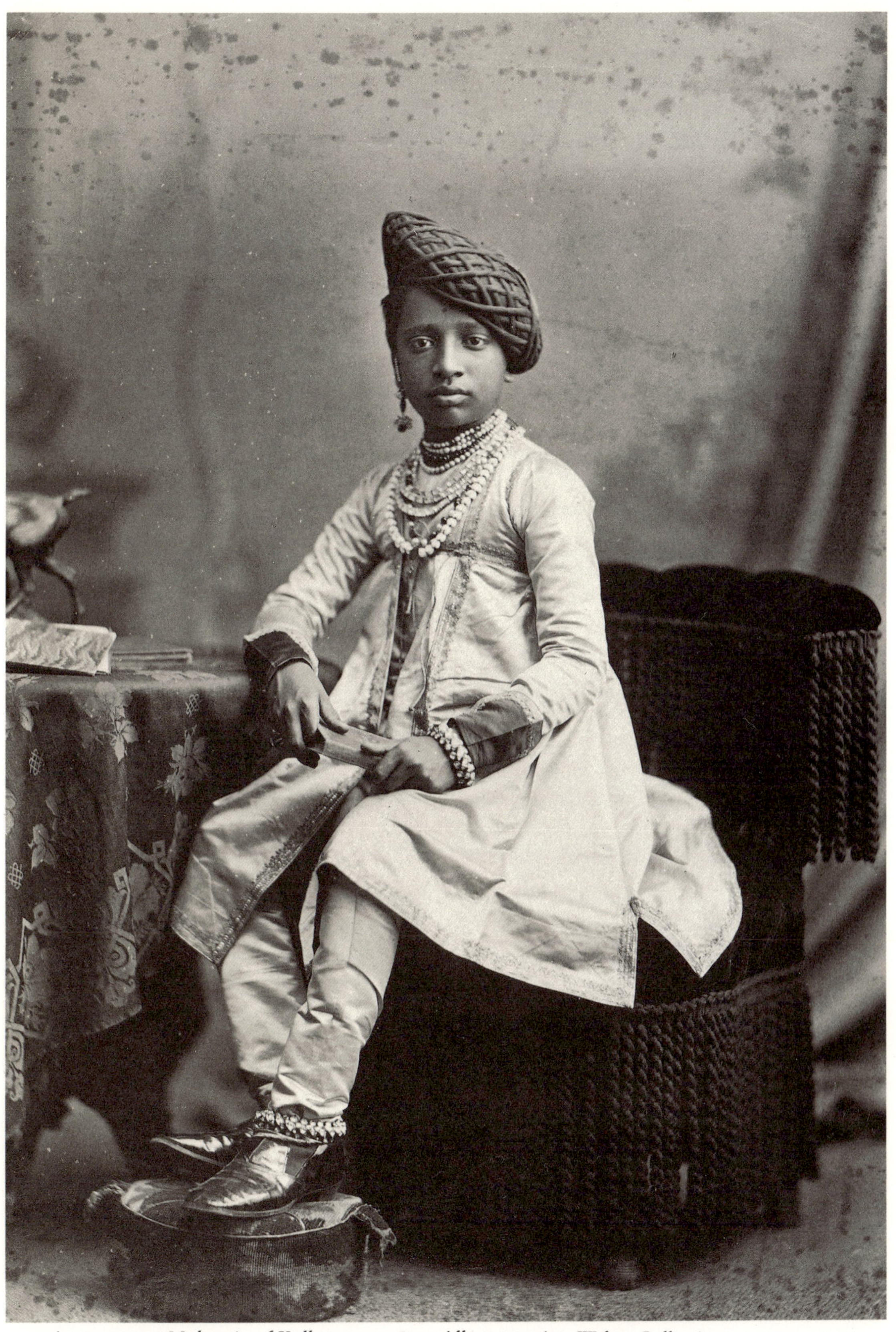

212. Anonymous. *Maharaja of Kolhapur*. c. 1890. Albumen print. Walter Collection.

on native women. Frith, one of the leading land-scape photographers of the collodion and glass plate period who was best known for his spectacular photographs of Egypt and the Nile valley, established his photographic publishing company in 1860. While Frith himself never traveled to India, it appears that he was interested in views of that country, and commissioned photographers to go there. These anonymous photographs were published as *Indian Photographic Views* in the 1870s. The volume includes some fine compositions of temples, mosques, and ruins. More striking, however, are the photographs of the people, including the Kulu tribal women of the Himalayan regions with their typical rough woollen blankets (fig. 218), and the traditionally garbed high-class Maharashtrian women of the western coastal region, with shawls elegantly draped around their shoulders. Samuel Bourne seems to have been familiar with Frith's work and may even have been inspired by it.[50]

VI

THE field of news reportage was irreversibly altered by the camera which could record events that neither attracted the artist, nor were capable of being instantaneously documented by him. Italian-born Felice Beato, who became a British citizen, was the most remarkable news photographer to visit India (in India 1858–61). Together with James Robertson, he had documented the war in Crimea, making a detailed record of the fall of Sebastopol. On hearing of the Indian Munity of 1857, Beato, eager to be on the front line, moved on to India and arrived in time to witness the aftermath. He took a series of photographs highlighting the brutality of war, with many scenes of death and destruction. A group of views of Lucknow and the ruins of the Residency that shows only the shells of the buildings speaks graphically of the horrors that must have preceded Beato's arrival. Beato's picture of the ruins of Sikander Bagh, showing the skeletons in the midst of rubble, is an unforgettable document of war (fig. 73); his photographs of two hanging mutineers is frequently

reproduced in books on the history of that troubled period. The anonymous photograph of the *Hanging Tree* from about 1860–65 focused on the same subject (fig. 219).

Beato traveled throughout India and his eye generally lighted on newsworthy items. His *Tinnevelly Bridge at Flood* shows four spans totally washed away (fig. 220). Such spontaneous photographs of disasters were of interest to news photographers and introduced a new dimension of realism into reportage.

Beato rarely photographed monuments purely for their architectural interest; one of these unusual views is of the Kutub Minar, a tall, slender tower a few miles north of Delhi (fig. 221). Visiting the Minar in 1874, some twenty years later, artist Edward Lear wrote:

Without doubt a most wonderful specimen of what man can raise by way of a perpendicular monument . . . the beautiful proportions of this wonderful column are not more surprising than the infinite delicate and fresh-looking details in every part of it. At the

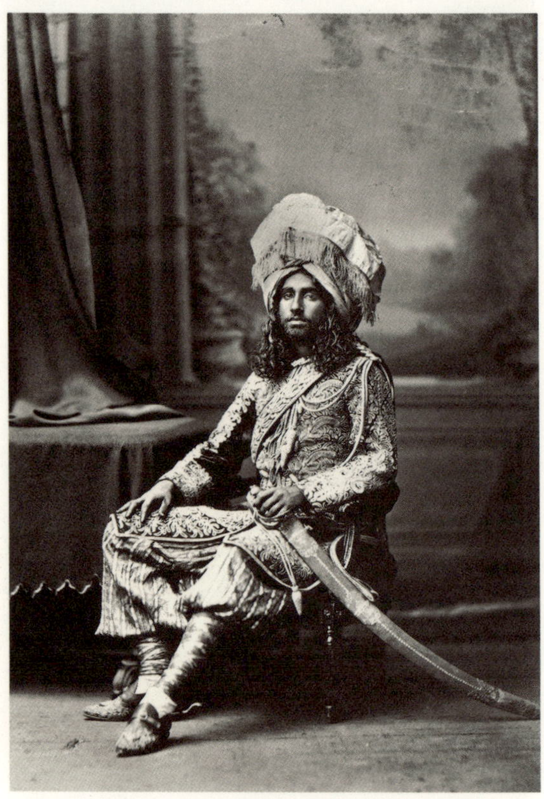

213. Anonymous. *Maharaja of Bhawalpur*. c. 1890. Albumen print. Walter Collection.

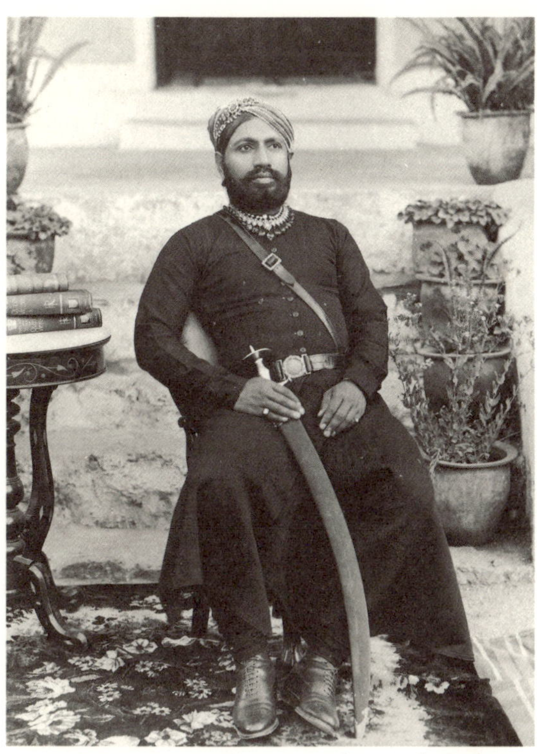

214. Anonymous. *The Raj Dhiraj of Shahpura (Dholpur)*. c. 1890. Gelatin-silver print. Walter Collection.

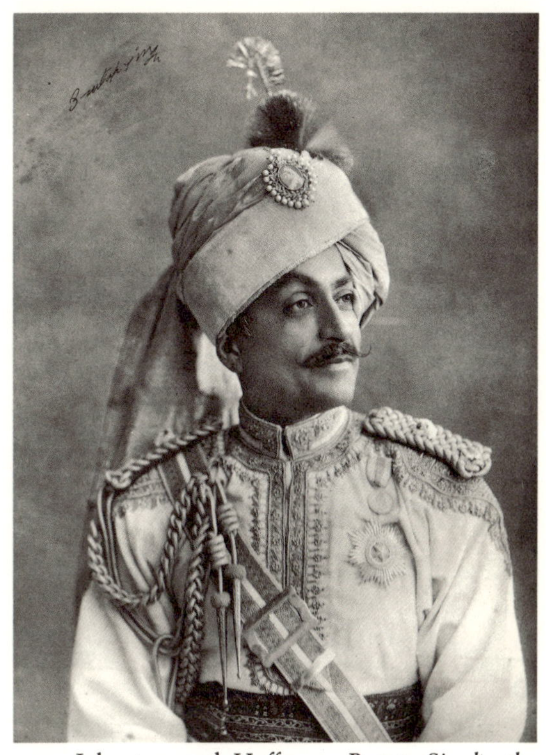

215. Johnston and Hoffman. *Pratap Singh, the Maharaja of Idar*. c. 1900. Gelatin-silver print. Walter Collection.

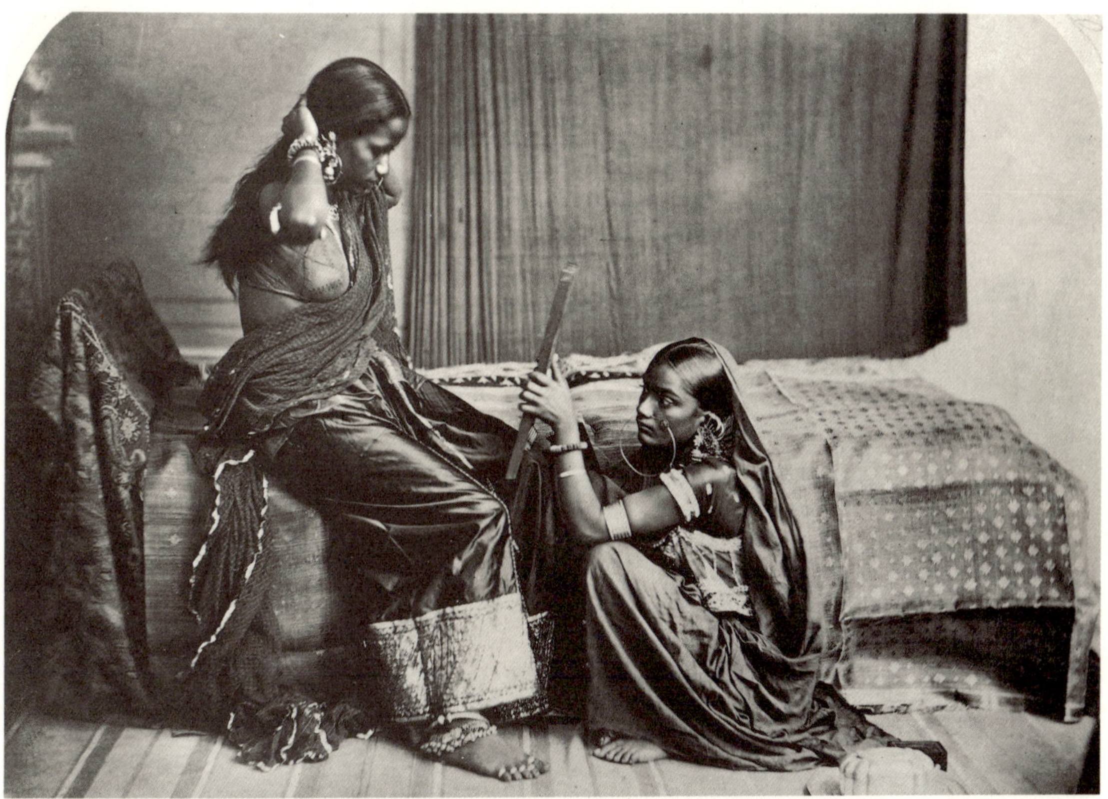

216. Anonymous. *Courtesan*. c. 1865. Albumen print. Walter Collection.

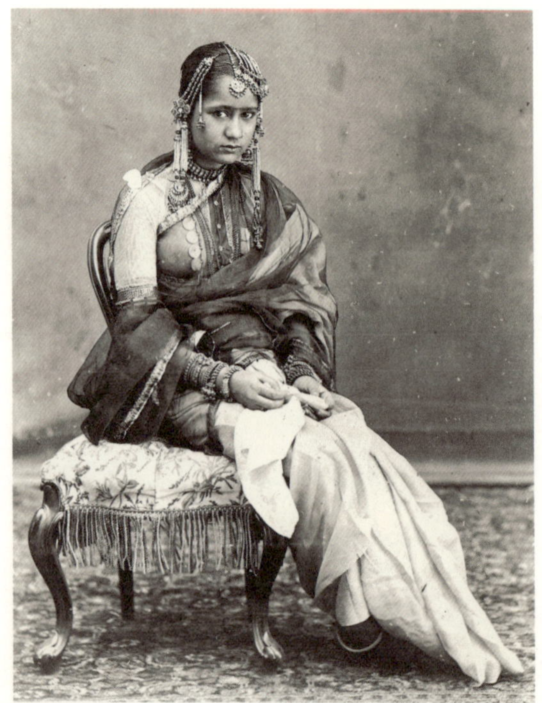

217. Anonymous. *Nautch Girl.* c. 1875. Albumen print. Walter Collection.

foot of the Kootab, and all about the ground near it, are trees—mostly of the Mimosa or Acadia kind . . . . The aspect of the whole scene is pleasing, all the more that the colour of the great Minar is so beautiful, a pale red.[51]

Beato's angled view of the Minar makes it seem even taller than it actually is. Two negatives were placed vertically to accommodate the height of the tower. In 1862, after he returned to London, Beato exhibited a large group of his photographs and *The Athenaeum* was enthusiastic in its review:

At Mr. Hering's, Regent Street, may be seen a large collection of photographic views and panoramas taken by Signor Beato during the Indian Mutiny and the Chinese war . . . . As photographs, these leave nothing to be desired; while some of the panoramas . . . which are in no less than six pieces each, must have demanded extraordinary care in production.[52]

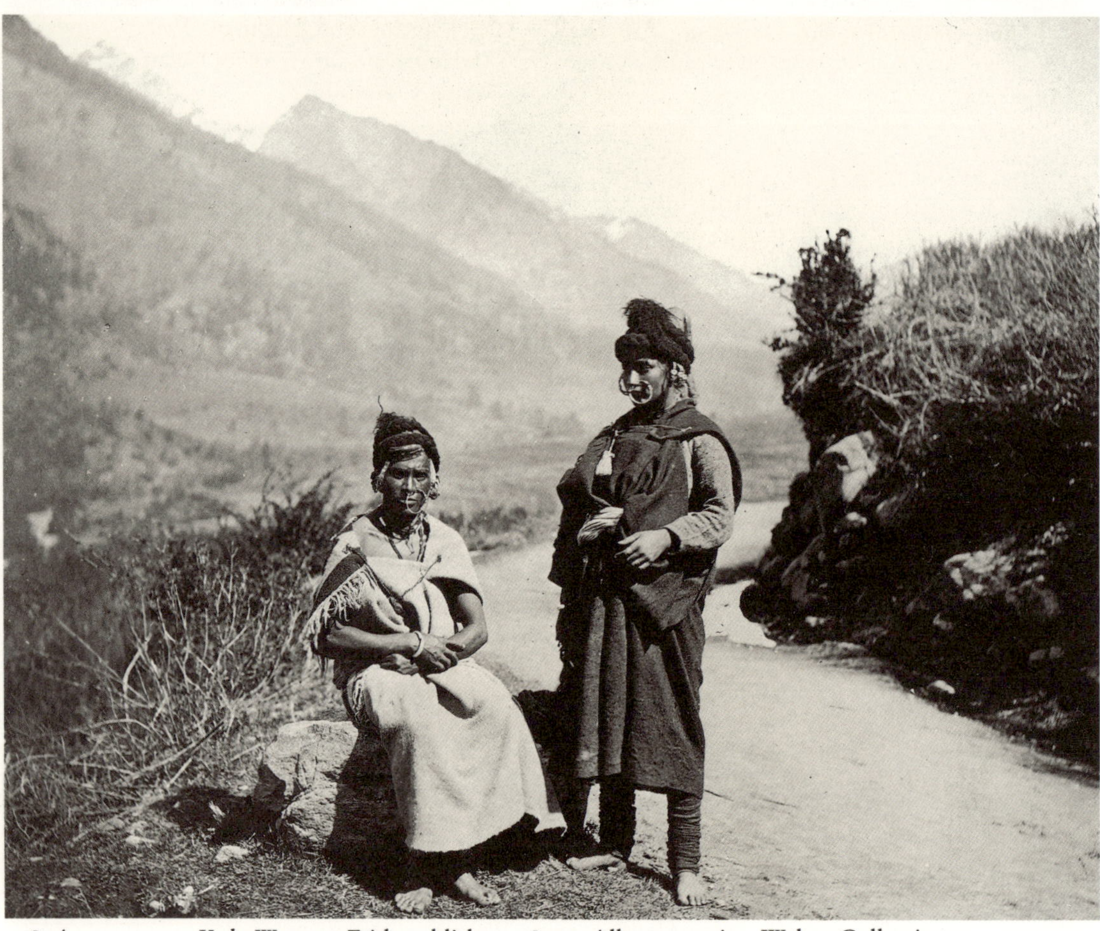

218. Anonymous. *Kulu Women.* Frith publisher. 1870s. Albumen print. Walter Collection.

The view of the Kutub was evidently displayed in this exhibition.

Beato used albumen plates for his photography—glass plates coated with egg white that could be prepared well in advance. He wrote that plates he prepared in Athens were not exposed until several months later in India. At first the albumen plate required exposures as long as three hours, but by 1886, Beato had invented a special developing technique that enabled him to reduce exposure time to a mere four seconds.[53] Beato left India in 1861 and went to China and Japan; he eventually settled in Burma where he opened a store that sold Burmese crafts in Rangoon and Mandalay by mail order catalogue.[54]

Captain Willoughby Hooper, an amateur photographer, took a series of pictures of the devastating famine of Madras of 1877–78. Hooper

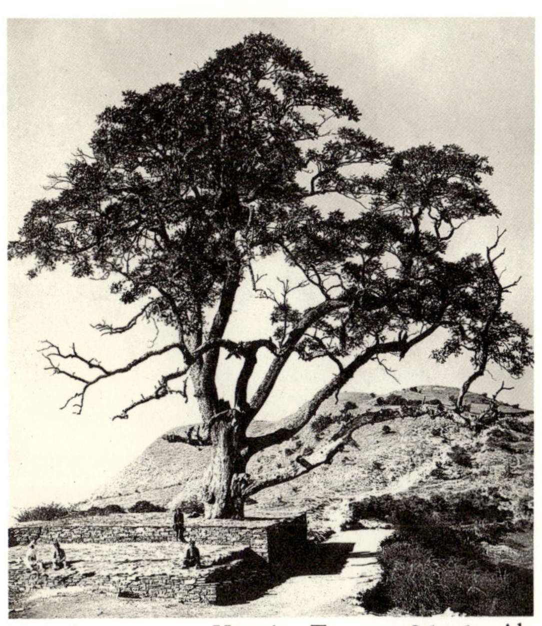

219. Anonymous. *Hanging Tree*. c. 1860-65. Albumen print. Walter Collection.

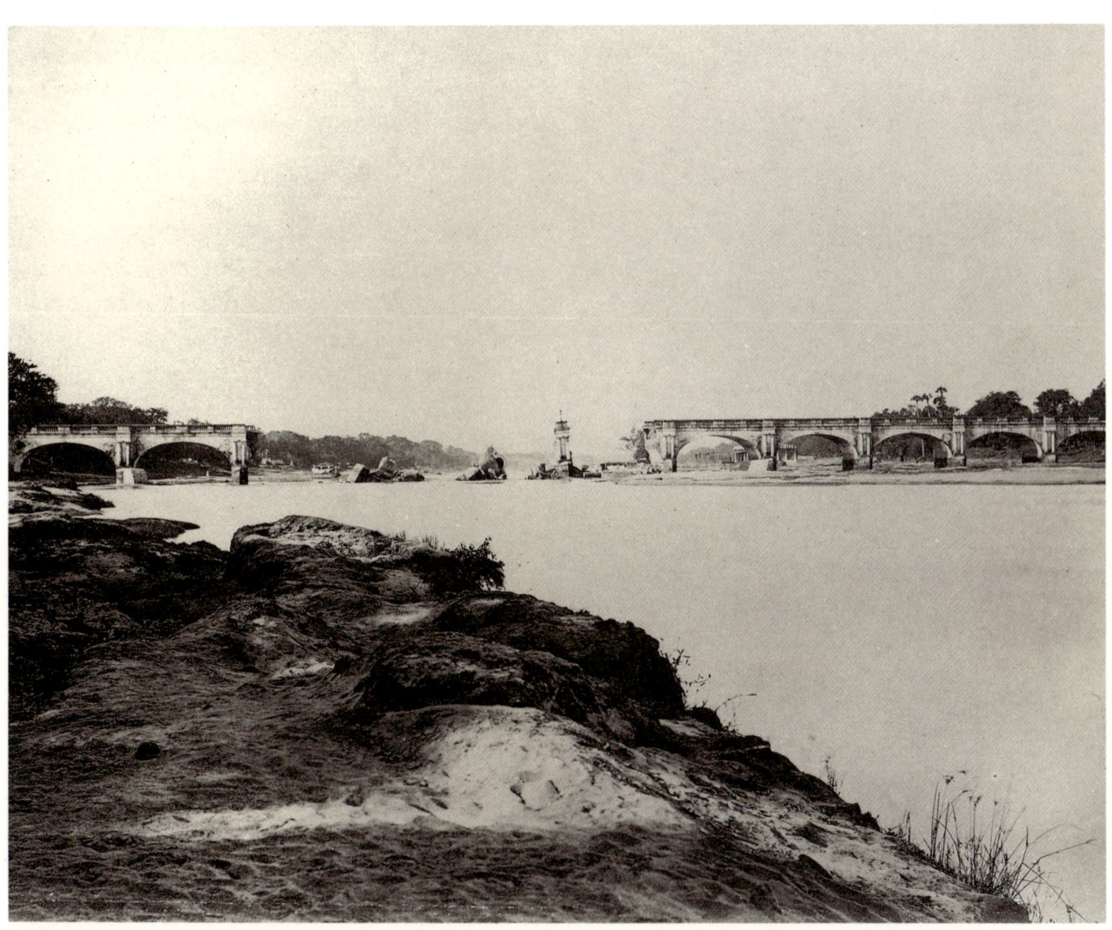

220. Felice Beato. *Tinnevelly Bridge at Flood*. c. 1860. Albumen print. Walter Collection.

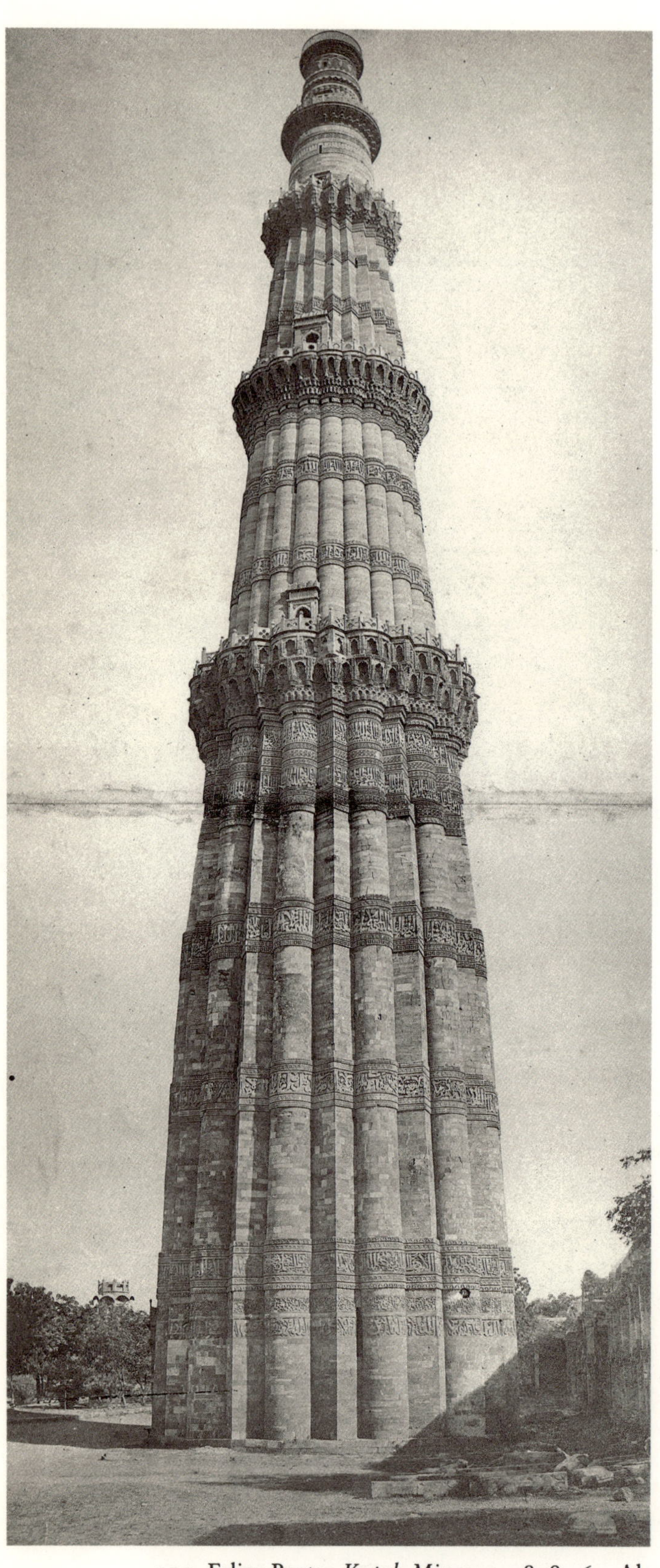

221. Felice Beato. *Kutub Minar*. c. 1858–60. Albumen print. Walter Collection.

was an army officer stationed in southern India. Hooper's horrifying photographs of the starving made the tragedy of the famine widely known (fig. 222).

The anonymous photograph in figure 223 shows the incredibly huge crowd that gathered for a major religious festival at the Kumbakonam temple in southern India. This amazing photograph of the 1870s recalls the accounts of British visitors present on similar occasions: "Until you have looked upon one of these tremendous gatherings of humanity many aspects of Indian life and character must be hidden from you." Sidney Low, correspondent for the *Standard*, remarked upon the "complete absence of violence, of drunkenness, of disorder" in "this vast assemblage, swept up from a continent," and spoke of the "swarming, shifting, variegated crowd."

Even as I gazed, the sun . . . burst into the sudden splendour of the Eastern day, and under that radiant light the rustling throng seemed like a giant horde of gay tropical beetles, settling upon a flower-bed with scintillating scales and quivering pinions.[55]

VII

FROM the very introduction of the camera into India, a number of Indians, including maharajas, had become interested in photography. Bourne wrote of the pride with which the raja of Chamba regarded the camera, lenses, and chemicals that he owned, although the Englishman did not think highly of the raja's photographic ability.[56] The maharaja of Jaipur, who bought his first camera in 1862, was another Indian who displayed both interest and talent in the field. He became an avid photographer and kept in close touch with the work produced by British firms.[57]

From the 1870s onwards, Indian firms, like the famous Raja Deen Dayal and Sons, increasingly assumed a position of importance in the realm of photography. Deen Dayal was the official court photographer of the Nizam of Hyderabad and his duties included taking photographs of innumerable princes and princesses. However, Dayal also photographed the British

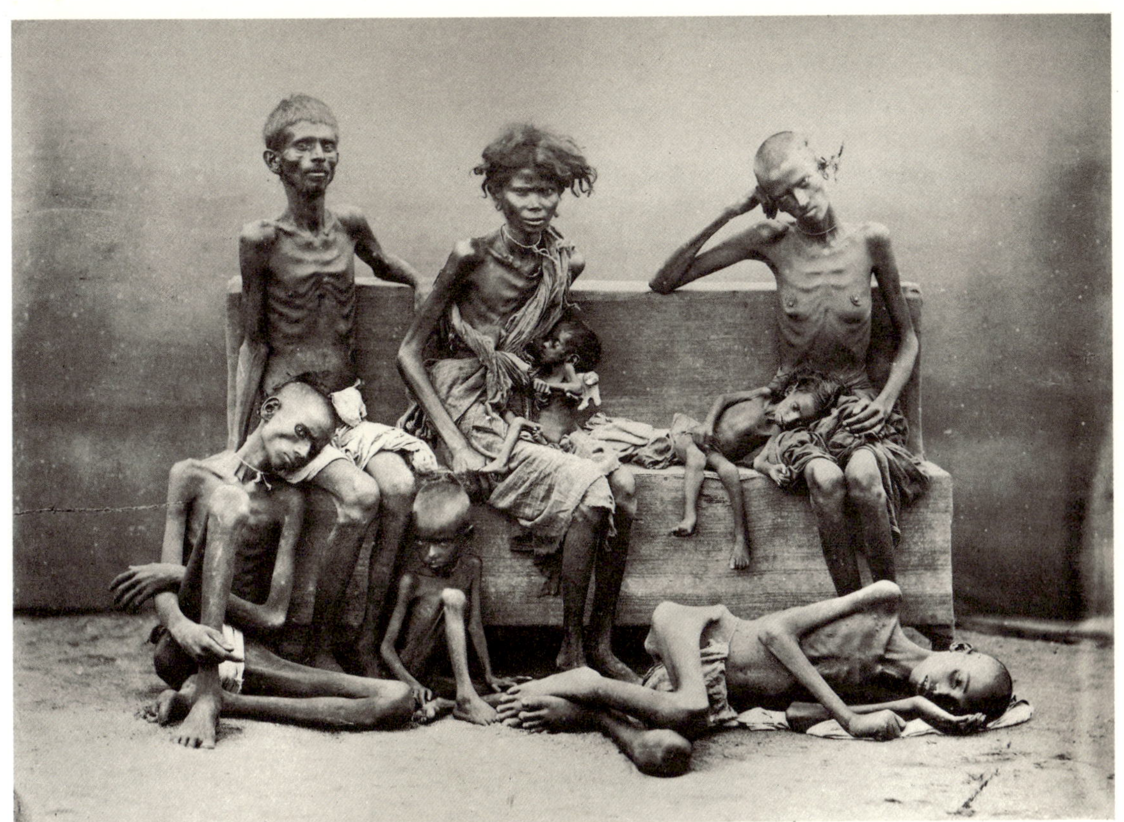

222. Captain Willoughby Hooper. *Madras Famine.* 1877–78. Albumen print. Walter Collection.

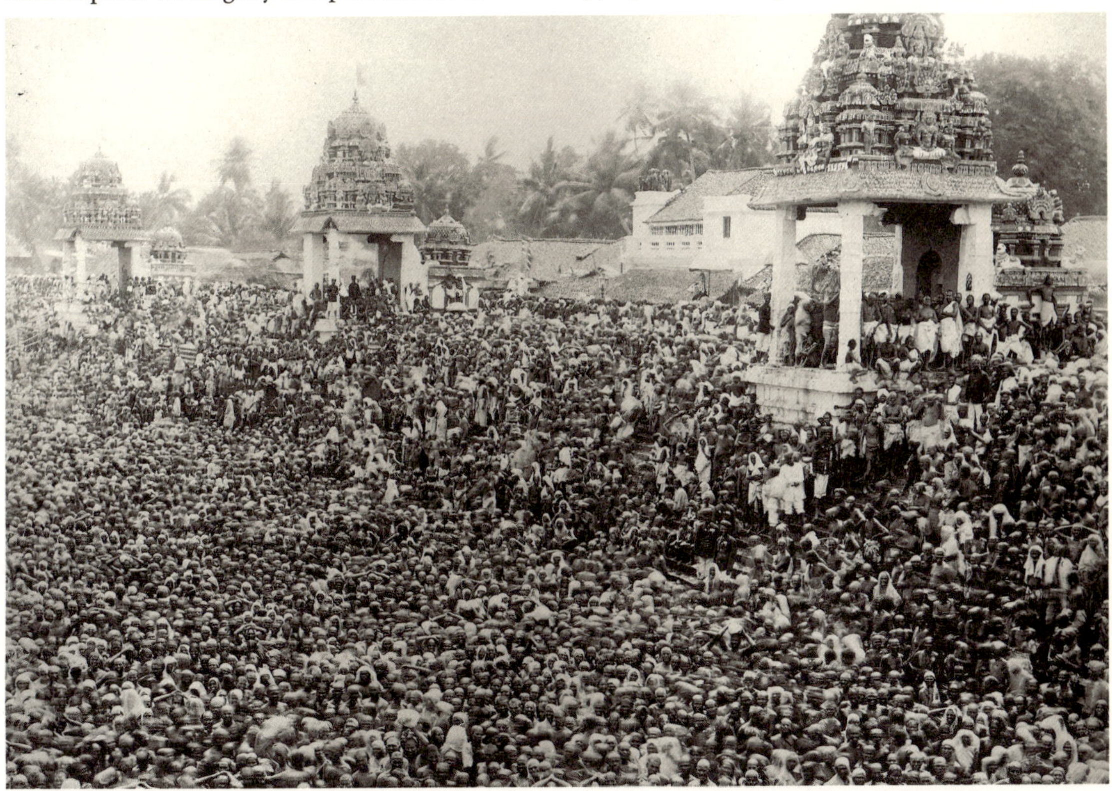

223. Anonymous. *Crowds at Kumbakonam Tank.* 1870s. Albumen print. Walter Collection.

in their leisure time. He portrayed them on the polo field, pulling on tug-of-war ropes, playing badminton or croquet, or merely standing around drinking gimlets. It would appear that he was as welcome at the British clubs as at the residences of the maharajas. In order to capitalize on the large clientele of women that existed, he opened a special *zenana* or womens' studio at Hyderabad, with an Englishwoman in charge. *The Journal of the Photographic Society of India* for January 1892 commented:

As this studio is for photographing native ladies only, special arrangements had to be made to protect them from the gaze of the profane and the stern. So the place is surrounded by high walls, and all day long within this charmed enclosure Mrs. Kenny-Levick, aided by native female assistants, takes the photographs of the high-born native ladies of the Deccan. How lovely! One revels in the thought of the Arabian Nights . . . .[58]

The 1895 catalogue of the studio advertises several photographic albums of views of India, Indian princes, and the visits of various foreign dignitaries to the nizam's court. "These albums will be found very useful for drawing rooms, palaces, and for presentation."[59] Deen Dayal received the ultimate in patronage: "By Appointment, Photographer to Her Imperial Majesty, Queen Victoria." While Deen Dayal and Sons was undoubtedly the best known of the Indian photographic firms, several others existed and by the 1880s, the number of Indian photographers listed in the *Bombay Directory*, for instance, was equal to that of European photographers. The glorious reign of the British photographer in India was coming to an end.

Notes

INTRODUCTION

1. Carey, 1964, p. 210. The Victorian artist Val Prinsep also wrote at about the same time: "As a field for artists, India has been of late years sadly neglected. While the more fortunate countries of the East–Turkey, Syria, Egypt and Arabia–have been frequently depicted India has remained almost unknown to the painter. Zoffany and Daniel, both Royal Academicians, in the old time, when the voyage alone to India was an affair of six months or more, thought it worth their while to visit the unknown land of Hind. Now in six months much of India may be seen, and yet since the time of these two artists no painter of note has thought it worth his while to convey to his countrymen an impression of our Eastern empire." (Prinsep, 1879, p. 350)
2. *Ibid.*
3. For a survey of British portraiture in India see M. Archer, 1979a.
4. *Ibid.*, p 381.
5. Archer, 1969b, *passim*.
6. Dyson, 1978, p. 136.
7. Nilsson, 1970, pp. 140–41.
8. Patten, 1983, p. 331.

CHAPTER 1

1. As quoted in M. Archer, 1979a, p. 395.
2. Woodruff, 1963, vol. I, p. 100.
3. Quennell, 1975, p. 240.
4. Spear, 1963, p. 23.
5. Cotton, 1980, p. 7.
6. Carey, 1964, p. 77.
7. As quoted in M. Archer, 1979a, p. 121.
8. *Ibid.*
9. *Ibid.*, p. 145.
10. Carey, 1964, pp. 237–38.
11. As quoted in M. Archer, 1979a, pp. 133, 145.
12. *Ibid.*, pp. 357–86.
13. *Ibid.*, p. 190.
14. *Ibid.*, p. 192.

15. This and the following quotations from M. Archer, 1979a, p. 230.
16. *Ibid.*, p. 255.
17. Carey, 1964, p. 211.
18. M. Archer, 1979a, p. 239.
19. Carey, 1964, p. 215.
20. M. Archer, 1979a, p. 262.
21. *Ibid.*, pp. 363-64.
22. *Ibid.*, p. 260.
23. *Ibid.*, p. 124.
24. Das Gupta, 1959, pp. 170–71.
25. Mahajan, 1983, p. 53.
26. *Ibid.*, p. 94.
27. Hodges, 1793, p. 149.
28. M. Archer, 1980, fig. 52.
29. Fraser, 1820, p. 439.
30. M. Archer, 1980, p. 224.
31. M. Archer and Lightbown, 1982, p. 84.
32. *Ibid.*, pp. 86-7.
33. *Ibid.*, p. 88.
34. Eyre-Todd, 1903, p. 91.
35. *Ibid.*, p. 92.
36. This and the following quotations from Hodges, 1793.
37. M. Archer and Lightbown, 1982, p. 25.
38. *Ibid.*, p. 101.
39. M. Archer, 1980, fig. 57.
40. *Ibid.*, fig. 79.
41. Hodges, 1793, pp. *iii-iv*.

CHAPTER 2

1. Rosselli, 1974, p. 146.
2. Moorhouse, 1983, p. 94.
3. Ackerley, 1983, p. 22.
4. Edwardes, 1970, p. 209.
5. Allen, 1977, p. 174.
6. Carey, 1964, pp. 78-9.
7. M. Archer, 1979a, p. 417.
8. *Ibid.*, p. 176.
9. *Ibid.*, p. 421.
10. Murphy, 1953, p. 46.
11. *Ibid.*, p. 51.
12. Carey, 1964, p. 37.

13. As quoted in Dyson, 1978, p. 81.

14. Carey, 1964, p. 74.

15. Quennell, 1975, p. 233.

16. As quoted in M. Archer, 1979a, p. 148.

17. Gould, 1957, p. 53.

18. This and the following quotation from Allen, 1979, pp. 93, 97.

19. Orwell, *Burmese Days*, 1935, as quoted in Allen, 1977, p. 219.

20. Allen, 1977, p. 76.

21. Hibbert, 1980, p. 49.

22. *Ibid.*, pp. 55–6.

23. *Ibid.*

24. *Ibid.*

25. For Lundgren and the Mutiny see Nilsson, 1970.

26. Hibbert, 1980, p. 192.

27. *Ibid.*

28. *Ibid.*, p. 341.

29. *Ibid.*, p. 366.

30. *Ibid.*, p. 191.

31. As quoted in Magnus, 1979, p. 177.

32. Kopf, 1969, p. 63.

33. Magnus, 1979, p. 176.

34. Moorhouse, 1983, p. 200.

35. From a letter in the collection of Mr. Paul F. Walter.

36. Magnus, 1979, p. 177.

37. Morris and Winchester, 1983, p. 35.

38. Prinsep, 1879, p. 264.

39. Morris and Winchester, 1983, p. 80.

40. *Ibid.*

41. *The Delhi Sketch Book*, 1852, as quoted in Edwardes, 1970, p. 210.

CHAPTER 3

1. As quoted in Clarke, 1981, p. 31.

2. As quoted in Barbier, 1963, p. 100.

3. *Ibid.*, p. 115.

4. Gilpin wrote: "Whenever I sit down with a pencil and paper before me, ideas of rocks and mountains and lakes always crowd into my head. . . . I conceive of no other kinds of landscape, but of this sublime kind, to be worth recording." *Ibid.*, pp. 107f.

5. *Ibid.*, p. 114.

6. As quoted in Mahajan, 1984, p. 67.

7. *Ibid.*, p. 49.

8. *Ibid.*, p. 54.

9. *Ibid.*, p. 50.

10. *Ibid.*, p. 76.

11. *Ibid.*, pp. 77–8.

12. Forbes, 1813, vol. I, p. 26.

13. Mahajan, 1984, p. 117.

14. Hodges, 1793, p. 33.

15. Hodges, 1785–88, vol. II, plate 8 text.

16. M. Archer, 1980, p. 89.

17. Hodges, 1793, pp. 1f.

18. *Ibid.*, pp. 25f.

19. *Ibid.*, *passim.*

20. *Ibid.*, pp. 59f.

21. In a 1786 letter to the Duke of Rutland, as quoted in Steube, 1979, p. 86.

22. Sutton, 1954, p. 92.

23. *Ibid.*, p. 97.

24. *Ibid.*, p. 144.

25. Hardie and Clayton, 1932, pp. 5, 16, 27.

26. Daniells, 1795–1807, vol. I, plate 2 text.

27. Grant, 1957–61, vol. IV, p. 277.

28. M. Archer, 1980, p. 232.

29. *Ibid.*, drawing on p. 230.

30. M. Archer, 1970a, p. 101.

31. Lear, 1873–74, Dec. 14, 1873.

32. As quoted in M. Archer, 1980, plates 35, 36 text.

33. Roberts, 1837, p. 237.

34. For instance, *The British Critic*, 1805, p. 230: "The union of engraving with colouring cannot we conceive, certainly will not easily, be carried to higher excellence."

35. For a thorough discussion of Zoffany's portraits see M. Archer, 1979a. Most of the pictures discussed here but not illustrated may be found there, pp. 130–77.

36. Hardie and Clayton, 1932, p. 16.

37. This painting only recently emerged from oblivion. See *Realism Through Informality*, Leger Galleries (London, 1983), no. 18.

38. M. Archer, 1979a, p. 168.

39. *Ibid.*, p. 177.

40. *Ibid.*, p. 381.

41. *Ibid.*, p. 382.

42. M. Archer 1969b, vol. I, p. 6.

43. M. Archer, 1970c, p. 179.

44. Man Ray, as quoted in Sontag, 1973, p. 186.

45. Eyre-Todd, 1903, p. 92.

46. Rev. V. Caunter who published *Oriental Annual* in 1834 which contained 24 drawings by William Daniell with commentary, as quoted in Mahajan, 1984, p. 105.

47. Eyre-Todd, 1903, p. 103.
48. Hofer, 1967, p. 12.
49. Lear, 1873–74, Nov. 28, 1873.
50. *Ibid.*, Nov. 22, 1873.
51. *Ibid.*
52. *Ibid.*, Dec. 10, 1873.
53. *Ibid.*, Dec. 13, 1873.
54. *Ibid.*, April 5, 1874.
55. *Ibid.*, Oct. 16, 1874.
56. *Ibid.*, Dec. 27, 1874.
57. *Ibid.*, Sept. 10, 1874.
58. Salaman, 1925, pp. 296–97.
59. As quoted in Mahajan, 1984, p. 50.
60. As quoted in Dyson, 1978, p. 194.
61. *Idem.*
62. Spencer, 1918, p. 284.
63. Anonymous ballad, M. Archer and Lightbown, 1982, p. 38.
64. Prinsep, 1879, p. 76.
65. Eden, 1866, p. 45.
66. *Ibid.*, p. 59.
67. *Ibid.*, p. 74.
68. Dickinson, 1919, p. 264.
69. *Ibid.*, p. 278.
70. As quoted in M. Archer and Lightbown, 1982, p. 84.
71. *Calcutta Gazette*, May 18, 1826, as reported in M. Archer, 1969a, p. 15.
72. As quoted in M. Archer and Lightbown, 1982, p. 85.
73. *Ibid.*
74. *Ibid.*, p. 67.
75. As reported in Dyson, 1978, p. 101.
76. M. Archer, 1979a, p. 126.
77. Mahajan, 1984, pp. 120–21.
78. Roberts, 1837, pp. 328–29.
79. Paviere, 1950, p. 130.
80. Forbes, 1813, vol. I, p. *vi.*
81. *Ibid.*, p. *xi.*
82. *Ibid.*, p. 43.
83. *Idem.*
84. *Ibid.*, p. 49.
85. *Ibid.*, vol. III, p. 275.
86. *Ibid.*, vol. I, p. 30.
87. Falkland, 1857, p. 32.
88. M. Archer, 1963, p. 480.
89. Lear, 1873–74, June 7 and 18, 1874.
90. Murphy, Dec. 23, 1873, p. 50.
91. *Ibid.*, p. 53.
92. Bellew in 1843, as quoted in Brown, 1948, pp. 18f.

CHAPTER 4

1. M. Archer, 1972, p. 10.
2. *Ibid.*
3. *Ibid.*, p. 4.
4. Prinsep, 1879, pp. 47–8.
5. M. Archer, 1972, p. 4.
6. As quoted in M. Archer, 1979a, p. 389.
7. *Ibid.*, p. 331.
8. M. Archer, 1972, p. 5.
9. Prinsep, 1879, pp. 47–8.
10. Falk and Archer, 1981, plates 379–400.
11. Nilsson, 1970, p. 141.
12. This and the following quotations from Trevelyan, 1866, pp. 210–13.
13. "Goddess, Great Lady of Tollus, Calie [Kali] Goddess Lady let all your smell be far away from my face, I entreat you. Lead from here the other smelling ones. Lead away the other putrid ones." (Translated by Aditya Dehejia)
14. Ghose, 1926, p. 98.
15. W. G. Archer, 1971, p. 1.
16. Knizkova, 1975, *passim.*
17. See Gangoly and Goswami, 1959, plates 14–50.
18. *Indian Charivari Album*, 1875, preface.
19. Paul, 1983, p. 14.
20. *Ibid.*
21. W. G. Archer, 1959, pp. 24–5.
22. *Ibid.*
23. Prinsep, 1879, pp. 89–90.
24. W. G. Archer, 1959, p. 26.
25. *Ibid.*, p. 29.

CHAPTER 5

1. Sontag, 1973, p. 148.
2. Kahmen, 1974, p. 13.
3. *Ibid.*, p. 16.
4. *Ibid.*, p. 14.
5. *Ibid.*
6. Prinsep, 1879, p. 47.
7. Murphy, 1953, p. 46.
8. Prinsep, 1879, p. 48.
9. Newhall, 1964, p. 19.
10. Gernsheim, 1969, p. 72.
11. Goldberg, 1981, p. 46.
12. Thomas, 1979, p. 221.
13. *Ibid.*
14. *British Journal of Photography*, Feb. 1, 1864, p. 50.

15. Thomas, 1979, p. 216.
16. As quoted in Newhall, 1964, p. 88.
17. *British Journal of Photography*, Jan. 4, 1867, p. 4.
18. *Ibid.*, July 1, 1863, p. 268.
19. *Ibid.*, Sept. 1, 1863, p. 346.
20. *Ibid.*, July 1, 1863, p. 268.
21. *Ibid.*, Sept. 1, 1863, p. 345.
22. As quoted in Brown, 1948, p. 27.
23. Herrmann, 1973, p. 12.
24. Quoted by Bourne in *British Journal of Photography*, Oct. 5, 1866, p. 474.
25. *British Journal of Photography*, Jan. 4, 1867, p. 4.
26. *Ibid.*, Jan. 25, 1867, p. 39.
27. *Ibid.*, April 1, 1870, p. 150.
28. *Ibid.*, Nov. 23, 1866, pp. 559f.
29. *Ibid.*, p. 560.
30. *Idem.*
31. *Ibid.*, Feb. 1, 1864, p. 51.
32. *Ibid.*, p. 70.
33. *Ibid.*, Jan. 11, 1867, p. 17.
34. *Ibid.*, Jan. 14, 1870, p. 16.
35. *Ibid.*
36. *Ibid.*
37. Bourne and Shepherd, n.d., p. 1.
38. *British Journal of Photography*, Feb. 1, 1864, p. 51.
39. *Idem.*
40. Heathcote, April 1982, pp. 107f.
41. As quoted in Desmond, 1976, p. 17.
42. *Ibid.*, p. 14.
43. *The London Times*, Nov. 16, 1869, p. 4a.
44. As quoted in Desmond, 1976, p. 23.
45. *The London Times*, April 5, 1869, p. 7e.
46. *Ibid.*, Jan. 18, 1861, p. 7a.
47. Bayer et al., 1981, p. 28.
48. *British Journal of Photography*, July 1, 1863, p. 269.
49. Douglas, 1913, pp. 287, 290.
50. Sprague, 1977, p. 28.
51. Lear, 1873–74, March 11, 1874.
52. As quoted in Pare, 1982, p. 245.
53. *British Journal of Photography*, March 19, 1886, p. 181.
54. Lowry, 1975, pp. 659f.
55. Sidney Low in 1905 as quoted in Mahajan, 1984, pp. 122–23.
56. *British Journal of Photography*, Nov. 2, 1866, p. 524.
57. Das, 1985, *passim*.
58. As quoted in Worswick, 1980, p. 149, n. 13.
59. *Ibid.*, p. 150.

Glossary

ATTAR: concentrated perfume.

AYAH: a native lady's maid or a nursemaid.

BABA: a young child.

BABU: Bengali gentleman; among the British, often used with slight sense of disparagement to characterize a superficially cultivated Bengali. Also a clerk.

BEGUM: a Moslem lady of rank; also applied to a Moslem princess.

BHAU: honorific title.

BIBI: wife; applied to unofficial native "wives" of British officers.

BRAHMAN: member of the Hindu priestly (highest) caste.

BURRA-KHANA: a big dinner party.

BURRA SAHIB: British officer recognized as the head of a district; also used for the head of a family.

CANTONMENT: military area of a British Indian settlement.

CHARAK: hook-swinging; a Hindu religious custom in which a hook suspended from a pole is passed through the muscle along the shoulder blades of the performer who is then whirled through the air.

CHOTA: small or little.

CIVIL LINES: civilian area of a British Indian settlement.

DAK BUNGALOWS: originally a stopping place for the post (*dak*); later used as inspection bungalows by British officers inspecting the district.

DUBASH: native broker conducting business for the British with the natives; literally, "speaker of two languages," hence interpreter.

DURBAR: specially convened court for major ceremonial or political occasion; originally used to mean executive government of a native state.

DURGA PUJA: festival of worship of the Hindu goddess Durga.

FAKIR: native devotees and naked ascetics.

GHAGRAS: long gathered skirt worn by native women.

GHAT: a path of descent to a river generally lined with steps; hence, bathing ghats; also a landing place for river craft.

GYMKHANA: sports club primarily for ball games.

HOOKAH: the Indian pipe for smoking through water, the elaborated hubble-bubble; normal smoking compound of tobacco, spice, molasses, and fruit; native smoking practice adopted by the British in the early days of the empire.

JHULA BRIDGE: swinging suspension bridge made from thick ropes and timber and used to ford rivers and ravines in Himalayan region.

KHELAT: a gift given by the British to natives of rank in recognition of their distinction.

KSHATRIYA: member of princely or ruling class; second level in caste system, after the Brahman.

MAHANT: chief priest in a Bengal Hindu temple.

MAHARAJA: major Indian king, generally Hindu.

MAHOUT: the driver and tender of an elephant.

MAHRATTA: Hindu ruling chieftains of western India; originally meant "great warrior"; a resident of Maharashtra on the west coast and a speaker of Mahratti language.

MAIDAN: open parklike ground in the British area of the city.

MEMSAHIB: respectful form of address for married European woman.

MOFUSSIL: the rural and remote areas of a district.

MOGUL: the famous Islamic dynasty founded in 1526 by Babar; among the great Moguls were the emperors Akbar, Shah Jehan, and Aurangzeb; in modern usage, refers to wealthy tycoons.

MORCHA: a fly whisk made of peacock's feathers.

MUNSHI: European term for a native teacher of languages.

NABOB: An Englishman who returned with fortunes from India; corruption of the Indian word nawab, meaning "ruler."

NAUTCH: dance performed by native women.

NAWAB: Indian term for a Moslem ruler.

NAZRANA: a gift or tribute offered by the natives

when calling upon a British representative.

ODHNIS: long, transparent scarflike garment draped loosely across the body.

PARSI: person of Persian stock following Zoroastrian (fire worship) religion, long settled in India, primarily in the Bombay region.

PATUA: native village painter of scrolls.

PILLAW: a rice dish mixed with spices and meat, of Islamic origin.

PUKKA: proper, as in pukka sahib = proper gentleman; also a term for a building of brick and mortar as opposed to one of inferior materials, such as mud, matting, and timber.

PUNKHAH: in Anglo-Indian colloquial, a large swinging fan, formed of cloth stretched on a rectangular wooden frame, and suspended from the ceiling and pulled to and fro with a rope by a "punkhah wallah."

PURDAH: literally "curtain"; term used for a screenlike garment worn by Moslem women to shelter them from the gaze of men.

RAJ: rule, as in British Raj = British rule.

RUDRAKSHA: a rosary of beads from berries of the sacred *rudraksha* tree.

SADHU: a sage or religious mendicant.

SEPOY: a native soldier disciplined and dressed in European style.

SHIKAR: a hunt.

SUDRA: manual laborer and lowest strata of caste system.

SUNYASEE: a Hindu religious mendicant.

SUTTEE: ancient ritual of voluntary self-immolation of Hindu widows on their husband's funeral pyres; custom outlawed by the British.

SYCE: groom for horses; primarily used in Bengal.

TATTY: a screen or mat made of the roots of fragrant grass (*khus-khus*), usually kept wet in front of doors and windows; as the dry wind blows against these screens, a fragrant cool air refreshes the house.

VAISHNAVA: follower of Hindu god Vishnu.

VAISYA: member of the trading community; third level in the caste system, after the *Kshatriya* (ruling class).

WALLAH: a suffix following a stated profession that means follower of that profession, as in *punkhah-wallah* or "fan-puller."

ZENANA: apartments of the house in which the women of the family are secluded; originally an Islamic custom.

Ackerley, J. R. *Hindoo Holiday*. Harmondsworth: Penguin, 1983.

Allen, C., ed. *Plain Tales From the Raj*. London: Futura Publications Limited, 1977.

———. *"Raj." A Scrapbook of British India: 1877–1947*. Harmondsworth: Penguin, 1979.

Archer, M. G. "Forgotten Painter of the Picturesque. Henry Salt in India, 1802–1804." *Country Life*, November 19, 1959, pp. 890–91.

———. "Sketches by the Daniells." *Apollo*, November 1962, pp. 689–92.

———. "Birds of India." *Geographical Magazine*, December 1963, pp. 470–81.

———. "British Painters of the Indian Scene." *Journal of the Royal Society of Arts*, October 1967, pp. 863–79.

———. "Balthazar Solvyns and the Indian Picturesque." *The Connoisseur*, January 1969a, pp. 12–18.

———. *British Drawings in the India Office Library*. 2 vols. London: Her Majesty's Stationery Office, 1969b.

———. "Benares through the Eyes of British Artists." *Apollo*, August 1970a, pp. 96–103.

———. "Indian Themes in English Pottery." *Apollo*, August 1970b, pp. 114–123.

———. "'The Talented Baronet': Sir Charles D'Oyly and His Drawings of India." *The Connoisseur*, November 1970c, pp. 173–81.

———. *Company Drawings in the India Office Library*. London: Her Majesty's Stationery Office, 1972.

———. "Renaldi and India. A Romantic Encounter." *Apollo*, July–September 1976, pp. 98–105.

———. *India and British Portraiture: 1770–1825*. London: Sotheby's, 1979a.

———. "Pictures of Note by British Artists in the Collection of the Royal Asiatic Society: Works by William Alexander and James Wales." In *The Royal Asiatic Society: Its History and Treasures*. Edited by Stuart Simmonds and Simon Digby. Leiden: E. J. Brill, 1979b.

———. *Early Views of India. The Picturesque Journeys of Thomas and William Daniell: 1786–1794*. London: Thames and Hudson, 1980.

Archer, M. G., and Lightbown, R. *India Observed. India as Viewed by British Artists: 1760–1860*. London: Victoria and Albert Museum, 1982.

Archer, W. G. *India and Modern Art*. London: George Allen and Unwin, Ltd., 1959.

———. *Kalighat Paintings*. London: Her Majesty's Stationery Office, 1971.

Ballhatchet, K. *Race, Sex, and Class Under the Raj*. New York: St. Martin's Press, 1980.

Barbier, C. P. *William Gilpin. His Drawings, Teaching and Theory of the Picturesque*. Oxford: Clarendon Press, 1963.

Barr, P. *The Memsahibs: The Women of Victorian India*. London: Secker & Warburg, 1976.

Bayer, J. *The Panoramic Image*. Southhampton: John Hansard Gallery, 1981.

Bell, L. "Artists and Empire: Victorian Representations of Subject People." *Art History*, March 1982, pp. 73–86.

Berry-Hill, H. and S. *George Chinnery, 1774–1852, Artist of the China Coast*. Leigh-on-Sea: F. Lewis, 1963.

Boase, T. S. R. *English Art, 1800–1870*. Oxford: Clarendon Press, 1959.

Bourne and Shepherd. "A Permanent Record of India." Calcutta, n.d.

British Journal of Photography, 1863–1870.

Brown, H., ed. *The Sahibs. The Life and Ways of the British in India as Recorded by Themselves*. London: W. Hodge, 1948.

Carey, W. H. *The Good Old Days of Honourable John Company*. Calcutta: Quins Book Company, 1964.

Clark, K. "On the Painting of English Landscape." *Proceedings of the British Academy* 21 (1935): 185–200.

Clarke, M. *The Tempting Prospect. A Social History of English Watercolours*. London: British Museum Publications, 1981.

Cohn, M. B. *Wash and Gouache. A Study of the Development of the Materials of Watercolor.* Cambridge, MA: Fogg Art Museum, 1977.

Cotton, H. E. A. *Calcutta Old and New.* Edited by N. R. Ray. Calcutta: General Printers and Publishers, 1980.

Cummings, F., and Staley, A. "On the Painting of English Landscape." *Proceedings of the British Academy* 21 (1968): 185–200.

Das, A. K. *The Photographer Prince Maharaja Sawai Ram Singh II.* Jaipur: Jaipur Museum, 1985.

Das Gupta, A. C., ed. *The Days of John Company.* Calcutta: West Bengal Government, 1959.

Desmond, R. "Photography in India During the Nineteenth Century." *India Office Library and Records. Annual Report for 1974,* pp. 5–38.

Dickinson, V., ed. *Miss Eden's Letters.* London: Macmillan, 1919.

Douglas, O. *Olivia in India. The Adventures of a Chota Miss Sahib.* London: Hodder and Stoughton, 1913.

Dunbar, J. *Golden Interlude. The Edens in India 1836–1842.* London: J. Murray, 1955.

Dyson, K. K. *A Various Universe.* Delhi: Oxford University Press, 1978.

Eden, E. *Up the Country.* 2 vols. London: R. Bentley, 1866.

Edkins, D. *Panoramic Photography.* New York: New York University Press, 1977.

Edwardes, M. *Bound to Exile. The Victorians in India.* New York: Praeger, 1970.

Edwards, P. I. *Indian Botanical Paintings.* Pittsburgh: The Hunt Institute for Botanical Documentation, Carnegie-Mellon University, 1980.

Eyre, G. "Art: Vintage Photographs of an Opulent Era. Indian Ambience of Royal Grandeur." *Architectural Digest,* April 1984, pp. 106–11.

Eyre-Todd, G., ed. *The Autobiography of William Simpson.* London: T. Fisher Unwin, 1903.

Fabian, R. and Adam, H. *Masters of Early Travel Photography.* New York: Vendome Press, 1983.

Falk, T. and Archer, M. *Indian Miniatures in the India Office Library.* London: Sotheby's, 1979.

Falkland, V. *Chow-Chow. Being Selections from a Journal Kept in India, Egypt and Syria.* 2 vols. London: Hurst and Blackett, 1857.

Foster, W. Sir. "British Artists in India: 1760–1820." *Walpole Society* 19 (1930–1931): 1–88.

Furber, H. *Rival Empires of Trade in the Orient, 1600–1800.* Minneapolis: University of Minnesota Press, 1976.

Gangoly, A. C. and Goswami, A. *Indian Terracotta Art.* New York: George Wittenborn, 1959.

Gernsheim, H. *The History of Photography.* New York: McGraw-Hill, 1969.

Ghose, B. *Selections from English Periodicals of 19th Century Bengal.* Vol. 1 Calcutta: Papyrus, 1978.

Ghosh, S. C. *The Social Condition of the British Community in Bengal.* Leiden: E. J. Brill, 1970.

Goldberg, V., ed. *Photography in Print. Writings from 1816 to the Present.* New York: Simon and Schuster, 1981.

Gould, B. J. *The Jewel in the Lotus.* London: Chatto & Windus, 1957.

Graham, M. *Journal of a Residence in India.* Edinburgh: A. Constable and Company, 1813.

Grant, M. H. *Old English Landscape Painters.* 8 vols. Leigh-on-Sea: F. Lewis, 1957–61.

Guichard, K. M. *British Etchers 1850–1940.* Portland: A. Prior, 1977.

Gutman, J. *Through Indian Eyes.* New York: Oxford University Press & International Center of Photography, 1982.

Hardie, M. and Clayton, M. "Thomas Daniell, R. A. and William Daniell, R. A." *Walker's Quarterly* 35–36 (1932): 2–34.

Haworth-Booth, M., ed. *The Golden Age of British Photography.* Philadelphia: Philadelphia Museum of Art, 1984.

Head, R. "An Endless Source of Amusement." *The Connoisseur,* February 1980, pp. 93–101.

Heathcote, P. F. "Samuel Bourne of Nottingham." *History of Photography.* April 1982, pp. 99–112.

Herrmann, L. *British Landscape Painting of the Eighteenth Century.* London: Faber & Faber, 1973.

Hershkowitz, R. *The British Photographer Abroad. The First Thirty Years.* London: Hershkowitz, 1980.

Hibbert, C. *The Great Mutiny.* Harmondsworth: Penguin, 1980.

Hodges, W. *Select Views of India.* London: J. Edwards, 1785–88.

———. *Travels in India During the Years 1780, 1781, 1782, and 1783.* London: J. Edwards, 1793.

Hofer, P. *Edward Lear as a Landscape Draughtsman.* Cambridge, MA: Belknap Press, 1967.

Irving, R. G. *Indian Summer.* New Haven: Yale

University Press, 1981.

Kahmen, V. *Art History of Photography*. Translated by Evan Tubb. New York: Viking, 1974.

Kaye, M. M., ed. *The Golden Calm*. New York: Viking, 1980.

Kedleston, Marquess Curzon of. *A Viceroy's India*. Edited by Peter King. London: Sidgewick & Jackson, 1984.

Knizkova, H. *The Drawings of the Kalighat Style*. Prague: National Museum, 1975.

Kopf, D. *British Orientation and the Bengal Renaissance*. Berkeley: University of California Press, 1969.

Lear, E. *Journals in India*. 2 vols. (unpublished manuscript), 1873–74.

Lowry, J. "Victorian Burma by Post. Felice Beato's Mail-Order Business." *Country Life*, March 1975, pp. 659–660.

Magnus, P. *King Edward the Seventh*. New York: Penguin, 1979.

Mahajan, J. *Picturesque India*. Delhi: Lustre Press Private, Ltd., 1983.

———. *The Ganga Trail*. London: Books from India (UK), Ltd., 1984.

Milner, J. D. "Tilly Kettle, 1735–1786." *The Walpole Society* 15 (1927): 47–103.

Moorhouse, G. *India Britannica*. London: Harvill Press, 1983.

Morris, J. *The Spectacle of Empire*. New York: Doubleday, 1982.

Morris, J., and Winchester, S. *Stones of Empire*. Oxford: Oxford University Press, 1983.

Murphy, R., ed. *Edward Lear's Indian Journal*. London: Jarrolds, 1953.

Newhall, B. *The History of Photography*. New York: The Museum of Modern Art, 1964.

Nilsson, S. "Egron Lundgren: Reporter of the Indian Mutiny." *Apollo*, August 1970, pp. 138–43.

Ollman, A. *Samuel Bourne. Images of India*. Carmel: Friends of Photography, 1983.

———. "Samuel Bourne. The Himalayan Images 1863–69." *Creative Camera*, October 1983, pp. 1122–25.

Panter-Downes, M. *Ooty Preserved. A Victorian Hill Station in India*. New York: Farrar, Straus & Giroux, 1967.

Pare, R. *Photography and Architecture: 1839–1939*. New York: Callaway Editions, 1982.

Parris, L. *Landscape in Britain c. 1750–1850*. London: The Tate Gallery, 1973.

Parry, B. *Delusions and Discoveries*. Berkeley: University of California Press, 1972.

Patten, R. L. "Conventions of Georgian Caricature." *Art Journal*, Winter 1983, pp. 331–38.

Paul, A., ed. *Woodcut Prints of Nineteenth-Century Calcutta*. Calcutta: Seagull Books, 1983.

Paviere, S. H. *The Devis Family of Painters*. Leigh-on-Sea: F. Lewis, 1950.

Piper, D., ed. *The Genius of British Painting*. New York: W. Morrow, 1975.

Prinsep, V. C. *Imperial India*. London: Chapman & Hall, 1879.

Quennell, P., ed. *Memoirs of William Hickey*. London: Purnell Book Services, 1975.

Reynolds, G. "British Artists in India." *The Art of India and Pakistan. A Commemorative Catalogue of the Exhibition Held at the Royal Academy of Arts, London, 1947–8*. Edited by Sir Leigh Ashton. London: Faber & Faber, 1950.

Roberts, E. *Scenes and Characteristics of Hindostan with Sketches of Anglo-Indian Society*. 2 vols. London: W. H. Allen and Co., 1837.

Rosselli, J. *Lord William Bentinck*. Berkeley: University of California Press, 1974.

Salaman, M. C. "Masterly Etchings by E. S. Lumsden." *Apollo*, July–December, 1925, pp. 296–97.

Shellim, M. *India and the Daniells*. London: Inchape & Co., Ltd., 1979.

Solkin, D. H. *Richard Wilson*. London: The Tate Gallery, 1982.

Sontag, S. *On Photography*. Harmondsworth: Penguin, 1973.

Spear, P. *The Nabobs*. London: Oxford University Press, 1963.

———. *The Nabobs: A Study of the Social Life of the English in Eighteenth-Century India*. Gloucester, MA: P. Smith, 1971.

Spencer, A. *Memoirs of William Hickey*. 4 vols. London: Hurst & Blackett, Ltd., 1918.

Sprague, S. "Samuel Bourne. Photographer of India in the 1860's." *British Journal of Photography*, January 14, 1977, pp. 28–32.

Stafford, B. "Rude Sublime: The Taste for Nature's Colossi During the Late Eighteenth and Early Nineteenth Centuries." *Gazette des Beaux-Arts*, April 1976, pp. 113–26.

———. "Toward Romantic Landscape Perception: Illustrated Travels and the Rise of 'Singularity' as an Aesthetic Category." *The Art Quarterly* I,

Autumn 1977, pp. 89–124.

Stanford, J. K., ed. *Ladies in the Sun*. London: The Galley Press, 1962.

Steube, I. "William Hodges and Warren Hastings: A Study in Eighteenth-Century Patronage." *The Burlington Magazine*, October–December 1973, pp. 659–66.

———. *The Life and Works of William Hodges*. New York: Garland, 1979.

Sutton, T. *The Daniells: Artists and Travellers*. London: Bodley Head, 1954.

Thomas, G. "The First Four Decades of Photography in India." *History of Photography*, July 1979, pp. 215–26.

Tindall, G. *City of Gold*. London: Temple Smith, 1982.

Trevelyan, G. O. *Competition Wallah*. London: Macmillan, 1866.

Watkin, D. "Some Dufour Wallpapers: A Neoclassical Venture into the Picturesque." *Apollo*, June 1967, pp. 432–35.

———. *The English Vision: The Picturesque in Architecture, Landscape, and Garden Design*. London: John Murray, 1982.

Webster, M. *Johan Zoffany: 1733–1810*. London: National Portrait Gallery, 1976.

Williams, S. I. *Samuel Bourne: In Search of the Picturesque*. Williamstown: Sterling and Francine Clark Art Institute, 1981.

Wilton, A. *J. M. W. Turner. His Art and Life*. New York: Rizzoli, 1979.

Woodruff, P. *The Men Who Ruled India*. 2 vols. London: Jonathan Cape, 1963.

Worswick, C. *Princely India. Photographs by Raja Deen Dayal, 1884–1910*. New York: Knopf, 1980.

Worswick, C., and Embree, A. *The Last Empire. Photography in British India, 1855–1911*. Millerton, NY: Aperture, 1976.

Wurgaft, L. D. *The Imperial Imagination*. Middletown, CT: Wesleyan University Press, 1983.

Yule, Col. H., and Burnell, A. C. *Hobson-Jobson*. London: John Murray, 1903.

Index

Black-and-white illustrations designated by italic page numbers.
Colorplates face page numbers printed in bold.
Titles of works of art and of books are in italic type.

Ackerley, J. R., 11, 46, 83
advertisement, 30, 31, 34–36
Agnew of Manchester, Thomas and Sons, 17
Akbar, 21, 42, 153–54
albumin, 199, 209
Allahabad, from the Right Bank of the Jumna (Simpson), 123, 124, *124*
Allan, Sir Alexander, 118–19; *Tritteny Pagoda*, 118–19, *119*
Allegorical Picture of Fortitude (attr. Basawan), 153–54, *154*
Amateur Artist at Work (Hunter), *13. See also Picturesque Scenery in the Kingdom of Mysore*
Amherst, Lady, 20
Ancient Excavations at Carli (Salt), 113, *115*
Anonymous, British: *Bengal Army on the March*, 37, *38*; *Bengal Soldier's Defence of a Hot Climate*, 61, *63*; *Burke Photographing the Ameer Yakoob Khan*, 183, *186*; *Calcutta with St. Paul's Cathedral in the Background*, 90, 182, *182*; *Camera Obscura*, 105, 126, *182*; *Captain Simpson's Children with their Ponies*, 64, *66*; *Cheyt Syng's Ghost*, 55, *59*; *Clive as Roman Emperor*, 48, *50*; *Courtesan*, 204, *207*; *Crowds at Kumbakonam Tank*, 210, *211*; *Elphinstone Circle*, 92, 198, *200–202*; *Emigration of the Clergy, or a Translation to India to Convert the Innocent Indoos*, *77*; *Hanging Tree*, 207, *209*; *H. E. Lord Curzon, taken at Chamba*, *87*; *Hot Quarters for the Tenth, or a Curiosity for India*, 61, *63*; *Imperial Assemblage, Delhi*, *86*; *Investiture of the Raja of Oodeypore*, 84, *85*; *Maharaja of Bhawalpur*, 199, *206*; *Maharaja of Kolhapur*, 199, *203*; *Maharashtrian Women*, 184, *188*; *Nabob Rumbled, or A Lord Advocates Amusement*, *58*; *Nabobs*, *60*; *Native Merchant in the English Costume*, *70*; *Nautch Girl*, 204, *208*; *Parliament House, New Delhi*, 90, *91*; *Political Banditti Assailing the Saviour of India*, 55, *59*; *Queen at Work*, *85*; *Raj Dhiraj of Shapura*, 199, *206*; *Sale of English Beauties in the East Indies*, 23, *32*; *Scene from San Toy Performed at Poona*, *68*; *Sir David Ochterlony Watching a Nautch*, *71*; *Suttee*, 138, *139*; *Taj* 198, *200–1*; *View of the Imperial Assemblage*, *88*; *View of the Secretariat, New Delhi*, 94, *95*; *Visit to the Jail*, *49*; *Warren Hastings*, 48, *50*
Anonymous, Indian: *Border with Flower Studies*, *169*; *Caricature of General Stuart, the British Governor, Madras*, 174, *174*; *Coconut Seller and Woman Vendor*, 158, *159*; *Hook-Swinging*, 161, 162, *163*; *Indian Artist at Work*, *19*; *Interior of the Tomb of Itimad-ud-daula*, 159, *160*; *Kali*, *171*; *Krishna-lila Scroll*, *172*; *Merchant Srimanta Sees a Vision of the Goddess*, 177, *177*; *Mirza Bidar Sandhar Khan and Wife*, 157, *159*; *Mohunt and the Seduced Girl Tête-à-Tête*, 171, 175, *176*; *Mohunt Forcing the Seduced Girl to Drink some Liquor*, 173, 175, *176*; *Mohurrum*, 161, 162, *163*; *Murder of Elokeshi by Nabin*, 175, *176*; *Nawab Ghazi-ud-din Haidar of Oudh*, 156, *158*; *Nawab Wajid Ali Shah Embracing Lord Hardinge*, 159, *160*; *Nude*, 161, *162*; *Portrait of a Lady* (after Tilly Kettle), 155, *156*; *Portrait of an Englishwoman*, 156, *158*; *Portrait of Sir Charles Metcalfe*, 154, *155*; *Principal Monuments of India, including the Taj Mahal*, *161*; *Savitri Pleading with Yama, the God of Death, for the Life of her Dead Husband* (Calcutta Art Studio), 179, *179*; *School in Calcutta*, 174, *175*; *Shah Jehan with Two Princes and an Attendant*, *167*; *Six Afghans*, 162, *164*; *Stork*, 166, *167*; *Tilly Kettle Painting a Portrait of Shuja-ud-daula, Nawab of Oudh, with Ten Sons*, 12, 156, *157*; *Trooper of Skinner's Horse*, 162, *176*; *Tumblers*, 161, *162*; *Vaishnava Priest at a Woman's Breast*, 174, *175*; *White Lotus*, 167, *169*
Archer, Mildred, 26, 32, 50, 153, 159
Archer, William G., 171–72, 180
architecture, 89, 90, 92, 95, 96, 182
art: British, 27, 97, 98, 101, 111, 129, 130–31, 140; influence on Indian artists, 20, 118, 153–58, 166, 172–73, 176–77, 179–80
artist, amateur, 13, 117–20, 140–41, 155

Asuf-ud-daula, 26, 33
Assaburdar or Long Silver-Stick Bearer (D'Oyly),
24. *See also* D'Oyly, *European in India*
Atkinson, G. F., *Curry and Rice*, 18, 53, 54, 64, 65,
66, 67, 68, 72, 173
Atkinson, James, 138; *Suttee*, 138
Auckland, George Eden, Earl of, 14, 132
auction, 30, 35, 36
Aurangzeb, 21, 22

B

Bacon, John, 48
Baden-Powell, B. H., 159, 160; *Our Bhisti, Water-
man*, 199, 204
Bamboos (Lear), 143, 145
Banyan Tree (Clark), 120, 121
Banyan Tree, Barrackpore (Bourne), 193, 194
Bartelozzi, F., *Lord Clive*, 23
Basawan, 153–54; *Allegorical Picture of Fortitude*,
154
Baudelaire, Charles, 181
Beato, Felice, *Interior of the Secundra Bagh, the
Spot where 1700 Rebels were Killed by H. M.'s
and Greens' 4th Punjab Infantry*, 80, 81, 188,
207–9; *Kutub Minar*, 207–210; *Tinnevelly
Bridge at Flood*, 207, 209
Beechy, George, 32, 33, 155
Benares, 40, 98, 99, 102, 107, 121, 127–29, 188
Benares (Lear), 126
Benares, Vishnu Pud (Bourne), 197, 199
Bengal Army on the March (Anon. Br.), 37, 38
Bengal Remedy for the Bile (Rowlandson), 62, 64
Bengal Soldier's Defence of a Hot Climate (Anon.
Br.), 61, 63
Bentinck, Lord William Cavendish, 45, 65, 138
Bhawanidas, 165
bibi, 46, 131–32
Blair Conversation Piece (Zoffany), 110, 111
Black Town of Calcutta (Solvyns), 39, 145. *See
also* Solvyns, *Two Hundred and Fifty Coloured
Etchings . . .*
Bombay, 28, 92, 95, 145, 178–79, 184, 198
Border with Flower Studies (Anon. In.), 169
Bordwine, J. F., *Southeast Front of the New Govern-
ment House*, 92, 93
Bourne, Samuel, 99, 186, 188–95, 197–98, 206;
Banyan Tree, Barrackpore, 193, 194, *Benares,
Vishnu Pud*, 197, 199; *Dal Lake, Kashmir*, 185,
188–89, 191; *Jhula Bridge at Spiti*, 193; *Kaiser
Pasund, Lucknow*, 92, 93, 197; *Memorial Well,
Cawnpore*, 80, 81; *Nainital*, 96, 187, 188, 191;
Ootacamund, A Peep from near Bombay House,
96, 184, 188–89; *Snowy Heights at Wangtu*,
190, 192; *View from New Tibet Road near
Cheenee*, 189, 191–92; *View of Khuds and Val-
leys of Simla*, 95, 96; *Village of Dunkar, Spiti*,
192, 193
Bourne and Shepherd, 188, 193, 199; *Post Office,
Calcutta*, 90, 90; *Statue of General Sir James
Outram, Calcutta*, 25
Branch of a Gul-mohr Tree (Lear), 144, 145
Brief History of Ancient and Modern India (Orme),
14, 26, 27, 89, 146
British Journal of Photography, 186, 194
Brown, Mather, 52, 53; *Departure of the Sons of
Tipu from the Zenana*, 54
Bulwer-Lytton, Edward Robert, 1st Earl of Lytton
(Owen Meredith), 189
Burke Photographing the Ameer Yakoob Khan
(Anon. Br.), 183, 186
Byron, Robert, 96

C

Calcutta, 22–25, 27, 28, 36, 45, 66, 67, 70, 71, 90,
92, 145–46, 167, 169, 170–72, 177–79, 182,
185, 188
Calcutta Bhisti (Sache), 199, 204
*Calcutta with St. Paul's Cathedral in the Back-
ground* (Anon. Br.), 90, 182, 182
calotype, 182, 185, 195–96
Camera-Obscura (Anon. Br.), 105, 126, 182
Canning, Charles John Canning, Earl, 47, 82,
184–85
Captain Simpson's Children with their Ponies
(Anon. Br.), 64, 66
Carey, W. H., *The Good Old Days of Honourable
John Company*, 11, 12
*Caricature of General Stuart, the British Governor,
Madras* (Anon. In.), 174, 174
Carpenter, Percy, 73; *Charge—Pig-sticking*, 75;
Tent Club at Tiffin, 72, 73
Carter, George, 30, 34, 52
cartoons, 17, 18, 23, 55, 57, 61, 62, 173–74. *See
also* individual works
caste, 20, 47, 77. *See also* society, Indian
Cawnpore, 79, 80, 127
Charge—Pig-sticking (Carpenter), 75
Cheyt Syng's Ghost (Anon. Br.), 55, 59
Chinnery, George, 12, 14, 25, 28, 29, 31, 110–13,
117, 138; *River Scene with Figures and a Fishing
Boat Moored Beside Ruins*, 112, 114; *Ruins of
a Temple, Sunset*, 112, 113, 114; *Self-Portrait*,
13; *Surf Boats on the Beach, Madras*, 31; *Two
Thatched Indian Huts*, 113
Chitpore Road (Daniells), 145–46, 147
Churchill, Lieutenant, 198; *Snake Charmers*, 203
cityscapes, 145–52
Clark, Captain Melville, 119–20; *Banyan Tree*,
120, 121
Clive, Robert, Baron Clive of Plassey, 22, 24, 32,
49, 54
Clive as Roman Emperor (Anon. Br.), 48, 50

Clive Receiving a Legacy from the Nawab of Murshidabad (Penny), 30, 49, *51*

Clive Receiving the Grant of the Diwani of Bengal from the Mogul Emperor Shah Alam (West), 49, *52*

Cobra de Capello, or the Spectacle Snake (Forbes), *141, 142. See also* Forbes, *Oriental Memoirs*

Cockfight (Zoffany), 27, 73, *73*

Coconut Seller and Woman Vendor (Anon. In.), 158, *159*

Colebrook, Robert Hyde, 24, 25, 118; *Southern Countryside*, *118*

collodion, 184–86, 197, 206

Colonel Antoine Polier with his Friends Claud Martin, John Wombwell and the Artist (Zoffany), *34*, 110

Company school, 20, 153–67, 172, 174

Cook, Captain James, 101–2, 110

Cornwallis, Charles, Cornwallis, 1st Marquess, 31, 50–52

Costumes of India. See D'Oyly, Sir Charles

Courtesan (Anon. Br.), 204, *207*

Coward, Noel, 48

Crimean War, 17, 80, 121, 207

Crowds at Kumbakonam Tank (Anon. Br.), 210, *211*

Cunningham, Sir Alexander, 185

Curry and Rice. See Atkinson, G. F.

Curzon Investing the Maharaja of Cochin at the Coronation Durbar, Delhi (Prior), 86, *87*

Curzon of Kedleston, George Nathaniel, Marquess, 84, 86, 98

D

daguerreotype, 182, 184–85

Dalhousie, James Andrew Broun Ramsey, 1st Marquess of, 78, 79

Dal Lake, Kashmir (Bourne), *185*, 188–89, *191*

Dance, Nathaniel, *Lord Clive*, 23

dancers (nautch), 70, 71, 132, 188, 204, 208

Daniell, Thomas and William, 12, 28, 30, 37, 38, 42, 44, 90, 100, 102, 104–10, 121, 135, 155, 176; *Chitpore Road*, 145–46, *147*; *Dhuah Koonde*, 43; *Great Pagoda, Trichinopoly*, 109; *Hindoo Temple in the Fort at Rhotas, Bihar*, 110; *Hindoo Temples at Bindrabund on the River Jumna*, 106, *112*; *Jai Singh's Observatory, Delhi*, *108*; *Jama Masjid, Delhi*, 107, *108*; *Oriental Scenery; Twenty-four Views in Hindoostan*, 15, 43, 104, 109; *Picturesque Voyage to India by the Way of China*, 39; *Portrait of a Sporting Artist, possibly W. B. Daniell*, 12; *Sacred Tree of the Hindoos at Gyah*, 106, *108*; *Views of Calcutta*, 105, 135; *Warren Hastings*, 25

Davis, Samuel, 105, 108, 109, 176; *In India, On the March*, *36*

Dawn at Beylah (Lundgren), 80

Day and Son, 42, 121, 124

Death of Tippoo, or Besieging the Haram (Rowlandson), *58*

Decoyed Elephants Leaving the Male Fastened to a Tree (Williamson), *116*, 117

Delaroche, Hippolyte, 181

Delhi/New Delhi, 76, 84, 86, 87, 95, 96, 102, 161

Departure of the Sons of Tipu from the Zenana (Brown), 52, 53, *54*

Desolation Hall, Futtehpore (French), 76, *76*

Devis, Arthur William, 12, 24, 27, 29, 30, 31, 52, 131, 136–37; *Native Women from Bengal Grinding Flour Outside a Hut*, *137*; *Portrait of a Holy Man Seated Under a Tree*, 140, *141*; *Pottery with Various Utensils in General Use*, 136, *137*

Dhuah Koonde (Daniell), 43. *See also* Daniell, *Oriental Scenery . . . Discovery of the Body of Tipu Sultan* (Porter), 53, *55*

Dissertation on the Prototypes of Architecture, Hindoo, Moorish, and Gothic (Hodges), 41

Dixon, Captain, *Great Temple at Bhubanesvar*, 197

Dixon, John, *Omdut-ul-Mulk, Nawab of Arcot*, 131, *131*

Douglas, Olivia, 198

D'Oyly, Sir Charles, 13, 14, 39, 64–66, 111, 117–18, 130–31, 144–46, 156, 173; *Assaburdar or Long Silver-Stick Bearer*, 24; *Costumes of India*, 16, 64, 65, 130; *English Gentleman and his Munshi or Native Professor of Languages*, 65, 66, 67; *European Couple Watching Snake-Charmer*, 139; *European in India*, 24, 65, 66, 67, 139; *Female Attendants*, 64, 65; *Fishers of Small Fry* (after Chinnery), 130; *Fort and Town of Calcutta*, 146, 148–49; *Ibis* (with Webb-Smith), 142, 145; *Suspension Bridge at Alipore over Tolly's Nulla*, 117; *Taylor's Emporium, Calcutta*, 35; *View of a Street in the City of Patna*, 146, 150; *Views of Calcutta Environs*, 146, 148–49

durbar, 42, 84, 86, 87

Dust Storm Coming On, near Jeypore Rajportana (Simpson), 122, *123*

Dying Hindoo Brought to the Ganges (Zoffany), 110, *112*

E

Earlson, Richard. *See* Zoffany, *Embassy of Hyderbeck*

East, G. B., *Madras, Embarking*, 62

East India Company (John Company), 11, 14, 17, 21, 22, 27, 29, 30, 55, 57, 65, 77, 84, 115, 159–60, 165, 195

Eastman, George, 186

Eden, Emily, 13, 14, 16, 20, 84, 132–33, 140; *Group of Tibet Tatars*, 132, *133*; *Lord Auckland Receiving the Raja of Nahun in Durbar*, 84, 104;

Portraits of the Princes and Peoples of India, 16;
Up the Country, 132
education: in Britain, 14, 115, 133, 195; in India,
64–66, 174
Edward VII, 42, 61, 83, 84, 86, 88, 124, 176
Elliot, Captain Robert, 98, 99
Elphinstone, Lord Monstuart, 162, 184, 198
Elphinstone Circle (Anon. Br.), 92, 198, 200–2
Embassy of Hyderbeck (Zoffany), 50, 53
*Emigration of the Clergy, or a Translation to India
to Convert the Innocent Indoos* (Anon. Br.), 77
*English Gentleman and his Munshi or Native Pro-
fessor of Languages* (D'Oyly), 65, 66, 67. *See also*
D'Oyly, *European in India*
Entrance Gateway to Akbar's Mausoleum, Sikandra
(Hodges), 41. *See also* Hodges, *Dissertation on
the Prototypes of Architecture . . .*
European Couple Watching Snakecharmer (D'Oyly),
139. *See also* D'Oyly, *European in India*
European in India. See D'Oyly
Exhibition of a Battle between a Buffalo and Tiger
(Williamson), 75
Exotic Insect: Two Views (Seetu Ram), 166, 168

F

Falkland, Viscountess, 144
Famine in India (Simpson), 17, 121–22, 122
Fancy Dress Ball at Mrs. Casement's (Prinsep, W.),
69
Farington, George, 33, 34, 138
Female Attendants (D'Oyly), 64, 65. *See also*
D'Oyly, *Costumes of India*
Festival of the Goddess Durga at Calcutta (Sol-
tykoff), 70, 71, 72. *See also* Soltykoff, *Indian
Scenes and Characters*
Fishers of Small Fry (D'Oyly, after Chinnery), 130,
130. *See also* D'Oyly, *Costumes of India*
Forbes, James, 13, 39, 99, 100, 130, 133, 141–45;
Cobra de Capello, or the Spectacle Snake, 141,
142; *Oriental Memoirs*, 15, 22, 41, 43, 141,
142, 144, **144**, 145, 147; *Red, Blue and White
Lotuses of Hindostan*, 142, 144; *Surat on the
Banks of the Tappee*, 22; *Taylor Birds and Fruit-
Bearing Convolvulus*, 144, **144**; *View of Bombay
Green*, 145, 147
Forrest, Colonel Charles Ramus, 40, 41, 98; *Pictur-
esque Tour along the Rivers Ganges and Jumna*,
40, 98
Forster, Edward Morgan, 83, 108
Forster, Johann Reinhold, 110
Fort and Town of Calcutta (D'Oyly), 146, 148–49.
See also D'Oyly, *Views of Calcutta Environs*
Fraser, James Baillie, 38, 39, 44, 99, 162
Fraser, William, 162
French, P. C., *Desolation Hall, Futtehpore*, 76, 76;
Lays of Agra—Poems and Sketches, 78; *Sahib

*Being Carried in a Palanquin, Corner of Writers'
Building*, 49
Frith, Frances, 204, 206; *Kulu Women*, 206, 208

G

Gainsborough, Thomas, 12
Ganges, 37, 39, 40, 42, 98–102, 121
Ganges (Simpson), 122, 123
gelatin (photographic), 186
genre, 16, 24, 30, 31, 129–40, 140–45, 152
George V (George Frederick Ernest Albert), 86, 87
Ghose, Ajit, 171
Ghulam 'Ali Khan, 162, 165; *Harem Scene*, 165
Gilpin, William, 97, 98
Gold, Captain Charles, 38, 135–36; *Hanuman
King of Apes*, 135, 136; *Itinerant Traders*, 134,
136; *Oriental Drawings*, 134, 135, 136; *Tents
Blowing Up in a Storm*, 38
Good Old Days of Honourable John Company
(Carey), 11, 12
Gould, Sir Basil, 76
Granville, Walter, 90
Great Pagoda, Trichinopoly (Daniell), 109, 109
Great Temple at Bhubanesvar (Dixon, Captain),
197
Green, James, *Indian Jugglers*, 140
Griffiths, John, 20, 120, 131, 152, 178; *Mid–day
Sun—Camels Before a Shrine in Western India*,
151, 152; *Woman Labourer*, 130, 131
Grindlay, Robert, 13
Group of Tibet Tatars (Eden), 132, 133

H

Haig, Axel Herman, *Victoria Railway Terminus,
Bombay*, 91, 92
Hanging Tree (Anon. Br.), 207, 209
Hanuman King of Apes (Gold), 135, 136. *See also*
Gold, *Oriental Drawings*
Hardinge, Charles Stewart Hardinge, 2nd Viscount,
87, 95, 119, 159; *Kote Kangra*, 119, 120
Harem Scene (Ghulam 'Ali Khan), 165, 165
Hastings, Warren, 23, 25–27, 30, 32, 33, 48, 55,
102
Havell, Ernest Binfield, 178, 180
Heath, Charles. *See* Forbes, *View of Bombay Green*
Heber, Bishop, 98, 118
H. E. Lord Curzon, taken at Chamba (Anon. Br.),
87
Herrmann, Luke, 189
Herschel, Sir John, 182
Hibbert, C., 79
Hickey, Thomas, 25, 28–30, 32
Hickey, William, 23, 28, 30, 33, 46, 71, 131
hillstation, 95, 96, 184, 187, 188, 189, 191
Hindoo Temple in the Fort at Rhotas, Bihar

(Daniell), 110, *110*

Hindoo Temples at Bindrabuo on the River Jumna (Daniell), 106, *112*

Hindustani Family (Renaldi), 46, *47*

Hodges, William, 11, 12, 17, 30, 38, 39, 42–44, 90, 100–4, 109, 129, 186; *Dissertation on the Prototypes of Architecture, Hindoo, Moorish, and Gothic,* 41; *Entrance Gateway to Akbar's Mausoleum, Sikandra,* 41; *Select Views in India,* 15, 100, 102, 103, 105; *Storm on the Ganges with Mrs. Hastings Braving the Eddies near the Col-Gon Rocks,* 102, *104; View of an Insulated Rock in the River Ganges at Jangerah,* 99; *View of the Island of Jangerah at Sultanganj with Figures in the Foreground,* 101; *View of Musjid, or the Tomb at Jaunpur,* 102, *103; View of Part of the City of Benares,* 102, *103*

Holland, William, 55

Home, Robert, 12, 33, 52, 155–57

Hookah-Bearer (Solvyns), *133*

Hooker, William, 141, 142, **144**. *See also* Forbes, *Oriental Memoirs*

Hook-Swinging (Anon. In.), 161–62, *163*

Hooper, Captain Willoughby, 17, 188, 210; *Madras Famine,* (a) *15, 17,* 188, *209;* (b) 188, 210, *211*

Horse and Groom (Shaikh Muhammad Amir of Karraya), 166, *168*

Hot Quarters for the Tenth, or a Curiosity for India (Anon. Br.), 61, *63*

Humphry, Ozias, 28, 33, 155; *View from John Wombwell's House Across the River Gumti,* 29

Hunter, James, *Picturesque Scenery in the Kingdom of Mysore,* 13

Hunting Jackals (Williamson), 74, *117*

I

Ibis (D'Oyly and Webb-Smith), 142, *145*

illustrated books, 13, 15, 16, 105, 152, 176, 177. *See also* individual works

Imperial Assemblage, Delhi (Anon. Br.), 86

Impey, Lady, 20, 165–66

Impey, Sir Elijah, 20, 57, 165

India, Ancient and Modern (Simpson), 124

Indian Artist at Work (Anon. In.), *19*

Indian Charivari Album, 18, 173, *174*

Indian Girl in an Interior (Renaldi), 46, *46,* 131

Indian Jugglers (Green), 140, *140*

Indian Scenes and Characters Soltykoff), 72

Indo-British relations, 11, 24, 45–48, 73, 76–80, 82–84, 87–89. *See also* society, Anglo-Indian

Ingres, Jean Auguste Dominique, 181

In India, On the March (Davis), 36

Interior of the Secundra Bagh, the Spot where 1700 Rebels were Killed by H. M.'s and Greens' 4th Punjab Infantry (Beato), 80, 81, 188, 207–9

Interior of the Tomb of Itimad-ud-daula (Anon.

In.), 159, *160*

Investiture of the Raja of Oodeypore (Anon. Br.), 84, *85*

Isaacs, Martha, 23, 30

Isherah—Water Procession of the Image of Doorga Previous to her Immersion at Sunset (Prinsep, W.), 136, *140*

Itinerant Traders (Gold), 134, *136. See also* Gold, *Oriental Drawings*

J

Jahangir, 154, 166

Jaipur (Mempes), 151, *152*

Jai Singh's Observatory, Delhi (Daniell), 108, *108*

Jama Masjid, Delhi (Daniell), 107, 108

Jhula Bridge at Spiti (Bourne), 193, *193*

Johnston and Hoffman, *Pratap Singh, the Maharaja of Idar,* 199, 204, *206*

Jones, Sir William, 29, 34, 65

K

Kaiser Pasund, Lucknow (Bourne), 92, *93,* 197

Kali (Anon. In.), *171*

Kalighat school, 20, 167–74, 176–77

Kettle, Tilly, 21, 22, 25, 26, 33, 46, 155–56

Khan, Ismael, 154, 161, 181

Kipling, Lockwood, 20, 170, 178

Kipling, Rudyard, 20, 146, 170

Kittoe, Markham, 159

Knizkova, H., 172

Kodak, 186

Kote Kangra (Hardinge), 119, *120*

Krishna-lila Scroll (Anon. In.), 172, *172*

Kulu Women (Frith), 206, *208*

Kutpootlee Nautch, Alis Fantoccini—on My Verandah (Prinsep, W.), 48, *64*

Kutub Minar (Beato), 207–210

L

Lady Impey's Bird (Shaikh Zayn-al-din), *166*

landscape, 16, 97–129, 152

Lawrence, Honoria, 98

Lays of Agra—Poems and Sketches (French), 78

Lear, Edward, 42, 62, 107, 120, 124–29, 145, 152, 181–82, 207–8; *Bamboos,* 143, *145; Benares,* 126; *Branch of a Gul-mohr Tree,* 144, *145; Marble Rocks, Nerbudda,* 125, *126; Trichinopoly,* 127, *128; View of Calicut,* 125

Lord Auckland Receiving the Raja of Nahun in Durbar (Eden), 84, **104**

Lord Clive (Bartelozzi after Nathaniel Dance), 23

Lucknow, 28, 33, 73, 79–81, 121, 145, 155, 207. *See also* Oudh

Luggar Falcon (Webb-Smith), 142, *144*

Lumsden, Ernest Stephen, 120, 129; *Art of Etching*, 129; *River Craft, Benares*, 128, 129
Lundgren, Egron, 17, 80, 169; *Dawn at Beylah*, 80
Lutyens, Sir Edwin Landseer, 88, 90, 95
Lyon, Captain E. D., 196–97

M

Mabon, Robert, 28, 33, 176–77; *Mahratta Peshwa and his Ministers*, 33; *Sepoy Punishment*, 79
Macauley, Thomas Babington, 65
Madras, 25, 28, 90, 145, 178–79, 185, 196
Madras, Embarking (East), 62
Madras Famine (Hooper), (a) 15, 17, 188, 209, (b) 188, 210, 211
Magnus, Philip, 84
Mahabharata (Ramtaran Das), 177, 178
Maharaja of Bhawalpur (Anon. Br.), 199, 206
Maharaja of Kolhapur (Anon. Br.), 199, 203
Maharashtrian Women (Anon. Br.), 184, 188
Mahratta Peshwa and his Ministers (Mabon), 33
Mahrattas, 33
Marble Rocks, Nerbudda (Lear), 125, 126
Marochetti, Charles, 80
Martin, Major Claud, 33, 34
Memorial Well, Cawnpore (Bourne), 80, 81
Mempes, Mortimer, 120, 152; *Jaipur*, 151, 152
Merchant Srimanta Sees a Vision of the Goddess (Anon. In.), 177, 177
Mid-day Sun—Camels Before a Shrine in Western India (Griffiths), 151, 152
Mirza Bidar Sandhar Khan and Wife (Anon. In.), 157, 159
Misdirected Energy (Anon.), 174. *See also Indian Charivari Album*
Moffat, James, 57, 176; *Rival Candidates at Calcutta*, 17; *Scene in the Writers' Buildings, Calcutta*, 57, 61
Moguls, 21, 49, 64, 70, 84, 86, 153–56, 161, 166–67
Mohunt and the Seduced Girl Tête-à-Tête (Anon. In.), 171, 175–76
Mohunt Forcing the Seduced Girl to Drink some Liquor (Anon. In.), 173, 175–76
Mohurrum (Anon. In.), 161, 162, 163
Mohurrum (Sewak Ram), 162, 164
Mordaunt, John, 34
Morris, Jan, 89, 95
Muhammad Ali, Nawab of Arcot, 32
Muhammad Ali, Nawab of Arcot (Smart), 32, 156
Murder of Elokeshi by Nabin (Anon. In.), 175, 176
Murray, Dr. John, *Principal Street, Agra*, 195, 196
Murshidabad, 32, 33
Mutiny, Indian, 16, 17, 42, 77–82, 120–21, 145, 207
Mysore, 50–53. *See also* Tipu Sultan

N

nabob, 23, 27, 54, 55, 57, 90, 92
Nabob Rumbled, or a Lord Advocates Amusement (Anon. Br.), 58
Nainital (Bourne), 96, 187, 188, 191
Native Merchant in the English Costume (Anon. Br.), 70
Native Women from Bengal Grinding Flour Outside a Hut (Devis), 127, 137
Nautch Girl (Anon. Br.), 70, 71, 132, 188, 204, 208
Nawab Ghazi-ud-din Haidar of Oudh (Anon. In.), 156, 158
Nawab Wajid Ali Shah Embracing Lord Hardinge (Anon. In.), 159, 160
Newland, J. W., 182
Nilsson, Sten, 17
Nude (Anon. In.), 161, 162

O

Old Courthouse, Calcutta (Orme), 89. *See also* Orme, *Brief History of Ancient and Modern India*
Omdut-ul-Mulk, Nawab of Arcot (Dixon, J.), 131, 131
Ootacamund. *See* hillstation
Ootacamund, A Peep from near Bombay House (Bourne), 96, 184, 188–89
Oriental Field Sports (Williamson), 16
Oriental Memoirs (Forbes), 15, 22, 41, 43, 141, 141, 142, 142, 144, 144, 145, 147
Oriental Scenery; Twenty-four Views in Hindoostan (Daniell), 15, 43, 104, 109
Orme, Edward, 145; *Brief History of Ancient and Modern India*, 14, 26, 27, 89, 146; *Old Courthouse, Calcutta*, 89; *Tipu Sultan*, 50, 53; *View of Part of St. Thome Street, Fort St. George*, 146
Orwell, George, 76
Oudh, 26, 33, 80, 81, 155–57. *See also* Lucknow
Our Bhisti, Waterman (Baden-Powell), 199, 204
Our Burra-Khanah (Atkinson, G. F.), 68. *See also* Atkinson, G. F., *Curry and Rice*
Our Coffee House (Atkinson, G. F.), 72. *See also* Atkinson, G. F., *Curry and Rice*
Our Cook Room (Atkinson, G. F.), 64, 65. *See also* Atkinson, G. F., *Curry and Rice*
Our Moonshee (Atkinson, G. F.), 66, 67. *See also* Atkinson, G. F., *Curry and Rice*

P

Paget, Sir Edward, 111
Parks, Fanny, 98
Parliament House, New Delhi (Anon. Br.), 90, 91
Paterson, George, 32
patronage: of British artists, 16, 24–28, 31, 32, 42;

by the East India Company, 29, 30; by Indian
    rulers, 26, 32, 33; of Indian artists, 153–62,
    165–67, 174
Penny, Edward, 30, 49; *Clive Receiving a Legacy
    from the Nawab of Murshidabad*, 30, 49, *51*
photography, 16, 99, 120, 145, 152, 159, 181–212
picturesque, 39, 97–129, 186, 188, 191
Picturesque Scenery in the Kingdom of Mysore
    (Hunter), *13*
*Picturesque Tour along the Rivers Ganges and
    Jumna* (Forrest), 40, 98
Picturesque Voyage to India by the Way of China
    (Daniell), *39*
Place, George, 33, 155
Plassey, Battle of, 15, 22, 32
Polier, Colonel Antoine, 33, 34, 155
Political Banditti Assailing the Saviour of India
    (Anon. Br.), 55, *59*
Porter, Captain John Young, *Sir Thomas Strange's
    House*, **64**, *76*
Porter, Sir Robert Kerr, 52, 53; *Discovery of the
    Body of Tipu Sultan*, 53, *55*; *Storming of Se-
    ringapatam*, 53, *56*
Portrait of a Holy Man Seated Under a Tree (Devis),
    140, *141*
Portrait of a Lady (Anon. In.), *155*, *156*
Portrait of an Englishwoman (Anon. In.), 156, *158*
Portrait of a Sporting Artist, possibly W. B. Daniell,
    12
Portrait of Sir Charles Metcalfe (Anon. In.), 154,
    155
Portraits of the Princes and Peoples of India (Eden),
    16
portraiture, 12, 30–33, 76, 110–11, 113, 131,
    154–57, 180, 182
Post Office, Calcutta (Bourne and Shepherd), 90, *90*
Pottery with Various Utensils in General Use
    (Devis), *136*, 137
Pratap Singh, the Maharaja of Idar (Johnston and
    Hoffman), 199, 204, *206*
*Principal Monuments of India, including the Taj
    Mahal* (Anon. In.), *161*
Principal Street, Agra (Murray), 195, *196*
Prinsep, James, 138–39
Prinsep, Valentine, 42, 84, 95, 132, 154, 161, 179,
    181–82
Prinsep, William, 64, 139–40; *Fancy Dress Ball at
    Mrs. Casement's*, *69*; *Isherah—Water Procession
    of the Image of Doorga Previous to her Immer-
    sion at Sunset*, 136, *140*; *Kutpootlee Nautch,
    Alias Fantoccini—On My Verandah*, **48**, *64*
prints, 15, 20, 105, 117, 129, 135, 153, 176–79
Prior, Melton, *Curzon Investing the Maharaja of
    Cochin at the Coronation, Durbar, Delhi*, 86, *87*
Pyne, W. H., 97

Q

Queen at Work (Anon. Br.), *85*

R

Raja Deen Dayal, 210–11
Raj Dhiraj of Shapura (Anon. Br.), 199, *206*
Ramdas, 165
Ramtaran Das *Mahabharata*, 177, *178*
Read, Catherine, 25
Red, Blue and White Lotuses of Hindostan (For-
    bes), 142, *144*. See also Forbes, *Oriental
    Memoirs*
Renaldi, Francesco, 12, 33, 46, 131, 155; *Hin-
    dustani Family*, 46, *47*; *Indian Girl in an Interior*,
    46, *131*
Repton, Humphrey, 106
*Residency, Lucknow, Showing the Room where Sir
    Henry Lawrence was Mortally Wounded* (Shep-
    herd and Robertson), 81, *83*
Reynolds, Sir Joshua, 104, 111
Rival Candidates at Calcutta (Moffat), *17*
River Craft, Benares (Lumsden), 128, *129*
*River Scene with Figures and a Fishing Boat
    Moored Beside Ruins* (Chinnery), 112, *114*
Roberts, Emma, 98, 99, 108, 140
Rosburgh, William, 166–67
Rowlandson, Thomas, 62; *Bengal Remedy for the
    Bile*, 62, *64*; *Death of Tippoo, or Besieging the
    Haram*, *58*
Royds, Mabel, 129
Ruins of a Temple, Sunset (Chinnery), 112–13, *114*
Rungia Raju, 167
Russell, William Howard, 80, 82

S

Sache, *Calcutta Bhisti*, 199, *204*
Sacred Tree of the Hindoos at Gyah (Daniell), 106,
    108
Sadler, J. C. *See* Hunter, James
*Sahib Being Carried in a Palanquin, Corner of Writ-
    ers' Building* (French), *49*
Salaman, M. C., 129
Sale of English Beauties in the East Indies (Anon.
    Br.), 23, *32*
Salt, Henry, 113; *Ancient Excavations at Carli*, *115*
*Savitri Pleading with Yama, the God of Death, for
    the Life of her Dead Husband* (Anon. In./Calcutta
    Art Studio), 179, *179*
Scene from San Toy Performed at Poona (Anon.
    Br.), *68*
Scene in the Writers' Buildings, Calcutta (Moffat),
    57, *61*
School in Calcutta (Anon. In.), 174, *175*
schools, art, 20, 36, 170, 176, 178–80

Scott, Mrs. W. L. L., *Sunset View of a Temple among Cedars near Simla*, *191*, *192*
Seetu Ram, *166*; *Exotic Insect: Two Views*, *168*
Self-Portrait (Chinnery), *13*
Select Views in India (Hodges), *15*, *100*, *102*, *103*, *105*
Sepoy Punishment (Mabon), *79*
Seringapatam, *24*, *51*, *53*. *See also* Mysore; Tipu Sultan
Sewak Ram, *Mohurrum*, *162*, *164*
Shah Jehan with Two Princes and an Attendant (Anon. In.), *167*
Shah Nujeef, Lucknow (Simpson), *82*
Shaikh Muhammad Amir of Karraya, *166*; *Horse and Groom*, *168*
Shaikh Zayn-al-din, *165–66*; *Lady Impey's Bird*, *166*
Shepherd, Charles. *See* Bourne and Shepherd
Shepherd and Robertson, *Residency, Lucknow, Showing the Room where Sir Henry Lawrence was Mortally Wounded*, *81*, *83*
Shuja-ud-daula, *12*, *26*
Simla. *See* hillstation
Simpson, William, *17*, *42*, *99*, *120–24*, *145*, *148*, *152*; *Allahabad, from the Right Bank of the Jumna*, *123*, *124*; *Dust Storm Coming On, near Jeypore Rajportana*, *122*, *123*; *Famine in India*, *17*, *121*, *122*; *Ganges*, *122*, *123*; *India, Ancient and Modern*, *124*; *Shah Nujeef, Lucknow*, *82*; *Street Scene in Bombay*, *16*, *148–49*; *Village Well* (Rajasthan), *149*, *150*, *152*
Siraj-ud-daula, *32*
Sir David Ochterlony Watching a Nautch (Anon. Br.), *71*
Six Afghans (Anon. In.), *162*, *164*
Skinner, James, *162*
Sleeman, Sir William, *138*
Smart, John, *32*; *Muhammad Ali, Nawab of Arcot*, *32*, *156*
Smith, Charles, *28*, *33*, *155*
Snake Charmers (Churchill), *198*, *203*
Snake Festival (Solvyns), *134*, *135*
Snowy Heights at Wangtu (Bourne), *190*, *192*
society: Anglo-Indian, *13*, *15*, *18*, *20*, *23*, *24*, *27*, *28*, *32*, *36*, *46–49*, *53*, *54*, *57*, *61*, *62*, *64–67*, *69–71*, *73*, *76*, *84*, *89*, *92*, *96*, *133*, *145*; Indian, *20*, *131–32*, *173–75*, *177*, *179*, *188*, *204*, *212*
Solvyns, Balthazar, *24*, *25*, *40*, *133*, *135*, *140*, *145*; *Black Town of Calcutta*, *39*, *145*; *Hookah-Bearer*, *133*; *Snake Festival*, *134*, *135*; *Two Hundred and Fifty Coloured Etchings Descriptive of the Manners, Customs and Dresses of the Hindoos*, *39*, *133*, *134*, *135*, *145*, *170*; *View of the Pagoda of Calleegut*, *145*, *170*
Soltykoff, Prince Alexis, *70*; *Indian Scenes and Characters*, *72*; *Festival of the Goddess Durga at Calcutta*, *70*, *71*, *72*

Sontag, Susan, *181*
Southeast Front of the New Government House (Bordwine), *92*, *93*
Southern Countryside (Colebrook), *118*, *118*
South Front of the Viceroy's House (Walcot), *94*, *95*, *96*
Spear, Percival, *23*
Statue of General Sir James Outram, Calcutta (Bourne and Shepherd), *25*
Stork (Anon. In.), *166*, *167*
Storming of Seringapatam (Porter, R. K.), *53*, *56*
Storm on the Ganges with Mrs. Hastings Braving the Eddies near the Col-Gon Rocks (Hodges), *102*, *104*
Sir Thomas Strange's House (Porter, J. Y.), **64**, *76*
Street Scene in Bombay (Simpson), *16*, *148–49*
Sunset View of a Temple among Cedars near Simla (Scott), *191*, *192*
Surat on the Banks of the Tappee (Forbes), *22*. *See also* Forbes, *Oriental Memoirs*
Surf Boats on the Beach, Madras (Chinnery), *31*
Suspension Bridge at Alipore over Tolly's Nulla (D'Oyly), *117*, *117*
Suttee (Anon. Br.), *138*, *139*
Suttee (Atkinson, J.), *138*, *138*
Symes, Michael, *154*

T

Taj (Anon. Br.), *198*, *200–1*
Taj Mahal, *42*, *99*, *161*, *188*, *198*, *200–1*
Talbot, William Henry Fox, *182*
Taylor Birds and Fruit-Bearing Convolvulus (Forbes), *144*, **144**. *See also* Forbes, *Oriental Memoirs*
Taylor's Emporium, Calcutta (D'Oyly), *35*, *35*
Tent Club at Tiffin (Carpenter), *72*, *73*
Tents Blowing up in a Storm (Gold), *38*, *38*
Tilly Kettle Painting a Portrait of Shuja-ud-daula, Nawab of Oudh, with Ten Sons (Anon. In.), *12*, *156*, *157*
Tinnevelley Bridge at Flood (Beato), *207*, *209*
Tipu Sultan, *50–53*
Tipu Sultan (Orme), *50*, *53*
travel, *27*, *37–39*, *57*, *98*, *102*, *104–6*, *113*, *119*, *121*
Trevelyan, Sir Charles Edward, *196*
Trevelyan, Sir George Otto, *170–71*
Trichinopoly (Lear), *127*, *128*
Tripe, Captain Linneaus, *196*, *197*; *Unfinished Gopuram*, *196*
Tritteny Pagoda (Allan), *118–19*, *119*
Trooper of Skinner's Horse (Anon. In.), *162*, **176**
Tumblers (Anon. In.), *161*, *162*
Turner, Joseph Mallord William, *13*, *102*, *104–5*, *111*
Two Hundred and Fifty Coloured Etchings Descrip-

tive of the Manners, Customs and Dresses of the Hindoos (Solvyns), *39, 133, 134, 135, 145, 170*
Two Thatched Indian Huts (Chinnery), *113*

U

Unfinished Gopuram (Tripe), *196*

V

Vaishnava Priest at a Woman's Breast (Anon. In.), *174, 175*
Varma, Ravi, *180*
Victoria (Alexandrina Victoria), *22, 42, 47, 82, 84, 88, 121*
Victoria Memorial, Calcutta, 92, 92
Victoria Railway Terminus, Bombay (Haig), *91, 92*
View from John Wombwell's House across the River Gumti (Humphry), *29*
View from New Tibet Road near Cheenee (Bourne), *189, 191–92*
View of a Street in the City of Patna (D'Oyly), *146, 150*
View of an Insulated Rock in the River Ganges at Jangerah (Hodges), *99, 100*
View of Bombay Green (Forbes), *145, 147. See also* Forbes, *Oriental Memoirs*
View of Calicut (Lear), *125*
View of Khuds and Valleys of Simla (Bourne), *95, 96*
View of Musjid, or the Tomb at Jaunpur (Hodges), *102, 103*
View of Part of St. Thome Street, Fort St. George (Orme), *146. See also* Orme, *Brief History of Ancient and Modern India*
View of Part of the City of Benares (Hodges), *102, 103*
View of the Imperial Assemblage (Anon. Br.), *88*
View of the Island of Jangerah at Sultanganj with Figures in the Foreground (Hodges), *101, 101*
View of the Pagoda of Calleegaut (Solvyns), *145, 170. See also* Solvyns, *Two Hundred and Fifty Coloured Etchings . . .*
View of the Secretariat, New Delhi (Anon. Br.), *94, 95*
Views of Calcutta Environs (D'Oyly), *146, 148–49*
Village of Dunkar, Spiti (Bourne), *192, 193*
Village Well (Rajasthan) Simpson, *149, 150, 152*

W

Walcot, William, *South Front of the Viceroy's House, 94, 95, 96*
Wales, James, *12, 28, 33, 106; Mahratta Peshwa and his Ministers, 33*
Ward, Francis Swain, *32*
Warren Hastings (Anon. Br.), *48, 50*
Warren Hastings (Daniell), *25*
Webb-Smith, Christopher, *144, 145; Luggar Falcon, 142, 144;* (and D'Oyly) *Ibis, 142, 145*
Wellesley, Richard Colley Wellesley, Marquess, *22, 84, 92, 160, 167*
Wellington, Arthur Wellesley, 1st Duke of, *51*
West, Benjamin, *49; Clive Receiving the Grant of the Diwani of Bengal from the Mogul Emperor Shah Alam, 49, 52*
Westmacott, Sir Richard, *48*
White, Lieutenant-Colonel George Francis, *100, 139*
White Lotus (Anon. In.), *167, 169*
Wilkie, Sir David, *52*
Williamson, Captain Thomas, *Decoyed Elephants Leaving the Male Fastened to a Tree, 116, 117; Exhibition of a Battle between a Buffalo and Tiger, 75; Hunting Jackals, 74, 117; Oriental Field Sports, 16*
Willison, George, *25, 30, 32*
Wilson, H. H., *32*
Wilson, Richard, *101–2*
Woman Labourer (Griffiths), *130, 131*
women: British, *23, 67, 69, 70;* Indian, *131–32, 157, 188*
Woodruff, Phillip, *22*

Y

Yule, Sir Henry, *80*

Z

Zoffany, Johann, *12, 26, 28, 30, 33, 34, 73, 110, 155; Blair Conversation Piece, 110, 111; Cockfight, 27, 73; Colonel Antoine Polier with his Friends Claud Martin, John Wombwell and the Artist, 34, 110; Dying Hindoo Brought to the Ganges, 110, 112; Embassy of Hyderbeck, 50, 53*